John X Evans

Erasmian Foll
Moreau XXVII

hierarchy of allusions
diegetic and extradiegetic
damnable iteration

spectrum

allegory ————————————— "damnable" iteration
                        literal reference
                    ironic + contrastive (270)

THE BIBLE IN SHAKESPEARE

The Bible in Shakespeare

HANNIBAL HAMLIN

OXFORD
UNIVERSITY PRESS

OXFORD
UNIVERSITY PRESS

Great Clarendon Street, Oxford, OX2 6DP,
United Kingdom

Oxford University Press is a department of the University of Oxford.
It furthers the University's objective of excellence in research, scholarship,
and education by publishing worldwide. Oxford is a registered trade mark of
Oxford University Press in the UK and in certain other countries

© Hannibal Hamlin 2013

The moral rights of the author have been asserted

First Edition published in 2013

Impression: 4

All rights reserved. No part of this publication may be reproduced, stored in
a retrieval system, or transmitted, in any form or by any means, without the
prior permission in writing of Oxford University Press, or as expressly permitted
by law, by licence or under terms agreed with the appropriate reprographics
rights organization. Enquiries concerning reproduction outside the scope of the
above should be sent to the Rights Department, Oxford University Press, at the
address above

You must not circulate this work in any other form
and you must impose this same condition on any acquirer

British Library Cataloguing in Publication Data

Data available

ISBN 978–0–19–967761–0

Printed in Great Britain by
CPI Group (UK) Ltd, Croydon, CR0 4YY

Links to third party websites are provided by Oxford in good faith and
for information only. Oxford disclaims any responsibility for the materials
contained in any third party website referenced in this work.

In memory of my father,
Cyrus Hamlin (1936–2011)

Acknowledgments

This book is the product of many years of reading, thinking, and discussion. At an early stage in my research on *The Bible in Shakespeare*, I received generous support from The Ohio State University (Mansfield Campus) and The Francis Bacon Foundation at the Huntington Library. A Frederick Burkhardt Residential Fellowship for Recently Tenured Scholars (from the American Council of Learned Societies) and a National Endowment for the Humanities Fellowship enabled me to spend two years at the Folger Shakespeare Library. At The Ohio State University (Columbus), Valerie Lee (then Chair of English) and John Roberts (then Dean of the College of Humanities) made it possible for me to take these two years of research leave.

This was a scholar's fantasy come true, and I am deeply grateful to these people and institutions, and to the superb Folger staff for their assistance, encouragement, and warm collegiality. I thank in particular Gail Kern Paster, Richard Kuhta, Steve Ennis, Georgianna Ziegler, Steve Enniss, Carol Brobeck, Kathleen Lynch, Elizabeth Walsh, LuEllen DeHaven, Camille Seerattan, Rosalind Larry, and Harold Batie. The Folger is like the Grand Central Station of international early modernists, and I benefited greatly from the valuable insights and interest in this project expressed by many of these new friends and colleagues. My co-fellows during the first year were Katherine Eggert, Linda Levy Peck, Julia Rudolph, and Wolfram Schmidgen. We were an especially close and collegial group, and the teas, lunches, drinks, and dinners we shared, full of true conviviality—intellectual, cultural, social, personal—seem to me the ideal of scholarly society. In my second year, Jonathan Gil Harris, Caroline M. Hibbard, Erik Midelfort, Alec Ryrie, and David Schalkwyk were also stalwart companions in the tea room and beyond. Others whose company I enjoyed and benefited from include Kim Coles, Thomas Freeman, Gerard Kilroy, Tobias Gregory, Anne McKeithen, Robert Miola, Jason Rosenblatt, Rebecca Totarro, and the late Marshall Grossman, who prophesied then that this book would take longer to complete than those two years, and I am sorry he did not live to see how right he was.

Portions of this book have been published previously, and I am grateful to Notre Dame University Press for permission to reprint, as Chapter 8, "The Patience of Lear" from Arthur F. Marotti and Ken Jackson (eds), *Shakespeare and Religion: Early Modern and Postmodern Perspectives* (Notre Dame: Notre Dame University Press, 2011), 127–62; and to the

Beinecke Library for permission to reprint, as part of Chapter 5, "The Bible, *Coriolanus*, and Shakespeare's Modes of Allusion," from Jennifer Lewin (ed.), *Never Again Would Birds' Song Be the Same: New Essays on Poetry and Poetics, Renaissance to Modern* ([New Haven]: Beinecke Library, 2002): 73–91.

Many of my ideas about Shakespeare's biblical allusions have been tested in conference papers and discussions, and I am grateful for all those who listened and responded, including especially Sarah Beckwith, Arthur Marotti, Richard McCoy, Steve Mentz, and Annabel Patterson. After more than a decade, I am sure to be forgetting many others, for which I hope they will forgive me and accept my general thanks. In particular, though, I thank Mark Rankin and Erin E. Kelly for inviting me to participate in an SAA seminar in 2009 on Shakespeare and Religion; Nick Moschovakis for inviting me to lead, along with Joseph Pucci, a seminar on Allusion at the 2010 conference of the Association of Literary Scholars, Critics, and Writers; and Thomas Fulton for inviting me to join an SAA seminar in 2012 on Reading Shakespeare and the Bible. The members of all these seminars provided valuable feedback and stimulating discussion. Like anyone studying the Bible in Shakespeare, I owe an immense debt to the labors of Naseeb Shaheen. I regret never having met Professor Shaheen, who died in 2009, but I was pleased to be able to express my gratitude for his work posthumously in a 2012 lecture at the opening of the Naseeb Shaheen Antiquarian Bible Collection at the University of Tennessee-Knoxville. Heather Hirschfeld and Jennifer Benedetto Beals were the best of hosts at that event.

My colleagues at The Ohio State University have been uniformly supportive and intellectually stimulating, but I would like especially to thank Barbara McGovern, Norman W. Jones, John N. King, Richard Dutton, Alan Farmer, Jennifer Higginbotham, Christopher Highley, and Luke Wilson. Like many scholars, I have probably taken more good ideas from students than I am aware of, but I acknowledge in particular my graduate students in a rewarding seminar on Biblical Allusion in Renaissance Literature in 2010.

My editors at Oxford University Press have exhibited something like the patience of Job in waiting for this book. The tidal wave that was the 400th anniversary of the King James Bible and deaths in the family swept me away from this project, and it took some time to swim back to shore. Jacqueline Baker has been an exemplary editor, and my many questions about this and that were answered promptly and ably by Rachel Platt and Jenny Townsend. I would also like to thank my production editor Shereen Karmali, Prabhavathy Parthiban from SPi Global, and my copy-editor, Hilary Walford.

Finally, I dedicate this book to my father, Cyrus Hamlin, who was at various places (the University of Toronto and Yale) and at various times Professor of English, of German, and of Comparative Literature. Though I am not sure I remember it myself, he took me to see *Hamlet* in Oxford starring Derek Jacobi when I was 5 years old. Apparently, when the ghost appeared, I crouched down behind the seat in front, peering fearfully over the top. Though a specialist in German Romanticism, my father taught both Shakespeare (at Toronto, with Northrop Frye) and the Bible (at Yale, with Hans Frei), and he was keen on my work on the Bible in Shakespeare from its earliest days. Sadly, he did not live to see the book finished and in print. The rest of my family, both Hamlins and Martins, have lived with this book a long time, and I thank them for their patience. My wife, Cori Martin, has been as always my muse, my best editor, and my staunchest support. She will also be more pleased than anyone that this book is finally done.

Contents

List of Illustrations — xii
Editions and Abbreviations — xiii
Note to the Reader — xvii

Introduction — 1

PART I. SHAKESPEARE'S ALLUSIVE PRACTICE AND ITS CULTURAL AND HISTORICAL BACKGROUND

1. Reformation Biblical Culture — 9
2. A Critical History of the Bible in Shakespeare — 43
3. Allusion: Theory, History, and Shakespeare's Practice — 77

PART II. BIBLICAL ALLUSION IN THE PLAYS

4. Shakespeare's Variations on Themes from Genesis 1–3 — 127
5. Creative Anachronism: Biblical Allusion in the Roman Histories — 179
6. Damnable Iteration: Falstaff, Master of Biblical Allusion — 231
7. The Great Doom's Image: *Macbeth* and Apocalypse — 271
8. The Patience of Lear: *King Lear* and Job — 305

Conclusion — 334

Bibliography — 337
Index — 369

List of Illustrations

1.1. The flight into Egypt on a cushion cover	24
1.2. Adam, Eve, and the Serpent	25
4.1. Adam and Eve on a panel	131
4.2. The Virgin in a hortus conclusus	160
4.3. The Madonna on the Crescent Moon	165
5.1. The Pelican in her Piety	190
5.2. Christ shown to the people	206
5.3. The Woman and the Dragon with Seven Heads	227
6.1. The prodigal son among the swine	245
6.2. Dives and Lazarus	247
7.1. Guild Chapel "Doom," Stratford	273
7.2. Hell-mouth from a Doom	287
8.1. Tobit blinded by sparrows' droppings	317
8.2. Pietà/Lamentation over the dead Christ	325

Editions and Abbreviations

EDITIONS OF SHAKESPEARE PLAYS USED

Antony and Cleopatra *Antony and Cleopatra*, ed. John Wilders, Arden³ (Routledge, 1995; repr. London: Thomson Learning, 2002)

Coriolanus *Coriolanus*, ed. Philip Brockbank, Arden² (Methuen, 1976; repr. London and New York: Routledge, 1988)

Cymbeline *Cymbeline*, ed. Martin Butler, New Cambridge Shakespeare (Cambridge: Cambridge University Press, 2005; repr. 2006)

Hamlet *Hamlet*, ed. Harold Jenkins, Arden² (London and New York: Methuen, 1982)

Julius Caesar *Julius Caesar*, ed. David Daniell, Arden³ (Walden-on-Thames: Thomas Nelson and Sons, 1998)

King Henry IV, Part 1 *King Henry IV, Part 1*, ed. David Scott Kastan, Arden³ (London: Thomson Learning, 2002)

King Henry IV, Part 2 *King Henry IV, Part 2*, ed. A. R. Humphreys, Arden² (Methuen & Co., 1981; repr. London: Thomson Learning, 2005)

King Henry V *Henry V*, ed. T. W. Craik, Arden³ (Routledge, 1995; repr. London: Thomson Learning, 2001)

King Lear *King Lear*, ed. R. A. Foakes, Arden³ (Walton-on-Thames, Surrey: Thomas Nelson and Sons, 1997)

Love's Labour's Lost *Love's Labour's Lost*, ed. H. R. Woudhuysen, Arden³ (Walton-on-Thames, Surrey: Thomas Nelson and Sons, 1998)

Macbeth *Macbeth*, ed. A. R. Braunmuller, New Cambridge Shakespeare (Cambridge: Cambridge University Press, 1997)

The Merchant of Venice *The Merchant of Venice*, ed. John Drakakis, Arden³ (London: A & C Black Publishers Ltd., 2010)

The Merry Wives of Windsor *The Merry Wives of Windsor*, ed. Giorgio Melchiori, Arden³ (London: Thomson Learning, 2000)

Editions and Abbreviations

Othello	Othello, ed. E. A. J. Honigmann, Arden³ (Walton-on-Thames: Thomas Nelson and Sons Ltd., 1997)
Pericles	Pericles, ed. Doreen DelVecchio and Antony Hammond, New Cambridge Shakespeare (Cambridge: Cambridge University Press, 1998)
King Richard II	King Richard II, ed. Charles R. Forker, Arden³ (London: Thomson Learning, 2002)
Romeo and Juliet	Romeo and Juliet, ed. Jill L. Levenson, Oxford Shakespeare (Oxford and New York: Oxford University Press, 2000)
The Winter's Tale	The Winter's Tale, ed. Stephen Orgel, Oxford Shakespeare (Oxford and New York: Oxford University Press, 1996)
All other citations	The Complete Works, ed. Alfred Harbage, The Pelican Text Revised (New York: Viking Press, 1969; repr. 1977)

ABBREVIATIONS FOR REFERENCE WORKS AND JOURNALS

BCP	The Book of Common Prayer: The Texts of 1549, 1559, and 1662, ed. Brian Cummings (Oxford: Oxford University Press, 2011)
Bishops'	[The Bishops' Bible], The. holie. Bible conteynyng the olde Testament and the newe (London: Richard Jugge, 1568)
Bullough	Geoffrey Bullough (ed.), Narrative and Dramatic Sources of Shakespeare, 8 vols (London: Routledge and Kegan Paul; New York: Columbia University Press, 1957–75)
EEBO	Early English Books Online
ELH	English Literary History
ELR	English Literary Renaissance
EMLS	Early Modern Literary Studies
Geneva	The Geneva Bible: A Facsimile of the 1560 Edition, intro. Lloyd E. Berry (University of Wisconsin Press, 1969; repr. Peabody, MA: Hendrickson Publishers, Inc., 2007)

Editions and Abbreviations xv

Geneva–Tomson	*The Holy Bible conteyning the Olde Testament and the Newe* [Geneva–Tomson Bible] (London: Christopher Barker, 1595)
Hamlin	Hannibal Hamlin, *Psalm Culture and Early Modern English Literature* (Cambridge: Cambridge University Press, 2004)
HLQ	*Huntington Library Quarterly*
Homilies	*Certaine Sermons or Homilies Appointed to be Read in Churches In the Time of Queen Elizabeth I (1547–1571)*, facs. edn by Mary Ellen Rickey and Thomas B. Stroup, 2 vols, separately numbered (Gainesville, FL: Scholars' Facsimiles and Reprints, 1968). Online edn, by Ian Lancashire and based on the Scholar's Facsimile <http://www.library.utoronto.ca/utel/ret/homilies/elizhom.html>
JEGP	*Journal of English and Germanic Philology*
JMEMS	*Journal of Medieval and Early Modern Studies*
Jones	Emrys Jones, *The Origins of Shakespeare* (Oxford: Clarendon Press, 1977; repr. 1978)
KJV	The King James Version (or King James Bible, or Authorized Version) of the Bible
N&Q	*Notes and Queries*
Noble	Richmond Noble, *Shakespeare's Biblical Knowledge and Use of the Book of Common Prayer as Exemplified in the Plays of the First Folio* (London: Society for Promoting Christian Knowledge; New York: Macmillan Company, 1935)
ODNB	*Oxford Dictionary of National Biography*
OED	*Oxford English Dictionary*, 2nd edn
RES	*Review of English Studies*
RQ	*Renaissance Quarterly*
SCJ	*Sixteenth Century Journal*
SEL	*Studies in English Literature*
Shaheen	Naseeb Shaheen, *Biblical References in Shakespeare's Plays* (Newark, DE: University of Delaware Press; London: Associated University Presses, 1999)

SP   *Studies in Philology*
SQ   *Shakespeare Quarterly*
SS   *Shakespeare Survey*
SSt   *Shakespeare Studies*
STC   Short Title Catalogue

Vulgate   *Biblia sacra vulgata*, Clementine version,
           DRBO.ORG <http://www.drbo.org>

Note to the Reader

Given the enormous bibliography on Shakespeare and the Bible, stretching back over more than two hundred years, I have not attempted to cite the first critic to recognize each particular biblical allusion. Even if this were possible, which I doubt, it would be of limited use and would make an already sizeable body of footnotes overwhelming. I have tried to acknowledge particular debts when relevant, and the Bibliography provides a guide for those who might want to pursue the critical history in more detail than is provided in Chapter 2.

Original spelling of most early modern texts (apart from Shakespeare) has been maintained, though i/j, u/v, vv/w, and long "s" have been modernized, and abbreviations and contractions expanded. Alterations have been made in a small number of instances where confusion might otherwise result (for instance, "thee" for "the"). Given the increasing interest in printing and the history of the book, printers and publishers of early modern books have been provided where possible.

Introduction

This book is about allusions to the Bible in Shakespeare's plays. It argues that such allusions are frequent, deliberate, and significant, and that the study of these allusions is repaid by a deeper understanding of the plays. A supplementary argument, or perhaps a presupposition, is that Shakespeare's culture as a whole was profoundly and thoroughly biblical, a culture in which one could assume a degree of biblical knowledge that is difficult to imagine in today's mass-media global culture. One gropes for a modern analogy, but there is none. Imagine a television program that everyone in the country has been watching every week, sometimes more than once, for their entire lives, having seen some episodes dozens of times. Suppose your parents and grandparents had watched all the same episodes, and suppose further that millions of people in other neighboring countries had watched these episodes too, dubbed into their own languages. Suppose people had actually been watching this show, in still other languages, for over a thousand years, and that vast libraries had accumulated over the centuries full of books about how best to interpret the show. Suppose that it was illegal not to watch this show and, moreover, that your eternal salvation was understood to depend on it. Suppose that this TV show was the basis for your country's literature and art, its political theory, its history, its philosophy, its understanding of the natural world as well as human nature, and essential to most other fields of knowledge as well. In sixteenth- and seventeenth-century England, the Bible was that show; it was always in reruns, and it never went off the air.

It is no surprise, then, that Shakespeare, like most of his fellow writers—Christopher Marlowe, Edmund Spenser, Thomas Nashe, Ben Jonson, John Donne, George Herbert, among many others—exploited this pervasive common culture to make meaning in his work. This is not breaking news. As a later chapter will make clear, people have been aware of Shakespeare's biblical allusions for centuries and indeed since the plays were first performed and read. Though there is no surviving written record of Elizabethan and Jacobean playgoers noting or discussing biblical allusions, the allusions were obviously there to be recognized and interpreted, and presumably they were. As the Bibliography will make clear, many modern critics of Shakespeare have written about biblical allusion: there are excellent essays about the Bible and individual plays, several collections of such essays, and a few scholarly monographs that treat the subject of Shakespeare and the Bible within other contexts like early modern religion or political theory. Excellent books have also been written about biblical allusion in the poems of Edmund Spenser, George Herbert, and John Milton, and about Shakespeare's allusions to other sources like Virgil's *Aeneid*, Ovid's *Metamorphoses*, or Seneca's *Tragedies*. For whatever reason, however—and some are suggested in Chapter 2—no one has yet published a full-length critical study of Shakespeare's practice of biblical allusion and the implications of biblical allusion for our understanding of the plays. *The Bible in Shakespeare* is intended to address this deficiency.

The present book is not, however, about ferreting out Shakespeare's religious beliefs. Of course, the Bible was not just a source of characters and stories but the foundation of the Christian faith, especially for *sola scriptura* Protestants. Shakespeare, like everyone else, presumed this. Many of his biblical allusions are inevitably connected with religious ideas, even contemporary or long-standing theological or exegetical controversies: grace and forgiveness, providence and divine right, witchcraft and prophecy, even miracles and resurrection. Furthermore, such automatic associations with familiar Bible verses enabled Shakespeare to engage his audience on elemental matters of life and death, salvation and damnation. Thus, the interpretative stakes were higher with biblical allusions than with allusions to secular literature; no one in England was ever burned for misreading Ovid. So one may be curious to ask what Shakespeare himself believed. Indeed, many of Shakespeare's readers and viewers over the centuries have wanted to know. Arguments have been made for Shakespeare as Catholic, Protestant, Puritan, Atheist, even Jew.[1] Which is right? To paraphrase Stephen Booth's conclusion about Shakespeare's sexuality, it seems certain that Shakespeare subscribed either to one of these faiths, some combination of them, or none at all.[2] Beyond that, the plays offer little evidence. Furthermore, despite the current (or recurrent) vogue for the Catholic Shakespeare based on biographical or historical claims, there is no reliable external evidence for Shakespeare's personal beliefs, though there is evidence for his religious practice

---

[1] On the latter, see Ghislain Muller, *Was Shakespeare a Jew?: Uncovering the Marrano Influences in his Life and Writing* (Lewiston, NY: Edwin Mellen Press, 2001). For other arguments about Shakespeare's religion, see Ch. 2.

[2] "William Shakespeare was almost certainly homosexual, bisexual, or heterosexual. The sonnets provide no evidence on the matter" (Stephen Booth [ed.], *Shakespeare's Sonnets* [New Haven and London: Yale University Press, 1977], 548).

Introduction 3

(see Chapter 1). The question of Shakespeare's faith is not, in any case, one that this book seeks to answer.

My own personal faith, disbelief, or doubt is even less relevant. It has become common for writers about the Bible or religion to include a prefatory credo, often as a disclaimer of bias, perhaps to reassure the reader that the book is not a disguised sermon or religious polemic. Writers on Ovid feel no need to state whether they are practicing pagans, nor those on Seneca whether they are or ever have been card-carrying Stoics. It thus seems no more reasonable to require a statement of faith from scholars of the Bible or Christianity. The principal justification for this study is that it reveals the extent to which the works of early modern England's greatest playwright allude to and engage with the age's most important book. In addition, allusion was one of Shakespeare's most common rhetorical, dramatic, and poetic techniques. For instance, *Titus Andronicus* alludes to Ovid's account of Philomela, *The Tempest* to Ovid's Medea, *Hamlet* alludes to the Troy story, *As You Like It* to the Robin Hood legend, and *The Merry Wives of Windsor* to the schooltext *The Introduction of Grammar* by William Lilly and John Colet. All of Shakespeare's plays regularly allude to other works. Yet no book is alluded to more often, more thoroughly, or with more complexity and significance than the Bible. The explanation for this is simple: the Bible was the most important and most widely known book in Shakespeare's culture. In truth, knowledge of the Bible is necessary fully to understand Shakespeare's plays; understanding Shakespeare's use of biblical allusion also reveals a great deal about the nature of early modern English biblical culture. In other words, the plays mirror aspects of the culture out of which they are written, and the culture also mirrors aspects of the plays. Exploring the biblical culture, how and in what contexts English men and women knew the Bible, and what were the prevailing contemporary interpretations of key biblical characters and passages, provides an essential framework for reconstructing how Shakespeare's biblical allusions might have been interpreted in the theater.

The organization of *The Bible in Shakespeare* is intended to allow for maximum coverage of the topic, potentially a vast one, in a single volume. It is impossible to be encyclopedic, but most of Shakespeare's plays have been addressed, in greater or lesser degree. Selection has partly been guided by what has been done by previous critics. Thus *The Merchant of Venice*, for example, a play rich in biblical allusions, has not been studied as extensively here as it might otherwise have been, since the recent criticism of that play is substantial and excellent.[3] About other plays and

---

[3] See especially Janet Adelman, *Blood Relations: Christian and Jew in* The Merchant of Venice (Chicago and London: University of Chicago Press, 2008).

theoretical considerations there seemed much more left to be explored. As a result, the first three chapters address historical, theoretical, and methodological issues. Chapter 1 paints a backdrop of early modern English biblical culture, finding the Bible both in obvious places, like the church, and in places one would not expect, such as puppet plays, tavern wall paintings, popular ballads, and embroidered bed curtains. Chapter 2 traces the long and often peculiar critical history of Shakespeare and the Bible, from insightful comments by his earliest editors, through Victorian celebrations of Shakespeare and the Bible as the twin moral underpinnings of British culture, to twentieth-century "neo-Christian" studies of Shakespeare's plays. Chapter 3 describes the variety of ways in which Shakespeare manipulates his biblical allusions, but it also explores in detail, both historical and theoretical, the nature of "allusion" as one of literature's most essential tropes. One perhaps surprising discovery is that the English term "allusion" originates in the context of biblical exegesis, and that allusion has been a particular concern of Christian biblical interpreters from at least the sixth century.

The second part of the book looks more closely at how allusion functions in specific plays and how this affects their meaning. The chapters are organized so as to maximize the number of plays covered, in terms of genre and period, while also focusing on a range of different questions related to Shakespeare's practice of allusion. Chapter 4 thus takes a single brief biblical passage, the story of Adam, Eve, and the serpent in Eden and the Fall of Man (Gen. 1–3), and traces the variety of ways in which Shakespeare alludes to it in plays throughout his career, from *Love's Labour's Lost* through *Richard II* and *Hamlet* to *The Winter's Tale*. Shakespeare uses these allusions to illuminate questions about gender, sex, childbirth, and marriage, providence and right rule, sinfulness and corruption, and renewal and restoration. Gardens too. Chapter 5 looks at Shakespeare's Roman plays, *Julius Caesar*, *Coriolanus*, and *Antony and Cleopatra*, all of which allude in significant ways to the Crucifixion story as well as (in *Antony and Cleopatra*) the Book of Revelation. Since it seems peculiar for pre-Christian Romans to be alluding, even unconsciously, to the Christian Bible, this chapter provides an opportunity to explore the relationship between allusion and anachronism. Chapter 6 also addresses several plays, but this time all of them involve a single character: Falstaff. Falstaff is one of the most brilliant practitioners and manipulators of biblical allusion in Shakespeare. This chapter takes up the question of characters' self-conscious versus unconscious allusion. It also uses biblical allusions as a means to track the metamorphosis of Falstaff's character from *Henry IV Parts 1 and 2* through to *The Merry Wives of Windsor*. Finally, Chapters 7 and 8 each focus on the workings of biblical allusion in a single play. Chapter 7 studies the allusions to Revelation in *Macbeth*, showing how they help establish the apocalyptic atmosphere of the play. Further allusions to the gospels and Samuel are similarly apocalyptic but also suggest Macbeth's defeat and death as a kind of grotesque parody of the Crucifixion. Chapter 8 focuses on *King Lear* and Job. There is a long history of comments on the similarity of these two works, but it has not been fully recognized how deeply Shakespeare's play wrestles with its biblical precursor. Allusions to Job and related passages engage the audience of *King Lear* with basic existential questions of providence, justice, and the meaning of suffering. The lack of any divine intervention, the voice from the whirlwind, makes Shakespeare's play in some ways even bleaker than the biblical Job.

This book shares its title, *The Bible in Shakespeare*, with the 1903 publication by William Burgess, also the author of *Land, Labor, and Liquor* and *The World's Social Evil*. Unlike Burgess (I assume), I now and again enjoy a little wine (or even a couple of martinis) for the stomach's sake. I am also not convinced that Shakespeare advocated temperance. Like Burgess, however, though I might put it differently, I am convinced that Shakespeare "drew largely from the Bible for his loftiest thoughts and noblest inspirations."[4] He also drew from it less lofty thoughts and rather ignoble inspirations. In fact, Shakespeare drew from the Bible constantly and alluded to it in all of his plays in an extensive variety of contexts, high, low, and middle ground. The Bible needs to be included alongside—though actually ahead of—Ovid's *Metamorphoses*, Holinshed's *Chronicle*, and Plutarch's *Lives* as one of the works essential to understanding Shakespeare's plays. That is the argument of this book.

---

[4] William Burgess, *The Bible in Shakspeare: A Study of the Relation of the Works of William Shakespeare to the Bible* (1903; repr. New York: Haskell House, 1968), p. vii.

PART I

SHAKESPEARE'S ALLUSIVE PRACTICE AND ITS CULTURAL AND HISTORICAL BACKGROUND

1
Reformation Biblical Culture

William Shakespeare was born into a biblical culture. His generation of English men and women born in the 1560s was the first to be able to take the reality of an English Bible for granted.[1] In 1564, Shakespeare's birth year, there were already a number of English versions of the Bible in circulation, the most recent being the Geneva Bible, first printed in Geneva in 1560, and translated by English Protestants in exile there during the reign of Catholic Queen Mary. Earlier translations had been made, both unofficial (William Tyndale's complete New Testament and partial Old Testament, and Miles Coverdale's 1535 Bible) and official (the Great Bible, a combination of Tyndale and Coverdale, edited by the latter). But the development of the English Bible had been suppressed in Mary's reign, although she seems to have left alone copies already owned by churches.[2] The Geneva Bible was to become the most popular English Bible for most of the next century, and Shakespeare clearly had a copy that he read at home, possibly a medium-sized quarto like the first edition, or else a more inexpensive octavo.[3] When Orlando at the beginning of *As You Like It* says to his brother, "Shall I keep your hogs and eat husks with them?" (1.1.37–8), he alludes to the Parable of the Prodigal Son: "And he wolde faine have filled his bellie with the huskes, that the swine ate: but no man gave them him" (Luke 15:16). Shakespeare here is alluding to the Geneva Bible translation, since it was the first to use the word

---

[1] Debora Shuger calls religion "the master-code of pre-capitalist society" and "the cultural matrix for explorations of virtually every topic," and "religion," for English Protestants, meant the Bible. Shuger, *Habits of Thought in the English Renaissance: Religion, Politics, and the Dominant Culture* (Berkeley and Los Angeles: University of California Press, 1990), cited in Patrick Collinson, "Biblical Rhetoric: The English Nation and National Sentiment in the Prophetic Mode," in Claire McEachern and Debora Shuger (eds), *Religion and Culture in Renaissance England* (Cambridge: Cambridge University Press, 1997), 15–45, 17.

[2] David Daniell, *The Bible in English: Its History and Influence* (New Haven: Yale University Press, 2003).

[3] This size was unusual; most English Bibles were first published in large folio for use in churches. That the Geneva was first published in a smaller edition suggests it was intended for personal reading as well as liturgical use.

"huskes" in this passage.[4] The Bishops' Bible was the other most common translation in Shakespeare's lifetime, published in 1568 for the official use of the Elizabethan Church. Instead of "huskes" it has "cods." But again, Othello alludes to Proverbs in the Geneva version when he rails against Desdemona for her supposed adultery:

> Yet could I bear that too; well, very well:
> But there where I have garnered up my heart,
> Where either I must live or bear no life,
> The fountain from the which my current runs
> Or else dries up to be discarded thence!
> Or keep it as a cistern for foul toads
> To knot and gender in! (4.2.56–62)

The use of fountain and cistern as metaphors for marriage derives from Proverbs 5:15,

Drinke the water of thy cisterne, and of the rivers out of the middes of thine owne well. Let thy fountaines flowe forthe, and the rivers of waters in the stretes. But let them be thine, even thine onely, and not the strangers with thee. Let thy fountaine be blessed, and rejoyce with the wife of thy youth.

As the marginal note in the Geneva Bible informs the reader, this whole chapter of Proverbs is about "an harlot which giveth her self to another then to her husband," which indicates its relevance to Shakespeare's play about jealousy and (imagined) adultery. And it is to the Geneva translation that Shakespeare alludes, since it is the only translation to include the fountain and cistern; the Bishops' Bible has "well" in both places.

There were further printings of the Geneva Bible in Geneva in 1562 and 1570, as well as separate editions of the New Testament, but Geneva Bibles were not printed in England until after the death of Archbishop of Canterbury Matthew Parker in 1575. Thereafter they were produced in huge numbers in every available format. In 1576 an edition was published with revisions to the New Testament by Laurence Tomson, scholar, linguist, member of parliament, and secretary to Sir Francis Walsingham. Tomson also added new marginal notes, some his own, and some translated from those of Calvin's successor in Geneva, Theodore Beza. Tomson's revisions to the biblical text were also based partly on Beza's edition of the

---

[4] I take this example from Shaheen, 593–4. Shaheen also lists the eighty-odd references that he determines to be translation-specific, i.e., specific to Geneva, Bishops', or Coverdale (pp. 38–48). Like any scholar studying Shakespeare's use of the Bible, I am in constant debt to Shaheen. For the most part, however, I will not cite his catalogue whenever an allusion I mention is included there. Such citations would be cumbersome and not very useful, since many if not most of the references Shaheen himself includes were included in earlier studies by Richmond Noble, Thomas Carter, and others. On these works, see Ch. 2.

Greek New Testament. There is some evidence that Shakespeare had read one of these Geneva–Tomson editions, perhaps one of the New Testaments published separately in large quantities.[5] He may also (or alternatively) have known the later edition known as Geneva–Tomson–Junius (1599), which added extensive, highly anti-Catholic, notes on the Book of Revelation, translated from the Latin version of Francis Junius.

The Geneva Bible was popular with the hotter sort of English Protestants, given its association with Calvin's Geneva and the evangelical zeal of some of its marginal notes. These copious notes made this Bible popular with everyone, however, since most of them were not polemical but interpretative. Such notes were designed for private reading, of course, and occasional signs that Shakespeare was aware of them reinforce the argument that he knew the Geneva Bible from his own reading.[6] This was the first Study Bible for the ordinary reader, packed with a helpful interpretative apparatus: maps, genealogies, chronologies, editorial summaries, tables of the interpretation of biblical names, and an index, as well as those thousands of marginal notes. The text, for the first time (and following the practice of Bibles printed in Geneva in other languages), was in Roman type, which, even though a novelty, was probably easier to read than the black letter type for the average person.[7] For further ease of reference, the Geneva Bible also divided the biblical text into chapters and, for the first time in an English Bible, verses. Chapter divisions had been introduced into Latin (Vulgate) Bibles by Archbishop of Canterbury Stephen Langton in the thirteenth century, but verse numbers were added to Bibles only in the mid-sixteenth century, by the French printer Robert Estienne, and these were adopted by William Whittingham for his 1557 New Testament and then for the complete Geneva Bible. The Geneva Bible was the most user-friendly edition that had ever been published. It was also the first complete English Bible translated from the original languages, Hebrew and Greek.[8]

---

[5] Naseeb Shaheen, "Shakespeare and the Tomson New Testament," *N&Q* 42/3 (1995), 290–1. In *Othello*, if the Folio reading of 5.2.348 is correct and Othello says that "like a base Judean" he threw away a pearl "richer than all his tribe," Shakespeare may be drawing on Tomson's note to Matt. 10:4, which explains that Judas, like Jesus whom he betrayed, was of the tribe of Judah. As Shaheen notes, this is slim evidence, but possible.

[6] See, for instance, Beatrice Groves, "Shakespeare's Sonnets and the Genevan Marginalia," *Essays in Criticism*, 57/2 (2007), 114–28.

[7] There is some question about this, since, while Roman type seems clearer to modern readers, early modern readers, especially those less familiar with the classical and humanist texts printed in Roman, may actually have found the black letter more familiar. See Femke Molekamp, "Using a Collection to Discover Reading Practices: The British Library Geneva Bibles and a History of their Early Modern Readers," *Electronic British Library Journal* (2006), 1–13, 3.

[8] Tyndale translated from original languages, but he died before he could translate all of the Old Testament. Coverdale translated the entire Bible, but from Latin and German not Hebrew and Greek.

The domestic printing of Geneva Bibles was for some reason prevented during the lifetime of Matthew Parker. It is not clear that he himself was responsible, but he was the principal editor and translator of its main rival, the Bishop's Bible.[9] First published in 1568, it is called the "Bishops" ' because it was the bishops (including Parker) who translated it. Many English Bishops had resisted a vernacular Bible in the 1530s and 1540s, but, after the Great Bible of 1539, officially sanctioned by Henry VIII, the English Bible was an unavoidable fact. The 1560 Geneva Bible drove this home. Its occasionally strong Calvinist leanings, however, rankled with more conservative churchmen, and it was a translation produced outside the authority of the Established Church (though of course, at the time it was begun, that Church, under Mary, was Catholic). The Bishops' Bible was essentially a revision of the earlier Great Bible, produced quickly, and published in a huge, lavish, and richly illustrated folio edition for use on church lecterns. That it was not principally designed for private reading is indicated by the instruction to the translators (from Parker) to mark dangerous parts of the text that should not be read in public.[10] The controversial illustrations in this Bible might suggest it was aimed at readers, since images can hardly be communicated orally from the pulpit, but the readers Parker had primarily in mind were those who would consult the book independently in churches.[11] Bishops' Bibles were printed in smaller formats, but they were never as popular as the Geneva for personal use.[12] Nevertheless, it was the Bishops' Bible that most English men and women heard read in church every week, and this is no doubt primarily how Shakespeare came to know it.

---

[9] Margaret Aston notes the letter from Parker and Edmund Grindal to William Cecil, stating that it shall "nothing hinder but rather do moche good to have diversitie of translacions and readings" ("The Bishops' Bible Illustrations," in *The Church and the Arts* (Oxford and Cambridge, MA: Published for the Ecclesiastical History Society by Blackwell Publishers, 1992), 267–85, 269.

[10] Parker's letter to Cecil, cited in Daniell, *The Bible in English*, 343.

[11] Bibles of the largest size were required to be placed in churches not just for reading during worship but for parishioners to consult on their own. This is not the kind of private or domestic reading facillated by personal Bibles, however. The educational function of the Bishops' illustrations, "instructive pictures, dispersed up and down the book," was noted by John Strype in his life of Matthew Parker. See Elizabeth Evenden, *Patents, Pictures and Patronage: John Day and the Tudor Book Trade* (Aldershot and Burlington, VT: Ashgate, 2008), 105–7.

[12] In the 1580s, there were four editions of the Bishops' Bible compared to twenty of the Geneva; in the 1590s, the figures were two versus twenty-one. See Ian Green, *Print and Protestantism in Early Modern England* (Oxford: Oxford University Press, 2000), 52, table 2.2. On formats, see T. H. Darlow and H. F. Moule, rev. A. S. Herbert, *Historical Catalogue of Printed Editions of the English Bible 1525–1961* (London: British and Foreign Bible Society; New York: American Bible Society, 1968). Quartos of the Bishops' were printed from 1569, and New Testaments were available in octavo.

Church attendance was required by law every Sunday and on major holidays. Failure to attend risked one's being listed by the wardens as a recusant, which might result in fines and even imprisonment.[13] Shakespeare's father, John, was entered on the Stratford recusant rolls in 1592, when William was 28 and established in the London theater world. Though proponents of a Catholic Shakespeare (see Chapter 2) have tried to argue otherwise, the reason for John Shakespeare's non-attendance seems not to have been latent Catholic beliefs, but debt—he was on a list of those who avoided church "for feare of procésse for Debtte."[14] As Stanley Wells, among many others, has pointed out, John Shakespeare was buried, and his children (including William) were baptized, according to the rites of the Church of England.[15] There is no reason to think that William did not attend regular services at Holy Trinity Church, where he himself was buried, along with his parents (John died in 1601 and Mary in 1608), his sister, and two of his brothers, his wife, Anne, his son Hamnet, and his daughters Judith and Susanna, as well as Susanna's husband John Hall. Shakespeare would almost certainly have attended the funerals of his parents, siblings, and son, who all predeceased him, and also the baptism of his children in 1583 and 1585. But these were only the most intensely personal rites of passage he celebrated at the church. He would have been in regular attendance, every Sunday and every holiday, from as soon as he could be brought to church, until he left to make his name in London. Even then, he was back regularly, and for some long periods, as when the theaters were closed for plague in 1592–3. The standard narrative until recently has been that Shakespeare spent most of his time in London and returned to Stratford only a few years before his death in 1616. Jonathan Bate has suggested, however, that not only did Shakespeare perhaps return to Stratford more often than has been thought, but that he may have effectively "retired" there shortly after James I came to the throne.[16]

---

[13] On recusancy, see Alexandra Walsham, *Church Papists: Catholicism, Conformity, and Confessional Polemic in Early Modern England* (Woodbridge: Published for the Royal Historical Society by Boydell Press, 1993). As Walsham's main argument makes clear, however, mere church attendance is no reliable marker of belief. For both Protestants and church papists, though, attendance would have resulted in familiarity with the Bible.

[14] Peter Holland, "William Shakespeare," *ODNB*, citing Samuel Schoenbaum, *William Shakespeare: A Documentary Life* (New York: Oxford University Press, in association with The Scolar Press, 1975), 39. See also Robert Bearman, "John Shakespeare: A Papist or Just Penniless?" *SQ* 56/4 (2005), 411–33.

[15] Stanley Wells, *Shakespeare for All Time* (Oxford: Oxford University Press, 2003), 25.

[16] Jonathan Bate, *Soul of the Age: A Biography of the Mind of William Shakespeare* (New York: Random House, 2009), 333–42.

Even when in London, Shakespeare was expected to attend church. The tax records for the parish of St Helen's Bishopsgate show Shakespeare living there (and presumably attending church) sometime before October 1596. Between 1598 and 1599, he moved to Southwark, in the liberty of the Clink.[17] Many of his theatrical colleagues attended St Saviour's (now Southwark Cathedral), near the Globe (and Rose), and Shakespeare may have attended services there too. The actors Augustine Phillips and Robert Gough from Shakespeare's company had children baptized at St Saviour's, and playwrights John Fletcher and Philip Massinger were buried there, along with the theater entrepreneur Philip Henslowe.[18] It is telling that Shakespeare's brother, Edmund, also an actor, was buried there in a prominent place in the choir, very likely at William's expense.[19] Between 1603 and 1605, Shakespeare was living on Silver Street, which means he probably attended St Olave's across the street.[20] Shakespeare would also have attended some services at court, when the Chamberlain's (and later King's) Men were called to perform there. James Shapiro notes one such instance, when the Chamberlain's Men performed at Richmond on February 20. It was an evening performance, so the players stayed for the night, and probably thus went to the Chapel Royal the next morning for the Ash Wednesday service and to hear the preaching of Lancelot Andrewes.[21]

Shakespeare, like everyone else, attended hundreds of church services throughout his life, with the Bible at the center of all of them: in the famous phrase of William Chillingworth, "the Bible, the Bible only I say, is the religion of Protestants," which echoes the principal of *sola scriptura* ("by scripture alone") championed by Martin Luther and early Reformers.[22] Yet the experience of the Bible in church was complex and various. Most obviously, there were the Proper Lessons, consisting of a reading from the Old Testament and one from the New Testament for each Morning and Evening Prayer, or, for Communion and feast days, a reading from the Epistles and one from the Gospels. (Early modern practice favored Morning and Evening Prayer, with Communion held infrequently; many communicated only once a year.)[23] All of these were prescribed in the Table of Lessons in

---

[17] Charles Nicholl, *The Lodger Shakespeare: His Life on Silver Street* (New York: Viking, 2008), 38–42.

[18] See Andrew Gurr's *ODNB* biographies of Phillips and Gough (in "Lord Chamberlain's Men").

[19] Bate, *Soul of the Age*, 42–3.

[20] Nicholl, *Lodger*, 58–60.

[21] James Shapiro, *A Year in the Life of William Shakespeare: 1599* (New York: Harper-Collins, 2005), 77–81.

[22] Patrick Collinson, *The Religion of Protestants: The Church in English Society 1559–1625* (Oxford: Clarendon Press, 1982), pp. vii–viii.

[23] Arnold Hunt, "The Lord's Supper in Early Modern England," *Past and Present*, 161 (1998), 39–83.

the Book of Common Prayer, and they were read from the large lectern Bibles present in most churches. Shakespeare would probably have heard these readings, from 1568 or relatively soon after, in the translation of the Bishops' Bible.

The Bishops' was intended by Parker to be the "official" Bible, so most churches would have used it. However, there was never an official injunction from either the Church or Queen Elizabeth I requiring all churches to acquire a copy, as there had been with Henry VIII's Great Bible. Such instructions would have been given at the diocesan level by individual bishops, so the speed and universality of acquisition probably varied from diocese to diocese. Records from after 1611 indicate the same process for the acquisition of the King James Bible, and, since some of these note churches still using the Great Bible or the Geneva Bible, the same must have been true before 1611 as well.[24] Such resistance to change increased with distance from London and other urban centers, however. In London, the parish churches Shakespeare attended, let alone the royal chapels, would certainly have used the Bishops', and the same was probably true in Stratford too, especially since the town fell under the jurisdiction of the Bishop of Worcester. Edwin Sandys held the see from 1559 to 1570 and Nicholas Bullingham from 1571 to 1576; both had been Marian exiles, and Bullingham was one of the Bishops' Bible translators.[25]

That Shakespeare did hear the Bishops' Bible in church is indicated by his occasional use of the translation in references or allusions in the plays. In *Love's Labours Lost*, for example, Shakespeare alludes twice to Romans 13:9–10, "Thou shalt love thy neighbour as thy selfe. Charitie worketh no ill to his neyghbour, therefore the fulfilling of the lawe is charitie." Longaville says to Dumaine in act 4, "Thy love is far from charity" (4.3.125). Later in the scene, Berowne picks up on his friend's phrase in his argument advocating breaking their vow to avoid women, and makes the biblical allusion more prominent:

> It is religion to be thus forsworn,
> For charity itself fulfills the law,
> And who can sever love from charity? (4.3.360–2)

---

[24] For this information I rely on a talk by Kenneth Fincham, "The King, the Bishops, the Parishes and the KJV," at the conference "An Anglo-American History of the KJV," Folger Shakespeare Library, Washington, September 30, 2011.

[25] See Patrick Collinson, "Edwin Sandys," and Julian Lock, "Nicholas Bullingham," *ODNB*. The situation of Holy Trinity, Stratford, was complex, since it was a collegiate church, with the appointment of its vicar under the control of the lord of the manor, who in the 1560s and 1570s was the staunchly Protestant Ambrose Dudley, Earl of Warwick. For a meticulous study of religion and church in sixteenth-century Stratford, see Robert Bearman, "The Early Reformation Experience in a Warwickshire Town: Stratford-upon-Avon, 1530–1580," *Midlands History* (2007), 68–109.

"Charity," from the Latin *caritas* (the word used in the Vulgate Bible), is used only in the Bishops' Bible; Geneva, following William Tyndale, has "love."[26] Shakespeare probably favored the Bishops' in this instance because it allowed him to play wittily (or have Berowne do so) with the difference between "love" and "charity."[27] Shakespeare alludes to the same passage from Romans, again in the Bishops' translation, in *The Merchant of Venice*, when Portia says facetiously of the Scottish lord that "he hath a neighborly charity in him" (1.2.74). Most of the time, however, when the specific translation can be identified (and many passages are indeed identical among the various translations), Shakespeare had the Geneva in mind.

Another feature of the Book of Common Prayer liturgy was the recitation of Psalms, according to a set calendar, with the entire book being completed each month. The question of which English translations of the Psalms Shakespeare heard in the services he attended is more difficult than one might think, since there were several possibilities. The Psalms of Miles Coverdale, from his Great Bible of 1539, were commonly bound together with the Book of Common Prayer, whether by printers or at the request of purchasers, and treated as a single book, though they were not adopted as fully part of it until 1662. Even after the publication of new Bible translations like the Bishops' and the King James, the Coverdale Psalms remained as the psalter attached to the Book of Common Prayer. Thus, when at Morning Prayer it is instructed that "Then shal folowe certeyn Psalmes in order, as they bene appoincted," it could be the Coverdale Psalms that were recited.[28] Yet, in many parishes, psalms were sung by the congregation, and the Coverdale translations, being in

---

[26] This was one of those translation choices that had featured in the battle between Tyndale and Sir Thomas More. Tyndale preferred words, like "love," which were both plain and free of associations with the Established Church. More defended the traditional language, based on the Vulgate, and thought "love" would encourage lasciviousness. See *A dyaloge of syr Thomas More knyghte... Wyth many othere thyngys touching the pestylent sect of Luther and Tyndale, by the tone bygone in Sarony* [sic], *and by tother laboryed to be brought in to Englond* (London: [J. Rastell], 1529), fo. 80ᵛ.

[27] It may also be relevant that when people were in quarrels or disputes with neighbors or others, such that they were unfit to take Communion, they were described, and described themselves, as being "out of charity." See Hunt, "The Lord's Supper," 47–8. Also, for example, the visitation articles of the Bishop of London, John Aylmer, *Articles to be enquired of within the dioces of London, in the visitation of the Reverend Father in God, John Bishop of London* (London: [T. Orwin], 1589), sig. A2ᵛ–A3ʳ. The question is asked whether anyone has been admitted to Communion, "any malicious person that is notoriously knowne and detected to bée out of charitie, or detected to haue done any open wrong to his neighbour by word or déede, without due reconciliation first made to the partie that is wronged." This usage seems ultimately to derive from the English Bible, in the fourteenth-century Wylciffite translation of the Vulgate for 1 Cor. 8:1 and 13:13 (see *OED*).

[28] *BCP* 105.

prose, were poorly suited to this purpose. As Luther, Calvin, and other reformers recognized, for good communal singing the Psalms needed to be rendered into metrical verse, like other popular song lyrics. By far the most popular metrical Psalms in England were those of the Sternhold and Hopkins Psalter, first printed complete in 1562, and then reprinted in vast numbers through the seventeenth century.[29] Like the Coverdale Psalter, the Sternhold and Hopkins Psalter was also frequently bound with the Book of Common Prayer, and also with English Bibles. Since the Bishops' Bible was the translation used in most churches for Bible readings, however, it is also possible that Psalms were read from that translation in those parishes too—that is, if the Psalms were read aloud rather than sung. Knowing exactly what went on in any one English church service is as difficult as knowing what precisely went on in the theater on any specific afternoon. The Book of Common Prayer, like many published playtexts, is like a script for performance.[30] Any actual performance may have varied considerably from the text, the official rubrics, in ways that we cannot now know.

In any case, the evidence from the language of the plays shows that Shakespeare was familiar with the Coverdale Psalter from the Book of Common Prayer. Indeed, Shakespeare alludes to the Psalms more often than to any other biblical book, and, as Naseeb Shaheen notes, "whenever it is possible to trace Shakespeare's reference to the Psalms to a particular version, it is almost always to the Psalter."[31] For instance, in *The Winter's Tale* 1.2.110–11, when Leontes says, "My heart dances | but not for joy, not joy," he alludes to Psalm 28: "Therefore my heart danceth for joy" (Ps. 28:8). Shakespeare has the Coverdale version in mind here, since Bishops' has "skippeth for joy" and Geneva "mine heart shal rejoice" (28:7). In another example, Psalm 39 has the memorable description of human life: "as it were a span long" (Ps. 39:6). Shakespeare alludes to this verse in two plays, *Timon of Athens* ("Timon is dead, who outstretched his

---

[29] See Hamlin, chs 1 and 2; Beth Quitslund, *The Reformation in Rhyme: Sternhold, Hopkins and the English Metrical Psalter, 1547–1603* (Aldershot and Burlington, VT: Ashgate, 2008).

[30] Playtexts are even more complicated, of course, since they may reflect the text of the play composed by the author or authors before the performance and, in the case of prompt copies, used for it, but they may also reflect later, post-performance, alterations of the text, or any combination thereof. The point, however, is that neither playtexts nor the Book of Common Prayer liturgies necessarily represent exactly what was performed on any specific occasion. Little is specified in terms of action or costume, and it seems to have been possible to insert sung music (including psalms) at several different points in the service. See Anthony M. Cummings, "Toward an Interpretation of the Sixteenth-Century Motet," *Journal of the American Musicological Society*, 34 (1981), 43–59.

[31] Shaheen, 20.

span," 5.3.3) and *Othello* ("A soldier's a man; | O, man's life's but a span," 2.3.71–2). Geneva and Bishops' have "hand breadth" rather than "span," so the source is Coverdale from the Book of Common Prayer. Similarly, the reference to the "horned heard" of "Basan" in *Antony and Cleopatra* 3.13.127–8 seems also specific to Coverdale, since the place name is spelled "Bashan" in both Bishop's and Coverdale. Yet it must be said that this is a distinction that would be barely audible, if at all (there is no way of ascertaining whether the spelling reflects a different pronunciation).

It is possible, even likely, that Shakespeare owned a copy of the Book of Common Prayer, bound with the Coverdale Psalms. Just as likely, however, is that the Coverdale Psalms were familiar to him from hearing them read and chanted in church.[32] Shakespeare also knew the Sternhold and Hopkins metrical Psalms (properly *The Whole Book of Psalms*), and these he almost certainly knew from singing them and hearing them sung.[33] In *Henry IV, Part 2*, Prince Hal says, "the spirits of the wise sit in the clouds and mock us," a phrase derived from Psalm 2, in which God in heaven laughs at the heathen kings. It is only Sternhold and Hopkins, however, that has the key verb, "mock":

> But he that in the heaven dwelleth,
>   their doinges will deride:
> And make them all as mocking stockes,
>   throughout the world so wide.[34]

In both Coverdale and Bishops', God will "laugh them to scorn" and "shall have them in derision." There are other instances where the word choices of Sternhold and Hopkins stuck in Shakespeare's ear, and even one place where a mangled version of the metrical Psalm itself is sung, when, in *The Merry Wives of Windsor*, Parson Evans scrambles Sternhold and Hopkins's Psalm 137 with Christopher Marlowe's seduction poem "The Passionate Shepherd to His Love":

---

[32] Peter le Huray suggests that churches may have used John Merbecke's *The Book of Common Prayer Noted* or perhaps tunes like those featured in it (Merbecke's volume was not reprinted after its initial publication in 1550). Parish records at Ludlow suggest the use of adaptations of the Sarum tunes for the Psalms. *Music and the Reformation in England 1549–1660* (London: Herbert Jenkins, 1967; repr. Cambridge: Cambridge University Press, 1978), 157–59. Hyun-Ah Kim agrees with the consensus that Merbecke was little used in the sixteenth century. *Humanism and the Reform of Sacred Music in Early Modern England: John Merbecke the Orator and* The Booke of Common Praier Noted *(1550)* (Aldershot and Birmingham, VT: Ashgate, 2008), 2.

[33] Shaheen notes a number of these allusions or borrowings, but see also Richard Waugaman, "The Sternhold and Hopkins *Whole Book of the Psalms* is a Major Source for the Works of Shakespeare," *N&Q* 56/4 (2009), 595–604.

[34] *The Whole Booke of Psalmes* (London: John Day, 1562), sig. Cii[r].

Melodious pirds sing madrigals
Whenas I sat in Pabylon,—
And a thousand vagram posies. (3.1.23–5)

The Psalm text is "When as we sate in Babilon, | the rivers round about." No original music for *Merry Wives* survives, but presumably the joke would depend on the audience recognizing not only the Psalm text, inappropriately inserted into a love song, but some form of the familiar church tune as well.[35]

Lessons and Psalms are the most visible (and audible) readings from the Bible in the Book of Common Prayer. But numerous other biblical excerpts are interspersed throughout the liturgies at various points. At the beginning of Morning Prayer, for instance, the minister is instructed to read "some one of these sentences of the Scriptures that folowe": Ezekiel 18, Psalm 51, Psalm 51, Psalm 51, Joel 2, Daniel 9, Jeremiah 2, Matthew 3, Luke 15, Psalm 142, and 1 John 1.[36] The Lord's Prayer (Matt. 6:9–13) is recited at both Morning and Evening Prayer. Among the sung canticles at Morning Prayer are the *Venite* (Ps. 95) and *Jubilate Deo* (Ps. 100), and at Evening Prayer the *Magnificat* (Luke 1:46–55) and *Nunc dimittis* (Luke 2:29–32). Other alternative canticles are biblical too: the *Benedicite* (from the apocryphal Song of the Three Children),[37] the *Benedictus* (Luke 1:68–79), and Psalms 93 and 67. The other major canticle, the *Te Deum laudamus* (traditionally ascribed to Saints Augustine and Anselm), contains many verses from biblical texts: "Holy, holy, holy, Lorde God of Sabaoth" (Isa. 6:3), "Thou syttest on the ryght hand of God" (Col. 3:1 and elsewhere in the Epistles), and "O Lorde have mercy upon us" (Ps. 123:3).[38] The same is true of much of the language of the liturgy. The opening of the responses ("O Lord, open thou our lippes," with the answer "And our mouthe shall shewe furth they praise") comes from Psalm 51:15.[39] The address of the opening prayer of Morning Prayer, "Dearly beloved Brethren," echoes Phillipians 4:1, and the later phrase, "when we assemble

---

[35] Though it has not survived, there may have been a familiar tune for Marlowe's poem/song as well, and Evans may have blended tunes as well as words. For more on Marlowe's "Passionate Shepherd," see Hannibal Hamlin, "Replying to Raleigh's 'The Nymph's Reply': Allusion, Anti-Pastoral, and Four Centuries of Pastoral Invitations," in Christopher M. Armitage (ed.), *Sir Walter Raleigh: Literary and Visual Raleigh*, forthcoming from Manchester University Press.

[36] *BCP* 102–3.

[37] This was part of the book of Daniel (3:24–90) in the Septuagint version, but it was not in the Hebrew/Aramaic text. Roman Catholic Bibles, originating with Jerome's Vulgate, followed the Septuagint, but Protestants placed the Song in the Apocrypha.

[38] *BCP* 106–7.   [39] *BCP* 104.

and mete together, to rendre thankes," draws on Matthew 18:20.[40] When the congregation admits in the General Confession that "we have erred and straied from thy waies, lyke lost shepe,"[41] the metaphor is from the Parable of the Lost Sheep (Matt. 18:12–14). The third collect in Evening Prayer begins, "Lyghten our darckenesse, wee beseche thee (O Lorde),"[42] which is adapted from David's song in Samuel 22 (22:29).

The other major services in the Book of Common Prayer are also rich in biblical excerpts. The Communion Service begins with the reading of the ten commandments from Exodus 20, and the Communion proper includes the repetition of Jesus's words at the Passover in Matthew 26:26–9 (and other gospels). The statement in the Prayer of Humble Access, "we be not worthy so muche as to gather up the crommes under thy Table,"[43] echoes several passages in the gospels: the woman of Canaan who compares herself to a dog eating up Jesus's words like crumbs fallen from a table (Matt. 15:27 and Mark 7:28), and the poor man Lazarus who desires to eat the crumbs fallen from the rich man's table (Luke 16:21). In addition, the rite of Baptism includes the story in Mark 10 of Jesus, saying "Suffre the lytle children to come unto me." Also, the marriage service refers to Christ's first miracle at the wedding at Cana, Paul's praise of marriage, God's joining of Adam and Eve, and the married life of Isaac and Rebecca, and before the communion the minister reads a long pastiche of Ephesians 5, Colossians 3, and 1 Peter 3.[44] And the Burial Service begins with verses from John and Job, followed by a prayer that paraphrases Job 14:1–2, "Man that is borne of a woman, hathe but a shorte tyme to lyve, and is full of miserye: he commeth up, and is cut doune lyke a floure."[45] The Lesson in the Burial Service is 1 Corinthians 15: "Now is Christ risen from the dead, and become the first-fruits of them that slept." The Litany ("to be used upon Sondaies, Wednesdaies, and Fridayes, and at other tymes, when it shalbe commanded by the Ordinarye") incorporates, without citation, many Bible verses, as when the precentor says, "In al tyme of our tribulacion, in al tyme of our welth, in the house of death, and in the daye of judgement," to which the people add, "good Lorde deliver us."[46] In Judges, god commands the Israelites who have turned to false gods, "Go, and crye unto the gods which ye have chosen: let them save you in the time of your tribulation." The Israelites respond: "We have sinned: do thou unto us whatsoever please thee: onely we pray thee to deliver us this day" (Judg. 10:14–15). The prayer to "defende and provide for the fatherless children and widowes" takes language from James 1:27:

[40] *BCP* 103. [41] *BCP* 103. [42] *BCP* 114.
[43] *BCP* 136. [44] *BCP* 162–4.
[45] *BCP* 171. [46] *BCP* 118.

"Pure religion and undefiled before God, even the Father, is this, to visit the fatherless, and widdowes in their adversitie."[47] And the prayer "By thyne agonie and bloudy sweate, by the crosse and passion, by thy precious deathe and burial, by thy glorious resurrection, and ascension, and by the commynge of the holy Ghoste" is a précis of the New Testament, from Luke's description of Christ in Gethsemane—"being in an agonie, he prayed more earnestly: and his sweate was like droppes of blood" (Luke 22:44)—to Pentecost in Acts 2, where, as the Geneva headnote puts it, "The Apostles having received the holie Gost, make their hearers astonished."[48]

Like any other churchgoing Englishman, Shakespeare knew these services well, key phrases and passages clearly having been embedded in his memory. There are dozens of allusions to the marriage service in his plays, and to the rites of baptism and burial as well.[49] R. Chris Hassell, Jr, has argued that Shakespeare and his fellow dramatists were highly aware of the coincidences of their performances with the church calendar and its liturgies. This was especially true during the court celebrations of the twelve days of Christmas, which featured plays among other revels, but which also included the services for the major religious feast days: Christmas (December 25) and Epiphany or Twelfth Night (January 6) at either end, but also St Stephen's Day (December 26), St John the Apostle and Evangelist's (December 27), Holy Innocents' Day (December 28), and the Circumcision (January 1) in between. Depending upon the annual calendar, one or two of the days between December 25 and January 6 were also Sundays, when regular services would be held. *Measure for Measure* and *King Lear* were performed at court on St Stephen's Day (1604 and 1606 respectively), *The Comedy of Errors* on Holy Innocents' (1604 at court, and also at Grey's Inn in 1594). *A Midsummer Night's Dream* was performed in 1604 at New Year's (the Circumcision).[50] *Twelfth Night*, with its battle between Carnival and Lent, is obviously associated with Epiphany. Hassel notes the relevance of the proper lessons for Epiphany to Malvolio's imprisonment in a "dark house." At Matins, the First Lesson was from Isaiah 60, "For beholde, darkenes shal cover ye earth, and grosse darkenes the people," and at Evensong Isaiah 49, "That thou maiest say to ye prisoners, Go forthe: and to them that are in darkenes, Shewe your selves."[51] The players at court, at whichever palace the queen happened to be, attended services at the Chapel Royal, and the playwrights (Jonson, Middleton, and others, as well as

---

[47] *BCP* 119. [48] *BCP* 118. [49] Shaheen, 51–6; Noble, *passim*.
[50] R. Chris Hassell, *Renaissance Drama & the English Church Year* (Lincoln, NE: University of Nebraska Press, 1979), 22–53.
[51] Hassell, *Renaissance Drama*, 84–5.

Shakespeare) sometimes also wrote with an awareness of the liturgical–biblical contexts in which their plays would be performed. Listening to the related Bible readings in worship services informed and enriched the audience's experience of hearing the plays.

The Bible was not encountered only in the liturgy, however. Despite the ravages of Reformation iconoclasts, some images derived from Bible stories survived in English churches.[52] Ironically, though, biblical images were more common outside of churches than inside them. For example, tapestries often depicted biblical characters and stories, and these were well represented in the massive collection of Henry VIII. He had sets of tapestries telling the story of David and Bathsheba, the history of Abraham, the Passion of Christ, and the life of St Paul.[53] For the less wealthy, painted cloths served the same twin functions of keeping out cold air and decorating a room. Such cloths were common, though almost none has survived.[54] One pair that does, no doubt because it was painted on leather, consists of scenes from Esther.[55] Four remarkable painted cloths by the artist John Balechouse survive in Hardwick Hall, Derbyshire, the home of Bess of Hardwick, Countess of Shrewsbury. Painted *c.*1600–1, they depict in vivid detail and in colors still rich the conversion of Paul on the road to Damascus and other episodes from Acts.[56] These are from the high end of the market, however. According to Tessa Watt, the four most popular Bible stories for painted cloths in the late sixteenth century were Susanna and the Elders (the apocryphal addition to Daniel), Tobias (from Tobit), Dives and Lazarus (Luke 16:19–31), and the Prodigal Son (Luke 10:11–32). A Prodigal Son painting is among the possessions of Mistress Quickly at the Boar's Head Tavern in *2 Henry IV* and another decorates Falstaff's room at the Garter Inn in *The Merry Wives of Windsor*. The story was also painted on a series of wall panels that still

---

[52] Alison Shell, *Shakespeare and Religion* (London: Arden Shakespeare, 2011), 5–6, remarks, "a surprising number of statues, stained glass windows and wall paintings had survived the waves of iconoclasm under Henry VIII and Edward VI," citing Margaret Aston, *England's Iconoclasts* (Oxford and New York: Clarendon Press, 1988).

[53] Thomas P. Campbell, *Henry VIII and the Art of Majesty: Tapestries at the Tudor Court* (New Haven and London: Yale University Press, 2007).

[54] For a late-seventeenth-century example in the collection of the Shakespeare Birthplace Trust, illustrating the marriage of Isaac and Rebecca, see the feature in *Shakespeare's World in 100 Objects* <http://findingshakespeare.co.uk/shakespeares-world-in-100-objects-number-15-a-painted-cloth> (accessed December 15, 2011).

[55] The set (*c.*1600) was sold from Walsingham Abbey in 1916, but came to the Abbey from an unknown country house. Anthony Wells-Cole, *Art and Decoration in Elizabethan and Jacobean England: The Influence of Continental Prints, 1558–1625* (New Haven and London: Yale University Press, 1997), 97–8, fig. 127.

[56] Wells-Cole, *Art and Decoration*, 275–89, figs 477, 482, 487, 494. As Wells-Cole's volume makes clear, Hardwick Hall preserves many examples of biblical domestic arts and crafts, including embroideries, wall hangings, marble reliefs, and decorative plasterwork.

survive at Knightsland Farm in Hertfordshire (*c*.1600). Scenes from Dives and Lazarus were painted on two panels at Pittleworth Manor, Hampshire (1580), and in *1 Henry IV* Falstaff's description of his soldiers as "ragged as Lazarus in the painted cloth" indicates the subject's popularity.[57] In Francis Beaumont's *The Knight of the Burning Pestle*, the grocer's wife asks her husband if the painted hanging at the theater (where they both supposedly are) is "the confutation of Saint *Paul*." The grocer says it is actually "*Raph* and *Lucrece*." She confuses "confutation" with "conversion" (as he does "Raph" and "Rape"); she gets the image wrong too, but presumably the exchange suggests the subject might be Paul, or that she had seen such a cloth elsewhere.[58] Susanna and the Elders was a titillating subject, with the voyeuristic old men spying on the naked maiden, and it was featured in a set of painted cloths at Vaston Manor in Wiltshire (now lost), and on wall panels at Little Moreton Hall in Cheshire (*c*.1575?). In George Wilkins's 1607 play *The Miseries of Enforced Marriage*, a thieving butler describes his quaking companions as "more miserable then one of the wicked Elders picturd in the painted cloth."[59] The White Swan Hotel in Stratford, a tavern in Shakespeare's day, still has wall paintings of the story of Tobit (*c*.1570–80).[60] A carved and painted panel from Yeovil in Somerset (*c*.1600) depicts both Adam and Eve, with the serpent and the forbidden tree, and Abraham and Isaac.[61] The Victoria and Albert Museum has a set of twenty-five painted panels featuring Old Testament stories, including the Fall, Moses and Joshua, and Ezekiel and Elias (*c*.1600). Tara Hamling suggests they once formed part of the paneling of a gallery.[62] A stunning set of bed valances from late-sixteenth-century England or Scotland at the Metropolitan Museum of Art represent the story of Adam and Eve in several scenes.[63]

---

[57] Tessa Watt, *Cheap Print and Popular Piety, 1550–1640* (Cambridge: Cambridge University Press, 1991), 202–11. Dives and Lazarus are also featured on a frieze on the west front of Lincoln Cathedral. See <http://www.beyond-the-pale.org.uk/zxMondonedo.htm#lincoln> (accessed December 2, 2011).

[58] Cited in Andrew Gurr, *Playgoing in Shakespeare's London*, 3rd edn (Cambridge: Cambridge University Press, 2004), 123.

[59] George Wilkins, *The miseries of inforst mariage* (London: George Vincent, 1607), sig. F2ʳ.

[60] Watt, *Cheap Print*, 209.

[61] Tara Hamling, *Decorating the "Godly" Household: Religious Art in Post-Reformation Britain* (New Haven and London: Yale University Press, 2010), 242–3.

[62] Hamling, *Decorating*, 180–2.

[63] Andrew Morrall and Melinda Watt (eds), *English Embroidery from the Metropolitan Museum of Art, 1580–1700* (New Haven and London: Yale University Press, 2008), 258–9. The images are based on Bernard Solomon's woodcuts in *Quadrins Historiques de la Bible* (Lyons, 1553), an English edition of which was published in the same year. Morrall and Watt (pp. 264–5, fig. 74) also include a multicolored embroidered book cover (*c*.1607) for a Bible and Book of Common Prayer that features Adam and Eve and the serpent with the four rivers of Eden and various animals (including a unicorn).

Fig. 1.1. Biblical subjects were commonly depicted on early modern domestic objects. Here, the flight of the holy family into Egypt appears on a hard-wearing wool cushion cover. Joseph, on the right, is shown with his carpentry tools, while Mary and the infant Jesus ride a donkey. (Tapestry woven in wool, silk, and metal thread; Sheldon Tapestry Workshop, England, 1600–15.) © Victoria and Albert Museum, London.

The Victoria and Albert collections testify to the ubiquity of biblical images in sixteenth- and seventeenth-century English culture. Cushion cover tapestries (1600–10 and 1600–15) feature the Prodigal Son and the Flight into Egypt (see Fig. 1.1), a needlework lace panel (1600–50) shows the temptation of Adam and Eve, and an oak column (1600–20), possibly a newel post, is carved with Adam, Eve, and the serpent (see Fig. 1.2).[64] Another embroidered cushion cover shows the Crucifixion, along with

---

[64] Victoria and Albert Museum numbers T.1-1933, T.191-1926, T.17-1909, and W.25-1959, respectively. Viewed online <http://collections.vam.ac.uk> (accessed October 1, 2008).

Fig. 1.2. Adam, Eve, and the Serpent are carved on a column, possibly part of a staircase newel post. Eve holds an apple in her right hand, while her left hand pulls the long hair of the serpent, who has the head of a woman. On the reverse, an elderly, bearded Adam ("Old Adam") holds a spade. (Oak, carved, with gesso and traces of pigmentation; Devon, England, 1600–20.) © Victoria and Albert Museum, London.

the citation "Mark 15" (late sixteenth century).[65] Biblical images could appear on almost any kind of everyday object. A wooden knife sheath survives dated 1602 inscribed with six illustrations of the parable of the Prodigal Son on one side, and the Works of Mercy on the other. A sixteenth-century oak chest (*c*.1575) is decorated with both classical and

---

[65] Hamling, *Decorating*, 213, fig. 148. Fig. 146 (p. 212) shows a long cushion cover from the late sixteenth century, now at the Shakespeare Birthplace Trust in Stratford, showing several scenes from the story of Joseph.

biblical figures: Lucretia, Mars, and Judith. A German stoneware jug from the same century shows the Feast of Herod with Salome presenting the head of John the Baptist.[66] An early sixteenth-century stamped brass bowl depicts the Fall. It was made in Germany but imported into England.[67] Domestic objects and decoration featured not only biblical images but texts as well, perhaps particularly among the more godly Protestants. For instance, a set of sixteenth-century wooden trenchers is inscribed with Bible verses or paraphrases, like "Sette an order in thy house for thou dye and not lyve leves [live lives]" (2 Kgs 20:1 and Isa. 38:1).[68] Bible verses were also painted on walls for domestic edification; the Ten Commandments were especially popular.[69] Tara Hamling cites Richard Braithwaite's *The English Gentleman* (1630), which urges that God's word be written "upon the posts of thine house, and upon thy gates," paraphrasing Deuteronomy 6:4–9.[70]

Prints were also used to decorate the house or its gates. They were tacked to the walls of taverns, pinned up at home, and on display for anyone to see at the many booksellers in Paul's Churchyard.[71] These circulated widely and in quantity, though they are difficult to track today. Not all prints were entered in the Stationers' Register, since rolling presses (as opposed to letter presses) were unregulated.[72] Given that they were loose single sheets of paper, many perhaps cheaply made, it is not

---

[66] These last three artifacts are in the collection of the Shakespeare Birthplace Trust and are featured in *Shakespeare's World in 100 Objects* (see above n. 54). For more on pottery, see Andrew Morrall, "Protestant Pots: Morality and Social Ritual in the Early Modern Home," *Journal of Design History*, 15/4 (2002), 263–73. The pots Morrall examines are made in Germany, but these were often exported to England. He describes the variety of biblical themes on pottery, many copied from prints, which "bears out how deeply this didactic culture of vernacular Bible reading entered into the mentality and everyday experience of the age, and the extent to which the Bible provided exemplary metaphors for many areas of public and personal experience" (p. 268).

[67] Victoria and Albert Museum number M.336-1924. See above n. 64.

[68] Mary Anne Caton, "'Fables and fruit trenchers teach as much': English Banqueting Trenchers, c.1585–1662," *Magazine Antiques* (June 1, 2006). Caton's title cites a line from John Donne's verse epistle "To Sir Henry Goodyere," in which he offers Goodyere religious lessons that he then admits are commonplace, even on "fruit trenchers."

[69] Hamling (*Decorating*, 106–8) describes the Ten Commandments and psalm verses painted above a fireplace in an upstairs room in a house in Canterbury (c.1550s), the same carved on a screen over an entrance way at Hangleton Manor in Sussex (sixteenth century), and the Commandments, illustrated by biblical characters who violated them, in a town house in Hereford (c.1600). See also Adam Fox, *Oral and Literate Culture in England, 1500–1700* (Oxford: Clarendon Press, 2000), who notes the practice of writing proverbial, especially biblical, wisdom on walls (pp. 146–7).

[70] Hamling, *Decorating*, 106.

[71] Michael Hunter, 'Introduction', in Hunter (ed.), *Printed Images in Early Modern Britain: Essays in Interpretation* (Farnham and Burlington, VT: Ashgate, 2010), 1.

[72] Malcolm Jones, *The Print in Early Modern England: An Historical Oversight* (New Haven and London: Yale University Press, 2010), 1–2.

surprising that few of them survive. Moreover, prints circulated easily, and London print shops sold continental prints as well, though which ones, how many, and when, is not known.[73] Malcolm Jones lists the biblical prints that were recorded in the Stationers' Register: from the sixteenth century, *The Creation of the Worlde*, *the pycture of Saloman the wyse*, *The story of the iii children*, *the historye of the prodigall chylde*, *The pycture of Paule the appostell*, and *a picture made upon the vth of saynte Pawle to the Romaynes*. All of these were printed in the 1560s by the Huguenot printer Giles Godet; only the series of Prodigal Son woodcuts survives, in a single copy at the Bibliothèque Nationale.[74] An engraved print of Jonah sitting under the gourd, by Philips Galle after Maarten van Heemskerck, was inserted by an early English owner into a Geneva Bible now in the Huntington Library.[75] Many more biblical prints circulated and disappeared without a trace. One that survives is a Nativity, again from the 1560s, by John Bettes the Elder. Like many such images, Bettes's had a long afterlife, included in another larger image in 1631, and then reappearing in various forms into the eighteenth century.[76] Printed images were also included in books, including some Bibles, like the lavishly illustrated Bishops' Bible.[77] John Day's *Christian Prayers and Meditations* (London, 1569) included many Old and New Testament images in the borders around the text. Some of these seemed rather Catholic (including the Pietà and God represented as an old man), so they were altered in Richard Day's 1578 *Book of Christian Prayers* (many times reprinted) but the number of images was not reduced.[78] The plaster decorations of biblical subjects that were in vogue in later seventeenth-century homes were often based on earlier printed images like those in *Christian Prayers*, and continental volumes like *Vita, Passio, et Resurrectio Jesu Christi* (Antwerp: Adriaen Collaert, 1566).[79]

---

[73] Jones, *Print*, 3.   [74] Jones, *Print*, 401–2, app. IV.
[75] Femke Molekamp, "'Of the Incomparable Treasure of the Holy Scriptures': The Geneva Bible in the Early Modern Household," in Matthew Dimmock and Andrew Hadfield (eds), *Literature and Popular Culture in Early Modern England* (Farnham and Burlington, VT: Ashgate, 2009), 121–36, 130. The print is dated 1562.
[76] Jones, *Print*, 176–7, and fig. 159.
[77] Aston, "Bishops' Bible Illustrations." The first edition (1568) featured 124 woodcuts throughout the text, derived ultimately from Virgil Solis, *Biblische Figuren des Alten und Newen Testaments* (Frankfurt, 1560). The 1572 edition replaced these with a smaller number of images, in a larger format, and from a different source.
[78] On these books and their images, see Richard L. Williams, "Censorship and Self-Censorship in Late Sixteenth-Century English Book Illustration," in Hunter (ed.), *Printed Images*, 43–63.
[79] Tara Hamling, "Guides to Godliness: From Print to Plaster," in Hunter (ed.), *Printed Images*, 65–85.

Another aspect of biblical culture, both visual and aural, was popular ballads based on Bible stories. As Watt points out, the Protestant authors of these ballads were aiming "to replace the saints' lives and miracles of popish piety with characters and events from the Old Testament."[80] She notes ballads about "Patient Job," "David and Bathsheba," the "Proverbs of Salomon," "Jeffa [Jephtha] Judge of Israell," "Tobias of Ninive," "Aballett of Adam and Eve," "The overthrow of proud Holofernes, and the triumph of virtuous Queene Judith," and "The prayer of Daniel turned into metre and applied unto our tyme."[81] Ballads about New Testament stories were popular too, such as "When Jesus Christ was 12," "Joseph and Mary," "Resurrection of Christ," and others featuring the familiar stories of "the excellent parable of the prodigal child" and "Dives and Lazarus." As the inclusion of "David and Bathsheba" might suggest, the appeal of some of these ballads may have been less than perfectly spiritual. Not surprisingly, there was also a ballad of "Susanna." These broadsides were printed, and their visual appeal was sometimes enhanced by illustrative woodcuts, as in the many-times-reprinted ballad of Tobias, which featured not only Tobias himself but his dog.[82] As Bruce R. Smith points out, illustrated ballads, just like prints, could substitute for painted wall cloths or panels.[83] In Ben Jonson's *Bartholomew Fair* (1614), for instance, the young and foolish country gentleman Cokes asks, "O sister, do you remember the ballads over the nursery chimney at home o' my own pasting up? There be brave pictures!"[84] But ballads were sung and heard as well as read and viewed, and once they passed into the singer's memory, they ceased to be printed texts at all. The soundscape of early modern England, bustling London especially, must have included a good deal of biblical singing. In addition to biblical ballads, English Protestants sang metrical psalms too, not just at church, but on the way to and from services, at home, and even in the streets.[85] That Shakespeare was part of this aural culture is clear from his ballad peddler Autolycus in *The Winter's Tale*, from Parson Evans's muddling of Psalm 137 and the song of

---

[80] Watt, *Cheap Print*, 116.
[81] Watt, *Cheap Print*, 333–44, apps A–C. See also Green, *Print and Protestantism*, 454–8.
[82] David Norton observes that this is the only domestic pet in the Bible. It may be the popularity of this story that led to the tradition of naming dogs Toby (actually a popular early modern spelling of Tobit). Norton (ed.), *The Bible: King James Version with The Apocrypha* (London: Penguin Books, 2006), 1902.
[83] Bruce R. Smith, *The Acoustic World of Early Modern England: Attending to the O-Factor* (Chicago and London: University of Chicago Press, 1999), 168. Jones, 5–6.
[84] Ben Jonson, *Bartholomew Fair*, ed. G. R. Hibbard, New Mermaids (London: A&C Black; New York: W. W. Norton, 1977; repr. 1994), 3.5.43–5, cited in Watts, *Cheap Print*, 148–9.
[85] See Hamlin, 29–41.

Marlowe's "Passionate Shepherd," and from his many references to ballads in other plays.

Shakespeare heard the Bible but he read it too. He probably read it first as a schoolboy at King Edward IV grammar school in Stratford. Though no written evidence for Shakespeare's enrollment survives, the scholarly consensus is that this was where he was educated. T. W. Baldwin, who explored Elizabethan education extensively, notes the prominent role of the Bible in the boys' learning of Latin and Greek. In the grammar school curriculum lower forms, focused on Latin, Shakespeare would have labored over classical texts, as well as Proverbs, Ecclesiastes, Ecclesiasticus, and Psalms, translating them into Latin from the English of the Bishops' Bible.[86] Erasmus had recommended these books in his *Institutio Principis Christiani*, as did Thomas Elyot and John Cheke, and this accorded with the curricula at St Paul's and Winchester, which were widely influential. Gabriel Harvey described these books (minus Ecclesiasticus) among the typical reading of English schoolboys. As Wisdom books, they served to instill biblical values as well as aid in learning Latin grammar, and they had the merit of consisting largely of short pithy phrases. They were the biblical equivalent of classical sententiae. Baldwin suggests that Shakespeare read Genesis and Isaiah at this stage too, also among the books listed by Harvey, and among those to which Shakespeare most often alludes.[87] In further evidence of Shakespeare's early biblical reading and translating, Baldwin adds that Shakespeare's allusions to "the books of Solomon are prevailingly from the Bishops' Bible."[88] This corresponds to Noble's argument that early in Shakespeare's career he alludes largely to the Bishops' and later to the Geneva.[89] He even suggests Shakespeare might have owned a Bishops' quarto; they were available until 1584. Noble's evidence is thin, however, and Shaheen takes a more skeptical approach. The overwhelming majority of Shakespeare's allusions are not identifiable exclusively as either version. Yet even without the claim for Shakespeare's indebtedness to the Bishops' version, Baldwin's evidence for the centrality of the Bible to grammar school education is conclusive.

More intriguing are Baldwin's examples of Shakespeare alluding not just to the English of the Bishop's or Geneva, but to Latin translations of the Bible, and to problems in translation that he seems likelier to have

---

[86] T. W. Baldwin, *William Shakspere's Small Latine and Lesse Greeke* (Urbana, IL: University of Illinois Press, 1944), i. 682–5, ii. 707; online reprint http://durer.press.illinois.edu/baldwin/ (accessed September 21, 2012). See here i. 684–5.

[87] Baldwin, *William Shakspere's Small Latine*, i. 684–5. Baldwin bases this claim on Noble.

[88] Baldwin, *William Shakspere's Small Latine*, i. 687.

[89] Noble, 58–89.

learned from classroom exercises than from his own reading. For example, in *Love's Labours Lost*, the play in which Shakespeare's grammar school learning is most evident, Sir Nathaniel, the curate, indulges in pedantic badinage with Holofernes, the schoolmaster, saying at one point, "But, *omne bene*, say I, being of an old father's mind, | Many can brook the weather that love not the wind" (4.2.31–2). Baldwin, following Noble, reads the proverbial last line as a version of Ecclesiasticus 21:18, "As reedes that are set up on hie, can not abide the winde, so the feareful heart with foolish imaginacion can indure no feare." This is the Geneva version, however, the Bishops' being, as Baldwin notes, "not so likely to have suggested Shakspere's phraseology." Baldwin goes on to argue that "*omne bene*" is biblical too, an imperfect recollection (either Nathaniel's or Shakespeare's, from his youthful exercises) of Mark 7:37 in the Vulgate: "*Bene omnia fecit*" ("he hath done all thyngs well" in Bishops').[90] This seems unlikely, since the phrase "*omne bene*" appears in a 1590 sermon by William Burton as a stock ministerial formula for the forgiveness of sin, as well as in the anonymous *The Taming of a Shrew*, as Sly praises his ale, surely mocking the confessional formula.[91]

Somewhat more plausible is an argument based on Nathaniel's approval of Holofernes's proposal to compose an epitaph on a dead deer. Holofernes asks if he "will hear an extemporal epitaph on the death of the deer." Nathaniel responds, "perge [proceed], so it shall please you to abrogate scurrility" (4.2.48–51). Baldwin's argument is as abtruse as anything Holofernes himself might come up with, but he is after all a schoolmaster, of a sort Shakespeare no doubt encountered. In Ephesians, Paul condemns a variety of wicked behaviors: 'But fornication, and all uncleannesse, or covetousnesse, let it not be once named among you, as it becommeth saintes: Neither fylthynesse, neither foolyshe talking, neither jestyng, which are not comely: but rather gevyng of thankes' (Eph. 5:3-4, Bishops'). For the Vulgate Bible, Jerome chose to translate the Greek word *eutrapelia* ("jestying" in the Bishops') as "*scurrilitas*." In his translation from the Greek, the 1565 *Novum testamentum*, Beza took issue with Jerome's choice, noting Erasmus's substitution of "*urbanitas*" in his Latin New Testament; Beza decided instead on "*dicacitas*."[92] The

---

[90] Baldwin, *William Shakspere's Small Latine*, ii. 627–9.
[91] See William Burton, *A sermon preached in the Cathedrall Church in Norwich, the xxi. day of December, 1589* (London, 1590), sig. A3ʳ: "But if he wil sooth them vp in their sins with an omne bene, or a nihil dicit, he is the best preacher that euer they heard"; and anon., *A pleasant conceited historie, called The taming of a shrew* (London: Peter Short to be sold by Cutbert Burbie, 1594).
[92] Beza, *Novum testamentum* (Stephanus, 1565), part 2, 397, and Bishops' as cited in Baldwin, *William Shakspere's Small Latine*, ii. 631.

question is, what exactly is Paul condemning? Thomas Cooper defined these three terms as, respectively, "Saucie scoffyng," "pleasant jesting," and "Scoffyng or bourdyng" (to bourd is to mock).[93] Beza, who seems to have been relying on the definitions in Ambrogio Calepino's *Cornucopiae* (according to Baldwin the most widely used Latin dictionary at the time), felt the Vulgate was too narrow but Erasmus too broad. Baldwin's argument is that Nathaniel is not simply echoing Ephesians here—the curate following Paul in his injunction to "abrogate scurrility"—but also this "disputed point in translation," something Shakespeare learned from his early Latin lessons.[94] Indeed, the only way "abrogate scurrility" could be perceived as an allusion to Ephesians 5:4 is if one has the Vulgate's "*scurrilitas*" in mind, since the English Bibles, beginning with Tyndale, all have "jesting."[95] The "point" seems impossibly erudite for a schoolboy today, but the argument seems less stretched when one knows that Greek instruction, in upper forms, included the translation of the New Testament, and that Beza's Latin translation (with notes) was probably used for the purpose.[96] Shakespeare may have had "small Greek," according to the university-educated and learned Ben Jonson, but what Greek he had was rooted in the New Testament, and the translation studies of an Elizabethan schoolboy were remarkably sophisticated by today's standards. The lesson from Baldwin most valuable to this study is that parts of the Bible were embedded in Shakespeare's memory from working over them, in several languages, in school. Robert Miola also notes that the practice of oral repetition involved in the rote learning of the grammar schools, along with the habit of reading aloud, "developed acute inner ears that could appreciate sonic effects which are lost on moderns." This "aural sensitivity led to delight in wordplay of all kinds, repartee, double

---

[93] Thomas Cooper, *Thesaurus linguae Romanae & Britannicae* (London: [Henry Denham], 1578), s.v.

[94] Baldwin, *William Shakspere's Small Latine*, ii. 630–5.

[95] As so often, however, Shakespeare's memory of this passage from Ephesians might be mediated by its use or adaptation in other non-biblical works. Robert Parsons's *Christian Directory*, for instance, a book that Shakespeare read (see Ch. 8), writes of men hindered from resolution by "slothe, negligence, and hardnes of harte." "These men praye never. Christs Apostle saieth, that covetousnes, uncleanesse, or scurrilitie should not be so muche as once named amongest Christians." The note in the margin provides the citation, "Ephe. 5." *Robert Persons, SJ, The Christian Directory (1582)*, ed. Victor Houliston (Leiden, Boston, and Cologne: Brill, 1998), 304, 313.

[96] Baldwin, *William Shakspere's Small Latine*, ii. 625–6, 636, 645. Baldwin notes the remarkable coincidence that the University of Illinois copy of a 1587 London edition of Beza contains a manuscript note of ownership placing it in Stratford in the seventeenth century. Baldwin indulges in a bit of (indirect) fancy: "Since it was printed in Vautrollier's shop, with Richard Field, Shakspere's Stratford schoolmate, working upon it, some romancer may put it in Shakspere's pocket on his first return to Stratford after he had been chased away for deer-stealing" (ii., 634–5, no. 39).

entendre, puns, and quibbles."[97] Miola does not include it, but one of the principal kinds of wordplay reading aloud encouraged was allusion, especially for a playwright creating new texts, also to be read aloud.

One of the many aids to the reader provided in the Geneva Bible was a page-long guide called "Howe to take profite in reading of the holy Scriptures," by one T. Grashop.[98] Grashop advises the reader how to approach the biblical text itself, but especially interesting is his final injunction: "Take opportunity to: Read interpreters[,] Conferre with such as can open the Scriptures[,] Heare preaching." So, despite all of the helps in the Geneva Bible itself—summaries, marginalia, tables—the reader is urged to go elsewhere too for insights into its interpretation. Writers and publishers made sure the reader did not need to go far, producing numerous paraphrases, commentaries, concordances, sermons, and other aids. The early modern Bible was, to borrow a term from biblical scholar James Kugel, an "interpreted Bible."[99] For Protestants, the Word was essential to both salvation and a godly life, but the Word required interpretation, and interpretation required supplementary words. The scriptural justification for the necessity of interpretation and of authoritative interpreters was cited by Grashop. In Acts 8:26–40, the apostle Philip is commanded by an angel to travel to Gaza, where he meets an Ethiopian, a eunuch of Queen Candace, who is sitting in his chariot reading Isaiah. Philip asks him if he understands what he is reading, and the Ethiopian replies, "How can I, except I had a guide?" Philip then "preached unto him Jesus" and baptized him. Grashop is suggesting that all Bible readers are in the position of the Ethiopian eunuch, in need of an interpretative guide.

The proliferation of interpretative aids might be seen as an attempt by the clergy to control lay reading, which might lead in dangerous directions

---

[97] Robert S. Miola, *Shakespeare's Reading* (Oxford and New York: Oxford University Press, 2000), 2–3, cited in Mark Robson, "Looking with Ears, Hearing with Eyes: Shakespeare and the Ear of the Early Modern," *EMLS* 7/1 (2001), 10.1–23.

[98] Several scholars have been interested in Grashop's guidelines, including William H. Sherman, *Used Books: Marking Readers in Renaissance England* (Philadelphia: University of Pennsylvania, 2008), 73; Peter Stallybrass, "Books and Scrolls: Navigating the Bible," in Jennifer Andersen and Elizabeth Sauer (eds), *Books and Readers in Early Modern England: Material Studies* (Philadelphia: University of Pennsylvania Press, 2002), 42–79; and Patrick Collinson, "'The Coherence of the Text: How it Hangeth Together': The Bible in Reformation England," in W. P. Stephens (ed.), *The Bible, the Reformation, and the Church* (Sheffield: Sheffield Academic Press, 1995), 84–108. Collinson (p. 92, n. 22) notes that neither he nor Christopher Hill was able to find anything out about Grashop, though he might have been connected to the Canterbury schoolmaster John Gresshop. Lewis Lupton provides the most information about Grashop, assuming the references he cites (to Gresshope, Greshop, Gresshop, Gressop) are to the same man. He may have preached in London and may have been in Geneva with the Marian exiles. Lupton, *A History of the Geneva Bible*, vi. *Hope's Anchor* (London: Olive Tree, 1974), 14–16.

[99] James Kugel, *The Bible As It Was* (Cambridge, MA: Harvard University Press, 1997), 5.

if unchecked by the Church.[100] There is an element of this, certainly, as evidenced by the official injunctions to make available in churches not just English Bibles, but also Erasmus's *Paraphrases*, John Foxe's *Acts and Monuments*, and (after 1609), the works of Bishop Jewel.[101] Yet too much can be made of the argument that exegetical works were attempts at interpretative suppression. The Geneva notes, for instance, were written by exiles, hardly representatives of the Established Church. Many members of the establishment, James I included, saw them as inherently subversive, not conservative. Parker refers to them famously as the "bitter notes," and interpretive marginalia were purposely omitted from the Bishops' as well as the King James Version (KJV) of 1611.[102] Most of the Geneva notes, however, were not polemical one way or another, but genuinely aimed to guide the earnest reader through difficult passages, to offer alternative translations of problematic words or phrases, or to provide cross references to relevant passages elsewhere in the Bible. The same honest desire to help the reader was surely shared by many authors of commentaries and sermons. Moreover, these works were not imposed upon unwilling lay readers but eagerly sought out by them, as the number of editions suggests. Whether they had read Grashop or not, Bible readers were keen to "read interpreters," most obviously because they wanted to understand what they read. As stated earlier, evidence in his writing suggests that Shakespeare read not only the Geneva Bible but its notes. Later chapters will offer further arguments for Shakespeare's reading of biblical interpreters, insofar as it can be determined from the language of the plays.

Studies of Shakespeare's reading have seriously neglected religious books. Religious books constituted by far the majority of publications before and during Shakespeare's lifetime, and many of the bestsellers—even apart from Bibles and the Book of Common Prayer—were devoted to religious topics. It would be strange if such works were not part of his reading. Yet Henry R. D. Anders's *Shakespeare's Books: A Dissertation on Shakespeare's Reading and the Immediate Sources of his Works* (Berlin, 1904)

---

[100] Green, *Print and Protestantism*, 43–4, shows that, despite their different religious confessions, Henry VIII, Mary, and Elizabeth I all tried to control Bible reading through legislation and injunction.

[101] For the Bible and Erasmus, see *Injunctions geven by the Quenes Majestie anno Domini MD.LIX.* (London: Richard Jugge and John Cawood, 1559), sig Aiii^r (renewing the earlier injunctions of Edward VI). For Bancroft's effort to place Jewel in all churches, and earlier efforts along these lines by individual bishops, see John Craig, "John Jewel," *ODNB*. See also Fiona Kisby, "Books in London Parish Churches before 1603: Some Preliminary Observations," in Caroline M. Barron and Jenny Stratford (eds), *The Church and Learning in Later Medieval Society: Essays in Honour of R. B. Dobson*, Proceedings of the 1999 Harlaxton Symposium (Donington: SHAUN TYAS, 2002), 305–26.

[102] See Maurice Betteridge, "The Bitter Notes: The Geneva Bible and its Annotations," *SCJ* 14/1 (1983), 41–62.

has only one short chapter among eight on religious works, and this focuses entirely on the Bible, the Book of Common Prayer, and metrical Psalms. Virgil Whitaker's *Shakespeare's Use of Learning* (1953) makes a case for Shakespeare having read Hooker (along with the Bible), but is otherwise focused on secular works. Miola's *Shakespeare's Reading* (Oxford, 2000) does not include the Bible, since, as he writes, it is treated in another volume in the Oxford Shakespeare Topics. Yet that other volume, Steven Marx's *Shakespeare and the Bible*, also ignores biblical commentaries and religious literature. Jonathan Bate, in his recent *Biography of the Mind of William Shakespeare*, includes the Geneva Bible and the Book of Common Prayer among his speculative list of books on Shakespeare's shelves (or in his trunk), but not a single other religious title.[103] Bate notes that Shakespeare could have had access to books through his Stratford schoolmate Richard Field, who was apprenticed to the printer Thomas Vautrollier, and who later published Shakespeare's own *Venus and Adonis*. Vautrollier printed an Italian grammar that Shakespeare might have used, Bate notes, without also noting that the majority of Vautrollier's stock was composed of religious titles: among others, Calvin's *Institutes* (*The institution of the Christian religion*), Luther's *A right comfortable treatise containing fourteene pointes of consolation for them that labor and are laden*, and John Knox's *History of the Reformation*. Field himself, once he took over from Vautrollier, printed Luther's commentary on Galatians, Peter Moffett's on Proverbs, George Abbott's on Jonah, William Perkins's lecture on Revelation 1–3, Hugh Broughton's translation and exposition of Daniel, Guillaume du Vair's biblical meditations (*The holy love of heavenly wisdom*), Henry Lok's verse paraphrase of Ecclesiastes, and sermons by Henry Smith, George Gifford, and William Burton. Shakespeare could have obtained a copy of Plutarch or Timothy Bright's *Treatise of Melancholy* through Field, but there were many other titles available too, the majority being religious in nature.

Shakespeare read widely; Leonard Barkan describes Shakespeare the reader as "voracious; more middle-brow than high-brow; heterodox; philosophically not of the avant-garde; anglo-centric in certain ways."[104] In terms of religion, Shakespeare seems to have read across confessional lines, looking (presumably) for what was most interesting or helpful as he explored particular Bible passages or questions they raised for him in the context of his plays. This was easy enough to do, within limits, since, not

---

[103] Bate, *Soul of the Age*, 132–9.
[104] Leonard Barkan, "What did Shakespeare Read?" in Margreta de Grazia and Stanley Wells (eds), *The Cambridge Companion to Shakespeare* (Cambridge: Cambridge University Press, 2001), 31–48, 40.

only were some prominent Catholic writers printed in England, but many continental publications were easy to lay hands on.[105] He read Calvin, certainly the Sermons on Job (*Sermons of Master John Calvin, upon the Booke of Job. Translated out of French by Arthur Golding* (London, 1574); see Chapter 8), and perhaps also those on Psalms and Ephesians (*The Sermons of M. John Calvin, upon the Epistle of S. Paule too the Ephesians. Translated out of French into English by Arthur Golding* (London, 1577); and *The Psalmes of David and others. With M. John Calvins Commentaries*, trans. Arthur Golding (London, 1571); see Chapter 4). Calvin's works were popular and an obvious place to go for biblical exegesis, but the fact that these were translated by Arthur Golding, who also translated Ovid's *Metamorphoses*, another of Shakespeare's favorite books, may have had a specific appeal. Also in the context of Job, Shakespeare seems to have read the Jesuit Robert Parsons's *The First Book of Christian Exercise* ([Rouen], 1582), or he may have known it in the somewhat revised form of *A Booke of Christian Exercise… by R.P. Perused and accompanied now with a Treatise tending to Pacification: by Edm. Bunny* (London, 1584). Bunny's Protestantized version was a best-seller, published in over thirty editions between 1594 and 1630. Parsons's original went through multiple editions too, those after 1585 revised to respond to Bunny, as did his *Seconde Parte* (thirteen editions 1590–1627).[106] Though Parsons's *First Booke* was initially printed at the Catholic College in Rouen, it was later published frequently in Oxford and London. The popularity of these volumes cannot, then, have been attributed to their exclusive appeal to one confession or another, and Shakespeare's reading of Parsons (via Bunny or not) is no reliable indicator of his own religious views.[107] As Stephen Greenblatt has shown, Shakespeare also read Samuel Harsnett's *Declaration of Egregious Popish Impostures* (1603), a popular book reprinted in 1604 and 1605, which provided demonic names used by Poor Tom in *King Lear*.[108] Shakespeare obviously found Harsnett's exploration of the theatricality of

---

[105] The works of Catholic authors like Juan Luis Vives were printed many times in England, for instance.

[106] Victor Houliston argues that, if all the different versions are included, *The Christian Directory* was "probably the most popular devotional work to appear in English before 1650" (*Robert Persons, SJ, The Christian Directory*, ed. Houliston, p. xi).

[107] Gary Kuchar, for instance, in *The Poetry of Religious Sorrow in England* (Cambridge: Cambridge University Press, 2011), makes a strong case for Shakespeare reading the Catholic priest and poet Robert Southwell, who was a popular writer among Protestants as well as Catholics (pp. 48–61). Eight editions of Southwell's *Saint Peters Complaint*, to cite only one of his publications, were printed in London between 1595 and 1615, with a further edition in Edinburgh.

[108] Stephen Greenblatt, *Shakespearean Negotiations: The Circulation of Social Energy in Renaissance England* (Berkeley and Los Angeles: University of California Press, 1988), ch. 4, "Shakespeare and the Exorcists."

exorcism fascinating, but there is no evidence he shared the author's fierce animus against Catholicism. Harsnett was listed as a source in Geoffrey Bullough's compendious *Narrative and Dramatic Sources* of Shakespeare, along with Reginald Scott's *The Discoverie of Witchcraft* (1584) and Foxe's *Acts and Monuments*.[109] If Shakespeare read Calvin, Parsons/Bunny, and Harsnett, it seems reasonable to think he read other biblical and religious works as well, given their ubiquity, especially if they caught his interest in conjunction with what he was composing.

Whatever religious books he read, much of Shakespeare's experience of biblical exegesis, as well as theology, came from sermons. It was impossible to avoid Grashop's final injunction to "heare preaching"—ranging from the officially promulgated *Book of Homilies*, to the regular preaching at his local parishes, to the virtuosic performances of Lancelot Andrewes and other stars at court or at the public pulpits in London.[110] Shakespeare probably heard better preaching than many of his contemporaries. The vicar at Holy Trinity in Stratford was described in a 1584–5 survey of Warwickshire ministers as "learned, zealous and godly, and fit for the ministry; a happy age if our Church were fraught with many such."[111] John Flint, the minister at St Olave, Silver Street, was known in college (Christ's Cambridge) as a "great preacher"; presumably he still preached a good sermon when Shakespeare heard him.[112] At St Saviour's Southwark, Edward Philips gave sermons and weekday lectures that were compelling enough to draw listeners from across the river.[113] At court, as mentioned above, Shakespeare could have heard Lancelot Andrewes, renowned as one of the greatest preachers of the day, as well as other pulpit luminaries like Thomas Dove, Richard Fletcher (father of Shakespeare's collaborator, John Fletcher), and John Buckeridge.[114] Shakespeare could also have attended the public sermons at Paul's Cross, which were among the major entertainments in London life. These drew crowds as large as six thousand, and were intended to be an extra Sunday sermon, featuring the very best preaching: regular

---

[109] Geoffrey Bullough (ed.), *Narrative and Dramatic Sources of Shakespeare*, 8 vols (London: Routledge and Kegan Paul; New York: Columbia University Press, 1957–75).

[110] On the homilies, see Natalie Mears, "Public Worship and Political Participation in Elizabethan England," *Journal of British Studies*, 51/1 (2012), 4–25.

[111] Patrick Collinson, *The Elizabethan Puritan Movement* (Oxford: Clarendon Press, 1967), 281; cited in Bryan Crockett, *The Play of Paradox: Stage and Sermon in Renaissance England* (Philadelphia: University of Pennsylvania Press, 1995), 17. According to J. Harvey Bloom, *Shakespeare's Church* (London: T. Fisher Unwin, 1902), 144, the vicar at this time was Richard Barton.

[112] Nicholl, *Lodger*, 59, citing John Venn and J. A. Venn, *Alumni Cantabrigienses* (1922–7).

[113] Arnold Hunt, *The Art of Hearing: English Preachers and their Audiences, 1590–1640* (Cambridge: Cambridge University Press, 2010), 218.

[114] See Peter E. McCullough, *Sermons at Court: Politics and Religion in Elizabethan and Jacobean Preaching* (Cambridge: Cambridge University Press, 1998).

morning prayer was meant to end by 9 a.m., and the Paul's Cross sermons started an hour later, at 10:00.[115] Thomas Playfere, for instance, preached *Hearts Delight* (on Ps. 37:4) at Paul's Cross in 1593. Thomas Nashe wrote of him, "Seldome have I beheld so pregnant a pleasaunt wit coupled with a memorie of such huge incomprehensible receipt, deepe reading and delight better mixt than in his Sermons."[116] Others chosen to preach there included Thomas Bilson, Bishop of Winchester; William Barlow, Bishop of Rochester and Lincoln; Arthur Lake, Bishop of Bath and Wells; and John Jewel, John Foxe, Richard Hooker, and John Donne.[117]

There were other open-air sermons for large audiences held elsewhere in the city too. On Monday, Tuesday, and Wednesday of Easter week, for instance, sermons were delivered in the churchyard of St Mary's Spital, attended by the Lord Mayor and alderman, along with the governors and children of Christ's Hospital and other London hospitals.[118] The audience was about two thousand. Indeed, London was a city of preaching, as described by Anthony Maxey in a sermon at court in 1606:

How generally is [the Sabbath] observed, how religiously sanctified, even in this great and busie Citie, wherein the streets may often be seene in a manner desolate, and few stirring upon the Saboth, in the time of divine prayer and preaching: The painfull preaching frequented with infinite congregations, and mightie assemblies in this famous Citie; the diligent and daylie prayers, the devotion and thanksgiving, the readiness and attention in hearing the word of God both preached and reade even in this place where I stand, doth witness what I say.[119]

Such statements need to be born in mind when considering the conventional complaints by preachers about congregants lured away from sermons to plays. (Plays were technically banned on Sundays and holidays, but antitheatrical polemicists like Philip Stubbes nevertheless complained about Sunday playing.)[120] Finally, sermons constituted a substantial body of the printed books in the period; like plays, they could be read as well as heard.

---

[115] Hunt, *Art of Hearing*, 212. For the figure of six thousand, see Alan Fager Herr, *The Elizabethan Sermon: A Survey and a Bibliography* (Philadelphia: University of Pennsylvania, 1940; repr. New York: Octagon Books, 1969), 24.

[116] Thomas Nashe, *Works*, ed. from the original texts by Ronald B. McKerrow; repr. from the original edn with corrections and supplementary notes, ed. F. P. Wilson (Oxford: Blackwell's, 1958), i. 314, cited in P. E. McCullough, "Thomas Nashe," *ODNB*.

[117] Mary Morrissey, *Politics and the Paul's Cross Sermon, 1558–1642* (Oxford and New York: Oxford University Press, 2011).

[118] William Gifford, "Time and Place in Donne's Semons," *PMLA* 82/5 (1967), 388–98, 394.

[119] Anthony Maxie, *The Churches Sleepe, Expressed in a Sermon Preached at the Court* (1606), cited in Hunt, *Art of Hearing*, 204.

[120] See, e.g., Peter Lake with Michael Questier, *The Antichrist's Lewd Hat: Protestants, Papists & Players in Post-Reformation England* (New Haven and London: Yale University Press, 2002), 429.

The critical aspect of sermons for this study, though, is that they expounded upon biblical texts. Not only was their primary purpose to interpret biblical verses and passages, but they did so partly by means of citing and explicating additional related biblical verses and passages (as Grashop suggested). John Dove, for instance, preached at Paul's Cross on November 4, 1594, on the text "Little children, it is the last houre, and as ye have heard that Antichrist shal come, even nowe are there many Antichristes, whereby we know that it is the last houre" (1 John 2:18).[121] The printed text of the sermon features Revelation 1:7 on the title page ("Beholde, he commeth in the Clouds, and everye eye shall see him"), and the margins of almost every page are crammed with biblical citations. On page 2, for instance, the marginal notes are John 12, Mark 14, John 13, Romans 13, and Matthew 10. The biblical passages in Dove's text are marked by italics:

My soule is troubled: father, save me from this houre. [John 12:27]

Father if it be possible let this houre passe away from me. [Mark 14:36]

He knew that his hour was come that he should depart out of this World unto his father. [John 13:1]

Now the houre is come that we should awake out of sleepe, for our redemption draweth nearer then when we first beleeved. [Rom. 13:11]

When they shall deliver you up, take no thought, howe, or what ye shall answere, for, *vobis dabitur in illa hora, it shall be given you in that houre.* [Matt. 10:19][122]

The density of biblical reference in another of Dove's sermons was remarked by one in the congregation: "We had plenty of preaching here this Christmas. The bishop and the Deane performed their parts very well, and Dr Pasfield was not much behind them, but your brother Dove swept the scriptures together upon heapes, as one man told me in that very phrase."[123] Henry "silver-tongued" Smith's sermon, *Jacobs ladder, or The high way to heauen* (1595), is even thicker with biblical citations than Dove's. On a single page (sig. B3^v), he cites Agge [Haggai] 1:2, 2 Corinthians 6:2, Matthew 25:15, Luke 19:13, Genesis 1, Genesis 1:14, Matthew 3:2, Matthew 10, and Matthew 4:10. It is impossible to know

---

[121] John Dove, *A sermon preached at Pauls Crosse, the 3 of Nouember 1594* (London: V.S. for William Jaggard, [1594?]).

[122] Dove, *A sermon*, sigs A2^r–A2^v. Chapter and verse added. Interestingly, Dove's citations correspond to neither the Bishops' Bible nor the Geneva, and the inclusion of the Latin in the verse from Matthew suggests he may have been using his own translation. The Latin seems to be from the Junius–Tremellius Bible, since the Vulgate has *dabitur enim vobis in illa hora*.

[123] John Chamberlain, letter to Dudley Carleton, January 8, 1608, in Peter McCullough, Hugh Adlington, and Emma Rhatigan (eds), *The Oxford Handbook to the Early Modern Sermon* (Oxford: Oxford University Press, 2011), 539.

how these sermons were actually delivered, and whether the text was read as written, without the biblical passages being specifically identified, or whether book, chapter, and verse were somehow included for the listeners. The context usually makes clear at least that the Bible was being cited, even if chapter and verse were not provided. Many ministers encouraged their congregation to review the sermon together afterward, and to note and look up the biblical passages referred to.[124] Some members of the congregation were so keen to locate the biblical citations that it irritated the preachers, who criticized those who "tosse the leaves of their Bibles to and fro (to seeke the place he nominates)."[125] Preachers came under fire too, however, for too abundant and arbitrary biblical references. Thomas Nashe wrote that "heede must be taken, that theyr whole Sermons, seeme not a banquet of broken fragments of Scripture":

> Scripture we hotch-potch together, and doe not place it like Pearle and Gold-lace on a garment, heere and there to adorn, but pile it, and dunge it upon heapes, without use or edification. We care not howe we mispeake it, so we have it to speake. Out it flyes East and West; though we loose it all it is nothing, for more have we of it, then we can well tell what to doe withal. Violent are the most of our pack-horse Pulpit-men, in vomiting they'r duncery. Their preachings seeme rather pestilential frenzies, then anything els. They writhe Texts lyke waxe, and where they envie, Scripture is theyr Champion to scold.[126]

It became common for members of the congregation to take notes during sermons, even in shorthand, and volumes containing blank leaves were printed for this purpose, sometimes bound together with liturgical texts like the Book of Common Prayer and Sternhold and Hopkins.[127] George Webbe instructed parishioners to bring Bibles to church, to "marke the Text, observe the division; marke how every point is handled: quote the places of Scripture which he alledgeth for his Doctrine proofe, fold down a leafe in your Bible from which the place is recited, that so at your leasure after your returne from the Church, you may examine it."[128] Stephen

---

[124] Hunt, *Art of Hearing*, 60–116. The Bible was also read aloud among groups. Heads of households were to read aloud to their families, and there are numerous records of people gathering in churches, where Bibles were made available, to listen to one of their group read. See Fox, *Oral and Literate Culture*, 37–8.

[125] James Warre, *The Touch-stone of Truth, wherein Veritie, by Scripture is Plainely Confirmed, and Error Confuted* (1630), cited in Hunt, *Art of Hearing*, 68–9.

[126] Thomas Nashe, *Christes Teares over Jerusalem* (London: James Roberts, 1593), fos. 64ᵛ–65ʳ.

[127] On shorthand, see Hunt, *Art of Hearing*, 139–47.

[128] George Webbe, "A short Direction for the daily exercise of a Christian," cited in Sherman, *Used Books*, 75–6. Webbe's original is printed in *A garden of spirituall flowers. Planted by Ri. R. Will. Per. R. Gree. M.M. and Geo. Web.* (London, 1609), reprinted in dozens of editions through the century. Sherman notes that the "frequent cases, found

Egerton urged his fellow-preachers not to "swarve from the words of the common Translation," since the listeners would look up the references, and the authority of the preacher might be undermined by an inaccurate citation.[129]

A number of scholars have pointed out some fundamental similarities of the church and the theater as cultural institutions, despite the familiar body of anti-theatrical rhetoric that might suggest the opposite. Bryan Crockett, for instance, reads complaints like Edwin Sandys's—"Will not a filthy play with a blast of a trumpet sooner call a thousand than an hours tolling of the bell bring to the sermon an hundred"—as underscoring the competition between church and theater, which drew on roughly the same population for their audiences.[130] Even the outdoor performing spaces were similar, as Millar MacLure notes of Paul's Cross:

> If we look at the scene as a whole, it reminds us of the Elizabethan theatre: groundlings and notables, pit and galleries, and, in the midst, the pulpit as stage. Indeed it was a theatre; to borrow a term from the young Spenser, "a Theatre, wherein be represented as wel the miseries and calamities that follow the voluptuous worldlings as also the greate joyes and pleasures which the faithfull do enjoy." Sermons, proclamations, processions, and penances were all theatrical, and many a preacher of the Puritan persuasion acknowledged and fulminated against the competition from the Bankside.[131]

Both sermons and plays were primarily auditory experiences, heard rather than simply seen.[132] Yet there was in fact much to see as well. For one

---

especially but not exclusively in printed sermons, where a reader notes [in the margin] the precise reference for an unidentified scriptural passage, suggests how thoroughly familiar many lay readers had become with the Bible (to the point where they could cite, as the phrase now goes, 'chapter and verse')" (p. 80).

[129] Stephen Egerton, *The Boring of the Eare* (1623), cited in Hunt, *Art of Hearing*, 77.

[130] Edwin Sandys, *Sermons* (London, 1585), cited as the epigraph in Herr, *Elizabethan Sermon*. Crockett, *Play of Paradox*, 2. "Competition," Crockett argues, "implies kinship." New Historicists like Stephen Greenblatt and Louis Montrose have also argued for the parallels between Church and theater, though their argument is that the theater takes up the cultural functions of the Church after its (Catholic) rituals have been emptied of their transcendent meaning, an argument that has come to seem increasingly limited both historically and theoretically. See Greenblatt, *Shakespearean Negotiations*, 94–128, and Montrose, *The Purpose of Playing: Shakespeare and the Cultural Politics of the Elizabethan Theatre* (Chicago: University of Chicago Press, 1996). For a critique of the New Historicist approach to religion, focusing especially on Greenblatt, see Sarah Beckwith, "Stephen Greenblatt's *Hamlet* and the Forms of Oblivion," *JMEMS* 33/2 (2003), 261–80.

[131] Millar MacLure, *The Paul's Cross Sermons, 1534–1642* (Toronto: University of Toronto Press, 1958), 4.

[132] Ramie Targoff, among others, notes "the shift of emphasis from a visual to an auditory register" in the liturgical changes brought about by the Reformation. *Common Prayer: The Language of Public Devotion in Early Modern England* (Chicago: Chicago University Press, 2001), 22.

thing, preachers were encouraged to use dramatic gestures to drive home their words, and to appeal as strongly as possible to the emotions of their auditors.[133] The best preachers were, in effect, acting, and their popularity depended as much on their power as performers as on their learning and godliness. Churches and playhouses even shared some of the same distractions. Young gallants took seats for the play on the stage or in the gallery in order to be seen and show off their fashions, and they did the same in church, as the preacher Robert Shelford complained: "these [vain and ostentatious people] take more care for braverie, the newest fashions, and the finest allures that can be bought for money; for here [in church] we are lookt upon. We should come hither to serve God: but these come to shew themselves."[134]

Most important for the study of Shakespeare's use of biblical allusion is the similar experience of hearing the Bible in the church and the theater. In fact, the experience of hearing the Bible in worship conditioned early modern audiences to recognize biblical allusion in plays.[135] Sermons contained scores of quotations, from single words and phrases to longer passages, compiled from throughout the Bible; it was the preacher's job to make these scattered references relevant to the interpretation of his principal text and to his religious message, but the audience was obviously engaged in this too, noting Bible references either mentally or in a note book, looking them up afterward, and discussing their meaning. The services in the Book of Common Prayer, as described above, were similarly a pastiche of biblical texts, some of them longer, some shorter, some clearly identified, some subtly interwoven with the rest of the liturgical texts. The question has sometimes been asked whether a theater audience could reasonably have perceived and processed allusions in the rapid course of a performance.[136] Modern audiences have little trouble with the dense allusions of television shows like *The Simpsons*, *South Park*, or *The Daily Show*, but critics are more skeptical when it comes to Shakespeare's theater, perhaps

---

[133] See anon., *The Practice of Preaching* (London, 1577), fo. 41ʳ: "The Preacher shall not employe his least care in moving of affections." On preacher's gestures, see Herr, *Elizabethan Sermon*, 46.

[134] Robert Shelford, "A Sermon shewing how we ought to behave our selves in Gods house," in *Five pious and learned discourses* (Cambridge: [Thomas Buck and Roger Daniel], 1635), 48. For the theatrical practice, see Gurr, *Playgoing*, 46–51.

[135] Frank Kermode makes a similar suggestion in *Shakespeare's Language* (New York: Farrar, Straus, Giroux, 2000), 4, cited in Hunt, *Art of Hearing*, 10.

[136] Gurr, *Playgoing*, 99–102, though he then goes on to note important (non-biblical) allusions in Webster, and later on notes a correspondence between Sir John Harington and Robert Cecil demonstrating their "facility with allusion," in this case to Jaques's Seven Ages speech in *As You Like It* (pp. 117–18). For a more strongly skeptical argument against the perception of allusion, see Richard Levin, "The Relation of External Evidence to the Allegorical and Thematic Interpretation of Shakespeare," *SSt* 13 (1980), 1–29.

because to a modern audience biblical allusions do seem obscure.[137] To Shakespeare's audience, however, the Bible was common, and popular, culture. There was obviously, then as now, a range of education, intelligence, and perceptiveness among audiences, even in the more exclusive venues of the private theaters or the court. Some audience members probably no more understood Shakespeare's biblical allusions than they did his classical allusions, complex puns, and other figures of speech. Many others surely did, however, aided by long familiarity with biblical stories and texts from schooling, catechism, churchgoing, sermons, family and community discussion, personal reading, and the biblical texts and images that surrounded them in their daily lives. In this thick biblical culture Shakespeare could communicate, complicate, and enrich the meanings of his plays by manipulating allusions to biblical texts, characters, narratives, and images.

---

[137] See, e.g., Jonathan Gray, *Watching with the Simpsons: Television, Parody, and Intertextuality* (New York: Routledge, 2006); " 'Simpsons Did It!': South Park and the Intertextuality of Contemporary Animation," *Studies in American Humor*, 3/17 (2008), 19–34.

2
A Critical History of the Bible in Shakespeare

Given the vast proliferation of Shakespeare studies especially since the twentieth century, why has there not yet been a satisfactory full-length critical study of Shakespeare's use of the Bible? Certainty is impossible when explaining why something does not exist, but exploring the history of criticism on Shakespeare and the Bible may help provide some answers. This history is longer, richer, and quirkier than might be expected. Some of the quirks in particular may be responsible for giving serious scholars qualms about entering the field. Inevitably, for instance, the study of Shakespeare and the Bible overlaps with the study of Shakespeare and religion, since the Bible is at the center of at least Protestant Christianity. Claims for Shakespeare's Christian values or special pleading for his own Catholic or Protestant faith have produced some particularly poor and potentially offputting scholarship over the past two centuries, and some of these have included arguments about Shakespeare's use of the Bible. As far as possible, this chapter's critical history will focus on studies of the Bible rather than religion more broadly. The latter has been explored well by a variety of recent studies, but it is a distinctly different topic, even if studies of religion sometimes refer to the Bible, and studies of the Bible refer to religious belief and practice.[1]

EARLIEST IMPRESSIONS

It is not surprising that Shakespeare's biblical allusions were not remarked on by his earliest critics. In the seventeenth and eighteenth centuries, the critical preoccupation was with character and moral value rather than

---

[1] See, e.g., Alison Shell, *Shakespeare and Religion* (London: Arden Shakespeare, 2011); Phebe Jensen, *Religion and Revelry in Shakespeare's World* (Cambridge: Cambridge University Press, 2008); Arthur F. Marotti and Ken Jackson (eds), *Shakespeare and Religion: Early Modern and Postmodern Perspectives* (Notre Dame, IN: University of Notre Dame Press, 2011). The bibliography is large and growing.

close reading of tropes and schemes. Furthermore, while biblical knowledge was deep and widespread, it may not have occurred to anyone to note what was obvious to most readers and audience members. Samuel Johnson was certainly aware of the nature of allusion, noting that, at the opening of *Twelfth Night*, Orsino "evidently alludes to the story of Actaeon," when Orsino states that "when my eyes did see Olivia first, |...| That instant I was turn'd into a hart" (1.1.20–2). He notes too that, when Orlando describes the moon as "Thrice crowned Queen of Night" in *As You Like It* (3.2.2), he is "alluding to the triple character of *Proserpine, Cynthia* and *Diana*."[2] Johnson is particularly interested in topical allusion, which he suspects to be running through the plays, albeit undetected and undetectable by readers who have lost the necessary frames of reference:

> Of the books which [Shakespeare] read, and from which he formed his style, some perhaps have perished, and the rest are neglected. His imitations are therefore unnoted, his allusions are undiscovered, and many beauties, both of pleasantry and greatness, are lost with the objects to which they were united, as the figures vanish when the canvass has decayed.[3]

In his first note on *The Merchant of Venice*, Johnson writes, "I am always inclined to believe, that *Shakespear* has more allusions to particular facts and persons than his readers commonly suppose."[4] Presumably he did not consider Shakespeare's allusions to the Bible lost and undiscoverable; he makes no reference to the Bible in all his notes on the plays, perhaps expecting that his readers could perceive these for themselves.

Not all of Shakespeare's eighteenth-century editors ignored biblical allusion. Lewis Theobald, in his riposte to the Shakespeare edition of Alexander Pope, argued that Gratiano in the first scene of *The Merchant of Venice* says, of those who are "reputed wise | For saying nothing,"

> I'm very sure
> If They should speak, would almost DAMN those Ears,
> Which, hearing them, would call their Brothers Fools.
> (1.1.97–9, as in Theobald)[5]

Pope's edition had "DAMM" (i.e., stop up) instead of "DAMN." Theobald explains his emendation in terms of biblical allusion:

---

[2] Samuel Johnson, *Johnson on Shakespeare*, ed. Walter Raleigh (London: Oxford University Press, 1908; repr. 1952), 83.
[3] *Johnson on Shakespeare*, ed. Raleigh, 2–3.
[4] *Johnson on Shakespeare*, ed. Raleigh, 81.
[5] Lewis Theobald, *Shakespeare restored: or, a specimen of the many errors, as well committed, as unamended, by Mr Pope in his late edition of this poet* (London, 1726), 144.

Critical History of the Bible in Shakespeare

The Author's Meaning is directly this; That some People are thought wise, whilst they keep Silence; who, when they open their Mouths, are such stupid Praters, that their Hearers cannot help calling them *Fools*, and so incur the Judgment denounced upon them in the *Gospel*. It is very familiar with *Shakespeare* to allude to Passages of Scripture; and it is plain to me, even to Demonstration, that he had here before his Eye this Text of St MATTHEW, *Ch. 5.v.22. And whosoever shall say to his Brother,* Raca, *shall be in danger of the Council: But whosoever shall say, thou* Fool, *shall be in danger of Hell-fire.*

Because I would not assert any Thing, but what I would be willing to second with a Proof, I'll subjoin a few Instances, out of a great Number that may be collected, in which our Poet has an Eye to *Scripture-History*; and Others, in which he both alludes to, and quotes the very *Texts* from *Holy-Writ*.

In *All's well that ends well*, Page 445. he talks of *Nebuchadnezzar*'s eating Grass; in *Love's Labour lost*, Page 104. of *Sampson*'s carrying the City Gates on his Back; in the *Merry Wives of Windsor*, Page 308. of *Goliah*, and the Weaver's Beam; in K. *Richard* II. Page 162. Of *Pilate*'s Washing his Hands; in the *First* Part of K. *Henry* IV. Page 261, 262. *Falstaffe*'s Soldiers are compar'd to *Lazarus*, and to the *Prodigal Son*; and in the third Part of *Henry* VI. Page 7. And in *Hamlet*, Page 391. there is an Allusion to *Jephthah*'s Daughter.[6]

Theobald quotes further passages from the plays, indicating in the margin the biblical passage alluded to in each case. In a note to *The Merchant of Venice* 1.1 in his edition of Shakespeare's *Works*, Theobald repeats his argument for the allusion to Matthew 5:22, noting that "Mr Pope, in his last Edition, has vouchsafed to borrow the Correction [of 'dam' to 'damn'] and Explanation."[7] Pope's edition of 1728 does indeed use "damn" and notes, "It alludes to the saying in St. Matth. v. 22. Whosoever shall say to his brother, Thou fool, shall be in danger of Hell-fire."[8]

Theobald's remarks on biblical allusion proved influential. In *The Morality of Shakespeare's Drama Illustrated*, the playwright Elizabeth Griffith quoted the Gentleman's description to Kent of Cordelia's grief on hearing of King Lear's ill treatment and noted: "Theobald hints that Shakespeare had borrowed this fine picture of Cordelia's grief, from Joseph, *in Holy Writ*, who being no longer able to restrain his affections, ordered his retinue from his presence, and then wept aloud."[9] Theobald does indeed make this suggestion in his note to King Lear 4.3.[10] Griffith

---

[6] Theobald, *Shakespeare restored*, 14, emphasis in original.
[7] Lewis Theobald (ed.), *The Works of Shakespeare in Seven Volumes* (London, 1733), ii. 6.
[8] *The Works of William Shakespeare. In ten volumes. Publish'd by Mr. Pope and Dr. Sewell*, ii (London: A. Bettesworth and C. Hitch, J. Tonson, F. Clay, W. Feales, and R. Wellington 1728), 156.
[9] Elizabeth Griffith, *The Morality of Shakespeare's Drama Illustrated* (London: T. Cadell, 1775), 368. Griffith dedicated the volume to David Garrick.
[10] Theobald (ed.), *Works of Shakespeare*, v. 186–7.

also notes the allusion to Matthew 5:22 that Theobald claimed for *The Merchant of Venice* 1.1, as well as others not noted by Theobald.[11] In the first scene of *Henry V*, for instance, the Archbishop of Canterbury describes the prince's reformation after his misspent youth, remarking that he "whipt the offending Adam out of him; | leaving his body as a paradise" (1.1, as in Griffith). Griffith's note exclaims: "What a beautiful and poetical allusion is here made to the circumstance of our first parents being exiled from Eden!"[12] Of the Gentleman's comment in *A Winter's Tale* on the reconciliation of Leontes and Perdita—"they looked as they had heard of a world ransomed, or one destroyed" (5.2.14–15)—Griffith again links its beauty to its biblical basis, going on to make a general claim for Shakespeare similar to Theobald's:

This description not only contains the beautiful and the sublime, but rises to a still higher sublimity, or, to speak in the style of the Psalmist, to the most highest, in the allusion to sacred writ, relating to the two principal articles in the Old and New Testament, the fall of man, and his redemption. Shakespeare makes frequent references to the sacred text, and writes often, not only as a moralist, but as a divine.[13]

The leap from Shakespeare as a writer who alludes to the Bible to Shakespeare as "moralist" or "divine" became commonplace in the nineteenth century.

THE BARD AND THE VICARS

Interest in Shakespeare's use of the Bible developed in tandem with the rise of what George Bernard Shaw called Bardolatry, the almost cultish elevation of Shakespeare not only as the greatest writer in the English language, but as a source of moral and spiritual wisdom. The seeds of this development were planted in the seventeenth- and eighteenth-century claims for Shakespeare's moral stature. This is already evident in John Dryden's prefaces to his own plays, for instance, which state, in heroic verse, that "*Shakespear's* pow'r is sacred as a King's" and that the author feels that, in spite of his modest pride, "a secret shame | Invades his breast at *Shakespear's* sacred name."[14] Johnson, despite his carping about Shakespeare's occasionally indecorous language, claimed that "it may be

---

[11] Griffith, *Morality*, 53.   [12] Griffith, *Morality*, 255.
[13] Griffith, *Morality*, 114–15.
[14] John Dryden, *From the Prologue to* The Tempest, or The Enchanted Island, 1667, *published* 1670, and *From the Prologue to* Aureng-Zebe, 1675, *published* 1676, in D. Nichol Smith (ed.), *Shakespeare Criticism: A Selection, 1623–1840* (London: Oxford University Press, 1916; repr. 1964), 22, 23.

said of *Shakespeare*, that from his works may be collected a system of civil and oeconomical prudence."[15] After David Garrick's production of the Shakespeare Jubilee in Stratford-upon-Avon in 1769, the cult of Shakespeare attracted devotees across the English-speaking world. The Jubilee supposedly celebrated the 200th anniversary of Shakespeare's birth, though it was actually five years late (the town, at the time hardly a tourist mecca, came up with the plan only in 1768).[16] The events included a banquet at which a 327-pound turtle was consumed, as well as speeches, and dramatic and musical performances—most notably by Garrick, whose song, "Shakespeare's Mulberry-Tree," presented Shakespeare as saint and god:

> Behold this fair goblet, 'twas carv'd from the tree,
> Which, O my sweet Shakespeare, was planted by thee;
> As a relick I kiss it, and bow at the shrine,
> What comes from thy hand must be ever divine![17]

Garrick's veneration of the mulberry was not just poetic hyperbole; objects carved from the sacred mulberry, supposedly planted by Shakespeare, were indeed sought after and venerated as relics. Proliferating like the fragments of the true cross, such artifacts would have required a forest, not just a single tree. The goblet referred to in the song was presented to Garrick by the town of Stratford, along with a cassolette ostensibly carved from the tree, and a remarkable number of other objects were said to be made from the same source.[18] Washington Irving remarked that the tree had "extraordinary powers of self-multiplication."[19] Garrick's song went on to claim that "law and gospel in Shakespeare we find, | And he gives the best physic for body and mind."

By the nineteenth century, Shakespeare's status as a moral and spiritual authority was secure. In 1840, Thomas Carlyle compared Shakespeare to Dante, the "melodious Priest of Middle-Age Catholicism":

May we not call Shakespeare the still more melodious Priest of a *true* Catholicism, the "Universal Church" of the Future and of all times? No narrow superstition, harsh asceticism, intolerance, fanatical fierceness or perversion: a Revelation, so

---

[15] *Johnson on Shakespeare*, ed. Raleigh, 12.
[16] Isabel Roome Mann, "The Garrick Jubilee at Stratford-Upon-Avon," *SQ* 1/3 (1950), 128–34.
[17] David Garrick, *Shakespeare's Garland* (London: T. Becket and P. A. de Hondt, 1769), 9–10.
[18] The Folger Shakespeare Library has a tea-caddy that was at one time thought to have come from the same wood <http://www.folger.edu/html/exhibitions/fakes_forgeries/FFF-mulberry.asp> (accessed December 15, 2011).
[19] Irving's *Sketch Book*, cited in *The Complete Works of William Shakespeare; Revised from the original editions: with a Memoir, and Essay on his Genius by Barry Cornwall*, iii (London: London Printing Company, 1870), 216.

far as it goes, that such a thousandfold hidden beauty and divineness dwells in all Nature; which let men worship as they can! We may say without offence, that there rises a kind of universal Psalm out of this Shakespeare too; not unfit to make itself heard among the still more sacred Psalms. Not in disharmony with these, if we understood them, but in harmony!—I cannot call this Shakespeare a "Sceptic," as some do; his indifference to the creeds and theological quarrels of his time misleading them. No: neither unpatriotic, though he says little about his Patriotism; nor sceptic, though he says little about his Faith. Such "indifference" was the fruit of his greatness withal: his whole heart was in his own grand sphere of worship (we may call it such); these other controversies, vitally important to other men, were not vital to him.[20]

John Milton had written of Shakespeare as a force of Nature, "warbling his native wood notes wild," and Garrick's claim for Shakespeare was also rooted in an argument about his connection to Nature, contrasting his peculiar (and superior) "law and the gospel" with the "learning and knowledge" of "the well-letter'd birch" that "supplies law and physic, and grace for the church."[21] Carlyle builds on this idea, implicitly combining it with both a Romantic celebration of Nature and the traditional Christian notion of Nature as the second book of God's Revelation. Because Shakespeare is so in tune with this "book" of Nature, he can pass its "Revelation" on to his audience and readers. The development of these attitudes to Shakespeare, like Romanticism, were international. In Goethe's novel *Wilhelm Meisters Lehrjahre* (1795–6), the young protagonist experiences Shakespeare as an epiphany, a magical possession, and he likens his plays to "a great ocean of nature."[22] Across the ocean in the opposite direction, Ralph Waldo Emerson wrote in *Representative Men* (1850) that

Shakespeare is as much out of the category of eminent authors, as he is out of the crowd. He is inconceivably wise; the others, conceivably... He is wise without emphasis or assertion; he is strong, as nature is strong, who lifts the land into mountain slopes without effort and by the same rule as she floats a bubble in the air, and likes as well to do the one as the other. This makes that equality of power in farce, tragedy, narrative, and love-songs; a merit so incessant that each reader is incredulous of the perception of other readers.[23]

---

[20] Thomas Carlyle, "The Hero as Poet," in Carlyle, *On Heroes, Hero-Worship, and the Heroic in History*, ed. John C. Adams (Boston and New York: Houghton, Mifflin and Company; Cambridge, MA: Riverside Press, 1907), 157.

[21] John Milton, "L'Allegro," l. 134, in *The Riverside Milton*, ed. Roy Flannagan (Boston and New York: Houghton Mifflin, 1998), 71; Garrick, *Shakespeare's Garland*, 9.

[22] Cited in Simon Williams, *Shakespeare on the German Stage*, i. *1586–1914* (Cambridge: Cambridge University Press, 1990, repr. 2004), 2.

[23] Ralph Waldo Emerson, "Shakespeare, or, The Poet," in Emerson, *Representative Men*, in *The Complete Works of Ralph Waldo Emerson*, iv (Boston and New York: Houghton, Mifflin and Company, 1903–4), 187–219, 211–13.

Critical History of the Bible in Shakespeare 49

From the mid-nineteenth century on, there was a proliferation of publications premised upon and supporting the claim that Shakespeare had somehow tapped directly into God's revelation, and that his works provided wisdom and spiritual knowledge equivalent to the Bible. The format of gathering extracts from Shakespeare's plays was derived from the popular anthologies of "beauties" in the previous century.[24] William Dodd's was the most successful of these: *The beauties of Shakespear, regularly selected from each play: with a general index, digesting them under popular heads: illustrated with explanatory notes, and similar passages from ancient and modern authors* (1752). The first of the "Bible and Shakespeare" collections was Sir Frederick Beilby Watson's *Religious and Moral Sentences Culled from the Works of Shakespeare, Compared with Sacred Passages Drawn from Holy Writ* (1843), dedicated to "the Shakespeare Society by a member; and compiled for the benefit of the Benevolent Fund of the Theaters Royal Drury Lane and Covent Garden."[25] The 120 pages of parallel extracts cover everything from "Abel" and "Ability" to "Witchcraft" and "World's Dissolution." Methodologically, the parallels are a hodge-podge. Some are direct quotations or references, some genuine allusions, some intriguing parallels, some just free associations. Under "Wisdom," for example, is found "Wisdom cries out in the streets, but no man regards it," from *1 Henry IV* 1.2, and the verse from Proverbs, "Wisdom crieth without; she uttereth her voice in the streets" (Prov. 1:20). Hal is clearly alluding here, albeit playfully, to Proverbs, and an awareness of the biblical source is necessary to a full understanding of the scene. Watson identifies none of the speakers, however, let alone the dramatic contexts, so the implication is that Shakespeare's writings are simply, as is claimed, "conformable to the Holy Scripture."[26] In fact, both Hal and Falstaff play fast and loose with Scripture in a way that is dramatically delightful and perhaps meaningful, but hardly morally edifying by any doctrinal standard (for Falstaff, see Chapter 6). Under "Grafted," Watson includes a passage from *All's Well That Ends Well*:

---

[24] See Charles LaPorte, "The Devotional Texts of Victorian Bardolatry," in Travis DeCook and Alan Galey (eds), *Shakespeare, the Bible, and the Form of the Book: Contested Scriptures* (New York and Abingdon: Routledge, 2012), 143–59.
[25] Sir Frederick Beilby Watson, *Religious and Moral Sentences Culled from the Works of Shakespeare, Compared with Sacred Passages Drawn from Holy Writ* (London: Calkin & Budd, 1843). The book appeared anonymously. Watson was a Member of the Royal Society and, in 1827–38, Master of the Royal Household. *Religious and Moral Sentences* was published by Calkin & Budd, "Booksellers to Her Majesty." It was reprinted many times in both Britain and America.
[26] Watson, *Religious and Moral Sentences*, 140.

Methinks I hear him now,—his plausive words
He scatter'd not in ears, but *grafted* them
To grow there, and to bear. (1.2.53–5)

Across, on the next page, is a quotation labeled "Liturgy": "Grant, we beseech *Thee, Almighty God*, that the words which we have heard this day with our outward ears, may, through *Thy grace*, be so *grafted* inwardly in our hearts, that they may bring forth in us the fruit of good living." This seems another case where one might argue for a conscious allusion, since the "liturgy" here is one of the collects that would have been familiar from the close of Morning Prayer, Evening Prayer, Communion, or the Litany, in the Book of Common Prayer.[27] Yet, without identifying the specific contexts of both passages (in the play, the King of France is speaking of Helena's father), and furthermore the way in which the King's invoking the liturgy might be significant in *All's Well*, the comparison is meaningless. Under "Sabbath," Watson places, from *The Merchant of Venice*, "By our holy Sabbath have I sworn" (4.1.35) together with Exodus, "This is that which the Lord hath said, To-morrow is the rest of the holy Sabbath unto the Lord" (16:23). But there are countless biblical references to the Sabbath, and Shakespeare's usage seems commonplace. Under "Fears" the relationship between the two parallel texts seems entirely arbitrary. The Shakespeare extract is from *A Midsummer Night's Dream*:

Their sense, thus weak, lost with their *fears*, thus strong,
Made senseless things begin to do them wrong. (3.2.27–8)

Watson's related biblical passage is from Wisdom: "*Fear* is nothing else but a betraying of the succours which reason offereth" (17:12). Both passages describe fear, but any similarity between them may be ascribed simply to common human experience, since all they share verbally is the key noun "fear." A final selection from Shakespeare, without biblical analogues, was designed by Watson to show "how copiously he drew from the pure source of his own all-gifted mind, sentences of high morality and true religion."[28]

T. R. Eaton's *Shakespeare and the Bible: Showing How the Great Dramatist Was Indebted to Holy Writ for his Profound Knowledge of Human Nature* (1858) aimed to demonstrate "the vastness of Shakespeare's Bible lore," which he no doubt, according to Eaton, learned from his mother.[29] Eaton's format abandons the thematic catalogue of parallels, opting instead for a

---

[27] *BCP* 139.   [28] Watson, *Religious and Moral Sentences*, 141.
[29] T. R. Eaton, *Shakespeare and the Bible: Showing How the Great Dramatist Was Indebted to Holy Writ for his Profound Knowledge of Human Nature* (London: James Blackwood, 1858), 9–10.

series of chapters focusing on one or more plays, but his loose associative method is much the same as Watsons's. Chapter one presents an extract from *Macbeth* 4.3, in which Malcolm tries unsuccessfully to comfort Macduff, followed by lines from *King John* in which Constance rebuffs the comforts of Pandulph. Then follows,

So Job—
I also could speak as ye do: if your soul were in my soul's stead, I could heap up words against you, and shake mine head at you. But I would strengthen you with my mouth, and the moving of my lips should assuage your grief (Job 16:4–5).[30]

How these are "so" is left to the reader, but the intended point of comparison seems the difficulty of comforting the afflicted, especially those who have lost children. Shakespeare hardly needed the Bible to learn this. And yet Eaton is at least open about his critical practice:

Shakespeare perpetually reminds us of the Bible; not by direct quotation, indirect allusion, borrowed idioms, or palpable imitation of phrase and style, but by an elevation of thought and simplicity of diction which are not to be found elsewhere. A passage, for instance, rises in our thoughts, unaccompanied by a clear recollection of its origin. Our first impression is, that it *must* belong *either* to the *Bible* or to *Shakespeare*. No other author excites the same feeling in an equal degree.[31]

Eaton himself demonstrates the inadequacy of his methodology, however, since some of the passages that rise in his thoughts clearly *are* allusions. The Painter in *Timon of Athens*, for instance, says "you shall see him [Timon] a palm in Athens again, and flourish with the highest" (5.1.11–12). Eaton provides as Bible text Psalm 92:12, "The righteous shall flourish like a palm-tree," and this is obviously the passage Shakespeare had in mind and what his more attentive audience members would recognize in the painter's language.[32]

Although the tradition of "Bible and Shakespeare Compared" books began with a lay author (Watson), Eaton was the first of many clergymen to have been drawn to the genre, including the Revd Alfred Pownall (*Shakespere Weighed in an Even Balance*, London, 1864), the Revd Charles Wordsworth, Bishop of St Andrews (*Shakspeare's Knowledge and Use of the Bible*, London, 1864), the Revd Charles Bullock (*Shakspeare's Debt to the Bible*, London, 1879), the Revd George S. Goodspeed (two articles on "Shakespeare and the Bible," 1892, in the journal *The Old Testament Student*), the Revd James Bell (*Biblical and Shakespearean Characters Compared*,

---

[30] Eaton, *Shakespeare and the Bible*, 9. [31] Eaton, *Shakespeare and the Bible*, 13.
[32] Eaton, *Shakespeare and the Bible*, 99.

Hull and London, 1894), and the Revd William Procter (*Shakespeare and Scripture*, London, 1929). In addition, G. Q. Colton's *Shakespeare and the Bible: Parallel Passages* (New York, 1888) is introduced by the Revd Robert Collyer, and the American editions of Watson's *Religious and Moral Sentences* contain an extra preface by Frederick D. Huntington, Bishop of New York.[33] Christian Ginsburg, the Bible scholar and missionary (and convert from Judaism), wrote "Shakespeare's Use of the Bible" for the *Athenaeum* in 1883. To this list one might also add the annual Shakespeare's birthday sermons preached in Stratford-upon-Avon, some of which were collected and published by the Revd George Arbuthnot in 1900 (*Shakespeare Sermons*). Another birthday sermon, not included in Arbuthnot's volume, was given on the tercentenary by Archbishop Richard Chenevix Trench, "Every Good Gift and Every Perfect Gift is from Above and Cometh Down from the Father of Light."[34]

But not all the authors of such books were ordained. *Bible Truths with Shakespearean Parallels* was published in 1862 by J. B. Selkirk, but "Selkirk" was the pseudonym of James Brown of Selkirk, a Scots poet and essayist (author of *Ethics and Aesthetics of Modern Poetry*, 1878). *Bible Truths* was popular enough to be published in a Swedish translation in 1863 (Stockholm), and in at least three further editions before the end of the century. It was cited as a major influence by the Revd Bullock, who plagiarized it freely in his *Shakspeare's Debt to the Bible*, as well as by Charles J. Plumptre, in his *The Religion and Morality of Shakespeare's Works* (London, 1873). Brown praises the "sterling biblical morality" of British literature in general, but in particular commends Shakespeare's plays, "perfectly impregnated with the leaven of the Bible."[35] The parallels are arranged in 116 short chapters, each focused on some moral topic: "The Danger of an Ungoverned Tongue," "Spiritual Blindness," "Mercy Attributed to God," and so forth. Like so many such compilers, Brown lists passages from both the Bible and Shakespeare out of all context and does not attribute the Shakespearean quotations to particular characters. A list of "Shakespeare's Allusions to Scripture Characters, Incidents, Etc." seems to promise greater specificity, but it consists almost entirely of references to proper names. Finally, Brown lists passages in Shakespeare that he

---

[33] This seems to have misled Charles LaPorte ("The Bard, the Bible, and the Shakespeare Question," *ELH* 74 (2007), 609–28), who attributes the book to Huntington.
[34] On Trench, see Richard Foulkes, "'Every Good Gift from Above': Archbishop Trench's Tercentenary Sermon," *Shakespeare and Religions, SS* 54, ed. Peter Holland (Cambridge: Cambridge University Press, 2001), 80–8.
[35] James Brown ("J. B. Selkirk"), *Bible Truths with Shakespearean Parallels* (London: Hodder and Stoughton, 1862; 3rd edn, 1872), v–vi. Brown's language is itself biblical, echoing verses like Gal. 5:9, "A little leaven leaveneth the whole lump" (KJV).

admits cannot be called allusions, but that he claims strongly recall biblical ideas or language. Helen's speech to the King about "Inspired merit" in *All's Well That Ends Well* 2.1.148–58, for instance, is described as a "comprehensive ramification of biblical allusion."[36] There are no actual verbal allusions in the passage, and it is more likely that Shakespeare's speech is simply rooted in commonplace religious ideas.

Another contribution to the genre by a layman was *Sacred & Shakespearean Affinities, being analogies between the writings of the Psalmists and of Shakespeare* (1890), by Charles Alfred Swinburne (unrelated to the poet Algernon Charles), who was also the author of *Life and Work of J. M. W. Turner* (1902). Swinburne begins with a lengthy and learned discourse on the Psalms as one of the great "building" projects of David and Solomon, along with Jerusalem and the Temple. The bulk of the book consists of the texts of the Psalms, in order and in the King James Version, with brief extracts from Shakespeare inserted where the author feels an "affinity." These extracts are unidentified, though in the Folger Shakespeare Library copy an early reader penned in play, act, and scene for at least the first fifty-two Psalms.[37] Swinburne intended only to juxtapose, stating his interest in selecting "from the writings of such a man ['not only a poet, great among the greatest poets, but the greatest of dramatists, and a moralist and philosopher of high order'] passages containing ideas and illustrations more or less apposite to, and not unworthy to be placed side by side with, extracts from the Psalms themselves."[38] This results in such analogies as that between Psalm 6:5, "For in death no man remembereth thee: and who will give thee thanks in the pit?" and *Measure for Measure* 3.1.117–18: "To die, and go we know not where; | To lie in cold obstruction, and to rot." The passages are connected only in so far as both describe death as generally unpleasant. The Psalmist focuses on oblivion, Shakespeare on mystery and decay. And, as so often with such parallels, the dramatic context is ignored. The language of Claudio's meditation on death is almost as powerful as Hamlet's, but it surely ought to affect our interpretation somewhat that he is speaking to his sister Isabella, who is about to enter the Convent of the Poor Clares, and is asking her to get his death sentence dropped by having sex with Angelo. In other places, however, Swinburne's affinities point to actual allusions, though he leaves it up to the reader to recognize specific verbal relationships. He cites some verses of Orlando from *As You Like It*, for instance:

---

[36] Brown, *Bible Truths*, 218. [37] Folger call number, Sh. misc. 102.
[38] Charles Alfred Swinburne, *Sacred & Shakespearean Affinities, being analogies between the writings of the Psalmists and of Shakespeare* (London: Bickers and son, 1890), xxxiii.

> See, how brief the life of man
> Runs his erring pilgrimage
> That the stretching of a span
> Buckles in his sum of age. (3.2.126–9)

These probably do allude to Psalm 39:6, at least in describing man's life with the keyword "span" ("Behold, thou hast made my days as it were a span long"). Another use of words freighted with biblical resonance occurs in Macbeth's soliloquy, "Tomorrow, and tomorrow, and tomorrow," when he calls life a "tale | Told by an idiot, full of sound and fury | Signifying nothing" (5.5.17, 25–6). Swinburne inserts this speech after Psalm 90:9, "we spend our years as a tale that is told," to which Shakespeare is here alluding and adapting, along with other verses from the Psalms (see Chapter 7). A stronger allusion is marked at Psalm 137, "By the rivers of Babylon, there we sat down, yea, we wept, when we remembered Zion":

> We hanged our harps upon the willows in the midst thereof.
>   .   .   .   .   .
> If I forget thee, O Jerusalem, let my right hand forget her cunning.
> If I do not remember thee, let my tongue cleave to the roof of my mouth.
> (Ps. 137:2, 5–6)

Swinburne here inserts Mowbray's speech from *Richard II*:

> And now my tongue's use is to me no more
> Than an unstrung viol or a harp,
> Or like a cunning instrument cased up. (1.3.161–3)

This speech is one of the play's several allusions to Psalm 137, which is part of an allusive pattern that both reflects and expresses the play's preoccupation with exile.[39] Other of Swinburne's affinities do constitute biblical allusions, but not to the Psalms as he claims. Adam's prayer in *As You Like It*, "He that doth the ravens feed, | Yea, providently caters for the sparrow, | Be comfort to my age!" (2.3.43–5), has nothing to do with Psalm 29, as Swinburne suggests, but it does allude to Job and Matthew:

> Who prepareth for the raven his meat, when his byrdes crye unto God, wandering for lacke of meat? (Job 39:3)

> Are not two sparrowes solde for a farthing, and one of them shal not fall on the ground without your Father? (Matt. 10:29)

Pericles 2.1.58–60 does not allude to the Psalms either. Pericles describes himself to the fishermen as

---
[39] See Hamlin, 242–4.

> A man whom both the water and the wind,
> In that vast tennis-court, hath made the ball
> For them to play upon, entreats you pity him.

Swinburne's suggested parallel is Psalm 42:9, "One deep calleth another, because of the noise of the water-pipes: all thy waves and storms are gone over me." Apart from the water—common enough in oceans—there is little basis for comparison. The tennis-ball metaphor, however, comes ultimately from Isaiah 22:18, "He wil surely rolle & turne thee like a ball in a large contrey," perhaps via Calvin's sermon on Job 1:9–12, where he refers to God sporting with us "as with a tennis ball."[40] Swinburne had a good ear for biblical language, but he unnecessarily handicapped himself by focusing only on the Psalms.

G. Q. Colton's slightly earlier *Shakespeare and the Bible: Parallel Passages Suggested by the Bible with the Religious Sentiments of Shakespeare* (1888) demonstrates the necessity of considering the entire Bible: Shakespeare did seem to have some favorite books, such as Psalms and the Wisdom books, but there is almost no book in the Bible, including those in the Apocrypha, that he does not allude to somewhere in the plays or poems. Like other compilers of parallels, Colton lumps allusions, references, quotations, and free associations together indiscriminately, but at least, like the best of them, he does root out some genuinely important intertextual relationships. Some of these are allusions, like Orlando's allusive representation of himself as the Prodigal Son in *As You Like It*: "Shall I keep hogs, and eat husks with them? What Prodigal portion have I spent, that I should come to such penury?" (1.1.34–6). As mentioned in Chapter 1, Shakespeare's use of "husks" is not only an allusion to Luke 15:16 ("And he wolde faine have filled his bellie with the huskes, that the swine ate"), but also proof that he had the Geneva translation in mind here. Of the Bibles available to Shakespeare, only the Geneva has "husks," though Colton is oblivious to this, using the anachronistic King James Version as his reference throughout (in this passage the KJV happens to follow the Geneva, but the KJV was printed only in 1611, after most of Shakespeare's plays had been

---

[40] John Calvin, *Sermons of Master John Calvin, upon the Booke of Job. Translated out of French by Arthur Golding* (London: Henry Bynneman for] Lucas Harison and George Byshop, 1574), 23. The same metaphor is used in George Wilkins's 1608 *The Painfull Adventures of Pericles Prince of Tyre* (London: T. P[urfoot] for Nat: Butter, 1608): ("At last, Fortune having brought him here, where she might make him the fittest Tennis-ball for her sport"). Wilkins either remembered it from Shakespeare's play, or contributed the metaphor to the play himself, if the arguments for Wilkins's co-authorship are correct (see Doreen DelVecchio and Antony Hammond's introduction to their edition of *Pericles* (Cambridge and New York: Cambridge University Press, 1998), 8–15). Either way, the allusion is to the "ball" in Isaiah, updated in conformity with the Renaissance sport of tennis.

written). Others of Colton's parallels might better be called theological commonplaces, though these are inevitably allusive when they are derived from biblical texts. In Portia's mercy speech in *Merchant of Venice*, for instance, she urges Shylock to consider that, "in the course of justice, none of us | Should see salvation" (4.1.195–6). This is good Protestant theology, based on Paul's seminal Epistle to the Romans: "Therefore by the workes of the Law shal no flesh be justified in his sight" (3:20).[41] Shakespeare's lines are not precisely an allusion to Paul, since there is no specific textual relationship to the biblical source, but Paul's emphasis on "flesh" suggests that this may be more than simply a coincident parallel, given the critical importance of flesh in Shakespeare's scene.

Nuggets of useful criticism can be found in many of the Victorian "Bible and Shakespeare" volumes, but in most there is far more dross than gold. Analyzing Shakespeare's use of allusion was not, after all, what most of these writers were most interested in. Theirs was primarily a religious agenda, which also partly explains the predominance of clergymen among them. Charles LaPorte has argued that bardolatrous nineteenth-century ideas about Shakespeare were intertwined with ideas circulating about the Bible generated by the German Higher Criticism.[42] It is difficult to extract a straightforward narrative from the complex history of ideas—William B. Hesseltine famously decribed writing intellectual history as "like trying to nail jelly to the wall"—but it is notable that the rise of bardolatry coincided with the rise of what David Norton has called "AVolatry," the veneration of the Authorized Version (King James Bible) as a masterpiece of English prose. The elevation of and devotion to the King James Bible may have been partly an attempt to hold onto something timeless and solid in the face of biblical studies that were demythologizing the Bible, fragmenting the biblical text into separate narrative strands, written and redacted by various human authors over centuries, most of them unreliable as historical documents.[43] For those committed to Christian belief, especially under the auspices of the Church of England, the King James Bible became essential to both English religious and national identity. Shakespeare was similarly revered as both a national literary treasure and a moral–spiritual icon, leading in the most extreme cases to hagiography or even deification. In 1854, B. S. Naylor called Shakespeare "one of the

---

[41] G. Q. Colton, *Shakespeare and the Bible: Parallel passages and passages suggested by the Bible with the religious sentiments of Shakspeare* (New York: Knox, [*c.*1888]), 41, 22.

[42] LaPorte, "The Bard."

[43] This was certainly the origin, to cite a more extreme case, of the "King James Only" movement of the later twentieth century, an offshoot of American Fundamentalism.

greatest Moral-philosophers that ever lived."[44] In 1865, the author of *An Imaginary Conversation between Mr Phelps and Dr Cumming* gave Phelps the lines, "Oh! the Bible is a grand book, that is very true, but when you say there is only one book in the world, I go further than you, for I say there are two, the Bible and Shakespeare. The Bible the book of God— Shakespeare the book of Man."[45] In 1880, J. F. Timmins quoted the Revd Canon Boyle as saying, "there is scarcely to be found in any other book such a digest of the Christian faith as in the writings of Shakespeare."[46] Charles Downing perhaps represents the extreme development of this line of thought. Writing under the pseudonym "Clelia," he published *God in Shakespeare* in 1890, in which he promised, "I will show that the profane play-actor was a Holy Prophet—'Nay, I say unto you, and more than a Prophet,' the Messiah. Heine, a Hebrew, first spoke of Stratford as the northern Bethlehem. I will show that Heine, a poet, spoke more truly than he knew."[47] "Clelia" followed up in 1901 with *The Messiahship of Shakspeare: A Symbolic Poem*, which takes the Shakespeare cult to its pinnacle:

The Tempest, like the Sonnets, is a work of a religious nature by unmistakable marks. It is imbued throughout with high moral passion, it presents in Prospero a worker and teacher of the moral law, a God-man, a Logos, a Trinity in Unity, which, moreover, is the Christian Trinity in Unity. And observe, Prospero is not the mere artistic presentation of a God-man. He is the proclamation of the eternal significance of a *rôle* that has been lived. For twelve years previous to the proclamation, Shakspeare, at one with the Spirit and with God, at one with Christ the Judge, in a series of great tragedies had judged the world.[48]

Deranged as Downing sounds, his *God in Shakespeare* was published, and reprinted, by the respectable publisher T. Fisher Unwin, and it obviously sold well enough to justify the publication of *Messiahship* eleven years

---

[44] B. S. Naylor, *Time and Truth reconciling the moral and religious world of Shakespeare; the greatest Poet and Dramatist, the greatest Moral-philosopher and Philanthropist, that ever lived in the tide of times: whose greatness, like an Alpine-avalanche, continues increasing and increasing and increasing, as the wonderful revelations of his overwhelming Genius roll down the steep of time* (London: W. Kent & Co., 1854), 2.

[45] Anon., *An Imaginary Conversation Between Mr. Phelps and Dr. Cumming. By the Ghost of Walter S. Landor* (n.p., 1865?), 5.

[46] J. F. Timmins, *The Poet-Priest: Shakespearian Sermons Compiled for the Use of Students and Public Readers* (London: J. Blackwood & Co., 1880), 13.

[47] Clelia [Charles Downing], *God in Shakespeare: The Course of the Poet's Spiritual Life with his Reflections thereon and his Resultant Conception of his World-Personality Inductively Established by the Text*, 2nd edn (London: T. Fisher Unwin), 15.

[48] Clelia [Charles Downing], *The Messiahship of Shakespeare Sung and Expounded* (London: Greening, 1901), 61.

later by Greening & Co., publishers of serious criticism on Walter Raleigh, Rudyard Kipling, Arthur Pinero, and Oscar Wilde.[49]

Not all of those interested in the Bible and Shakespeare were committed to religious faith, however. Some welcomed the demystification of the Bible, along with the humanizing of Jesus in works like David Strauss's *Life of Jesus* (in German 1835–6, translated by George Eliot in 1846), and their celebration of the King James Bible and Shakespeare's plays as secular scripture was decidedly non-religious. Thus F. J. Furnivall's statement in his preface to W. H. Malcolm's *Shakspere and Holy Writ* (1880): "It is but natural for an Englishman, whether he believes in the full inspiration of the Bible or not, to couple it and Shakespere's works together; for these books are the two which have most influenced the English mind."[50] The poet Algernon Charles Swinburne wrote of the volume of Shakespeare's works that "it would be better for the world to lose all others and keep this one than to lose this and keep all other treasures bequeathed by human genius to all that we can conceive of eternity."[51] Swinburne's hyberbole is almost identical to that of Thomas Babington, Lord Macaulay, eighty years earlier, praising the "book which if everything else in our language should perish, would alone suffice to show the whole extent of its beauty and power."[52] Yet Macaulay was writing of the English Bible (in 1828 almost certainly the King James Version).

Religious faith was a factor in the proliferation of studies of the Bible and Shakespeare in another way too. An explicit purpose of Watson's *Religious and Moral Sentences* was to prove "from *Shakespeare's own writings*, that he lived and died a *true Protestant*."[53] Claims for Shakespeare's Catholicism date back to the seventeenth century, when John Speed referred to Robert Parsons and Shakespeare as "this papist and his poet" (1611) and Richard Davies claimed Shakespeare died a papist.[54] Much was also made of a Catholic document supposedly discovered in the rafters of the Shakespeare house in Stratford, signed by John Shakespeare,

---

[49] Downing also published *Great Pan Lives* in 1892 (London: Luzac and Co.), a study of "the Evolution of the Ideal" in Sonnets 20–126.

[50] W. H. Malcolm, *Shakspere and Holy Writ: Parallel Passages, Tabularly Arranged*, with foreword by F. J. Furnivall (London: Marcus Ward & Co., 1881), 1.

[51] Swinburne, *Shakespeare* (1909), cited in LaPorte, "The Bard," 612.

[52] Thomas Babington, "John Dryden (January 1828)," in *Miscellaneous Writings and Speeches of Lord Macaulay*, ii. Online text prepared by Mike Alder and Sue Asscher, Project Gutenberg <http://www.gutenberg.org/ebooks/25903> (accessed 11November 21, 2012).

[53] Sir Frederick Beilby Watson, *Religious and Moral Sentences*, p. xix.

[54] E. K. Chambers, *William Shakespeare: A Study of Facts and Problems*, 2 vols (Oxford: Clarendon Press, 1930), ii. 257, 217.

Shakespeare's father. Edmund Malone published this in his 1790 edition of Shakespeare, persuaded that it was genuine and that it indicated that John Shakespeare was a Catholic recusant, but he changed his mind and omitted it from the 1796 edition. The document itself subsequently disappeared, but arguments for a Catholic Shakespeare persisted. A steady stream of articles in Catholic periodicals like the *Rambler*, the *American Catholic Quarterly Review*, the *New Ireland Review*, and the *Month* made the case, and gained some continental support from A. F. Rio's biography, *Shakespeare* (Paris, 1864), followed by his *Shakespeare catholique* (Paris, 1875).[55] Richard Foulkes has argued that the movement for a Catholic Shakespeare gained impetus with Catholic Emancipation in Britain in 1829, its proponents wrestling with the champions of the Anglican Shakespeare for control of the "national" poet.[56] In any case, the debate about Shakespeare's personal faith stimulated further comparison of his plays with the Bible, though generally from the Protestant side, Catholic apologists focusing instead on biographical evidence and matters like the plays' representations of priests and good Catholics like Katherine of Aragon (in *Henry VIII*).[57]

WILLIAM SHAKESPEARE, BIBLE TRANSLATOR

One very peculiar idea that evolved out of the semi-intellectual soup of Victorian writing on Shakespeare and the Bible was the notion that Shakespeare himself wrote the Bible, or rather that he was involved in the translation of the King James Version. Where this originated is impossible to determine, but it appears in print in the first years of the twentieth century. Rudyard Kipling explores the idea fancifully in his last short story, "Proofs of Holy Writ," published in 1934.[58] The story features

---

[55] Rio's thesis in the biography is that "Shakespeare était mort catholique romain" (Shakespeare died a Roman Catholic). *Shakespeare* (Paris: Charles Douniol, 1864), 335.
[56] Richard Foulkes, "William Shakespeare: The Model Victorian Protestant," *Shakespeare* 5/1 (2009), 68–81.
[57] An interesting anomaly in this debate is William J. Birch, author of *An Inquiry into the Philosophy and Religion of Shakspere* (London: C. Mitchell, 1848). Birch writes that "Shakspere treated religion with even less respect than Marlowe. He introduced obscenity, and went beyond him in profanity" (p. 3). Birch sees Shakespeare as a skeptical atheist, critical of all religion. In his play-by-play exposition of Shakespeare's irreligion, however, Birch does examine a number of significant instances of biblical allusion, as in *Richard II* (Richard's attempt to cast himself as Christ) and *The Merchant of Venice* (Shylock's use of the story of Jacob and Laban).
[58] Rudyard Kipling, "Proofs of Holy Writ," *The Strand* (April 1934), repr. in December 1947. See David Norton, " 'Proofs of Holy Writ': Myths of the Authorized Version: Kipling and the Bible," *Kipling Journal* (December 1989), 18–27.

60   *Shakespeare's Allusive Practice*

Shakespeare and Ben Jonson talking over pints of ale, discussing fine points of the translation of Isaiah 40 ("Arise, shine, for thy light is come") after Shakespeare recounts his being called in by Miles Smith to doctor the King James translation. Anthony Burgess was another fiction writer who enjoyed this idea; he included it in his novels *Enderby's Dark Lady* and *Earthly Powers*. Burgess was particularly fascinated by an apparent cipher in the KJV's Psalm 46. It is true that if you count 46 words from the beginning of this Psalm, in the King James Version, you find the word "shake." If you count 46 words from the end, ignoring the Hebrew word *selah*, which nobody any longer understands, you find "spear."

Who first noticed this no one knows; its origins recede into the mists of folklore. One writer attributes it to an Eton schoolboy, another to the Irish Classicist Yelverton Tyrrell.[59] The earliest appearance in print seems to be in 1901 in *The Flaming Sword*, the publication of the Koreshan Unity, an American utopian sect founded in the 1870s by Cyrus Teed. The editor cites the "wonderful cryptogram in the Bible" along with other mysteries like the pyramids and phrenology.[60] In 1902, there is a brief paragraph on "The Cipher Theory" in the *Cambrian*, a monthly published by and for the Welsh in America, and apparently a similar notice the same year in the *Book-Lover*.[61] In 1913, there was a note on "The Baconian Method Applied to the Psalms" in New York's the *Independent*. The *Independent* credits an earlier article in the *Fortnightly Review* of St Louis.[62] Eventually, in 1976, after bouncing around lesser periodicals, the cipher ended up in *The Times*, in a Shakespeare's Birthday piece by Mark Hodson, former Bishop of Hereford but in his retirement Assistant Bishop of London.[63] For Hodson, the cipher was a tribute to Shakespeare by one of the KJV translators. However, most "breakers" of the code argue that it is a signature, a mark of Shakespeare's own covert involvement in the translation. Some more energetic amateur cryptographers find even more in Psalm 46. They note, for instance, that Shakespeare was 46 during at least part of 1610, as the finishing touches were made to the KJV. Some observe that, if you spell Shakespeare's name without the final "e," it contains 10 letters, 4 consonants and 6 vowels.

---

[59] For the argument for Tyrrell, see the letter to *The Times* from the Canon C. B. Armstrong (April 29, 1976), 17. A letter to the same paper two days earlier from Noel Fermor, Chairman of the Francis Bacon Society (*The Times*, April 27, 1976, 15) claims the cipher was known to Baconians as early as 1886.

[60] Anon., "In the Editorial Perspective," *Flaming Sword*, 15/14 (February 22, 1901), 10.

[61] Anon., "The Cipher Theory," *Cambrian*, 22 (Utica, NY, 1902), 247–8. The article cites "a writer in a London newspaper."

[62] Anon., "The Baconian Method Applied to the Psalms," *Independent*, 74 (New York, January–June, 1913), 48.

[63] Letter to the Editor, *The Times* (April 24, 1976), 12.

Critical History of the Bible in Shakespeare 61

The Baconians, not surprisingly, read the cipher as the signature of Bacon, not Shakespeare. Henry Seymour, in a 1924 lecture to the Baconian Society, noted that the sixth and seventh words from the beginning of the tenth verse of Psalm 46 are "I am," and the sixth and seventh from the end are "will I." Hence, "William," crushed a little bit in the manner of Malvolio. But if you take the name "William Shakespere" (spelled "ere") anagrammatically, it reads "We are like his psalm." Since "William Shakespeare" is merely the pseudonymous "signature" of Bacon, however, it is invaluable to discover that the number 46 can be deciphered by cabalistic numerology as "S. Alban." (Bacon was the first Viscount St Alban.) The mystery unfolds.[64]

The so-called cipher in Psalm 46 has been debunked many times, most notably by the genuine cryptanalysts William and Elizebeth Friedman, in *The Shakespearean Ciphers Examined* (Cambridge: Cambridge University Press, 1957).[65] It is also notable that the words "shake" and "spear" (neither uncommon) appear in earlier English Bibles, at approximately the same positions. The slight shift in the KJV is due to the omission of two words—"then" and "the"—both of which are easily explained as attempts at greater faithfulness to the Hebrew, as was pointed out in a later letter to *The Times* by the philosopher D. D. Raphael.[66] The 46 count also depends on omitting the word *selah*; as noted above, biblical scholars are not sure what this Hebrew term means, but it is clearly there in the text. Coincidence is less sexy than conspiracy, but it is sometimes the better explanation.[67] Some of the other codes are even more tenuous: for example, the deciphering of Shakespeare's name depends upon particular spellings, though we know Shakespeare signed his name several ways. Of course, the greatest problem with the idea of Shakespeare as Bible translator is that it just does not make sense. He was not a scholar, he was not a clergyman (as were all but one of the KJV translators), and he did not have the necessary languages. The idea that he should be part of the KJV team would have been preposterous to everyone, including Shakespeare. Moreover, the styles of Shakespeare and the KJV are as different as can be, the one spare, minimalistic, and limited in its vocabulary, the other florid, densely metaphorical, and full of neologisms. And the KJV translators were not especially interested in literary excellence anyway; they aimed to

---

[64] Henry Seymour, "Illustrations of Baconian Cyphers," *Baconiana*, 3rd edn, 17 (1924), 256–75.
[65] William Friedman worked for US intelligence and was instrumental in founding the National Security Agency.
[66] Letter to the Editor, *The Times*, April 30, 1976, 17.
[67] For another debunking, see R. H. Robbins, "Shakespeare and Psalm 46: An Accumulation of Coincidences," *N&Q* 50/1 (March 2003), 58–60.

be accurate, not "poetic."[68] Despite the claims of reason, however, the Psalm cipher has continued to spread more widely than ever, cropping up in a remarkable range of books and across the Internet: not just studies of Shakespeare and the Bible, but books on science and numbers, works on mysticism, intuition, and psychoanalysis, and collections of literary curiosities. The story is a curiosity of cultural history, but it testifies further to the close link that was felt and possibly still is felt between Shakespeare and the Bible.

BIBLICAL REFERENCES

Out of the confusion of nineteenth-century volumes on the Bible and Shakespeare, most deservedly forgotten, a line of genuine scholarship emerges that is increasingly independent of confessional partisanship. For one thing, J. O. Halliwell established in 1867 that Shakespeare primarily used the Geneva Bible, citing numerous examples of biblical borrowings or allusions whose language clearly derives from that translation: he included the "husks" reference from *As You Like It*, as well as examples of biblical allusions from other plays, testing them against various sixteenth-century Bible translations.[69] Nevertheless, most of the Bible and Shakespeare compilations had quoted the King James Bible, since it is the English version lauded as a national monument, even though it was published too late (1611) to be of any significant influence on Shakespeare.

The identification of borrowings or allusions continued to be haphazard and shallow for many writers, but Bishop Charles Wordsworth's *Shakespeare's Knowledge and Use of the Bible* (1864) represents an advance in critical methodology. Wordsworth divided his chapters into "noticeable Forms of Speech in the English Bible found also in Shakespeare," "noticeable Words in the English Bible found also in Shakespeare," "Allusions in Shakespeare to the Historical Facts and Characters of the Bible," a long section on "Shakspeare's Religious Principles and Sentiments derived from the Bible," and finally "the Poetry of Shakespeare as derived from the Bible." Wordsworth was obviously aiming at something more systematic than most of the "Bible and Shakespeare Compared" compilers. Wordsworth's first two chapters are sophisticated and original. The first

---

[68] David Norton, *A History of the English Bible as Literature* (Cambridge: Cambridge University Press, 2000), 56–75, and throughout.

[69] J. O. Halliwell, *An Attempt to Discover Which Version of the Bible Was That Ordinarily Used by Shakespeare* (London: Privately Printed, 1867).

compares peculiar or antiquated idioms in Shakespeare, including grammar and syntax, with similar usages in the English Bible (he checks Geneva and Bishops', obviously aware that the KJV is not relevant). Shakespeare uses the phrase "die the death" with its seemingly superfluous article, for instance, in several plays (*Measure for Measure* 2.4, *Midsummer Night's Dream* 1.1, *Cymbeline* 4.2), and Wordsworth suggests it derives from (English) biblical language like "sick to the death" (2 Chron. 32:24) and "unto the death" (Acts 22:4).[70] Shakespeare also used a "double comparative" as in "more richer," "more worthier," "more worse" in *King Lear*, which are similar to the biblical "most highest" (Book of Common Prayer Psalms) and "most straightest" (Acts 26:5).[71]

Wordsworth's second chapter tracks the use of rare or obsolete words in Shakespeare that are also used in sixteenth-century English Bibles, including, for instance, "atone" meaning "reconcile" in *Othello* 4.1 and Acts 7:26; or "cunning" as "knowledge" or "skill" in *Antony and Cleopatra* 2.3 and *Taming of the Shrew* 1.1 and Psalm 137:5 and Exodus 38:23; or "man-child" in *Coriolanus* 1.3 and Leviticus 7:2.[72] The value of Wordsworth's conclusions is qualified by his inattention to the history of English usage, considering neither the extent to which Shakespeare's usage was that of his contemporaries nor the extent to which English Bible translations might simply be reflecting popular sixteenth-century usage, but Wordsworth was working long before the advent of the *OED*. Wordsworth's "Facts and Characters" chapter is much more solid, noting references to biblical characters like Adam (*Hamlet* 5.1, *As You Like It* 2.1) and Cain and Abel (*Richard II* 1.1, *1 Henry VI* 1.3), and unambiguous references to biblical stories like the Creation (*The Tempest* 1.2, "the bigger light" and "the less") or the Fall (*Henry V* 2.1, "another fall of man"). Wordsworth's section on "Religious Principles and Sentiments" is less concerned with biblical allusion, since it covers broader ideas such as divine kingship, immortality, mercy, angels, sin, and repentance. Unlike others who made similar claims for Shakespeare's use of religious–biblical ideas, however, Wordsworth was careful to cite the dramatic context of all of his quotations, attributing such ideas not to Shakespeare but to the characters who utter them. His final chapter explores Shakespeare's use of certain images from the English Bible. Some of these are too vague or commonplace to be convincing, but others clearly do constitute genuine allusions, like Faulconbridge's ironic inversion of Isaiah's beating "swords into

---

[70] Charles Wordsworth, *Shakespeare's Knowledge and Use of the Bible*, 4th edn, rev. (London and Sydney: Eden, Remington & Co Publishers, 1864), 10–12.
[71] Wordsworth, *Shakespeare's Knowledge*, 20–1.
[72] Wordsworth, *Shakespeare's Knowledge*, 29–30, 32, 36.

ploughshares" and "spears into pruning-hooks" (Isa. 2:4, and also Mic. 4:3; for the contrary image, see Joel 3:9–10). In *King John*, Faulconbridge speaks of ladies who "Their thimbles into armed gauntlets change, | Their needles to lances, and their gentle hearts | To fierce and bloody inclination" (5.2.156–8).[73]

The next major step forward in the study of Shakespeare's biblical allusions was taken by Thomas Carter. Carter was a Presbyterian minister from Birmingham who launched a salvo against the proponents of the Catholic Shakespeare with *Shakespeare, Puritan and Recusant* (Edinburgh and London, 1897). There was little new here, though Carter did assert, based on specific citations, Shakespeare's tendency to use the Geneva Bible, which apparently convinced William Ewart Gladstone.[74] In 1905, however, Carter published *Shakespeare and Holy Scripture with the Version he Used*, which is the major precursor to the twentieth-century studies by Richmond Noble and Naseeb Shaheen. Like those later scholars, Carter treats each play in a separate chapter, for each one listing all the passages, scene by scene, which show a verbal relationship to the Bible. Carter favors the term "reference" to describe these intertextual relationships, though he occasionally uses "allusion" and even (twice) "echo." Often, Carter refers simply to Shakespeare's "use" of a biblical word or phrase. There are almost 500 pages of these references, with virtually no other text or apparatus, apart from an introductory chapter reiterating the argument for Shakespeare's use of Geneva, citing Halliwell, and a brief chapter on "Shakespeare and Puritanism." This is really a scholarly reference work, designed for maximum utility for anyone wanting to see what references to the Bible Shakespeare makes in any given play, or for those suspecting a biblical reference but wanting to know the source. Despite his claims for the Geneva, Carter also sometimes lists variants among different English Bibles, as when he cites Matthew 5:44 ("praye for them which hurt you, and persecute you") as referred to by Rivers in *Richard III* 1.3.316, "To pray for them that have done scath to us." Carter gives the passage in Wyclif, Tyndale, the Great Bible, the Rheims New Testament, and the Authorized Version, as well as the Geneva.[75]

Carter's *Shakespeare and Holy Scripture* established the format that was followed in 1935 by Richmond Noble. Noble's *Shakespeare's Biblical*

---

[73] Wordsworth, *Shakespeare's Knowledge*, 265–6.
[74] The Folger copy (PR3012 .C3) contains newspaper clippings citing a letter from Gladstone to Carter in which he makes this admission.
[75] Thomas Carter, *Shakespeare and Holy Scripture with the Version He Used* (London: Hodder and Stoughton, 1905), 127–8. "Cranmer" (as Carter calls the Great Bible) is the same as Geneva in this passage, but the others are different. The Bishops' Bible is also identical to Geneva (and Great), though for some reason Carter does not cite it.

Knowledge and Use of the Book of Common Prayer became a standard reference work, cited by editors and scholars for the next half century. The inclusion of the Book of Common Prayer reflected Noble's particular interest in exploring Shakespeare's use not only of Coverdale's Psalms but of the Church liturgy. Noble's scholarship was more systematic than any of his predecessors. Introductory chapters provide a history of English translations of the Bible in the Tudor period and a thorough assessment of which version Shakespeare used (Geneva but also Bishops', as well as the Book of Common Prayer). Noble also suggests how Shakespeare acquired his biblical knowledge, offering five means—reading the Bible, listening to it read in church, hearing sermons and liturgies, general reading, and general conversation—but also exploring whether the English Bible was used in Tudor schools. Most importantly, Noble describes his methodology and its relationship to previous studies, including those of Wordsworth and Carter. Chapter 7, which takes up 151 of the book's 303 pages, is entitled "List of Biblical and Liturgical References," using the same neutral term "reference" favored by Carter, but Noble explores the terminology for intertextual relations more precisely in an earlier chapter. He describes his classification of "quotation and allusion," dividing them into three classes: "passages in the plays which can positively be stated to contain Biblical or Liturgical quotations or allusions"; "other passages containing probable references, which would commend themselves as such to any reasonable man conversant with the Bible and with the plays"; and "those that on a rational showing could possibly be held to be quotations or allusions but about which no one could be dogmatic one way or the other."[76] Noble provides examples of each, but also notes the more problematic case of "parallels," which "contain no quotation of Scripture, yet exhibit a more or less close resemblance in thought to some Biblical passages." These parallels are admitted, he notes, only "with discretion and for some particular reason."[77] Noble also considers the phenomenology of allusion, noting that "the dramatist is limited in his use of literary allusion as compared with ordinary writers." The problem, as he sees it, is that an allusion must not interfere with the progress of the drama and that a passage that is allusive must be comprehensible and enjoyable to the audience whether they perceive the allusion or not. Noble cites the example of Bottom's speech in *A Midsummer Night's Dream*, "The eye of man hath not heard, the ear of man hath not seen . . ." (4.1.211–13). The deeper understanding of the passage requires audience recognition of the allusion to (and muddling of) Paul's First Epistle to the Corinthians (see

---

[76] Noble, 24.   [77] Noble, 35–6.

Chapter 3). But many readers and theatergoers have also enjoyed Bottom's synaesthetic nonsense without knowing its engagement with the biblical text—"If nobody noticed, Shakespeare did not care, everything went on as though no allusion had been made."[78] Noble also suggests that "literary allusion involves the reader or spectator in a working partnership with the author," which moves further than any previous critic toward an understanding of the function of allusions (biblical or otherwise) in the plays.[79]

The line of scholarship from Wordsworth to Carter to Noble culminates in the work of Naseeb Shaheen, who is as authoritative for Shakespeare scholars today as Noble was for those in the earlier twentieth century. Shaheen began his career by publishing *Biblical References in The Faerie Queene* (1976), but then published a sequence of volumes cataloguing such references in Shakespeare's plays: *Biblical References in Shakespeare's Tragedies* (1987), *Biblical References in Shakespeare's History Plays* (1989), and *Biblical References in Shakespeare's Comedies* (1993). The three volumes were combined in *Biblical References in Shakespeare's Plays* (1999). Shaheen amassed a substantial personal collection of early modern Bibles, including over 115 copies of the Geneva, and this was the basis for his tracking of references.[80] Like Noble, however, Shaheen was very much aware of his predecessors; Noble cited Wordsworth and Carter, Shaheen cites Carter and Noble, and provides a thorough bibliography of earlier criticism. Shaheen also follows Noble's format, listing references chronologically, play by play (though he lists them by genre, not in order of composition, as Noble did), providing an index of biblical passages referred to, and setting out in introductory chapters a history of the English Bible, a consideration of the liturgy, and a methodological chapter, "Considerations for a Valid Reference." Noble's three classes of allusion are the same as Shaheen's categories of reference, the certain, the probable, and the possible. Shaheen looks for clear verbal parallels, though he allows into his third category passages where "the borrowing from Scripture is not so much verbal as it is the borrowing of an idea."[81] Unlike Noble, Shaheen does not address how biblical references might work in drama or their effect on the reader. His approach is bibliographical rather than interpretative, leaving it to his readers what to make of all of the references

---

[78] Noble, 22–3.   [79] Noble, 23.
[80] The majority of Shaheen's Bibles, along with his notes and annotated copies of Shakespeare's plays, are now housed in the Shaheen Antiquarian Bible Collection at the University of Tennessee, Knoxville.
[81] Shaheen, 70. The example used is the description of Coriolanus, "I have seen the dumb men throng to see him, and | The blind to hear him speak" (2.1.262–3). On this allusion, which I would argue is actually verbal, see Ch. 5.

he points out. For each play, however, Shaheen provides a useful introduction, beginning with dating and then describing the play's sources, noting whether any of Shakespeare's biblical references were already present in the works on which he based his play. Shaheen also takes into account different versions of the play in quarto and folio. Despite its avoidance of interpretation or theories of intertextuality, *Biblical References* is an exceptionally thorough and useful reference work, not likely to be superseded soon.

WARS OF RELIGION

Twentieth-century Shakespeare critics continue the struggle to claim Shakespeare for one Christian denomination or another. For the most part, however, these arguments tend to be based on biography and religious themes rather than on biblical allusions. Shakespeare criticism of all sorts grows exponentially, however, and, rather than my attempting a thorough catalogue of scholarship that includes discussion about biblical allusions, it might be most useful to offer some representative samples from among leading proponents of different critical approaches. G. Wilson Knight is the major proponent of what William Empson called, with contempt, the neo-Christian school. Knight's *The Wheel of Fire* was published in 1930, with an approving introduction by T. S. Eliot. Most of Knight's essays on Shakespeare's tragedies do not directly concern the Bible (though he notes that "*King Lear* is analogous to the *Book of Job*," on which see Chapter 8), with the striking exception of "*Measure for Measure* and the Gospels."[82] Knight begins this essay by asserting "a clear relation existing between the play and the Gospels," based on the title's allusion to Matthew 7:1, which he cites in the King James Version:

Judge not, that ye be not judged. For with what judgement ye judge, ye shall be judged: and with what measure ye mete, it shall be measured to you again.[83]

Given that this is the only play Shakespeare wrote whose title alludes to the Bible—and critics of all sorts agree on this—it is not surprising to find other biblical allusions in the text. The problem with Knight's approach, however, is that his identification of allusions (not a term he uses) is

---

[82] G. Wilson Knight, *The Wheel of Fire: Interpretations of Shakespearian Tragedy* (London: Methuen, 1930; repr. 1964). The comment on *King Lear* is in "The *Lear* Universe," 191.
[83] The Geneva translation is essentially the same, but Knight's spelling suggests he is using the King James.

largely subjective and that his interpretation of them is skewed by his reading of the play as a Christian allegory.

Sometimes Knight's claims for intertextual relationships seem persuasive, as when he cites the Duke's words to Escalus, "Look, the unfolding star calls up the shepherd. Put not yourself into amazement how these things should be: all difficulties are but easy when they are known" (4.2.194–97). Knight states that the first sentence "derives part of its appeal from New Testament associations." He does not spell these out, but surely what he has in mind is a conflation of the Nativity stories in Matthew and Luke, with the "star in the east" from the former and the shepherds from the latter. Such conflation was traditional, as in the many artistic renderings of the Nativity that combine both the three kings and the shepherds (not to mention the ox and ass from Isa. 1:3), and for any Christian audience shepherds and a star will probably suggest the Nativity to some degree. Knight continues, "the second sentence holds the mystic assurance of Matthew, x.26: '. . . for there is nothing covered, that shall not be revealed; and hid, that shall not be known.'"[84] The only claim here is for some sort of mystic analogy, and the suggestion is not unreasonable, given other New Testament references to hidden mysteries and eventual revelation (Paul's darkling vision in 1 Cor. 13, for instance). When, earlier in the play, the Duke tells Angelo,

> Heaven doth with us as we with torches do;
> Not light them for themselves; for if our virtues
> Did not go forth of us, 'twere all alike (1.1.32–4),

we can agree that "the thought is similar to that of the Sermon on the Mount":

Ye are the light of the world. A city that is set on a hill cannot be hid. Neither do men light a candle, and put it under a bushel, but on a candlestick; and it giveth light unto all that are in the house. (Matt. 5:14)[85]

These are familiar Christian metaphors, and, as Shaheen notes, it is all the more likely that Shakespeare had them in mind, since the Duke is speaking of Heaven's (that is, God's) will. Knight is not interested in analyzing these passages in depth, considering the dramatic context, or in asking whether, if they do constitute genuine allusions, the effect is straightforward or ironic. Instead, they are meant to support his larger allegorical reading. The Duke's language sometimes sounds like Jesus's, because "the Duke, like Jesus, is the prophet of a new order of ethics" and "a symbol of the same kind as the Father in the Parable of the Prodigal Son (Luke xv)

---

[84] Knight, *Wheel of Fire*, 81.   [85] Knight, *Wheel of Fire*, 77.

or the Lord in that of the Unmerciful Servant (Matthew xviii)." *Measure for Measure* "must be read in the light of the Gospel teaching," and "on the analogy of Jesus' parables."[86] This simply licenses his free associations, and Knight follows through, likening the play's denouement, with the Duke's various sentencings, as the "last act of judgement... heralded by trumpet calls," with his condemnation of Lucio to marriage with a whore as a fulfillment of Matthew 12:36: "every idle word that men shall speak, they shall give account thereof in the day of judgment."[87]

Studies like Knight's generated considerable ire from critics, like Empson, who were unsympathetic or hostile to Christianity in particular or religion in general, as well as critics who were simply more skeptical about Shakespeare's religious beliefs and the implications of biblical allusions or echoes in the plays. Roland Mushat Frye, for instance, lambasted the "School of Knight" in his 1963 *Shakespeare and Christian Doctrine*. Frye's argument, essentially, is that there is no Christian doctrine, *per se*, in Shakespeare, except insofar as he puts theological ideas or language into the mouths of his characters for the dramatic purposes of a play. A particular source of irritation for Frye was the attempt by critics such as Knight, Paul N. Siegel, J. A. Bryant, and others to read "Christ-figures" everywhere in Shakespeare's plays. The Duke in *Measure for Measure* is a case in point (for Knight), but Frye also cites Siegel's argument for Timon as an exemplum of "Christ's boundless generosity and love" and Bryant's claim for Antonio in *The Merchant of Venice* that nowhere in Renaissance literature is there "a neater parallel to Christ's voluntary assumption of the debt that was death to repay."[88] Other Christ-figures include Desdemona in *Othello* and Cordelia in *King Lear* (Siegel), and Hermione in *The Winter's Tale* (Bryant). This proliferation of Christ-figures also bothered William R. Elton, who cited in his 1966 *King Lear and the Gods* Knight's sweeping statement that every Shakespearian tragic hero is "a miniature Christ."[89] Elton throws other critics onto the pyre as well: J. Dover Wilson, for whom it is "impossible to contemplate the death of Lear without thinking of Calvary," as well as Geoffrey L. Bickersteth, John M. Lothian, John F. Danby, S. L. Bethell, and Edgar I. Fripp (and Siegel again).

---

[86] Knight, *Wheel of Fire*, 82–3.   [87] Knight, *Wheel of Fire*, 89–91.
[88] Roland Mushat Frye, *Shakespeare and Christian Doctrine* (Princeton: Princeton University Press, 1963), 34, citing Paul N. Siegel, *Shakespearean Tragedy and the Elizabethan Compromise* (New York: New York University Press, 1957), and J. A. Bryant, *Hippolyta's View: Some Christian Aspects of Shakespeare's Plays* (Lexington, KY: University of Kentucky Press, 1961).
[89] William R. Elton, *King Lear and the Gods* (San Marino, CA: Huntington Library, 1966), 8, citing G. Wilson Knight, *Principles of Shakespearian Production with Especial Reference to the Tragedies* (London: Faber and Faber, 1936), 231.

After the critiques of Frye, Elton, and others, Christian readings of Shakespeare's plays fell into some disrepute, though Knight himself continued publishing and lecturing into the 1980s, Siegel and Bryant into the 1990s. The term "Christ-figure" became for many an embarrassment. This is unfortunate, since it is actually a rather useful term, and it is also clear that, despite the excessive claims of Knight et al., there are in fact a number of major characters in Shakespeare's plays who might be so designated, Cordelia included (see Chapter 8). Richard Levin in a characteristically witty and scathing *PMLA* article condemned all hunting for Christ-figures from Knight on, likening their critical practice to Fluellen's comparison of a river in Macedon and the river Wye as "both alike" in that "there is salmons in both."[90] Levin never names the critics he cites and dismisses, but they are relatively easy to identify with the advent of GoogleBooks: Nevill Coghill, Knight, Howard C. Cole, David L. Stevenson, Norman Holland, Mary Lascelles, [one other critic I have not traced], William B. Toole, A. D. Nuttall, Burton R. Pollen, Bryant, Carl Dennis, Bryant (again), Jarold W. Ramsey, Siegel, Roy W. Battenhouse, Barbara K. Lewalski, and Ramsey (again, same article).[91] Levin's objection to Fluellenists and Fluellenism, as he names them, is that any characters can be described as a Christ-figure, given the numbers of possible points of comparison (from actions mentioned in the gospels to characteristics like sacrifice, resistance of temptation, love, and so forth), and that such comparisons are always selective, leaving out whatever else in Shakespeare or the Bible does not fit. The problem with Levin's argument is that it throws out the baby with the bathwater, rejecting not only the specious claims of Knight, Siegel, Bryant, and others, but biblical allusion altogether.

---

[90] Richard Levin, "On Fluellen's Figures, Christ Figures, and James Figures," *PMLA* 89/2 (1974), 302–11. For Fluellen, see *Henry V* 4.7.24–51.

[91] Nevill Coghill, "Comic Form in *Measure for Measure*" *SS* 8 (1955), 14–27; Knight, *Wheel of Fire*; Howard C. Cole, "The Christian Context of *Measure for Measure*," *JEGP* 64/3 (1965), 425–51; David L. Stevenson, *The Achievement of Shakespeare's* Measure for Measure (Ithaca, NY: Cornell University Press, 1966); Norman Holland, "*Measure for Measure*: The Duke and the Prince," *Comparative Literature*, 11/1 (1959), 16–20; Mary Lascelles, *Shakespeare's* Measure for Measure (London: University of London, Athlone Press, 1953); William B. Toole, *Shakespeare's Problem Plays: Studies in Form and Meaning* (The Hague and New York: Mouton, Humanities, 1965); A. D. Nuttall, "*Measure for Measure*: Quid Pro Quo?" *SSt* 4 (1968), 231–51; Burton R. Pollen, "Hamlet, a Successful Suicide," *SSt* 1 (1965), 240–60; J. A. Bryant, "Shakespeare Allegory: 'The Winter's Tale,'" *Sewanee Review*, 63/2 (1955), 202–22; Carl Dennis, "'All's Well that Ends Well' and the Meaning of 'Agape,'" *Philological Quarterly*, 50/1 (1971), 175–84; Bryant, *Hippolyta's View*; Jarold W. Ramsey, "Timon's Imitation of Christ," *SSt* 2 (1966), 162–73; Paul N. Siegel, "Echoes of the Bible Story in Macbeth," *N&Q* (April 1955), 142–3; Roy W. Battenhouse, *Shakespearean Tragedy: Its Art and Christian Premises* (Bloomington and London: Indiana University Press, 1969); Barbara K. Lewalksi, "Biblical Allusion and Allegory in 'The Merchant of Venice,'" *SQ* 13/3 (1962), 327–43.

As later chapters will demonstrate, Shakespeare does in fact create "Christ-figures," insofar as he uses biblical allusion to suggest comparisons or, more often, contrasts between certain of his characters and Christ. Cordelia is one such, as is Lear, Julius Caesar, Brutus, Coriolanus, Antony, Antonio (in *Merchant*), Richard II, and others. This is not to say that all characters are Christ-figures, nor is it to condone critical free association. Levin attacks Bryant's comparison of Richard II's death at Pomfret to Christ's Crucifixion, noting that Bryant "fails to mention that Richard's manifestation of regality, in which he kills two of his would-be executioners and consigns them to a 'room in Hel' and the 'never-quenching fire,' is just the opposite of Jesus's ('Father, forgive them; for they know not what they do')."[92] But, as will be clear throughout this book, Shakespeare's biblical allusions are often ironic, setting up parallels in order to emphasize their differences. This point would seem to be addressed by Levin's subsequent critique of "falling back upon the convenient concept of 'parody.'" But because it is convenient does not mean it is automatically false. The best reason for thinking of Richard II in terms of Christ, as discussed in Chapter 4, is that Richard makes this comparison himself, explicitly likening those at his deposition to Judases and Pilates, and thus implicitly identifying himself as the betrayed Christ. *Richard II* is a play especially rich in biblical allusion, and some of these allusions are to the gospels, suggesting Richard as a potential "Christ-figure." This is not to say that Richard *is* Christ, or is even very much *like* Christ, as do pious but critically naive studies like George H. Morrison's *Christ in Shakespeare* (1928). It is simply that one of the ways in which Shakespeare is exploring Richard's character and story is through comparisons to another character and story that he and his audience knew exceptionally well. To see Christ-figures everywhere in sixteenth- and seventeenth-century English culture is not a delusion nor the result of "neo-Christian" bias. Christ *was* everywhere, since everyone was (in some sort) Christian, and Christ was the essential model for living and essential to eternal salvation. Moreover, the Bible itself provided the pre-eminent model for comparing people to Christ. To take only a single work among the many that use the term, Erasmus's *Paraphrases* describe as a "figure of Christ," Isaac, David, Jeremiah, Joseph (father of Jesus), and Joseph (son of Jacob).[93] Other preachers and commentators apply the same term to Adam, Abel, Melchisedech, Moses, Aaron, Noah, Samson, Solomon, and Jonah. The term "figure" is used interchangeably with "type." Adam is a figure of

---

[92] Levin, "On Fluellen's Figures," 307.
[93] *The first tome or volume of the Paraphrase of Erasmus upon the Newe Testamente* (London: Edwarde Whitchurche, 1548), fos 21ʳ, 21ᵛ, 87ᵛ, 192ʳ, 197ᵛ.

Christ, in Christian thinking, in a different way from what any dramatic character could be, but the practice of reading the Bible typologically nevertheless encouraged comparisons beyond the Bible. Christ and the Christian story were at the center of every worship service. Christ was the ultimate model for self-sacrifice, turning the other cheek, betrayal (as the one betrayed), and human suffering, not to mention more peculiar phenomena such as incarnation and resurrection. It would be more surprising *not* to find references to him throughout the culture, and specifically in Shakespeare's plays.

The same is true, to a lesser degree, for other familiar biblical characters and stories. The Parable of the Prodigal Son also pervaded the culture, for instance, perhaps because primogeniture created so many prodigals in England's younger sons. Richard Helgerson argued for the Prodigal Son as an essential paradigm for the careers of Elizabethan authors such as George Gascoigne, John Lyly, and Sir Philip Sidney; Alan Young and others have shown how the story of the Prodigal Son shaped (in ways large or small) many Elizabethan plays, including Shakespeare's (*As You Like It, 1 Henry IV, King Lear*) as well as the anonymous *The Prodigal Son* and *The London Prodigal*, George Chapman, Ben Jonson, and John Marston's *Eastward Ho*, Middleton's *Michaelmas Term*, Jonson's *The Staple of News*, and many others through the 1630s.[94] Levin might call this just another type of Fluellenism, but, as a Yale University Art Gallery exhibition, *Prodigal Son Narratives, 1480–1980*, made clear, the Prodigal Son was everywhere in the culture, not just on stage. As curator Ellen G. D'Oench points out, the story of the Prodigal Son was "the most frequently illulstrated biblical parable in Western art," available in prints by Albrecht Dürer, Sebald Beham, Lucas van Leyden, Adriaen Collaert, Johannes Sadeler, as well as in many anonymous Reformation woodcuts and engravings.[95] Tessa Watt notes that the Prodigal Son was

---

[94] Richard Helgerson, *The Elizabethan Prodigals* (Berkeley, Los Angeles, and London: University of California Press, 1976); Alan R. Young, *The English Prodigal Son Plays: A Theatrical Fashion of the Sixteenth and Seventeenth Centuries* (Salzburg: Institut für Anglistik and Amerikanistik, Universität Salzburg, 1979); Ervin Beck, "Terence Improved: The Paradigm of the Prodigal Son in English Renaissance Comedy," *Renaissance Drama*, 6 (1973), 107–22; Dieter Mehl, "The London Prodigal as Jacobean City Comedy," in Mehl, Angela Stock, and Anne-Julia Zwierlein (eds), *Plotting Early Modern London: New Essays on Jacobean City Comedy* (Aldershot: Ashgate, 2004), 165–76; Darryl Tippens, "Shakespeare and the Prodigal Son Tradition," *Explorations in Renaissance Culture*, 14 (1988), 57–77; Susan Snyder, "*King Lear* and the Prodigal Son," *SQ* 17/4 (1966), 361–9.

[95] Ellen G. D'Oench, *Prodigal Son Narratives 1480–1980* (New Haven: Yale University Art Gallery, 1995), 3. See also Robert W. Baldwin, "A Bibliography of the Prodigal Son Theme in Art and Literature," *Bulletin of Bibliography*, 44 (September 1987), 167–71.

sung in popular ballads, and illustrated on painted walls and cloth wall hangings.[96] As with the story of Christ, the Prodigal Son so pervaded Elizabethan culture that it would be surprising if it had not influenced popular drama.

Steven Marx's *Shakespeare and the Bible* in some ways hearkens back to Victorian collections of biblical and moral analogies, including many legitimate and significant biblical allusions in Shakespeare's plays but also what seem more like free associations. Marx presents himself as a modern midrashist, his book "combining wordplay, storytelling, and interpretations to blend typological readings of Shakespeare and the Bible into a composite narrative of its own, a tale with a beginning, middle, and end."[97] So Marx plays with the peculiar notion that the Bible, in order from Genesis to Revelation, is formally analogous to Shakespeare's first Folio. Marx does hit upon important intertextual relations, as in his discussion of comic and ironic allusions in *The Merchant of Venice*, but he is less concerned with Shakespeare's own allusive practice than with fashioning his own creative narratives.

A more methodologically rigorous, yet modest, study of Shakespeare and the Bible is James H. Sims's 1966 *Dramatic Uses of Biblical Allusions in Marlowe and Shakespeare*, following on his earlier study of *The Bible in Milton's Epics*.[98] The two chapters on Shakespeare consist of only forty-seven pages, yet Sims makes a smart, systematic case for Shakespeare's use of biblical allusion, situating Shakespeare's practice within a broader perspective in which, as we might expect, playwrights like Thomas Dekker, Thomas Heywood, Jonson, and especially Marlowe allude to the Bible too. Particularly interesting is Sims's argument that Shakespeare learned from Marlowe the ironic or even parodic use of biblical allusions, a point that will be explored in the next chapter. Sims treats the comedies separately from the histories and tragedies, covering a wide range of plays, offering numerous examples of Shakespeare's meaningful use of biblical allusions. In each case, Sims show how the allusion functions in context, generating comedy, developing character or theme, and always enriching the play. In the chapter on comedies, the treatments of *Love's Labour's Lost*, *Measure for Measure*, and *The Tempest* are more extended, showing how biblical allusions are used by three key characters: Biron (Berowne), Angelo, and Prospero. The chapter on histories and tragedies

---

[96] Tessa Watt, *Cheap Print and Popular Piety, 1550–1640* (Cambridge: Cambridge University Press, 1991), 120, 202–0.
[97] Steven Marx, *Shakespeare and the Bible* (Oxford and New York: Oxford University Press, 2000), 16.
[98] James H. Sims, *Dramatic Uses of Biblical Allusions in Marlowe and Shakespeare* (Gainesville, FL: University of Florida Press, 1966).

again focuses on character, this time selecting six: Juliet and Desdemona, Prince Hal and Hamlet, and Claudius and Iago. Some of the allusions Sims includes are familiar and relatively obvious, like the reference to Cain and Abel in *Hamlet* ("the primal eldest curse...| A brother's murder," 3.3.37–8), but Sims's interpretation is always useful. In this instance, he cites Bryant's comment that here and at 1.2.103–6, Claudius's allusions to the first, fratricidal murder are inadvertent.[99] He also connects these allusions to others that link Claudius with the sinful and penitent David (3.3) and Esau, who "was reprobated: for he found no place of repentance, though he sought it carefully with teares" (Heb. 12:17).[100] The allusions develop, one into another: like Cain, Claudius has killed his brother, like David, he prays for forgiveness, but, since his contrition is not genuine, he fails, being reprobated like Esau. Noble references the allusions to Cain and David, but the point about Esau is original. It is more tentative, perhaps, since there is no clear verbal link, but its plausibility is increased by the fact that, like Cain and Abel, Jacob and Esau represent an essential biblical model for fraternal competition and hostility.

Much of the criticism of Shakespeare and the Bible since Sims will be referenced throughout this book, so there is no need to include it all here. The late tragicomedies or Romances have received particular attention in terms of Shakespeare's exploration of apocalyptic themes and language (for example, Cynthia Marshall's *Last Things and Last Plays: Shakespearean Eschatology*), and the exploration of providence in the English histories has also generated studies of their use of biblical allusion (see, for instance, chapter 2 of Maurice Hunt's *Shakespeare's Religious Allusiveness: Its Play and Tolerance*, or Jean-Christophe Mayer, *Shakespeare's Hybrid Faith: History, Religion, and the Stage*). There is also a growing number of excellent articles and book chapters on Shakespeare's use of the Bible in individual plays. What has been described as the "turn to religion" in the study of early modern English literature has perhaps generated some increased interest in the Bible and Shakespeare, yet less than one might expect.[101] New Historicists like Stephen Greenblatt and Jeffrey Knapp are interested in religion as an extension or manifestation of politics, and the texts of the Bible tend to figure only peripherally in their work.[102] The same is true of studies of political theology, many of which apply modern philosophical

---

[99] Sims, *Dramatic Uses*, 59, citing Bryant, *Hippolyta's View*, 119.
[100] On the contrastive allusive link between Claudius and David, see Hamlin, 215–17.
[101] Ken Jackson and Arthur F. Marotti, "The Turn to Religion in Early Modern English Studies," *Criticism*, 46/1 (2004), 167–90.
[102] See Stephen Greenblatt, *Hamlet and Purgatory* (Princeton: Princeton University Press, 2001); Jeffrey Knapp, *Shakespeare's Tribe: Church, Nation, and Theater in Renaissance England* (Chicago and London: University of Chicago Press, 2002).

studies of St Paul by Giorgio Agamben and Paul Badiou, but are not really interested in the Bible as such, let alone the full range of Shakespeare's biblical allusion.[103]

The battle for Shakespeare's faith continues, with arguments for his Catholicism gaining the ascendancy. Claims for Shakespeare spending his lost years in Lancashire, in the household of the recusant Houghton family, have gained in popularity.[104] Some New Historicist critics like Greenblatt and Richard Wilson have added their voices to those of Catholic scholars, liking the notion of Shakespeare as a marginal, oppressed, and possibly subversive recusant.[105] But the Catholic Shakespeare remains especially popular among Catholic scholars. The Jesuit, Peter Milward, the most prolific proponent of the Catholic Shakespeare, published *Shakespeare's Religious Background* in 1973 and continued into the new millennium with *The Catholicism of Shakespeare's Plays* (2000) and *Shakespeare the Papist* (2005). Some Catholic studies consider Shakespeare's use of the Bible. David Beauregard's *Catholic Theology in Shakespeare's Plays* (2008), for instance, tracks religious and biblical allusions in *The Winter's Tale*, *Hamlet*, and other plays, asserting that they demonstrate Shakespeare's adherence to the Old Faith.[106] Most, however, still focus on biography and the representation of characters (especially monks and friars) and religious ideas and practices. Arguments for a Protestant Shakespeare have dwindled, perhaps because it is the consensus view assumed by many critics of Shakespeare and religion, or Shakespeare and the Bible.[107] Most recently, several scholars have made persuasive arguments for a skeptical or even atheist Shakespeare.[108]

---

[103] See Debora Shuger, *Political Theologies in Shakespeare's England: The Sacred and the State in* Measure for Measure (Basingstoke: Palgrave, 2001); Julia Reinhard Lupton, *Citizen–Saints: Shakespeare and Political Theology* (Chicago and London: University of Chicago Press, 2005).

[104] See Richard Dutton, Alison Findlay, and Richard Wilson (eds), *Region, Religion, and Patronage: Lancastrian Shakespeare* (Manchester and New York: Manchester University Press, 2003), and *Theatre and Religion: Lancastrian Shakespeare* (Manchester and New York: Manchester University Press, 2003). These volumes grew out of the seminal 1999 conference on Lancastrian Shakespeare at Lancaster University.

[105] Stephen Greenblatt, *Will in the World: How Shakespeare became Shakespeare* (New York: W. W. Norton, 2004); Richard Wilson, *Secret Shakespeare: Studies in Theatre, Religion, and Resistance* (Manchester and New York: Manchester University Press, 2004).

[106] For a largely negative review, see Hannibal Hamlin, "Review of *Catholic Theology in Shakespeare's Plays*, by David Beauregard," *SQ* 59/4 (2009), 24–6.

[107] One of the few recent Protestant Shakespeare studies is Daniel L. Wright, *Anglican Shakespeare: Elizabethan Orthodoxy in the Great Histories* (Vancouver, WA: Pacific-Columbia Books, 1993).

[108] John D. Cox, *Seeming Knowledge: Shakespeare and Skeptical Faith* (Waco, TX: Baylor University Press, 2007); Jean-Christophe Mayer, *Shakespeare's Hybrid Faith: History, Religion, and the Stage* (Basingstoke and New York: Palgrave Macmillan, 2007); Eric S. Malin, *Godless Shakespeare* (London and New York: Continuum, 2007).

What is certain is that Shakespeare knew the Bible extremely well, and that he alluded to it very frequently in the plays. The present book is based on the assumption that these allusions deserve thorough, systematic, critical—and confessionally unbiased—study.

3

Allusion: Theory, History, and Shakespeare's Practice

> There are some enterprises in which a careful disorderliness is the true method.
>
> (Herman Melville, *Moby Dick*)[1]

As is evident from the previous chapter, critics have discussed Shakespeare's integration of the Bible into his works in a variety of terms. Shaheen uses the word "reference," while others prefer "quotation," "allusion," or "echo." Some write instead of "influence," "borrowing," or "sources," while others prefer the term "imitation." The preferred basic term in this book is "allusion," which is applied broadly, as including any instance of a work that refers to, quotes, points to, echoes, evokes, or parallels an earlier work. For reasons that will be explained below, it is best to keep the scope broad, since attempts to narrow the definition invariably prove reductive and untenable.

Allusion is one of the most basic and ubiquitous of literary devices, though it is by no means confined to literature. Newspapers and magazines regularly incorporate allusions into their headlines. *The Times* [London] of August 12, 2012, for instance, included a story entitled "The Good, the Bad, and the Olympic Spirit." The implication is that the Olympic Spirit is ugly, but to understand this the reader must catch the allusion to the western film *The Good, the Bad, and the Ugly*. *The New York Times*, also in coverage of the 2012 Olympics, featured a special report called "The Good, the Bad, and the Unforgettable" (August 13, 2012). Advertisers also capitalize on allusion, as in the many television commercials adapting the story of Adam and Eve in Eden. In one of these by the Frito Lay company, apparently a finalist for their Superbowl ad competition, a seductive-looking Eve offers Adam the apple, but he prefers to stick with

---

[1] Herman Melville, *Moby Dick* (London: Penguin, 2003), 395.

his Doritos chips.[2] A print ad for the Hamburg Fire Brigade features Dürer's painting of Adam and Eve and the fatal apple, with the caption "Removal of Dangerous Substances."[3] These are relatively unsophisticated allusions, since they do not engage the text alluded to in any complexity; knowing more than the title of the Sergio Leone film will not make the newspaper stories any more meaningful, and all one needs to know about Eve's apple is that it is forbidden and connected with sex. But they are allusions none the less. Allusions appear at all levels of culture, from high art to popular television and comics, and they function in a variety of media. Paintings allude to prior paintings, films to films (and paintings), and symphonies and operas to earlier musical works.[4] Finally, allusions have a history as old as human culture. The High Modernism of T. S. Eliot, James Joyce, and Ezra Pound is exceptionally allusive, but so too are the poems of Virgil and Catullus, Pindar and Callimachus.

Given the regular use of allusion among classical writers, it is peculiar that classical rhetorics included no term for the device. Since they depended so devotedly on their Greek and Roman precursors, it is perhaps less surprising that there is also no term for allusion in Renaissance rhetorics. Yet, again, the near-universal allusive practice of Renaissance writers makes such a deficiency puzzling. Allusion is often involved in poetic imitation, and *imitatio* was a common and highly self-conscious classical and Renaissance literary practice.[5] An essential component of rhetorical training in Aristotle, Horace, Cicero, and their Renaissance counterparts involved the studious imitation of great writers, reproducing their style, their diction, their characteristic figures of speech, their generic conventions. Renaissance Latinists learned to write like Cicero, perhaps excessively, as Erasmus complained. Poets wrote pastoral lyrics in

---

[2] *YouTube* <http://www.youtube.com/watch?v=zHSjpezHHcw> (accessed September 3, 2012).

[3] *Coloribus* http://www.coloribus.com/adsarchive/prints/hamburg-fire-brigade-adam-eve-2338105/ (accessed September 3, 2012).

[4] For a few sample studies, see Christopher A. Reynolds, *Motives for Allusion: Context and Content in Nineteenth-Century Music* (Cambridge, MA: Harvard University Press, 2003); *Foirades/Fizzles: Echo and Allusion in the Art of Jasper Johns* ([Los Angeles]: Grunwald Center for the Graphic Arts: Wight Art Gallery, University of California, Los Angeles, 1987); Stephanie Ross, "Art and Allusion," *Journal of Aesthetics and Art Criticism*, 40/1 (1981), 59–70; William Irwin and J. R. Lombardo, "The Simpsons and Allusion: 'The Worst Essay Ever,'" in Irwin, Mark T. Conrad, and Aeon J. Skoble (eds), *The Simpsons and Philosophy: The D'Oh of Homer* (Chicago: Open Court, 2001): n.p.; Stacey Harwood, "Poetry in Movies: A Partial List," *Poets.org* <http://www.poets.org/viewmedia.php/prmMID/19359> (accessed October 12, 2012).

[5] Thomas M. Greene, *The Light in Troy: Imitation and Discovery in Renaissance Poetry* (New Haven and London: Yale University Press, 1993); G. W. Pigman III, "Versions of Imitation in the Renaissance," *RQ* 33/1 (1980), 1–32.

imitation of Theocritus or Virgil (or, later, Mantuan and Sannazaro), tragedies in imitation of Seneca, love poems in imitation of Catullus or Petrarch, epics in imitation of Homer and Virgil (later, Ariosto, Boiardo, and Tasso). Imitation often included allusion, but the two terms are not synonymous. Sir Thomas Wyatt's "Whoso list to hunt," for example, is an imitation of Petrarch's Rime 190, "*Una candida cerva.*" Since Wyatt was also translating, as well as adapting, the poem into English, however, it is difficult to speak of actual allusion, except in the case of the words inscribed around the neck of the deer/woman, "*Noli me tangere*, for Caesar's I am, | And wild for to hold, though I seem tame."[6] Petrarch's deer has a similar phrase on her collar, in Italian, "*Nessun mi tocchi*," though the collar is differently described and the rest of the inscription is different from Wyatt's. Nevertheless, "*Noli me tangere*" does allude to "*Nessun mi tochi*," especially if one knows that commentators on Petrarch cited the original inscription on Caesar's deer as "*Noli me tangere quia Caesaris sum.*"[7] Thus, Wyatt is alluding to Petrarch by way of his commentators. More interesting still, by using the Latin phrase rather than the Italian, and by quoting only the first three words, Wyatt seems also to allude to Jesus's statement to Mary Magdalene after his resurrection, "Touche me not: for I am not yet ascended to my Father" (John 20:17), "*Noli me tangere*" in the Vulgate Bible. Wyatt's allusions are complex, interwoven, and difficult fully to sort out, perhaps intentionally so in this hazardous poem that may also allude topically to Wyatt's affair with Anne Boleyn before she drew the attention of Henry VIII.[8] Yet Wyatt's decision to write an imitation of Petrarch did not necessitate allusion, as evidenced by the many more simplistic imitations of his contemporaries. Both Wyatt and the Earl of Surrey wrote imitations of Petrarch's Rime 140 ("*Amor, che nel penser mio vive et regna*"), for instance, but neither English poem specifically alludes to the Italian original. They each follow Petrarch fairly closely throughout, but this is not the same as specifically referencing the earlier poem by importing a portion of its language or content into a new and different context, which is what allusion entails. Knowing the Petrarchan original may be useful for understanding Wyatt's and Surrey's versions, but neither of those

---

[6] Sir Thomas Wyatt, "Whoso list to hunt," in *Sir Thomas Wyatt: The Complete Poems*, ed. R. A. Rebholz (Harmondsworth: Penguin, 1978), 77.
[7] Patricia Thomson, "Wyatt and the Petrarchan Commentators," *RES* ns 10:29 (1955), 225–33, cited in Adrienne Williams Boyarin, "Competing Biblical and Virgilian Allusions in Wyatt's 'Who So List to Hounte,'" *N&Q* 53:4 (2006): 417–21, 418.
[8] See Boyarin, "Competing Biblical and Virgilian Allusions," who also detects allusions to Virgil. For the argument about Anne Boleyn, see Stephen Greenblatt, *Renaissance Self-Fashioning: From More to Shakespeare* (Chicago and London: University of Chicago Press, 1980), 145–50.

directs the reader to specific details in the Italian, and in neither case is Petrarch's poem essential for a full understanding of the imitation.⁹

Some definitions of allusion have stressed its covert nature, but "covert" is the wrong term.¹⁰ For one thing, as stated above, many allusions are perfectly overt, such as direct references or outright quotations. But more subtle allusions are not covert either: to constitute allusions they must to some extent be recognizable to some readers, and, furthermore, they must be intended by the author to be recognized. The question of authorial intention has been a minefield ever since W. K. Wimsatt and Monroe C. Beardsley's "Intentional Fallacy" of 1954 and more so, though for different reasons, since the announced "death of the author" by Roland Barthes and Michel Foucault.¹¹ It may be impossible to prove categorically, and one can imagine instances where a reader perceives an allusion that the author did not actually intend (though genuinely meaningful examples of this must be rare), yet allusion seems nevertheless a phenomenon in which authorial intention is to some extent clear and demonstrable.¹² The reader perceives an allusion based on some kind of trigger,

---

⁹ There is a general sense, perhaps, in which a translation or paraphrase of a poem alludes to its original, in that its status as a translation inevitably encourages comparison to that which it translates. But allusion generally involves a more local phenomenon, a word, phrase, or scene, within a larger work, rather than the work as a whole.

¹⁰ As Joseph Pucci notes, the definitions of "allusion" in the 1965 and 1993 editions of *The Princeton Encyclopedia of Poetry and Poetics* differ on the matter of covertness. According to the former, allusion is a "tacit reference to another literary work [etc.]," while in the latter it is a "poet's deliberate incorporation of identifiable elements from other souces." Pucci, *The Full-Knowing Reader: Allusion and the Power of the Reader in the Western Literary Tradition* (New Haven and London: Yale University Press, 1998), 3–4. In the latest, fourth edition, R. Wetzsteon's article on "allusion" also leaves out the tacitness or covertness, though she does stress, as does Pucci, the dependence on an "intelligent reader." *The Princeton Encyclopedia of Poetry & Poetics*, 4th edn (Princeton and Oxford: Princeton University Press, 2012), 42–3. The *OED* (4) defines "allusion" as a "covert, implied, or indirect reference," but many other theorists of allusion allow overt references into the category. See Ziva Ben-Porat, "The Poetics of Literary Allusion," *PTL* 1 (1976), 105–28, 107; Carmella Peri, "On Alluding," *Poetics*, 7 (1978), 289–307, 290; William Irwin, "What Is an Allusion?" *Journal of Aesthetics and Art Criticism*, 59/3 (2001), 287–97, 287. Christopher Ricks states simply, "Allusion need not be covert or indirect" (*Allusion to the Poets* (Oxford: Oxford University Press, 2002), 157).

¹¹ W. K. Wimsatt Jr. and Monroe C. Beardsley, "The Intentional Fallacy," in Wimsatt, *The Verbal Icon: Studies in the Meaning of Poetry* (Lexington, KY: University of Kentucky Press, 1954), 3–20. Roland Barthes, "The Death of the Author," in *Image, Music, Text*, trans. Stephen Heath (New York: Hill and Wang, 1977), 142–8. Michel Foucault, "What is an Author?" in Donald F. Bouchard (ed.), *Language, Counter-Memory, Practice: Selected Essays and Interviews by Michel Foucault* (Ithaca, NY: Cornell University Press, 1977), 113–38.

¹² Irwin puts the point most strongly, stating that "without the author's intent to allude, we have no allusion" ("What Is an Allusion?" 290). He does acknowledge the epistemological problem that we cannot finally know the author's intention, but, if we understand allusion as involving "reference" or "pointing to," then the reader must infer the intention.

Allusion 81

something identifiable in the text—a word, a phrase, a familiar rhythm, a portion of narrative—that brings to mind a prior text.[13] Knowing the prior text enriches the later one, perhaps only in a small way, or perhaps quite significantly. The reader will not simply have made a connection between two texts independently; he or she will also have made a connection with the author, who first made the connection. This seems one of the most profound experiences available in reading, the realization of Alberto Manguel's fanciful notion that, in a library, "One book calls to another unexpectedly, creating alliances across different cultures and centuries."[14] Charming as it is to think of books conversing with each other, it is only people, readers and writers, who can do this, though books provide a medium for, as Stephen Greenblatt hauntingly put it, speaking with the dead.[15]

The dependence of allusion on authorial intention distinguishes it from the phenomenon known as "intertextuality," in the sense given the term by its originator, Julia Kristeva.[16] Kristeva coined the term to describe the way in which literary works, like language itself, participate in a discursive field, connecting in infinitely complicated ways to other works in ways that will inevitablly be unique for every reader, indeed every reading, as the words in a given text, so arranged, resonate outward to connect to and interact with the same or similar words in countless other texts that have been experienced, just as future encounters with yet other texts will resonate back to this one. All readers and reader–writers bring to bear, in every act of reading (or writing), all that they have read, and since all that they have read depends upon and connects to countless other works they have not yet read, the whole set of interconnections is an impossibly, yet fascinatingly, intricate web of language and meaning. Kristeva was

---

[13] As Gregory Machacek points out, the terminology for allusion is limited in that it cannot distinguish between the element in a work that alludes, the prior text alluded to, and the whole phenomenon, all of which are called "allusion." For the former, I opt for the term "trigger," introduced by Richard Garner, *From Homer to Tragedy: The Art of Allusion in Greek Poetry* (London: Routledge, 1990), 6. Machacek lists several other terms that have been proposed—"marker" and "signal," for instance—but neither seems appreciably better, and Machacek's own term, "reprise" (with the text alluded to as "spur"), seems awkward. Gregory Machacek, "Allusion," *PMLA* 122/2 (2007), 522–36, 529.

[14] Alberto Manguel, *The Library at Night* (New Haven and London: Yale University Press, 2006), 14.

[15] Greenblatt opens his *Shakespearean Negotiations* with the sentence, "I began with the desire to speak with the dead." Stephen Greenblatt, *Shakespearean Negotiations: The Circulation of Social Energy in Renaissance England* (Berkeley and Los Angeles: University of California Press, 1988), 1.

[16] Julia Kristeva, "Word, Dialogue, and the Novel," in Leon S. Roudiez (ed.), *Desire in Language: A Semiotic Approach to Literature and Art*, trans. Thomas Gora, Alice Jardine, and Leon S. Roudiez (New York: Columbia University Press, 1980), 64–92.

building upon the earlier work of Mikhail Bakhtin, particularly his notion of dialogism, which described the novel as a genre especially rich in these kinds of intertextual discourses, which he termed "heteroglossia."[17] Kristeva ultimately abandoned the term "intertextuality" in favor of "transposition," in part because "intertextuality" was adopted by critics interested in matters of allusion, something quite alien to the original concept.[18] However, "intertextuality" continues to be used, quite logically, as inclusive of the deliberative, rhetorical phenomenon of allusion. So it is used, occasionally, in this book.

The one aspect of this study that extends beyond allusion to something like Kristeva's and Bakhtin's understanding of intertextuality is its consideration of other works—sermons, commentaries, other literature, visual arts—in order better to determine how the Bible might have been interpreted by Shakespeare and his audience by tracking the range of interpretations available. Some of these other works are identifiable sources for Shakespeare's language, plots, or ideas; others are not identifiable as such, though they were in circulation and available for Shakespeare to read, and they provide parallels to the plays suggesting that he would have found them compatible with his own thinking, had he read them. Turning to the audience's perspective, these works establish that certain biblical interpretations were available, either by reading or by participating in the broader public discourse, and that they could then have been used to interpret Shakespeare's own biblical allusions. Source study has had a bad name for some decades. Stephen Greenblatt called it "the elephant's graveyard of literary history," and Harold Bloom called source hunters "those carrion-eaters of scholarship."[19] Yet Greenblatt's statement came at the opening of one of the late twentieth century's most influential source studies of Shakespeare, and Bloom's in his seminal *The Map of Misreading*, which might, despite his gnashing of teeth, be described, like Greenblatt's, as source study new and improved. For the purposes of exploring Shakespeare's biblical allusions, source study can be invaluable. The precise intentions of an author may be ultimately unknowable, as epistemologists tell us, but we can at least approach such knowledge by

---

[17] Mikhail M. Bakhtin, "Discourse in the Novel," in Michael Holquist (ed.), *The Dialogic Imagination: Four Essays*, trans. Caryl Emerson and Michael Holquist (Austin, TX: University of Texas Press, 1981), 259–422.

[18] Julia Kristeva, *Revolution in Poetic Language*, trans. Margaret Waller (New York: Columbia University Press, 1984).

[19] Stephen Greenblatt, "Shakespeare and the Exorcists," in Patricia Parker and Geoffrey Hartman (eds), *Shakespeare and the Question of Theory* (New York and London: Methuen, 1985), 163–86, 163. When Greenblatt republished the essay as chapter 4 of his *Shakespearean Negotiations*, he omitted the elephants. Harold Bloom, *The Map of Misreading* (New York: Oxford University Press, 1975; repr. 2003), 17.

studying how an author has used and adapted other works in creating his own. Comparing Shakespeare's English history plays with the chronicles of Edward Hall and Raphael Holinshed shows what he included and excluded, what he altered and compressed, and this gives us hints as to what he had in mind in writing, including matters of theatrical expedience as well as ideology and interpretation. Similarly revealing is the evidence of Shakespeare's recourse to Robert Parsons's interpretation of Job in his *Christian Directory*, since it gives us hints about his reading of and thinking about the biblical original, or at least evidence of interpretations available to him (see Chapter 8). The English Reformation Bible was, to quote James Kugel, an "interpreted Bible."[20] In *The Bible as it Was*, Kugel combs through the surviving writings of ancient exegetes in order to reveal how they read the stories of Adam and Eve, Cain and Abel, even individual verses or words. This study takes a similar approach to early modern Bible reading, in an attempt, however limited, to reveal how Shakespeare and his contemporaries may have interpreted their Bible. This is intertextual study of a kind Kristeva and Kristevans might find more congenial, but it is done in aid of the study of Shakespeare's allusions.

Studies of intertextuality often discuss the differences between a diachronic and a synchronic approach to literary works. As Gregory Machacek puts it, "The broad distinction is between approaches that study the text diachronically, in connection with earlier works of literature, and those that examine the text synchronically, in connection with a contemporaneous semiotic field made up of literary and nonliterary texts."[21] The distinction dates back to Ferdinand de Saussure, who advocated a structuralist, synchronic approach to language as opposed to the diachronic, historical philology of earlier linguists.[22] In terms of the study of literature, however, this is a false distinction, or at least one that can be maintained only in the abstract, since "prior" literary works (or indeed other "texts") are as much part of the present as the past, in that they by and large remain available to any contemporary who cares to read them (apart from cases of absolute loss, as of Lucretius's *De rerum natura* until its rediscovery in 1417). This is especially true of reprinted works, like the important editions of Chaucer published in the sixteenth century. Chaucer was a past author for Shakespeare and his contemporaries, dead for two centuries, but he

---

[20] James Kugel, *The Bible As It Was* (Cambridge, MA: Harvard University Press, 1997), 5. For more on the sixteenth-century interpreted Bible, see Ch. 1.
[21] Machacek, "Allusion," 524.
[22] The key work is Ferdinand de Saussure, *Cours de linguistique générale* (in *Revue des Langues romanes*, 59 [1916]), published posthumously by his students.

was also "present" in the sense that he was available at the London booksellers (as well as in older editions in circulation) and was thus an active part of Tudor culture. In terms of the availability of books and experience of reading, Chaucer was no more part of the past than Spenser, for whom he was a powerful influence.[23] The same is true all the more of the Bible, which was at once ancient and also continually present, both in its ongoing meaning for Christian lives, and (more materially) in the new Bible translations and editions that regularly came off the presses.

As noted above, modern terminology for the phenomenon of allusion is varied, and each term comes with different implications. "Imitation," for instance, implies the subordination of the alluding work to the work alluded to, even, with Renaissance educational systems in mind, a subordination like that of pupil to teacher. The greatest imitations may equal or even surpass their originals, but this cuts against the relational implications of the term. "Reference" is fine as far as it goes, but it fails to capture allusion's dynamism, its production of meaning by the continuing back-and-forth resonation between the two literary works: recognition of the allusion to the earlier work makes us think back to the meaning of the "trigger" in its original context; we then return to the current work, which is enriched by the additional context; but then we may turn again to the earlier work, which may in turn be illuminated for us (even if anachronistically) by the later author's reading of it—and so forth. The same is true of "borrowing," which also implies a one-way process. Moreover, an allusion is not really a borrowing at all; T. S. Eliot said that great poets do not borrow, they steal, but they do not steal either, since what they "steal" remains where it always was.[24] Many critics favor "echo," but neither is that term neutral. Most importantly, it leaves out the author of the allusion and any question of intention. We may speak of an author echoing an earlier one, but the natural acoustic phenomenon of echo works in one direction only, generating from the original source outward, in partial and fading repetitions. We can hear an echo but not make one; even if we make a sound that echoes, the echo itself is a natural occurrence. By analogy, then, one would think that one literary work "echoed" in another independently of any human authorial agency. One great advantage of the term "echo" for allusion studies, however, as evident pre-eminently in John Hollander's *The Figure of Echo*, is that it allows for nuances of

---

[23] For a superb study of the survival, printing, and reading of medieval books in sixteenth-century England, see Jennifer Summit, *Memory's Library: Medieval Books in Early Modern England* (Chicago: University of Chicago Press, 2008).
[24] T. S. Eliot, "Philip Massinger," in *Selected Essays*, new edn (New York: Harcourt, Brace & World, Inc., 1960), 182 ("Immature poets imitate; mature poets steal"); Christopher Ricks, "Plagiarism," in *Allusion to the Poets*, 219–40.

volume. Echoes may be louder or softer, and this is a useful metaphor for the degrees of obviousness in allusions.

"Allusion" seems to me the best all around term, though others are used at various points in this study if they seem useful and appropriate. It is useful to think about the etymological origin of "allusion" in the Latin verb *ludere*, "to play." The first sense of "allude" in the *OED* is "To play with, make game of, mock" (from 1535), and an "allusion" seems often to have meant a kind of joke or wordplay. The complex history of the term is discussed below, but the lingering sense of play is valuable. The play of allusion may be serious or frivolous, but in play there is a degree of improvisation, and the excitement of the game depends upon the interaction of the players, which can be unpredictable. Joseph Pucci introduces the useful notion of the "space" of allusion to describe the mental playing field where this game takes place.[25] Both works and both writers and the reader meet in this space. The meaning of an "allusion" (in its broadest sense of play and interplay) is generated by all these players—texts, authors, reader—interacting together.

The etymological playfulness of allusion may also explain why literary allusions are so often contrastive, subversive, ironic, or even parodic. But this may be a feature of any trope, which is defined etymologically (back to the Greek) as a "turning." Not every turning is so sharp as to parody or undercut, but there is always with allusions some sense of adaptation or adjustment to a new context, which is one of the creative aspects that makes allusion interesting. Shakespeare's biblical allusions are almost always contrastive or ironic; they sometimes may seem almost blasphemous. The Bible was a particularly rich source for allusion, because, not only was the book familiar to Shakespeare and his audience, but it came with deeply ingrained ideological baggage. The Bible *mattered* to a superlative degree, which gave consequence to biblical allusions in literature.

HISTORY

The first citation in the *OED* for "allusion" in the modern literary sense ("a covert, implied, or indirect reference; a passing or incidental reference") is from Michael Drayton's *Poly-Olbion* in 1612. The passage was actually written by John Selden, who provided the notes, or "illustrations," covering matters historical and philological: "What the Verse oft, with

---

[25] Pucci, *Full-Knowing Reader*, 43–4. Pucci also stresses the importance of play in allusion.

allusion, as supposing a full knowing Reader, lets slip; or in winding steps of Personating Fictions (as some times) so infolds, that suddaine conceipt cannot abstract a Forme of the clothed Truth, I have, as I might, *Illustrated.*"[26] Selden "illustrates," or interprets, Drayton's allusions (which "the Verse oft...lets slip"), as well as other complexities of figurative language. The term was actually in use earlier. The first citation in the *OED* for the verb "allude" is from Thomas More's *Apologye* (1533), in which More cites a passage from the 1532 *Treatise concerning the Division between the Spirituality and Temporality*, and observes that the words of the passage "allude unto certayne wordes of Tyndale, wyth whych he argueth agaynst me."[27] The next *OED* citation is from 1711, but in fact the term was often in print during the sixteenth century. For instance, Martin Luther, in the translation of John Hollybush, interprets a passage in Luke where Zacharius, father of John the Baptist, sings of the coming of the "day spring from an [on] high" (Luke 1:78):

The day sprynge doth Zachary call here Christe, as thoughe he were buddynge and spryngynge, lyke a braunch of a tre, alludynge to the sayenge of Jeremy in hys. xxiii. chap. sayenge: I wyll rayse up the ryghteous braunch of David, which shall beare rule, and discusse matters with wysedom, and shal set up equite and ryghteousnesse agayne in the earth.[28]

In addition, Erasmus wrote of Alexander that, "when his leggue was wounded with an aroe in battaille, and many came rennyng about hym, whiche had of a custome ofte tymes used to call hym a God, he with a bolde and a mery countenaunce alludyng to a verse of the Poete *Homere*, saied: 'This that ye see, is blood withouten oddes[|] Even such like, as cometh from the Goddes.'" Erasmus then specifies that "the allusion that he made, was to a place of Homere in the fifth volume of his werke entitled Ilias, where it is tolde howe Venus was wounded of Diomedes."[29]

Erasmus's secular use of "allusion" is uncharacteristic, however. The term tended to be used in religious and, as in the example from Luther, biblical contexts. Nicholas Udall, for instance, who translated the *Apopthegmes*, was also the principal translator of Erasmus's *Paraphrases*, the second volume of which uses "allusion" in a biblical context: "We embrace

---

[26] Michael Drayton, *Poly-Olbion* (London: M. Lownes, J. Browne, J. Helme, J. Busbie, 1612), sig. A2r.
[27] Sir Thomas More, *The apologye of syr Thomas More knyght* (London: W. Rastell, 1533), fo. 52r.
[28] Martin Luther, *An exposicion upon the songe of the blessed virgine Mary*, trans. John Hollybush ([Southwark: J. Nicholson], 1538), sigs M4r–M5v.
[29] Desiderius Erasmus, *Apophthegmes*, trans. Nicholas Udall (London: Richard Grafton, 1542), fo. 188v.

Jesus our sacrifice and hie [high] priest, who, as it were alludyng to the figure of the lawe, would be crucified without the gate of the citie of Jerusalem, there to pourge his people with his most precious bloude." (Erasmus elsewhere explains his use of the term "figure," writing, "man is made righteous through fayth in Jesus Christ the sonne of God, whom the lawe promised, and in figure represented.")[30] Further examples of "allusion" in terms of references to scripture can be found in Stephen Gardiner's *An explication and assertion of the true Catholique fayth* (1551), Nicholas Ridley's *A brief declaracion of the Lordes Supper* (1555), Roger Edgeworth's *Sermons very fruitfull, godly, and learned* (1557), Nicholas Sanders's *The supper of our Lord* (1566), and John Jewel's *A defence of the Apologie of the Churche of Englande* (1567).

Some writers (or translators) seemed especially fond of the term "allusion." In *A Harmonie upon the three Evangelists* (1584) John Calvin, translated by E.P., suggests that the "daye spring" of Luke 1:18 is "an allusion to the 4. Chap. 2.v. of Mal [Malachi]." Of Luke 4:19, he notes that "it seemeth to many to be an allusion to the yeere of Jubile." Calvin explains Matthew 5:19 ("Whosoeuer therfore shall breake one of these least commaundements and teache men so, he shall be called the least in the kingdome of heauen") by clarifying that when Jesus "sayeth he shall be called least, [it] is an allusion to that was sayde before of the commaundementes."[31] "Allusion" is used five more times in similar contexts, and nine times in *A commentarie vpon the Epistle of Saint Paul to the Romanes*, published the previous year (translated by Christopher Rosdell). In some of these instances, "allusion" is used in the sense of a play on words or pun, or else a "reference or likening; a metaphor, parable, allegory" (*OED* 2 and 3). In others, however, an intertextual reference is clearly meant. A marginal note in Rosdell's translation of the Romans commentary helpfully explains, "Allusion, is when we in respect the saying or writing of another, that we also borrow some words thence, or els touch them in our own words."[32]

It is not an accident that "allusion" in the sense of a "covert, implied, or indirect reference" enters English and is most commonly used in biblical commentaries, sermons, and religious tracts, just as the first Latin use of *allusio* in the sense of a "hidden level of reference" is in

---

[30] Desiderius Erasmus, *The seconde tome or volume of the Paraphrase of Erasmus upon the Newe Testament* (London: Edward Whitchurch, 1549), fols 26ʳ, 2ʳ.

[31] John Calvin, *A Harmonie upon the three Evangelists*, trans. E.P. (London: George Bishop, 1584), 49, 139, 169.

[32] Calvin, *A commentarie vpon the Epistle of Saint Paul to the Romanes*, trans. Christopher Rosdell (London: John Harison and George Bishop, 1583), fo. 143ʳ.

Cassiodorus's sixth-century *Exposition on the Psalms*.[33] Commentators need "allusion" because allusion is so prominent and essential in the Bible; it is simply unavoidable that the Bible alludes in this way, as discussed next. This is not to say, of course, that "allusion" was the only term that could have been adopted to refer to this intertextual phenomenon, nor that the phenomenon of allusion originates or exists only in the Bible. There is an independent secular tradition of allusion, which seems for some time to have done without any rhetorical term for the phenomenon at all. Nevertheless, the history of "allusion" as a rhetorical term and the history of the practice of biblical allusion seem to have developed in parallel.

The biblical writers allude to each other (and themselves) frequently. For example, when the Flood has subsided, God tells Noah to leave the ark and to "Bring forthe with thee everie beast that is with thee, of all flesh, bothe foule and cattel, and everie thing that crepeth and moveth upon the earth, that thei maie brede abundantly in the earth, and bring forthe frute and increase upon the earth" (Gen. 8:17). The power of this moment depends largely upon its allusion to the creation story, when God spoke on the sixth day, "Let the earth bring forthe the living thing according to his kinde, cattel, and that which crepeth, and the beast of the earth," and when he created man and told them (male and female) to "bring forthe frute and multiplie, and fil the earth" (Gen. 2:24, 28). God's language in Genesis 8 alludes to his language in Genesis 2, the point being that the preservation of Noah, his family, and the animals is a second creation, after the failure of the first, and moreover that, like the first, it begins with the containing of the waters. Later in Genesis, God says to Jacob, "I am God all sufficient[,] growe, and multiplie: a nation and a multitude of nations shal spring of thee, and Kings come out of they loynes" (Gen. 35:11). The command to "multiply" signals the renewal of the covenant between God and man, alluding to the original command to "bring forthe frute and multiplie" ("Be fruitful and multiplie" in the Bishops' Bible). A similar allusion is at work in Jacob's prophecy to his son Joseph that he "shalbe a fruteful bough, even a fruteful bough by the wel side" (Gen. 49:22). The metaphor is clear enough on its own, but Joseph's fruitfulness is more meaningful in the context of God's similar commands to Jacob and his forebears.

Parallelism or repetition is a feature of the Jewish Scripture (Tanakh) or Christian Old Testament at the level of narrative as well as language.[34] The

---

[33] Pucci, *Full-Knowing Reader*, 41–2; the description of Cassiodorus's sense is Pucci's.

[34] Robert Alter includes the following examples, among many others, in "Allusion and Literary Expression," in *The World of Biblical Literature* ([New York]: Basic Books, 1992), 107–30.

story of Jephthah and his daughter in Judges 11, for instance, gains a layer of complexity in the context of the story of Abraham and Isaac in Genesis 22, which it parallels and to which it thus alludes. Both Jephthah and Abraham are faced with the terrible prospect of sacrificing their children to God. Abraham has been commanded to do so by God himself, and he obeys the command, only to be prevented at the last moment and praised for his obedience. Jephthah makes a rash vow to God to sacrifice the first thing he sees on returning home from victory in battle, and he goes through with the sacrifice of his daughter on the understanding that this is what he owes God. The similarities in the narrative to the Abraham and Isaac story—a defining one for Judaism, called the *Akedah* after the "binding" of Isaac—underscore the crucial differences: as commentators tended to point out, one is not obligated to fulfil a bad or wicked promise, which Jephthah's certainly is. God at no point asks Jephthah to sacrifice his daughter, and the narrator never claims that Jephthah's actions are in accord with God's will. God once tested a man (Abraham) by asking him to sacrifice his child, but did not permit him to go through with the sacrifice; Abraham's willingness and obedient intention were enough. And surely nothing but a direct command from God should be sufficient to persuade anyone to sacrifice a child, or indeed any human being. This is made clear in the *Homily against Swearing and Perjury*: "Thus doeth GOD shew plainely how much hee abhorreth breakers of honest promises bound by an oath made in his Name. And of them that make wicked promises by an oath, and will performe the same, wee haue example in the Scriptures, chiefely of Herod, of the wicked Jewes, and of Jephtah."[35]

A similar narrative repetition occurs later in Judges, when the Levite goes in search of his wayward concubine. He finds her at her father's house, and they return home, stopping on the way in Gibeah, where they stay in the house of an old man they meet. The "wicked men" of the city come to the door at night, demanding to see the Levite so that they "may know him" (Judg. 19:22). The master of the house offers them instead his virgin daughter and the Levite's concubine, the latter of whom they take and rape to death. This leads ultimately to full-scale civil war among the Israelites and the near destruction of the tribe of Benjamin. The allusion in the narrative is to the story of Sodom and Gomorrah, when Lot hosts the angels who have come to destroy the city. There, the "men of the citie" come to the door demanding the strangers, again "that we maie know them," but Lot instead offers them his two virgin daughters (Gen. 19:4–8). Once again, the similarities in the narratives serve to emphasize their differences: the angels blind the men of Sodom and destroy the city, apart

[35] *Homilies*, i., 49.

from Lot and his family; there are no saving angels in the Judges story, and the concubine is raped and killed. The destruction of Sodom is an unambiguous case of divine judgment. The bloody consequence of the Judges story is much harder to interpret, since, while the war results from the genuine offence of the Gibeans, it is nevertheless a lawless and destructive bloodfeud.

If repetition, parallelism, and allusion are favored devices of the authors of the Jewish Scriptures, these become almost ubiquitous in the Christian writings of the New Testament. Indeed, Christianity might be said to be a fundamentally intertextual religion. Although some early Christians proposed doing away with the Jewish Scriptures, orthodoxy ultimately adopted them as the Old Testament of the Christian Bible. Since those books were all pre-Christian, however, some means needed to be found for making them relevant to the Christian reader. The means hit upon by Paul, the gospel writers, and subsequent Christian writers and artists was typology, interpreting Old Testament "types" as anticipations or prophecies of their New Testament "antitypes," which fulfilled the types and gave them meaning. Thus many Old Testament figures were seen as types of Christ:[36] Adam's fall was redeemed by the sacrifice of the "new Adam," Christ; Moses led the people of Israel out of Egypt and gave them the Law, while Jesus led all humanity out of sin and gave them the gospel; David was anointed king over Israel, while Christ was the king of the heavenly kingdom. Typology is not quite the same as allusion, but they are close cousins, and typological relations in the Bible are often signaled by allusions. The "New Jerusalem" of Revelation 21, for instance, is an obvious antitype of the physical Jerusalem, but John's statement "I sawe the holie citie new Jerusalem come downe from God out of heaven, prepared as a bride trimmed for her housband" (Rev. 21:2) makes the typological relationship clearer by alluding to prophecies in Isaiah. There, God promises, "I will creat new heavens and a newe earth," and he tells Zion (Jerusalem), "as a bridegroom is glad of the bride, so shal thy God rejoice over thee" (Isa. 65:17, 62:5).[37]

---

[36] All these Old Testament characters might thus be termed in a special sense "Christ-figures." The critical controversy about this perhaps overused literary term is discussed in Ch. 2.
[37] One particular problem presented by biblical allusion is that of distinguishing between an allusion to a specific verse and a *topos* repeated many times. There is a further distinction to be made between a biblical topos, recurring frequently, and a typological pairing. The distinctions are impossible to maintain perfectly, since multiple passages may be linked in typological chains. The best one can do is be aware of the problem and aim for as much accuracy as possible, case by case. Perhaps this is another place where one should keep the "play" of allusion in mind.

To take an even more obvious example, Matthew's account of Jesus's birth and childhood is an extended allusion to the story of Moses in Exodus. Like Moses, Jesus is born to humble Jewish parents, and, like him, he narrowly escapes death at the hands of a tyrant. Herod has all the male children of Bethlehem slain, just as Pharaoh did the children of the Israelites. Jesus's parents flee to Egypt, so that, as Matthew notes, "it might be fulfilled, which was spoken of the Lord by the Prophet, saying, Out of Egypt have I called my Sonne" (Matt. 2:15). The reference is to Hosea 11:1, "When Israel was a childe, then I loved him, and called my son out of Egypt," but Hosea himself is clearly alluding to the Exodus of Israel out of Egypt led by Moses (as in Psalm 114:1, "When Israel came out of Egypt"). Hosea's allusion looks backward to Exodus, but Matthew interprets it as looking forward in time (turning it into prophecy) to refer to the second Moses, Jesus. One might add the further parallel that both Moses and Jesus are raised by adoptive parents. Moses is cast onto the river and found, then adopted, by the daughter of Pharaoh; Jesus is not abandoned, but he is raised by Joseph, rather than his true father, God. After the Exodus, Moses and the Israelites wandered in the wilderness for forty years before crossing Jordan into Canaan (Num. 32:13). Jesus, returned again out of Egypt, is led into the wilderness for forty days and forty nights, to be tempted by the devil (Matt. 4). As so often, there are contrasts as well as parallels: Moses is not allowed to come into the promised land; Jesus promises that, "after I am risen againe, I wil go before you into Galile" (Matt. 26:32).

Still more obvious are moments when Jesus and Paul explicitly mention Old Testament figures and stories in order to reinterpret them in Christian terms. For example, Jesus tells the scribes and Pharisees, "as Jonas was thre dayes, and thre nights in the whales bellie: so shal the Sonne of man be thre dayes and thre nights in the heart of the earth" (Matt. 12: 40). Jonah is reinterpreted by Jesus as a type of himself, and the allusion is again contrastive: Jonah is the pre-eminent reluctant prophet, cast into the whale for disobedience, whereas Jesus sacrifices himself willingly. Another example appears in Galatians, where Paul radically reinterprets the story of Abraham's sons, Ishmael and Isaac, reading them as symbolic, respectively, of Jews and Christians, the Law and the Promise:

For it is written that Abraham has two sonnes, one by a servant, and one by a free woman. But he which was of the servant, was borne after the flesh: and he which was of the fre woman was borne by promes. By the which things another thing is ment: for these mothers are the two Testaments, the one which is Agar of mounte Sina, which gendreth unto bondage, (For Agar or Sina is a mountaine in Arabia, and it answereth to Jerusalem which now is) and she is in bondage with her children. But Jerusalem, which is above, is fre: which is the mother of us all. For it is written, Rejoyce thou barren that bearest no children: breake forthe, and crye, thou that travailest not: for the desolate hathe many mo children, then she which hathe an housband. Therefore, brethren, we are after the manner of Isaac, children of the promes. But as then he that was borne after the flesh, persecuteth him that was borne after the spirit, even so it is now. But what saith the Scripture? Put out the servant and her sonne: for the sonne of the servant shal not be heire with the sonne of the fre woman. Then brethren, we are not children of the servant, but of the fre woman. (Gal. 4:22–31)

Paul is playing fast and loose with Scripture. After Isaac's birth, Sarah (not named by Paul) does say, "God hath made me to rejoice: all that heare wil rejoyce with me" (Gen. 21:6), but this is not the writing about rejoicing Paul alludes to. Rather, it is written in Isaiah, "Rejoyce, o barren that didest not beare: breake forthe into joye and rejoice, thou that didest not travaile with childe: for the desolate hathe mo children then the married wife, saith the Lord" (Isa. 54:1). This is another instance of the "Jerusalem as God's bride" metaphor, but Isaiah's point is hardly that God has turned from the Jews to the Gentiles. The non-Israelites (the "barren") are bearing more children than Israel (the "married wife"), but this is a temporary affliction for Israel's sins; as in the passage cited above, Isaiah later promises that God the bridegroom will reunite with his bride. Paul hammers the square peg of Isaiah's verse into the round hole that is his reading of Genesis, in which Christians are children of the free woman (Sarah, the New Testament, the Promise), and the Jews, children of the servant Hagar, remain in bondage to the Law.

As Pucci has argued, drawing on the work of Sarah Spence, the advent of Christianity thus revolutionized the role of the reader. The Bible was not open and straightforward, but difficult, requiring the reader to penetrate below the mysterious surface to the deep truths lying beneath. This is the lesson of the story of the Eunuch of Queen Candace of the Ethiopians whom the apostle Philip meets in the desert (Acts 8:26–40). The Eunuch is intently reading Isaiah, but cannot understand what he reads until Philip interprets it for him (in Christian terms). It is no surprise that early Christians also favored the new format of the codex over the scroll, since the codex greatly facilitated the cross-referential reading necessary to their understanding of the Bible.[38] As shown above, Jewish Scriptures themselves were internally allusive, and there were important parallels between one story and another. For Christians, however, the Bible became a massive hypertext. Paul and the gospel-writers refer fre-

---

[38] See Peter Stallybrass, "Books and Scrolls: Navigating the Bible," in Jennifer Andersen and Elizabeth Sauer (eds), *Books and Readers in Early Modern England: Material Studies* (Philadelphia: University of Pennsylvania Press, 2002), 42–79.

quently (usually without citation) to the Pentateuch, the Psalms, the Prophets, and other books, but cross references appear in the margins even of verses that would not otherwise seem to require them. It is simply regular practice to interpret a biblical text by referring to another text elsewhere in the Bible. As Augustine, the most important early proponent of this reading practice, wrote, "it is with delight that we experience some trouble in searching for divine truth...for some passages from Scripture are easier, and they relieve our hunger; in the ones that are harder...practically nothing is dug out which is not discovered to be said more plainly in another place."[39] Such arguments lie behind George Herbert's "The H. Scriptures (II)," in which he describes a practice of associative or (in theological terms) typological reading like that advocated by Augustine. Addressing the Scriptures themselves, he writes,

>   Oh that I knew how all thy lights combine,
>   And the configurations of their glorie!
>   Seeing not onely how each verse doth shine,
>   But all the constellations of the storie.
>   This verse marks that, and both do make a motion
>   Unto a third, that ten leaves off doth lie:
>   Then as dispersed herbs do watch a potion,
>   These three make up some Christians destinie.[40]

This is the practice schematized by T. Grashop's "Howe to take profite in reading of the holy Scriptures" (see Chapter 1), and which is reflected in the tradition of filling the margins of the Bible with cross references, a feature common to all early modern English Bibles, from Tyndale's through the Geneva to the King James. The reader of the Geneva Bible is not puzzled long by Paul's cryptic reference in Galatians 4:27 to "what is written," because the margin cites the original, "Isa 64:1." Likewise, when Matthew writes of "the Prophet, saying, Out of Egypt," the margin provides the citation "Hose 11.1." In many places, however, the uneducated reader might have no idea that a prior text was relevant, or was being alluded to, as in Gabriel's announcement to Mary that "thou shalt conceive in thy wombe, and beare a sonne, and shalt call his name Jesus" (Luke 1:31). There is no obvious indication that these words are not original to Gabriel at this moment, yet the margin cites "Isa.7.14": "Beholde, the virgine shal conceive and beare a sonne, and she shal call his name Immanuel." The Geneva margin to Isaiah's verse does not in turn cite

---

[39] Augustine, *De doctrina Christiana*, cited in Pucci, *Full-Knowing Reader*, 79.
[40] *The Works of George Herbert*, ed. F. E. Hutchinson (Oxford: Clarendon Press, 1941), 58.

Luke, but it makes clear Isaiah's prophecy refers to Christ. The angel Gabriel's speech is in fact a pastiche of allusions. For instance, when he says that Jesus "shal reigne over the house of Jacob for ever, and of his kingdome shalbe no end" (Luke 1:33), the margin cites "Dan 7.14," in which Daniel dreams of "one like the Sonne of man" whose "dominion is an everlasting dominion, which shal never be taken awaie: and his kingdome shal never be destroyed."[41] These are allusions, rather than sources, since the New Testament writers were not simply borrowing from the Old; it was essential for Christians to recognize that the Old Testament prophecies were fulfilled in the New; their verbal borrowings confirmed this.[42]

There is more to be said about marginalia and allusion, especially but not exclusively in the Bible. In the Geneva and other Bibles allusions are noted in the margins (as they are in modern scholarly editions of poetry), but it is striking that the term "allusion" itself first appears in English in the margins rather than the text. In Abraham Fleming's translation of Synesius's *Paradoxe, Proving by reason and example, that Baldnesse is much better than bushie haire* (1579), a marginal note to a remark that "it would fare with me, as with *Thrasymachus*" reads, "The allusion is to one *Thrasymachus*, who maintained, more impudently than learnedlie, that justice is to be counted among evill things, and injustice among good: which opinion of his, *Socrates* made him, with shame enough, to recant."[43] In a more serious (religious) publication, *A Bright Burning Beacon, forewarning all wise Virgins to trim their lampes against the coming of the Bridegroom* (1580), also translated by Fleming, a reference to the thief in the night

---

[41] The marginalia here also make clear that Daniel's dream prophesies the coming of Christ. No doubt somewhere in the vast body of Christian commentary there is a gloss on the numerical coincidence of 7:14 in both Isaiah and Daniel, but I have not seen it.

[42] From the standpoint of faith, it may be that these are not exactly allusions. Gabriel speaks what he does because that is what he must speak, because Isaiah and Daniel write of his words before the fact, because God knows what will be said (and done) from eternity. In human terms, however, these *are* allusions, Luke self-consciously crafting Gabriel's speech out of snippets of Old Testament prophecy. That it is so crafted is supported by the alternative Old Testament allusions made by Matthew and Luke in their different Nativity stories. On the other hand, one might argue that the Christian faith allows for a unique kind of allusion. Since God is the author of both Creation and the Word, one might see typological relationships as a form of divine allusion, alluding in the media both of language and of reality itself. Moreover, since types look forward to their antitypes, divine allusions of the typological sort can, uniquely, move forward as well as backward in time. Thus, the Jonah story alludes (typologically) to Christ in a way that, in secular literature, no earlier text can to any later one.

[43] Synesius of Cyrene, Bishop of Ptolemais, *Paradoxe, Proving by reason and example, that Baldnesse is much better than bushie haire*, trans. Abraham Fleming (London: H. Denham, 1579), sig. b2ʳ.

(1 Thess. 5:2) is accompanied by the marginal note, "An allusion made to the example which Christ himself useth in the Gospell."[44] The Rheims New Testament (1582) uses "allusion" in two marginal notes. The first explains that the statement of the angel in Revelation that "we signe the servants of our God in their foreheads" (Rev. 7:3) is "an allusion to the signe of the Crosse which the faithful beare in their foreheads, to shew they be not ashamed of Christ." The second, also in Revelation (or The Apocalypse, as it is in Rheims), explains that the "woman clothed with the sunne" (Rev. 12:1) is "properly and principally spoken of the Church: and by allusion, of our B. Lady also."[45] *The Summe of the Conference betwene John Rainoldes and John Hart*, which uses "allusion" twice in its text, also uses it in the margins. Rainoldes remarks that "the Popes have stretched out their owne fringes," and the marginal note explains that this is "Spoken by allusion to the Scribes and the Pharises, who enlarged the Phylacteries and frindges of their garments."[46]

Marginal notes provide commentary on the text, offering explication, either through paraphrase, or explanation, or through cross references to other biblical texts that serve an explanatory function. Since allusion depends upon recognition and interpretation by the reader, it is logical that the term would appear in commentaries designed to aid the reader in these tasks. In fact, the first appearance of "allusion" in Latin to designate a literary figure is in a work of biblical commentary, Cassiodorus's exposition of the Psalms, mentioned above. Similarly, the first English citation of "allusion" in the *OED* (though not in fact, as shown above, its first printed use) is also in a commentary, John Selden's "illustrations" on Drayton's *Poly-Olbion*. The term "allusion" arises in the context of biblical reading, which necessitates cross referencing, intertextual referencing on the part of the Christian reader, and in the marginal glosses and more extended commentaries written to instruct the reader in this essential skill—essential because in reading the Bible with understanding lay the key to eternal salvation.[47]

---

[44] Friedrich Nausea, *A Bright Burning Beacon, forewarning all wise Virgins to trim their lampes against the coming of the Bridegroom*, trans. Abraham Fleming (London: Henrie Denham, 1580), sig. K3ᵛ.
[45] *The New Testament of Jesus Christ* (Rheims: John Fogny, 1582); marginal notes at Rev. 7:3 and Rev. 12:1.
[46] *The Summe of the Conference betwene John Rainoldes and John Hart* (London: [John Wolfe], 1584), 633.
[47] See Pucci, *Full-Knowing Reader*, on Christianity's shift in emphasis, departing from the classical rhetorical tradition, from the skilled speaker to the "full-knowing reader."

DRAMATIC PRECEDENTS TO SHAKESPEARE'S ALLUSIVE PRACTICE

The flowering of Shakespeare's practice of biblical allusion grew from the deep roots of this traditional Christian understanding and reading of the Bible, but there were also more recent models of biblical allusions in the works of his dramatic forebears. The greatest popular sensations of the Elizabethan stage in the years before Shakespeare's own plays hit the boards, while he was possibly apprenticing in the London theater world, were by Christopher Marlowe and Thomas Kyd, young playwrights who knew each other well, wrote together, and at one time lived together.[48] Shakespeare probably knew both of them personally; he certainly knew their plays.[49] Kyd's *The Spanish Tragedy* and Marlowe's *Doctor Faustus* and *The Jew of Malta* were smash hits and all three contain important biblical allusions that create irony, provide contrast between a stage character and a biblical one, or even parody a familiar biblical passage.[50] These were methods of biblical allusion that Shakespeare came to use frequently.

The Spanish Tragedy was probably written in the late 1580s and set the pattern for the Elizabethan revenge tragedy, greatly influencing *Hamlet*, among many lesser plays.[51] The Knight Marshall of Spain, Hieronimo, is the protagonist seeking revenge for the murder of his son, Horatio. As he pursues his vengeance, his mind, in good Senecan fashion, begins to deteriorate until he is completely mad. The denouement is the staging of a bizarre play, written by Hieronimo, apparently performed in a variety of

---

[48] See Jeffrey Masten, "Playwrighting: Authorship and Collaboration," in John D. Cox and David Scott Kaston (eds), *A New History of English Drama* (New York: Columbia University Press, 1997), 357–82, 360–6.

[49] Park Honan asserts that Marlowe and Shakespeare must have known each other, though there is no specific evidence of it. *Christopher Marlowe: Poet and Spy* (Oxford and New York: Oxford University Press, 2005), 2. Lois Potter concurs, noting that the world of London theater was a small one. She also cites the arguments of some critics that on *1 Henry VI* Shakespeare collaborated with Kyd (according to Brian Vickers and Marina Tarlinskaya) and Marlowe (according to Hugh Craig). *The Life of William Shakespeare: A Critical Biography* (Malden, MA: Wiley-Blackwell, 2012), 79.

[50] On the popularity and influence of these plays, see G. K. Hunter, *English Drama 1586–1642: The Age of Shakespeare* (Oxford: Clarendon Press, 1997), 66–7, 71–9. Marlowe had other successes, most notably the *Tamburlaine* plays, but these two are representative of his practice of biblical allusion. For a brief but solid study of Marlowe's biblical allusions, see James H. Sims, *Dramatic Uses of Biblical Allusions in Marlowe and Shakespeare* (Gainesville, FL: University of Florida Press, 1966).

[51] The play must have been written by 1592, when it was staged and entered in the Stationers' Register, but it may date from five to ten years earlier. See J. R. Mulryne (ed.), in Thomas Kyd, *The Spanish Tragedy*, New Mermaids, 2nd edn (London: A&C Black; New York: W. W. Norton, 1989, repr. 2000), pp. xiii–xiv. Citations are from this edition.

different languages. Included among the actors are Balthazar, the villain who murdered Horatio, and Bel-Imperia, who loved Horatio and is loved by Bathazar. The climax of the play-within-the-play is Hieronimo's stabbing of Lorenzo, son of the Duke of Castile and another of Horatio's murderers, and Bel-Imperia's stabbing of Balthazar, followed by herself. Hieronimo, after biting out his own tongue, stabs the Duke of Castile and then kills himself. The body count is impressive. Near the end, as Hieronimo anticipates his revenge, he says, alone, "Now shall I see the fall of Babylon,| Wrought by the heavens in this confusion" (4.2.195–6). The reference to Babylon is obvious, but its significance is more complex. First, the destruction of Babylon was the archetype of divinely ordained vengeance for both Christians and Jews. Babylon had conquered Israel in 587 BCE and taken many of the Jews into captivity, where they longed for revenge and restoration to their homeland. Psalm 137 expresses the desire of the captive Jews, sitting "by the waters of Babylon," for bloody retribution:

O daughter of Babylon, wasted with misery: yea, happy shall he be that rewardeth thee as thou hast served us.

Blessed shall he be, that taketh thy children: and throweth them against the stones. (Ps. 137:8–9)

But Hieronimo's allusion to Babylon does more than provide biblical justification and precedence for his personal vengeance; it adds an apocalyptic resonance to the ensuing slaughter, since, at the last moment of the Last Times in Revelation, an angel cries, "It is fallen, it is fallen, Babylon that great citie, and is become the habitation of devils" (Rev. 18:2). In his madness, Hieronimo sees the achievement of his own purpose as the very end of Creation. Moreover, Babylon is etymologically connected to Babel, both words being identical in Hebrew (*Babel*). The biblical Tower of Babel was the place where God punished human over-reaching by confusing their language, making people unintelligible to each other. "Therefore," Genesis explains, "the name of it [the tower they were building] was called Babel" (Gen. 11:9). The Geneva marginal note elucidates, "Or, confusion." Hence Hieronimo's otherwise puzzling association of the fall of Babylon with a "confusion" that is "wrought by the heavens." He is conflating various biblical associations with Babel/Babylon, as most Bible readers already did. The "confusion" Hieronimo has in mind in this case is his own play-within-the-play, "in sundry languages," the sort of babbling play that might have been staged in Babel after the confusion of tongues.

Marlowe puts biblical allusion to equally complex uses, often scandalously. In *Dr Faustus*, to which Shakespeare specifically alludes in *Troilus and Cressida*, we expect Faustus to quote the Bible, since among his areas of scholarly expertise is theology, and Valdes tells him that he will need for his conjuring "The Hebrew Psalter, and New Testament" (sc. 1.155).[52] Like a good humanist scholar, however, Faustus cites his text in Latin. "*Consummatum est*," he says after he has signed his soul to the devil (sc. 5.74). A more contrastive allusion would be hard to imagine, since these are Christ's last words on the cross in John: Faustus quotes the Vulgate translation of the verse, which in the Geneva Bible reads "it is finished" (John 19:30). Faustus is being deliberately blasphemous, having little to lose, given that he has just damned himself. Two other allusions are more subtle, citing the Bible in fragments, so that the significance of the allusions require the audience to fill in the missing text. Early in the play Faustus cites "Jerome's Bible":

> *Stipendium peccati mors est*: ha! *Stipendium*, etc.
> The reward of sin is death? That's hard.
> *Si peccasse negamus, fallimur, et mulla est in nobis veritas.*
> If we say that we have no sin,
> We deceive ourselves, and there's no truth in us. (sc. 1.39–43)

Faustus concludes, "Why then belike we must sin, | And so consequently die" (sc. 1.44–5). This conclusion depends upon the incompleteness of Faustus's quotations; as so often with sophisticated allusions, the full significance depends upon knowing the surrounding context of the passage alluded to. "The reward of sin is death" is indeed hard, but the lesson is mollified by the second half of the verse from Romans: "but the gift of God is eternall life, through Jesus Christ our Lord" (Rom. 6:23). The second allusion works the same way, quoting 1 John 1:8 but omitting the essential verse 9: "If we acknowledge our sinnes, hee is faithfull and just, to forgive us our sinnes, and to cleanse us from all unrighteousnesse." Edmund Spenser picked up this deliberately manipulative trick from Marlowe, using similarly truncated allusions in *The Faerie Queene*, such as when Despaire tries to attack Redcrosse Knight. Despair gives Redcrosse a lesson on divine justice to tempt him to suicide:

> Is not his lawe, Let every sinner die:
> Die shall all flesh? what then must needs be donne,
> Is it not better to doe willinglie,

---

[52] Christopher Marlowe, *Dr Faustus: Based on the A Text*, ed. Roma Gill, New Mermaids (London: A&C Black; New York: W. W. Norton, 1968; 2nd edn, 1989). Further citations are from this edition. The play is divided only into scenes, not acts. In *Troilus and Cressida*, Troilus says of Cressida, "Why, she is a pearl | Whose price hath launched above a thousand ships" (2.2.81–2), alluding to Faustus's famous description of Helen: "Was this the face that launched a thousand ships, | And burnt the topless towers of Ilium?" (sc. 12).

Then linger, till the glas be all out ronne?
Death is the end of woes: die soone, O faeries sonne. (1.9.47, ll. 5–9)[53]

Despaire is paraphrasing Romans 6:23, "For the wages of sinne is death." Yet, for all the terror of this clause, it is only a preparation for the more essential one that follows, completing the biblical verse: "but the gifte of God is eternall life through Jesus Christ our Lord." Una, Redcrosse's companion, saves him by paraphrasing this second clause, asking "In heavenly mercies hast thou not a part?" (1.9.53, l. 4).

Marlowe's biblical allusions in *The Jew of Malta* are overtly parodic. The titular Jew, Barabas, opens the play in his counting-house surrounded by piles of gold. He speaks of making "a miracle of thus much coin," heaping up "pearl like pebble-stones," as well as "seld-seen costly stones of so great price," which "May serve in peril of calamity | To ransom great kings from captivity" (1.1.13, 23, 28, 31–2).[54] Together, these phrases constitute a grotesque allusion to Christ, whose miraculous birth and willing sacrifice served to ransom humanity from its sins, and who described the kingdom of heaven as "like to a merchant man, that seketh good perles, Who having found a perle of great price, went and solde all that he had, and boght it" (Matt. 13:45–6). Jesus came "to give his life for the ransome of manie" (Matt. 20:28), he "led captivitie captive" (Eph. 4:8), and he is the "King of Kings" (1 Tim. 6:15) who has "made us unto our God Kings and Priests" (Rev. 5:10). Even Barabas's description of his treasure as "Infinite riches in a little room" (1.1.37) is a blasphemous burlesque of the incarnation. In one of the most well-known medieval English carols, Mary is described as a rose in which "conteynyd was | Heven and erthe in lytyl space."[55] Even if Marlowe is not deliberately alluding to this carol, which survives in a commonplace book at Trinity College, Oxford, he is debasing the miracle of the incarnation to a "miracle" of material wealth.[56] "Infinite riches" was not an unusual phrase, but was used commonly in translations of Calvin and Luther (among others) to refer to the wealth of God's goodness and mercy. It is also biblical: "And great pleasure is in her [Wisdom's] friendshippe, and that in the workes of her hands are infinite riches" (Wis. 8:18).[57]

---

[53] Edmund Spenser, *The Faerie Queene*, ed. A.C. Hamilton, text ed. Hiroshi Yamashita and Toshiyuki Suzuki (London and New York: Longman, 2001).

[54] Marlowe, *The Jew of Malta*, ed. Roma Gill, in *The Complete Works of Christopher Marlowe*, iv (Oxford: Clarendon Press, 1995). Further citations are from this edition.

[55] "Ther is no rose of swych vertu," no. 173 in Richard L. Greene (ed.), *The Early English Carols* (Oxford: Clarendon Press, 1935), 130–1.

[56] Trinity MS O.3.58. This manuscript dates from the early fifteenth century (Greene, *Early English Carols*, 343–4).

[57] The phrase goes back to the Coverdale Bible (1535). In the Geneva Bible, the phrase also appears in a note on Nahum 2:9: "God commandeth the enemies to spoile Nineveh, and promiseth them infinite riches, and treasures."

A more obvious allusion occurs in scene 2, when Barabas has been stripped of all his wealth by the Maltese. His friend, "First Jew," counsels, "remember Job" (1.2.181). The reference seems appropriate, pointing to a model for coping with unmerited suffering. Yet the explicit reference alerts the audience to more allusions to the book of Job in the scene. For one thing, "First Jew" is accompanied by two others, paralleling the three friends of Job, who try to console and advise him in his downfall. Barabas picks up the Job reference and riffs on it. First, he boasts that he has far more wealth than Job's "seven thousand sheep, | Three thousand camels, and two hundred yoke | Of labouring oxen," so Barabas reasons that he is far more entitled than Job to "curse the day, | Thy fatal birthday, forlorn Barabas" (1.2.183–5, 192–3). The animal count is nearly right (Job actually has five hundred oxen, as well as five hundred "she asses"), and Job "opened his mouth and cursed his day" (Job 1:3, 3:1). The second Jew urges Barabas to "be patient," and Barabas replies, "Pray leave me in my patience" (1.2.200–1). The point of the story of Job (at least by the orthodox interpretation) is that Job is, as the Geneva Bible headnote puts it, "the example of a singular patience." After they have gone, Barabas castigates them for thinking him "a senseless lump of clay" (1.2.218). Job similarly says to his friends, "Your memories may be compared unto ashes and your bodies to bodies of clay" (Job 13:12), and the description of man as "clay" recurs throughout the book (Job 4:19, 10:9, 27:16, 33:6, 38:14). This allusive re-enactment of Job is a travesty of the original, since Barabas is in fact most impatient, and he is the antithesis of "an upright and juste man, one that feared God, and eschewed evil" (Job 1:1). But this is Marlowe's point. It is also impossible to miss that Barabas is named after the thief whom the Jews asked to be released instead of Jesus (Matt. 27). According to Christian tradition, Job in his suffering is seen as a type of the suffering Christ. Barabas's name thus suggests this Jew of Malta is much more like the biblical thief than the crucified Jesus.

SHAKESPEARE'S ALLUSIVE PRACTICE

Like Kyd's and Marlowe's, Shakespeare's allusions are often ironic or parodic; these can be comical, serious, or both. One serious example is Iago's statement in *Othello*, "I am not what I am" (1.1.65). The allusion is to God's name, at least as much of a name as God admits to, in Exodus 3. Having been given his mission to bring Israel out of Egypt, Moses asks God by what name he should be identified. God replies, "I AM THAT I AM" (Exod. 3:14), which is the English rendering (in the Geneva Bible) of the Hebrew Tetragrammaton, the four letters that are also rendered as "YHWH," "Yahweh," and "Jehovah." Though in the latter renderings this may seem to be a name, it is in fact the denial of a name. God has no name, or rather no need of a name, because he is "God," the one and only God, who does not need to be differentiated from other "gods." God's answer to Moses also indicates God's eternal immutability; in the Hebrew, verbs have no tense, so YHWH could also mean, "I am what I was," "I will be what I am," and every other possible permutation of tense. Thus, God is, has been, and always will be just what he is. Iago's allusion inverts this. Not only is Iago never what he seems to be, in keeping with his prior admission that his "outward action" does not "demonstrate | The native act and figure of my heart" (1.1.61–2), but he actually *is* not what he is. This is, on the one hand, a logical impossibility, but on the other an expression of utter negation and vacuity.[58] If God is ultimate plenitude, then Iago is absolute emptiness. All this meaning is packed into Iago's brief, blasphemous allusion, and considerably enriches the scene for the attentive audience member. Such auditors (or readers) will still have this line in mind at the end of the play when Othello, finally disillusioned, says of Iago, "I look down towards his feet; but that's a fable" (5.2.286). Othello half-expects to see the cloven hooves commonly associated with the Devil.[59] For the audience, Iago's devilish nature has already been established. As the one who is not what he is, Iago is the opposite of God: the Devil. Iago cannot literally be the Devil, of course, but the allusions representing him as such greatly deepen our perception of his wickedness.

By contrast, an example of a comical allusion occurs in *The Winter's Tale*, when the Clown (country bumpkin) says to the conman Autolycus,

---

[58] Iago's statement is thus quite different from Viola's in *Twelfth Night*, "I am not that I play" (1.5.179), which refers simply to her disguised state. She does say later, however, "I am not what I am" (3.1.139), but in the context this statement seems to be about social rank (Viola also says to Olivia, "you are not what you are"), as well as the ongoing disguise. Keir Elam in the Arden edition (3rd series) suggests that there may be an echo of Paul's statement in 1 Cor. 15:10, "But by the grace of God, I am that I am," which is glossed in the Geneva Bible: "For he was but the instrument, and minister and giveth the whole glorie to God." There might perhaps be a sense, analogous to the Corinthians passage, in which Viola is not acting as an independent agent but is wooing by the "grace" of Orsino. In any case, in the very different context of *Othello*, the phrase alludes not to Corinthians but to the more familiar verse in Exodus.

[59] E. A. J. Honigman in the Arden[3] *Othello* cites a proverb in Tilley, D252, "The Devil is known by his cloven feet." Tilley offers limited evidence, however, citing only an example from Thomas Dekker's *Honest Whore* (1604) before *Othello*. Morris Palmer Tilley, *A Dictionary of the Proverbs in England in the Sixteenth and Seventeenth Centuries* (Ann Arbor: University of Michigan Press, 1950). As the *OED* points out, though, the devil's cloven hooves derived ultimately from the Greek God Pan, who had the feet of a goat. In the same year as *Othello* (1606), William Perkins writes of "the plaiers and the painters Divels, some blacke horned monster with broad eies, crooked clawes or cloven feet." *The combat betweene Christ and the Divell displayed* (London: Melchisedech Bradwood for E. E[dgar], 1606), sig. A2ᵛ.

"We are but plain fellows, sir." Autolycus replies, "A lie; you are rough and hairy" (4.4.721–2). The Clown and his Shepherd father probably respond to this badinage with blank stares, but the Jacobean audience would grasp not only the obvious physical insult, which puns on the two senses of "plain" (both simple and smooth-skinned), but the allusion to the story of Jacob and Esau. Jacob says to his mother Rebecca, "Beholde, Esau my brother is a heary man, and I am smoothe" (Gen. 27:11; here Shakespeare is blending together the Bishops' Bible and the Geneva, perhaps from memory, since the former has "heary" and the latter "rough"). The allusion is not frivolous, since Jacob's statement comes just before he tricks his brother out of his birthright; Rebecca puts animal skins on Jacob's arms to make him seem "heary" to his blind father, Isaac. Since Autolycus is a trickster too, and a master of disguise, the allusion is especially fitting.

A case of allusions that are simultaneously playful and serious, as well as scandalous, is in *The Merchant of Venice*, a play deeply indebted to Marlowe's *Jew of Malta*. As a Jew, Shylock might well be expected to know and cite Hebrew Scripture, and he does. In 1.3 Shylock recounts to Antonio and Bassanio, at considerable length, the story of Jacob and Laban from Genesis 30:31–43:

> Mark what Jacob did:
> When Laban and himself were compromised
> That all the eanlings which were streaked and pied
> Should fall as Jacob's hire, the ewes, being rank,
> In end of autumn turned to the rams;
> And when the work of generation was
> Between these wooly breeders in the act,
> The skilful shepherd peeled me certain wands,
> And, in the doing of the deed of kind,
> He stuck them up before the fulsome ewes,
> Who, then conceiving, did in eaning time
> Fall parti-coloured lambs, and those were Jacob's.
> This was a way to thrive, and he was blest:
> And thrift is blessing, if men steal it not. (1.3.73–86)

In other words, after Laban and Jacob have agreed that, at the next lambing, Laban will take the solid colored lambs and Jacob the spotted ones, Jacob places a spotted or streaked stick in front of the mating sheep, and this produces an unusually large percentage of spotted lambs.[60] As in *The*

---

[60] From the perspective of modern science, this seems strange animal husbandry, but similar beliefs survived into the Renaissance. Pregnant women were warned not to look at ugly animals, lest they give birth to horse- or ape-faced children. See Simona Cohen, *Animals as Disguised Symbols in Renaissance Art* (Leiden: Brill, 2008), 133–4.

Winter's Tale, just discussed, Jacob is similarly a trickster, but are his tricks laudable cleverness or despicable deceit? For Shylock, Jacob is a precedent for seizing opportunity; he has turned to this passage in response to Antonio's apparent criticism of lending money at interest ("I do never use it," Antonio says at 1.3.66, punning on the financial sense of "use" or usury).[61] Before Shylock begins his extended account, Antonio questions Jacob's relevance: "what of him, did he take interest?" Shylock responds, "No, not take 'interest,' not as you would say | Directly interest," and this is the extent of the explanation for his lengthy account of Jacob's peculiar breeding of livestock (1.3.71–3). Antonio again challenges the relevance:

> This was a venture, sir, that Jacob served for,
> A thing not in his power to bring to pass,
> But swayed and fashioned by the hand of heaven.
> Was this inserted to make interest good?
> Or is your gold and silver ewes and rams? (1.3.87–91)

Shylock responds simply, "I cannot tell, I make it breed as fast" (1.3.92). Antonio turns from interpretative debate to contempt, noting to Bassanio how "the devil can cite Scripture for his purpose" (1.3.94). This remarkable scene of exegetical debate signals the centrality of the Bible to *Merchant*'s exploration of usury and Jewish–Christian relations, which has been the focus of much critical attention.[62] This and other allusions to the Jacob story, for instance, raise questions about fathers and sons, inheritance and birthright, that adumbrate deeper questions as to whether Jews or Christians are the true sons of Abraham, the chosen people of the Book (not to mention the greatest tricksters).

Shylock is also surprisingly familiar with the Christian New Testament. For example, he alludes to Jesus's healing of the man possessed by a demon (Matt. 8:28–32) in his mockery of the idea that he might ever dine with Christians: "to smell pork, to eat of the habitation which your prophet the Nazarite conjur'd the devil into" (1.3.33–5). Jesus exorcises the demon Legion by driving him (them?) into a herd of swine, who promptly rush into the sea and drown. For Shylock to claim that the Jewish avoidance of pork might be due to Jesus having driven demons into pigs, or even that

---

[61] The word also puns on the "ewes" that are the subject of Jacob's breeding experiment. Marc Shell works out these and other puns in intricate detail. See "The Wether and the Ewe: Verbal Usury in *The Merchant of Venice*," *Kenyon Review*, 1/4 (1979), 65–92.

[62] Barbara K. Lewalski's seminal article "Biblical Allusion and Allegory in *The Merchant of Venice*," *SQ* 13/3 (1962), 327–43, has been considerably complicated and superseded by both major and minor studies, especially James Shapiro, *Shakespeare and the Jews* (New York: Columbia University Press, 1996), and Janet Adelman, *Blood Relations: Christian and Jew in* The Merchant of Venice (Chicago: University of Chicago Press, 2008).

his driving the demon into this particular animal indicates Jesus's recognition of its impurity by Jewish dietary law, is ingenious though obviously dubious from a Christian perspective. Shylock also comments that Antonio looks "like a fawning publican" (1.3.41), which seems to allude to the penitent publican in Luke 18:10–14, who is contrasted with a proud hypocritical Pharisee. Both pray to God, but, while the Pharisee is full of self-righteous pride, it is the sinful publican who is genuinely humble and penitent. Shylock reverses the characters, apparently, seeing the publican as "fawning" rather than praying in earnest. Shylock's allusions to the gospels are usually parodic; he knows the texts, but interprets them mischievously. Shylock's reference to the publican cuts two ways, however, since in the Christian reading the publican is the righteous one, while the Pharisee (to whom Shylock obviously corresponds because of his strict emphasis on the law) is condemned; so is Shylock.

Since the Bible was everywhere in Shakespeare's culture, his allusions to the Bible sometimes come indirectly by way of the language of the church liturgy, sermons, biblical commentaries, literature, drama, or even religious art. When Hamlet condemns the players who "out-Herod Herod," for instance (3.2.14), he is referring to the Jewish King Herod from Matthew's Nativity account. More specifically, though, he is thinking of the traditionally bombastic representations of Herod in the English Mystery plays.[63] In *The Play of Sir Thomas More*, in the scene generally acknowledged to be by Shakespeare, More warns the crowd against rebellion and disobedience, saying, "'tis a sin | Which oft th'apostle did forewarn us of, | Urging obedience to authority."[64] The "apostle" is Paul, and the forewarning is in Romans 13, "Let everie soule be subject unto the higher powers: for there is no power but of God: and the powers that be, are ordained by God" (Rom. 13:1). Many Elizabethans would have recognized this passage also as mediated by the "Homily on Disobedience and Willful Rebellion," which, along with the "Homily on Obedience," was required by law to be read in every church nine times a year during Elizabeth's reign:[65]

---

[63] Emrys Jones, *The Origins of Shakespeare* (Oxford: Clarendon Press, 1977; repr. 1978), ch. 2, "Shakespeare and the Mystery Cycles." For an interesting early study, see Roscoe E. Parker, "The Reputation of Herod in Early English Literature," *Speculum*, 8/1 (1933), 59–67. See also Michael O'Connell, "Vital Cultural Practices: Shakespeare and the Mysteries," *JMEMS* 29/1 (1999), 149–68. Further Shakespeare allusions to biblical material by way of the Mystery plays are explored in Chs 5 and 7.

[64] Anthony Munday, Henry Chettle, et al., *Sir Thomas More*, ed. John Jowett, Arden (London: Methuen Drama, A&C Black, 2011), [scene 6,] 105–7.

[65] Paul N. Siegel, "English Humanism and the New Tudor Aristocracy," *Journal of the History of Ideas* 13/4 (1952), 450–68, 461.

The holye scriptures do teach most expresly that our saviour Christe him selfe, and his apostle saint Paul, saint Peter, with others, were unto the magistrates and higher powers, which ruled at their beyng uppon the earth, both obedient them selves, and dyd also diligently and earnestly exhort all other Christians to the lyke obedience unto their princes and governours.[66]

Among the marginal references is "Ro.13.a.1."

Another example of the mediation of biblical texts is in *The Taming of the Shrew*, when, in Kate's final speech about husbands and marital duty, she pronounces, "Thy husband is thy lord, thy life, thy keeper, | Thy head, thy sovereign" (5.2.151–2). Paul writes that "the housband is the wives head" (Eph. 5:23) and that "the man is the womans head" (1 Cor. 11:3). But Kate's "thy head" is probably only indirectly Pauline, since in the *Fourme of Solempnizacion of Matrimonye* in the Book of Common Prayer, the priest quotes Paul extensively, including the statement from Ephesians that "the housbande is the wyves headde, even as Christe is the headde of the Churche."[67] Shaheen also points out that the phrase "the husband is the head of the woman" is also quoted in the *Homily of the State of Matrimony*.[68] That Kate should be alluding to the marriage service or the homily in this speech is of course entirely appropriate. A similar example occurs in *Hamlet*, when Hamlet responds to Rosencrantz's question about what he has done with Polonius's body, "Compounded it with dust, whereto 'tis kin" (4.2.5). In his Arden[2] note, Harold Jenkins cites Genesis 3:19, "Dust thou art, and unto dust shalt thou return." (This is, inappropriately, the KJV; the Bishops' Bible has "dust thou art, and into dust shalt thou be turned agayne.") In this persistently funereal play, however, it seems likely that Hamlet is not alluding directly to the verse from Genesis but to its use in *The Order for the Buriall of the Dead*: "we therefore committe hys bodye to the grounde, earthe to earthe, ashes to ashes, dust to dust."[69] Dust appears six times in *Hamlet* in similar contexts: for example, "Seek for thy noble father in the dust" (1.2.71); "this quintessence of dust" (2.2.308); "Alexander returneth unto dust" (5.1.202–3). In each case it is the Book of Common Prayer Burial Service that is alluded to, though the original verse from Genesis is in the deeper intertextual background, as most audience members (and churchgoers) would have been aware.

On the other hand, the Bible, mediated or not, was only one of the literary sources flowing into Shakespeare's imagination, and his allusions to biblical stories and characters can exist alongside, or even be intertwined with, those from classical or Renaissance literature or English folklore.

---

[66] *Homilies*, ii. 308. [67] *BCP* 163.
[68] Shaheen, 97. [69] *BCP* 172.

It was an age of syncretistic thinking, when people could believe both that England was the new Israel, God's chosen Protestant kingdom on earth, and also that it was founded by Brute, the grandson of Aeneas, hero of Virgil's *Aeneid* and survivor from the fall of Troy. Thus Marc Antony in *Antony and Cleopatra* can be read allusively as an avatar of Hercules, Aeneas, Christ, and perhaps Satan, all at once, or at least at various points in the play.[70] Similarly, Posthumus, in *Cymbeline*, who has a dream vision of Jupiter on an eagle, is at the same time allusively connected to both Moses and Jesus. A gentleman recounts what happened to the infant Posthumus, both of whose parents died before his birth:

> The King he takes the babe
> To his protection, calls him Postumus Leonatus,
> Breeds him and makes him of his bedchamber,
> Puts to him all the learnings that his time
> Could make him the receiver of… (1.1.40–4)

Acts 7:21–2 describes the similar royal adoption of the infant Moses:

And when he was cast out, Pharaos daughter toke him up, and nourished him for her owne sonne. And Moses was learned in all the wisdom of the Egyptians, and was mightie in words and in dedes.

The gentleman goes on to praise the young Posthumus's development:

> Most praised, most loved,
> A sample to the youngest, to th'more mature
> A glass that feated them, and to the graver
> A child that guided dotards. (1.1.47–50)

Shaheen notes the parallel with Jesus in Luke 2:40–7:

And the childe grewe, and waxed strong in Spirit, and was filled with wisdome, and the grace of God was with him…And when he was twelve yere olde…they founde him in the Temple, sitting in the middes of the doctours, bothe hearing them, and asking them questions. And all that heard him, were astonied at his understanding, and answers.

In this case, the verbal triggers of the allusion are small, "learnings" and "learned" in the first case, and perhaps, more obliquely (and punningly), "dotards" and "doctours" in the second, as well as the commonplace noun "child." But Jesus and Moses were already linked typologically for Christians, however, as emphasized in Matthew's Nativity narrative of Jesus as another Moses, escaping the slaughter of the innocents, coming out of Egypt, and spending forty days in the wilderness, as discussed

---

[70] For more on Marc Antony, see Ch. 5.

above. The double allusion underscores the promise of young Posthumus and foreshadows his role as (secular) savior of his people. At the same time, Jupiter himself confirms both Posthumus's special potential and also, more surprisingly, reinforces the allusions to Christ, prophesying to the ghosts of Posthumus's parents that "Your low-laid son our godhead he will uplift" and noting that "Our Jovial star reigned at his birth" (5.4.103, 105). Jesus is correspondingly "low-laid": "I am meke and lowlie in heart" (Matt. 11:29). Also, he will be uplifted first on the cross and afterward in heaven: "And as Moses lift up the serpent in the wilderness, so must the Sonne of man which is in heaven" (John 3:14). Finally, Jesus's birth, like Posthumus's, is marked by the "starre in the East" (Matt. 2:2).

Classical and biblical allusions merge again in *The Merchant of Venice*, when Portia says, "I stand for sacrifice" (3.2.57). She has just explicitly identified herself with Hesione, "The virgin tribute paid by howling Troy | To the sea monster" (3.2.56–7), who is rescued by Hercules; Portia, "sacrificed" to her father's peculiar marriage lottery, hopes to be "rescued" by Bassanio. Portia's statement takes on quite a different sense in retrospect, however, after Shylock announces dramatically, "I stand here for law" (4.1.141). As many readers have noted, Shylock and Portia "stand" for opposed values of Justice versus Mercy, or for the Jewish and Christian principles, respectively, of Law versus Sacrifice.[71] This dichotomy is represented on the title page of a number of English Bibles, including both the Geneva and the Bishops', where two female figures sit atop the architectural frame, standing for Justice (left, with sword and scales) and Mercy (right, with a book, presumably the New Testament).[72] Thus Portia's allusion to sacrifice simultaneously encompasses both classical and biblical sources.

One of Shakespeare's most syncretistic, or culturally scrambled, plays is *A Midsummer Night's Dream*, which takes place in ancient Athens, and combines characters out of Greek myth (Theseus and Hippolyta), young lovers out of Greece by way of Renaissance Italy (Demetrius and Lysander, Hermia and Helena), fairies from English folklore (Oberon and Titania,

---

[71] See Lewalski, "Biblical Allusion and Allegory." The equation of Judaism with Justice and the Law is the Christian perspective, of course, hardly representing a Jewish self-understanding.

[72] The same title page appears in Geneva Bibles in 1578 (STC 2123) and 1583 (STC 2136) and the Bishops' in 1588 (STC 2149), 1591 (STC 2156), and 1595 (STC 2167). See R. B. McKerrow and F. S. Ferguson, *Title-Page Borders Used in England and Scotland, 1485–1640* (London: Printed for the Bibliographical Society at the Oxford University Press, 1932), 132. That these figures are Justice and Mercy is confirmed by the first quarto edition (1589, STC 2105) of the Bishops', which includes the same figures, posed slightly differently, but prominently labeled as such. Curiously, this 1589 title page was reused for John Ward's *First Set of English Madrigals* in 1613, perhaps because it includes a "Mourning Song in memory of Prince Henry."

but especially Robin Goodfellow, the Puck), and tradesmen seemingly from the streets of Elizabethan London (the "rude mechanicals"). One of the latter, Bottom the Weaver, is magically given the head of an ass in order that Titania may fall in love with him (also by enchantment) as part of Oberon's revenge plot. As Jonathan Bate points out, "this is one of the few moments in Shakespeare at which Ovidian metamorphosis actually seems to be taking place on stage."[73] After much magical amusement, Bottom is put to sleep, his body is restored to normal, and he wakes up to reflect on his midsummer night's "dream":

> I have had a most rare vision. I have had a dream, past the wit of man to say what dream it was. Man is but an ass, if he go about t' expound this dream. Methought I was—there is no man can tell what. Methought I was, and methought I had—but man is but a patch'd fool, if he will offer to say what methought I had. The eye of man hath not heard, the ear of man hath not seen, man's hand is not able to taste, his tongue to conceive, nor his heart to report, what my dream was. (4.1.205–14)

Bottom's speech is on the surface nonsensical, but its meaning and its humor are clearer if one recognizes its allusion to Paul's First Epistle to the Corinthians:

> The eye hath not seen, and the eare hath not heard, neither have entred into the heart of man, the thynges which God hath prepared for them that love hym. (1 Cor. 2:9, Bishops' Bible)

Bottom is not simply scrambling senses, or mixing up nouns and verbs; his "dream" is a parody of Paul's description of the wondrous mysteries of God's love.

Of course, Bottom cannot himself be conscious of either the biblical allusion or the parody, since, despite his English appearance and language, he is at the same time living in ancient, pre-Christian Athens. (This makes any self-consciousness of Ovid impossible too.) Yet, if the audience catches the allusion, the scene benefits in quite complex ways. Shakespeare's tone with respect to the mechanicals is always subtle. Bottom is an ass, of course, even without the actual head of one, and his "vision" speech is a delightful muddle. Yet, when he says that he will call the ballad of his dream "'Bottom's Dream,' because it hath no bottom" (4.1.214–15), his statement is deep as well as shallow. A "bottom" can also be an "ass,"

---

[73] Jonathan Bate, *Shakespeare and Ovid* (Oxford: Clarendon Press, 1993; repr. 2001), 142–3. Bate notes the specific allusion to Midas, the "rich fool" given ass's ears for misjudging a singing contest. Deborah Baker Wyrick shows that ass's ears were standard iconography for the fool in Renaissance emblems. "The Ass Motif in *The Comedy of Errors* and *A Midsummer Night's Dream*," *SQ* 33/4 (1982), 432–48. Critics have noted another classical source in Bottom's metamorphosis in Apuleius's *The Golden Ass*.

and Bottom both is, and has, an ass in this sense.[74] And yet his experience was genuinely magical, and was legitimately "bottomless" in the sense of being "unfathomable" (a seafaring word that means the same thing: infinite and unknowable). In one sense, then, his dream is nonsense, since eyes never *can* hear, nor ears see. In another sense, however, Bottom's experience could be said to be more transcendent than the one described by Paul. In Paul's description, the mysteries of God's love are beyond anything the eye has seen or the ear has heard; in Bottom's description, his dream goes beyond even what we can conceive, let alone experience, since we simply cannot imagine eyes hearing, ears seeing, or hands tasting. Bottom's Dream is extrasensory.

Here is another case where an allusion takes on additional resonance from the biblical context around the text specifically alluded to. The language of Bottom's allusion to 1 Corinthians 2:9 is closest to the Bishop's Bible, but Thomas Stroup points out that, in the Geneva New Testament of 1557, Paul continues, "But God hath opened them [the things prepared for them that love him] unto us by his Sprite, for the Sprite searcheth all things, yea, the *bottom of Goddes secretes*."[75] By the 1560 complete Geneva Bible, "bottom of Goddes secretes" was replaced by "deepe things of God," but "bottom" was actually in Tyndale's translation, followed by Coverdale, and also by the translator of Erasmus's *Paraphrases*. The phrase was repeated, moreover, in numerous religious writings of Franz Lambert, Roger Hutchinson, Thomas Paynell, David Chytraeus, and even Thomas More (in *The confutacyon of Tyndales answere*, 1532, which obviously generally refutes Tyndale, but takes no issue with his translation of Paul's phrase, which More himself repeats). That "Goddes secretes" had a "bottom" would thus have been a familiar idea to Elizabethans.[76]

---

[74] It has been usual for Shakespeare critics to claim that the word "ass" did not include the meaning "bottom" (in the anatomical sense) in the sixteenth century, but this is disproved by Cedric Watts, "Fundamental Editing: In *A Midsummer Night's Dream*, Does 'Bottom' Mean 'Bum'? And How about 'Arse' and 'Ass'?," *Anglistica Pisana*, 3/1 (2006), 215–22. It is unfortunate that this journal is somewhat inaccessible to many English and American scholars. Annabel Patterson also accepts that "ass" and "arse" (and "bottom") were interchangeable, based on Frankie Rubinstein, *A Dictionary of Shakespeare's Puns and their Sexual Significance* (Houndsmills and London: Macmillan, 1984). Patterson, "Bottom's Up: Festive Theory in *A Midsummer Night's Dream*," in Dorothea Kehler (ed.), A Midsummer Night's Dream: *Critical Essays* (New York: Garland, 1998), 165–78, 173.

[75] 1 Cor. 2:10 (Geneva NT 1557), emphasis added, cited in Thomas B. Stroup, "Bottom's Name and his Epiphany," *SQ* 29/1 (1978), 79–82, 80. Robert F. Wilson takes issue with Stroup ("God's Secrets and Bottom's Name: A Reply," *SQ* 30/3 (1979), 407–8), reasserting that the name "Bottom" derives from a weaver's tool and that Bottom's dream has nothing to do with "God's secrets." This is unnecessarily reductive, since both of these senses may obviously be significant at the same time.

[76] Linda Shenk, *Learned Queen: The Image of Elizabeth I in Politics and Poetry* (New York: Palgrave Macmillan, 2010), comments on Shakespeare's allusion to 1 Cor. 2:9, finding allusions

Stroup also notes, citing Frank Kermode, that Bottom is an exemplar of Christian foolishness described still later in 1 Corinthians: "if anie man among you seme to be wise in this worlde, let him be a foole, that he may be wise" (1 Cor. 3:18).[77] The most popular Renaissance meditation on the notion of Christian folly was Erasmus's *The Praise of Folly*, printed first in Latin (1511) and translated into English by Sir Thomas Chaloner in 1549. Erasmus's brilliant satire closes with a citation of 1 Corinthians (*"was never mans eie sawe, nor eare heard, nor thought of hert yet compassed, what, and how great felicitee god hath prepared unto suche as dooe love him"*) in support of Folly's claim that "spirituall thynges [are] to be preferred before flesshely thinges, and the invisible before the other visible."[78] That Shakespeare probably had Erasmus in mind when alluding to the same passage from Corinthians is indicated by Folly's reference a few lines earlier to Plato's claim that "*the passion and extreme rage of fervent lovers was to be desired and embrased, as a thing above all others most blisfull.*" In fact, the whole final section of *The Praise of Folly* develops the idea that the "*Christian Religion* seemeth to have a certaine sybship [kinship] with simplicitee, and devoute foolisshenesse, in nothyng agreyng with worldly wysedome."[79] Folly's description of those who have a foretaste of God's secrets through some ecstatic experience of madness is worth quoting extensively, since it parallels Bottom's experience of "translation" remarkably closely and also suggests what Shakespeare had in mind in his allusion to Paul:

Who so ever therefore have suche grace (whiche sure is gevin to few) by theyr life tyme to tast of this saied felicitee, they are subjecte to a certaine passion muche lyke unto madnesse or witravyng, whan ravisshed so in the sprite, or beyng in a traunce, thei dooe speake certaine thyngis not hangyng one with an other, nor after any earthly facion, but rather dooe put foorth a voyce they wote never what, muche lesse to be understode of others: and sodeinely without any apparent cause why, dooe chaunge the state of theyr countenaunces. For now shall ye see theim of glad chere, now of as sadde againe, now thei wepe, now thei laugh, now they

---

to the same passage in the speeches of Elizabeth I, at Oxford (1592), and to Parliament (1601), part of her self-creation as a divine Queen of Love, a strategy recognized by the Earl of Essex and Francis Bacon when they incorporated a similar allusion in the royal entertainment *Of Love and Self-Love*.

[77] Stroup mistakenly claims this passage is in 1 Cor. 2. Kermode makes this point in "The Mature Comedies," in *Shakespeare, Spenser, Donne* (first edn, 1971; repr. Abingdon: Routledge, 2005), 200–18, 209. See also R. Chris Hassel Jr., *Faith and Folly in Shakespeare's Romantic Comedies* (Athens, GA: University of Georgia Press, 1980), 53–58.

[78] Desiderius Erasmus, *The praise of Folie, Moriae Encomium, a booke made in latine by that greet clerke Erasmus Roterodame* (London, 1549), sig. T3ʳ. Thelma N. Greenfield pursues some further connections between *Midsummer* and *The praise of Folie*. "*A Midsummer Night's Dream* and *The Praise of Folly*," *Comparative Literature*, 20/3 (1968), 236–44.

[79] Erasmus, *The praise of Folie*, sig. S2ᵛ.

sighe, for briefe, it is certaine that they are wholy distraught and rapte out of theim selues. In sort that whan a little after thei come againe to their former wittes, thei denie plainly thei wote where thei became, or whether thei were than in theyr bodies, or out of theyr bodies, wakyng or slepyng: remembring also as little, either what they heard, saw, saied, or did than, savyng as it were through a cloude, or by a dreame: but this thei know certainely, that whiles their mindes so roved and wandred, thei were most happie and blisfull, so that they lament and wepe at theyr retourne unto theyr former senses, as who saieth, nothyng were leefer unto theim than continually to rave and be deteigned with suche a spece of madnesse. And this is but a certaine smacke or thinne taste of theyr blisse to come.[80]

Despite its biblical allusions, *A Midsummer Night's Dream* is not a "Christian play" in any meaningful sense. The Pauline allusion, after all, describes Bottom's experience among Fairies, as he and his fellow mechanicals prepare for the wedding in Athens of an Amazon Queen and the half-son of the god Poseidon. Yet Paul's description of holy mysteries adds a suggestion of the sacred to Bottom's "dream," even if it remains ultimately secular. Furthermore, while Shakespeare may not allude directly to Erasmus, it does seem that his allusion to Paul may have been suggested by *The Praise of Folly*; in any case, Erasmus's allusion to 1 Corinthians 2:9, and the context in which it appears, serves as a useful guide to interpreting the allusion in Shakespeare's play and the manner in which an alert and educated audience member might have interpreted it. Erasmus links dreams, madness, and spiritual rapture in the context of 1 Corinthians 2:9, as Shakespeare does in his Dream play. With Erasmus in mind, we can recognize that Theseus' unimaginative rejection of lunatics, lovers, and poets is misguided, and that Bottom, wise in his folly, has had an inkling, a "certaine smacke or thinne taste" of something like a spiritual experience. Or at least we can recognize that, in the experience of art, of theater, as in the experience of madness, love, and dreams, one may for a time transcend the mundane world of "flesshely things."

There is also a political dimension to the allusion to 1 Corinthians 2:9, which has been pursued by Annabel Patterson and Louis Montrose.[81] Verses 7 and 8 of this passage read,

But we speake the wisdome of God in a mysterie, even the hid wisdom, which God had determined before the worlde, unto our glorie. Which none of the

---

[80] Erasmus, *The praise of Folie*, sigs T3^r–T3^v.
[81] Patterson, "Bottoms Up"; Louis Montrose, *The Purpose of Playing: Shakespeare and the Cultural Politics of Elizabethan England* (Chicago: University of Chicago Press, 1996), esp. 190–9.

princes of this worlde hathe knowen: for had thei knowen it, thei wolde not have crucified the Lord of glorie. (1 Cor. 2:7–8)

That it is Bottom, a weaver from the bottom rung of the social ladder, who has the "rare vision" is thus not surprising. Nor is it surprising that this vision is denied to Duke Theseus, who "never may believe | These antique fables, nor these fairy toys" (5.1.1–2). (That Theseus is himself, for Shakespeare's audience, an "antique fable" makes his position all the more untenable.)

Shakespeare's familiarity with the Bible was extensive. There is no biblical book, including the Apocrypha, to which he does not allude. However, he was particularly drawn to certain books. Some, like Genesis, Exodus, Samuel, Job, and the gospels, are the richest ones in character and narrative, and have been perennial favorites with artists of all sorts. Others of Shakespeare's favorites, like Psalms, Proverbs, Ecclesiastes, the Apocryphal wisdom books Wisdom and Ecclesiasticus, and the New Testament epistles, indicate an interest in ideas or (as in the Psalms) powerful poetic language as well. Apart from the intrinsic appeal of the various biblical books, some books or passages within them were natural loci for topics of particular interest in early modern England or for themes that Shakespeare was exploring in particular plays. Any discussion of love, marriage, or relationship between the sexes, the core subject of comedy, was bound to consider the story of Adam and Eve in Genesis 1–3, as well as perhaps some of the pertinent writings of Paul (see Chapter 4). The subject of kingship or government, on the other hand, the focus of Shakespeare's English Histories, would naturally lead to consideration of the books of Samuel with its stories of kings Saul and David (as well as those of other Old Testament rulers).[82] Similarly, Shakespeare and his contemporaries considered suffering and persecution, in various configurations the subject matter of tragedy, through the lens of Jesus's Passion in the gospels, as well as the story of Job, traditionally an Old Testament type of Christ (see Chapter 8). But, whatever his favorite books, Shakespeare knew the Bible thoroughly, in several English versions, and returned to it consistently to the end of his career.

Shakespeare alludes to the Bible in a variety of modes, resulting in a variety of effects. First, the most obvious allusions are outright quotations from or references to the Bible, in which the character making the allusion is fully conscious of and intentional in making it. For example, when

---

[82] See Steven Marx, "Historical Types: Moses, David, and Henry V," ch. 3 in *Shakespeare and the Bible* (Oxford and New York: Oxford University Press, 2000); David Evett, "Types of King David in Shakespeare's Lancastrian Tetralogy," *SSt* 14 (1981), 139–61.

Henry V orders "Let there be sung *Non nobis* and *Te Deum*" after the battle of Agincourt in *Henry V* (4.8.124), it is obvious that he means the Book of Common Prayer canticle *Te Deum* and Psalm 115, which begins (in the Vulgate) "*Non nobis domine, non nobis.*"[83] Also, in *Henry VI, Part 3*, Clarence, who had fought with the Lancasters against his York brothers, swears that he has repented and changed sides again. He tells King Edward and Richard of Gloucester that he cannot maintain his former "holy" oath, since it was impious to fight against his family: "To keep that oath were more impiety | Than Jephthah when he sacrificed his daughter" (5.1.90–1). Clarence knows, as did Shakespeare's audience, that Jephthah's vow (Judg. 11:30–9) was often cited as the kind of rash and wicked oath that was not therefore binding.[84] In addition, if Othello does indeed compare himself to "the base Judean" just before he kills himself (5.2.347 in the Folio; this is a notorious textual crux), and if "Judean" refers to Judas Iscariot, who betrayed Christ, this would be another example of a character's intentional, overt allusion. Othello, realizing he has betrayed the person who most loved him, compares himself to the biblical exemplar of treachery and betrayal. (The comparison, by a kind of allusive logic, reinforces Desdemona's innocence by aligning her with Christ.) Shylock's recounting of the story of Jacob and Laban's sheep in *The Merchant of Venice* (1.3.71–90) is another example of a self-conscious and intentional allusion (see above). Similarly, in *Two Gentlemen of Verona*, Launce comes on stage with his dog and says, "I have received my portion, like the prodigious son" (2.1.2–3). Launce has gotten the parable's title wrong, of course, comically substituting "prodigious" for "prodigal," but he is making the allusion knowingly, however ineptly. On the other hand, Hamlet's biblical allusions can be strange, but the strangeness is deliberate, part of his "antic disposition." For instance, after killing Polonius, Hamlet is asked by Claudius where he has hidden the body:

KING   Now, Hamlet, where's Polonius?
HAMLET   At supper.
CLAUDIUS At supper? Where?

---

[83] This and the following verses that constitute Ps. 115 in Protestant Bibles were actually part of Ps. 113 in the Vulgate (Ps. 113:9–26), since Catholics and Protestants numbered the Psalms differently. Shakespeare might simply be remembering the Latin heading of Ps. 115, taken from the Vulgate, in Coverdale's translation in the Book of Common Prayer, but he would have known that both Edward Hall and Raphael Holinshed state that Henry called for the Psalm "In exitu Israel de Egipto," which is Ps. 114 for Protestants, and Ps. 113 in the Vulgate, which includes the "*Non nobis.*" See Shaheen, 469–70. The *Te Deum*, an ancient hymn, also retained its Latin title in the Book of Common Prayer, though the rest of the text was printed in English.

[84] See the discussion of Jephthah earlier in this chapter.

HAMLET	Not where he eats, but where 'a is eaten. A certain convocation of politic worms are e'en at him. Your worm is your only emperor for diet...
CLAUDIUS	Where is Polonius?
HAMLET	In heaven. (4.3.16–32)

That Polonius is at supper in heaven is Hamlet's playful allusion to the ultimate meal promised in Revelation: "Blessed are they which are called unto the Lambes supper" (Rev. 19:9). The allusion has followed upon Hamlet's topical allusion to the Diet of Worms, convened by the Emperor Charles V to address Martin Luther and his movement for reform of the Church. Though the chronology of the play is somewhat confused, judging from some obvious anachronisms, Hamlet is presumably as conscious of his topical allusion as his biblical one; after all, one would expect a student at Wittenberg to be aware of the career of its most illustrious professor, Martin Luther.[85]

While there are examples of such overt biblical references, many of Shakespeare's allusions to the Bible are, if not covert, at least less obvious, incorporated seamlessly into ordinary speech, and requiring the audience first to recognize and then to interpret them. Iago's allusion to Exodus, "I am that I am," for example, could be self-conscious, since he is proud of his devilish villainy, but he gives no verbal indication that he is alluding, so the audience must identify it on their own. The same is true of Katherine of Aragon's statement that, "Like the lily | That once was mistress of the field and flourished, | I'll hang my head and perish" (*Henry VIII*, 3.1.151–3). The audience might readily understand the sense of mortality and mutability in the commonplace image of a flower that flourishes, withers, and dies, but they could also hear the more specific allusion being made. The allusion is to the well-known passage in Matthew, where Jesus places the lily above kings: "Learne, how the lilies of the field do growe: they labour not, nether spinne: Yet I say unto you, that even Solomon in all his glorie was not arayed like one of these" (Matt. 6:28–9). The Queen's verb "flourished" is probably taken from Psalm 103:15–16, "The daies of man are but as grass: for he flourisheth as a flower of the field." Katherine's personal emblem was a pomegranate, but the lily is more appropriate as a symbol of purity and innocence, traditionally associated with the Virgin Mary. Virginity was the key question

---

[85] The University of Wittenberg was founded in 1502, and the Diet of Worms took place in 1521, though the original story on which *Hamlet* is based is medieval, as indicated by Claudius's reference to England being in awe of and paying homage to the "Danish sword" (4.3.60).

Allusion 115

in Henry's case for annulment, insisting that Katherine's marriage with his brother Arthur had been consummated. The lily was also, in the form of the fleur-de-lis ("flower of the lily"), a prominent part of the coat of arms of the kings of England from Henry IV to George I. The surface of a coat of arms is known in heraldic terms as a "field" (*OED* III.17.a). Katherine's statement is thus about more than flowers.

Naturally, anachronistic allusions cannot be made self-consciously by a character, and it would thus be nonsensical for the characters to give any verbal signal that they are alluding, like the gospels' frequent "as it is written." For example, when Aaron in *Titus Andronicus* chastises Tamora's sons as "white-limed walls" (4.2.98), he cannot know that he is alluding to the "whited tombes" of Matthew 23:27. Yet, without knowing that this is Jesus's metaphor for the hypocritical Pharisees, "which appeare beautiful outward, but are within ful of dead mens bones, and of all filthiness," the audience could understand Aaron's insult only superficially, as a slur against Demetrius's and Chiron's white skin. Similarly, when Apemantus refuses the food of Timon of Athens, saying, "It grieves me to see so many dip their meat in one man's blood" (*Timon* 1.2.38–9), the audience needs to recognize the anachronistic allusion to the Last Supper when Jesus says, "He that dippeth his hand with me in the dish, he shal betraye me" (Matt. 26:23). John's account is clearer, with Jesus saying instead: "He it is, to whom I shal give a soppe, when I have dipt it" (John 13:26). He dips the sop and gives it to Judas. The allusion, of which neither Apemantus nor Timon could be historically conscious, foreshadows Timon's betrayal by his friends. Apemantus drives the point of the allusion home, continuing, "The fellow that sits next him now, parts bread with him, pledges the breath of him in a divided draft, is the readiest man to kill him" (1.2.44–6). Since the characters speaking the allusions are unaware of them, there is dramatic irony in the *audience*'s awareness of a further significance beyond the awareness of the characters on stage.[86]

Any recognizable allusion requires a trigger of some sort, a signal perceptible to readers or the audience that directs them to the text being alluded to. In most cases, triggers are specifically verbal, consisting of a

---

[86] The current critical consensus is that *Timon* is a collaborative play, and the Arden³ editors assign 1.2 to Thomas Middleton. While this is important to acknowledge, it does not appreciably affect the analysis of this biblical allusion, which works in the same way whoever wrote it. The process of collaboration is sufficiently complex, as well as undocumented, that we cannot entirely determine who was responsible for what. Shakespeare was surely the senior writer, and the Arden³ editors note that "collaborators have a way of harnessing each other's ways of thinking, of adopting their partner's verbal patterns." If Apemantus's biblical allusion is Middleton's, then he has written it in an entirely Shakespearian manner. *Timon of Athens*, ed. Anthony B. Dawson and Gretchen E. Minton, Arden³ (London: Cengage Learning, 2008), 5–6.

shared word or phrase. In some cases, though, the trigger seems less specifically verbal than contextual, constituting shared settings, characters, and narrative elements. In a few instances, Shakespeare alludes even syntactically, signaling not with shared words but with shared sentence rhythms. For instance, as noted above, Henry V calls for the singing of "*Non nobis*," which in the English version in the Book of Common Prayer begins, "not unto us, O Lord, not unto us, but unto they name give the praise."[87] Earlier in *Henry V*, Henry offers a different prayer:

> Not today, O Lord,
> O not today, think not upon the fault
> My father made in compassing the crown. (4.1.289–91)

This speech precedes the battle, and Henry is anxious that his father's sin in usurping the crown of Richard II not be weighed against him, resulting in defeat by the French. Henry's prayer is for forgiveness and deliverance, the later "*Non nobis*" a prayer after deliverance and victory have been achieved, giving the credit to God. The parallel between the two prayers is made by the syntactical resemblance of the earlier one to the later. "Not today, O Lord, O not today," and "Not unto us, O Lord, not unto us." The two repeated negatives, "Not X," bracketing "O Lord," the three short phrases separated by commas, create the allusion, and the trigger in this case is as much rhythmic as specifically verbal.

Another example of syntactic allusion can be detected in *The Tempest*, when Prospero describes his power, saying, "graves at my command | Have wak'd their sleepers, op'd, and let 'em forth" (5.1.48–9). Most editions of the play note that this speech adapts Medea's words in Ovid's *Metamorphoses*.[88] Shaheen suggests also an allusion to the description of the extraordinary events following Jesus's death: "And the graves did open them selves, and many bodies of the Sainctes which slept, arose, And came out of the graves after his resurrection" (Matt. 27:52–3). Shaheen's suggestion is based on shared content, the opening of graves. An additional argument can be made based on sentence rhythm. "Have wak'd their sleepers, op't, and let 'em forth"; "bodies of the Sainctes which slept, arose, And came out." Each has a clause including "sleepers" or "slept," comma, participle, comma, clause beginning with "and" expressing exit ("let 'em forth," "came out"). One can also hear the similar clipped sound of "op't" and "slept." Allusion of this phonetic subtlety is more common in poetry than staged drama, but Shakespeare after all was a poet–playwright.

---

[87] *BCP* 579. [88] See Bate, *Shakespeare and Ovid*, 239–63.

Shakespeare employed another kind of allusive trigger, unavailable to poets, since plays in performance are not only verbal but visual. Such visual allusions are obviously difficult to trace retrospectively, since we do not have access to Shakespeare's original stagings. We cannot see precisely what his audience saw. But we can make informed conjectures. Possible visual allusions in *Coriolanus* and *King Lear* are discussed in Chapters 4 and 8. There is also an unusually clear visual allusion in *Henry VIII*, in the astonishing angelic vision of Katherine of Aragon. The stage direction, atypically extensive, tells us what we would have seen on stage:

Enter, solemnly tripping one after another, six personages clad in white robes, wearing on their heads garlands of bays, and golden vizards on their faces, branches of bays or palms in their hands [etc.]. (4.2.82, s.d.)

Katherine sees what John of Patmos saw, as he described it in Revelation: "After these things I behelde, and lo, a great multitude, which no man colde number, of all nacions and kindreds, and people, and tongues, stode before the throne, and before the Lambe, clothed with long white robes, and palmes in their hands" (Rev. 7:9). Katherine's vision (shared by the audience) is less crowded and less international, but the white robes and palms are distinctive. The visual allusion, the fact that it corresponds in key particulars to the authoritative vision of heaven in Revelation, confirms the genuineness of Katherine's experience, which imbues her with as much saintliness as a Protestant theater might allow.[89]

Of course, Shakespeare's culture was so Bible oriented that some instances of biblical language in the plays are simply cases of biblical idioms having become commonplace in English speech. In *Timon of Athens*, for instance, Timon curses young people, calling on "Lust, and liberty" to infect them, so that "'gainst the stream of virtue they may strive, | And drown themselves in riot!" (4.1.25–8). Ecclesiasticus does urge readers, "strive thou not against the streame," but there was also a contemporary English proverb, "It is hard to strive against the stream," so the passage may or may not be a specifically biblical allusion.[90] Similarly, Queen Margaret's reference to her son being in "the shade of death" might evoke the verse about "the valley of the shadow of death" in Psalm 23, but the phrase also occurs in Job, and the gospels, and thus may have been so common as not to constitute a specific allusion on its own (*Richard III*, 1.3.266). In Robert Armin's *The history of the two maids of More-clacke*

---

[89] This scene has been cited in arguments for Shakespeare's Catholicism, and it certainly shows admiration for Katherine, yet the play is ultimately a celebration of Elizabeth, daughter of Katherine's successor as queen.
[90] Shaheen, 677.

with the life and simple maner of John in the hospital, a character uses the same phrases without any apparent biblical sense, vowing a "reconciled amitie, | Which violated, doos command my life | To yeeld his intrest to the shade of death."[91] An image in *Titus Andronicus* may also be commonplace, when Bassianus declares, "I will…|…| Commit my cause in balance to be weighed" (1.1.56–8). The idiom of being weighed in the balance is biblical, as in Job's "Let God weigh me in the just balance" (Job 31:6) and Daniel's "thou are wayed in the balance" (Dan. 5:27), but, as Shaheen notes, it was also a common English expression since at least Chaucer, who uses it in "The Monk's Tale."[92] Yet an *EEBO* search shows that the majority of sixteenth-century printed uses were in a biblical or religious context, so Shakespeare's audience might have heard the phrase as generally biblical. Even so, neither the Job nor the Daniel passage seems especially relevant to the scene in *Titus*.

Some of Shakespeare's biblical allusions have limited significance, illuminating or affecting only one particular speech or short scene in a play. Others have a substantial impact, connecting to predominant themes of the whole play, especially insofar as they are linked to additional allusions to the same, or closely related, biblical passages. One fairly localized allusion, for example, occurs in *All's Well That Ends Well*, when Lavatch, the Countess's clownish servant, says to Lafew, "I am no great Nebuchadnezzar, sir; I have not much skill in grass" (4.5.18–19). The discussion has been about Helena, whom they think is dead, and whom they compare to a rare herb among common salad greens. Lavatch gets his herbs muddled, and calls her "sweet marjoram of the sallet, or rather, the herb of grace." Lafew chastises him for confusing "nose herbs" with salad herbs, since the "herb of grace," rue, was strongly scented but bitter. Lavatch's retort draws on the story of Nebuchadnezzar, king of Babylon, who for his sins is driven mad and made "to eat grasse, as the oxen" (Dan. 4:29). This is a long explanation for a small joke, but its wit might be appreciated by anyone who knew the story. Another allusion limited in scope occurs in *Romeo and Juliet*, when Juliet, on hearing that Romeo has killed her cousin Tybalt, calls her lover a "wolvish ravening lamb" (3.2.76). The image of hypocrisy from the Gospel of Matthew reads: "Beware of false Prophets, which come to you in sheepes clothing, but inwardely they are ravening wolves" (Matt. 7:15). Juliet's allusion is ironic, in that Romeo is not a wolf in lamb's clothing but a lamb that ravens like a wolf. This amounts to

---

[91] Robert Armin, *The history of the two maids of More-clacke with the life and simple maner of John in the hospital* (London: N.O. for Thomas Archer, 1609), sig. B2ᵛ. The play was probably performed *c.*1597–8. See Martin Butler's life of Armin in the *ODNB*.

[92] Shaheen, 499.

much the same thing—the lamb does not behave as it is supposed to and endangers other lambs—but perhaps Juliet chooses this wording, because she cannot quite bring herself to call her Romeo a wolf, or perhaps she cannot imagine the fiery Tybalt, Romeo's victim, as a lamb. In any case, while adding poignancy to Juliet's bitter outburst, the allusion has no significance beyond the scene (other than that the Nurse has called Romeo as "gentle as a lamb" in an earlier scene, 2.5.44); even within a few lines, Juliet's love for Romeo reasserts itself. By contrast, though, Shakespeare's allusions are more often complex, forming significant patterns with other biblical allusions to the same or different biblical texts that develop important themes relevant to the play. These are the type of allusions explored in later chapters of this book.

Sometimes Shakespeare's biblical allusions suggest parallels between one of his dramatic characters and one in the Bible. The allusions that connect Julius Caesar, Coriolanus, and Richard II with Christ are examples of this technique, which is typically used to emphasize the contrasts within their superficial similarities (see Chapters 4 and 5). As discussed in Chapter 2, the so-called Christ-figure is the most common of these sorts of allusion. Christ is the most important character in the Christian Bible, of course, but some Old Testament characters were also perceived to be types of Christ: Adam, Melchizedek, Jacob, Moses, Isaac, David, Job, Jonah. Shakespeare's "Christ-figures" are compared to or contrasted with Christ, either briefly or extensively, depending upon the dramatic context. Such allusions in *Timon* and *Cymbeline* were mentioned above, to which might be added *Henry VI, Part 3*. Richard of Gloucester (the future Richard III) has an aside following his expression of love to the king: "To say the truth, so Judas kissed his master | And cried 'All hail!' when as he meant all harm" (5.7.33–4).[93] In casting himself as a Judas, Richard implicitly identifies King Henry with Christ, a suitable identification given his piety and innocence, and himself with the ultimate betrayer. An allusion to King David, rather than Christ, occurs in *Hamlet*. Claudius, thinking he is alone, meditates on his murderous crime and weighs the possibility of being forgiven by God:

> What if this cursed hand
> Were thicker than itself with brother's blood,
> Is there not rain enough in the sweet heavens
> To wash it white as snow? (3.3.43–6)

These lines allude to Psalm 51, "thou shalt wash me, and I shall be whiter then snow" (Ps. 51:7). The authorship of Psalm 51 was traditionally

---

[93] On this cry as an allusion to the Mystery plays, and on its appearance elsewhere in Shakespeare, see Chs 4 and 5.

attributed to King David, being his expression of guilt and contrition after having committed adultery with Bathsheba and having commissioned the murder of her husband Uriah (2 Sam. 11). In a way, Shakespeare's allusion is appropriate, since Claudius is similarly a king, guilty of murder, and (perhaps) adultery with Gertrude, the wife of his victim. Yet, while David expresses genuine contrition, Claudius feels only a bit guilty, and, significantly, he is not willing to give up the spoils of his crime, Gertrude and the throne. Therefore, the biblical allusion is contrastive again, setting up a parallel that ultimately highlights the profound dissimilarity between Claudius and David.[94] This scene contains another visual allusion if Claudius kneels at a prie-dieu as he prays, mirroring the iconographic pose of the penitent King David in prayer.[95]

Similarly, Shakespeare's protagonists are often paralleled with biblical characters. For instance, a series of allusions to Jonah occurs in *Pericles*.[96] The shipwrecked Pericles is cast up on the shores of Pentapolis, while three fishermen discuss the wreck of his ship, which they have just witnessed. They compare human society to the world of the sea they know so well, and one describes a miser as being like a whale:

I can compare our rich misers to nothing so fitly as to a whale: 'a plays and tumbles, driving the poor fry before him, and at last devours them all at a mouthful. Such whales have I heard on a'th'land, who never leave gaping till they swallowed the whole parish, church, steeple, bells, and all. (2.1.28–32)

To this the second fisherman replies that "if I had been sexton I would have been that day in the belfry," explaining further,

Because he should have swallowed me too, and when I had been in his belly, I would have kept such a jangling of bells that he should never have left till he cast bells, steeple, church, and parish up again. (2.1.37–40)

The social satire is clear enough, but the fisherman's little allegory also suggests the seminal story of a man being in the belly of a fish (or whale) and then cast up again: Jonah. The fishermen cannot be consciously alluding to Jonah (the time of the ancient story is unclear but seems pre-Christian), and Jonah seems to have nothing to do with their story, but Pericles, who is listening unseen, has just been through an experience somewhat similar to the Old Testament prophet's. Pericles is not a

---

[94] For more on Ps. 51 in the Renaissance, including this allusion, see Hamlin, ch. 6.
[95] See Hamlin, 190–217.
[96] See Peter Womack, "Shakespeare and the Sea of Stories," *JMEMS* 29/1 (1999), 169–87; Maurice Hunt, *Shakespeare's Romance of the Word* (Lewisburg: Bucknell University Press, 1990), 18–41.

prophet, of course, and he is not swallowed by a fish, but both characters have a misfortune at sea, yet are ultimately rescued by being tossed up on land.

Later in *Pericles*, Shakespeare alludes again to Jonah. Pericles is back on the sea, this time with his new wife Thaisa, pregnant with his child. Once again, a storm blows up that threatens to sink their ship, and Pericles, following the traditional interpretation of a storm as the voice or hand of the divine, calls on the powers behind the storm to break it off.[97] The excitement sends Thaisa into premature labor, and she gives birth to a girl, seemingly at the cost of her own life. Alerting the audience to the symbolic implications of his own journey—the life-as-a-sea-voyage metaphor—Pericles refers to his "poor infant," soon to be named Marina after the sea that gave her birth, as "this fresh new seafarer" (3.1.42). Without giving him time to grieve, however, the superstitious sailors insist that the body of Thaisa must be cast overboard, since

> the sea works high,
> The wind is loud and will not lie till the ship
> Be cleared of the dead. (3.1.48–50)

As subsequent allusions confirm, the sailors see the body of Thaisa as a Jonah, calling down the storm on them just as the presence of the errant prophet did for the biblical mariners. The use of "Jonah" as a term for any person bearing bad luck, especially on board ship, seems to have been current by the time of *Pericles*, especially among sailors (see *OED*). In his preface to *The Travels of Certaine Englishmen*, for instance, Theophilus Lavender tells the story of a sea voyage from 1605 that ran afoul of a storm. After quoting Psalm 107:27 ("They were tossed to and fro, and staggered like drunken men, and all their cunning being gone"), Lavender writes that "every man called upon his god (like the Mariners in *Jonas* ship)." The superstitious sailors then decide that an English preacher, whom they have seen with various books, is in fact a conjurer, and they "thought it best to make a *Jonas* of him, and to cast both him and his books into the Sea." Fortunately, they change their minds, and "by the providence of God, they came all safely to their desired Port."[98] Thaisa's

---

[97] Calvin saw thunder as the voice of God, and, as the author of *The Whipper of the Satyre* (1601) writes, "But let the Heavens frowne, the Welkin thunder,/Perhaps weele feare a little, and minde our God." William R. Elton, King Lear *and the Gods* (San Marino: Huntington Library, 1966), 197–212, citing *The Whipper* on 202, 204.

[98] Theophilus Lavender's preface to [William Biddulph], *The travels of certaine Englishmen into Africa, Asia, Troy, Bythinia, Thracia, and to the Blacke Sea* (London: Thomas Haveland for W. Aspley, 1609), sigs B2ᵛ–B3. It is hard not to think that Theophilus Lavender is a nom de plume.

body, however, is jettisoned, and Pericles's eulogy makes the parallel with Jonah explicit:

> A terrible child-bed hast thou had, my dear:
>
> . . . . .
>
> The air-remaining lamps, the belching whale,
> And humming water must o'erwhelm thy corpse
> Lying with simple shells. (3.1.56–64)

Though she does not actually end up in the belly of whale, Thaisa is belched up out of the "belly" of the sea, as Cerimon, the physician who saves her, puts it:

> If the sea's stomach be o'ercharged with gold,
> 'Tis a good constraint of fortune it belches upon us. (3.2.53–4)

Yet Thaisa, dead or alive, does not on the surface seem like a Jonah figure, any more than Pericles had earlier; what do these allusions mean? The key lies in biblical typology. The traditional Christian interpretation of Jonah's time in the whale was as a foreshadowing of Christ's death and resurrection. This interpretation was reinforced in the marginal glosses to Jonah in the Geneva Bible, but the ultimate source for reading Jonah as a type of Christ is Jesus himself:

Then answered certeine of the Scribes and of the Pharises, saying, Master, we wolde se a signe of thee.

But he answered, and said to them, An evil and adulterous generacion seketh a signe, but no signe shal be give unto it, save the signe of the Prophet Jonas.

For as Jonas was thre dayes, and thre nights in the whales bellie: so shal the Sonne of man be thre dayes and thre nights in the heart of the earth. (Matt. 12:38–40)

Given the typological association of Jonah's "resurrection" with Christ's, then, the allusions to Jonah in Pericles seem significant not only for Pericles himself but for Thaisa. Thaisa's body is the "Jonah," the offensive passenger, which must be cast overboard into the "belly" of the sea in order to satisfy the "god of this great vast" (3.1.1). Like Jonah, she is cast up on shore, and, like Jesus, whom Jonah prefigures, she "dies" and is miraculously brought back to life. Thaisa is not Jonah or Christ, of course, and in reality she never truly dies. But this chain of allusions reinforces the sense that these are miraculous and mysterious events, by exploiting the audience's conditioned typological associations with the stories of Jonah and Christ. At the same time, we remain in the fantastical, and secular, realm of Romance.

Only one of Shakespeare's plays has an overtly biblical title—*Measure for Measure*. It is derived from Matthew 7:2: "with what measure ye meate, it shalbe measured to you agayne." But every one of Shakespeare's plays contains biblical allusions. Some of them, like *The Comedy of Errors*, *The Merchant of Venice*, and *Hamlet*, can hardly be comprehensible without some understanding of the allusions. Shakespeare alludes to the Bible not for any detectable doctrinal reasons, but primarily because it was a vast, readily available storehouse of powerful stories, characters, and language that everyone knew. As critics like Jonathan Bate and Heather James have shown, Shakespeare's allusions to Ovid and Virgil work similarly to his biblical allusions.[99] But many more members of his audience knew the gospels than the *Metamorphoses*, popular though it was. The stakes with biblical allusion may also have been higher than with classical literature, since no one expected the *Metamorphoses* or the *Aeneid* to be a sufficient guide to godly living and final salvation. Biblical allusions were pre-eminently recognizable, they tapped into the audience's deepest concerns, and they thus proved one of the most effective devices in Shakespeare's rhetorical toolbox for engaging his audience and enriching the significance of his plays.

---

[99] Bate, *Shakespeare and Ovid*; Heather James, *Shakespeare's Troy: Drama, Politics, and the Translation of Empire* (Cambridge and New York: Cambridge University Press, 1997).

PART II

BIBLICAL ALLUSION IN THE PLAYS

4

Shakespeare's Variations on Themes from Genesis 1–3

"God Almighty first planted a garden."[1] So Francis Bacon's essay "On Gardens" begins, stating what his readers already knew from the Bible: that "the Lord God planted a garden Eastwarde in Eden" (Gen. 2:8). The story of the Creation of the World, of Adam and Eve in the Garden of Eden, of their disobedience in eating the forbidden fruit, and of their Fall—recounted in Genesis 1–3—was among the most familiar of all biblical stories. It was recounted annually during the Proper Lessons of Morning and Evening Prayer on the Sundays leading up to Lent (Septuagesima and Sexagesima). It reminded Christians of their fallen state and their inheritance of the sinful nature of Adam and Eve. Furthermore, at every baptism the community heard the prayer: "O merciful God, grant that the old Adam in these children may be so buried, that the new man may be raised up in them."[2] In this case, Genesis was being conveyed through a double interpretative lens. In his Epistle to the Romans, Paul wrote: "Knowing this, that our old man is crucified with him, that the body of sinne might be destroyed, that henceforth we should not serve sinne" (Rom. 6:6). The gloss on this same verse by Beza and Camerarius, translated by Laurence Tomson in the Geneva Bible (the "Geneva–Tomson" editions post-1576), added: "All our whole nature, as we are conceived and borne into this world with sinne, which is called old, partly

---

[1] Francis Bacon, "Of Gardens," in *Francis Bacon: A Critical Edition of the Major Works*, ed. Brian Vickers (Oxford and New York: Oxford University Press, 1996), 430–5, 430. "Of Gardens" first appeared in the expanded 1625 edition of Bacon's *Essays*.

[2] In this instance, Brian Cummings's *Book of Common Prayer* is misleading. His text of the 1559 version of the Baptism Service does not include this prayer, but instead one that prays that the child "maye crucify the old man, and utterly abolyshe the whole bodye of synne" (*BCP* 146). A full bibliography of the Book of Common Prayer is far beyond the scope of this study, but, while Cummings's text is accurate for editions in 1580 (STC 16307), 1582 (STC 16309.5), 1592 (STC 16316), and 1594 (STC 16318), a different edition of the Book of Common Prayer was in simultaneous circulation, with the "old Adam" prayer: 1559 (STC 16293.3), 1570 (STC 16299), 1579 (STC 16306.9), 1586 (STC 16311.4), 1595 (STC 16320.3), 1596 (STC 16321), and 1603 (STC 16326). This is not a complete list of editions, but it seems the "old Adam" edition may have been more common than the one reflected in Cummings.

by comparing that olde Adam with Christ, and partly also in respect of the deformities of our corrupt nature, which wee change with a newe."[3]

In addition, the marriage service reminded the congregation that matrimony was "instytuted of God in Paradise, in the time of mannes innocencie." In the same service, the priest returned to Genesis, invoking "Almighty God, which at the beginnyng did create our firste parentes Adam and Eve, and did sanctifie and joyne them together in mariage." At the end of the ceremony, he repeated Adam's response to the creation of Eve, his helpmeet: "For this cause shall a man leave father and mother, and shalbe joined unto his wife, and thei two shalbe one flesh" (cf. Gen. 2:14).[4] A more subtle reminder of the Genesis story was featured in the liturgy for the Visitation of the Sick: "Remembre not Lorde oure inquities, nor the iniquities of our forefathers" (our ultimate forefather being Adam, whose iniquity was original sin).[5] In the Burial Service, the phrase "dust to dust" recalled Adam's creation out of the earth ("dust of the grounde" in Gen. 2:7), and the Funeral Lesson from 1 Corinthians 15, "For as by Adam al die, even so by Christ shal al be made alive," asserted the typological connection between Adam, the first sinner, and Christ, who atones for Adam's sin.[6] In the rite for the Churching of Women, the minister gave thanks for the woman's delivery "from the great paine and peril of childe birthe," which congregants would have understood as God's punishment for Eve's sin: "In sorowe shalt thou bring forthe children" (Gen. 2:16).[7]

The story of Adam and Eve would have been familiar too from many of the hundreds of sermons the churchgoer heard, like the Elizabethan *Homily against Disobedience*, which cites the first couple as the first to commit this sin:

---

[3] Geneva–Tomson Bible (London, 1595). In the Arden[3] *Henry V*, T. W. Craik is incorrect in stating that "old Adam" is in the biblical text of Romans, but it was an almost ubiquitous phrase, perhaps most importantly (after the Book of Common Prayer) in the English translation of Erasmus's *Paraphrases on the New Testament*, which was required to be placed in all churches alongside the Bible: faith "killeth the olde Adam, and maketh us altogether newe" and our consciences are "bound and in daunger to the law under old Adam the flesh, as long as he liveth in us" ("A prologe upon the Epistle of Sainct Paule to the Romaynes," in *The seconde tome or volume of the Paraphrase of Erasmus upon the Newe Testament* [London: Edward Whitchurch, 1549], sigs + + i, + + iiii). For more on Erasmus's *Paraphrases*, see Ch. 1, and Gregory D. Dodds, *Exploiting Erasmus: The Erasmian Legacy and Religious Change in Early Modern England* (Toronto: University of Toronto Press, 2009), chs 1–2. The phrase is also used in Calvin's *Institutes*, sermons by Thomas Becon, John Knox, and John Jewel, Matthew Parker's Psalter, Thomas à Kempis, John Bale, John Foxe's *Actes and Monuments*, Robert Southwell's *Epistle of Comfort*, and dozens of other printed texts.

[4] *BCP*, "The Fourme of Solempnizacion of Matrimonie," 157, 162, 163.
[5] *BCP* 164.   [6] *BCP* 172.   [7] *BCP* 176.

As God the Creatour and Lord of all things appointed his Angels and heavenly creatures in all obedience to serve and to honour his majesty: so was it his will that man, his chiefe creature upon the earth, should live under the obedience of his Creatour and Lord: and for that cause, GOD, assoone as hee had created man, gave unto him a certaine precept and law, which hee (being yet in the state of innocency, and remayning in Paradise) should observe as a pledge and token of his due and bounden obedience, with denunciation of death if hee did transgresse and breake the sayd Law and commandement.[8]

In the *Homily on the Misery of All Mankind*, congregants were reminded that man's misery originated in the punishment of Adam and Eve:

In the booke of Genesis, Almighty GOD giveth us all a title and name in our great grandfather Adam, which ought to warne us all to consider what wee bee, whereof wee bee, from whence we came, and whither we shall, saying thus, In the sweat of thy face shalt thou eat thy bread, till thou bee turned againe into the ground, for out of it wast thou taken, in as much as thou art dust, into dust shalt thou be turned againe. Heere (as it were in a glasse) wee may learne to know our selves to be but ground, earth, and ashes, and that to earth and ashes we shall returne.[9]

Modern Christmas revelry and cheer is in stark contrast to the manner in which the Nativity was marked in Shakespeare's lifetime. Early modern worshippers were asked to meditate on sin. Human corruption derived from the disobedience of Adam and Eve, which necessitated the Incarnation of Christ and, more importantly, his sacrifice:

Saint Paul in the fift Chapter to the Romanes sayth, By the offence of onely Adam, the fault came upon all men to condemnation, and by one mans disobedience many were made sinners. By which wordes wee are taught, that as in Adam all men universally sinned: so in Adam all men universally received the reward of sinne, that is to say, became mortall, and subject unto death, having in themselves nothing but everlasting damnation both of body and soule.[10]

Naturally enough, the homilies returned to the subject of original sin during Holy Week, leading up to the Easter celebration of Christ's Crucifixion, death, and resurrection:

When our great grandfather Adam had broken GODS commandement, in eating the apple forbidden him in Paradise, at the motion and suggestion of his wife, he purchased thereby, not only to himselfe, but also to his posterity for ever, the just wrath and indignation of GOD, who according to his former sentence pronounced at the giving of the commandement, condemned both him and all his to everlasting death, both of body and soule.[11]

---

[8] *Homilies*, ii. 275. [9] *Homilies*, i. 7.
[10] *Homily on the Nativity*, *Homilies*, ii. 168.
[11] *Second Homily on the Passion for Good Friday*, *Homilies*, ii. 181.

The Elizabethan Homilies were published, as the 27th injunction of Elizabeth to her clergy explained, "Because through lack of preachers in many places of the queen's realms and dominions the people continue in ignorance and blindness," and therefore "all parsons, vicars, and curates shall read in their churches every Sunday one of the homilies, which are and shall be set forth for the same purpose by the queen's authority, in such sort, as they shall be appointed to do in the preface of the same."[12] Thus, in many English churches, the homilies would have been regular fare, and there were probably few parishes where they were not read at least occasionally.

Even for the illiterate or inattentive, the story of Adam and Eve was unavoidable, since it was a common subject for church art, featured in stained-glass windows, wood carvings, and wall paintings (see Fig. 4.1).[13] Adam and Eve, conventionally portrayed as flanking the Tree of the Fruit of the Knowledge of Good and Evil with the serpent winding up the trunk, could also be found in domestic wall paintings, in embroidered fabrics (used in private chambers), and on clothing, furniture, and tableware.[14] The tale of Adam and Eve was sung in popular ballads like "When Father Adam first did flee" or "A ballet of Adam and Eve," and played in popular entertainments like puppet shows and parish plays.[15] Some among Shakespeare's audience might have seen the Adam and Eve plays

---

[12] Ian Lancashire, "A Brief History of the Homilies" (Toronto: Web Development Group, University of Toronto, 1994, 1997) <http://www.library.utoronto.ca/utel/ret/homilies/elizhom3.html> (accessed September 21, 2012.)

[13] Catherine Belsey includes images of Adam and Eve and the Fall on a marriage chest, bedheads, a betrothal dish, and bed hangings, in *Shakespeare and the Loss of Eden* (New Brunswick, NJ: Rutgers University Press, 1999). A set of images representing the Creation of Adam and Eve, the Fall, their Conviction, and the Expulsion, survives in the south clerestory of the nave in the Great Malvern Priory Church in Worcestershire. G. McN. Rushforth, *Medieval Christian Imagery as Illustrated by the Painted Windows of Great Malvern Priory Church Worcestershire* (Oxford: Clarendon Press, 1936), figs 62–6. An image of Adam delving is part of the genealogy of Christ, originally in the clerestory of the choir in Canterbury Cathedral. Herbert Read, *English Stained Glass* (London and New York: G. P. Putnam's Sons, 1926), 49. There are carved images of Adam and Eve, the serpent, and the tree, as well as the Expulsion, on misericords at Ely and Worcester. Francis Bond, *Wood Carvings in English Churches*, i. *Misericords* (London, New York, etc.: Henry Frowde, Oxford University Press, 1910), 130–3.

[14] Adam and Eve appear under the Tree, among other Old Testament images, on a plaster ceiling at Lanhydrock, Cornwall (dating from *c.*1640). Geoffrey Beard, *Decorative Plasterwork in Great Britain* (London: Phaidon, 1975), fig. 17. They are also painted on walls in a Buckinghamshire farmhouse (*c.*1627) and a property owned by Wassell Wessells (1575). Tessa Watt, *Cheap Print and Popular Piety, 1550–1640* (Cambridge: Cambridge University Press, 1991), 201–2.

[15] For the ballads, see Watt's list of godly ballads registered with the Stationers' Company (*Cheap Print*, app. C, 342–4). On biblical puppet plays, see Margaret Rogerson, "English Puppets and the Survival of Religious Theatre," *Theatre Notebook*, 52/2 (1998), 91–111.

Fig. 4.1. Probably the most commonly reproduced scene from the Bible was that of Adam, Eve, and the Serpent in the Garden of Eden. (Oil on oak panel; Plymouth, England, c.1600.) © Victoria and Albert Museum, London.

in the great Corpus Christi cycles performed at York, Chester, Coventry, and elsewhere.

The narrative of Adam and Eve's Creation and Fall was fundamental to the Christian theology of Atonement, based on a principle of retributive justice. Adam sinned, and was himself unable to make sufficient recompense to God; to redeem humanity, Christ sacrificed himself in Adam's place.[16] A number of late medieval carols express the idea metaphorically:

> Adam our fader was in blis,
> And for an appil of lytil prys

---

[16] This is a theological commonplace. The doctrine of the atonement was first worked out in terms of retributive justice by Anselm in *Cur deus homo* (1098).

> He loste the blysse of Paradys,
>   *Pro sua superbia* [For his pride].
>
> . . . .
>
> Than these profetes prechyd aforn
> That a child xuld [should] be born
> To beye [buy] that Adam hadde forlorn
>   *Sua morte propria* [By his own death].[17]

Another carol is even more explicit about the benefit of Adam's sin:

> Adam lay ybounden,
> Bounden in a bond;
> Four thousand winter,
> Thought he not too long.
>
> And all was for an apple,
> An apple that he took.
> As clerkes finden,
> Written in their book.
>
> Ne had the apple taken been,
> The apple taken been,
> Ne had never our ladie,
> Abeen heav'ne queen.[18]

Or, as the crucified Christ himself says in a sixteenth-century ballad,

> How deepe a danger was thou in,
>   inwrapt through Adam's fale [fall],
> Whome none but I could freedome winne,
>   and my hartes blood recalle.[19]

Adam and Eve's "original sin" was thus inherited by all humanity, and Christ's sacrifice was required for their redemption.

The lessons of Genesis 1–3 for English Christians were not only theological. Since Adam and Eve were believed to be literally humankind's first parents, the history of the world began with them, and their Fall

---

[17] "Adam our fader was in blisse," stanzas 1 and 3, no. 68, in Richard L. Greene (ed.), *The Early English Carols* (Oxford: Clarendon Press, 1935), 42.

[18] Sloane MS 2593. Edith Rickert (ed.), *Ancient English Christmas Carols, 1400–1700* (New York: Duffield and Company, 1915), 163–4. Spelling slightly altered.

[19] "Behold our Saviour crucified," (from BL Add. MS 15,2225), stanza 18, lines 1–4, in Hyder E. Rollins (ed.), *Old English Ballads, 1553–1625* (Cambridge: Cambridge University Press, 1920), 124. George Herbert, in the voice of Christ, expresses the same theological idea with marvelous succinctness: "Man stole the fruit, but I must climbe the tree" ("The Sacrifice," in *The Works of George Herbert*, ed. F. E. Hutchinson [Oxford: Clarendon Press, 1941], 33).

provided the same kind of moral lesson found in the falls of later men and women, collections of which, like *The Mirrour for Magistrates*, were popular reading for Elizabethans. Adam and Eve were also the first couple, and their relationship, before and after the Fall, influenced later thinking on gender, marriage, sex, and childbirth.

Shakespeare's allusions to the Genesis story both reflect and manipulate these traditional interpretations, adapting his emphases according to dramatic genre. In the English history plays, for instance, a political reading of the Fall of mankind from Eden provides a model for the later political fall of the English people and the corruption of their own "Eden." On the other hand, in the comedies, preoccupied as they are with relations between the sexes, Shakespeare often suggests comparisons between his secular stories and that of Adam and Eve, exploring the nature of love and marriage both in a state of innocence and after the Fall. The tragedies, by contrast, emphasize human corruption, carnal degradation, and the misogyny generated by some traditional views of Eve. In the Romances, Shakespeare's allusions to Genesis are complex, as one would expect in tragicomedy. The dark legacy of the Fall is still present, but the possibilities for some kind of redemption seem real.

HISTORY

That Shakespeare should allude to Adam and Eve in Eden in his English Histories should come as no surprise, since in many Elizabethan histories the narrative commenced with Genesis, including Scripture as part of the historical record. This was encouraged within English Bibles themselves: the Bishops' Bible, for instance, included the Roman emperors within its genealogy of Adam through to Christ. Sir Walter Raleigh began his famous *History of the World* (1614) with several chapters analyzing various historical problems posed by Genesis 1–3. Where exactly was Eden? Why was it no longer to be found? What was the nature of the two most important trees? (What kind of fruit did they bear?) If Adam was made in God's image, in what precisely did this resemblance consist? (Was it physical? spiritual? moral?) Many other commentators on Genesis asked these questions too, but Raleigh approached them as a historian not a theologian. Even Raleigh's famous title-page engraving featured the familiar image of Adam, Eve, the tree, and the serpent, located on the map of the world (seemingly somewhere north of the Black Sea). But Raleigh was not the first to begin with "In the beginning." William Camden's *Brittania* (1590) traced the origins of the Britons back to Brute, the great-grandson of Aeneas, who thus linked Britain to Troy, then stretched back further to

Old Testament history, linking all Europeans to Japhet: son of Noah. Readers of the Bible genealogies could then calculate the ultimate link to Adam: Noah–Lamech–Methusaleh–Henoch–Jered–Mahalaleel–Kenan–Enosh–Sheth–Adam (Gen. 5).[20] In addition, the chronicle history begun by Thomas Lanquet and completed by Thomas Cooper and Robert Crowley opened with the Creation of the World. It paid particular attention to the story of Adam and Eve, since not only were they considered part of recorded history, but

> the holy scryptures, besydes that they make us certayne of the wyll and woorde of God, and also of the spyrytuall kyngedome of Chryste, teache us polyticall administracion, and set forth many notable examples, which in rulynge a publyke weale be necessary to bee knowen, and whereby the myndes of pryncs maye be styerred to the study of true nobilitye and vertue.[21]

Adam was, as Joshua Sylvester put it, "King of Eden," which was why his story was featured along with those of other historical rulers in Boccaccio's *De casibus virorum illustrium* (1355–74), translated into English by John Lydgate, and reprinted as late as 1554 by Richard Tottel (*A Treatise excellent and compendious, shewing and declaring, in maner of Tragedye, the falles of sondry most notable Princes and Princesses*).[22] The lessons of Genesis were also applied to events in *The seconde part of the Mirrour for magistrates* (1578), as in "The Complaynt of Carassus":

> Sith men be borne by Nature naked all,
> With their estates why are not men content?
> Why doo they deeme the want of wealth a thral?
> Why shoulde they lothe the lot, which God hath sent?
> Adam him selfe I finde, at fyrst was sent,
> As one who did disdaine his poore estate,
> To disobay, with God to be a mate.[23]

A few lines later, Carassus, a husbandman, describes himself as "the sonne of Adam by descent," a genealogy he shares with all humanity.

---

[20] These are the spellings in the Geneva Bible. The more familiar KJV versions are Seth (Sheth), Enos (Enosh), Cainan (Kenan), Jared (Jered), Enoch (Henoch). Many Bibles, including the Geneva, provided such genealogies as part of the apparatus designed to aid the reader.

[21] Thomas Lanquet, Thomas Cooper, and Robert Crowley, *An epitome of chronicles Conteyninge the whole discourse of the histories as well of this realme of England, as al other cou[n]treys* (London: [William Seres for] Thomas Marshe, 1559), fo. 1ʳ.

[22] Guillaume de Salluste Du Bartas, *Du Bartas his devine weekes and workes translated: and dedicated to the Kings most excellent Majestie by Josuah Sylvester* (London: Humfrey Lounes, 1611), 149.

[23] Thomas Blenerhasset, *The seconde part of the Mirrour for magistrates* ([London]: Richard Webster, 1578), fos 10ʳ, 10ᵛ.

Shakespeare's allusions to Genesis 1–3 are more complex than those in the chronicle histories, and sometimes ambiguous, but they are based on similar assumptions: Old Testament history is real history, and the story of Adam and Eve offers valuable moral and political lessons to later rulers and their subjects. Shakespeare also applies the story of Eden to English history symbolically, interpreting Eden as a "state" of innocence in multiple senses. England was felt by many, not just John of Gaunt, to be "this other-Eden, demi-paradise" (*Richard II* 2.1.42). In 1604, for example, Alexander Craig put such a comparison into the mouth of Queen Elizabeth. Her ghost celebrates England as the "onely earthly Eden now for pleasure and delighte" (that it was Eden only "now" is an obvious compliment to James I from this Scots poet).[24] A year earlier, John Lane had eulogized Elizabeth and described the national mourning across the "Paradice and *Eden* of our Land."[25] Joseph Hall added an additional level to the comparison, celebrating his native county of Suffolk that is "Englands Eden hight | As England is the worlds."[26] John Speed apologized if his "affection passe limits," but stated that "England's Climate, Temperature, Plentie and Pleasures, make it to be as the very Eden of Europe."[27] Thomas Lodge, in his *Alarum against Usurers* (1584), was more qualified:

> Once *Albion* cald, next *Britaine Brutus* gave,
> Now *England* hight, a plot of beautie brave,
> Which onely soyle, should seeme the seate bee,
> Of Paradise, if it from sinne were free.

Theologically, England could no more be said to have escaped the consequences of the Fall than any other nation, but the metaphor of the homeland as earthly paradise was still strongly felt and proved useful for describing the history of England's many rises to and falls from states of relative political or moral grace.

One of the most cataclysmic of such "falls" in the English history recent to Shakespeare's contemporaries was that which resulted in the Wars of the Roses. Appropriately, the history of the wars begins in a garden, where supporters of the two contenders in the conflict, Lancaster and York,

---

[24] Alexander Craig, "Eliazabeth [*sic*], Late Queene of England, her Ghost," in *The Poeticall Essayes* (London: William White, 1604), sig. C4r.

[25] J.L. [John Lane], *An elegie upon the death of the high and renowned princesse* (London: [W. White] for John Deane, 1603), sig. A4r.

[26] Joseph Hall, *The Kings Prophecie* (London: Symon Waterton, 1603), stanza 45, sig. B6r. In an earlier stanza, Hall writes, "As for that tree of life faire *Edens* pride, | Hee set it in our mids, and every side," stanza 24, sig. A8v.

[27] John Speed, "To the well-affected and favourable reader," in *The theatre of the empire of Great Britaine* (London: [William Hall] for John Sudbury and Georg Humble, 1612), sig. 3r.

pluck red and white roses, respectively, as badges of their allegiance (*1 Henry VI* 2.4). This garden setting was not invented by Shakespeare, nor is the potential biblical symbolism of the garden exploited in his first tetralogy of English histories. (An isolated exception is the rebel Jack Cade's defense of himself and his low social status to Sir Humphrey Stafford, stating that even "Adam was a gardener" [*2 Henry VI* 4.2.125]. In this context, Shakespeare's audience would surely have recalled the famous rallying cry of Wat Tyler's 1381 Peasant's Revolt: "When Adam delved and Eve span, who was then the gentleman?").[28] But Shakespeare seems to have become alert to the political resonance of the Genesis story when he turned to *Richard II*. Shakespeare finds the cause of England's fall was prior to the Temple Garden scene. For John of Gaunt, it is Richard himself who has turned the "sceptred isle," the "other Eden," into a "tenement or pelting farm" because of his personal corruption (2.1.40, 42, 60). Yet, despite Richard's failings as a man and a monarch, one might argue that it is actually his deposition as divinely appointed king, and his subsequent murder, that marks England's fall. From this perspective it is thus Bolingbroke's sin from which the country and the monarchy require redemption. Shakespeare explores the relative culpabilities of the Plantagenet cousins, Richard and Bolingbroke, in terms of biblical allusion.

For example, Shakespeare returns to the Genesis story in *Richard II* 3.4, an entirely invented scene that takes place in a garden. That this garden is to be taken allegorically is suggested by the overtly allegorical thinking of the Queen, her ladies, and the gardeners. When the Gardener and his men enter, he refers to dangling apricots as "unruly children" with "prodigal weight" (alluding to that most famous unruly child, the Prodigal Son of Luke 15:11–32), and to the "fast-growing sprays" as over-reachers in the arboreal "commonwealth," needing their heads cut off (3.4.29–36). The political allegory of the garden gradually incorporates specific allusions to the garden of Genesis. For instance, the First Worker's reference to England as "our sea-walled garden" overrun with weeds and caterpillars (a standard metaphor for court flatterers) echoes John of Gaunt's speech. The Gardener describes Richard in similar terms:

> He that hath suffered this disordered spring
> Hath now himself met with the fall of leaf. (3.4.48–9)

[28] Robert Greene quotes these lines in *A quip for an upstart courtier* (London: John Wolfe, 1592), describing them as "old wives logick" (sig. B2ʳ). Thomas Walsingham (*Historia Anglicana*) identifies this as the text of a speech by John Ball to Tyler's rebels, though the text itself comes from Richard Rolle (see Mark T. Elvins, *Catholic Trivia: Our Forgotten Heritage* [Leominster: Gracewing, 2002; first pub. Harper Collins 1992], 55). See also Mark O'Brien, *When Adam Delved and Eve Span: A History of the Peasant's Revolt of 1381* (Cheltenham: New Clarion, 2004).

The leaf's fall is primarily part of the Gardener's seasonal metaphor, but, with Gaunt's "other-Eden" in mind, the metaphor also becomes an allusion to the biblical Fall that by tradition introduced the four seasons to the world.[29] The biblical Fall is also a more appropriate metaphor here, since, like Adam, Richard has, to a large extent, brought about his own undoing. The Gardener's instructions on apricots have already suggested that this is an orchard as well as a garden. His reference to "fruit trees" further identifies this orchard–garden, a political microcosm of England, with the one in Eden, especially given that these trees are in danger of being "over-proud" (3.4.58–9)—many commentators on Genesis argued that the principal sin of Adam and Eve was pride.[30] The Queen drives home the Edenic aspect of the garden in her chastisement of the Gardener:

> Thou, old Adam's likeness,
> Set to dress this garden, how dares
> Thy harsh rude tongue sound this unpleasing news?
> What Eve, what serpent hath suggested thee
> To make a second fall of cursed man?
> Why dost thou say King Richard is deposed? (3.4.72–7)

Of course, it is not the Gardener as much as Richard who is like Adam, not in his digging but in his sinfulness and his fall. Nor is Richard's fall the Gardener's doing. Richard and Bolingbroke have jointly brought it about, and the complexity of this joint responsibility is represented in the Queen's muddled allusions. The Gardener refers to Richard's fall, which presumably is also the "second fall" to which the Queen refers. But the Queen's question about the Gardener's report of Richard's deposition complicates the Genesis allusion, since Adam was not deposed but expelled for transgressing God's command.[31] Furthermore, the Queen likens the Gardener himself to Adam, whose "sin," she suggests, is the false reporting of Richard's downfall, with Eve and the serpent figured as sources of rumor or misinformation. Like so many characters in this play, especially Richard himself, the Queen is keen to use biblical allusions but has trouble deciding to whom they properly apply.

The moral vector of *Richard II* shifts with Richard's deposition. In the first part of the play, Richard is a self-indulgent tyrant whose bad kingship brings about his own downfall; in the second part, he is the anointed king unjustly deposed and murdered. This shift in the play's perspective on

---

[29] Arnold Williams, *The Common Expositor* (Chapel Hill: University of North Carolina Press, 1948), 135.
[30] Williams, *Common Expositor*, 120–5.
[31] One might perhaps argue that Adam was deposed, by God, but this is not an argument that seems to have been made by commentators.

Richard is, of course, more ambivalent than this generalized distinction suggests, and the ambivalence is marked by biblical allusions that continue to challenge interpretation, especially when misapplied by the characters who make them. Richard is first represented as another fallen Adam undone by his own sin, but post-deposition he also takes on qualities of Christ, in that he is a man, yet king by divine right (the king's two bodies mirroring Christ's two natures, human and divine), unjustly punished. Or perhaps this is simply what Richard himself would like to think, since he is the one who self-consciously alludes to Christ's Passion. Richard calls his already executed supporters "three Judases," mistakenly thinking they have betrayed him (3.2.132). Later, in the deposition scene, he returns to this analogy, saying of the men around Bolingbroke,

> Yet I well remember
> The favours of these men. Were they not mine?
> Did they not sometimes cry "All hail" to me?
> So Judas did to Christ, but He in twelve
> Found truth in all but one; I, in twelve thousand, none. (4.1.168–72)[32]

If these men are Judases, however, they are also Pilates, washing their hands of reponsibility—Richard seems happy to cast them in either role, so long as he can play Christ:

> Though some of you, with Pilate, wash your hands,
> Showing an outward pity, yet you Pilates
> Have here delivered me to my sour cross,
> And water cannot wash away your sin. (4.1.239–42)

Indeed, Bolingbroke has previously, though apparently unconsciously, compared himself to Pilate. He explains to Bushy and Green the crimes for which he is executing them, because he wishes "to wash your blood | From off my hands" (3.1.5–6).[33] Bolingbroke's final allusion to Pilate is perhaps more self-conscious; after learning of Richard's murder, he vows,

---

[32] Phyllis Rackin interestingly suggests, though without explanation, that the deposition scene, like the garden scene earlier, "alludes to medieval mystery cycles and also to providential history" ("Temporality, Anachronism, and Presence in Shakespeare's English Histories," *Renaissance Drama*, 17 [1986], 101–23, n. 16). Some support lies in Richard's use of "All hail" as the greeting of Christ by Judas, since this phrase is used similarly in *Julius Caesar* as well as in the York cycle (see Ch. 5). See Rowland Wymer, "Shakespeare and the Mystery Cycles," *ELR* 34/3 (2004), 274.

[33] John W. Velz notes the possibility that the "vegetative names" "Bushy" and "Green" may have encouraged Shakespeare to explore imagery of "fertility and infertility"—and gardens—in the play. "England as Eden in *Richard II*," in Beatrice Batson (ed.), *Shakespeare's Second Historical Tetralogy: Some Christian Features* (West Cornwall, CT: Locust Hill Press, 2004), 130.

"I'll make a voyage to the Holy Land | To wash this blood off from my guilty hand" (5.6.49–50).

Shakespeare's allusions are complex, though, and, even if Bolingbroke may seem like a Pilate, the venal if sympathetic Richard still resembles the fallen Adam more than the self-sacrificing Christ, and his efforts to represent himself as a Christ-figure are strained. For instance, at Barkloughly Castle, Richard proclaims,

> This earth shall have a feeling, and these stones
> Prove armed soldiers, ere her native king
> Shall falter under foul rebellion's arms. (3.2.24–6)

These lines recall Christ's statement to the Pharisees, who have urged him to stop his disciples from praising him as king: "I tel you, that if these shulde holde their peace, the stones wolde crye" (Luke 19:40).[34] It is hard to tell if Richard is self-consciously alluding; if he is, the allusion is self-serving and inaccurate, since Christ's kingdom is pointedly not of this world, and the stones in Luke, even if they were to cry out, would not "prove armed soldiers," since Christ repudiates violence. If Richard utters the allusion unconsciously, its rhetorical effect is still ironic and for the same reason. Richard is similarly overreaching in his analogies later in this scene when he claims to his remaining followers that,

> For every man that Bolingbroke hath pressed
> To lift shrewd steel against our golden crown,
> God for his Richard hath in heavenly pay
> A glorious angel. (3.2.58–61)

The allusion here is to yet another garden, the garden of Gethsemane in which Christ is betrayed by Judas and arrested. Jesus says to Peter, who has drawn his sword to defend him, "thinkest thou, that I can not now pray to my Father, and he wil give me mo then twelve legions of Angels?" (Matt. 26:53). Given the practice of reading the Bible typologically, one biblical garden almost inevitably evokes the others, just as Adam and Christ, type and antitype, naturally implicate each other. Thus, Richard's words in 3.2 may also allude to the temptation in the wilderness, when Satan calls on Jesus to save himself from falling, if he can, since God ought to "give his Angels charge over thee, and with their hands they shal

---

[34] These lines may also allude to the metamorphosis of stones into soldiers in the Cadmus story in Ovid. The allusions to Ovid and Luke enhance each other, rather than canceling each other out. As Jonathan Bate observes, Shakespeare often enjoys alluding in several directions at once; see Bate, *Shakespeare and Ovid* (Oxford: Clarendon Press, 1993), 200, n. 46 (Bate is writing about the synthesizing of sources, but the same is true of allusion).

lifte thee up" (Matt. 4:6). (Richard's subsequent reference to falling—"if angels fight, | Weak men must fall"—reinforces the allusion to the temptation.) Again, if Richard's allusions are conscious, he has missed the point of both passages; if they are unconscious, they are deeply ironic. For example, Christ pointedly does not call the angels in response to Satan's suggestion, because "Thou shalt not tempt the Lord thy God" (Matt. 4:7). He does not call them when he is on trial either, because "How then shulde the Scriptures be fulfilled, which say, that it must be so?" (Matt. 26:54). Richard, by contrast, seems rather eager to call on the angels and tempt God. Ultimately his stance is vain, of course, since, although he is an anointed king, he is no Christ; nor is he sacrificing himself for others but clinging to the shreds of his own, misused power. Once again, Richard has the wrong biblical model in mind, because Christ does not "fall" as a result of his temptation, but Adam certainly does. Shakespeare's shifting allusions allow us to recognize that, while Bolingbroke has betrayed his king—as a Judas or Pilate—Richard, like Adam, is nevertheless the author of his own fall.

In *Richard II* the allusions to the Passion and the Fall of Adam are further interwoven amongst allusions to various classical "falls"—the fall of Troy (5.1.11),[35] the fall of Phaëton (3.3.178)—coloring our response to the "true king's fall" (4.1.318), since they are both tales of the wages of sin: Paris's rape of Helen and the overweening pride of Phaëton. A repentant Bolingbroke (now Henry IV) casts Richard also in the role of Abel, when he bids the murderous Exton "with Cain go wander thorough shades of night" (5.6.43). (As Richard's blood cousin and the instigator of Exton's act, Bolingbroke fits the role of Cain better himself.) Shakespeare again uses multiple allusions to set up a complex set of points of comparison for his characters and his plot, avoiding the one-to-one equivalent of simple allegory: as Richard says, "Thus play I in one person many people" (5.5.31).

A different cluster of biblical allusions represents England itself as fallen, exiled from its original happy state, as Jerusalem was after its fall, when it was mourned by Jeremiah and the Psalmist in exile following the Babylonian conquest.[36] *Richard II* features several characters in exile. The first is Mowbray, banished for life because of his involvement in the

---

[35] Though a little muddled, the Queen's reference to "old Troy" seems actually to be to Troynovant (on the site of London), which stood where the Tower ("Julius Caesar's ill-erected tower") now stands. But ill-erected towers fall, and the "old Troy" of Troynovant suggests the yet older Troy by whose survivors (Brute) it was legendarily settled. Moreover, the fall of the "topless towers of Ilium" (Troy) was in everyone's ears, especially Shakespeare's, after Marlowe's great speech in *Doctor Faustus*.

[36] I have explored these allusions to Ps. 137 more fully in Hamlin, ch. 7.

murder of Thomas of Woodstock.[37] Mowbray laments his enforced exile in terms of Psalm 137 ("By the waters of Babylon"), the psalm of the Jewish exile:

> My native English, now I must forgo,
> And now my tongue's use is to me no more
> Than an unstringed viol or a harp,
> Or like a cunning instrument cas'd up. (1.3.160–3)

The Psalmist, having hanged his harp "up on a tree" (and in some versions of the Psalm the harp is also "unstrung") and refusing to "sing the Lord's song in a strange land," vows that, if he forgets Jerusalem, "let my right hande forget her cunning" (Ps. 137:2, 4, *BCP*). Another allusion to the psalm of exile occurs shortly after Gaunt's speech about the "other Eden," when Northumberland reports Gaunt's death: "His tongue is now a stringless instrument" (2.1.149). Gaunt's "exile," if this is what the allusion suggests his death constitutes, is different from Mowbray's. On the one hand, he is most obviously "exiled" from life, which is why his tongue is silent. But for Christians from Augustine on, death was not an exile but a return home from exile on earth. Instead, the implicit conjunction between the allusion to Gaunt's exile and Gaunt's previous lament for England's fall suggests rather that the country is itself in exile from its proper state. Just as Adam's fall brings about a corresponding "fall" for all Creation, so does Richard's double fall—first from the proper behavior of a king, then from the throne itself—result in a fallen kingdom. This reading of England as a type of both fallen Creation and fallen Jerusalem is supported by an earlier allusion to Lamentations, wherein Gloucester's widow laments the effects of Richard's sins—her personal bereavement, her fallen manor of Plashy, and the country's general misery:

> Alack, and what shall good old York there see
> But empty lodgings and unfurnish'd walls,
> Unpeopled offices, untrodden stones?
> And what hear there for welcome but my groans?
> Therefore commend me; let him not come there
> To seek out sorrow that dwells everywhere.
> Desolate, desolate, will I hence and die!
> The last leave of thee takes my weeping eye. (1.2.67–74)

Like Jerusalem, personified in Lamentations as a widow who "wepeth continually in the night," the weeping, widowed duchess is England's ruin

---

[37] This is the historical reason, as many in Shakespeare's audience would know, though in the play the ostensible cause is his participation in the trial by combat with Bolingbroke.

personified. The word she repeats, "desolate," is a recognizable keyword in Lamentations, in which repeatedly the gates of Jerusalem "are desolate," "made...desolate" by God, and the Israelites her children "are desolate" (Lam. 1:4, 13, 16).[38]

The confluence of biblical allusions to the fallen Jerusalem in *Richard II* may have occurred to Shakespeare independently, but he may also have followed the suggestion of a work he knew well, Thomas Nashe's *Christ's Teares over Jerusalem*, published a year or two earlier in 1593.[39] Nashe's lament was intended for "purblind London," but he too holds up Jerusalem as a mirror to his contemporaries, arguing that "as great a *desolation* as *Jerusalem*, hath *London* deserved":

> The Lord by a solemne oath bounde himselfe to the Jewes; yet when they were oblivious of him, he was oblivious of the covenant he made with their forefathers, and left theyr Citty *desolate* unto them. Shall he not then (we starting from him, to whom by no bonde he is tyde) leave our house *desolate* unto us?[40]

As Nashe attempts to impress upon God, in a combination of patriotic zeal and moral outrage, "No image or likenes of thy *Jerusalem* on earth is there left, but London." Nashe also links both London and Jerusalem back to Eden, in that they are guilty of the same pride that "hast disparradiz'd our first Parent *Adam*," as well as even greater injustice: "If the stealing of one Apple in Paradise brought such an universall plague to the worlde, what a plague to one soule will the robbing of a hundred Orphans of theyr possessions and fruite-yards bring?"[41] Thus, through biblical allusion Shakespeare links the fall of Jerusalem, the fall of England, and the fall of its king, Richard II, while simultaneously linking all of them with their model and the ultimate cause of all subsequent falls, that of Adam and Eve and their expulsion from the Garden of Eden.

If *Richard II* alludes to England's paradise lost caused by Richard's fall from grace and Bolingbroke's deposition of the rightful king, then *Henry V* represents paradise regained, at least for a while. As Henry IV, Bolingbroke struggles to reverse the fall he has caused throughout both eponymous plays. For instance, he longs to make a pilgrimage to Jerusalem, which he hopes might atone for his sin. But he gets only as far as the

---

[38] Some translators of Ps. 137 incorporated the word "desolate" as a means of recalling Lamentations. See Hamlin, 222–3.

[39] See the many articles by J. J. M. Tobin, including "*Macbeth* and *Christ's Teares over Jerusalem*," *Aligarh Journal of English Studies*, 7/1 (1982), 72–8, and "*Hamlet* and *Christ's Teares over Jerusalem*," *Aligarh Journal of English Studies*, 6/2 (1981), 158–67. For more on Nashe and Shakespeare, see Ch. 6.

[40] Thomas Nashe, *Christes Teares over Jerusalem* (London: James Roberts, 1593), fos 90ʳ, 38ʳ–38ᵛ, 91ʳ.

[41] Nashe, *Christes Teares*, fos 91ᵛ, 38ᵛ, 48ᵛ.

"Jerusalem Chamber" of Westminster Abbey, the room in which he dies. Reinforcing Henry's failure to atone, reminders of the Genesis story recur at several points in *Henry IV, Part 1*, in comic contexts. In one such, Hal jokes that he is "of all humours that have showed themselves humours since the old days of Goodman Adam" (2.4.90–2), and it may be telling that, while he is currently engaged upon a harmless practical joke, Hal has also just been party to highway robbery: some of Hal's humours are seriously out of balance. Later in the play, Falstaff defends his own lies with another reference to Adam: "Thou knowest in the state of innocency Adam fell, and what should poor Jack Falstaff do in the days of villainy? Thou seest I have more flesh than another man and therefore more frailty" (3.3.163–7). Shaheen points out that Falstaff's allusion to Adam comes by way of the *Homily against Disobedience*, which refers to man, just after God creates him, as "being yet in the state of innocency."[42]

The prevailing allusive structure in *Henry IV, Part 1* is based, not on Genesis, however, but on Paul's Epistle to the Ephesians: "Take hede therefore that ye walke circumspectly, not as fooles, but as wise, Redeming the time" (Eph. 5:15–16).[43] To summarize briefly, various redemptions are at issue in the play. King Henry takes issue with Hotspur over the redeeming of prisoners of war: "Shall our coffers, then, | Be emptied to *redeem* a traitor home?" (1.3.85–6). Hotspur longs to redeem his honor, and tells his Percy relatives, "yet time serves wherein you may *redeem* | Your banish'd honours" (1.3.179–80). He also speaks of his desire to pluck up "drowned honour by the locks, | So he that doth *redeem* her thence might wear, | Without corrival, all her dignities" (1.3.204–6). Perhaps most importantly, Hal is concerned to redeem his character, promising his father, "I will *redeem* all this on Percy's head" (3.2.132). In his first soliloquy, Hal promises to redeem time, in lines that allude to the key passage from Ephesians: "I'll so offend to make offence a skill, | *Redeeming* time when men think least I will" (1.2.206–7). By "time," Hal seems to mean primarily the time he has spent wasting his youth like a Prodigal Son, among the denizens of Eastcheap. He does eventually fulfill this promise, as his father Henry acknowledges ("Thou hast *redeem'd* thy lost opinion," 5.4.47). Just what kind of redemption has been achieved by Hal so far—financial, proprietal, honorial, soteriological—is a question Shakespeare keeps open. But Paul's final words in the passage from Ephesians are that we should redeem the time "for the dayes are evil," which implies something more than just personal reformation.

---

[42] Shaheen, 420. "Flesh is frail" was proverbial, but may derive from Matt. 26:41, "The flesh is weake." The use of "frailty" in *Hamlet* is discussed later in this chapter.

[43] See Paul Jorgensen, *Redeeming Shakespeare's Words* (Berkeley and Los Angeles: University of California Press, 1962), 52–69. For more on these allusions, see Ch. 6.

Something like the redemption of England—restoring this "other Eden" to its state of relative grace before the fall into Civil War—does seem to occur in *Henry V*. Hal has thrown off Falstaff and his madcap ways and become the next King Henry. The Archbishop of Canterbury describes this transformation in the familiar terms of Genesis 1–3:

> yea, at that very moment,
> Consideration like an angel came
> And whipped th'offending Adam out of him,
> Leaving his body as a paradise
> T'envelop and contain celestial spirits. (1.1.27–31)

Despite the familiarity of the Pauline idea of "old Adam" in the late sixteenth century, it seems clear that Canterbury has a particular "old Adam" in mind: Falstaff may not have been whipped, but he was decisively rejected by Henry at the end of *Henry IV, Part 2*.[44] But, if the king's body has been reimparadised, his country has not been, for a few scenes later Henry uncovers a plot against him by Cambridge, Scroop, and Grey, which he compares to "Another fall of man" (2.2.142). The political fruit of original sin—rebellion—continues to flourish as it had in the reign of Henry IV. This notion of the origins of rebellion is seen in Sylvester's popular translation of Guillaume Du Bartas's *Divine Weeks and Works*, which explained that God created Man, "th'Earths sole Potentate," last, "because he should have made in vain, | So great a Prince, without on whom to Raign" (that is, Man is a Prince, a Prince requires subjects, therefore God created the subjects and the kingdom first).[45] If Man was Prince of Eden, then the Fall was understood partly as a case of misrule, of rebellion against God, since, while Man reigned over Earth, God reigned over all Creation. Hence the prominence of the Genesis story in the *Homily against Disobedience and Willful Rebellion*, since Adam introduced rebellion to the world (see above). Hence also the recurrent references to Adam in Wilfrid Holme's verses on *The fall and evil successe of rebellion from time to time* (London, 1572), which examines rebellions throughout history, including that of "the Archbishop of Yorke with the Earl Marshall of England," the subject of *Henry IV, Part 2*. "Then may we consider Adams disobedience," he writes, "By whose transgression hath given death eternal," and that "disobedience hath given death and

---

[44] Hal's expulsion of his "old Adam," whether that be Falstaff, Hal's old sinful nature, or both, is also accompanied by a name change from Prince Hal to King Henry, a baptism of sorts. It is in the baptismal service of the Book of Common Prayer that the phrase "old Adam" appears.

[45] Du Bartas, *Du Bartas his devine weekes and workes*, 157, 156.

damnation, | And how the law was given to know to reconcile agayn."[46] Thus, if earthly, political rebellion is a consequence of the Fall, it might be inescapable in this fallen world. But with a wise king, enforcing "the law," rebellion might perhaps be kept at bay. The ever-pragmatic Henry V recognizes (as indeed his father does) that what England really needs is to take its wars abroad, uniting all diverse factions against a common enemy: France.

Interestingly, when the play shifts to France Shakespeare reintroduces the image of a nation as a garden, although France's, like England's, is in a fallen state. As the Duke of Burgundy puts it, challenging Gaunt's argument for England as Eden, France is the "best garden of the world," but without peace it is "corrupting in it [*sic*] own fertility" (5.2.36, 40). The Chorus finally tells us that, after negotiations were over, Henry achieved "the world's best garden" (Epilogue 7), echoing Burgundy's earlier description. Yet if England, as Gaunt believes, is another Eden, how can France be the "world's best garden"? Curiously, Burgundy's long description of the French Eden contains mostly English plants, both good and bad: this garden formerly grew "freckled cowslips, burnet and green clover," but now "hateful docks, rough thistles, kecksies, burrs" (5.2.49, 52).[47] Similarly nasty plants also feature in Richard's curse in *Richard II*. He calls upon the earth to "Yield stinging nettles to mine enemies" and to protect each flower with a suspiciously serpentlike "lurking adder" (3.2.18, 20). So is the France Burgundy praises just a metaphor for England? Technically, of course, after Henry V's conquest, France and England are united under one crown, and even Elizabeth I was officially (in England) considered to be Queen of France as well as England, Wales, and Ireland. It might be, then, that Shakespeare's allusions to Eden were designed to reflect this union of kingdoms on either side of the Channel, as well as to emphasize Henry's achievement in restoring the national (and imperial) "paradise," however briefly.

As Richard Dutton points out, however, there are actually two texts of *Henry V*, the First Quarto of 1600 and the Folio of 1623, and the differences between the two texts may reflect the different political contexts in which they were written, published, or performed. The later version is considerably darker than the earlier, adding the cynical scheming of the churchmen in 1.2, making Henry personally responsible for Falstaff's

---

[46] Wilfrid Holme, *The fall and evill successe of Rebellion* (London: Henry Binneman, 1572), sigs D^v and E4^r.
[47] All of these plants are described in John Gerard, *The herball or Generall historie of plantes* (London: [Edm. Bollifant for Bonham Norton and] John Norton, 1597), but Shakespeare has also made sure to use obviously Anglo-Saxon, rather than Latinate, names, some of them (like "kecksies") dialectal.

decline in 2.1, adding a motive beyond bribery for Cambridge's betrayal (according to Holinshed, he supported the Mortimer claims to the throne), and intensifying the brutality of Henry's speech in 3.3.[48] Burgundy's "best garden" speech is also a Folio addition, and, as Dutton concludes, it "ties in with the folio's altogether more complex and questioning approach to Henry's achievements than we find in the quarto: here it is the implication that warfare may ruin what it seeks to conquer."[49] Part of this "complex and questioning approach" involves biblical allusion, since all of the allusions to Eden and the Fall—"th'offending Adam" (1.1.29), "Another fall of man" (2.2.142), the "best garden of the world" (5.2.36)—are in the Folio text, not in the Quarto.

If Dutton is right that the Folio represents additions to the original play, then Shakespeare added a set of biblical allusions that not only linked *Henry V* more firmly to the allusive patterns of *Richard II* and *1 Henry IV*, but also increased the play's political and moral ambivalence. Norman Rabkin famously compared *Henry V*'s political perspectivism, in which Henry is irresolvably both populist hero and brutal Machiavel, to the familiar drawing that is both a rabbit and a duck, depending upon which animal one wants to see.[50] Subsequent critics have elaborated on this interpretation: Paola Pugliatti, for instance, sees *Henry V* as Shakespeare's "most conspicuous achievement in the reasoning *in utremque partem*," reading it in the context of the rhetorical tradition that trained debaters to argue both sides of a question; John S. Mebane summarizes decades of critical opinion, ultimately agreeing with Graham Bradshaw that the play is a "dramatization of conflicting political positions," no one of which the play ultimately endorses.[51] Mebane cites a prominent biblical allusion as evidence that we cannot easily applaud Henry's French campaign: apart from the general bloodthirstiness of Henry's threatening speech to the citizens of Harfleur, in which he prophesies the defiling of "shrill-shrieking daughters," the dashing of the "most reverend heads" of aged fathers, and

---

[48] Richard Dutton, "'Methinks the Truth Should Live from Age to Age': The Dating and Contexts of *Henry V*," *HLQ* 68/1–2 (2005), 173–204. Dutton cites the summary of such additions by Gary Taylor in his Oxford edition of the play.

[49] Dutton, "'Methinks the Truth,'" 203.

[50] Norman Rabkin, "Either/Or: Responding to *Henry V*," in Harold Bloom (ed.), *Modern Critical Interpretations: Shakespeare's* Henry V (New York, New Haven, and Philadelphia: Chelsea House, 1988), 35–59. Originally published in Rabkin, *Shakespeare and the Problem of Meaning* (Chicago and London: University of Chicago Press, 1981). The image is taken from E. H. Gombrich, *Art and Illusion: A Study of the Psychology of Pictorial Representation* (Princeton: Princeton University Press, 1969).

[51] Paola Pugliatti, *Shakespeare the Historian* (New York: St Martin's Press, 1996), 137. John S. Mebane, "'Impious War': Religion and the Ideology of Warfare in *Henry V*," *SP* 104/2 (2007), 250–66, 251. Melbane paraphrases Graham Bradshaw, *Misrepresentations: Shakespeare and the Materialists* (Ithaca, NY: Cornell University Press, 1993).

the spitting of "naked infants on pikes," the wailing of "mad mothers" that will result is likened to that of the "wives of Jewry | At Herod's bloody-hunting slaughtermen" (3.3.35–41). This allusion too is present only in the Folio, and there is no way to take positively a comparison between Henry and his troops to Herod and the Slaughter of the Innocents, Herod's primary motive being to kill the infant Jesus. The allusions to Genesis are less pointed, but they also complicate our perspective on Henry and his foreign war. Can the restoration of England's "other Eden" really depend upon the destruction of the "world's best garden?" And, if France is also an "other Eden" for the French, what does this imply about biblically based nationalism in general? Perhaps the point is that these allusions are a species of metaphor; the theological reality is that all the world is equally fallen, and Eden is forever lost.

It has been argued that "in *Richard II* biblical allusions, echoes, and derivative imagery create a unity that one would not realize without an awareness that the play is permeated with the spirit of man's fall and first fratricide," the latter being dependent upon the former.[52] In addition, allusions to Old Testament laments of exile and the fallen Jerusalem, as well as the Passion narrative from the New Testament, similarly create unity not just in *Richard II* but in the sequence of four plays that tell the rest of this part of English history.[53] This is not to say that Shakespeare's histories are biblical dramas or are to be read as tidy allegories. An awareness of the allusions nevertheless is part of Shakespeare's conception of English history, from the fall of Richard II (both sinning Adam and martyred king) to the redemption of England's throne and of fallen Eden by Henry V. Shakespeare's biblical allusions might seem to support the traditional providential view of history, in which everything happens according to divine plan, insofar as the allusions tie the Wars of the Roses to the Genesis narrative, as one critic has argued. Yet the allusions may actually have the opposite effect. Linking Richard to Adam underscores the sense in which England falls along with its king, but it also places much of the blame for that fall on Richard's individual actions.[54] Furthermore, as the final Chorus of *Henry V* reminds us, Henry's success is not only ambivalent but temporary. England will again be plunged into Civil War after his death, to be finally redeemed (if we accept the Tudor myth) only by Henry VII.

---

[52] Stanley R. Maveety, "A Second Fall of Cursed Man: Bold Metaphor in *Richard II*," *JEGP* 72 (1973), 175–93, 187.

[53] The allusions are recurrent but not consistent. *Henry IV, Part 2* contains few traces of the allusive pattern, and in *Henry V* the garden imagery of the last act is not explicitly edenic, but seems to take on this quality primarily in the context of earlier allusions to Genesis in the play and earlier still in *Richard II*.

[54] John Wilders, *The Lost Garden* (Totowa, NJ: Rowman and Littlefield, 1978).

COMEDY

Dramatic comedy conventionally concerns love, marriage, and gender relations; the story of the Fall was crucial to the Elizabethan understanding of these topics. Given the tendency of comedies to end happily, however, Shakespeare's comedies hold out the possibility for at least some amelioration of the consequences of Adam's and Eve's original sin, of a return to the Garden. Luther and Calvin would have denounced the notion that humanity can ever return to a prelapsarian state of innocence. The notion of a return to the Garden, though, may be a case where Christian thought was complicated by an infusion of classical myth. Andrew Wallace-Hadrill describes the powerful influence of Virgil's fourth, "messianic" Eclogue, with its vision of a return of the Golden Age, on Western Christian thought.[55] Whatever its source, however, the question of how this return might be achieved is critical. For Virgil, as perhaps for Shakespeare in the history plays, the solution required effective rulers like Augustus or Henry V. But the goal in comedy is not good rulers but happy couples.

In this respect the King and his friends in *Love's Labour's Lost* seem perhaps not to understand the genre they are in. Their plan for improving themselves is to shun the opposite sex entirely, to retreat to their "little academe" (1.2.13). Elizabethan students of the classics knew that the original "academe," or academy, was a garden, specifically the grove near Athens where Plato taught—hence Horace's *silvas Academi*, which Milton translated as the "Olive Grove of *Academe*."[56] The desire of Shakespeare's French king to create an entirely male retreat was shared in the next century by the speaker of Andrew Marvell's "The Garden," who muses longingly about the period Adam lived alone in Eden before the creation of his "helpmeet":[57]

> Such was that happy garden state,
> While man there walked without a mate:

---

[55] Andrew Wallace-Hadrill, "The Golden Age and Sin in Augustan Ideology," *Past and Present*, 95 (1982), 19–36.

[56] Horace, *Epistulae* 2.2.45, *The Epistles of Horace: A Bilingual Edition*, trans. David Ferry (New York: Farrar, Straus and Giroux, 2001), 134; Milton, *Paradise Regained*, 4.244, in *The Riverside Milton*, ed. Roy Flannagan (Boston and New York: Houghton Mifflin Company, 1998), 771. Given the ostensibly French setting of *Love's Labour's Lost*, the more immediately relevant model for Shakespeare's "little Academe" was the fictional French Academy described by Pierre de la Primaudaye (translated into English in 1586 as *The French Academie*), but the ultimate model was the more famous Athenian grove.

[57] As the *OED* notes, "helpmeet" is actually a word created by a misreading of Gen. 2, where God creates "an helpe mete for" Adam, in other words, a helper appropriate for him. The translators did not intend that Eve be described as a "helpmeet."

> After a place so pure, and sweet,
> What other help could yet be meet?
> But 'twas beyond a mortal's share
> To wander solitary there:
> Two Paradises 'twere in one
> To live in Paradise alone.[58]

In such a view, the key to a true paradise is (male) solitude. The biblical resonance of the noblemen's plan in *Love's Labour's Lost* is established by allusions to the Genesis story elsewhere in the play. For instance, Don Armado's grandiloquent letter accusing Costard of being "taken with a wench" is peppered with biblical language, describing Jaquenetta, for example, as "a child of our grandmother Eve" (1.1.274, 252). It may also be apt that the transgressing couple is discovered in a place "north-north-east and by east from the west of [the King's] curious-knotted garden" (1.1.238–9). Armado's directions are themselves curiously knotted and impossible to chart, but the prevailing direction seems to be easterly, which corresponds to the garden God planted "Eastwarde in Eden" (Gen. 2:8), in which he put man, woman, and the forbidden tree. The gate through which the fallen Adam and Eve are expelled is also "at the Eastside of the garden of Eden" (3:24). In another example, Dull poses Holofernes and Nathaniel a riddle about the moon and Cain, which Holofernes solves with a reference to Adam (4.2.33–42).[59] In addition, Berowne later says mockingly of Boyet and his powers over women, "Had he been Adam, he had tempted Eve" (5.2.322). (In other words, Boyet's rhetorical powers are such that the traditional roles of Adam and Eve as tempted and tempter would have been reversed.) But, for most of the play, it is Berowne and his comrades who think themselves tempted by Rosaline and the other children of Eve, as when Berowne remarks to the King that "Devils soonest tempt, resembling spirits of light" (4.3.253), identifying Rosaline with Satan, who was "an Angel of light" (2 Cor. 11:14). Furthermore, Armado provides a list of heroes undone by the temptations of women, including Samson and Solomon, and he yokes Satan and Cupid together (and by implication Delilah, the Queen of Sheba, and all women) in concluding that "there is no evil angel but Love" (1.2.165–7).

Yet in *Love's Labour's Lost* it is not the women but the men who are tempters—as well as oath-breakers. The *Homily on Swearing and Perjury*

---

[58] Andrew Marvell, "The Garden," ll. 57–64, in *The Poems of Andrew Marvell*, ed. Nigel Smith, rev. edn, (Harlow and New York: Pearson Longman, 2007), 158.

[59] Interestingly, this passage contains Shakespeare's only two uses of the word "allusion." Though he uses it in the sense of "riddle" (*OED* 2), the riddle in question depends on allusions (in the more familiar rhetorical sense) to Genesis.

condemns "breakers of honest promises," but it also cites Herod and Jephtha as examples of those who "make wicked promises by an oath, and will performe the same," their foolish oaths resulting in the deaths, respectively, of John the Baptist and Jephthah's own daughter.[60] The King and his friends may not be wicked, exactly, but they do make a foolish oath, since they vow not to speak to any women, even though the Princess is expected shortly on a visit of state. Later, Berowne provides the men with a lengthy justification for breaking their vow, arguing that

> It is religion to be thus forsworn,
> For charity itself fulfils the law,
> And who can sever love from charity? (4.3.347–9)

This contorted logic is based on self-serving appropriations of Romans 13:8 ("he that loveth another, hathe fulfilled the Law" in Geneva) and 13:10 ("therfore the fulfyllyng of the lawe is charitie" in Bishops') as well as the English Reformation controversy over whether the Greek *agapē* should be rendered as "love" or "charity."[61] Despite Berowne's Falstaffian appropriation of scripture, however (see Chapter 6), it is clear that Berowne is right about love at least. Even apart from the King's specific arrangements with the Princess, any arrangement that enforces an unnatural separation of men and women would be seen as misguided, since it attempts to put asunder those whom God himself had originally joined together (Mark 10:9), and perhaps even smacks of Catholic monasticism.

Longaville sees oath-breaking as the lesser evil to forgoing the pleasures of women, asking himself, "what fool is not so wise | To lose an oath to win a paradise?" The King throws his words back at him—"You would for paradise break faith and troth" (4.3.70, 140). Berowne suggests this line of argument is "pure idolatry," though one might prefer to call it casuistry; actually, however, it is sound theology. Wicked oaths, as the homily states, should not be kept. Furthermore, the real false paradise in the play is not the love of the women but the "little academe," whose purpose is, in vivid contrast to the original biblical paradise, the pursuit of knowledge. In case we miss the point, Berowne jokes that he will "study so, | To know the thing I am forbid to know" (1.1.60). The humour depends upon our awareness of the incongruity of pursuing paradise by studying

---

[60] *Homilies*, i. 149.
[61] See Noble, 146, as well as T. W. Baldwin, *William Shakspere's Small Latine and Lesse Greeke* (Urbana, IL: University of Illinois Press, 1944), ii 643; online reprint <http://durer.press.illinois.edu/baldwin/> (accessed September 21, 2012). The translation of *agapē* as "love" or "charity" was one of the points of fierce debate between Thomas More and William Tyndale.

forbidden knowledge, since eating the forbidden fruit of the Tree of Knowledge was just what got Adam and Eve expelled. Berowne's desired course of "study"—good food and pretty girls—is also implicitly called into question by the Genesis allusions, since the original sin involved eating and (in the traditional interpretation) resulted in carnal knowledge. But Berowne's joke reflects back on the King's plan to fast and remain abstinent in order to seek intellectual fame that will "grace us in disgrace of death" (1.1.3). The pursuit of lasting fame is a Renaissance commonplace, derived from classical literature, and Shakespeare is not condemning this desire in itself (a desire that he articulates in his own sonnets), nor the pursuit of knowledge or "living art," but he is calling into question the pursuit of these goals by means of a "war against your own affections" (1.1.14, 9).

The young men's first plan is cast aside upon the arrival of the women. They then pursue a different kind of "paradise"—love, in Longaville's terms—but this too proves a fool's paradise. While the men are larking about dressed like Muscovites and trying to tempt the women to satisfy their desires, their plans are once again interrupted. Death enters the garden in the form of Marcadé, whose very name may refer to his role in "marring Arcadia" or disrupting paradise.[62] He announces the death of the Princess's father and concludes, "my tale is told," alluding to Psalm 90's familiar statement of the limits of human life: "we brynge our yeares to an ende, as it were a tale that is tolde" (Ps. 90:8, *BCP*). The young men's efforts to avoid the realities of human life, either by retreating to their study or by abandoning themselves in adolescent games of love, ultimately prove inadequate. They must live in the real world. To the King's final request for her love, the Princess responds with the sobering observation that the time left to them is "too short | To make a world-without-end bargain in" (5.2.783).[63] Shakespeare's comedy points up the false idealism of romantic comedy. In a fallen world, no perfect return to paradise is possible; death is inevitable. And yet we find consolation in love, even if it must wait for a year until Berowne and the others have completed their "reformation" (5.2.857). But that is too long for a play.

---

[62] The significance of this name has been much debated. See, e.g., René Graziani, "M. Marcadé and the Dance of Death: *Love's Labour's Lost* V.2.705–711," in Felicia Hardison Londré (ed.), *Love's Labour's Lost: Critical Essays* (New York and London: Garland Publishing, 1997), 301–4, and also H. R. Woudhuysen's introduction to *Love's Labour's Lost*, 34, 65–6.

[63] This is an allusion to the lesser doxology, the *Gloria patri* ("Glory be to the father"), which concludes, "As it was in the beginning, is nowe and ever shalbe. Worlde without ende. Amen." *BCP* 104. This was repeated many times throughout the liturgy, including in the wedding service.

As You Like It is most obviously a Prodigal Son play, a genre already popular on the Elizabethan stage.[64] Orlando trumpets this to the audience in the opening scene, when he alludes to the parable's "hogs" and "husks" and complains about his "prodigal portion" (1.1.35–6; see Chapter 3). But, as usual, Shakespeare's allusions overlap and intermix, and here Orlando speaks his lines about prodigality to his old servant "Adam." Adam is a common name, but it becomes clear as the play progresses that this particular Adam's name is intentionally allusive. (Notably, Shakespeare omits Adam's surname "Spencer" from the play's source, Thomas Lodge's *Rosalynde*.) Like so many of Shakespeare's comedies, *As You Like It* features a trip to the green world, in this case the Forest of Arden. This forest is more symbolic than geographical, doubling as both the French Ardennes and the Forest of Arden near Stratford. The former suits the ostensibly French setting, but the forest seems to be translated in spirit back across the Channel to England when the wrestler Charles describes the "merry men" flocking to the banished Duke in the woods, where "they live like the old Robin Hood of England" (1.1.109–11). In Charles's next simile, however, the forest becomes the Ovidian "golden world" (1.1.13). It is a short step from Ovid to Genesis, especially with Golding's syncretic introduction to the *Metamorphosis* in mind:

> Moreover, by the gold age what other thing is meant
> Than Adam's time in Paradise, who, being innocent,
> Did lead a blest and happy life until that thorough sin
> He fell from God?[65]

The Duke himself declares that in the forest "feel we not the penalty of Adam," as if he and his company have managed to re-enter prelapsarian Eden itself (2.1.5). What he means by Adam's penalty is not immediately obvious, however. Since he goes on to describe the winter, though cold and painful, as free from flattery, it seems the Duke connects the Fall specifically with the hypocrisy and corruption of the court. Ironically, though, the Duke is living in the edenic forest because his usurping brother banished him. (Can one be banished into, rather than out of,

---

[64] See Alan R. Young, *The English Prodigal Son Plays: A Theatrical Fashion of the Sixteenth and Seventeenth Centuries* (Salzburg: Institut für Anglistik und Amerikanistik, Universität Salzburg, 1979), John Doebler, "*The Knight of the Burning Pestle* and the Prodigal Son Plays," *SEL* 5/2 (1965), 333–44, and Susan Snyder, "*King Lear* and the Prodigal Son," *SQ* 17/4 (1966), 361–9. Shakespeare himself was for many years credited with one such play, *The London Prodigal* (1605). According to Noble, the Parable of the Prodigal Son is the parable most often alluded to in Shakespeare's plays (eight times, although Shaheen cites fifteen references).

[65] Arthur Golding, Epistle of 1567, ll. 469–72, in *Ovid's Metamorphoses Translated by Arthur Golding*, ed. Madeleine Forey (Baltimore: Johns Hopkins University Press, 2002), 18.

Eden?) Since Cain and Abel, fraternal conflict had been interpreted as a prominent consequence of the Fall (see the discussion of *Hamlet* below), so it seems that, despite his protests to the contrary, in terms of fraternal conflict and political rebellion the Duke feels Adam's penalty rather sharply.[66]

Shakespeare underscores this in a wonderfully ironic visual image. As if in a living emblem, illustrating the seventh of Jaques's ages of man—the geriatric "*sans* teeth, *sans* eyes, *sans* taste, *sans* everything" (2.7.167)—Orlando enters, bearing on his back his exhausted old servant, Adam. Critics have read this scene in conjunction with Geoffrey Whitney's emblem for filial piety, which features an image of Aeneas bearing his aged father Anchises out of Troy on his back.[67] Yet, if the audience remembers that this old man is named Adam, and remembers too that "old Adam" is an Elizabethan commonplace for original sin, the emblem suggests not just loyalty and filial piety, but also the "penalty of Adam" that Orlando, another victim of fraternal violence, bears along with the Duke. In his sermons on Ephesians (to which Shakespeare also alludes in *Hamlet*, written a year after *As You Like It*; see below), Calvin writes that "wee carrie the old Adam continually about us, who cannot bee put quyte and cleane away but by death."[68] Orlando also describes his Adam as a gardener, just as the original was, although this Adam symbolically tends the growth of his young master: "poor old man, thou prun'st a rotten tree" (2.3.63).[69] Orlando also notes that Adam "sweats" (albeit "for duty not for meed")

---

[66] See also Michael Taylor, "'As You Like It': The Penalty of Adam," *Critical Quarterly*, 15/1 (1973), 76–80.

[67] Raymond Waddington, "Moralizing the Spectacle: Dramatic Emblems in *As You Like It*," *SQ* 33/2 (1982), 156. Waddington cites John Doebler, *Shakespeare's Speaking Pictures* (Albuquerque: University of New Mexico Press, 1974), 33–4, and Rosalie Colie, *Shakespeare's Living Art* (Princeton: Princeton University Press, 1974), 258.

[68] Calvin, *The Sermons of M. Iohn Calvin, upon the Epistle of S. Paule too the Ephesians. Translated out of French into English by Arthur Golding* (London: [By Thomas Dawson] for Lucas Harison and George Byshop, 1577), sig. *6. Interestingly, Calvin's next sentence talks of wrestling, between the flesh and the spirit: "And the flesh not onely lusteth, but also wrestleth and fyghteth so myghtily ageinst the spirit, that oftentymes it weakeneth, woundeth, overthroweth, yea and (as sayeth Saint Paule) leadeth us captive to the lawe or service of sinne." This may be a coincidence, but Orlando, in addition to carrying old Adam, is also a wrestler. Orlando wrestles physically with Charles, but perhaps also morally and spiritually, in a sense, with the legacy of the Fall and its implications for his family.

[69] Shakespeare may also be playing with the idea of Orlando as a tree when Touchstone remarks of the verses Rosalind finds on a tree, "Truly, the tree yields bad fruit" (3.2.113). Since the "fruit," Orlando's verses, actually comes from Orlando, he is in a sense the tree here (perhaps also recalling the proverb derived from Matt. 12:33, "the tre is known by the frute"). This occasions a series of puns on medlars from Rosalind, apparently mocking Touchstone as a "meddler." Somewhere in the background, however, may be the more familiar other sense of "medlar," the female genitals or a prostitute; the association of sex and fruit has an obvious biblical origin.

and remarks on his "pains and husbandry" (2.3.58, 65), recalling God's curse that the first Adam must earn his bread from the soil "in the sweat of thy face" (Gen. 3:9). This Adam, like the original, digs in a fallen world. The biblical allusions establish Arden's landscape as postlapsarian, outside of Eden, and reinforce the anti-pastoral elements of Arden, in which the shepherds work for absent landlords and the sheep are for sale to the highest bidder. Though this is a forest, providing a respite from the dangers of court, it is no simplistically idealized Garden of Eden.

TRAGEDY

The standard trajectory of tragedy is a fall, according to both Aristotle and the *de casibus* model of *The Mirrour for Magistrates*, so it is natural that Shakespeare's tragedies should also allude to the biblical Fall. In terms of allusions to Genesis, the richest of Shakespeare's tragedies is *Hamlet*. For one thing, Cain and Abel are an explicit parallel for Claudius and Old Hamlet,[70] but the play also alludes to the Fall, in which the role of the serpent is taken by Claudius. As the Ghost of his father tells Hamlet, "'Tis given out that, sleeping in my orchard, | A serpent stung me," but "The serpent that did sting thy father's life | Now wears his crown" (1.5.35–6, 39–40). Shakespeare adds to the scene its orchard setting (not in the extant sources), which in combination with the serpent clearly represent this as a re-enactment of the Fall—as the Ghost laments, "O Hamlet, what a falling off was there" (1.5.47). Of course, the fall the Ghost laments is more immediately that of Gertrude, a type of Eve seduced by the "serpent" Claudius. In this scenario, since he has also killed Hamlet Sr, Claudius is both woman-seducing serpent and fratricidal Cain, while Hamlet Sr is both duped Adam and murdered Abel. Shakespeare's allusive doubling and variations on Genesis stories complicate our response to the play, not least because they make it difficult to get a moral bearing on the three principals. For example, is Hamlet Sr guilty like Adam or an innocent victim like Abel? Claudius is unambiguously guilty like the serpent and Cain, but is he primarily guilty as a seducer or a murderer, or both equally? Is Gertrude, like Eve, implicated in her husband's fall or simply weak-willed or oversexed?

The story of the Fall also underlies Hamlet's apparent misogyny, manifested in his relationships with both Gertrude and Ophelia. "Frailty thy

---

[70] Most explicitly, Hamlet refers in the graveyard scene to "Cain's jawbone, that did the first murder" (5.1.76), but Claudius's reference to the "first corse" in 1.2 would also have been recognized to invoke Cain and Abel, since, according to biblical history, the first corpse was Abel's.

name is woman," Hamlet exclaims, in his first soliloquy (1.2.146). The Ghost has not yet revealed to him Claudius's crime, so Hamlet focuses here on his mother's inadequate mourning of her husband and her too-hasty marriage to Claudius, her husband's own brother. But why is the Ghost's blame focused on Gertrude rather than Claudius? As a number of critics have observed, Renaissance Christians commonly interpreted the first murder as a direct consequence of the Fall.[71] In a sense, then, thinking typologically, if misogynistically, the fault for Old Hamlet's murder is really Gertrude's, insofar as she, as a woman, inherits the blame of Eve, just as the blame for Abel's death (following this very male line of thought) was Eve's.

For Shakespeare's audience, Hamlet's railing on the frailty of women was a complaint not just about Gertrude but about all the daughters of Eve, the "weaker vessel" (1 Pet. 3:7).[72] In fact, Hamlet's word "frailty" seems actually to have originated in English in conjunction with the biblical notion of the frailty of human nature, both in flesh and in will.[73] References to the frailty of human nature in the sixteenth century are commonplace, and fleshly frailty is often represented as specifically sexual, as in Spenser's *Faerie Queene*, when Amavia explains the seduction of her love Mordant by Acrasia, "For he was flesh: (all flesh doth frailtie breed)."[74] The connection of human frailty with the Fall was also common, as in Edward Hake's reference to "the verye frailtye of olde rebellious Adam."[75] William Perkins makes the same connection:

> Thus much touching mans fall into sinne by Gods just permission: Nowe followes the good use which we must make thereof. First by this we learne to acknowledge and bewaile our owne *frailtie*. For Adam in his innocencie beeing created perfectly righteous, when hee was once tempted by the devill, fell away from God: what shal we doe then in the like case which are by nature sold under sinne, and in our selves a thousand times weaker then Adam was?[76]

---

[71] Catherine Belsey, *Shakespeare and the Loss of Eden*, 131; Heather Hirschfeld, "Hamlet's 'First Corse': Repetition, Trauma, and the Displacement of Redemptive Typology," *SQ* 54/4 (2004), 424–48, 424–5.

[72] Shakespeare uses Peter's phrase "weaker vessel" to refer to women in *Love's Labour's Lost* (1.1.258), *Romeo and Juliet* (1.1.14–15), *Henry IV, Part 2* (2.4.59), and *As You Like It* (2.4.6).

[73] A keyword search on *EEBO* supports this, with citations in Tyndale, More, Erasmus (in translation), and others. The first citations in the *OED* of the two senses of "frailty" (physical and moral) are both biblical, from Wyclif's translation of Hebrews 7:28 and Richard Rolle's Ps. 21:2. The same sources provide first citations for "frail."

[74] Edmund Spenser, *The Faerie Queene*, ed. A. C. Hamilton, text ed. Hiroshi Yamashita and Toshiyuki Suzuki (London and New York: Longman, 2001), 2.1.52, l. 6.

[75] E.H. [Edward Hake], *A touchestone for this time present expresly declaring such ruines, enormities, and abuses as trouble the Churche of God and our Christian common wealth at this daye* (London: [W. Williamson] for Thomas Hacket, 1574), sig. A3ᵛ.

[76] William Perkins, *An exposition of the Symbole or Creed of the Apostles* (Cambridge: John Legatt, 1595), 117, emphasis added.

Hamlet's identification of "frailty" specifically with women is less common (the word, not the general notion of weakness). But there is precedent in Anthony Munday's translation of the Romance *Palmerin D'Oliva* (1588), in which the Great Turk acknowledges "what frailtie commonly is in women," or in George Pettie's rant on the "fraylty and fraud of women."[77] Hamlet would perhaps have sympathized with Pettie's opinion of marriage:

And as *Eve* caused *Adam* to bee deprived of Paradise, so I think her sexe is ordained to deprive *Adams* posteritie of prosperiti. Yea in mariage it self where only they are counted necessarie, I see not but that they are accompanied with more care then commoditie, more cost then comforte, more paine then gaine, more greife their good.

Pettie writes that he will "conclude with scripture": "I thinke best for man not to touche a woman."[78] Thus, although it is no longer obvious to modern readers, Hamlet's use of "frailty" to describe woman invokes the origins of the English word in the specific context of the biblical Fall.

That Shakespeare has this in mind is indicated by his use of another word that has similar biblical associations, though this word also constitutes *Hamlet*'s most notorious textual crux. Hamlet's first soliloquy meditates on flesh, either "solid," "sallied," or "sullied," the relative merits of which textual scholars have debated endlessly. The debate will no doubt continue, but support for the editorial emendation "sullied," punning on "solid," might be found in its etymology.[79] The *OED*'s first citations for "sullied" and "sully" suggest that it was Shakespeare who brought this word (in its various forms—also "sully" as noun) into common English usage, in the Sonnets (15, "To change your day of youth to sullied night"), *Henry VI, Part 1* (4.4.6, "The over-daring Talbot | Hath sullied all his gloss of former Honor"), *Henry IV, Part 1* (2.4.84, "Look you Francis, your white | Canvas doublet will sully"), *The Winter's Tale* (1.2.327, "Sully the puritie and whiteness of my Sheetes?"), and elsewhere in *Hamlet* itself (2.1.39, "You laying these slight sullies on my son, | As 'twere a thing a little soil'd i'th' working"). These are all first citations, for various forms and senses. Of course, *OED* first citations are often not

---

[77] Anthony Munday, *Palmerin D'Oliva The mirrour of nobilitie* (London: J. Charlewood, for William Wright, 1588), sig. A4ᵛ; George Pettie, *A petite pallace of Pettie his pleasure* (London: R. W[atkins], 1576), 200.

[78] Pettie, *A petite pallace of Pettie*. By "conclude," Pettie means essentially "concur," and the Scripture he has in mind is 1 Cor. 7:1, "It were good for a man not to touche a woman," but the marginal note in Geneva points out that this is because of "mans corruption," which has tainted the institution of marriage God created before the Fall.

[79] The First Quarto has "sallied" and the Folio "solid." As the Arden³ editors note, many editors have emended to "sullied."

the earliest uses in print, and, not surprisingly, a word search in *EEBO* reveals pre-Shakespearian uses of "sullied." There are not many of them, however, and they date back only to the 1570s. Interestingly, the first citations in *EEBO* are all from translations of Calvin by Arthur Golding, translator of Ovid's *Metamorphoses*, one of Shakespeare's favorite books. In Golding's translation of the *Sermons on Job* (1574), humanity is described as "sullyed and full of all fylthe."[80] In the *Sermons on Ephesians*, Golding uses the word again, when Calvin writes that, if we give ourselves to God, we will "bee no more atteynted and sullied with the filthinesse of the worlde."[81] Another form of the word appears in a sermon on the Psalms: "Although the land were covered with solydnesse [i.e., "sulliedness"] throughe the troublous invasion of the enemies, yit... it recovered hir whiteness, so as it became as whyte as Snowe."[82] The relative merits of "solid" and "sullied" have been argued by Shakespeare's editors, but Golding's spelling of "solydnesse" indicates that even in print, let alone as delivered orally by an actor, the two words were sometimes indistinguishable, and that either might easily pun on the other. "Sullied" makes obvious sense in the context of Calvinist theology, in which all flesh is corrupt, but "solid" makes sense too, in the narrower context of Hamlet's image of solid flesh melting. But melting may take us back again to "sullied," if we have in mind Calvin's image of snow, white when new fallen, but increasingly dirty as it melts.

Though it digresses somewhat from the present focus on Genesis, a further comment about Calvin's influence on Hamlet's misogyny is warranted. As will be shown in a later chapter, Shakespeare read Golding's translation of Calvin's *Sermons on Job*, an extremely popular work (with six editions in only a decade). Given the strong verbal parallels, it seems hard to believe that he did not also read the *Sermons on Psalms*.[83] In addition, sermon 34 on Ephesians 5:3–5 offered Shakespeare background material for *Hamlet*. In the verses Calvin is explicating above, Paul fulminates against "fornication and all unclennes," "filthiness," and whoremongering.

---

[80] Calvin, *Sermons of Master John Calvin, upon the Booke of Job. Translated out of French by Arthur Golding* (London: [Henry Bynneman for] Lucas Harison and George Byshop, 1574), 188.

[81] Calvin, *Ephesians*, fo. 244ʳ.

[82] Calvin, *The Psalmes of David and others. With M. John Calvins Commentaries*, trans. Arthur Golding (London: [Thomas East and Henry Middleton: for Lucas Harison, and George Byshop], 1571), fo. 252ʳ.

[83] David C. Steinmetz notes that "Nowhere has Calvin's influence been more pervasive than in the English-speaking world." David C. Steinmetz, *Calvin in Context*, 2nd edn (Oxford and New York: Oxford University Press, 2010), 3. In addition to the editions of the *Sermons on Job*, he cites eleven editions of the *Institutes* (translated by Thomas Norton) by 1632.

A few lines before the "sullyed" passage from his Ephesians sermon (cited above), Calvin addresses the source of human corruption: "For what are we by nature? what is there in us? Even from our moothers womb wee bring nothing but disorder, wee bee cursed, we bee shaped in sine..." (fo. 244 ʳ⁻ᵛ). Calvin's own misogyny is even more intense earlier in the sermon, where he describes all women as "allurements of Satan," charging that, "if it be suffered, it cannot bee but the mayd must bee made a harlot, though shee were the honestest woman in the world" (fo. 241ᵛ). Hamlet's studies at Wittenberg are anachronistic, of course, but, if the Danish prince were to have studied at the Reformation university (at least from the 1550s on), he would have read Calvin. In fact, not only Hamlet's attitude to women but his specific language in conversation with Ophelia seems indebted to Calvin, as, for example, when the latter urges self-examination to avoid lust:

> let us take heede too our selves, and drive the enemie farre from us, and let us bee sure that where such lyghtnesse and leaudnesse have full scope, by and by there must needes bee a Brothelrie, or stewes set up, not in some one corner of a Citie or towne, but over all, so as no place shall bee cleane, as experience sheweth too much.[84]

While Hamlet tells Ophelia "get thee to a nunnery" (3.1.121), this also means, paradoxically, "get to a brothel."[85] Calvin's sermon on Ephesians suggests the difference between the two—nunnery and brothel—may be moot, if all the world is a brothel. Hamlet's remark here seems occasioned by his thinking that every mother, including his own, is a "breeder of sinners" (3.1.122); that is exactly the line of thought Calvin follows in his sermon. Hamlet thus plays one sense of nunnery against the other, essentially warning Ophelia that, if she does not get to a nunnery (a house of chaste virgins), she will end up in a nunnery (a brothel); in this view there is no difference between mother, wife, and whore.

Returning to the "solid/sullied" crux, a keyword search of *EEBO* reveals that only two other authors used the word "sullied" between Golding and Shakespeare—Richard Day (*A booke of Christian prayers*, 1578) and Edwin Sandys (*Sermons*, 1585). Golding's foundational Calvin translations may be the source of their usage as well, since they use "sullied" in the same biblical–theological context to refer specifically to either sinfulness or the state of the soul. That Shakespeare uses a form of the word ("sullies") a few scenes after the first soliloquy may be

---

[84] Calvin, *Ephesians*, fo. 243ʳ.
[85] On the various senses of "nunnery," see Harold Jenkins's long note in his Arden² *Hamlet*, 493–6.

significant, since Shakespeare often rings changes on certain keywords throughout his poems and plays. Finally, "sullied," with its theological senses of corruption and sinfulness, suits Hamlet's preoccupation in this soliloquy with the consequences of the Fall. Indeed, as a writer especially obsessed with words, Shakespeare may have had in mind that the etymology of "sullied" is derived from "soil" (both come from the French, *souiller*, and ultimately the Latin *solum*, "ground"). Adam is made out of dust and, after his sin, condemned both to earn his bread by tilling the earth and to return finally to the dust from which he came. Adam is sullied in manifold ways, all of which he has passed on to his heirs, including Hamlet.

The Fall is the theological explanation, then, for Hamlet's sullied flesh. However, a more immediate cause of his sulliedness is the flesh by means of which he inherited Adam's sin: Gertrude's. Like all women, she is a "breeder of sinners." Woman (Eve) was, after all, the reason the world is "an unweeded garden" in which things "rank and gross in nature | Possess it merely" (1.2.135–7). This garden is described as "rank and gross" not simply because it is untended but because in Nature itself "something is rotten." While Hamlet's garden metaphor applies to fallen Nature in the corrupt world, or more specifically Denmark, it also symbolizes his mother, the root of all his troubled meditations. The associative chain of his thoughts runs from his own sullied flesh to the unweeded garden to Gertrude as an avatar of Eve. Behind these connections lies not just the association of Eve with the Fall and Expulsion from the Garden; the garden was itself a metaphor for woman, and this notion was based on a traditional interpretation of the Bible.[86] Medieval images of the Virgin Mary often represented her within a walled, or enclosed garden, in Latin, a *hortus conclusus*. This was not just because such gardens were popular in the medieval world, as indeed they were in Shakespeare's London.[87] The enclosed garden symbolized Mary's virginity, an image derived from the description of the beloved in the Song of Solomon: "My sister my spouse is as a garden inclosed, as a spring shut up, and a fountaine sealed up" (4:12), or in the Vulgate, "*Hortus conclusus soror mea, sponsa, hortus con-*

---

[86] Compare also Northrop Frye's interpretation of Genesis 2–3 in which Adam is not alone before Eve's creation, but rather paired with the female Garden itself. Frye describes a "metaphorical identity between a paradisal environment and a female body, or, in Genesis, between Eden and Eve, a metaphor in which Eve is to Adam what the garden of Eden was to adam [i.e., simply the man, in the Hebrew, not the man named 'Adam'] preceding Eve" (*Words with Power: Being a Second Study of the Bible and Literature* [San Diego, New York, and London: Harcourt Brace Jovanovich, 1990], 195).

[87] See, e.g., C. Paul Christianson, *The Riverside Gardens of Thomas More's London* (New Haven and London: Yale University Press, 2005).

160   *Biblical Allusion in the Plays*

Fig. 4.2. The Virgin Mary with the infant Jesus in a hortus conclusus (walled or enclosed garden). The walled garden, as in the Song of Solomon 4:12, was a metaphor for virginity. (From the prayer book *Les Vingt quatre heures de la Passion*; Flemish, sixteenth century.) Princeton University Library.

clusus, fons signatus" (see Fig. 4.2).[88] The typological interpretation of this verse was complex: Protestants (as directed by the Geneva Bible marginalia) read the Song of Solomon as an allegory of Christ's marriage with the Church; Catholics (and some Protestants) read it in terms of God's "marriage" with the Virgin Mary as well. The verse's symbolism of virginity is obvious enough, but the garden simile also nicely suited the view of Mary as the antitype of Eve. What evil the seductive Eve did, the virginal Mary undid, by bearing Jesus Christ. One medieval carol playfully sings, *Ave fit ex Eva*—"Ave" (Gabriel's first word to Mary at the Annunciation) is made from "Eva"—what Mary makes (Jesus) unmakes what Eve made (sin).[89] So, if Eve brought humanity sin, corruption, and (as in Golding's Calvin)

---

[88] As Stanley Stewart points out, this passage from the Song of Solomon, or Song of Songs, was featured prominently in the Sarum liturgy for the feast of the Assumption of the Blessed Virgin, and was also part of the consecration of nuns (conceived of as a marriage with Christ) in the *Pontificale Romanum* (*The Enclosed Garden: The Tradition and the Image in Seventeenth-Century Poetry* [Madison: University of Wisconsin Press, 1966], 31).

[89] "Nova, nova: Ave fit ex Eva," in Greene (ed.), *Early English Carols*, 150–51.

"whoremongering," humanity was redeemed from these through the grace of a virgin, and in a garden no less.

Hamlet's world is utterly fallen, however, and remains subject to death and decay, as he observes in the graveyard scene, as the gravediggers simultaneously joke about holding "Adam's profession," since "Scripture says Adam digged" (5.1.33, 36). Hamlet's obsession with his mother's sexuality leads to his meditation upon a garden gone to seed, and Gertrude herself provides the associative links behind Hamlet's mental shifting from sullied flesh, to the unweeded garden, and to the name of woman. Gertrude is both Eve and the fallen garden itself, a "rank" garden that Hamlet perceives not as closed but all too open, a hortus non conclusus. Tellingly, the word "rank," which in the context of gardens or vegetation means "vigorous or luxuriant in growth," can also mean, applied to female animals, "in heat," as when Shylock speaks of Jacob's trick, with Laban's ewes "being rank" (*Merchant* 1.3.76; *OED* s.v. 6, 16).

In *Romeo and Juliet* Shakespeare exploits the association of the hortus conclusus with the Virgin Mary.[90] In Arthur Brooke's *Tragicall Historye of Romeus and Juliet* (1562), Shakespeare's principal source, Romeo meets Juliet at the Capulet Ball. Then the young lovers rendezvous by Juliet's house. A conveniently located "garden plot" discovered by Romeus enables him to approach his beloved's window.[91] However, in Shakespeare's version, the garden is explicitly surrounded by a wall, a point emphasized repeatedly. For instance, Benvolio notes that Romeo "ran this way and leapt this orchard wall" (2.1.6). Juliet later asks Romeo how he got on to the property, since the "orchard walls are high and hard to climb" (2.1.106). Romeo responds that "with love's light wings did I o'erperch these walls" (2.1.109). The point of Shakespeare's re-landscaping of the garden scene is that this garden is a hortus conclusus, enclosing Juliet in her virginal state. Shakespeare also notably converts the "garden" into an orchard, and this feature too is emphasized. Benvolio and Juliet both describe it as an "orchard," not just a garden, and Romeo later attempts to swear by the moon "that tips with silver all these fruit-tree tops" (2.1.151). (The moon, the sphere of Cynthia or Diana in classical myth, is also a symbol of virginity.)

The Capulet orchard is potentially "death" to Romeo (2.1.107). Literally, this is because there are Capulets close by with rapiers, but allusively

---

[90] To this play might be added *Twelfth Night*, when Olivia asks that the garden door be shut on her interview with Viola/Cesario, and, according to Helen Ostovich, in the garden scene in *Richard II*. For the latter, see "'Here in this garden': The Iconography of the Virgin Queen in Shakespeare's *Richard II*," in Regina Buccola and Lisa Hopkins (eds), *Marian Moments in Early Modern British Drama* (Aldershot: Ashgate, 2007), 21–34.

[91] l. 451, in Bullough, i. 297.

this mortal danger may also reinforce the associations of this garden with Eden: the latter is guarded by the cherubim with flaming sword after Adam and Eve are expelled, and their sin brings death into the world. But the primary threat in this scene is not to Romeo but to Juliet. It is her walled orchard-garden into which Romeo has intruded, and Romeo's further designs physically threaten Juliet's biological *hortus conclusus*, her virginity. Robert Watson and Stephen Dickey have pointed out the pervasive suggestion of rape in *Romeo and Juliet*, in the play's many allusions to classical rapists: Tereu, Hades, Tarquin, and Paris.[92] The love of Romeo and Juliet has typically been read as genuine and true, however rash and unlucky. Yet Watson and Dickey show that there is a strong undercurrent suggesting a darker reading. In the balcony scene, for instance, Juliet's alarmed, naive response to Romeo's complaint that he is left unsatisfied— "What satisfaction canst thou have tonight?" (2.1.169)—reflects the real vulnerability of her situation, a 13-year-old girl surprised by an intruder at her bedroom window. After Romeo and Juliet do consummate their love, Juliet's attempt to persuade Romeo that it is the nightingale, not the lark, that they hear adds a disturbing suggestion that he might be abandoning her after achieving his desires, because readers of Ovid would hear in this nightingale the mournful echo of Philomela, transformed into the bird after being raped by her brother-in-law Tereu. Watson and Dickey point out further that the tree in which Juliet describes the nightingale singing—the pomegranate—was associated with another Ovidian rape victim, Prosperpina, since it was the eating of pomegranate seeds that resulted in her having to spend half the year in the Underworld with Hades, her rapist–husband. None of the Ovidian allusions in the play are happy ones for Juliet. A further allusion to Ovid points, also unhappily, to Romeo as a Narcissus: Juliet calls him back to her balcony in 2.1, saying that, if she was not constrained to whisper, she would "tear the cave where Echo lies" (2.1.207), in other words she would shout so loudly that the echoes would shatter the cave in which the mythical Echo herself lives. In Ovid, however, the nymph Echo loves Narcissus but is ignored by him, since he loves only himself. He dies trying to embrace his own reflection in a pool, and she pines away into a disembodied voice.

The Ovidian allusions are reinforced by the biblical ones. For instance, Romeo climbs over the wall into the forbidden Capulet garden, but the allusions to Genesis represent this as, in a sexual sense, a re-enactment of original sin. The typological connection between the enclosed garden of

---

[92] Robert N. Watson and Stephen Dickey, "Wherefore Art Thou Tereu? Juliet and the Legacy of Rape," *RQ* 58 (2005), 127–56.

Eden (the word "paradise" in Latin, Greek, and ultimately Persian means a "walled garden") and the hortus conclusus ("garden enclosed") of the Song of Solomon encourages the disturbing thought that Romeo intends not just a violation of the Capulet's property but a violation of Juliet's virginity. Of course, he does intend this, and he achieves it later, though when it finally occurs it is not as a rape but as the consummation of holy matrimony, however secretive.

The allusions to the Fall and the hortus conclusus may also signify in tandem with the especially "rank and gross" language of Mercutio with which Shakespeare frames the garden scene. Though not the first to recognize them, Jonathan Goldberg has drawn attention to the visceral references to sex, genitalia, and the anus in the preamble to the garden scene.[93] Interestingly, several of the prominent puns are about fruit: the medlar, an apple-like fruit, which for Elizabethans was also slang for the vagina (further echoed in Mercutio's repeated "O"s) and which was also called by some the "open-arse"; and the "popp'rin pear," which apparently looked something like a penis and also supposedly punned on "pop her (i.e., the penis) in" (2.1.35–9). The identification of the "knowledge" of the forbidden fruit with carnal knowledge was traditional, and partly embedded in the Genesis text itself (awareness of the Hebrew wordplay connecting the "knowledge" of good and evil with Adam and Eve's first postlapsarian sex was what led English Bible translators to the utterly non-idiomatic "the man *knewe* Hevah his wife," Gen. 4:1).[94] Mercutio's bawdy puns confirm the sexual potential lurking in fruit, but they also serve as a critique of Romeo's idealized Petrarchan love language from earlier scenes. Indeed, Mercutio is explicit in his contempt for such talk:

> Romeo! Humours! Madman! Passion! Lover!
> Appear thou in the likeness of a sigh;
> Speak but one rhyme and I am satisfied.
> Cry but "Ay me," pronounce but "love" and "dove"... (2.1.11)

For Mercutio, love is just a contemptible mystification of sex.

But Mercutio's is not the only critique of Romantic love available. Petrarch himself was aware of its limits. The lyric sequence that began the European sonnet-craze, Petrarch's *Rime sparse*, closes by turning away from earthly desire—Petrarch's Laura, after all, is dead long since—toward

---

[93] Jonathan Goldberg, "Romeo and Juliet's Open Rs," in *Shakespeare's Hand* (Minneapolis: University of Minnesota Press, 2003), 271–85.

[94] Emphasis added. The same Hebrew root is used for the "knowledge" of Good and Evil and the verb expressing the first sexual act after the Fall, which the English translators render as "knew."

the chaste and divine love of the Virgin Mary.[95] In "*Vergine bella*," Petrarch addresses the Virgin, "clothed with the sun and crowned with stars," the "noble window of Heaven," the "star of this tempestuous sea," to "bend now to my prayer" and give him peace.[96] Romeo, having climbed over the wall of the hortus conclusus, sees the light cast by Juliet's open window, a light that is "the east, and Juliet is the sun." Although Goldberg suggests that Romeo's call to Juliet to "Arise, fair sun, and kill the envious moon" marks a shift from female (moon) to male (sun), the sun here is surely female, in its association with the Virgin Mary, identified with "woman clothed with the sunne" in Revelation 12:1, who also has "the moon...under her feete, and upon her head a crowne of twelve stars" (see Fig. 4.3).[97]

Juliet's eyes are "two of the fairest stars in all the heaven," in Romeo's enraptured hymn to "her eye in heaven" (2.1.58–65). Juliet is also a "saint," and Romeo even calls her "my lady," a phrase ordinarily commonplace but rather charged in the context of other allusions to the Virgin (2.1.69, 98, 53). This idolatrous language is already familiar from the first meeting of the young lovers, with their wordplay on pilgrimage and prayer, but the focus here is specifically on Juliet as a figure of the Virgin, even though later in the scene Juliet calls Romeo the "god of my idolatry" (2.1.157).[98] The point to be taken, as in so many of Shakespeare's biblical allusions, is not a religious one, certainly not a veiled celebration of Catholic devotion (which could hardly be directed to an ordinary young Italian girl, and could not safely be directed anywhere in Protestant England). The allusions serve instead, for those who recognize them, to highlight Juliet's virginal innocence, threatened by Romeo's intrusion into the walled garden, especially if the "love" he feels is like the raw sexual desire described by his friend Mercutio.

---

[95] On Shakespeare's reading of Italian, see William Kennedy, *The Site of Petrarchism: Early Modern National Sentiment in Italy, France, and England* (Baltimore: Johns Hopkins University Press, 2003), and Robert S. Miola, *Shakespeare's Reading* (Oxford and New York: Oxford University Press, 2000).

[96] *Petrarch's Lyric Poems: The* Rime sparse *and Other Lyrics*, trans. and ed. Robert M. Durling (Cambridge, MA: Harvard University Press, 1976), 574, 576, 580, 574.

[97] The Geneva editors again, as in the Song of Solomon, attempt to interpret this verse as an image of the Church, but the traditional Marian interpretation had been familiar for centuries, not least in countless images of the Virgin Mary with the sliver of a moon under her feet.

[98] Of course, for Juliet to call her lover a god might be symbolically appropriate, if blasphemous, since it is in some mysterious sense God who "impregnates" Mary in the Annunciation story. On the other hand, Juliet's language may simply reflect what Paul N. Siegel calls the religion of love. Paul N. Siegel, "Christianity and the Religion of Love in *Romeo and Juliet*," *SQ* 12/4 (1961), 371–92.

Fig. 4.3. The Virgin Mary is portrayed as the "woman clothed with the sunne" who has "the moon under her feete, and upon her head a crowne of twelve stars" described in Revelation 12:1. (From *The Life of the Virgin*; Albrecht Dürer, *c.*1511.) © Sterling and Francine Clark Art Institute, Williamstown, Massachusetts, USA. Photo by Michael Agee.

If Romeo represents a sexual threat to Juliet, on whatever level, another set of allusions suggests that she can hold her own. Despite Juliet's youth and inexperience, for instance, she seems consistently in the superior, more emotionally mature position in the encounters between the two lovers. Furthermore, in the balcony scene Juliet is not the only one to be represented as the Virgin Mary; ironically, Romeo briefly plays the part as well. He remarks that Juliet is a "bright angel"

> As glorious to this night, being o'er my head,
> As is a winged messenger of heaven
> Unto the white upturned wond'ring eyes
> Of mortals that fall back to gaze on him
> When he bestrides the lazy puffing clouds
> And sails upon the bosom of the air. (2.1.69–75)

This might be called an epic simile, since it describes a divine messenger's descent from heaven, like those conventional to Homer, Virgil, Ariosto, and others.[99] Yet, while in classical epic the descending figure is most often female (Iris, Athena, Thetis), the angel in Romeo's extended simile is a "he," and in the context of the other allusions to the Virgin the logical identity of the "winged messenger" is Gabriel (the Hebrew word translated in sixteenth-century Bibles as "angel" means "messenger"). Romeo's description then constitutes a bizarre parody of the Annunciation. The twist is that, despite Romeo's masculine pronoun, he is describing Juliet, who thus plays Gabriel to his Virgin Mary. Another further twist, perhaps confirming the speech's complication of gender roles, is that here it is Romeo, with the "upturned wond'ring eyes," who "falls back" submissively, just as the toddler Juliet did in the Nurse's description of her. Who, we might ask, is really on top in this play? Both, it seems, and neither, which is perhaps a positive sign that there is something genuinely reciprocal about this relationship. The love of Romeo and Juliet somehow transcends the darker implications of both the biblical and classical allusions. Jonathan Bate describes Shakespeare's allusions to Ovid in 2.1 as "dialectical imitations" (Thomas Greene's term) that transume their original context. He argues that Juliet is no passive figure of Echo, for instance, but rather "becomes her own Echo, symbolically liberating both herself and her mythical antetype":[100]

> Bondage is hoarse, and may not speak aloud,
> Else would I tear the cave where Echo lies,
> And make her airy tongue more hoarse than mine
> With repetition of my Romeo's name. Romeo!" (2.1.205–8)

The gender of pronouns is significant here, as it is in Romeo's "Annunciation" image; "Romeo" is, as Juliet asserts, "*my* Romeo's name," just as he is at the end of the play "*her* Romeo." She may ultimately stab herself like Lucrece, yet Juliet has not been raped but married, and she dies not to rid her family of shame but to join her husband.

The play ends in a very different enclosed and tree-filled plot, the churchyard with its yew trees around the Capulet tomb. The world is a fallen one after all—as Donne later put it, "this whole world is but an universal churchyard, but our common grave"—in which love and death are inextricably intertwined.[101] Hence Paris's "love in death," Romeo's

---

[99] Thomas M. Greene, *The Descent from Heaven: A Study in Epic Continuity* (New Haven and London: Yale University Press, 1963).
[100] Bate, *Shakespeare and Ovid*, 180.
[101] John Donne, "Death's Duell," in *Devotions upon Emergent Occasions together with Death's Duell* (Ann Arbor: University of Michigan Press, 1959), 171.

"womb of death," and Juliet who is "married to her grave," claimed, like Prosperina, by the "amorous Death" (4.4.84, 5.3.45, 3.5.139). In Romeo and Juliet's brief marriage, perhaps we do have at least a fleeting vision of what it would be like to get back to the garden, but the vision proves a fantasy.

ROMANCE

When Shakespeare returned to comedy late in his career, in that peculiar hybrid genre known as tragicomedy or Romance, he continued to rework allusions to Genesis, but these plays convey a sense of hope for some kind of redemptive return to the garden. *Pericles* begins with a contest: to win the princess, the prince must answer a riddle posed by the king, at peril of his life. Such dangers are conventional in Shakespearian comedy—we remember the Athenian law of *A Midsummer Night's Dream*, borrowed from Terence and Plautus—but in this case the plot takes a shockingly dark turn. The answer to the riddle reveals that the princess is in an incestuous relationship with her father, leaving Pericles with the equally unpleasant options of either answering the riddle and winning a debauched bride or refusing to answer and losing his life. Of course, since the answer would expose the crime of the king, Pericles would probably be executed in any case. The complexities of Pericles's dilemma are expressed partly through an allusion to a garden. On seeing the princess, Pericles expresses his "inflamed desire" to "taste the fruit of yon celestial tree | Or die in the adventure" (1.1.21–2). Antiochus responds with a similar reference to plucking fruit:

> Before thee stands this fair Hesperides,
> With gold fruit, but dangerous to be touched,
> For death-like dragons here affright thee hard. (1.1.28–30)

The classical allusion to the Garden of the Hesperides is appropriate to the ancient Mediterranean setting. It is natural for both Pericles and Antiochus to know the famous story of Hercules's labor of taking one of the golden apples of the daughters of Hesperus, guarded by a dragon.[102]

---

[102] Suzanne Gossett's note in the Arden³ *Pericles* states that "Shakespeare thought the Hesperides was the name of the garden," rather than that of the daughters of Hesperus, but this was a commonplace in the Renaissance. In *Love's Labour's Lost*, Shakespeare again confused the garden and its owners, with Holofernes declaring that "For valour, is not Love a Hercules, | Still climbing trees in the Hesperides?" (4.3.314–15). In *Friar Bacon and Friar Bungay*, Shakespeare's (would-be) rival Robert Greene wrote of "the fearful dragon... | That watched the garden called Hesperides, | Subdued and won by conquering Hercules."

The story of Hercules and the Hesperides was familiar, but, as a story of forbidden fruit, guarded by a dragon, and associated with women, it would also have been understood by the syncretic-minded Jacobeans as a pagan cognate of the Genesis story, like Ovid's Golden Age discussed above. The same cross-cultural association led Samuel Nicholson to link the stories in his *Acolastus* (1600), which describes the topsy-turvey wickedness of the city, in which

> Leacherie and Lucar strike a match,
> Making a compound of two deadly sinnes;
> And or'e the Hesperian fruite like dragons watch,
> Or as the Eden-keeping Cherubims;...[103]

Jeremy Taylor, in a popular sermon later in the century, urged readers of Scripture to "allow the literal sense" as well as the spiritual, otherwise "the Garden of *Eden* shall be no more then the *Hesperides*," presumably in that it would be rendered nothing more than a symbolic tale.[104] A few decades later the clergyman John Edwards argued that Eden actually "seems to be represented by the famous Garden of the Hesperides."[105] In *The Painfull Adventures of Pericles Prince of Tyre*, published shortly after the play by George Wilkins, Shakespeare's probable collaborator, the Hesperides myth is not mentioned by name, so references to Antiochus as one who "by stealth hath filched a taste from foorth a goodly Orchard" and as not being "satisfied with the fruite obtained by his former desire," and to his daughter being left like a "weeping braunch to wither by the stocke that brought her foorth," allude to the Genesis story without classical mediation.[106]

Thus, Shakespeare's allusion refers specifically to the Hesperides, but the comparison of the desired woman to dangerous fruit on a "celestial tree" evokes the biblical context as well. The "death-like dragons" are similarly ambivalent, alluding, on the one hand, to the dragon Hercules had

---

Robert Greene, *The honorable historie of frier Bacon, and frier Bongay* (London: [Adam Islip] for Edward White, 1594), sig. E4ʳ. Even the learned Thomas Elyot and Thomas Cooper made this conflation of place and persons, so "Hesperides" seems to have named both the daughters and their garden. But the reference in *Pericles* is actually more subtle, since it is both an allusion and a metaphor. The daughter of Antiochus is herself metaphorically the Hesperides, the garden with the golden fruit (her virginity?), but, since she is also a daughter, the metaphor in a sense restores the name to its proper designee, referring to both person and place at once.

[103] Samuel Nicholson, *Acolastus* (London: John Baylie, 1600), sig. H3ᵛ.

[104] Jeremy Taylor, *Dekas embolimaios* (London: R. Royston, 1667), 195, reprinted in several editions of the next decade.

[105] John Edwards, *A Discourse concerning the authority, stile, and perfection of the books of the Old and New-Testament* (London: Richard Wilkin, 1693), 115.

[106] Bullough, vi. 496–7.

to overcome, and, on the other, to the serpent (interpreted as Satan, the great dragon of Rev. 12:9), as well as recalling the punishment for eating the forbidden fruit: death. After realizing the truth of the father–daughter relationship, Pericles calls both of them "serpents" (1.1.133). If Shakespeare had been reading Robert Greene's bestselling *A Quip for an upstart Courtier* (six editions in 1592 alone), he might have found inspiration for this conflation of images and allusions in the misogynistic description of "a troupe of nice wantons, faire women that like to *Lamiæ* had faces like Angels, eies like stars, brestes like the golden frout in the Hesperides, but from the middle downwards their shapes like serpents."[107] Might Antiochus's daughter, then, be both the forbidden fruit and the dragon guarding it? Greene may himself have been indebted to Spenser's Errour,

> Halfe like a serpent horribly displaide,
> But th'other halfe did womans shape retaine,
> Most lothsom, filthie, foule, and full of vile disdaine.[108]

In Spenser, the creature combines woman and serpent, alluding to Genesis and placing the blame for the "original" error clearly with Eve. Greene makes a similar, symbolic point, while adding another allusive layer to the myth of the Hesperides. Shakespeare interweaves the elements of both the classical and the biblical stories and further complicates the monstrous figure.[109]

The final restoration of Pericles to his wife and child is miraculous, but the prevailing miracle is a resurrection not a return to Eden.[110] *Cymbeline* has a different kind of resolution that similarly depends in part on an allusion to Genesis. Posthumus says to Innogen, "Hang there like fruit, my soul, | Till the tree die" (5.5.263–4). Tennyson remarked that these were "among the tenderest lines in Shakespeare," and most editors add no interpretative gloss, though it seems hardly commonplace that Posthumus should represent himself as a tree and Innogen as both his soul and something fruitlike.[111] Martin Butler explains the lines with a reference to the

---

[107] Greene, *A quip for an upstart Courtier*, sig. A4ʳ. In the original, "front" is an obvious typo for "frout (fruit)."
[108] Spenser, *Faerie Queene*, 1.1.14, ll. 7–9.
[109] He returns to such a figure in *King Lear*, in Lear's "Down to the waist they're centaurs, | Though women all above. | But to the girdle do the gods inherit; | Beneath is all the fiend's" (4.5.120–3).
[110] Interestingly, although the possibility of a return to Eden may be a borrowing from classical myth, the Resurrection of Christ is linked typologically to Eden in John's Gospel: Christ's first post-Resurrection appearance in a garden and his being mistaken by Mary for the gardener. As the type of Adam, Christ has taken Adam's place.
[111] Tennyson is quoted in the note to the Arden³ *Pericles*, ed. Suzanne Gossett (London: Thomson Learning, 2004).

emblem of an elm wrapped about with a vine found in Geoffrey Whitney's *A Choice of Emblems* and other emblem books.[112] As Butler notes, even though Whitney's emblem symbolizes *amicitia*, citing Ovid on the friendship of Orestes and Pylades, Jonson and Milton both use the emblem "to betoken a good marriage." Shakespeare himself alludes to this emblem in *A Midsummer Night's Dream*:

> So doth the woodbine the sweet honeysuckle
> Gently entwist; the female ivy so
> Enrings the barky fingers of the elm. (4.1.41–3)

Yet the image in *Cymbeline* is actually quite different, involving not a vine wrapping round a tree, but a piece of fruit hanging on it. The obvious referent is a fruit tree rather than a grape vine growing on an elm, as in Whitney.[113] And, given the context in *Cymbeline* of love and marriage, the betrayal and renewal of vows, the specific fruit tree described by Posthumus is surely, although he is unconscious of it, identified with the one in Genesis that started all the trouble between men and women.

Cymbeline's addressing of Innogen in the next line as "my flesh, my child" reinforces this context, evoking the language of the first marriage: Adam calls Eve "flesh of my flesh" and announces that "man shal leave his father and his mother, and shal cleave to his wife, and they shalbe one flesh" (Gen. 2:23–4). Cymbeline's remark is gently ironic, reminding us that his flesh will now become Posthumus's (and Posthumus's Innogen's). In Posthumus's dream-vision, his dead brother praises him, asking where any is that could "stand up his parallel, or *fruitful* object be | In eye of Innogen" (5.3.137–8, emphasis added). When Posthumous tells Innogen to "hang there like fruit," the audience might also remember Belarius's account to his "sons" that in his days of prosperity he was "a tree | Whose boughs did bend with fruit" (3.3.60–1), an image deriving from Psalm 1's description of the blessed man who "shalbe lyke a tre planted by the watersyde, that wyll brynge forth hys frute in due season. His leafe also shall not wither" (Ps. 1:3). But Belarius does wither; his "mellow hangings, nay, my leaves" are stripped not by winter but by the "storm or robbery" of court slander (3.3.63, 62). Posthumus also ceases to be fruitful, but the fault is his own for trusting Iachimo and for putting his wife to a shameful test. Though necessarily unconscious of her own (anachronistic) biblical allusions, Innogen describes Posthumus's degeneracy in terms of Genesis, as a "great fall," which, like Adam's, will "lay the leaven on all proper men" (3.4.60–2).

---

[112] Butler is cited in the note to the Cambridge *Pericles*.
[113] Caroline Spurgeon, *Shakespeare's Imagery and What It Tells Us* (New York: Macmillan; Cambridge: Cambridge University Press, 1936), 292–93.

There is a specific biblical allusion in these lines to 1 Corinthians 5:6—"know ye not that a litle leaven, leaveneth the whole lump?"—as well as a general allusion to original sin. Posthumus's restoration to fruitfulness "in eye of Innogen" (as his brother puts it) coincides with his wish for her to "hang there like fruit." In other words, if the rift between man and woman resulted from the plucking of the forbidden fruit from the tree, then the restoration of marital union can be represented symbolically by the reattachment of fruit to tree, as in Posthumus's metaphor for embracing Innogen.

To call Innogen the fruit to Posthumus's tree might seem patriarchal. But the fruit-tree image seems to be gender equal, given the remark of Posthumus's brother that he is the "fruitful object" of Innogen's eye. Probing even further, might Shakespeare have picked up a copy of Augustine's *City of God*, first translated into English just as *Cymbeline* was being written (1610)? There he could have read Augustine's meditation on Matthew 7:17–18 ("So everie good tre bringeth forthe good frute, and a corrupt tre bringeth forthe evel frute. A good tre can not bring forthe evil frute: nether can a corrupt tre bring forthe good frute").[114] Augustine argues:

> So then God made man, upright, and consequently well-willed: otherwise he could not have beene upright. So that this good will, was Gods worke, man being there-with created. But the evill will, which was in man before his evill worke, was rather a fayling from the worke of God to [their] owne workes, then any worke at all. And therefore were the workes evill, because they were according to themselves, and not to God, this euill will being as a tree bearing such bad fruite, or man himselfe, in respect of his evill will.[115]

Turning back to the metaphor of tree and fruit as applied to Innogen and Posthumous with the verses from Matthew in mind, it may not matter which partner is tree or fruit; evil in one will naturally affect the other, and good in either requires good in both. Yet it is clear in the play that Posthumus has betrayed Innogen, not the other way around. Augustine's elaboration of Matthew offers one possible reading of Posthumus's metaphor: Posthumus's evil will is the tree that bears the evil fruit that nearly results in Innogen's death; the fruit of his restored, good will is (for him) Innogen herself or (for both) a fruitful marriage. The mutual embrace of Posthumous and Innogen, tree and fruit, marks a symbolic undoing of sin and a sense of return to the garden before the fruit was plucked.

The Winter's Tale is preoccupied with the Genesis story perhaps more than any of Shakespeare's plays and is the culmination of his career-long

---

[114] As mentioned above, Touchstone alludes to these verses from Matthew in *As You Like It*, 3.2.113.
[115] St Augustine, *Of the Citie of God*, trans. J.H. (London: George Eld, 1610), 512.

exploration through allusion of the implications of the Fall.[116] The first suggestion of a biblical subtext comes in the theologically charged conversation of Hermione and Polixenes regarding the latter's childhood with Leontes. It is represented as timeless: "Two lads that thought there was no more behind | But such a day tomorrow as today, | And to be boy eternal" (1.2.62–4). It was also innocent:

> We were as twinned lambs that did frisk i'th'sun,
> And bleat the one at th'other; what we changed
> Was innocence for innocence—we knew not
> The doctrine of ill-doing, nor dreamed
> That any did. Had we pursued that life,
> And our weak spirits ne'er been higher reared
> With stronger blood, we should have answered heaven
> Boldly, "not guilty," the imposition cleared
> Hereditary ours. (1.2.66–74)

The "doctrine of ill-doing" and the "imposition" of "hereditary" guilt refer to original sin, from which Polixenes imagines himself and his childhood friend to have been free in their state of innocence. The "Fall" came, it seems, when the boys encountered women, since Polixenes says that in the earlier "unfledged days was my wife a girl," and Hermione had not yet "crossed the eyes" of Leontes (1.2.77–8). Hermione responds to Polixenes's playful misogyny with a phrase that confirms the relevance of Genesis: she interrupts him, she says, before he can say that his "queen and I are devils" (1.2.80–1). The biblically rooted language of misogyny is familiar from *Love's Labour's Lost*, and we know from that play both that sin is hardly the exclusive fault of women and that paradise is not to be found in an all-male world. Any Protestant theologian would have pointed out that even children, of both sexes, are guilty of original sin.

Sure enough, the real fall comes with the onset of Leontes's inexplicable and characteristically masculine jealousy. His fall is accompanied by the play's first specific verbal allusion to Genesis 3. Leontes claims to Hermione that, in looking on Mamillius, he has seen his own childhood:

> Looking on the lines
> Of my boy's face, methoughts I did recoil
> Twenty-three years, and saw myself unbreeched,
> In my green velvet coat, my dagger muzzled

---

[116] One might argue that *The Tempest* concerns returning to the garden, as represented by Prospero's island and mediated by thinking about Genesis in response to contemporary discoveries of "brave new worlds" overseas. Shakespeare's exploration of Genesis in *The Tempest* is thematic rather than involving specific allusions, however, so it properly lies beyond the scope of this study.

Lest it should bite its master and so prove,
As ornaments oft do, too dangerous. (1.2.152–7)

"Unbreeched," meaning too young to wear a man's breeches ("breeching" in the period marked the passage from boy to man), is also a subtle allusion to Genesis 3:7, in which, according to a famous passage in the Geneva Bible translation, Adam and Eve realize they are naked and "made themselves breeches."[117] Just as Polixenes did, Leontes imagines a prelapsarian boyhood, not just before he wore breeches, but one of innocence before wearing them was necessary.[118] (His "dagger muzzled" might then be read in proto-Freudian terms as his prepubescent penis, linking individual sexual development to sin and the Fall.) Of course, the fact that, even if "unbreeched" (in the biblical sense), Leontes is nevertheless wearing his "green velvet coat" suggests there is something askew with his paradisal recollection. Indeed, if one has the Genesis story in mind, the color of the coat might suggest the fig leaves donned by Adam and Eve after their sin. Furthermore, Leontes has been reading Mamillius's face for signs of resemblance to his own, not because he is thinking wistfully of his own childhood, but because he suspects his wife of adultery.

Hermione goes off with Polixenes, telling Leontes, "If you would seek us, | We are yours i'th'garden" (1.2.175–6), providing the prototypical biblical setting for all falls, real or imagined. Even Leontes's bitter comment to Mamillius that Hermione plays "so disgraced a part, whose issue | Will hiss me to my grave" may have biblical resonance, if we hear in this mortal hissing the sound of the serpent (1.2.186–7). (Similarly, the "forked one" Leontes refers to could be read as the deceitful serpent's tongue as well as Leontes's own cuckhold's horns; the more passionate he gets, the more ambiguous, even convoluted, his language becomes, 1.2.184.) Polixenes observes that

> The King hath on him such a countenance
> As he had lost some province, and a region
> Loved as he loves he himself. (1.2.364–6)

That this lost province is a kind of lost Eden is supported by Leontes's own complaint that he would rather remain ignorant of his cuckoldry, "Alack for lesser knowledge!" (2.1.38). Also, Antigonus's protest that "every dram of woman's flesh, is false | If she be" is a misogynistic comment Hamlet would have readily comprehended (2.1.138–9). Shakespeare's plot plunges into a rapid succession of crises, as Hermione is imprisoned,

---

[117] For this reason, the Geneva translation became popularly known among book collectors as the "Breeches Bible."
[118] For a stranger allusion to Adam and Eve's "breeches" in *Macbeth*, see Ch. 7.

gives birth, is tried, and seemingly dies, her infant is given to Antigonus to dispose of, the Oracle of Apollo pronounces Hermione innocent and wronged, and Antigonus and his crew, after leaving the baby in Sicily, are respectively eaten by a bear and drowned. After sixteen years, the story recommences in the green-world of pastoral.

Much ink has been spilled over Shakespeare's violation of Aristotelian unities in *The Winter's Tale*, and of the problematic relationship between the two parts of the play, one in the dark, winter world of the Bohemian court, the other in the rural summer of Sicilia many years later. One link between these worlds may be found in the common application of the Genesis story to ideas about procreation and childbirth, and about gardening. As Mary Fissell observes, "the central narrative about reproduction in late medieval England was a sacred one: the story of Mary's miraculous conception of Christ."[119] Interestingly, popular retellings of the Nativity, like those in the pageant plays connected with York and Coventry, featured a jealous Joseph initially unwilling to accept his wife's explanation for her pregnancy.[120] Of course, Joseph's doubts are more reasonable than Leontes's, since Mary claims to be a pregnant virgin; Hermione has already had one son, so, unlike Mary and Joseph, she and Leontes have consummated their marriage. Fissell further argues that "writings about the mechanics of conception and pregnancy had religious connotations in England in the 1540s," but that, with the advent of Protestantism, "women were to connect their suffering in childbirth not with the Virgin Mary but with Eve."[121] In a prayer in Thomas Raynalde's *A Newe Boke* (1548), women acknowledged the justice of their pain in childbirth as punishment for Eve's "original transgression," expressed by God himself in Genesis 3:13.[122] Since in early modern England (and Europe) childbirth recalled Eve's sin, Leontes's misogyny has precedent.

It was also standard terminology in early modern medical texts to refer to the fetus as a "fruit," a practice in English that originates in Bible translations as an attempt to render in English a Hebraic idiom (as in "the

---

[119] Mary E. Fissell, "The Politics of Reproduction in the English Reformation," *Representations*, 87 (2004), 43–81, 44.
[120] Chester N. Scoville, *Saints and the Audience in Middle English Biblical Drama* (Toronto: University of Toronto Press, 2004), ch. 4, "Joseph, Pathos, and the Audience."
[121] Fissell, "Politics of Reproduction," 66.
[122] Fissell, "Politics of Reproduction," 66, quoting Thomas Raynalde, *A Newe Boke, Conteyninge an Exhortacio[n] to the Sycke. The Sycke Mans Prayer. A Prayer With Thankes, at the Purification of Women. A Consolacion at Buryall* ([London], [1548]). Raynalde was the publisher of the most popular book on childbirth in the period, *The byrth of mankynde, otherwyse named the womans booke* (1545), translated by Richard Jonas from a German text of 1513.

fruite of the wombe," Gen. 30:2 and elsewhere).[123] Thus, when Hermione laments being separated from Mamillius, the "first-fruits of my body" (3.2.95), the metaphor is not only a complex biblical allusion but the technical language of obstetrics. Hermione's allusion is specifically to the phrase "first-fruits," as an agricultural term in the Old Testament for the first crops of harvest, which were offered to God (as Lev. 2:12). More generally, however, the reference to a child as a fruit evokes the context of Genesis 3. Only after the Fall did Eve bear a child, the very "first" fruit of all, and by some interpretations actually one of the "fruits" (consequences) of original sin. There is an additional biblical reference to "first frutes" that may be important for *The Winter's Tale*. In his First Epistle to the Corinthians Paul writes that "now is Christ risen from the dead, and was made the first frutes of them that slept" (1 Cor. 15:20). Paul is explaining not only that Christ has been resurrected but the importance of that Resurrection for everyone else. As the Geneva gloss puts it: "As by the offring of the first frute the whole frute is sanctified, so by Christ which is the first that is raised, all have assurance of resurrection." Indeed, *The Winter's Tale* ends with Hermione's seeming resurrection. One might argue that Hermione is not resurrected but simply revealed to be alive. Nevertheless, this revelation is powerfully restorative, for Leontes, for his family (now extended by marriage into that of Polixenes), and for his kingdom. All are resurrected, all are reborn (except Mamillius and Antigonus, whose permanent deaths mark the play as a tragicomedy). The theatrical experience of this renewal is dramatically enhanced by allusions to the Resurrection and rebirth that Shakespeare's audience best knew.[124]

The pastoral world of Acts 4 and 5 does not allude to Genesis specifically, but the debate between Perdita and Polixenes (disguised) about grafting flowers evokes the same biblical context as Leontes's bitter musings on sex and children. Perdita disdains carnations and gillyvors as "nature's bastards," the product of artificial cultivation (4.4.82). Polixenes responds that "art itself is nature," or at least that art mends nature's defects (4.4.97). As for gillyvors, he says, "do not call them bastards" (4.4.99). Their discussion is obviously about more than flowers. For one thing, we have already seen that the consequences of bastardy can be severe, since Perdita herself was judged a bastard and condemned to die

---

[123] On this usage in European medical texts, see Kathleen Crowther-Heyck, "'Be Fruitful and Multiply': Genesis and Generation in Reformation Germany," *RQ* 55/3 (2002), 904–35.

[124] These are intertwined, of course, with the great metamorphosis of the Pygmalion story in Ovid, as Jonathan Bate, Leonard Barkan and others have pointed out. Bate, *Shakespeare and Ovid*, 234–8. Barkan, *The Gods Made Flesh: Metamorphosis and the Pursuit of Paganism* (New Haven and London: Yale University Press, 1990), 283–7.

for it. For another, the art versus nature debate has implications for the socially transgressive love of Perdita and Florizell. Polixenes seems unaware of these implications, since he makes an argument that appears to justify the marriage he is soon to reject:

> You see, sweet maid, we marry
> A gentler scion to the wildest stock,
> And make conceive a bark of baser kind
> By bud of nobler race. (4.4.92–5)

Perdita seems oblivious to the obvious implications too, since she is the "wilder stock" who desires to marry the "gentler scion." Or does Polixenes know what he is doing: is he testing both Perdita's cleverness as well as her designs upon his son? In any case, the question of superior breeding ultimately proves moot (as so often in Renaissance pastoral), since the country maid proves to be a long-lost princess, gentle after all.

Clearly there are implications for human interrelations, marriage, and breeding lurking behind the discussion of gardening. But this is not surprising, since early modern discussions of procreation and childbirth were often couched in the language of agriculture (as in the use of "fruit" mentioned above).[125] Furthermore, like books on childbirth, books on gardening commonly featured references to the original Garden, similar to Bacon's with which this chapter began. In *The Gardeners Labyrinth* (1577), for instance, Henry Dethicke offers a dedication to William Cecil that links earthly and heavenly gardens:

I wish unto your honour by dayly Prayer, the fruition of the Heavenly Paradise, craving of the Omnipotent and provident God, the guider of that gorgeous Garden, that hee would vouchsafe to graunte unto you, the sweete savour of his chiefe fragrante floures, that is, his comfort cleave fast unto you, his mercy to keepe you, and his grace to guyde you, nowe and evermore.[126]

Another reference to Genesis (3:19) is found in the epigraph to *Foure Bookes of Husbandry, collected by M. Conradus Heresbachius*, translated by Barnabe Googe (1577): "In the sweate of thy face shalt thou eate thy bread, tyll thou be turned agayne into the ground, for out of it wast thou taken: yea, dust thou art, and to dust thou shalt returne."[127] This verse

---

[125] Crowther-Heyck, "'Be Fruitful and Multiply,'" 917–22, citing also Carolyn Merchant, *The Death of Nature: Women, Ecology, and the Scientific Revolution* (San Francisco: Harper and Row, 1980).

[126] Henry Dethicke, "To the righte honourable and his singular good Lord, Sir William Cecill," in Dydymus Mountaine [Thomas Hill], *The gardeners labyrinth* (London: Henry Bynneman, 1577), sig. a3ʳ.

[127] Conrad Heresbach, *Foure Bookes of Husbandry*, trans. Barnabe Googe (London: Richard Watkins, 1577), title page.

explains why husbandry manuals are necessary: husbandry itself was unnecessary before the Fall. In John Gerard's *Herball* (1597), also dedicated to Cecil, whose son Robert was to create one of the greatest English gardens at Theobalds, the author explains to his readers the biblical precedent for his vocation of herbalist:

> I list not to seeke the common colours of antiquitie; when notwithstanding the world can brag of noe more ancient monument than Paradise, and the garden of Eden: and the fruits of the earth may contend for seignioritie, seeing their mother was the first creature that conceived, and they themselves, the first fruit she brought foorth. Talke of perfect happinesse or pleasure, and what place was so fit for that, as the garden place where *Adam* was set, to be the Herbalist? Wherefore did the Poets hunt for their sincere delights, but into the gardens of *Alcinous*, of *Adonis*, and the orchards of *Hesperides*? Where did they dreame that heaven should be, but in the pleasant garden of *Elysium*?[128]

As Rebecca Bushnell summarizes, it was a commonplace of early modern gardeners that "through gardening we could restore some part of that paradise we lost with the fall, which condemned us to sweat for our food."[129] If *The Winter's Tale* is in one sense about the consequences of the Fall—the rift between men and women, betrayal and sexual jealousy, pain, sorrow, and death—it also contemplates the possibility of reversing the Fall. The play's exploration of these possibilities unites the otherwise seemingly disparate languages of procreation, grafting, and gardening, of marriage, and childbirth with overlapping allusions to Genesis.

One of the characters in Philip Pullman's novel *The Golden Compass* explains that Adam and Eve are "like an imaginary number, like the square root of minus one: you can never see any concrete proof that it exists, but if you include it in your equations, you can calculate all manner of things that couldn't be imagined without it."[130] Early modern Christians believed that Adam and Eve and their story, recounted in Genesis 1–3, were not imaginary but historically real. Nevertheless, the story of the creation of the first man and woman, their temptation by the serpent, eating of the forbidden fruit, fall into sin and death, and expulsion from the garden of Eden did allow them to "calculate all manner of things," as Pullman describes. Shakespeare's calculations involved matters of history and politics, desire, love, and marriage, temptation, murder, and corruption. He seems never to have exhausted his fascination with the Genesis story and

---

[128] Gerard, *The herball or Generall historie of plantes*, sig. B5^v.
[129] Rebecca Bushnell, *Green Desire: Imagining Early Modern English Gardens* (Ithaca, NY: Cornell University Press, 2003), 101.
[130] Philip Pullman, *The Golden Compass* (New York: Dell Laurel-Leaf, 1995), 327. Originally published in the United Kingdom as *Northern Lights*.

its implications. Furthermore, the vast number of early modern commentaries, paraphrases, visual representations, and allusions relating to the story of Adam and Eve attest that Shakespeare was tapping into one of the richest and most widely recognized sources of his culture. Indeed, it might be said of the Genesis story that early modern English culture "couldn't be imagined without it."

5
Creative Anachronism: Biblical Allusion in the Roman Histories

While watching a film of the "sword and sandals" variety in a tenth-grade history class, proud of the sophistication of our historical understanding, my classmates and I howled at spotting a wristwatch on a Roman soldier. Today, websites such as *Total Film* ("40 Historical Movie Errors") delight in providing lists of such anachronistic errors on film.[1] Literary critics have a different attitude to anachronism, however, though it has been slow in developing. It used to be that the chiming clock in *Julius Caesar* and the anachronistic pastiche of political systems in *Titus Andronicus* were passed off either as insignificant slips by a historically inexpert playwright, or as evidence of a fundamentally unhistoricized sensibility on the part of Elizabethans of all sorts.[2] Of Douglas's pistol in *1 Henry IV*, Samuel Johnson wrote dismissively that "Shakespeare never has any care to preserve the manners of the time."[3] Edward Dowden attempted to rescue Shakespeare from such charges by means of a peculiarly historicizing Platonism: "While Shakespeare is profoundly faithful to Roman life and character, it is an ideal truth, truth spiritual rather than truth material, which he seeks to discover."[4] Dowden's rather Romantic argument has at least the merit of placing anachronism back under Shakespeare's control as a deliberate artistic strategy. Many, more recent, critics agree that Shakespeare's apparent historical slips are (for the most part) deliberate rhetorical strategies, reflecting not a naive lack of proper historicism but a sense that the best use of history is in comparison to the present. Sigurd

---

[1] George Wales, "40 Historical Movie Errors" (January 10, 2011), in *Total Film: The Modern Guide to Movies* <http://www.totalfilm.com/features/40-historical-movie-errors> (accessed September 23, 2012).

[2] See Dennis Kezar, "*Julius Caesar*'s Analogue Clock and the Accents of History," in Horst Zander (ed.), *Julius Caesar: New Critical Essays* (New York and London: Routledge, 2005), 241–55.

[3] Cited in Phyllis Rackin, *Stages of History: Shakespeare's English Chronicles* (Ithaca, NY: Cornell University Press, 1990), 86.

[4] Edward Dowden, *Shakspere: A Critical Study of His Mind and Art* (1875), cited in John W. Velz, "The Ancient World in Shakespeare: Authenticity or Anachronism? A Retrospect," *SS* 31 (1978), 1–12, 1.

Burckhardt, for example, points out that in 1599 Europe was undergoing a chronological disruption similar to one undergone in Julius Caesar's Rome: Caesar introduced the "Julian" calendar in 46 BCE; Pope Gregory XIII abolished the Julian in favor of the Gregorian calendar in 1582:

> The striking clock is not only a metaphor; it is a touchstone. Proud classicists, sure of their learning, will mark it as evidence that Shakespeare had, in Ben Jonson's words, "small Latin and less Greek." But in the very act of doing so they betray their blindness, their refusal fully to surrender to the actually given—in this case to the carefully wrought pattern of time references by which Shakespeare defines the precise meaning of his anachronism.[5]

As Jacques Amyot argued in the preface to his 1559 French translation of Plutarch (translated into English in 1579 by Sir Thomas North), history "is a certain rule and instruction which by examples past teacheth us to judge of things present and to foresee things to come, so as we may know what to like of, and what to follow, what to mislike, and what to eschew."[6] Including a few obvious "things present" in the historical representation may simply have highlighted the essential relationship with "examples past."

Anachronism does not originate with Shakespeare, of course. It is a regular feature of Renaissance art, as in the *Weimar Altarpiece* (1553–5) by Lucas Cranach the Elder and Lucas Cranach the Younger, which features the crucified Christ with Cranach the Elder (onto whose head blood streams from Christ's wounded side) and Martin Luther, pointing to an open Bible in his hand.[7] Pieter Brueghel the Elder's *Way of the Cross* (1564) sets the Crucifixion in a sixteenth-century Netherlandish scene, in which the wife of Simon of Cyrene wears a rosary. Cranachs and Brueghel knew perfectly well that their paintings violated historical verisimilitude, but they were less interested in that kind of accuracy than in bringing biblical stories into their own present time and place. Even in the Middle Ages, Christians in their devotions had been enjoined to imagine themselves present at the Crucixifion, but the Cranach and Brueghel paintings demand a more sophisticated historical consciousness. In Brueghel, for instance, the viewer needs to recognize that the red-coated soldiers on horseback riding across the middle of the painting, taking Christ to

---

[5] Sigurd Burckhardt, *Shakespearean Meanings* (Princeton: Princeton University Press, 1968), quoted in Kezar, "*Julius Caesar*'s Analogue Clock," 242–3. Steve Sohmer pursues in more detail the ways in which *Julius Caesar* relates to calendrical reform in *Shakespeare's Mystery Play: The Opening of the Globe Theatre 1599* (Manchester and New York: Manchester University Press, 1999).

[6] "Amyot, to the Reader," in Plutarch, *The Lives of the Noble Grecians and Romans*, trans. Sir Thomas North, ed. Roland Baughman (New York: Heritage Press, 1941), i, p. xxxi.

[7] On various aspects of anachronism in Renaissance art, see Alexander Nagel and Christopher Wood, *Anachronic Renaissance* (New York: Zone Books, 2010).

Golgotha, are identifiable as the Spanish troops of Emperor Charles V who under the command of the Duke of Alba occupied the southern Netherlands.[8] Thus, Brueghel's anachronisms have a political as well as devotional purpose. Furthermore, proper viewing of these paintings involves not confusing past and present but properly distinguishing them; for the present fully to engage with the past the present must recognize that the past *is* past. Thomas M. Greene distinguished Renaissance anachronism from medieval practice in terms of its level of historical awareness, comparing Gavin Douglas's naive description of maenads as "nuns of Bacchus" in his translation of Virgil's *Aeneid* with the self-conscious "creative" anachronism of Renaissance humanists, as in Sir Thomas Wyatt's imitation of a chorus from Seneca's *Thyestes* in his poem about the fall of Thomas Cromwell and the perilous world of the Tudor court, "Stond so who list upon the Slipper toppe."[9]

Greene's distinction might be applied to English drama too. On the one hand is the naive (though delightful) anachronism of *The Second Shepherds' Play*, in which Mak and other medieval English shepherds, who refer to Christ and the Rood, the Saints, the liturgy, and the town of Harbury near Wakefield, hear the angel's annunciation of Christ's birth and go to visit the holy family in the stable in Bethlehem, which seems to be within easy walking distance. On the other hand, Thomas Kyd, paraphrasing a French closet drama by Robert Garnier, puts into the mouth of Cicero the language of the gospels:

> Heaven delight not in us, when we doe
> That to another, which our selves dysdaine:
> Judge others, as thou would'st be judg'd againe.
> And do but as thou wouldst be done unto.
> For, sooth to say, (in reason) we deserve
> To have the self-same measure that we serve.[10]

---

[8] Michael Francis Gibson, *The Mill and the Cross: Peter Bruegel's "Way to Calvary"* (Lausanne: Acatos, 2000), ch. 3, "The Spaniards."

[9] Thomas M. Greene, *The Light in Troy: Imitation and Discovery in Renaissance Poetry* (New Haven and London: Yale University Press, 1982), 242–6, as well as ch. 2, "Imitation and Anachronism." See also Greene, "History and Anachronism," in Gary Saul Morson (ed.), *Literature and History: Theoretical Problems and Russian Case Studies* (Stanford: Stanford University Press, 1986), 205–20. Rackin similarly argues that "What distinguishes the Renaissance is the sense of anachronism, the recognition of temporal distance that alienated a nostalgic present from a lost historical past" (Rackin, *Stages of History*, 91).

[10] Robert Garnier, *Pompey the Great, his faire Corneliaes Tragedie*, trans. Thomas Kyd (London: Nicholas Ling, 1595), cited in Clifford Ronan, *"Antike Roman": Power Symbology and the Roman Play in Early Modern England, 1585–1635* (Athens, GA, and London: University of Georgia Press, 1995), 19–20. Ronan's first two chapters are devoted to anachronism.

In Matthew 7:1 (and Luke 6:37), Christ says, "Judge not, that ye be not judged," and in Matthew 7:2 (and Mark 4:24), "with what judgement ye judge, ye shal be judged, and with what measure ye mette [mete], it shall be measured to you againe" (the verse alluded to in the title of *Measure for Measure*). Kyd's biblical allusions, like those in *The Spanish Tragedy* discussed in Chapter 3, are deliberate and self-conscious.[11]

Richard Dutton has shown that English audiences had a ready capacity for "analogical reading," for recognizing and interpreting parallels between historical or fictional plots and characters and those making news in England. Jonathan Bate, similarly, refers to the "Renaissance habit of thinking in terms of parallels between present experience and mythological precedent."[12] For "mythological," one might easily substitute "historical," and, in the sixteenth and seventeenth centuries, the distinction was not always clear. An example of Shakespeare's analogical thinking occurs in *Henry V* (1601), when the Prologue describes the London crowds welcoming Henry, "their conqu'ring Caesar," and then compares this to how "the general of our gracious empress" may be received when he returns "from Ireland" (5.0, Chorus, 28, 30–1). This is usually read as an allusion to the Earl of Essex, though Dutton proposes an alternative in Charles Blount, Lord Mountjoy, Essex's successor as Lord Deputy of Ireland.[13] In either case, Henry V is being likened to Julius Caesar, and both are then compared, allusively, to a contemporary Elizabethan commander. As Dutton argues, such parallels were loose and suggestive, rather than strictly allegorical. This helped keep the censors at bay and also suited Shakespeare's predilection for exploring questions perspectivally rather than from any single position.

The Elizabethan habit of analogy also suggests why Shakespeare may have been drawn to Plutarch at the end of the 1590s. Plutarch's appeal for Shakespeare lay also no doubt in the Greek author's interest in the personality and character of his historical subjects; what intrigued Plutarch were their moral dilemmas and choices rather than the objective facts of their biography. Even though many of his subjects were involved in events decisive for the political development of their societies, Plutarch's focus was on how the principal characters responded to the events around them,

---

[11] Josephine A. Roberts and James F. Gaines argue that Kyd considerably "amends" Garnier's original, adding, among other things, numerous Christian references. "Kyd and Garnier: The Art of Amendment," *Comparative Literature*, 31/2 (1979), 124–33.

[12] Richard A. Dutton, *Licensing, Censorship, and Authorship in Early Modern England* (Basingstoke: Palgrave, 2000), pp. ix–xviii. Jonathan Bate, *Shakespeare and Ovid* (Oxford: Clarendon Press, 1993, repr. 2001), 151.

[13] Richard Dutton, "'Methinks the Truth should Live from Age to Age': The Dating and Contexts of *Henry V*," *HLQ* 68/1–2 (2005), 173–204, 197–201.

and what traits determined this response. According to T. J. B. Spencer, Plutarch "saw history in terms of human character; and interpreted Antiquity to the modern world as a state of existence in which outstanding men moulded events by their personal decisions and by the inevitable tendencies of their characters."[14]

Plutarch's *Lives* focuses on character, then, but its biographies are also comparative, most of the lives presented in pairs, one Greek and one Roman. They are followed by essays on points of similarity and difference. Such an arrangement was ideally suited to the analogical imagination. Plutarch's approach may have influenced Shakespeare's practice of biblical allusion as well as his use of anachronism. By means of biblical allusion, Shakespeare could add a further historical complication to his Roman plays, implicitly comparing the Rome he represents to an entirely different "example past"—the New Testament life of Christ—so that the two past times are set against each other as well as against Shakespeare's own times. Yet obviously these biblical allusions are completely anachronistic, since the Roman plays are set before the time of Christ. (The gospels set Christ's birth at the time of Augustus Caesar.) In addition to whatever analogies an Elizabethan audience might here draw between contemporary British politics and the stories of Caesar and Brutus, Antony and Cleopatra, or Coriolanus, they would also have recognized this third layer of historical analogy. In the case of Julius Caesar and Jesus Christ, moreover, the analogy may have been encouraged by the coincidence that two men with initials "JC" were declared gods at roughly the same historical period.[15] By means of anachronistic allusions, Shakespeare spins webs of analogies in which the tragedies of the protagonists are all measured against the tragedy (if it is one) of Christ. Furthermore, *Antony and Cleopatra* moves beyond tragedy in the transcendent Liebestod of its two lovers, and this is expressed in allusions to the Christian model of transcendence in the final book of the Bible, Revelation.

---

[14] T. J. B. Spencer (ed. and intro.), *Shakespeare's Plutarch* (Harmondsworth: Penguin, 1964), 7.

[15] Sohmer, *Shakespeare's Mystery Play*, 28. Augustus Caesar declared his predecessor Julius a god in 42 BCE, citing as proof of this a comet that appeared around the time of his death. Valerius Maximus, writing some seventy-five years after Caesar's death, added the story of the ghost of "*divus Julius*" (divine Julius) appearing to Cassius before Philippi, which seemed to confirm Augustus's pronouncement. Valerius Maximus, *Facta et dicta memorabilia* (1.8.8., cited in *Julius Caesar*, ed. David Daniell, 296 n. See also Nicholas Thomas Wright, *The Resurrection of the Son of God* (Minneapolis: Fortress Press, 2003), 57.

JULIUS CAESAR

Perhaps because of the anachronistic and contrastive nature of Shakespeare's biblical allusions in the Roman plays, literary critics have been tentative about acknowledging or explaining them; even David Daniell, author of *The Bible in English*, confines his remarks on Shakespeare's biblical allusions to a single page in his 147-page introduction to the Arden *Julius Caesar*. "It is not far-fetched to consider the Scripture, and especially the New Testament, as commonly in the minds of both playwright and audience in a way that is wholly alien to the late twentieth century," Daniell suggests cautiously. He states simply that "verbal echoes from the Bible in *Julius Caesar* will be noted in the commentary."[16] These are hardly faint echoes but deliberate and overt allusions, however, and there are a good many of them. Daniell notes only six, Arthur Humphreys in the Oxford only three, whereas Shaheen lists twenty-five, not including a few doubtful ones. The Bible—specifically the story of Christ—must have more importance to the play than Daniell's introduction and commentary suggest.[17] In fact, Shakespeare repeatedly draws Julius Caesar into parallel with Christ, by this means calling into question not only his divinity, but the sacrificial nature of his death, and its meaning for the people of Rome (and, in Shakespeare's own day, England).

The first time Caesar appears on stage, he is processing through the crowded streets of Rome with his followers when he is accosted by the Soothsayer: "Beware the Ides of March" (1.2.18). Shakespeare's scene is from Plutarch (the Soothsayer's warning, in fact, had become proverbial long before the 1590s).[18] But Shakespeare adds several biblical allusions. "Who is it in the press that calls on me?" Caesar asks, and says of the Soothsayer, "Set him before me. Let me see his face" (1.2.15, 20). The word Shakespeare uses for the crowd—"press"—is an unusual one, and it does not appear frequently in his plays. Used in this sense, it appears only in *King John* (5.7.19), *Henry VIII* (4.1.78 and 5.4.83), and *The Rape of*

---

[16] David Daniell, intro., *Julius Caesar*, 94–5.
[17] Humphreys notes biblical "parallels" at 1.2.152, 3.2.222–3, and 5.5.13; Humphreys's 83-page introduction does not mention the Bible at all. *Julius Caesar*, ed. Arthur Humphreys (Oxford: Clarendon Press, 1984). Marvin Spevack includes Noble in a list of source studies, but otherwise does not mention the Bible in his introduction to the updated Cambridge edition. Nor is it mentioned in Marga Munkelt's "Recent Film, Stage and Critical Interpretations," included in the Cambridge edition, and not a single Cambridge note references the biblical allusions.
[18] As early as 1534, English schoolboys were taught that "a southsayer hadde warned Cesar before to beware of the Ides of Marche" (Nicholas Udall, *Floures for Latine spekynge selected and gathered oute of Terence* [London: Tho. Bertheleti, 1534], fo. 136ᵛ).

Lucrece (ll. 1301 and 1408). As Daniell notes, however, the word is used five times in the gospels (Geneva) for the crowd that throngs around Jesus. The specific language of Caesar's entrance thus points to a number of similar biblical scenes. In Mark 5, for instance, Jesus is surrounded by a great crowd, and a sick woman "came in the preasse behind, and touched his garment." Like Caesar, Jesus becomes aware of this eager person among the "press," and turns and calls, "Who hath touched my clothes?" (Mark 5:27–30). Later in Mark, a blind man cries out to Jesus in the midst of a crowd. Jesus commands him to be called, "and they called the blinde, saying unto him, Be of good comfort: arise, he calleth thee" (Mark 10:47–9). Neither person who accosts Jesus is a soothsayer, nor do they warn of the Ides of March, but Jesus and Caesar are similarly men of fame and power, walking amidst the throng of common people, condescending to pay attention to one lowly voice among the multitude. In both cases, too, Jesus and Caesar are known (to the audience) to be heading ultimately for death, Caesar by assassination and Jesus by execution.

In the passages from Mark just cited, Jesus is ministering to the sick; he heals the woman who touches him and the blind man who calls him. Caesar cannot work such miracles, of course, but Cassius makes a suggestive and ironic remark (if we hear its biblical resonance). After declaring to Casca his intention to kill himself if Caesar is crowned king, Cassius says,

> I know where I will wear this dagger then:
> Therein, ye gods, ye make the weak most strong;
> Therein, ye gods, you tyrants do defeat. (1.3.89–92)

Cassius suggests that, in a perverse way, Caesar will make the weak strong should he become king, at least in so far as the weak Cassius will find strength then to kill himself. As in Christ's healing of the woman and the blind man, the weak are made strong repeatedly throughout the New Testament. Paul writes to the Corinthians that "the weaknes of God is stronger then men" (1 Cor. 1:25); "we are weake, and that ye are strong" (1 Cor. 4:10); "I take pleasure in infirmities... for when I am weak, then am I strong" (2 Cor. 12:10); "For we are glad, when we are weak, and ye are strong" (2 Cor. 13:9); and "out of weake were made strong" (Heb. 11:34). This paradoxical causal relationship between weakness and strength is distinctive to the New Testament; in the Old Testament, many men are described as strong, but weakness and strength are not juxtaposed in the same way. Cassius's "ye make the weak most strong" is a recognizable New Testament idiom, though Shakespare uses it to generate irony. For Cassius, "weakness" is the inability to kill, either Caesar or himself, whereas the strength of Christ and Christians lies in the ability to remain faithful and loving even while suffering and dying.

On the other hand, some genuine miracles are, in fact, attributed to Caesar. The night before the fatal March 15, Rome is full of supernatural portents familiar to readers of North's Plutarch: "fires in the element, and spirites running up and downe in the night, and also these solitarie birdes to be seene at noone days sittinge in the great market place," as well as "a slave of the soldiers, that did cast a marvelous burning flame out of his hande" and a sacrificed beast that, when opened up, is found to have no heart ("that was a straunge thing in nature, how a beast could live without a hart").[19] Shakespeare adds several more prodigies, including a group of "ghastly women," and a lion in the Capitol, that Calphurnia later says has whelped in the streets (1.3.3–32, 2.2.17). Calphurnia goes on to describe the storm in apocalyptic terms:

> And graves have yawned and yielded up their dead.
> Fierce fiery warriors fight upon the clouds...
> And ghosts did shriek and squeal about the streets. (2.2.18–26)

Shakespeare may have read the account of some of these portents in Virgil's *Georgics*, which similarly describes armies clashing in the sky (portending the Roman Civil War to come) and open graves.[20] Graves "yielding up their dead," however, would also have recalled the cataclysmic events accompanying Christ's death:

And the graves did open them selves, and many bodies of the Sainctes which slept arose,

And came out of the graves after his resurrection, and went into the holie Citie, and appeared unto many. (Matt. 27:52–3)

By contrast, the unnatural occurrences in *Julius Caesar* portend Caesar's death, while they follow Christ's, and what comes out of the Roman graves are old bones (and ghosts) rather than walking saints (which, for Protestants, means the godly in general, not those canonized by Church of Rome). Moreover, unlike Christ, Caesar will not be resurrected. The allusions are thus primarily contrastive. As the note to Matthew 27:52 in the Geneva–Tomson Bible explains, at Christ's death, "the stones clave in sunder, and the graves did open themselves, to shew by this token that death was overcome: and the resurrection of the dead followed the resurrection of Christ." The disturbed graves in *Julius Caesar* show only that Caesar is going to die, as will many other Romans too.

---

[19] Plutarch, "The Life of Julius Caesar," in Bullough, v. 83.
[20] Virgil, *Georgics*, I.461 ff. in *Virgil*, i, ed. H. Rushton Fairclough, Loeb Classic Library (Cambridge: Harvard University Press, 1965), 112–15. This possible source is mentioned by Daniell, in *Julius Caesar*, note to 2.2.17–24.

Meanwhile, though, Caesar's assassination and Jesus's execution do have some basic elements of character and plot in common: each is offered but rejects a kingship (Jesus tells Pilate that his kingdom is not of this world, John 18:36); each is betrayed by one of those closest to him; each is killed, ostensibly, for the greater good. A powerful cluster of allusions connecting Caesar with Christ is concentrated in the build-up to the scene that, significantly, Brutus would like to think of as Caesar's "sacrifice." ("Let's be sacrificers but not butchers," Brutus says to Cassius at 2.1.165, arguing against the additional murder of Antony.) Decius's greeting to Caesar on the day of the assassination, "Caesar, all hail," may seem unremarkable, but Shakespeare used this phrase in several plays to echo Judas's greeting to Jesus in the Garden of Gethsemane.[21] In *3 Henry VI*, for instance, the Judas-like Duke of Gloucester remarks in an aside,

> To say the truth, so Judas kiss'd his master,
> And cried "All hail!" when as he meant him harm. (5.7.33–4)

This precise wording is found in none of the English Bibles; the closest is Tyndale's 1534 New Testament, which has "hail Master." (Geneva has "God save thee.")[22] But, as Peter Millward and Rowland Wymer have noted, the exact phrase is used by Judas in the Cordewaners' play of the York Cycle: "All hayle, maister in faith, | And felawes all in fere."[23] Two other allusions to this phrase, discussed in chapters 4 and 7, are in *Richard II* (4.2.160–2), "Did they not sometime cry 'All hail!' to me? | So Judas did to Christ," and *Macbeth* (1.3.46), the "All hail" repeated several times by the witches. Paul Whitfield White and other historians of drama have recently complicated the history of drama, which had taught that the performance of religious plays ended with the last Mystery Cycle performance in Coventry in 1579. In fact, in small town and provincial venues the performance of religious drama, including parts of the Mystery cycles, continued well into the seventeenth century.[24] Since many of the inhabitants of London were, like Shakespeare, native to other parts of

---

[21] Emrys Jones, *The Origins of Shakespeare* (Oxford: Clarendon Press, 1977; repr. 1978), 31–84.

[22] In Tyndale, and in the Bibles of Miles Coverdale who followed him, Jesus greets his disciples after the Resurrection with an "All hayle" at Matt. 28. Shakespeare clearly has a different scene in mind, however.

[23] The Cordewaners play ("The Agony and the Betrayal"), in *York Plays*, ed. Lucy Toulmin Smith (New York: Russell & Russell, 1963), 251. Peter Millward, *Shakespeare's Religious Background* (1973), cited (and corrected) in Roland Wymer, "Shakespeare and the Mystery Cycles," *ELR* 34/3 (2004), 265–85, 274.

[24] Paul Whitfield White, *Drama and Religion in English Provincial Society, 1485–1660* (Cambridge: Cambridge University Press, 2008). See also Records of Early English Drama.

the country, it seems likely that many of them knew provincial religious drama first hand, as Shakespeare obviously did.[25]

Judas's greeting had also by this time become conventional. For instance, in a sermon preached at Paul's Cross in 1571, John Bridges asked, "Is not this Judas trayterouse kisse, openly to saye, *Ave rabbi,* all haile maister...".[26] John Field, in his 1581 *A caveat for Parsons Howlet concerning his untimely flighte*, castigates Howlett for an epistle he dedicated to Elizabeth: "for the maner of conceiving & penning that treatise, if it had ben done with such modesty and humility you speake of, you woulde not so haue betraied her majestye with a Judas Kysse, crying *All hayle* and yet putting her into her enemies handes."[27] John Norden's *A mirrour for the multitude* also includes Judas's greeting, noting that "the outwarde kysse of *Judas,* was outwardly a token of love, and yet it proceeded of an heart full of gall and bitternesse, of deceyte and murther, his words of all hayle master came as if his lippes had testified obedience to his master, but the poyson of Aspys was under his tong."[28] Judas is said to greet Jesus in the same words in Miles Coverdale's *Fruitfull lessons, upon the passion, buriall, resurrection, ascension, and of the sending of the holy Ghost* (1593), Samuel Rowlands's *The betraying of Christ. Judas in despaire. The seven words of our Savior on the crosse. With other poems on the Passion* (1598), and Francis Bacon's *A letter written out of England to an English gentleman remaining at Padua containing a true report of a strange conspiracie* (1599). Decius's "all hail" thus marks him as a Judas, the archetypal betrayer, and it implies that Caesar, the betrayed leader, stands somehow in the role of Christ.

After Caesar has finally been persuaded by the conspirators to attend the Senate, he invites them in to "taste some wine" (2.2.126). This is another of Shakespeare's inventions (it is not in Plutarch), and is perhaps, as one critic argues, "the classic symbol of betrayal: the murderers taking wine with the victim just before the killing."[29] But the symbol is "classic" primarily because it is established as a paradigm in the biblical account of the Last Supper (Matt. 26, etc.), at which Judas breaks bread and shares

---

[25] Lawrence Manley quotes the Corporation of London Civic Records for 1572–3, which state that the mobile population of the city was "by birth for the most part a mixture of all the countries" of the realm. *Literature and Culture in Early Modern London* (Cambridge: Cambridge University Press, 1995), 8.

[26] John Bridges, *A sermon, preached at Paules Crosse on the Monday in Whitson weeke Anno Domini. 1571* (London: Henry Binneman for Humfrey Toy, 1571), 129.

[27] John Field, *A caveat for Parsons Howlet concerning his untimely flighte* (London: Robert Waldegrave for Thomas Man and Toby Smith, [1581]), sig. A5.

[28] John Norden, *A mirrour for the multitude* (London: John Windet, 1586), 92.

[29] Norman Sanders (ed.), *Julius Caesar* (Harmondsworth: Penguin, 1967), cited in *Julius Caesar,* ed. Daniell, note to 2.2.126–7.

wine with Jesus, knowing full well that he will betray him.³⁰ That Shakespeare is shaping Caesar's assassination as a kind of Crucifixion scene is also indicated by the time that the Soothsayer announces to Portia in 2.4, while the murder is taking place. She asks, "What is't o'clock?" and he replies, "About the ninth hour, lady" (2.4.23). Not only is this the time that Jesus dies on the cross, but even the lack of precision in the phrase is allusive, since Jesus speaks his last words "at *about* the ninth houre" (Matt. 27:46, emphasis added). By contrast, Plutarch mentions no specific time.

Shakespeare's most striking biblically allusive additions to Plutarch are in the description of Calphurnia's dream and in the behavior of the conspirators immediately following the "sacrifice" of Caesar. In Plutarch, for instance, Calphurnia "dreamed that Caesar was slaine, and that she had him in her armes."³¹ But in Shakespeare her dream is more detailed and disturbing. Caesar says,

> Calphurnia here, my wife, stays me at home.
> She dreamt tonight she saw my statue,
> Which, like a fountain with an hundred spouts,
> Did run pure blood; and many lusty Romans
> Came smiling and did bathe their hands in it. (2.2.75–9)

It is not hard to see why Calphurnia might see in this dream "warnings and portents | And evils imminent," but Decius cleverly offers an entirely different interpretation (because, as Cicero observes, "men may construe things after their fashion | Clean from the purpose of the things themselves," 1.3.34–5):

> It was a vision fair and fortunate.
> Your statue spouting blood in many pipes
> In which so many smiling Romans bathed
> Signifies that from you great Rome shall suck
> Reviving blood, and that great men shall press
> For tinctures, stains, relics and cognizance. (2.2.84–90)

Decius knows Caesar will die, and so do we, even if Caesar somehow thinks he can give blood to the Roman population and remain alive. But Decius's reinterpretation represents Caesar's death in terms of the "sacrifice" Brutus wants it to be, and the sacrifice is conceived in traditionally Christian terms. The idea of Christ's saving blood is a biblical and theological commonplace (see, for instance, Acts 20:28, Eph. 1:7, Rev. 1:5),

---

³⁰ See also Sohmer, *Shakespeare's Mystery Play*, 27.
³¹ Plutarch, "The Life of Julius Caesar," in Bullough, v. 83.

190   *Biblical Allusion in the Plays*

> *Quod in te est, prome.*
> Ad eundem.
>
> THE Pellican, for to reuiue her younge,
> Doth peirce her breſt, and geue them of her blood:
> Then ſearche your breſte, and as yow haue with tonge,
> With penne proceede to doe our countrie good:
> Your zeale is great, your learning is profounde,
> Then helpe our wantes, with that you doe abounde.
>
> Parad. Poët.
> *Cor Pharius roſtro figit*
> *pelecanus acuto,*
> *Et ſe pronatis ſic nu-*
> *cat ipſe ſuis.*
>
> De par-

Fig. 5.1. According to ancient legend, the female pelican was thought to use her beak to prick her breast, feeding her young with her own blood. The pelican thus became a widely used symbol for Christ. This emblem shows the "pelican in her piety," and relates her story in the verse below. (From Geoffrey Whitney, *A choice of emblems, and other devises...*, 1586.) By permission of the Folger Shakespeare Library.

but Decius's statement that Romans will "suck" Caesar's "reviving blood" suggests a specific symbol of Christ: the Pelican in her Piety (see Fig. 5.1). Shakespeare refers in several plays to the "kind life-rend'ring Pelican" (*Hamlet* 4.5.147). According to a popular legend dating back at least to Isidore of Seville,[32] the Pelican feeds its young with its own blood, but Christians appropriated this bit of fictional zoology as a symbol of Christ, who feeds his "children" with his own blood, in the sacrifice of the Crucifixion and in its re-enactment in the Eucharist.[33] After Caesar has been

---

[32] P. J. Heather, "Animal Beliefs" (Continued) *Folklore* 52/3 (1941): 217.
[33] This feeding is literal as well as spiritual, at least in the Catholic theology of the Eucharist, in which Christians are believed to drink the actual blood of Christ, transubstantiated from wine during the Institution of the Mass. For an online image, see http://www.southwark.anglican.org/cathedral/tour/bosses.htm. Among other uses of the image, there is an elaborate carved baptismal font with the pelican feeding her young in the church of St. Lawrence, Diddington, and a similar pelican on a font in St. Peter and St. Paul, Norfolk. The image remains in wide use in churches today. Queen Elizabeth I also wears a

killed, Brutus almost seems to fulfill the prophecy of Calphurnia's dream, calling on the conspirators to "stoop" and "bathe our hands in Caesar's blood" (which Antony shortly calls "the most noble blood of all this world"), crying "Peace, Freedom and Liberty" (3.1.105–10). Cassius responds,

> Stoop, then, and wash. How many ages hence
> Shall this our lofty scene be acted over
> In states unborn and accents yet unknown. (3.1.111–13)

Washing in blood is a common metaphor for the spiritual effect of Christ's sacrifice, expressed in the Bible ("Unto him that loved us and washed us from our sins in his own blood," Rev. 1:5) and in countless extra-biblical writings. The Elizabethan *Homily of Repentance and True Reconciliation unto God*, for instance, states that "verily herein doth appeare how filthy a thing sinne is, sith that it can by no other meanes be washed away, but by the blood of the onely begotten Sonne of GOD."[34] And in one of his sermons on the Eucharist, the popular preacher Henry Smith speaks of baptism as "the true circumcision of the heart," because it representeth unto us the blood of Christ, which washeth our soules as the water in baptisme washeth our bodies."[35] Further uses of the commonplace are in poems by Thomas Churchyard:

> Who hath byn washed in thy Blood,
> is whiter than the Snoe.[36]

And by Edmund Spenser:

> This joyous day, deare Lord, with joy begin,
> and grant that we for whom thou diddest dye
> being with thy deare blood clene washt from sin,
> may live for ever in felicity.[37]

Although Christ's saving blood was a Christian commonplace, when writing this scene Shakespeare seems to have had in mind a specific biblical

---

pelican jewel in her "Pelican" portrait, painted by Nicholas Hilliard. See Roy Strong, *Portraits of Queen Elizabeth I* (Oxford: Clarendon Press, 1963). On the allusion to the pelican legend in *King Lear*, see chap. 8.

[34] *Homilies*, ii. 272.

[35] Henry Smith, *A treatise of the Lords supper in two sermons* (London: R. Field, 1591), 4.

[36] Thomas Churchyard, "A Dollfull Discourse of two Straungers, a Lady and a Knight," in *The Firste Parte of Churchyardes Chippes* (London, 1575), fol. 33. Churchyard additionally incorporates here an allusion to Psalm 51:7, "thou shalt wash me, and I shall be whiter than snow."

[37] *Amoretti* 68, lines 5–8. William A. Oram et al., *The Yale Edition of the Shorter Poems of Edmund Spenser* (New Haven and London: Yale University Press, 1989), 641.

passage dealing with blood, sacrifice, and several other relevant matters: during Holy Week, the center of the Christian liturgical year when the Passion of Christ is commemorated, the prescribed lectionary readings from the Epistles for Wednesday and Friday (Good Friday) were the ninth and tenth chapters of Hebrews. Chapter nine is concerned with distinguishing Old Testament blood sacrifice from the contrasting sacrifice of Christ: "Almost all things are by the law purged with blood [Brutus predicts at 2.1.179, 'we shall be called purgers'], and without the shedding of blood is no remission." But Christ's blood sacrifice is singular both in its saving power and in its historical singularity, in so far as the Jewish high priest "entereth into the holy place every year with strange blood," but Christ "appeared once, to put sin to flight by the offering up of himself." His sacrifice takes place once, just as "it is appointed unto all men that they shall once die."[38] The marginal notes in the Geneva Bible provided further related ideas.[39] Note "q" on Hebrews 9:23 ("the similitudes of heavenlie things" versus the "better sacrifices" of Christ) clarifies the relationship between pre-Christian sacrifices and that of Christ himself:

Albeit there is but one sacrifice, which is Christ him selfe once offered, yet because this true and eternal sacrifice is compared with all those which were figurative, and so more sufficient than all they, therefore he calleth it in the plural number, sacrifices.

By "figurative" the Geneva editors seem to mean those pre-Christian sacrifices that typologically pre-figured, but only imperfectly resembled, Christ's. The most obvious example might be Abraham's sacrifice of his son Isaac, who was traditionally interpreted as a type of Christ', even though Isaac is ultimately spared. Caesar's sacrifice is figurative in a different sense, in that Brutus describes his assassination of Caesar by the "figure," or metaphor, of sacrifice. The strain inherent in the metaphor is intensified and underscored by the contrastive allusions to the genuine Christian sacrifice. Rather than saving the Roman people, Caesar's death plunges Rome into a protracted and bloody civil war that results not only in thousands of human deaths but, ultimately, in the death of the Republic.

---

[38] Shaheen (526) notes Caesar's bravura remark that "the valiant never taste of death but once" (2.2.33) as a reference to Matt. 16:28, "There be some of them that stande here, which shall not taste of death," but Shakespeare may instead have had Hebrews in mind, though as a point of contrast.

[39] In addition to ideas and language about sacrifice, Shakespeare may have noticed comments in Hebrews about what one might call Christ's "will." Note "n" on Hebrews 9:15 ("the promes of eternal enheritance") states that Christ "by his death shulde make us his heires." Caesar likewise makes the humble citizens his heirs: Antony says coyly to the people "'tis good you know not you are his heirs" (3.2.146).

Caesar is also alluded to in terms of a kind of god or saint, an idea whose kernel Shakespeare probably derived from Plutarch's description of Caesar's funeral ("Nowe the Senate graunted generall pardonne for all that was paste, and to pacifie every man, ordained besides, that Caesars funerals shoulde bee honored as a god").[40] For example, at 1.2.10 Antony responds to Caesar's command that in his Lupercalia race he touch Calphurnia: "When Caesar says 'Do this,' it is performed," giving Caesar's utterances the same performative power as those of the biblical God, who can effect things merely by speaking them: "God said, Let there be light: and there was light" (Gen. 1:3). Caesar also has, at least in his own mind, the atemporal constancy of God: "always I am Caesar," he says, apparently giving his name the same eternal permanence as YHWH ("I AM THAT I AM," Exod. 3:14, glossed in Geneva as "The God which have ever bene, am and shal be"). Despite this claim, the mortal Caesar does die. However, Antony later suggests (anachronistically) that Caesar will be venerated as a saint:

> And they would go and kiss dead Caesar's wounds,
> And dip their napkins in his sacred blood,
> Yea, beg a hair of him for memory,
> And, dying, mention it within their wills,
> Bequeathing it as a rich legacy
> Unto their issue. (3.2.133–8)

Editors (like Daniell) gloss this speech by referring to the practice of gathering relics of martyrs. In England, at least into the 1580s, crowds (or presumably the still-Catholic members thereof) at the executions of Catholic priests and missionaries seized pieces of clothing, body parts (like Caesar's "hair of him for memory"), and even bloodstained ground as the holy relics of potential saints. In this period, "Handerkerchief-dipping was all the rage."[41] Decius's earlier reference, in his interpretation of Calphurnia's dream, to crowds pressing Caesar for "tinctures" and "relics" needs to be read in the same context (which suggests, though Decius obviously does not say this, that Caesar at that point will be dead). For a Protestant audience, of course, the Catholic practice of relics was to be condemned as idolatrous, and those who died were considered political traitors not martyrs.[42] Perhaps, then, the proper response to Antony's

---

[40] Plutarch, "The Life of Julius Caesar," in Bullough, v. 87.

[41] Peter Lake and Michael Questier, "Appropriation and Rhetoric under the Gallows: Puritans, Romanists and the State in Early Modern England," *Past & Present* 153 (1996), 64–107, 83.

[42] Lake and Questier describe the efforts of the English Protestant Church and State to secularize and criminalize the punishment of Catholics.

speech is to recognize the inappropriateness of worshipping Caesar or any other man, since he is no saint, and saints in the Catholic sense were in any case to be rejected by Shakespeare's original audience, at least by the Protestant majority.[43]

Two final allusions draw Caesar and Christ into parallel. First, in his oration over Caesar's body, Antony refers to the wounds visible in "Caesar's vesture" (3.2.194). The word "vesture" occurs only five times in Shakespeare, and in at least one other instance—in *Coriolanus*—it functions allusively as it does here (see below). The word significantly occurs in the biblical Crucifixion story, where soldiers "cast lots upon the vesture" of Christ (Matt. 27:35). Secondly, Antony says that, if he had Brutus's gift of oratory, he would

> Put a tongue
> In every wound of Caesar that should move
> The stones of Rome to rise and mutiny. (3.2.221–3)

Daniell (following Shaheen) identifies these lines as an allusion to Luke 19:40, where Jesus tells the Pharisees that, even if people should stop praising him as the "King that cometh in the Name of the Lord," the "stones wolde crye" to the same effect.[44]

Summing up, Brutus wants to be called a "sacrificer" or a "purger" rather than a "butcher," and wants Caesar's death to be not a squalid assassination but a necessary, noble sacrifice to redeem Rome. Caesar's blood, by this logic, should in fact save the Republic, whereas it paves the way for Rome's imperial era instead. Brutus and Cassius hope that the blood ritual they enact (or wish to think they are enacting) will be repeated by Romans in years to come, in commemoration of the original act, suggesting the sacrifice of Christ regularly commemorated when participants in the Eucharist consume the "saving blood" of Christ. But Caesar is no Christ, nor even a saint, because, though his death does superficially benefit the Roman citizens, they get only seventy-five drachmas and some public walks rather than eternal salvation. Caesar's

---

[43] Alison Shell usefully reminds us that Shakespeare's audience might well have included some Catholics, who would have responded to these and other religious and biblical allusions differently. Alison Shell, *Shakespeare and Religion* (London: Arden Shakespeare, 2011). Wymer ("Shakespeare and the Mystery Cycles," 278–84) argues that Shakespeare's use of the word "napkins" specifically echoes the veil of Veronica, which according to Catholic legend retained the image of Christ's face after she had wiped it for him on the way to Calvary. The scene was represented in the Mystery plays but was also more generally familiar. Such an allusion would strengthen the others to the Crucifixion, and would also, of course, be disturbing to Protestants.

[44] See Daniell's note in *Julius Caesar* and Shaheen, 530. Shakespeare alludes to the same passage from Luke in *Richard II* (3.2.24–6). See Ch. 4.

inadequacy is further argued by Cassius, who tells of a time Caesar almost drowned in the Tiber. The two men were swimming together, when Caesar was overcome with fatigue and cried, "Help me, Cassius, or I sink!" (1.2.111). That "this man | Is now become a god," as Cassius puts it bitterly, is all the more ironic if this is recognized as an allusion to Matthew:

> Then Peter answered him, and said, Master, if it be thou, byd me come unto thee on the water. And he said, Come. And when Peter was come downe out of the ship, he walked on the water, to go to Jesus. But when he sawe a mightie winde, he was afraied: and as he beganne to sinke, he cryed, saying, Master, save me. (Matt. 14:28–30)

As Daniell notes, Plutarch describes Caesar as a strong swimmer who saves himself without Cassius's help. Shakespeare alters the account both to compare Caesar to Christ and at the same time to undermine the comparison; it ought to be the disciple who sinks, not the master. This is a sorry "god" indeed. Furthermore, despite Brutus's desire to be seen as a "sacrificer" and "purger," he will ultimately be one of history's most notorious assassins, notably placed in the ninth circle of Hell in Dante's *Inferno*: right beside Brutus, among those who have betrayed lords and benefactors, is Judas.[45]

Shakespeare's plays almost always demonstrate a preference for ambivalence and ambiguity, and his use of biblical allusion supports this practice. Both Caesar and Brutus were as complex to him as they were, according to Geoffrey Bullough, in their earlier post-classical reputation:

> Julius Caesar appeared as a man of paradox. On the one hand there was general agreement on his martial skill, energy, endurance, power over his legions and the plebeians; on his kindness to friends and soldiers, his moderation in diet, his frequent clemency. On the other hand he was widely regarded as capable of great ruthlessness, a despiser of religion, lustful, guileful, above all ambitious....
>
> Brutus shared the double reputation of Caesar. He was noble in his Republican and Stoic principles, yet he killed his benefactor, and though he did it for the best political motives the result proved him wrong.[46]

---

[45] This juxtaposition from Dante may have been another prompt for Shakespeare to include allusions to the Crucifixion story in his play. There has been some debate about whether Shakespeare knew Dante, which was not available in English in Shakespeare's lifetime. Some scholars have detected textual and thematic influences, however. See, e.g., E. K. McFall, "*Macbeth* and Dante's *Inferno*," *N&Q* (December 2006), 490–4, and Frances Ferguson, *Trope and Allegory: Themes Common to Dante and Shakespeare* (Athens, GA: University of Georgia Press, 1977).

[46] Bullough, v., Introduction, 17–18.

Shakespeare's awareness of the ambivalence of these two antagonists and rival protagonists is evident in his allusive linking not only of Caesar but also of Brutus to Christ. It is Brutus, after all, who like Christ the healer plans a "piece of work that will make sick men whole." Ligarius by contrast immediately calls into question this prophesied miraculous healing, shifting focus from the greater good Brutus hopes for to the murder of Caesar that is the immediate plan: "But are not some whole that we must make sick?" (2.1.326–7). At Matthew 9:12, as at Mark 2:7 and Luke 5:31, Christ says to the Pharisees, in words that recall Ligarius', "The whole nede not a physicion, but thei that are sicke."

On the eve of the decisive battle of Philippi, Brutus experiences his own version of Christ's agony in the garden of Gethsemane. In a scene dramatized in the medieval cycle plays,[47] Jesus asks his disciples to "watch" with him, but they fall asleep, "for their eyes were heavie" (Matt. 26:43). "Colde ye not watch with me one houre?" he asks reproachfully (Matt. 26:40). Ultimately, Christ instructs the disciples to "Slepe henceforthe, and take your rest" (Matt. 26:45). Varrus and Claudio offer to "stand and watch your pleasure," but Brutus tells them to go to sleep (4.3.246–7). He does ask his servant Lucius (an invention of Shakespeare's) to stay awake with him ("Canst thou hold up thy heavy eyes a while?" 4.3.255) and to play a song to comfort him. Lucius is "willing," according to Brutus (4.3.257), but he soon falls asleep.[48] As with Christ's disciples, "the spirite in deede is *wyllyng*, but the fleshe is weake" (Matt. 26:41, Bishops' Bible, emphasis added).[49] The gospel and the play are paradoxical: Jesus is anxious at the thought of his impending death, which will cause him great pain but redeem the world; Brutus is anxious about the impending battle, part of a civil war that he himself caused by killing his friend and leader. Yet there are also notable similarities between Brutus's stoicism and Jesus's acceptance of suffering. Brutus's statement that he will arm himself "with patience | To stay the providence of some higher powers | Than us below" (5.1.107–9) expresses a similar idea to Jesus's "not as I wil, but as thou wilt" (Matt. 26:39), even if each has different "higher powers" in mind. Brutus's final

---

[47] In the Towneley Cycle, for instance, the scene takes up sixteen stanzas. Jesus first chastises the disciples when he finds them sleeping: "Symon, I say, slepys thou? | awake I red you all" (line 504–5), but he later gives up on them: "Slepe ye now and take youre rest" (l. 556). *The Towneley Plays*, ed. A. W. Pollard and Eugen Kölbing, Early English Text Society (London: Kegan Paul, Trench, Trübner & Co., 1897), XX *Incipit Conspiracio*, 220–1.

[48] There may be a further allusion in this scene to the boy David playing his harp for Saul to soothe his troubled spirit. 1 Sam. 16:14–23. Shakespeare often alludes in several directions at once.

[49] The Geneva Bible has "readie" instead of "willing," but Coverdale also has "willing," and the gospel reading on the Sunday before Easter was Matt. 26–7. Cummings (*BCP* 766) notes that ch. 26 was cut in the 1662 edition.

(unconscious) allusion to Christ is clear: as he prepares to die, he says to Volumnius, "I know my hour is come" (5.5.20). The phrase echoes Jesus, who repeatedly speaks about the coming of his destined hour:

Beholde, the houre is at hand. (Matt. 26:45)

And when the houre was come, he sate downe, and the twelve Apostles with him. (Luke 22.14)

Mine houre is not yet come. (John 2:4)

Now before the feast of the Passeover, when Jesus knewe that his houre was come, that he shulde departe out of the worlde unto the Father.... (John 13:1)

In Plutarch, Brutus knows that he will die. Might this too have suggested the biblical allusion to Shakespeare? Shakespeare builds on the similarity, giving Brutus a significant phrase that would have recalled the death of Christ to even the most apathetic churchgoer.

Shakespeare may have got the idea for comparing Brutus and Christ after he thought of comparing Caesar and Christ, having first decided to compare, in Plutarchan manner, Caesar and Brutus. The comparison in both cases is deeply ironic. Brutus thinks of himself as savior of the Republic, but he is also a betrayer and a murderer like Judas. Similarly, Caesar's followers, notably Antony and Octavius/Augustus, think of him as heroic and even divine, a martyr for Rome. But he is after all just a man, and an ambitious one at that. Plutarch writes that Caesar left behind him " a vaine name only, and a superficiall glory, that procured him the envy and hatred of his contrie."[50] If Renaissance culture was fashioned partly from that of classical Rome, early modern Christians still remained ambivalent about certain Roman values. "The Bible," as Cilfford Ronan argues, "helped increase Renaissance apprehension concerning power and the archeyptal secular repository of power, Rome."[51] The biblical allusions in *Julius Caesar* to Christ and the Crucifixion raise considerable apprehension about both Caesar and Brutus.

CORIOLANUS

Like *Julius Caesar*, *Coriolanus* is a play about pre-Christian Roman history that nevertheless contains Christian biblical allusions. Many of these allusions have been catalogued by Noble, Shaheen, and editors of the

---

[50] Bullough, "The Life of Julius Caesar," in Bullough, v. 88. The debate about whether Caesar was a hero or a tyrant continues. See Martin Jehne, "History's Alternative Caesars: *Julius Caesar* and Current Historiography," in Horst Zander (ed.), Julius Caesar: *New Critical Essays* (New York and London: Routledge, 2005), 59–70.

[51] Ronan, *"Antike Roman,"* 46. Ronan points out the many biblical passages criticizing monarchy as well as Jesus's rejection of the kingdoms of this world.

play, but critics have not much engaged with them. Philip Brockbank, for instance, in his Arden[2] *Coriolanus* notes that the remark about Coriolanus's success in battle, "in this city he | Hath unwidowed and unchilded many a one" (5.6.150–1) is an echo of Isaiah 47:9, "But these two things shal come to thee suddenly on one day, the losse of children and widdowehead." Yet the most Brockbank will say about this is that "like other Biblical echoes in the play, this one is highly suggestive without being in any way a controlled allusion."[52] Even Stanley Cavell, who takes biblical allusions seriously, is reluctant to commit himself, noting allusions that seem to suggest parallels between Coriolanus and Christ but calling such parallels "shadowy matters."[53] As in *Julius Caesar*, however, many biblical allusions in *Coriolanus* are indeed "controlled allusions" that would have been recognized by Shakespeare's audience as more than "shadowy matters." In fact, recognizing these allusions is essential for understanding Coriolanus's tragedy, which lies in the protagonist's failure to escape his humanity and achieve a kind of divinity.

Coriolanus, like Julius Caesar, is the central figure at a pivotal moment in Roman history. Caesar's assassination is the last gasp of the Republic, and it leads to the consolidation of power by Augustus and later emperors. In *Coriolanus*, an earlier political shift in the opposite direction is taking place: with the institution of the tribunes, elected representatives of the common people, constraints are being placed upon the power of the aristocracy in the Senate—constraints that Coriolanus himself finds intolerable. Shakespeare is exploring in both plays the political relationship between society and the individual, especially the remarkable individual. The Jacobean audience could easily perceive analogies to contemporary English politics in *Coriolanus*. For example, in 1608–10, when the play was performed, the Essex revolt of 1601 was still relatively recent, and Essex was certainly something of a Coriolanus figure. Sir Walter Raleigh, in the Tower at the time, was another. R. B. Parker cites

---

[52] *Coriolanus*, ed. Brockbank, 311.

[53] Stanley Cavell, "*Coriolanus* and the Interpretation of Politics," in *Disowning Knowledge in Six Plays of Shakespeare* (Cambridge: Cambridge University Press, 1987), 157. Published earlier as "'Who Does the Wolfe Love?': Coriolanus and the Interpretation of Politics," in Patricia Parker and Geoffrey Hartman (eds), *Shakespeare and the Question of Theory* (New York: Methuen, 1985) and "'Who Does the Wolf Love?': Reading Coriolanus," *Representations*, 3 (1983), 1–20. Bran Vickers also takes issue with Cavell's reference to "shadowy matters," but because he finds Cavell's essay and the very notion of biblical allusions in Coriolanus preposterous and irritating. While I take a different approach to *Coriolanus* from Cavell, I do agree with his suggestion that Coriolanus is a failed Christ. Like Vickers I find most Christianizing allegorical readings (which I explore in Ch. 3) wanting; unlike him, I obviously find the biblical allusions and parallels in *Coriolanus* essential. Brian Vickers, *Appropriating Shakespeare: Contemporary Critical Quarrels* (New Haven and London: Yale University Press, 1993), 378–84.

the relevance of the Midlands Uprising of 1607–8, a popular protest after a series of bad harvests produced a hunger crisis, as well as various other conflicts related to social class, popular franchise, and electoral procedures.[54] Other critics have pointed to the relevance of contemporary English concerns about civility and civic identity, James's conflicts with Parliament and Jacobean Republicanism.[55] But Shakespeare also seems to have had in mind a more universal political problem expressed in Aristotle's *Politics*: "But he that can not abide to live in companie, or through sufficiency hath need of nothing is not esteemed a part or member of a Cittie, but is either a beast or a god."[56] Man is by nature a social animal, according to Aristotle, essentially interdependent with his fellow humans, which makes a fiercely independent loner like Coriolanus an anomaly, with no legitimate place in the *polis*.

That Shakespeare had Aristotle in mind is evident in his comparisons of Coriolanus to a variety of both animals and divinities—beasts and gods. Coriolanus is associated at different points in the play with three models of divinity, none of which derives from Plutarch. The first model is Roman: Coriolanus is described as both Mars and Jupiter, the Roman gods of war and storm, respectively. In Act 2, for instance, a messenger describes how, upon Coriolanus' arrival in Rome, "the nobles bended | As to Jove's statue" (2.1.263–4). Menenius says that Coriolanus is so proud "He would not flatter Neptune for his trident, | Or Jove for's power to thunder" (3.1.254–5), but Titus Lartius's earlier account of the "thunder-like percussion of [his] sounds" suggests that Jupiter has nothing Coriolanus does not already have himself (1.4.59). Cominius describes how Coriolanus "struck Corioles like a planet"—presumably the planet Mars, Caius *Martius* Coriolanus' namesake (2.2.109, 113–14, emphasis added). Indeed, in Act 4 one of Aufidius' servants states that the Volscians treat Coriolanus "as if he were son and heir to Mars" (4.6.197). The second and third types of divinity in *Coriolanus* introduce a now-familiar anachronism:[57] these are the gods of the Old and New Testaments, Jehovah, the

---

[54] R. B. Parker (ed. and intro.), *Coriolanus* (Oxford and New York: Oxford University Press, 1994), 33–43.
[55] Cathy Shrank, "Civility and the City in *Coriolanus*," *SQ* 54/4 (2003), 406–23; Shannon Miller, "Topicality and Subversion in William Shakespeare's *Coriolanus*," *SEL* 32/2 (1992), 287–310; Alex Garganigo, "*Coriolanus*, the Union Controversy, and Access to the Royal Person," *SEL* 42/2 (2002), 335–59.
[56] *Aristotles Politiques*, translated by "I.D." from the French of Loys le Roy (1598), cited in Robert Miola, *Shakespeare's Rome* (Cambridge and New York: Cambridge University Press, 1983), 192.
[57] Technically, references to Jehovah are not anachronistic, since Coriolanus is said to have lived in the fifth century BCE and thus postdates the earliest Jewish prophets, not to mention Judaism itself. Much of Jewish scripture was not compiled, redacted, or even

destructive God of wrath who floods the world and burns Sodom and Gomorah, and Christ, the God (or Son of God) of love, who embodies humility, self-sacrifice, and mercy.[58] Whereas the comparison of Coriolanus to Roman gods is explicitly stated by characters in the play, however, the anachronistic comparisons to Christ and Jehovah are necessarily confined to the level of allusion, both verbal and visual.

As in *Julius Caesar*, Shakespeare's allusions in *Coriolanus* are comparative or analogical. Allusions to divinity, both explicit and implicit, provide a supplementary context for Shakespeare's exploration of the conflict between aristocratic and republican political values in terms of a parallel conflict between antithetical models of godhood. The military values of Coriolanus's Roman *virtus*,[59] embodied in the Roman pantheon by Mars the war god and Jupiter the god of thunder, are quite compatible with certain "virtues" of Jehovah: wrath, judgment, and vengeance. To be an effective politician, however, Coriolanus must demonstrate an entirely different set of virtues (less killing is required). He is called upon to show humility to the common people and mercy to the city of Rome, qualities embodied, for Christians, in Christ, a god who is significantly, simultaneously human.

Coriolanus is in his element in battle, and it is in this milieu that he is likened to the fierce Roman gods by whom he himself swears, but his anger and violence also evoke the wrathful god of the Old Testament familiar to Shakespeare's audience. The tribune Sicinius states that Coriolanus's hatred of the people

> Will be his fire
> To kindle their dry stubble; and their blaze
> Shall darken him forever. (2.1.255–7)

Though the tribune is, of course, unaware of it, his language echoes Isaiah's description of the judgment of Jehovah: "Therefore as the flame of

---

written until after the Babylonian Exile (post-538 BCE), however, and Coriolanus is a semi-legendary figure, so any precise chronology is problematic. Shakespeare in any case alludes to the "Old Testament" from a Christian perspective, and from that perspective they remain anachronistic.

[58] The Old Testament is, of course, the Christian designation for the Jewish Scriptures, restructured by the early Church according to Christian perspectives on the Bible and history. Thus, from the perspective of early modern English Christians, the "gods" of the Old and New Testaments might also be designated Jewish and Christian, though early moderns themselves would have designated them not as separate gods but rather as Father and Son, two parts of the Trinity.

[59] Plutarch writes that "in those days, valliantnes was honoured in Rome above all other virtues: which the class Virtus by the name of virtue selfe, as including in that generall name, all other speciall vertues besides. So that Virtus in Latin, was asmuche as valliantnes" (Plutarch, "The Life of Caius Martius Coriolanus," in Bullough, v. 506).

fyre devoureth the stubble, and as the chaffe is consumed of the flame....Therefore is the wrath of the Lord kindled against the people, and he hathe stretched out his hand upon them" (Isa. 5:24–5).[60] The godlike Coriolanus's wrathful disposition toward the people of Rome thus parallels that of Isaiah's wrathful god toward Israel. A similar parallel is suggested by the allusion to the Psalms in the description of Coriolanus by the Fourth Citizen in Act 2, scene 3: "You have been a scourge to her enemies, you have been a rod to her friends" (2.3.90–1). The allusion is to God's promise in the Psalms: "I will visit their offences with the rod, and their sin with scourges" (Ps. 89:32, *BCP*). In both cases, the allusions are subversive. In the first instance, Sicinius suggests that it is Coriolanus who will ultimately be destroyed; the implication of the metaphor within the allusive context seems to be that, as a man, unlike Isaiah's god, Coriolanus must stand in the midst of the human "stubble" he is setting alight. In the second allusion, Coriolanus's rage seems antithetical to the Psalm's statement of divine justice, since Coriolanus punishes indiscriminately both "enemies" and "friends" alike.

While Coriolanus is compared to multiple divinities throughout the play, the allusions that prompt comparisons to Christ are concentrated in several key scenes: 2.3, in which he must humbly seek the favor of the people; 3.3, when the crowd turns on him and calls for his death; 5.3, when he returns to Rome in judgment but shows mercy to the city after the intervention of his mother; and 5.6, which returns to the situation of 3.3 but with a different outcome. A connection between Coriolanus and Christ is suggested early in the play. After Coriolanus charges headlong through the gates of Corioles, one of his cowardly soldiers reports of his commander that "he is himself alone | To answer all the city" (1.4.51–2). Brockbank cites the Arden[1] note of R. H. Case, which identifies this as an echo of the Gospel of John: "When Jesus therefore perceived that they wolde come, and take him to make him a King, he departed againe into a mountaine him self alone" (John 6:15). The relatively commonplace phrase "himself alone" constitutes at best a faint echo on its own, but it increases in volume in the context of later allusions, and may have occurred to Shakespeare because of the parallel between Christ's rejection of

---

[60] Noted in Noble, 241, and Shaheen, 662. Shaheen suggests that Shakespeare's immediate source for this language is William Averell's *A Mervailous Combat of Contrarieties* (London: I. C[harlewood] for Thomas Hacket, 1588), but, since Averell is obviously himself alluding to Isaiah or similar biblical passages, no clear distinction seems either possible or necessary. It is ironic—and an irony Shakespeare was no doubt aware of—that the passage in Averell comes from his epistle against sedition, "To all true English heartes, that love God, their Queene, and Countrie" (sig. D4ʳ). This is another example of the complex intertextuality of Shakespeare's allusive practice.

kingship and Coriolanus's (later) attempted rejection of the Consulship, a political office for which he is unsuited. Erasmus explicates the verse from John in his *Paraphrases*:[61]

From theym that called hym to a kyngdome, he [Jesus] withdrewe hymselfe privelye all alone, so that no manne coulde perceive his goyng awaye, but of his owne free will he meteth theym that pulleth hym to the crosse, therein gevyng a playne exaumple to them that shoulde hereafter be his deputies. For he can never preache the ghospell purelye, that loveth a worldelye kyngdome and pompe, whiche thynges spirituall shepeherdes ought so litle to seeke for, that it behoveth them to refuse those thynges, though they be freelye geven them. For the kyngdome of the worlde agreeth not with the kyngdome of heaven, no more verilye then darkenesse and light accordeth.[62]

The irony of Shakespeare's allusion is that Coriolanus is much concerned with "the kyngdome of the worlde," but as a soldier he wants no part in its politics.

Allusive parallels between Coriolanus and Christ intensify as Coriolanus is eventually persuaded to enter the political arena. Brutus, for instance, describes the "pother" the citizens are making about Coriolanus in terms that recall Christ's unique combination of the human and divine:

> Such a pother
> As if that whatsoever god who leads him
> Were slily crept into his human powers,
> And gave him graceful posture. (2.1.216–19)

The tribune Brutus also describes the ritual Coriolanus must enact in order to gain the Consulship. According to the tribune, Coriolanus must don "the napless vesture of humility" and show "his wound s| To th'people" (2.1.232–4). In North's Plutarch, the clothing required by the ritual is a "poore gowne," a "simple gowne," and "mean apparel."[63] Shakespeare's "vesture of humility" extends the reference: "humility" may recall the injunction of 1 Peter, to "decke your selves inwardly in lowlines of minde: for God resisteth the proude and giveth grace to the humble" (1 Pet. 5:5). Humility is a consistent attribute of Christ, of course, but in Peter's text it is figuratively worn as a garment. Ironically, Coriolanus must wear his humility on the outside, unlike the Christian. Peter implies that decking oneself outwardly with humility is a form of pride; Coriolanus is hardly proud of his humility, but it is his pride that makes the humble garment

---

[61] For more on the *Paraphrases*, see Chs 1 and 4.
[62] *The first tome or volume of the Paraphrase of Erasmus vpon the Newe Testamente* (London: Edwarde Whitchurch, 1548), fo. 43ᵛ.
[63] Plutarch, *Lives*, trans. North, 331.

hateful to him. The term "vesture," as in *Julius Caesar*, alludes more specifically to the Crucifixion, when the soldiers cast lots over the "vesture" of Christ (Matt. 27:35). Finally, though accurately a Roman practice according to Plutarch, the showing of "his wounds | To th'people" echoes the Gospels (Luke 24:39–40 and John 20:20–8) in which the resurrected Christ must show his wounds to the disciples in order to gain their trust.[64]

Alexander Leggatt writes that, when Coriolanus is "translated from war to politics, he loses in translation."[65] While, as a soldier, Coriolanus can be an "army of one" (to cite the former US Army recruitment slogan), as a politician he must interact with and be responsible to and for others. This dilemma is represented partly in terms of contrastive, even parodic, allusions to Christ. For example, the Messenger to the tribunes describes Coriolanus's entry into Rome:

> I have seen the dumb men throng to see him,
> And the blind to hear him speak. (2.1.260–1)

As Brockbank notes, there is no equivalent for this passage in North's Plutarch, but the description alludes to that of Christ's miraculous healing in Matthew 15:30: "And great multitudes came unto him, having with them, halt, blinde, dome, maimed and manie other, and cast them downe at Jesus fete, and he healed them."[66] Matthew in turn alludes to Isaiah's messianic prophecy that "in that day shal the deafe heare the words of the boke, and the eyes of the blind shal se out of obscuritie, and out of darknes" (Isa. 29:18). But the allusion in Shakespeare's passage is parodic: if Coriolanus's "blind" *listeners* had seen and his "dumb" *viewers* spoken, his entry into Rome might have seemed more astonishing. As it is, this event, unlike the one recounted in Matthew, is decidedly unmiraculous.

Like *Julius Caesar*, *Coriolanus* also has its version of the Passion. Coriolanus's pointed silence through Act 2, scene 2 recalls the deliberate silence of Christ at his trial before Pilate:

And when he was accused of the chief Priests and Elders, he answered nothing.

Then said Pilate unto him, Hearest thou not how many things they lay against thee?

But he answered him not one worde. (Matt. 27:12–14)

---

[64] Cavell makes the same comparison, "*Coriolanus*," 158.
[65] Alexander Leggatt, *Shakespeare's Political Drama* (London and New York: Routledge, 1988), 192.
[66] *Coriolanus*, ed. Brockbank, 168.

Coriolanus's silence is not exactly an allusion in itself, since there is, of course, no verbal "trigger," but it seems to function as such in the context of other parallels to Christ's trial and *Coriolanus* 2.2. These further parallels are indicated by specific verbal allusions, and by visual allusions in the play's staging, costume, and gesture. Yet, as with all of the allusive parallels between Coriolanus and Christ, the differences between the Shakespearian and biblical scenes are marked. For example, Coriolanus is a nominee for the Consulship, and is listening to his own praises being sung, while Christ is accused as a criminal, and is listening to false charges being made against him. Nevertheless, the two scenes have strong similarities. Coriolanus must sit, against his will, to hear his "nothings monstered," and the Consulship is a position he is most reluctant to assume (2.2.77). Like Christ facing his trial and Crucifixion, Coriolanus dreads the forthcoming ritual in which he must submit to the people. Coriolanus begs Menenius (a surrogate for Coriolanus's strikingly absent father) to spare him this trial: "Please you | That I may pass this doing" (2.2.138–9). Similarly, in the garden of Gethsemane, Christ pleads, "O my Father, if it be possible, let this cup passe from me" (Matt. 26:39).

During the mandatory ritual, Coriolanus is, visually, at his most Christlike.[67] His emblematic clothing is again referred to as a "gown of humility" (2.3.41). When Coriolanus exclaims, referring to his battle scars, "Look, sir, my wounds!" (2.3.53), he echoes Christ's post-resurrection instruction to his disciples to witness his wounds: "Beholde me hands and my fete" (Luke 24:39).[68] However, Coriolanus speaks the phrase only in sarcastic mockery, stating that "I cannot bring | My tongue to such a pace" (2.3.52–3). Coriolanus's discomfort with the ritual is Shakespeare's invention: Plutarch writes that Coriolanus went through the ceremony dutifully, showing his wounds to all the people.[69] Shakespeare's scene may derive from a similar representation in the Mystery Plays as well as the biblical original. In the York Cycle, for instance, Christ shows his wounds

---

[67] Parker suggests that, at least in terms of the description of the "vesture of humility," Shakespeare has in mind the public humiliation of penitents in Elizabethan times (see *Coriolanus*, ed. Parker, 219). Bate describes a case of "white sheet penance" being imposed for adultery in 1616 upon Thomas Quiney, who was betrothed to Shakespeare's daughter Judith; Shakespeare would no doubt have been familiar with other such cases, both in Stratford and London (*Soul of the Age: A Biography of the Mind of William Shakespeare* [New York: Random House, 2009], 164, 179–80). The Elizabethan imitations were surely based on the humiliation of Christ, however, which was represented in countless printed images, as well as enacted in the Corpus Christi plays that Shakespeare seems to have seen.

[68] In Luke, Christ shows his hands and feet, but there is no mention of actual wounds; they seem to be implicit. This passage also tends to be conflated in the popular imagination with John 20, where Thomas actually places his hands in the nail holes and in Christ's side.

[69] Plutarch, *Lives*, trans. North, 332.

twice, first in the Scriveners Play, "The Incredulity of Thomas," and then finally in the Mercers' "The Judgment Day":

> Here may ye see my woundes wide,
> The whilke I tholed [suffered] for youre mysdede,
> Thurgh harte and heed, foote, hande, and hide,
> Nought for my gilte, butt for youre nede.
> Beholdis both body, bak, and side,
> How dere I bought youre brotherhede.[70]

Records of the original performance practice of the Mystery Plays have not survived, but it is likely that the actor playing Christ, whether on trial before Pilate, resurrected before the disciples, or returned for the final judgment, would have worn a costume like Coriolanus's "vesture of humility." Indeed, Jesus is almost always represented wearing a simple, long white robe, whether in contemporary paintings, woodcuts, or engravings, as in Albrecht Dürer's two sequences, the Large Passion and the Small Passion (see Fig. 5.2). Christ was, as Joseph Fletcher put it, the "Mirror of humility," and such a white robe was his traditional vesture, so a "vesture of humility" would naturally have been connected to Christ, especially in the context of the other allusions.[71]

Coriolanus's own description of the garment he must wear as a "wolvish toge" (3.2.114) alludes, in its combination of hypocrisy, humility, and animal disguise, to the warning from Matthew well known from anticlerical satires like Spenser's May eclogue in *The Shepheardes Calender*: "Beware of false prophetes, which comme to you in shepes clothing, but inwardly they are ravening wolves" (Matt. 7:15). The allusion seems once again contrastive, though complexly so: is Coriolanus a wolf in sheep's clothing or, as he suggests, just the opposite? In 2.1, Menenius, Brutus, and Sicinius wrestle with the wolf–sheep metaphor. Although the tribunes prefer the application the other way around, Menenius describes Coriolanus as a lamb to the citizens' wolves, which resonates with the biblical metaphor of Christ as the sacrificial Lamb of God (John 1:29 and elsewhere). A "gown of humility" is perhaps appropriate clothing for a lamb (if a lamb is going to wear anything), but Coriolanus insists the gown is a "wolvish toge." Perhaps, from Coriolanus's perspective, the clothing is "wolvish" in devouring its wearer in the same way that Nessus's robe did Hercules. (Menenius explicitly connects Hercules and Coriolanus at 4.6.100.[72]) In

---

[70] *York Plays*, 506, runes modernized.
[71] Joseph Fletcher, *Christes bloodie sweat, or the Sonne of God in his agonie* (London: Ralph Blower, 1613), 5.
[72] Cominius says, "He'll shake your Rome about your ears," and Menenius replies, "As Hercules | Did shake down mellow fruit."

Fig. 5.2. Coriolanus must abase himself, wearing the "napless vesture of humility" and showing "his wounds | To th'people" (2.1.232–4) in order to win their approval. The scene alludes to Christ's Passion in which Christ is similarly shown to the people who persuade Pilate to free a convicted criminal rather than the innocent Christ. Later, soldiers "cast lots" for Christ's "vesture" (Matt. 27). ("Christ shown to the people"; Jan Mostaert, oil on wood, Netherlands, c.510–15.) © The Metropolitan Museum of Art. Image source: ART Resource, New York.

any case, the incompatible wolf and lamb remain unreconciled, as one would expect if, like Shaheen, one hears Ecclesiasticus in Menenius' and Sicinius's discussion of the question "who does the wolf love?":[73] Everie beast loveth his like... How can the wolfe agre with the lambe? (Ecclus. 13.16, 18).

The wolf and the lamb—Coriolanus and the Roman populace, however configured—may therefore indeed be irreconcilable, and certainly Coriolanus is partly to blame, because of his utter lack of humility. The tribunes are also responsible, however, and their allusive role in 2.3, as in other scenes, is that of the "chief Priests and Elders" in the Crucifixion narrative, the manipulators behind the scenes who "had persuaded the people that thei shulde aske [for] Barabbas, and shulde destroy Jesus" (Matt. 27:20). The people condemn Coriolanus, but only after being persuaded to do so by Sicinius and Brutus, the "herdsmen of the beastly plebeians" (2.1.94–5; see also 3.1.32). This "priestly" role of the tribunes is confirmed in Coriolanus's "Crucifixion" scene. Like Christ's, Coriolanus's sentence has been predetermined. The people play the part of the biblical mob, crying, "To th'rock, to th'rock with him" (3.3.75; compare "Crucifie, crucife him," Luke 23:21). The voices of the people continue in the same fashion throughout the scene. The tribunes, specifically Sicinius, state:

> We need not put new matter to his charge.
> What you have seen him do, and heard him speak,
> . . . . .
> Deserves th'extremest death. (3.3.77–8, 83)

This speech alludes, in the variations on "What need we...," to the speech of the High Priest in Matthew, who asks, "He hathe blasphemed: what have we any more nede of witnesses?" (Matt. 26:65).[74]

Given the parallels to Christ's trial, we may expect Coriolanus's trial to lead to execution. Indeed, this is what the people and their tribunes initially insist upon. It is also what Coriolanus invites, daring the people to give him "Death on the wheel, or at the wild horses' heels" or on the "Tarpeian rock" (3.2.2–3). But Coriolanus is denied martyrdom. Although he has failed to be humble in begging the people's voices (2.3), and he has failed to speak "mildly" against their accusations (3.3), he is not killed but banished. Still, even his final words continue the parallel: he reverses the verdict against him, proclaiming, "I banish you!" and he condemns the

---

[73] Shaheen, 661.
[74] The Bishops' Bible version is: "He hath spoken blasphemie, what nede we of any mo witnesses?"

people for their "ignorance" (3.3.123, 129). In his procession to Calvary, Christ similarly reverses the sentence passed upon him: "Daughters of Jerusalem, wepe not for me, but wepe for your selves, and for your children" (Luke 23:28). Christ, however, is sincerely sorry for those who condemn him, and, even though he, like Coriolanus, calls them ignorant, he forgives them for it: "Father, forgive them: for they knowe not what thei do" (Luke 23:34). In Plutarch's depiction of Coriolanus's banishment, charges are brought against him by the tribunes that are not mentioned by Shakespeare. The verdict is assigned to the "voyces of the Tribes," but Plutarch does not note the actual words of the judgment.[75] Nor, in Plutarch, does Coriolanus have anything to say after his sentence is passed.

Coriolanus presents a poor imitation of Christ, yet the ironic allusions in Acts 2 and 3 might have suggested to Shakespeare's audience one reason for Coriolanus's political failure. As the tribune Brutus remarks, Coriolanus lacks the necessary humility, since, "With a proud heart he wore | His humble weeds" (2.3.151–2). The tribune astutely reads Coriolanus's true character in terms of divinity:

> You speak o'th' people
> As if you were a god to punish, not
> A man of their infirmity. (3.1.79–81)

Brutus is correct. Coriolanus fails because he is unable to abase himself to the common people. Coriolanus is the man so proud that he behaves like a god; Christ, on the other hand, is the god who so humbles himself that he becomes a man. And the kind of god on which Coriolanus models his behavior is, as Brutus recognizes, not the New Testament god of love but a "god to punish," a god of vengeance and warfare, like Mars or Jehovah.

Comparisons between Coriolanus and the latter types of divinity intensify following his banishment, as he becomes increasingly solitary and inhuman, ultimately being described as an "engine" or "a thing made for Alexander" (5.4.19, 22). In the play's last two acts, he abandons political aspirations and becomes a soldier again, obsessed by a desire for vengeance on Rome. Cominius reports Coriolanus's position with respect to the Volsces:

> He is their god. He leads them like a thing
> Made by some other deity than nature... (4.6.91–2)

Aufidius' Lieutenant has the same opinion of his new commander, remarking that he inspires such awe that the "soldiers use him as their grace 'for meat" (4.7.3). Cominius returns to the biblical harvest metaphor, reporting that Coriolanus no longer cares even for his friends and "could

---

[75] Plutarch, *Lives*, trans. North, 341.

not stay to pick them in a pile | Of noisome musty chaff" (5.1.25–6). The allusion builds on the earlier echo of Isaiah, likening Coriolanus to the wrathful Jehovah, except that in this case the language points not to Isaiah but to John the Baptist's modified use of the same metaphor to describe the coming of Christ, "Which hathe his fanne in his hand, and wil make cleane his floore, and gather his wheat into his garner, but wil burne up the chaffe with unquenchable fyre" (Matt. 3:12). Unlike Christ's, Coriolanus's fire is undiscriminating. As Cominius further reports, "He said 'twas folly, | For one poor grain or two, to leave unburnt" (5.1.26–7). As most editors note, this passage alludes to the agreement of Abraham's God to spare Sodom for the sake of a few righteous men (Gen. 18:23–33).[76] The significant point for the attentive listener is that Coriolanus is here even more vengeful than the Old Testament Jehovah at his angriest. The fire of Coriolanus's anger, a metaphorical expression of his literal plan to burn Rome, will become a recurring image in Acts 4 and 5: Coriolanus's army "consumed with fire and took | What lay before them" (4.6.81–2); Cominius describes Coriolanus not answering to any name until he has "forged himself a name of fire | In burning Rome" (5.1.14–15); Menenius accuses Coriolanus of "preparing a fire for us" (5.2.70). Although Plutarch describes "the fyer of his choler,"[77] allusions to the divine retributive fire of the Old Testament are exclusive to Shakespeare's version.

Act 5, scene 3, like the pivotal scenes 2.3 and 3.3, combines verbal and visual allusions, primarily to Christ. First, the key image of the scene is Coriolanus enthroned as judge, a visual tableau anticipated by Cominius's earlier description:

> I tell you, he does sit in gold, his eye
> Red as 'twould burn Rome... (5.1.63–4)

Cavell suggests an allusion to the figure of Christ in Revelation, who sits on a throne in heaven and whose "eyes were a flame of fyre" (Rev. 4:2, 1:14).[78] In this case, Coriolanus is likened to Christ in a manifestation that better suits his wrathful nature, that of his prophesied Second Coming on the Day of Judgment. Second, when in 4.6. Cominius anticipates Coriolanus's later arrival, he works another variation on the wolf–sheep metaphor. Cominius states of Coriolanus that

> the people
> Deserve such pity of him as the wolf
> Does of the shepherds. (4.6.111–12)

---

[76] See, e.g., *Coriolanus*, ed. Brockbank, 277; *Coriolanus*, ed. Parker, 322.
[77] Plutarch, *Lives*, trans. North, 343.   [78] Cavell, "*Coriolanus*," 159.

As in 2.1, one expects Coriolanus to be the wolf, yet again the term is unexpectedly applied to the Roman people. The comparison of Coriolanus to a shepherd recalls Christ the "good shepherd" of John 10:14, but in the gospels the shepherd represents care and protection, not punishment. (As Christ says, he "giveth his life for his shepe.") Third, Coriolanus's rejection of his family ties also parallels Christ's:

> Wife, mother, child I know not. My affairs
> Are servanted to others. (5.2.80–1)

Likewise, Christ asks, "Who is my mother? and who are my brethren?" (Matt. 12:48). Of course, while Coriolanus aims to renounce all bonds to family (and to Rome, and, despite his claim that his affairs are "servanted to others," that is, the Volscians, to humanity in general), Christ is embracing a more universal notion of family, extending to all mankind. This marks a contrast between Christ's broad humanity and Coriolanus's desire to

> stand
> As if a man were author of himself
> And knew no other kin. (5.3.35–7)

The last act's critical moment is Volumnia's petition to Coriolanus for "mercy" on behalf of Rome (5.3.137). Cominius sees Rome as entirely dependent upon Coriolanus's granting her request, stating, "We are all undone unless | The noble man have mercy" (4.6.108–9). Later, Menenius states that Coriolanus lacks "nothing of a god but eternity, and a heaven to throne in." But the ever-perceptive Sicinius replies, "Yes, mercy, if you report him truly" (5.4.24–6). Noble notes two references to Isaiah in Menenius's statement:[79]

For thus sayth he, that is hie and excellent, he that inhabiteth the eternitie, whose Name is the Holie one .... (Isa. 57:15)
Thus saith the Lord, the heaven is my throne. (Isa. 66:1)

These references constitute faint though perhaps genuine echoes. More relevant, perhaps, are the thirty-eight references to "throne" in Revelation (over twice as many as in all the rest of the New Testament), which book is in large part a pastiche of verses from Isaiah and other prophets. Combined with Cominius's description of Coriolanus sitting "in gold, his eye | Red" with fire, Menenius's comment reinforces the allusion to Christ's sitting in Judgment on the Last Day.[80] It is significant, in light of

---

[79] Noble, 242.
[80] On the Last Judgment as represented as the "Doom" in English churches, including the Guild Chapel in Stratford, see Ch. 7.

Shakespeare's variations on "lamb–wolf" imagery in Coriolanus, that the figure in Revelation who sits upon the throne is a lamb. This is a lamb with a difference, however, wrathful and capable of the defeat in battle of many kings and beasts (Rev. 6:16, 17:14). Sicinius's emphasis on the need for mercy evokes one of the most commonly espoused values of the New Testament. Brockbank compares Sicinius's response to the words of the Communion Prayer: "But thou art the same Lord, whose property is always to have mercy."[81] By contrast, Coriolanus has no such property.

Unbeknownst to Menenius and Cominius, however, Coriolanus has in fact already demonstrated the very quality Sicinius accused him of lacking. Volumnia is jubilant at the turn of events, and she predicts an exclamation from the people, "Be blest | For making up this peace!" (5.3.139–40), echoing the Beatitudes' declaration, "Blessed are the peace makers" (Matt. 5:9). This act marks a change for Coriolanus from wrath to mercy, making comparisons with Christ seem, for the first time, apt. St Paul's letter to the Ephesians also seems to lie behind this scene of transformation, signaled by Menenius's comparison of Coriolanus to the "cornerstone" of the Capitol (5.4.1–6). His intention is to emphasize Coriolanus's immovability, as well as his inhumanity; analogies to a "dragon," an "engine," and a "tiger" follow. Yet, ironically, in the previous scene Coriolanus *has* been moved, and has demonstrated human empathy after all. It is appropriate that "cornerstone" (Shakespeare's only use of the word in his works) alludes to the metaphor of Christ as the "chief corner stone" (Eph. 2:20). The emphasis in Ephesians 2 is on conversion, and St Paul welcomes the Ephesians, who are "no more strangers and foreigners: but citizens with the Saintes, and of the householde of God" (Eph. 2:19). The transformation from "stranger" to "citizen" is precisely the one Coriolanus himself undergoes at this point.

As Aufidius remarks, Coriolanus has also undergone a transformation of values from "honor" to "mercy." But this shift, Aufidius recognizes with delighted self-interest, will be Coriolanus's undoing:

> I am glad thou hast set thy mercy and thy honour
> At difference in thee. Out of that I'll work
> Myself a former fortune. (5.3.200–2)

In fact, Coriolanus also predicts his own downfall:

> Behold, the heavens do ope,
> The gods look down, and this unnatural scene

---

[81] *Coriolanus*, ed. Brockbank, 299. The quotation from the Book of Common Prayer Communion Service is a good one, but the language of mercy also runs throughout the Book of Common Prayer and the Gospels.

> They laugh at. O my mother, mother! O!
> You have won a happy victory to Rome;
> But for your son, believe it, O, believe it,
> Most dangerously you have with him prevail'd,
> If not most mortal to him. (5.3.183–9)

Shaheen notes in the opening lines of this speech a reference to Acts, "Behold, I se the heavens open, and the Sonne of man standing at the right hand of God" (Acts 7:56). If this is what Shakespeare had in mind, the allusion is highly appropriate, since these are the final words of St Stephen, the first Christian martyr. For Coriolanus at least, this "mortal" moment is indeed a kind of martyrdom, sacrificing himself for the good of Rome, or at least for his family. For the audience, however, the meaning of the allusion—whether it points to similarity or difference—is difficult to gauge. Although the word "mortal" is used by Plutarch in Coriolanus's speech to his mother,[82] it acquires a different connotation in Shakespeare's *Coriolanus*, with its allusive subtext. Volumnia has, on the one hand, persuaded her son to a "mortal" action, since, as Coriolanus senses, it will lead to his death. But she has also forced him to concede his common humanity, reducing him to the merely "mortal." At the end of the play, Coriolanus returns to Antium to be cut down by the mob, led on by Aufidius and his fellow conspirators, in a repetition of the earlier "Crucifixion" scene in Rome. The parallels this time seem more legitimate. Aufidius, whom Coriolanus trusted, has betrayed him and made false charges against him, and, like the crowd in Luke 23:21 ("Crucifie, crucifie him"), the Volscian crowd chants for his death: "Kill, kill, kill, kill, kill him" (5.6.130).

Coriolanus deals in part with the political problem of accommodating the exceptional individual—especially an outstanding warrior, whose skills are essentially antisocial—within an increasingly egalitarian society. Certainly, such accommodation is the last thing Coriolanus himself wants, and he struggles against community, against his humanity, against his ties to other people, even his family. In a sense, Sicinius is right when he accuses Coriolanus of wanting to "depopulate the city and | Be every man himself" (3.1.262–3). Furthermore, Coriolanus's monolithic integrity, his inability to "seem | The same you are not" (3.2.46–7), not only renders him politically impotent (great politicians in Shakespeare—Richard III, Henry V, Marc Antony—are always great actors); it also makes him seem inhuman. When Coriolanus asserts that he can only "play | The man I am" (3.2.15–16), although he expresses precisely the

---

[82] Plutarch, *Lives*, trans. North, 363.

opposite of Iago's nihilistic "I am not what I am" (*Othello*, 1.1.65) both statements nevertheless allude to and reformulate the same biblical passage: God's statement of absolute completeness and self-sufficiency, "I am that I am" (Exod. 3:14). But a human being cannot be entirely self-sufficient; if he cannot be "part or member of a Cittie," he must be either a beast or a god. Aristotle's point, of course, is that men cannot be gods, just as they cannot really be beasts. Men are inescapably, unavoidably human, and to be human means to be socially interdependent.

Like Christ, Coriolanus is "too absolute" for the world of politics (3.2.39). Certainly, like Christ, Coriolanus shows mercy to those that hate him when he halts his campaign against Rome. Like Christ, Coriolanus is finally a victim of the mob (set on by the conspiring Volcsian "Pharisees"), killed after false accusations have been laid to his charge. However, despite similarities suggested by Shakespeare's biblical allusions, Coriolanus is not a god and never can be. His defiant assertion, "There is a world elsewhere!" (3.3.135), recalls Christ's answer to Pilate, "My kingdome is not of this worlde" (John 18:36), but with considerable irony. Coriolanus's kingdom—his republic anyway—is very much of this world, and, for him, there is actually no world elsewhere, certainly not a transcendent one. Without a heaven, and dying with a curse rather than a blessing on his lips, Coriolanus makes a sad martyr. Kenneth Burke argued nevertheless that Coriolanus is a scapegoat sacrificed to ease "the pervasive unresolved tension typical of a given social order."[83] Coriolanus is ultimately destroyed by the people (though he is less a sheep devoured by wolves than, more pathetically, a wolf devoured by sheep). But, even if this is the case, a human scapegoat is a far lesser creature than Christ's sacrificial Lamb, the latter a manifestation of God, the former a mere beast.[84] On the other hand, just because Coriolanus is not a god, must he die like a beast? The problem with such an interpretation is that Coriolanus' downfall is the result of his one genuinely human gesture. What Harold Bloom calls Coriolanus' "solipsism" is defeated only by Volumnia, who alone is able to avert Coriolanus's attack.[85] Coriolanus never demonstrates fellow-feeling with the common people, but Volumnia prevails with him because she is his mother, his one undeniable link to humanity. Volumnia, who draws Coriolanus's attention to his "mother's womb | That brought thee to the world," is the physical proof that he is not "author of

---

[83] Kenneth Burke, "*Coriolanus*—and the Delights of Faction," in Harold Bloom (ed.), *Modern Critical Interpretations: William Shakespeare's* Coriolanus (New York: Chelsea House, 1988), 33–50, 48–9. One could apply Burke's argument to *Julius Caesar* as well, or at least this is how Brutus would like us to interpret Caesar's assassination.

[84] Burke, "*Coriolanus*," 49.

[85] Bloom (ed. and intro.), *Modern Critical Interpretations*, 5.

himself" (5.3.124–5, 36). By turning aside his attack, Coriolanus acknowledges her claim on him, but his acknowledgment of her kinship has wider implications as a tacit recognition of his kinship with his fellow Romans and with humanity as a whole. (In this context, Sicinius's earlier question to Volumnia, "Are you mankind?" takes on added significance [4.2.16].) It may be, finally, that Coriolanus dies as neither a god nor a beast, but as a man. However reluctant, partial, and contentious his admission of his own unself-sufficient humanity, Coriolanus does indeed make such an admission; perhaps his tragedy and his achievement are that this admission makes him truly, and in all senses, "mortal."

ANTONY AND CLEOPATRA

Like *Julius Caesar* and *Coriolanus*, *Antony and Cleopatra* contains significant anachronistic allusions to the Bible, but the anachronism in this play is even more radical than the others, amounting (perhaps) to a rejection of history itself.[86] Like them, *Antony and Cleopatra* represents a pivotal historical moment. In *Coriolanus*, Rome is on the brink of change from an aristocratic to a more democratic republic, the institution of the tribunes marking an increase in popular representation that to Coriolanus is an intolerable constraint on his noble prerogatives. *Julius Caesar* and *Antony and Cleopatra*, on the other hand, represent two consecutive phases in the death of the republic and the birth of empire. The conflict between Antony and (Octavius) Caesar marked the end of the long civil wars among the members of the two triumvirates—Julius Caesar, Pompey, and Crassus; and Octavius, Antony, and Lepidus—and the beginning of the imperial Golden Age under the Caesar who would become known as Augustus. Caesar's statement in Shakespeare's play that "the time of universal peace is near" refers to this *Pax Romana*, the Golden Age, the period of extended peace and prosperity that he will achieve after the defeat and death of Antony and Cleopatra (4.6.5). For Shakespeare's audience, however, the "time of universal peace" would have had an additional resonance from the Gospel of Luke, in which the angels sing to the shepherds, "Glorie be to God in the high heavens, and peace in earth, and towards men good wil" (Luke 2:14). This birth of Christ thus also ushers in a time

---

[86] Any statement about *Antony and Cleopatra* must remain tentative, since, as Janet Adelman demonstrates so well, "both the presentation of character and the dramatic structure work to frustrate our reasonable desire for certainty." Nothing in this play about "infinite variety" is certain. *The Common Liar: An Essay on* Antony and Cleopatra (New Haven and London: Yale University Press, 1973), 15.

of "universal peace." Historically, the Roman and Christian peaces coincided, since Luke's Jesus was born in the reign of Augustus Caesar (Luke 2:1), shortly after the events of Shakespeare's play. The tradition of aligning the *Pax Romana* and the *Pax Christi* goes back at least as far as the medieval interpretation of Virgil's fourth eclogue, only slightly modified by Renaissance humanists, according to which Virgil prophesied the return of the "Virgin" and the birth of a child "by whom the Age of Iron gives way to the Golden Age."[87] In his *Christian Directory* (1590), Robert Parsons wrote that Virgil had based the prophecy on "the Sibyls talking of the comming of Christ," and that both were examples of the revelation of Christ's coming to the Jews and Pagan Gentiles.[88] An intricate anachronistic web is at play: Shakespeare's *Antony and Cleopatra* alludes (anachronistically) to the birth of Christ; Virgil's Eclogue was understood to allude to (anachronistically) or to prophesy the birth of Christ; yet the real subject of Virgil's "prophecy" was the son of Antony and his wife Octavia, who would bring about the peace intended to result from this political marriage.[89] A further level of anachronism connects Augustus Caesar and James I, who saw his own reign as bringing in a time of peace, both by uniting England and Scotland and by ending the long war with Spain; James's coronation medal proclaimed him as the Caesar Augustus of Britain and references to Augustus were prominent in ceremonies welcoming James to London.[90]

Caesar's reference to "the time of universal peace" is not a precise biblical allusion and would not in itself constitute a strong evocation of a Christian context. However, the sense of the new Christian age on the horizon in *Antony and Cleopatra* is underscored by the number of references in the play to Herod, a name that for Christians automatically recalls the story of Christ's Nativity. References to "Herod" in *Antony and Cleopatra* designate explicitly Herod the Great (73 BCE–4 BCE), who is mentioned in Plutarch's "Life of Antony." For the Egyptians or Romans

---

[87] Virgil, Eclogue IV, in *The Eclogues of Virgil*, trans. David Ferry (New York: Farrar, Strauss and Giroux, 1999), 29. On Renaissance interpretations of Virgil's supposed prophecies or anticipations of Christianity, see Craig Kallendorf, "From Virgil to Vida: The Poeta Theologus in Italian Renaissance Commentary," *Journal of the History of Ideas*, 56/1 (1995), 41–62.

[88] Robert Parsons, *The seconde parte of the booke of Christian exercise, appertayning to resolution. Or a Christian directorie, guiding all men to their saluation* (London: John Charlwoode and [i.e. for] Simon Waterson, 1590), 248. For evidence that Shakespeare read Parsons's *Christian Directory*, see Ch. 8.

[89] See Guy Lee's translation and edition of *The Eclogues* (Harmondsworth: Penguin, 1980; rev. 1984), 25 and 115, note to IV.8–10.

[90] H. Neville Davies, "Jacobean 'Antony and Cleopatra'," in John Drakakis (ed.), *Antony and Cleopatra*, New Casebooks (New York: St Martins Press, 1994), 126–65, 128.

to refer to this Herod in Shakespeare's play is thus not anachronistic. The first reference to Herod in *Antony and Cleopatra*, however, suggests (anachronistically) not Plutarch but the Gospel of Matthew, and not Herod the Great but Herod Antipas, his son.[91] Charmian says to the Soothsayer, "Let me be married to three kings in a forenoon and widow them all. Let me have a child at fifty, to whom Herod of Jewry may do homage" (1.2.25–7). Logically, of course, this must be Herod the Great. Yet for anyone who has heard Matthew's Nativity story, the combination of "three kings" and a "child" to whom "Herod of Jewry" might do homage is an unmistakable allusion, however impossible historically, to the story of Jesus, Herod, and the Magi. Matthew tells of "Wisemen from the East" (traditionally three, based on the number of their gifts) who come to Jerusalem to ask Herod about the birth of "the King of the Jewes" (Matt. 2:1–2). The jealous Herod slyly asks them to tell him when they find the child, so that "I may come also, and worship him" (Matt. 2:8). The wisemen—wisely—do not give word to Herod, who proceeds to slaughter all the male infants of Israel in an attempt to kill the young rival and secure his crown. Later in Shakespeare's play, when Alexas tells Cleopatra that "Herod of Jewry dare not look upon you/But when you are well pleased," Cleopatra responds, "That Herod's head I'll have" (3.3.2–5). Historically, Herod kept his head, but Cleopatra's comment evokes the beheading of John the Baptist by Herod (Antipas again) at the request of Salome (Matt. 14:3–12),[92] though Cleopatra overreaches the biblical Salome in demanding the head of the king himself. Furthermore, in 3.6, Herod of Jewry ("the Great" this time) is one of the kings Caesar lists among the allies of Antony, and Herod's desertion is described later by Enobarbus (4.6.13–15). Herod the Great is part of Plutarch's narrative, but Shakespeare conflates him, anachronistically, with his far more familiar son.[93] As Hamlet's reference to "out Heroding Herod" indicates, Herod (Antipas) was a familiar character even outside the pages of the biblical text and the liturgy, a

---

[91] John Wilders suggests that Shakespeare confused the two Herods (*Antony and Cleopatra*, note to 3.3.3). But he seems to be purposefully conflating the two, referencing the older Herod in order to allude, anachronistically, to the younger one, whom his characters could not know but who was nevertheless part of the Christian story he wished to engage.

[92] Salome is not named in the gospel, being referenced simply as the daughter of Herodias, Herod's mistress and sister-in-law, but she is named in Josephus's *Antiquities of the Jews* and traditionally known as such.

[93] As Shaheen suggests (649), the same anachronistic effect might have occurred with the reference to "Archelaus | Of Cappadocia" in Caesar's list of kings on Antony's side (3.6.69–70). Some in the audience might have recalled the Archelaus mentioned in Matt. 2:22, who is the son and heir of Herod Antipas. News of Herod's death and Archelaus's inheritance brings Joseph and his family back to Israel from Egypt.

bombastic villain in the Corpus Christi plays, and a familiar subject in stained glass and sculpture.[94]

Antony and Cleopatra thus evokes the beginning of the Christian era, even though that era has not yet begun at the time the story is set. However, despite Shakespeare's allusions to the Nativity and the sense of imminent new beginnings they suggest, the most pervasive pattern of biblical allusions in *Antony and Cleopatra* is actually to the end of time, as decribed in the Book of Revelation. From the first scene, Antony expresses to Cleopatra the need for a "new heaven" and a "new earth," ones able to contain the infinite overflow of their love. A "new heaven" and "new earth" alludes to John's account in Revelation that he "sawe a new heaven, and a new earth: for the first heaven, and the first earth were passed away" (Rev. 21:1).[95] Indeed, of the more than sixty printed books on *EEBO* between Tyndale's 1534 New Testament and 1606 that reference a "new heaven" and "new earth," every one is either a version of Revelation, a comment on Revelation, or an application of John's prophecy to some other context.[96] Antony's desire that his sons may be "kings of kings" (3.6.13) is taken directly from Plutarch, but to a Christian audience, especially combined with Cleopatra's later address to Antony as "Lord of lords," this superlative is far more recognizable as an epithet for Christ: in Revelation, Christ appears with "KING OF KINGS, AND LORD OF LORDS" inscribed on his garment and his thigh (Rev. 19:16).[97] Another *EEBO* search reveals that, while the epithet "king of kings" is occasionally used to describe rulers like Alexander or Agamemnon, the vast majority of references (in 433 publications up to 1606) are to God or Christ. A further allusion to Revelation appears in Antony's description of his own downfall; he says that this is a time

> When my good stars that were my former guides
> Have empty left their orbs and shot their fires
> Into the abysm of hell. (3.13.149–51)

---

[94] Peter Richardson, *Herod: King of the Jews, Friend of the Romans* (Columbia, SC: University of South Carolina Press, 1996), 288. Herod features in two plays, for instance, in the N-Town or Coventry Cycle, *The Adoration of the Magi* and *The Slaughter of the Innocents*.

[95] John himself here alludes to God's prophecy in Isa. 65:17 that "I will create new heavens and a new earth"; Peter also states in 2 Peter 3:13 that "We looke for newe heavens, and a newe earth."

[96] Antony Colynet, for instance, applies John's apocalyptic prophecy ironically to the possibility of peace after the French Civil Wars. See *The true history of the civill warres of France* (London: [Thomas Orwin] for Thomas Woodcock, 1591). Colynet's is the most secular use of the phrase, and even he is self-consciously alluding to Revelation.

[97] Bullough, v. 290. Shaheen (648) also notes that the phrase "kings of kings" appears in Mary Sidney Herbert's *The Tragedie of Antonie*.

In his vision of the fifth angel in Revelation, John writes, "I sawe a starre fall from heaven unto the earth, and to him was given the keye of the bottomless pit. And he opened the bottomless pit, and there arose the smoke of the pit, as the smoke of a great furnace" (Rev. 9:1–2). The allusion is not marked by strict verbal parallels, but by the coincidence of stars falling, the fire (implied by the smoke and furnace), and the equivalence of "abysm" and "bottomless pit." (Shaheen notes that the Greek word in Revelation translated as "bottomless pit" is *abussos*, the root of both "abyss" and "abysm."[98]) The image of the fallen star returns in the guards' response to Antony's botched suicide: "The star is fall'n," says one, and the other responds, "And time is at his period." Both cry, "Alas, and woe" (4.14.8–10). Allusions to several additional passages from Revelation are combined here:[99]

> And there fell a great starre from heaven burning like a torch. (Rev. 8:10)
> And he sware... that time shulde be no more. (Rev. 10:6)
> Wo, wo, wo to the inhabitants of the earth. (Rev. 8:13)

As they did for Julius Caesar, Brutus, and Coriolanus, the biblical allusions here suggest parallel figures for Antony. In the first instance, Antony and Christ are linked, since both are (in their own ways) lords of lords. The references to falling stars, however, are more ambiguous; Revelation 9:1–2 was interpreted diversely by Shakespeare's contemporaries. The Geneva Bible (1560) glossed the star as "the Bishopes and ministers, which forsake the worde of God, and so fall out of heaven, & become Angels of darkenes," while the star with the key to the bottomless pit is said to be the Pope. However, John Napier, author of the popular *A plaine discouery of the whole Revelation of Saint John* (1593), argued that the falling star "must needs be the Mahomet, who fell from his former Christian profession, and became an Apostate, and out of the smoke of his heresie, stirred up the Turkes to be his armie."[100] Erasmus's *Paraphrases* interpreted the falling star as the devil, who "thorowe the judgement of god, he is

---

[98] Shaheen, 651.

[99] Ethel Seaton also noted the possible relevance of Rev. 9:6 to Antony's unfulfilled suicide: "Therefore in those daies shal men seke death, and shal not finde it, and shal desire to dye, and death shal flee from them" (Seaton, "*Antony and Cleopatra* and the Book of Revelation," *RES* 22/87 (1946), 219–24). An audience steeped in Revelation might have noticed the parallel with Antony's death attempt, but, rather than an allusion, this may be another example of a fruitful intertextual coincidence recognized by Shakespeare that led him to design his allusive subtext. Shakespeare's depiction of Antony's death follows Plutarch.

[100] John Napier, *A plaine discouery of the whole Revelation of Saint John* (Edinburgh: Robert Waldgrave, 1593), 5. Napier's commentary was reprinted several times in Edinburgh and London. Napier (1550–1617) was a Scottish mathematician who also studied and wrote on theology. His *plaine discovery*, dedicated to James VI of Scotland, was extremely popular, frequently reprinted and translated into several other languages. See the *ODNB* article by George Molland.

Creative Anachronism 219

fallen downe from heaven, unto the earthe, and hath received thorowe the judgement of god, and thorowe his permission, the key of hell and of the bottomless pyt of all wyckednesse."[101] This interpretation of Revelation 9:1–2 sees it as a fulfillment of Isaiah's prophecy, one of the few references to the devil (as it was interpreted) in the Old Testament: "How art thou fallen from heaven, o Lucifer, sonne of the morning?" (Isaiah 14:12). On the other hand, Francis Junius took an entirely different view:

> Whether thou take him [the star/angel] for Christ, who hath the keyes of hell himself, and by Princely authoritie, Chapter. 1.18 or whether for some inferior Angell, who hath the same key permitted unto him, and occupieth it ministerially, or by office of his ministrie; here and Chapter. 21. so the word *falling* is taken Gene.14.10. and 24.64 and Hebr. 6.6.[102]

Junius's commentary, reprinted many times, was also incorporated into the marginal glosses of many later editions of the Geneva Bible (the so-called Tomson–Junius editions published from 1599). In a later edition, *The Apocalyps*, additional commentary by "Fr Du Ion" explains Junius's gloss on "falling": "he fell from heaven, that is to say, that he threwe himself downe from above with such a vehemencie, as if he had tumbled downe and could not hold up himself."[103]

So do the allusions to Antony's falling star represent him as divine or diabolical? If the audience interprets John's falling star as the devil (Lucifer), the allusion would emphasize Antony's own fallenness and degeneracy (fitting Caesar's description of him as "a man who is the abstract of all faults | That all men follow" [1.4.8–9]). The allusion to Christ (as Lord of lords) would presumably then be parodic, pointing toward Antony as some kind of Antichrist or false messiah, an appropriate figure perhaps in the context of Revelation. Such an interpretation would jibe with readings of Cleopatra as a Whore of Babylon, also supported by biblical allusions.[104] Caesar tells his sister Octavia that Antony

> hath given his empire
> Up to a whore, who now are levying
> The kings o'th' earth for war. (3.6.67–9)

---

[101] Desiderius Erasmus, "A paraphrase or comentarie upon the Revelation of St. John faythfullye translated by Edmund Alen," fo. xi^v, in *The seconde tome or volume of the Paraphrase of Erasmus upon the Newe Testament* (London: Edward Whitchurch, 1549).

[102] Francis Junius, *Apocalypsis A briefe and learned commentarie upon the revelation of Saint John* (London: Richard Field for Robert Dexter, 1592), 28.

[103] Francis Junius, *The Apocalyps, or Revelation of S. John the apostle and evangelist of our Lord Jesus Christ* (Cambridge: John Leggat, 1596), 98.

[104] See, e.g., Clifford Davidson, "*Antony and Cleopatra*: Circe, Venus, and the Whore of Babylon," in Davidson, *History, Religion and Violence: Cultural Contexts for Medieval and Renaissance English Drama* (Aldershot: Ashgate, 2002), 64–94.

Later, after Cleopatra's fleet has failed to engage the enemy, Antony himself calls her "Triple-turned whore!" (4.12.13). In Revelation 17:1–2 one of the seven angels says to John, "Come: I wil shewe thee the damnacion of the great whore that sitteth upon many waters, With whome have committed fornication the Kings of the earth, and the inhabitants of the earth are drunken with the wine of her fornication." The "Kings of the earth" (on the righteous side this time) are gathered to battle the Beast in Revelation 19:19. Thus the conjunction of a "whore" with the "kings of the earth" suggests Cleopatra as the Whore of Babylon (properly, "A Mysterie, great Babylon, the mother of whoredomes, and abhominations of the earth," Rev. 17:5). Leeds Barroll also points out that Enobarbus's description of Cleopatra on her barge might have reminded the audience, especially in the context of other more explicit allusions, of "the whore that sitteth upon many waters" (Rev. 17:1).[105] The Whore famously holds a "cup of golde," and drink is a prominent feature of Cleopatra's Egyptian court, where Antony "fishes, drinks, and wastes | The lamps of night in revel" (1.4.4–5). Shakespeare was not the first to compare Cleopatra to the Whore of Babylon. William Fulke, in his *Praelections upon the sacred and holy Revelation of S. John* (1573), wrote,

This is therefore the greatest torment to the Babilonicall whore, that she whiche a litle before flowed in such abundance of all things whiche she abused to intemperance, that in riote she could compare with Cleopatra Quene of Egipt, now being naked and deserte should be oppressed with the scarcitie of all things that are good.[106]

Fulke interpreted Revelation, as did many Elizabethan Protestants, as a prophetic vision of the wickedness of the Pope and the Catholic Church. The Geneva Bible note (1560) explains the whore sitting on the beast (Rev. 17:3): "The beast signifieth the ancient Rome; the woman that sittenth thereon, the newe Rome which is the Papistrie." This is why many images of the Whore (following Lucas Cranach's engraving for the Luther Bible) represented her wearing a triple crown like the papal tiara. Thus, Antony's "Triple-turned whore" would have further suggested the Whore of Babylon in her role as a figure of the Pope, though of course the

---

[105] Leeds Barroll, "Enobarbus' Description of Cleopatra," *Texas Studies in English*, 37 (1958), 61–78; cited in Helen Morris, "Shakespeare and Dürer's Apocalypse," *SSt* 4 (1968), 252–62, 256.

[106] William Fulke, *Praelections upon the sacred and holy Revelation of S. John* (London: Thomas Purfoote, 1573), 121. Fulke's statement that the whore "flowed in abundance" resonates with the recurring images of overflowing in *Antony and Cleopatra*, connected both to Cleopatra's excesses and the annual flooding of the Nile on which Egypt's fertility depended.

"empire" he is said to give up to her is the classical, not the papal, Roman one.

Returning to the question of whether Antony is angel or devil, Christ or Antichrist, contrary to Erasmus and Napier, Junius provides important support for a positive interpretation of Revelation and its falling (not fallen) angels. After Antony's death, allusions to Revelation continue, and they too point toward Antony as divine hero. Cleopatra's eulogy for Antony describes him as a gigantic demigod:

> His face was as the heav'ns, and therein stuck
> A sun and moon, which kept their course and lighted
> The little O, the earth.
>
> . . . . .
>
> His legs bestrid the ocean; his reared arm
> As all the tuned spheres, and that to friends;
> But when he meant to quail and shake the orb,
> He was as rattling thunder. For his bounty,
> There was no winter in't; an autumn 'twas
> That grew the more by reaping. (5.2.78–87)

Ethel Seaton seems to have been the first to suggest a parallel between Cleopatra's speech and John's description of one of the angels in his apocalyptic vision:[107]

And I sawe another mightie Angel come downe from heaven, clothed with a cloude, and the raine bowe upon his head, and his face was as the sunne, and his feete as pillers of fyre...and he put his right fote upon the sea, and his left on the earth, and cryed with a lowed voice, as when a lyon roareth: and when he has cryed, seven thondres uttered their voices...And the Angel which I sawe stand upon the sea and upon the earth, lift up his hand to heaven, And sware...that time should be no more. (Rev. 10:1-6).

Both passages contain comparisons of their respective figures to the sun, heaven (or "the heav'ns"), a gigantic leg span measured by the ocean, and thunder, in both the figure raises an arm, and in both time stops. Seaton further argues that "the image of reaping that follows might well be suggested by the later vision in chapter 14, when the angel cries to Him that sat on the white cloud: 'Thrust in thy sickle and reap, for the time is come to reap, for the corn of the earth is ripe' (14:15)." The same verse may also have suggested to Shakespeare the language of Antony's command to Eros to kill him with a thrust sword: "Do't. The time is come" (4.14.68). The Geneva Bible (1560) is clear on the identity of the "mightie Angel" in Revelation 10:1—"Which was Jesus Christ that came to comfort his

---

[107] Seaton, *"Antony and Cleopatra."*

Church against the furious assaults of Satan and Antichrist"—and in this instance, Junius's note in the 1599 edition concurs. The figure on the cloud with the sickle is unambiguously "the Sone of man," that is, Christ (Rev. 14:14).

Supporting this group of allusions that link Antony to Christ is the single, oddly explicit allusion in Antony's wish to stand "Upon the hill of Basan, to outroar | The horned herd" (3.13.132–3). The bulls of Basan appear nowhere in ancient literature except in Psalm 22:12: "Manie yong bulles have compassed me: mightie bulles of Bashan have closed me about" (the "hill of Bashan" comes from Psalm 68:15, "As the hill of Basan, so is Gods hill"). In his Arden[3] note, John Wilders offers the reasonable gloss that "Antony sees himself as a cuckold, a horned beast, like one of the bulls of Bashan." But this does not seem adequate as an explanation of why Antony needs these particular biblical bulls to express his anger at being cuckolded. A crucial point is that Psalm 22 is strongly associated with Christ, who recites its first verse just before he dies on the cross (Matt. 27:47). Accordingly, the interpretative note at the beginning of this Psalm in the Geneva Bible (1560) explains, "here under his owne persone he [David] setteth forthe the figure of Christ." The Crucifixion in Matthew is narrated in self-conscious fulfillment of the prophecy (as interpreted messianically by Christians) in Psalm 22. The suffering figure in the Psalm complains, "they perced my hands and my fete," and "They parte my garments among them, and cast lottes upon my vesture" (Ps. 22:16, 18). Accordingly, in Matthew, "when they had crucified him, they parted his garments, and did cast lottes" (Matt. 27:35; Matthew makes the connection explicit, citing Ps. 22:18). And of course Jesus's hands and feet are pierced when he is nailed to the cross. Since Psalm 22 is the proper Psalm for Good Friday, in the service commemorating Christ's Crucifixion, Shakespeare's audience certainly heard the reference to the bulls of Basan. The reference is ironic, of course, since, while Christ is (figuratively) persecuted by the bulls ("enemies" in the Geneva note), Antony only feels like he is. Even the suggestion of cuckoldry is self-indulgent, since Cleopatra has only given Thidias her hand to kiss, nothing else. Any suggestion that this scene in the play is Antony's "crucifixion" is absurd. Yet Cleopatra's vision of Antony's divinity (though dismissed as fantasy by Dolabella), expressed in terms of Revelation's "mightie Angel," is not parodic for her.

Once a parallel between Antony and Christ has been established, however contrastive or ironic, further parallels are noticeable elsewhere in the play. Like Christ (and like Caesar, as noted above in relation to *Julius Caesar*), Antony is betrayed by a follower who loves him, Enobarbus. One might note further that, like Judas, Enobarbus is stricken with remorse after the fact. He does not commit suicide like Judas, but his weird death does seem somehow self-willed, after condemning himself as a "master leaver and a fugitive" (4.9.25). In fact, Judas hangs himself only in Matthew (27:3–10); in Acts, his death is differently described: "He [Judas] therefore hathe purchased a field with the rewarde of inquitie: and when he had thrown downe him selfe head long he brast a sondre in the middes, and all his bowels gushed out" (1:18). Enobarbus says to himself,

> Throw my heart
> Against the flint and hardness of my fault,
> Which, being dried with grief, will break in powder
> And finish all foul thoughts. (4.9.18–21)

He then falls to the ground and dies. Enobarbus abandons Antony after "one other gaudy night," recalling previous, more dissolute feasts like that on Pompey's barge, but also suggesting a kind of last supper. Antony orders, "Scant not my cups" (4.2.21), and states,

> Tomorrow, soldier,
> By sea and land I'll fight. Or I will live,
> Or bathe my dying honour in the blood
> Shall make it live again. (4.2.4–7)

"Let's to supper, come" he says as they exit (4.2.44). The image of resurrection through bathing in blood has Christian resonance (see the discussion above of sacrifice in *Julius Caesar*), though of course a violently active death in battle is the opposite of a passive death on the cross. Antony also says to his comrades, "Tend me tonight two hours—I ask no more" (4.2.32); like the scene of Brutus's late night before Philippi, this alludes to the Agony in Gethsemane, when Jesus asks Peter, James, and John to stay awake while he prays, and complains after they fall asleep: "colde ye not watche with me one houre?" (Matt. 26:36–40). Christ complains of his sleeping disciples "the spirit in dede is redie, but the flesh is weake"; Antony seems in the opposite condition, committed to the flesh, but with his mind and spirit in almost constant flux. And yet, the final meal with his men is unlike the earlier debauch on the barge. We see in this scene of conviviality why Antony's men love him, and in this Antony's and Christ's last suppers are similar. The similarities end there, however, since Antony's noble suicide is a failure, and his ultimate death is not a sacrifice in any Christian sense.

Though Antony remains alive after stabbing himself, the final scenes of the play are Cleopatra's, and the biblical allusions turn to the Bible's beginning and end, Genesis and Revelation. Before the remarkable denouement in which Cleopatra stages her own death, Shakespeare inserts one of his characteristic scenes of "comic relief," and, as is usually the case, the scene conveys more than comedy. A clown or rustic arrives, on instruction, with the means of Cleopatra's death, a poisonous asp. Cleopatra and the clown engage in some witty badinage, punning on the sexual implications of worms and dying, but there is also a serious subtext. The deadly "worm" is the final instance of a serpent motif that has run throughout the play. Cleopatra is herself Antony's "serpent of old Nile," and, after the drunken Lepidus remarks of Egypt that "you've strange serpents there," Antony makes fun of him by telling of the crocodile that is "like itself" but "transmigrates." Indeed "a strange serpent," as Lepidus concludes (1.5.26, 2.7.24–50). This final serpent is carried in a basket of figs, and, lest the audience miss the allusion to the serpent and fruit of Genesis, a guard later specifically mentions the fig leaves out of which Adam and Eve fashion "breeches" in Genesis (according to Geneva): "these fig leaves | Have slime upon them" (5.2.350).[108] The combination of figs and a serpent who offers a woman mortality points to this scene as, whatever else it is, a weird recapitulation of the Fall (and the latter word runs through the scene: "It smites me | Beneath the fall I have," says Cleopatra, or of the death of the great, "when we fall, | We answer others' merits in our name," and as Charmian dies, "Dost fall?" [5.2.170–1, 176–7, 292]).

Harold Fisch finds echoes of Genesis 1–3 in the Clown's speeches too:

I heard of one of them ["men and women"]—a very honest woman, but something given to lie, as a woman should not do but in the way of honesty—how she died of the biting of it, what pain she felt. Truly, she makes a very good report o'th' worm; but he that will believe all that they say shall never be saved by half that they do. (5.2.249–56)

You must not think I am so simple but I know the devil himself will not eat a woman. I know that a woman is a dish for the gods if the devil dress her not. But truly, these same whoreson devils do the gods great harm in their women, for in every ten that they make, the devil mar five. (5.2.271–6)

Fisch asserts that "the man who believed the good report that the woman brought of the worm but could not be saved by what she had done, is of course Adam; just as Cleopatra is Eve":

---

[108] "Slime" is a word that also evokes Genesis, since the dust out of which God created Adam was commonly referred to as "slime," as in Henry Smith's description of man as "a grosse lumpe of slime and clay" (*The sinfull mans search: or seeking of God* (London: [T. Scarlet] for Cuthbert Burby, 1592], sig. F3ʳ) or Hennoch Clapham's "the first man *Adam* was of the slime of the earth" (*Three partes of Salomon his Song of Songs, expounded* (London: Valentine Sims for Edmund Mutton, 1603), 196). The principle uses of the word "slime" in the sixteenth century are biblical—descriptions of Adam's creation and human corruption, the bricks that build Babel, built out of "slyme...in steade of morter" (Gen. 11:3), the kings of Sodom and Gomorrah fleeing to and dying in the "slyme pittes" of Siddim (Gen. 14:10), and Moses's mother daubing the ark she makes for him with slime (Exod. 2:3)—and there are no biblical uses of "slime" after Exodus.

Creative Anachronism 225

The serpent, from being a fertility symbol, possessing, like Cleopatra herself ("serpent of old Nile"), the chthonic potency or mana of the Nile mud, has now become the Tempter of Genesis, chapter 3, whilst Cleopatra is momentarily transformed into a figure in a morality play, a woman who might have been a dish for the gods but who has been unfortunately marred by the devil.[109]

One might add that Cleopatra and the serpent are weirdly intertwined in these allusions, reminiscent of images of the Genesis serpent with a woman's head (Fig. 1.2); it is not quite clear who is tempted by whom.

Weirder still, and stretching far beyond the simple moralism of the medieval mystery plays, is the image Cleopatra presents of herself and the serpent as a mother nursing her child:

> Dost thou not see my baby at my breast
> That sucks the nurse asleep? (5.2.308–9)

This is Shakespeare's invention; Plutarch reports the asp biting Cleopatra's arm.[110] The image of mother and child, following on the echoes of Eve and the serpent in Genesis 2–3, suggests a grotesque parody of the Madonna and Child.[111] Significantly, it was a Christian commonplace that the Virgin Mary was a type of Eve.[112] The serpent tempted Eve, whose sin brought her (and the world) death; by contrast, Mary brought Christ into the world who redeemed mankind and defeated death. In Cleopatra's image the serpent and child are merged; the asp at her breast gives fluid (poison) rather than taking it (as milk), bringing Cleopatra death rather than Cleopatra giving it life.

This scene is a scene of endings, and, while Genesis is evoked in the encounter with the Clown and his worm, biblical allusions thereafter return to Revelation and its description of the ultimate end. Cleopatra shifts again among her various mythical female roles, from Eve and Mary to Venus and Isis. For example, Cleopatra declares, "I am again for Cydnus," the river on which she appeared on her barge, described by Enobarbus as "o'erpicturing" Venus (2.2.210).[113] Also, Cleopatra and her court swear by Isis throughout the play, and Caesar describes her appearing

---

[109] Harold Fisch, *The Biblical Presence in Shakespeare, Milton, and Blake: A Comparative Study* (Oxford: Clarendon Press, 1999), 60. See also Leeds Barroll, "The Allusive Tissue of *Antony and Cleopatra*," in Sara Munson Deats (ed.), *Antony and Cleopatra: New Critical Essays* (New York and London: Routledge, 2005), 275–90, 278–80.

[110] As Wilders points out in his note to 5.2.308 in *Antony and Cleopatra*.

[111] Shakespeare may also have known of the iconographic tradition of Isis nursing Osiris. If so, this would be another instance of his characteristic syncretism, in which Cleopatra is both Isis and Mary simultaneously.

[112] See Ch. 4.

[113] Plutarch wrote only that Cleopatra was actually "attired like the goddesse Venus" (Bullough, v. 274).

earlier "in th'habiliments of Isis" (3.6.17). Thus the "robe" she dons at the end may suggest the Egyptian goddess too, but the female figures of Revelation are among the roles Cleopatra symbolically assumes as well.[114] As always in this most ambivalent of plays, however, the question is which one? Is Cleopatra still the Whore of Babylon, or has she become the Whore's opposite number, the woman clothed with the sun? (Rev. 12:1; see Fig. 5.3). The woman clothed with the sun was typically interpreted by Protestants as symbolizing the Church, as in the Geneva Bible gloss, but also as the Virgin Mary in her role as the avenger of Eve, since the woman clothed with the sun battles the red dragon in Revelation.[115] She is decribed as having the moon under her feet and is crowned with twelve stars; Cleopatra, as mentioned above, is associated with the moon (in connection with Isis), and Charmian is shortly to call her the "eastern star" (in astrological and mythical terms, Venus).

The sense of impending apocalypse is announced by Cleopatra herself: "when thou has done this chare [chore], I'll give thee leave | To play till doomsday" (5.2.230–1). Furthermore, the striking repetition of promises and entreaties to "come" in the final scenes of the play echo Revelation's penultimate verse: "Surely, I come quickly. Amen, even so come, Lord Jesus" (Rev. 22:20). (This second coming of Christ will mark the end of all time.) Antony calls, "Come Eros!" "Come, then!" and "Draw, and come" (4.14.55, 79, 85). Diomedes is sent by Cleopatra, who is worried that Antony may act rashly, but, as he says, "I am come, | I dread, too late," and he then calls to the guard, "Come, your lord calls!" (4.14.128–9, 132). The wounded Antony is taken to the monument, where Cleopatra calls "come, come Antony" (4.15.30). He replies, "O quick, or am I gone." "O come, come, come," she responds (4.15.32, 38). The many repetitions of the word culminate in Cleopatra's remarkable cry, "Husband, I come!" (5.2.286), which echoes Antony's similar cries earlier when he had thought Cleopatra was dead: "I come, my queen" (4.14.51). Shakespeare's use of the verb here includes all the ordinary senses of the word that John's translators employ, as well as his apocalyptic urgency. Shakespeare adds a sexual dimension that would ordinarily be bawdy, but here is weirdly transcendent. Cleopatra's cry, her only use of the word "husband" in the play, both calls for and verbally enacts a consummation with her lover that has behind it a favorite English sexual pun: she "dies" and "comes" at once,

---

[114] Wilders notes that Cleopatra's rejection of the "fleeting moon" may be a rejection of Isis the moon goddess, part of her desire to be "marble-constant" (*Antony and Cleopatra*, 5.2.238–9).

[115] Artistic representations of the Virgin Mary often show her standing on a sliver of a moon, with a crown of stars. See Fig. 4.3.

Fig. 5.3. The "woman clothed with the sunne" (Rev. 12:1) was typically interpreted by Protestants as symbolizing the Church, but also as the Virgin Mary in her role as avenger of Eve, since the woman clothed with the sun battles a dragon in Revelation. See also Fig. 4.3. (Woodcut from *The Apocalypse;* Albrecht Dürer, 1496–8.) Wetmore Print Collection, Connecticut College.

and the senses of both words intertwine in a peculiarly Shakespearian version of *Liebestod*.[116]

The biblical Apocalypse similarly concerns waiting for a husband to come (Christ the bridegroom), as emphasized in another passage describing the end of days, Matthew 25, in which Jesus likens the kingdom of heaven to "ten virgins, which toke their lampes, and went to mete the bridegroom" (Matt. 25:1). The virgins represent those believers who look to be admitted to heaven after death. Five virgins are wise, and keep their lamps lit and full of oil; five are foolish, and let their lamps run out. At midnight, "there was a cry made, Beholde, the bridegroom cometh: go out to mete him" (Matt. 25:6). The five wise virgins go in to the wedding, but the foolish ones are too late. As Barroll notes, the Clown with Cleopatra's asp alludes to the wise and foolish virgins of Matthew 25 when he states that "for every ten [women] that they [the gods] make, the devils mar five" (5.2.275–6).[117] Cleopatra also tells her women, after Antony's death, "Our lamp is spent, it's out" (4.15.89). Yet Cleopatra is no virgin, and she is also no fool. Characteristically, she does not wait for her bridegroom to come, but follows him into death. That she says, "I come" (not "come quickly") casts her in the role of the husband in terms of Revelation: such gender inversion (signifying dominance not masculinity itself) is typical of Cleopatra, as when she wore Antony's "sword Philippan" (2.5.23).

These biblical allusions do not by any means make *Antony and Cleopatra* a "Christian play," as some earlier critics argued.[118] But it is a play concerned with endings and beginnings, and this may provide the explanation for Shakespeare's imposition of a biblical subtext underneath the classical history. Ideas of Apocalypse were in the air in the early seventeenth century, in the tumultuous years after the Spanish Armada, the

---

[116] Dying and coming were both common puns for orgasm in English Renaissance literature, though only the latter continues in modern usage.

[117] Barroll, "Allusive Tissue," 286–7.

[118] John F. Danby argued the play was a Christian condemnation of both pagan Egypt and pagan Rome ("The Shakespearian Dialectic," *Scrutiny*, 16 [1949], 196–213). Roy Battenhouse (*Shakespearean Tragedy: Its Art and Christian Premises* [Bloomington and London: Indiana University Press, 1969], 161–83) reads the play instead as a "dark parody…of Christian beliefs and doctrines," as Fisch summarizes Battenhouse in his *Biblical Presence* (p. 62, n. 33). Battenhouse also goes beyond allusion to posit some numerological structures in *Antony and Cleopatra*, which are intriguing though perhaps far-fetched. The reign of evil in Revelation (11:2 and 13:5, echoing Daniel 7:25 and 12:7) is forty-two months. According to Battenhouse, this is approximately the number of months in the "usurped monarchy of Antony and Cleopatra" (34–30 BCE). He also notes that there are forty-two scenes in the play, divided equally before and after the pivotal battle of Actium. There are forty-two scenes in Arden³, but these are editorial, as Battenhouse acknowledges, according to the number of clearings of the stage. To make the neat division of two halves of twenty-one, however, one must ignore the fact that Antony and Cleopatra have arrived at Actium by 3.7, the nineteenth scene.

death of Elizabeth I, the Plague of 1603–4, and the Gunpowder Plot.[119] John Napier's commentary on Revelation, first published in 1593, was dedicated to James VI of Scotland, probably because James himself had written a commentary: *Ane fruitfull meditatioun contening ane plane and facill expositioun of ye 7.8.9 and 10 versis of the 20 chap. of the Revelatioun* was first printed in Edinburgh in 1588, then reprinted in London in 1603. Napier's and Junius's commentaries on Revelation were reprinted frequently in the 1590s. Other publications testifying to the interest in Revelation are George Gifford's *Sermons vpon the whole booke of the Revelation* (1596), Arthur Dent's *The ruine of Rome: or An exposition vpon the whole Revelation* (1603), William Perkins's *Lectures vpon the three first chapters of the Revelation* (1604), and William Symonds's *Pisgah evangelica By the method of the Revelation* (1605), which promised to interpret all of history from CE 97 to 1603 in terms of Revelation. The Armada may have inspired apocalyptic thinking, since there was a flurry of anti-Catholic commentaries on Revelation after 1588, including James's, arguing for the Pope as Antichrist: Lambert Daneau, *A treatise, touching Antichrist* (1589); Christopher Ocland, *The fountaine and wellspring of all variance, sedition, and deadlie hate* (1589); Laurence Deios, *That the pope is that Antichrist* (1590). All of these works were reprinted; the public clearly could not get enough information about the Apocalypse. The millennial mood and popular anti-Catholicism, further reinvigorated after the 1605 Gunpowder Plot, inspired Thomas Dekker's *The Whore of Babylon*, performed by Prince Henry's Men and printed in 1607. Dekker's play dramatized the conflict between the "Th'Empresse of *Babylon*: under whom is figured *Rome*" and "Titania the Faerie Queen: under whom is figured our late Queene Elizabeth," as explained in the printed *dramatis personae*. (Shakespeare's *Antony and Cleopatra* has been interpreted in similar terms, with Cleopatra as a figure for the late lamented Elizabeth, though some adjustment is required to align the Virgin Queen with the hypersexual Egyptian.[120]) Shakespeare's allusions to Revelation do capitalize on the interest in this biblical book at the turn of the century and the beginning of James's reign, encouraging, for instance, topical readings of *Antony and Cleopatra* in terms of James's providentialism, imperial ambitions,

---

[119] Joseph Wittreich, "'Image of that horror': The Apocalypse in *King Lear*," in C. A. Patrides and Joseph A. Wittreich (eds), *The Apocalypse in English Renaissance Thought and Literature* (Manchester: Manchester University Press, 1984), 175–206, esp. 182–3. For more on the late Elizabethan and Jacobean culture of Apocalypse, see Ch. 7.

[120] Helen Morris, "Queen Elizabeth I 'Shadowed' in Cleopatra," *HLQ* 32 (1969), 271–78; Keith Rhinehart, "Shakespeare's Cleopatra and England's Elizabeth," *SQ* 23 (1972), 81–6; Clifford Webber, "Intimations of Dido and Cleopatra in Contemporary Portrayals of Elizabeth I," *SP* 96/2 (1999), 127–43.

and commitment to peace.[121] Yet to overemphasize the historically topical may overlook the play's primary interest in Revelation—as a prophecy of history's end, when the world and time will be no more.

As Shakespeare often does, he here adapts spiritual or eschatological ideas for his own dramatic purposes. As Bate puts it in the context of *Othello*, "Shakespeare's plays use history, but they subsume geopolitics into interpersonal encounters."[122] Shakespeare is finally less interested in the theology of the Apocalypse, or the interpretation of Revelation, or even of millennial thinking in early Jacobean England, than he is in the last days of Antony and Cleopatra. Even when alive, they themselves claim to be out of time and history. "Eternity was in our lips and eyes," says Cleopatra (1.3.37), and time seems oddly stopped in Egypt, as in the apparently continuous action of 2.5 and 3.3, even though between them Pompey has entertained Octavius and Antony on his barge, Ventidius has triumphed over the Parthians, and Antony and Octavia have married.[123] Octavius and Roman history allow no place on earth for Antony and Cleopatra's Romantic eternity, however. For Caesar, Cleopatra can only "be eternal in our triumph" (5.2.66), led in chains through Rome, which, in defeat, leaves Antony and Cleopatra to seek eternity in another place. Of course, the lovers have no access to the heaven promised in Revelation, and, as ongoing critical debate about the end of the play indicates, it is not even clear whether Cleopatra's "immortal longings" are to be taken seriously. I think they must be, but that the transcendence and immortality she achieves are theatrical, not eschatological. Cleopatra's death is a theatrical *tour de force*, and the sense of apocalypse and transcendence borrowed from Revelation adds religious resonance to the aesthetic mystery that is achieved on stage. For a brief moment, in the theater, Shakespeare encourages his audience to imagine that Antony and Cleopatra have indeed triumphed over Octavius, over historical necessity, and even over death. But characters whose history has already been written can escape history only in a play. Cleopatra was worried that the "quick comedians | Extemporally will stage us and present | our Alexandrian revels," that "Antony | Shall be brought drunken forth" and that "Some squeaking Cleopatra [shall] boy my greatness | I'th' posture of a whore" (5.2.215–20). Instead, the tragedians, not the comedians, have directed the story, and Cleopatra has acted out the transcendent ending as she wished to stage it.

[121] Wittreich ("'Image of that horror'") shows the importance of Revelation to *King Lear* as well.
[122] Bate, *Soul of the Age*, 278.
[123] Cleopatra beats the messenger and chases him out in 2.5, but then calls him back at the end. At the beginning of 3.3, she is still calling, "Where is the fellow?"

6
Damnable Iteration: Falstaff, Master of Biblical Allusion

Many of the biblical allusions in Shakespeare's plays are uttered by characters who are unconscious of them. In some cases, such a consciousness would be historically impossible, as discussed in Chapter 5. Julius Caesar, Cleopatra, Coriolanus, as well as King Lear and Pericles lived before the time of Christ, and thus must be necessarily ignorant of the Christian Bible; it is highly unlikely historically that they knew Jewish scripture either. This also seems true of Bottom, since, although in speech and appearance he seems an ordinary English weaver, *A Midsummer Night's Dream* places him in a semi-mythical ancient Athens. Other Shakespearian characters live in Christian countries, and so might make self-conscious allusions to the Christian scripture. Nevertheless, it is often clear from the context in which such allusions occur that they are still unaware of the full implications of the words Shakespeare has put in their mouths. Othello, for instance, seems not to know that his statement, "Rude am I in my speech" (1.3.82), alludes to 2 Corinthians 11:6, "And thogh I am rude in speaking, yet I am not so in knowledge." That this is an allusion, and an ironic one, is confirmed by the relevance to *Othello* of earlier verses in 2 Corinthians 11:

For I am jelous over you, with godlie jalousie: for I have prepared you for one housband, to present you as a pure virgine to Christ: But I feare lest as the serpent beguiled Eve through subtilitie, so your minds shulde be corrupte from the simplicitie that is in Christ. (2 Cor. 11: 2–3)

Paul uses marriage and jealousy metaphorically to represent the fidelity of the Corinthians to Christ, but marriage and jealousy are literally central to Shakespeare's play, though Othello himself does not yet know it.

Similarly, in *The Merchant of Venice*, Launcelot Gobbo and his father seem unaware that they are acting out a parody of Isaac's blessing of Jacob in Genesis. Jacob tricks his father, Isaac, to receive the blessing properly due to his brother, Esau. Isaac is blind, so Rebecca, his wife and Jacob's mother, covers Jacob with "skinnes of the kyds of the goates" (Gen. 27:16), so that he will feel like his hairy brother Esau. Jacob tells his father that he is Esau and receives the blessing that Isaac intended for his eldest son. *Merchant* 2.2 is an extended allusion to this strange scene. In the street, Launcelot encounters his father, who is "sand-blind, high gravel blind" (2.2.32–3). Seeing that he "knows me not," Launcelot decides to "try confusions with him" (2.2.33). Launcelot says to his father, "Give me your blessing" (2.2.73). He does not put animal skins on his arms, but Gobbo does find him exceptionally hairy, since he mistakes the back of his head for his face: "Thou hast got more hair on thy chin than Dobbin, my thill-horse, has on his tail" (2.2.88). Gobbo's error seems to confirm Launcelot's previous statement that "it is a wise father that knows his own child" (2.2.71–2). All these allusions point to the biblical scene of Jacob tricking Isaac into blessing him. With the biblical background established, the audience may also hear in Gobbo's repeated references to "hair" a pun on the "heir" that the son becomes with the paternal blessing (the initial "h" in both words would probably have been silent). The dense pattern of allusions in the scene ties it in serious ways to important themes of the play like the bonds of parents and children.[1] That the Gobbos are ironically unconscious of the parody adds to the comedy of this almost slapstick scene.

Many other biblical allusions seem more or less self-consciously spoken. For instance, just before he plunges a dagger into his chest, Othello speaks of himself as

> one whose hand,
> Like the base Judaean, threw a pearl away
> Richer than all his tribe. (5.2.344–6)[2]

Assuming that the Folio reading of "Judaean" is legitimate,[3] Othello is surely conscious of labeling himself a Judas, who has betrayed and caused the death of the one he loved. According to the note in the

---

[1] Janet Adelman also ties the play's allusions to Jacob and Esau to *Merchant*'s exploration of the relationship between Christianity and Judaism, based on Paul's allegorical explication of Jacob and Esau as the two first Abrahamic faiths in Galatians (4:22–6). Adelman, *Blood Relations: Christian and Jew in* The Merchant of Venice (Chicago: University of Chicago Press, 2008), ch. 2.

[2] For reasons explained below, I substitute the Folio's "Judaean" for the Quarto's "Indian" in the Arden edition.

[3] The First Quarto reading, "Indian," is followed by E. A. J. Honigman in his Arden[3] edition, but the allusion to Judas would align with other biblical allusions like the kiss mentioned below. Shaheen (600–1) points out that, in the murder scene, Shakespeare departs from Geraldi Cinthio's *Hecatommithi* and follows a different story in Geoffrey Fenton's English translation of Matteo Bandello's *Novelle*, in which the murder is twice explicitly compared to the betrayal of Jesus by Judas. See also Bullough, vii. 204, 253–62.

Geneva Bible (in the "Tomson" New Testament), Judas was of the tribe of Judah.[4] The "pearl" Judas threw away was Jesus, whom he betrayed, and who was also of the tribe of Judah (Jesus himself refers to heaven parabolically as a "pearl of great price," Matt. 13:46). Because he has betrayed and murdered Desdemona, Othello, who is a Christian, is thus likening himself to the greatest betrayer in Christian history.[5] With his last breath, Othello says to Desdemona's body, "I kiss'd thee ere I kill'd thee" (5.2.356), an echo of Judas's kiss that identified Jesus to the soldiers of the chief priests and elders (as Richard of Gloucester says in *Henry VI, Part 3*, "So Judas kiss'd his master, | And cried 'All hail!' when as he meant all harm," 5.7.33–4). Some characters are exceptionally conscious in their use of biblical allusion, like Shylock, who repeatedly twists New Testament verses into attacks on his Christian oppressors. When Bassanio invites Shylock to dine with him and Antonio, Shylock replies, "Yes, to smell pork, to eat of the habitation which your prophet the Nazarite conjured the devil into" (1.3.30–1). This is a bitterly brilliant reinterpretation of Jesus's casting a demon out of a man and into a herd of swine, who rush into the sea and drown (Matt. 8:32–4). Shylock's reading of the gospel seemingly confirms the Jewish dietary prohibition of pork and implicitly asserts, in contradiction to explicit statements like Paul's that "there is nothing unclean of it self" (Rom. 14:18), Jesus's respect of Jewish food law.

The question of the self-consciousness or unself-consciousness of characters alluding to the Bible can be clarified by borrowing some terms from the discipline of film studies. "Diegesis," meaning literally "narrative" or "narration," is used by film critics to refer to elements included in the narrative of the film.[6] For instance, diegetic music is music played or heard within the narrative, such as when a character plays the piano; extradiegetic music is part of the soundtrack, which the audience hears but the characters in the film do not. By analogy, then, a diegetic allusion would thus be one that either a character is conscious of making or that

---

[4] Cited in Shaheen, 602–3.

[5] There is some debate as to whether Othello is a convert or a Christian by birth (see Honigman (ed.), *Othello*, introduction, 19–26). Even Iago, however, is clear that he is a Christian, referring to Othello's "baptism" at 2.3.338.

[6] See, e.g., Irena Paulus, "Stanley Kubrick's Revolution in the Usage of Film Music: *2001: A Space Odyssey* (1968)," *International Review of the Aesthetics and Sociology of Music*, 40/1 (2009), 99–127. Though film scholars tend to use "diegetic" and "nondiegetic," instead of the latter I will use "extradiegetic," which seems more precise and is the preferred term for narrative theorists. The term "diegesis" (diégèse) originates with the French narrative theorist Gérard Genette. See Remigius Bunia, "Diegesis and Representation: Beyond the Fictional World, on the Margins of Story and Narrative," *Poetics Today*, 31/4 (2010), 679–720.

another character recognizes; an extradiegetic allusion is one that the audience recognizes but the characters in the play do not or cannot. In the case of diegetic allusions, one may speak of both the author and the character alluding. Extradiegetic allusions, however, must be those of the author alone.

The master of diegetic allusion is Falstaff. No character alludes to the Bible more self-consciously, more frequently, or with more boldly revisionary misapplication. Biblical allusion is, in fact, one of his most characteristic features, along with other forms of verbal inventiveness, a universal irreverence for authority, massive girth, and insatiable appetite. Falstaff is also exceptional among Shakespeare's creations in being present in four different plays: *Henry IV, Parts 1 and 2, Henry V* (offstage, though notionally just upstairs), and *The Merry Wives of Windsor*. Since at least Maurice Morgann's early *Essay on the Dramatic Character of Sir John Falstaff* (1777), scholars have debated whether Falstaff is a wicked reprobate or an exuberant celebrant of life, whether he is cowardly or merely prudent, whether his rejection by Hal is logical and justified or cold and self-serving, and whether the Falstaff of the two parts of *Henry IV* and *The Merry Wives* is even the same character. Focusing on biblical allusion may not thoroughly resolve these questions, but it does offer some insights into this most ambivalent of Shakespearean personae.

HENRY IV, PART 1

The title page of the 1598 First Quarto of *The History of Henrie the Fourth* (later known as "Part 1") already indicates where the attention of the audience and readership is focused. In addition to "the battell at Shrewsburie, between the King and Lord Henry Percy, surnamed Henrie Hotspur of the North," the play is advertised to contain "the humorous conceits of Sir John Falstaff."[7] The play was a hit. A second edition was printed in the same year, and another in 1599, with three further editions before the Folio of 1623.[8] That Falstaff was a principal component of this popularity is suggested by a commendatory poem in Francis Beaumont and John Fletcher's folio *Comedies and Tragedies* (1647). Thomas Palmer, of Christ Church, Oxford, included a poem, "Master John Fletcher His Dramaticall Workes Now At Last Printed":

---

[7] William Shakespeare, *The History of Henrie the Fourth* (London: P[eter] S[hort] for Andrew Wise, 1598).

[8] David Scott Kastan points out that, of all the plays printed before 1640, only twelve achieved a second edition in the same year as the first. *King Henry IV, Part 1*, introduction, 106.

> I could praise Heywood now: or tell how long,
> Falstaffe from cracking Nuts hath kept the throng:
> But for a Fletcher, I must take an Age,
> And scarce invent the Title for one Page.[9]

Thus, even fifty years after his first appearance on stage, Falstaff's name was synonymous with popular audience appeal. Falstaff's impact is testified to much earlier in an anti-satirical pamphlet entitled *The Whipping of Satyre* (1601):

> I dare here speake it, and my speach mayntayne,
> That Sir John Falstaffe was not any way
> More grosse in body, then you are in brayne.
> But whether should I (helpe me nowe, I pray)
> For your grosse brayne, you like I, Falstaffe graunt,
> Or for small wit, suppose you John of Gaunt?[10]

The source of the anonymous author's consternation seems to be that Shakespeare's characterization of Falstaff has eclipsed the original history of Sir John Fastolf, a knight who fought with Henry V at Agincourt. That the author has Shakespeare's play specifically in mind is indicated by his use of the same pun on "Gaunt/gaunt"(proper name and adjective) made by Falstaff himself in *Henry IV, Part 1* ("Indeed I am not John of Gaunt," says Falstaff in response to Hal's calling him "Sir John Paunch," 2.2.64–5). The same concern to correct the historical record prompted the production of the play *The First Part of the True and Honorable Historie, the Life of Sir John Oldcastle* (1599), by Anthony Munday, Michael Drayton, and others, though the concern of these authors was not with Sir John Fastolf but with the man whose name Shakespeare originally gave his character.

As students of Shakespeare know, before Falstaff was "Sir John Falstaff" in *Henry IV, Part 1*, he was named Sir John Oldcastle. The original John Oldcastle, Baron Cobham, fought for Henry IV against the Scots and was close to the young Prince Henry.[11] Most famously, Oldcastle was a Lollard,

---

[9] Francis Beaumont and John Fletcher, *Comedies and Tragedies* (London: Humphrey Robinson and Humphrey Moseley, 1647), sig. f2ᵛ, cited in *King Henry IV, Part* 1, 38.
[10] Anon., *The Whipping of Satyre* (London: John Flasket, 1601), sig. D3ʳ.
[11] For information on Oldcastle, his descendants, and the history of the "Oldcastle Problem," see Alice-Lyle Scoufos, *Shakespeare's Typological Satire: A Study of the Falstaff–Oldcastle Problem* (Athens, OH: Ohio University Press, 1979). Also Gary Taylor, "The Fortunes of Oldcastle," *SS* 38 (1985), 85–100. Shakespeare could have found Oldcastle's story in Foxe's *Acts and Monuments* or Holinshed's *Chronicles*, which he knew well. John Bale wrote a *Brefe Chronycle concernynge the Examinacyon and death of the blessed martyr of Christ syr Johan Oldecastell the lorde Cobham* (1544), which was largely incorporated into Foxe.

an adherent of the heretical teachings of John Wyclif and his followers. Sixteenth-century Protestants saw the Lollards as their own precursors, and so Oldcastle, executed in 1417, became a Protestant martyr. Much has been written about why Shakespeare might have been drawn to this character, and what caused him to parody him so severely, but most agree that he changed the name to Falstaff in order to avoid offense to Oldcastle's descendants, especially William Brooke, the tenth Lord Cobham, Lord Chamberlain from 1596 to 1597. What is most important for the study of Falstaff's biblical language is Oldcastle's status as a proto-Protestant, a Protestant martyr, and a particular hero of the Puritans in the English Church.[12] Kristen Poole was the first to argue that Falstaff (or Oldcastle, in Shakespeare's characterization) is a parody of a peculiarly late-Elizabethan conception of the Puritan. As she pointed out, the popular sixteenth-century perception of Puritanism[13]—almost the opposite of the straight-laced fun-hater of American literature and Shakespeare's own Malvolio—was shaped by the Marprelate controversy of 1588–90, in which enterprising Puritan authors and printers produced a series of brilliant and savagely satirical pamphlets attacking certain high-ranking prelates and what they saw as the inadequately reformed Church establishment. So effective were these works, putatively authored by a "Martin Marprelate" and his sons, that the bishops were compelled to respond, both in their own right and by proxy, engaging such London wits as John Lyly, Thomas Nashe, Robert Greene, and Anthony Munday to attack Martin (as he was known) and defend the Church. Out of this pamphlet war emerged not only a new caricature of the English Puritan, a hypocritical hedonist of the kind Ben Jonson would later satirize through his character Zeal-of-the-Land Busy, but also a new genre of street-fighting ecclesiastical satire and an

---

[12] On Elizabethan Puritans who claimed a genealogy from the Lollards, see Stephen Brachlow, *The Communion of the Saints: Radical Puritan and Separatist Ecclesiology 1570–1625* (1988), cited in Kristen Poole, "Saints Alive! Falstaff, Martin Marprelate, and the Staging of Puritanism," *SQ* 46/1 (1995), 47–75, 48, n. 6.

[13] The term "puritan" is, like so many religious labels, problematic and has been much discussed by historians. The principal difficulties are to whom to apply it (if indeed it is legitimate at all) and from what date. It was initially a term of abuse, not one embraced by those to whom it apparently applied, and it included a large group of English Protestants, all of whom were inclined toward further reforms in the English Church, but not all of whom felt so strongly as to be separatists. The term naturally becomes more problematic still when considering parodies of Puritans. I use the term cautiously and with an awareness of its limitations. For two standard studies of the term, see Peter Lake, *Anglicans and Puritans? Presbyterianism and English Conformist Thought from Whitgift to Hooker* (London: Unwin Hyman, 1988), esp. 4–8, and Nicholas Tyacke, *Anti-Calvinists: The Rise of English Arminianism c.1590–1640* (Oxford: Clarendon Press, 1987), esp. 7–10. Also Patrick Collinson, "Ecclesiastical Vitriol: Religious Satire in the 1590s and the Invention of Puritanism," in John Guy (ed.), *The Reign of Elizabeth I: Court and Culture in the Last Decade* (Cambridge and New York: Cambridge University Press, 1995), 150–70.

original prose style, irreverent to the point of libel, casually yet blatantly learned, linguistically inventive, and lightening quick. Nashe cut his teeth on the anti-Martinist tracts, and not surprisingly, given the involvement of Lyly, Greene, and Munday, the controversy moved onto the stage as well. Francis Bacon complained of the pamphlet war that "it is more then Time, that there were an End, and surseance, made, of this Immodest, and Deformed, manner of Writing, lately entertained; whereby, Matter of Religion, is handled, in the stile of the Stage."[14] Ironically, however, the Martinist and anti-Martinist writings on religion clearly influenced the "stile of the stage." The original anti-Martinist plays, apparently staged by the Queen's Men, the Lord Strange's Men, the Lord Admiral's Men, and Paul's Boys, do not survive, but their influence, or perhaps the direct influence of the tracts, can be seen in the use of the same satirical style in plays by Greene, Dekker, Middleton, and especially Shakespeare.[15]

Falstaff is not the only source of biblical or religious allusion in *Henry IV, Part 1*, but he is responsible for about half of the total (twenty-three out of fifty-five, according to Shaheen). The play's language is pervasively biblical and religious. As already mentioned, King Henry opens by expressing his longing to embark on a crusade to the Holy Land, a plan he returns to regularly, without hope of success. Furthermore, the trajectory of Prince Hal's career is structured in terms of biblical allusion. In his famous first soliloquy, he promises a "reformation," "Redeeming the time when men think least I will" (1.2.203, 207). Whether Hal is aware of it or not, his language derives from Ephesians 5:15–16, "Take hede therefore that ye walke circumspectly, not as fooles, but as wise, Redeeming the time: for the days are evil."[16] Hal's promised redemption is a pointedly secularized version of Paul's, signaled by his repeated financial metaphors—he'll "pay the debt I never promised" (1.2.199). Hal will redeem his honor, not his or anyone else's soul, and he will redeem it as one "redeems" an empty soda bottle, exchanging his "indignities" for Percy's "glorious deeds" (3.2.146). Alternatively, though continuing the financial theme, Percy is his factor, buying up "glorious deeds" on behalf of Hal, who will then "call him to so strict account | That he shall render every glory up" (3.2.148–50). This is the chivalry of a shopkeeper. The

---

[14] Francis Bacon, "An Advertisement touching the Controversies of the Church of England," in *Resuscitatio* (London: Sarah Griffin for William Lee, 1657), 164. I owe this citation to Joseph L. Black (ed.), *The Martin Marprelate Tracts: A Modernized and Annotated Edition* (Cambridge: Cambridge University Press, 2008), p. xxvii.
[15] Black (ed.), *Martin Marprelate Tracts*, pp. lxiv–lxv.
[16] I am indebted to Paul A. Jorgensen's excellent study of Hal's "redemption" in *Redeeming Shakespeare's Words* (Berkeley and Los Angeles: University of California Press, 1962), ch. 4.

point, though, is that the biblical allusions underscore how both King Henry and his son Hal are preoccupied with teleologies, plans that will work out over time toward a specific goal: securing the English throne by a holy crusade, and securing inheritance by redeeming honor and reputation. Falstaff, on the contrary, has no interest in time, "unless hours were cups of sack, and minutes capons, and clocks the tongues of bawds, and dials the signs of leaping houses [brothels]" (1.2.6–8). Consequently, his playfulness with biblical allusion is about not future promise but present laughter.

Hal seems proud of his own keen twisting of Proverbs 1:20, 24 ("Wisdome cryeth without: she uttereth her voyce in the streete...and none would regarde") in response to Falstaff's remark on the criticism of Hal by a Council member he met in the street. Falstaff says, "I regarded him not; and yet he talked wisely and in the street too" (1.2.83–4). Hal retorts with "Thou didst well, for wisdom cries out in the streets and no man regards it" (1.2.85–6), which most editions do note as an allusion to Proverbs. Yet Hal is surely a bit thick, puffed up with his own cleverness but failing to notice that the allusion has already been made by Falstaff. The fat knight subsequently laments, "O, thou hast damnable iteration and art indeed able to corrupt a saint" (1.2.87–8). The joke is twofold. First, and most obviously, as everyone in England knows, it is Falstaff who is corrupting Hal, not the other way round. Second, it is actually Falstaff who is the master of "damnable iteration." Most editions gloss "iteration" as "repetition," which accords with the definition in the *OED*, where two areas of usage are distinguished: as a rhetorical figure involving repetition (as in George Puttenham's *Art of English Poesy*), and as the repeated use of a sacrament (the Mass, Baptism).[17] But Shakespeare seems to mean something more like "quotation" or even "allusion." Falstaff demonstrates damnable iteration a few lines later, defending himself against Hal's charge that he is a thief. "Why, Hal, 'tis my vocation, Hal; 'tis no sin for a man to labor in his vocation" (1.2.100–1). Falstaff's defense relies on a perverse application of Paul's injunction, "Let everie man abide in the same vocation wherein he was called" (1 Cor. 7:20).

The language of this scene is not just biblical, however, but specifically Puritan. Falstaff likens himself to a "saint" (1.2.88). As Poole notes, this is

---

[17] George Puttenham, *The Art of English Poesy: A Critical Edition*, ed. Frank Whigham and Wayne A. Rebhorn (Ithaca, NY, and London: Cornell University Press, 2007), 282–6. Puttenham includes such "iterative" figures as anaphora, antistrophe, symploche, and anadiplosis. William Perkins, to cite only one example of the sacramental usage, writes of the Catholics that, if they believe the Mass "is an iteration of Christs sacrifice, then also they speake blasphemie." *An exposition of the Symbole or Creed of the Apostles* (Cambridge: John Legatt, 1595), 265.

the Puritan term (appropriated and redefined from Catholic usage) for one of the elect, just as the damned are, in Puritan usage, the "wicked" (Falstaff moans, "now am I, if a man should speak truly, little better than one of the wicked," 1.2.90–1).[18] These terms derive ultimately from New Testament usage, especially Paul's: "To all you that be in Rome beloved of God, called to be saints" (Rom. 1:7); "take the shield of faith, that ye may quench all the fyrie darts of the wicked (Eph. 6:16)"; "the unclenlie conversation of the wicked" (2 Pet. 2:7). "Vocation" is another Puritan idiom. William Perkins in his popular *Golden Chaine*, for instance, writes, paraphrasing Paul, that "We ought not to vow the performance of that, which is contrarye to our vocation," and that the first effects of predestination are "vocation, election, and ordination to eternall life."[19] In this instance, however, Shakespeare could have derived Falstaff's mock-Puritan distortion of the Bible from an identical use of 1 Corinthians 7:20 in Nashe's *Christ's Tears over Jerusalem*:

Hee [Schimeon, "grand *Keysar* of cut-throtes"] held it as lawfull for him, (since all laboring in a mans vocation is but getting,) to get wealth as well with his sword by the High way side, as the Laborer with his Spade or Mattocke, when all are but yron.[20]

Christ's Tears, published in 1593, is a serious work, not part of the Marprelate exchange, but Nashe's style here shows signs of his earlier polemical writing, and Shakespeare obviously knew Nashe's work well.[21] Moreover, Nashe plays with the Puritan sense of "vocation" in his Marprelate tracts too. Cuthbert Curry-knave (a Nashe nom-de-plume) writes in *An Almond for a Parrat* of Martin's "limping brother. Pag." (Puritan preacher and author Eusebius Paget): "What woulde he doe my

---

[18] Poole, "Saints Alive!," 66. William Hopkinson, for instance, in his *A preparation into the waye of lyfe* (London: Robert Waldegrave, 1581), urges "buylding up the Lords Saints, the edification of the body of Christ, that we might be no more children caried about with every winde of doctrine, but that we mighte grow up into him which is the head, that is Christe" (sig. B^v). He also writes of "the judgement of God upon the wicked" (sig. Ciii^r), and references the saints and the wicked many times.
[19] William Perkins, *A golden chaine, or the description of theologie containing the order of the causes of salvation and damnation, according to Gods woord* (London: Edward Alde, 1591), n.p.
[20] Thomas Nashe, *Christes Teares over Jerusalem* (London: James Roberts, 1593), fo. 28^r.
[21] Neil Rhodes, "Shakesperean Grotesque: The Falstaff Plays," in Georgia Brown (ed.), *Thomas Nashe* (Aldershot: Ashgate, 2011), 47–93. Travis L. Summersgill, "The Influence of the Marprelate Controversy upon the Style of Thomas Nashe," *SP* 48/2 (1951), 145–60. On Nashe and Shakespeare, see the many articles by J. J. M. Tobin, for instance, "Nashe and Iago," *N&Q* 50/1 (March 2003), 47–50; "Antony, Brutus, and *Christ's Tears over Jerusalem*," *N&Q* 45/3 (September 1998), 324–31. A list of (non-biblical) borrowings from Nashe in *Henry IV, Part 1* is listed in *The First Part of the History of Henry IV*, ed. J. Dover Wilson (Cambridge: Cambridge University Press, 1964), 191–6. See also chap. 4.

maisters, if he had two good legges, that wil thus bestirre him in his vocation with one and a stump."[22] Nashe's fast and loose play with biblical texts often sounds exactly like Falstaff's. The following examples are from *Strange News of the Intercepting Certaine Letters* (1592):

Acts are but idle words, and the Scripture saith, wee must give account for every idle word [compare Matt. 12:36].

By this blessed cuppe of sacke which I now holde in my hand and drinke to the health of all Christen soules in, thou art a puissant Epitapher [compare Erasmus's Paraphrase of 1 Cor. 10:21, "drinke of the blessed cup of Christ"].[23]

Gentleman, by that which hath been already laid open, I doe not doubt but you are unwaveringly resolved, this indigested Chaos of Doctourship, and greedy pothunter after applause, is an apparant Publican and sinner [Matt. 9:10], a self-love surfeited sot, a broken-winded galdbacke Jade, that hathe borne up his head in his time, but now is quite foundred and tired.

It is a good signe of grace in thee, that thou hast confessest thou hast offences enough of thy owne to aunswere, though thou beest not chargd with thy Fathers. Once in thy life thou speaks true yet; I beleeve thee and pittie thee. God make thee a good man, for thou hast beene a wilde youth hitherto [Ps. 25:6 (BCP) or 2 Tim. 2:22].

Inke and paper, if they bee true Protestants, will pray that they may not be contaminated any more with such abhomination of desolation [Matt. 24:15], as the three brothers Apocripha pamphleting.[24]

Nashe's diatribe was written in anti-Martinist style against Gabriel Harvey. Lyly's *Pap with a Hatchet* had hinted that Harvey was connected to Marprelate. Harvey's brother Richard then weighed in, including Nashe in his counterattack. This opened up a new chapter in the pamphlet war, between the Harveys, principally Gabriel who leaped in to defend his brother, and Nashe. The Martinist/anti-Martinist tone and style was thus extended into the mid-1590s, long after Martin and his sons were silenced.

There are further similarities between Nashe and Falstaff in their choice of biblical allusions. When improvising the role of King Henry (to Hal's playing himself), for instance, Falstaff chastises Hal using a proverb from Ecclesiasticus popular with moralizing preachers:

There is a thing, Harry, which thou hast often heard of, and it is known to many in our land by the name of pitch. This pitch, as ancient writers do report, doth defile; so doth the company thou keepest. (2.4.400–4)

---

[22] Thomas Nashe, *An Almond for a Parrat* (London?: n.p., 1589), 11.

[23] *The seconde tome or volume of the Paraphrase of Erasmus upon the Newe Testament* (London: Edward Whitchurch, 1549), fo. 29ᵛ.

[24] Thomas Nashe, *Strange News of the Intercepting Certaine Letters*, in *The Works of Thomas Nashe*, ed. Ronald B. McKerrow; repr. with corrections and supplementary notes by F. P. Wilson, i (Oxford: Blackwell, 1958), 279, 288, 302, 323, 325.

The proverb is applied to the identical context in the Bible, warning against bad company:

> He that toucheth pitch, shalbe defiled with it: and he that is familiar with the proude, shal be like unto him. (Ecclus. 13:1)

This verse had become a naturalized English proverb by Shakespeare's day, but its frequent appearance in religious works suggests that those who used it remembered its biblical context. *The Schoole of Honest and Vertuous Lyfe*, for instance, asked its reader, "How can the Lambe and the Woolfe agree together? no more can the ungodly with the righteous: hee that toucheth Pitch, shalbe defiled therwith."[25] In *A Progresse of Pietie*, John Norden prays that God's children "not be intangled with false doctrine, nor defiled with the lothsome pitch of mans inventions."[26] Even Edmund Spenser uses the pitch proverb in *The Shepheardes Calender* in "May," his ecclesiastical eclogue. Palinode argues that worldly pleasures should be embraced ("Good is no good, but if it be spend;/God giveth good for none other end"), but is scolded by Piers: "Ah, *Palinodie*, thou art a worldes childe:/Who touches Pitch mought needes be defile."[27] Moreover, the proverb is used at least twice by Nashe, in *A Myrror for Martinists* (1590) and *Strange News* (1592).[28]

Shakespeare continues to borrow from Nashe in *Henry IV, Part 2*. The Lord Chief Justice calls Falstaff Hal's "ill angel," to which Falstaff responds that "your ill angel is light" (1.2.163–4). Falstaff is alluding to Corinthians again ("Satan him self is transformed into an Angel of light," 2 Cor. 11:14), but Shakespeare might have been remembering Nashe's *Pierce Penilesse his Supplication to the Divell* (a letter to Satan himself), in the preface to which Nashe calls himself the "evil Angel" of allegorizing interpreters. Also in *Part 2*, the Archbishop of York refers to the proverb from 2 Peter 2:22 (which in turn cites Prov. 26:11), "The dogge is returned to his owne vomit." The Archbishop chastises the fickle common people who "didst . . . disgorge/Thy glutton bosom of the royal Richard" but who now "wouldst eat thy dead vomit up" (1.3.97–99). Near the end of *Strange*

---

[25] [Thomas Pritchard], *The schoole of honest and vertuous lyfe profitable and necessary for all estates and degrees, to be trayned in* (London: [William How for] Richard Johnes, [1579]), 60.

[26] John Norden, *A Progresse of Pietie* (London: J. Windet for J. Oxenbridge, 1596), fo. 94–94ᵛ.

[27] Edmund Spenser, *The Yale Edition of the Shorter Poems of Edmund Spenser*, ed. William A. Oram et al. (New Haven and London: Yale University Press, 1989), 90.

[28] "Yea know, he that toucheth pitch shall be defiled therewith" (Nashe, *A myrror for Martinists, and all other schismatiques* (London: John Wolfe, 1590), 27). "Of pitch who hath any use at all, shall be abusd by it in the end" (Nashe, *Strange News*, in *Works*, i. 282).

News, Nashe writes that "a dogge will be a dogge, and returne to his vomit."[29] There is a clearer debt to Nashe in *Merry Wives*, when Parson Evans sputters at Page's news of Doctor Caius, "I had as life you would tell me of a mess of porridge" (3.1.58–59). As Shaheen notes, a chapter heading for Genesis 25 reads, "Esau selleth his birthright for a messe of pottage," the latter a phrase which became idiomatic.[30] Shaheen speculates that "mess of porridge" must also have been a common expression, but *EEBO* does not bear this out. Apart from a reference in Philip Stubbes's *The Anatomie of Abuses*, the only references before *Merry Wives* are from Nashe: "hee carries the poake for a messe of porredge in Christs Colledge" (*Have with You to Saffron-Walden*, sig. K3ʳ) and "he will sell his birthright in learning, with Esau, for a messe of porridge" (*Strange News*).[31] Whether Shakespeare was borrowing specific allusions or idioms from Nashe, consciously or unconsciously, is less important than the obvious indebtedness of Falstaff's biblical style to the style developed by Nashe and others in the Marprelate tracts, in which verses were ripped out of their original contexts and applied to any scandalous purpose that seemed fit.

Even in passages not apparently indebted to Nashe, Falstaff's language is peppered with biblicisms. "Watch tonight; pray tomorrow," he tells the Hostess (2.4.268–69), putting to the most mundane use the language of injunctions by Jesus ("Watch, and pray, that ye enter not into tentation," Matt. 26:41) and Paul ("And pray alwaise with all maner prayer and supplication in the Spirit: and watch thereunto with all perseverance and supplication for all Saintes," Eph. 6:18). Furthermore, Falstaff says of Gadshill, "if men were to be saved by merit, what hole in hell were hot enough for him?" (1.2.103–04), implicitly justifying his bad behavior by playing on the Protestant theology of faith over works, based on Romans 3:28 ("Therefore we conclude that a man is justified by faith without the works of the Law").[32] He later swears that if Gadshill, Peto, and Bardolph[33] don't corroborate his account of the robbery, they are "sons of darkness" (2.4.166), appropriating another verse from Paul ("Ye are the children of light, and the children of the day: we are not of the night

---

[29] Nashe, *Works*, i. 326.   [30] Shaheen, 198.   [31] Nashe, *Works*, i. 314.
[32] For the use of the word "merit" in this theological and biblical context, see John Calvin, *A commentarie vpon the Epistle of Saint Paul to the Romanes*, trans. Christopher Rosdell (London: John Harison and George Bishop, 1583), fo. 39ᵛ: "Therefore it followeth no merite of workes can bee admitted in the righteousnesse of faith."
[33] Kastan uses the name "Bardoll" in the Arden³ *Henry IV, Part 1*, arguing that this is the spelling of the early quartos. I substitute the Folio's "Bardolph," since it has become traditional, and since it is the spelling used in the subsequent plays. For the purposes of this chapter, it would be confusing to use both.

nether of the darkenes," 1 Thess. 5:5). He returns to this phrase later, calling Bardolph a "son of utter darkness" (3.3.37), the added adjective deriving from Jesus's frequent reference to "utter darkness" (Matt. 8:12, 22:13, 25:30). Again, in the improvised play about King Henry and Hal, Falstaff, as Henry, asserts that he sees virtue in that man Falstaff's looks, which means he is virtuous, since "the tree may be known by the fruit" (Luke 6:44, "For everie tre is knowen by his owne frute"). This (like the earlier reference to defiling pitch) is a more complex parody, since Falstaff is speaking as the king, who is using the biblical allusion seriously. Later, in his own voice, defending his girth, Falstaff draws on the dream of Pharaoh that Joseph interprets in Genesis. Pharoah dreams of "seven goodlie kine, and fatfleshed" who are eaten up by seven other kine, "evilfavoured and lean fleshed," which Joseph interprets to prophesy seven years of plentiful harvest followed by seven years of famine (Gen. 41:1–26). Falstaff pleads to Hal, "if to be fat be to be hated, then Pharaoh's lean kine are to be loved" (2.4.460–61). This would make little sense unless the audience understood that there were fat kine as well as lean, and that the fat represented plenty and the lean dearth.

Another of Falstaff's self-defenses relies on the story of the Fall: "Thou knowest in the state of innocency Adam fell, and what should poor Jack Falstaff do in the days of villainy?" (3.3.163–65). Falstaff continues on this theme: "Thou seest I have more flesh than another man and therefore more frailty" (3.3.165–67). As noted above (chap. 4), flesh and frailty were traditionally linked in English usage, and "frailty" entered English in conjunction with the biblical emphasis on human weakness, whether of the flesh or the will. Henry Lok's *Ecclesiastes* includes a sonnet on this theme in the section, "Sundry Affectionate Sonets of a Feeling Conscience":

> Since it hath pleasd the Lord to send such store
> Of blessings to the bodie, that it may,
> In peace and plentie spend one *joyful* day,
> (Which many want, and it long'd for before:)
> I not repin'd that it the same should use,
> But feard the *frailty* of the *flesh* (alas)
> Which made my soule, for safest way to chuse,
> (With Job) in feare and care my time to pas.[34]

There are a number of references to flesh in Job, but Lok may have in mind "Even when I remember, I am afraied, and feare taketh holde on my

---

[34] Henry Lok, *Ecclesiastes, otherwise called The preacher* (London: Richard Field, 1597), 131; emphasis added.

flesh" (21:6). Falstaff embraces and luxuriates in the flesh rather than fearing it, and it is hard to think of this "huge hill of flesh" (2.4.236–37) as frail, except of course in the moral sense.

FALSTAFF AND THE PARABLES

Two New Testament passages seem especially to preoccupy Falstaff: the Parable of the Prodigal Son from Luke 15, and the Parable of Dives and Lazarus in Luke 16. ("Dives" is not so named in the Bible, but the popular tradition gives him a name after the Latin for "rich" (*homo dives*) from the Vulgate.) These stories were among the most popular in English religious culture, explicated in sermons, sung in ballads, painted and carved on surfaces at church, at home, and at work. As mentioned in Chapter 1, they were popular subjects for wall paintings, like the one Falstaff refers to in *Henry IV, Part 2* (2.1.142–3) and the one in Falstaff's room in *Merry Wives* (4.5.6–7). There was in fact a whole subgenre of Elizabethan Prodigal Son plays, which included Shakespeare's *As You Like It* as well as others like the earlier *Nice Wanton, Lusty Juventus* and *The Disobedient Child*.[35] Richard Helgerson labeled an entire generation of Elizabethan authors prodigals—Lyly and Greene, as well as George Gascoigne, Philip Sidney, and Thomas Lodge—not only because they wrote variations on the Prodigal Son story but because the story reflected their own lives conflicted between filial duty and precocious rebellion.[36] Falstaff and Hal are both, in different ways, prodigals as well. Hal's prodigality is obvious, in his loose living in Eastcheap and later return to responsibility, asking his father's forgiveness. Falstaff is certainly dissolute, but his status as prodigal is more complex, and to some extent a parody of the original parable.

The Parable of the Prodigal Son tells of a younger son who asks his father in advance for his inheritance, and then squanders it on riotous living. He is impoverished and ends up in the low position of feeding swine (see Fig. 6.1). Deciding he has nothing to lose, he returns home and asks his father for forgiveness and for a position as a servant. The father embraces him, welcomes him, and celebrates his return. The parable is an appropriate point of comparison for Falstaff's troops, given their beggarly condition. "You would think," he says, "that I had a hundred and fifty

---

[35] Alan R. Young, *The English Prodigal Son Plays: A Theatrical Fashion of the Sixteenth and Seventeenth Centuries* (Salzburg: Institut für Anglistik und Amerikanistik, Universität Salzburg, 1979); G. K. Hunter, *English Drama 1586–1642: The Age of Shakespeare* (Oxford: Clarendon Press, 1997), 378–87. See also Ch. 4.

[36] Richard Helgerson, *Elizabethan Prodigals* (Berkeley, Los Angeles, and London: University of California Press, 1976).

Fig. 6.1. The Prodigal Son (Luke 15) was among the most popular biblical parables, often represented in visual images, and the subject of numerous plays. Here the prodigal is shown at his nadir, competing with swine for their food, after he has spent his inheritance on dissolute living. (Engraving; Albrech Dürer, probably 1496.) Museum of Fine Arts, Boston.

tattered prodigals lately come from swine-keeping, from eating draff and husks" (4.2.33–5). Falstaff refers to the same parable earlier, but more obliquely to modern ears. When he is asked to pay his debts to Mistress Quickly, Falstaff complains, "I'll not pay a denier. What, will you make a younker of me?" (3.3.79–80). A younker, as the Arden[3] edition notes, is Dutch for "young gentleman." The Arden[3] further glosses the word as pejorative, signifying a "novice" or "dupe," but this is not corroborated by the *OED*, which gives only the sense of "youngster," implying perhaps naivety but not gullibility. Furthermore, the context in *Henry IV, Part 1* seems to require a different sense. It is worth recalling that in *The Merchant of Venice*, as Shaheen notes, Gratiano compares a merchant vessel to the Prodigal Son:[37]

> How like a younger, or a prodigal,
> The scarfed bark puts from her native bay,
> Hugged and embraced by the strumpet wind!
> How like the prodigal doth she return,
> With overweathered ribs and ragged sails,
> Lean, rent and beggared by the strumpet wind! (2.6.15–20)

In the gospel, the Prodigal Son is also "the yonger" (Luke 15:22). Falstaff is thus accusing the Hostess of trying to reduce him to beggary, and it is relevant that the Prodigal Son lost much money, according to his older brother, "with harlots" (Luke 15:30). Falstaff later tells Hal that Quickly's house "is turned bawdy-house" (3.3.98–9).

The parable of Dives and Lazarus concerns a rich man who wallows in his wealth and indulges his appetites but denies even crumbs to the sick beggar at his gate (see Fig. 6.2). They both die, and while the beggar, Lazarus, ascends to heaven and rests in the bosom of Abraham, the rich man burns in hell. He asks that Lazarus be sent to "dippe the typ of his finger in water, and coole my tongue," but Abraham denies him: "thou in thy life time receivedst thy pleasures, and likewise Lazarus paines: now therefore is he comforted, and thou art tormented" (Luke 16: 19–31). What first reminds Falstaff of Dives is the brilliant red nose of the drunkard Bardolph: "I never see thy face but I think upon hell-fire and Dives that lived in purple: for there he is in his robes, burning, burning" (3.3.31–3). Dives was clothed "in purple and fine linen" (Luke 16:19). Presumably Falstaff also has Dives in mind when, as reported by the boy in *Henry V*, "'a saw a flea stick upon Bardolph's nose and 'a said it was a black soul burning in hell-fire" (2.3.38–40). Later, Falstaff recalls the poor man, Lazarus, when he looks on his pathetic conscripts, "slaves as ragged

[37] Shaheen, 420.

Fig. 6.2. This popular parable from Luke 16 tells of the rich man Dives and the beggar Lazarus who longs for crumbs from his table. Here, the naked Lazarus is beaten by a servant and licked by dogs, while Dives feasts in luxury. After death, Lazarus ascends to heaven and rests in the bosom of Abraham, while Dives burns in hell. (Georg Pencz in *The Illustrated Bartsch*, xvi.) © Victoria and Albert Museum, London.

as Lazarus in the painted cloth where the glutton's dogs licked his sores" (4.2.25–6). When Lazarus was at the rich man's gate, "the dogs came and licked his sores" (Luke 16:21).

In *Henry IV, Part 2*, Falstaff rails against a tailor who will not take his credit, wishing him the fiery damnation of Dives: "Let him be damned like the glutton! Pray God his tongue be hotter!" (1.2.34–5).[38] As noted above,

---

[38] He also calls him, oddly, a "whoreson Achitophel" (1.2.35). The Arden² note explains that Achitophel was "the treacherous counselor who deserted David for Absalom," which is accurate but does not seem very relevant. The tailor is hardly a traitor and even less a counselor. Falstaff may simply have latched onto a biblical villain, feeling betrayed. Perkins, for instance, lumps Achitophel together with Cain, Saul, and Judas as wicked suicides. *A treatise tending vnto a declaration whether a man be in the estate of damnation or in the estate of grace* (London: R. Robinson for T. Gubbin and I. Porter, 1590), 40. Perhaps Falstaff

Falstaff also says, in scathing response to the Hostess's complaint that his debts force her to pawn "the tapestry of my dining-chambers," that "the story of the Prodigal, or the German hunting,[39] is worth a thousand of these bed-hangers and these fly-bitten tapestries" (2.1.139–40, 142–5). The chain of Dives and Lazarus allusions culminates in the description of Falstaff's death in *Henry V*. On hearing that he is dead, Bardolph laments, "Would I were with him, wheresome'er he is, either in heaven or hell!" To which the Hostess responds, "Nay, sure, he's not in hell; he's in Arthur's bosom, if ever man went to Arthur's bosom" (2.3.7–10). This is a complexly muddled allusion that has been very diversely interpreted, as has Falstaff himself. Mistress Quickly presumably means "Abraham" rather than "Arthur," referring once again to the Dives and Lazarus story, with Falstaff the Lazarus who ascends to heaven to be comforted. Physically, and visually, this is absurd; the obese Falstaff is hardly a dead-ringer for the emaciated Lazarus. For some critics, it is also impossible to imagine Falstaff achieving salvation at all; despite his familiarity with Scripture, his behavior hardly conforms to any Christian norm of moral goodness. He drinks and eats to excess, spends time with whores (whether or not he can make use of them), commits highway robbery to pay for his indulgences, takes bribes to let off those of his conscripts who can pay, and sends those who cannot to be slaughtered in battle with no regret. He also lies prodigiously.

Paul Cubeta analyzes Falstaff's death in terms of the tradition of *ars moriendi*—the art of dying—in which the godly man, who has lived his life in constant remembrance of his end, embraces this end and dies gladly.[40] Certainly, Falstaff is continually expressing a desire to repent. He absurdly charges Hal with corrupting him (with his "damnable iteration"):

Before I knew thee, Hal, I knew nothing, and now am I, if a man should speak truly, little better than one of the wicked. I must give over this life, and I will give it over. By the Lord, an I do not, I am a villain. I'll be damned for never a king's son in Christendom. (1.2.89–94)

hopes his tailor will follow suit. Nashe blasts Achitophel and Judas as "two notable blemishes of the trade of rope-makers" (with a dig at the trade of Harvey's father), but this does not illuminate Falstaff's usage any further. *Have with You to Saffron-Walden* (London: John Danter, 1596), sig. I4ʳ. Roy Battenhouse tries to argue that Falstaff is aiming at Henry V (or IV), since "Achitophel was a vile politician who helped bring in Absalom on a 'reform' platform," but this seems too convoluted, and Hal is more obviously a David figure, not Absalom. Battenhouse, "Falstaff as Parodist and Perhaps Holy Fool," *PMLA* 90/1 (1975), 32–52, 43. For Hal as David, see Steven Marx, *Shakespeare and the Bible* (Oxford and New York: Oxford University Press, 2000), ch. 3.

[39] I.e., some hunting scene, presumably either set in or by an artist from Germany.

[40] Paul M. Cubeta, "Falstaff and the Art of Dying," *SEL* 27/2 (1987), 197–211. Cubeta (p. 201) quotes Thomas Lupset, "this dyenge well is in effecte to dye gladlye." *A compendious and a very fruteful treatyse, teachynge the waye of dyenge well* (London: Thomas Berthelet, 1541), fo. 11ᵛ. The book was first printed in 1531.

Damnable Iteration 249

Later, after the Gadshill robbery, Falstaff laments the "bad world" and expresses a desire for a humbler godly life: "I would I were a weaver; I could sing psalms or anything" (2.4.126–7). In *Part 2*, he claims he has lost his voice with the "singing of anthems" (1.2.189). The received truth that weavers were Puritan psalm-singers has recently been challenged by Beth Quitslund, who points out that there is little historical evidence for it before *Henry IV, Part 1*.[41] Most Protestants sang Psalms, not just the Puritans, and the theological leanings of weavers seem no more certain than any other trade. This is another case of the drama, especially Shakespeare's—especially Falstaff—shaping the popular conception of the "Puritan."

Still later, Falstaff returns to the subject of his future reformation, questioning Bardolph:

…am not I fallen away vilely since this last encounter? Do I not bate? Do I not dwindle? Why, my skin hangs about me like an apple-john. Well, I'll repent, and that suddenly, while I am in some liking. I shall be out of heart shortly, and then I shall have no strength to repent. An I have not forgot what the inside of a church is made of, I am a peppercorn, a brewster's horse. The inside of a church! Company, villainous company, hath been the spoil of me. (3.3.1–5)

But all this is part of Falstaff's mock-Puritan act. Immediately after swearing to give over Hal and his wicked life, he eagerly joins the robbery (claiming thievery is his vocation). After his longing for psalm-singing, and his condemnation of Hal's and Poins's cowardice, he lies about his "battle" with the men in "buckram suits," weasels his way out of exposure as a liar, but finally forgives the young men since they still have the loot: "by the Lord, lads, I am glad you have the money" (2.4.267). And rather than refresh his memory of the inside of a church, he asks Bardolph to "sing me a bawdy song, make me merry" (3.3.13–14). As for remembering his end, Falstaff says to his whore, "Peace, good Doll, do not speak to me like a death's-head, do not bid me remember mine end" (*Henry IV, Part 2*, 2.4.231–2). Even here, in his rejection of the memento mori, Falstaff distorts Psalm 39's "Lord, let me know mine end."[42]

---

[41] Beth Quitslund, *The Reformation in Rhyme: Sternhold, Hopkins, and the English Metrical Psalter, 1547–1603* (Aldershot and Burlington, VT: Ashgate, 2008), 268–73. Sternhold and Hopkins was sung in parishes across England. See also Hamlin, chs 1–2. For the received truth, see, e.g., Maurice Hunt, who quotes David Bevington, "many psalm-singing Protestant immigrants from the Low Countries were weavers" (*Shakespeare's Religious Allusiveness: Its Play and Tolerance* [Aldershot and Burlington, VT: Ashgate, 2004], 20).

[42] Ps. 39: 4, "Lord, let me know mine end, and the number of my daies: that I may be certified how long I have to live." Not surprisingly, this psalm is traditionally connected with meditations on death, as in Thomas Tuke, *A discourse of death, bodily, ghostly, and eternall* (London: William Stansbie for George Norton, 1613), 79. "And though *David* pray, *Lord let me know mine end, and the measure of my daies, what it is, and let me know how long I have to live*: yet he meanes (as I take it) not to begge the knowledge of the verie point

When Falstaff cries out on his deathbed, "God, God, God!," Mistress Quickly, always ready with the wrong word for every occasion, urges that "'a should not think of God; I hoped there was no need to trouble himself with any such thoughts yet" (2.3.18–21). And then she recounts how she felt under his bedclothes, "to his knees, and so up'ard and up'ard, and all was as cold as any stone" (2.3.25). Do we laugh or cry? The vibrant Falstaff, full of the fire of life, has gone cold. But Mistress Quickly, reaching up'ard and up'ard, must have found that, along with everything else, his "stones" were cold as stone.[43] Is this a eulogy or a testicle joke? Nym then chimes in that Falstaff "cried out of [i.e., against] sack," seemingly rejecting the beverage to which he recited a sublime hymn back in *Henry IV, Part 2*, and which it seems he could have used in his last hours, since "it warms the blood...and makes it course from the inwards to the parts' extremes" (*Part 2*, 4.3.101–6). Quickly's bad, unconscious puns continue, as she and the boy argue about whether Falstaff did or did not cry against women too. The boy reports that he said "they were devils incarnate," but Quickly responds that he "could never abide carnation, 'twas a colour he never liked" (2.3.30–2). Then Pistol calls the others to embark for the French wars, "the very blood to suck!" (2.3.54). No surprise that critics find it difficult to gauge this scene. Cubeta summarizes the interpretative dilemma:

Is Falstaff like Hal seeking a reformation that will glitter o'er his fault as he tries without parody to redeem the time? The fragmented and disconnected structure of his last words, the ambiguity of his observations, and the malapropisms of the Hostess deny resolution...And Falstaff cries out to God. But what does he mean? Is this only a feverish cry of fear? Is he trying to make an act of contrition and asking for divine forgiveness? Is this the cry of a man who believes that he has been abandoned by God—as by his friend and king—in his last hour?[44]

Certainly, Falstaff's last words allude to the Bible. It is Quickly who is sure he's "in Arthur's bosom," but Falstaff himself apparently "babbled of green fields" (2.3.16–17). The best argument for Theobald's emendation of these lines—apart from the fact that the alternative ("a Table of greene fields") makes no reasonable sense[45]—is that it makes perfect sense for Falstaff to die as he lived, quoting Scripture. The "green fields," as Dover

& article of his death, but desires God to give him grace to acknowledge, consider, and duely to acquaint himselfe with the shortnesse and frailtie of his life."

[43] Testicles were called "stones" since Anglo-Saxon times. Another example of Shakespeare playing on this usage is Dr Caius's threat about Sir Hugh Evans in *Merry Wives*: "By gar, I will cut all his two stones" (1.4.104).
[44] Cubeta, "Falstaff Dying," 206–7.
[45] The various over-ingenious arguments to make sense of the original (F: "Table of greene fields") are too convoluted to be convincing. The best summary of the critical and editorial history of this crux is George Walton Williams, "Still Babbling of Green Fields:

Wilson first argued, must be Falstaff's recitation of Psalm 23, "he shall feed me in a green pasture," perhaps (characteristically) muddled in the retelling by Quickly.[46] Psalm 23 remains the favorite psalm for consolation in distress, the expression of hope and trust in a protecting Lord even though one walks "through the valley of the shadow of death."[47] The psalm ends with a desire to "dwell in the house of the Lord for ever" (Ps. 23:6). As Calvin interprets this verse, "By this clause he sheweth openly, that he setleth not himself upon earthly pleasures or commodities: but that the marke which he shooteth at is in heaven, wher unto he leveleth all things."[48] Falstaff has not become a weaver, but at his death, as he departs this bad world, he is indeed singing (or at least saying) psalms.

But is he in Abraham's, or even Arthur's, bosom? Only the most dogmatic critics are willing completely to damn the prodigal Falstaff. Even Samuel Johnson, writing of "unimitated, unimitable Falstaff," could conclude only "that he is stained with no enormous or sanguinary crimes, so that his licentiousness is not so offensive but that it may be borne for his mirth."[49] Roy Battenhouse tried unpersuasively to make Falstaff into a kind of holy fool and he read the pattern of allusions to Dives and Lazarus parodically: "Battenhouse's reading of the conscription passage in *Henry IV, Part One*, is that Falstaff deftly transforms his Lazaruses into prodigals, which enables him to cast himself not as Dives but as the good father; Falstaff, Battenhouse argues, implies that King Henry is a Dives-figure who ignores his people's poverty."[50] Matthew Fike, whose summary this

Mr Greenfields and the Twenty-third Psalm," in Lois Potter and Arthur F. Kinney (eds), *Shakespeare: Text and Theater: Essays in Honor of Jay L. Halio* (Newark: University of Delaware Press; London: Associated University Presses, 1999), 45–61. The variant emendation, "talk'd of green fields," would not affect the allusion to Ps.23, but another argument for "babbled," not considered before, is that it hints at yet another psalm, the extremely popular "By the waters of Babylon we sat down and wept" (Ps. 137:1). The Hostess says that Falstaff (when he was rheumatic) would talk of "the whore of Babylon" (2.3.36). Babel and Babylon were frequently interchanged in the period, the names for the city and the tower are identical in Hebrew, and there was a folk etymology linking "to babble" with God's confusion of human languages at Babel. Parson Evans sings a muddled version of the psalm in *Merry Wives*. What would make a subtle allusion to the psalm appropriate in this context is that it is the quintessential biblical lament for exile, and Falstaff dies of heartbreak exiled from his Prince. On Ps. 137 and exile, see Hamlin, ch. 7.

[46] *Henry V*, ed. John Dover Wilson (Cambridge: Cambridge University Press, 1947).
[47] See Hamlin, ch. 5.
[48] *The Psalmes of David and others. With M. John Calvins commentaries*, trans. Arthur Golding (London: Thomas East and Henry Middleton: for Lucas Harison, and George Byshop, 1571), 87.
[49] Samuel Johnson, "From the Edition of Shakespeare's Works, 1765," in D. Nichol-Smith (ed.), *Shakespeare Criticism: A Selection 1623–1840* (London: Oxford University Press, 1916; repr. 1964), 117.
[50] Battenhouse, "Falstaff as Parodist," summarized by Matthew Fike, "Dives and Lazarus in *The Henriad*," *Renascence* 55/4 (2003), 279–91, 285.

is, points out that this argument ignores Falstaff's own exploitation of the poor and also that Falstaff's knowledge of the Bible does not signal a genuine Christian spirit. More than this, however, Battenhouse does not sufficiently recognize the full brilliant perversity of Falstaff's use of allusion.

Falstaff interweaves the two parables from Luke and turns them both upside down. What Lazarus and the Prodigal Son have in common is great expectations, Lazarus's in heaven and the prodigal's in his father's house, though of course that house is itself a metaphor for heaven; Jesus tells the two parables back to back in Luke to teach the same lesson about divine justice and mercy.[51] Falstaff's conscripts are thus either unlike both Lazarus and the prodigal, in that they have no expectations, or like them both, if we assume that they have such expectations in the world to come. In the latter case, Falstaff could not be the good father, since that role is God's; if the prodigality of the conscripts is an earthly one—they have "lately come from swine-keeping," which implies they are now at home or on their way there—Falstaff still does not seem the good father (or a bad one), since ultimately it is not Falstaff who is responsible for their conscription (or deaths) but the king. One might even argue that Falstaff has given them gainful employment and (presumably) regular meals, but the ultimate source is still the king. The role of Dives does not fit Falstaff much better than that of the good father. He is fat (like the damned "glutton" he mentions in *Part 2*), but he is hardly rich. He has taken bribes but from the men he lets go, not the ones he conscripts. Again, moreover, it is not clear that these men are much worse off in the army than out of it. At least they will not starve, and, despite Falstaff's grim prediction—"food for powder, food for powder" (4.2.64–5)—their death in battle is not certain. A few seem to have survived Shrewsbury (5.3.36–8), and Falstaff's entire troop survives in *Part 2*, thanks to his late arrival at the battle. (Of course, thanks to Prince John's Machiavellian strategy—he can lie as well as Falstaff can—there is no battle at all; the rebels surrender and the leaders are executed.)

It is important to note, when considering Falstaff's habitual lying, that not only does he never really deceive anyone, but he seems never to intend to.[52] We delight in his ingenious evasion of the truth, but the delight depends upon recognizing the evasion. "Is not the truth the truth?"

---

[51] In the margin to verse 20 in the Geneva Bible, for instance ("and when he was a great way off, his father sawe him"), the editor explains, "God preventeth [i.e., anticipates] us and heareth our gronings before we crye to him."

[52] Beatrice Groves, *Texts and Traditions: Religion in Shakespeare 1592–1604* (Oxford: Clarendon Press, 2007), 132.

Falstaff asks, but Hal is right that Falstaff's lies "are like their father that begets them, gross as a mountain, open, palpable" (2.4.218–19). As so often, the language here is biblical. Shaheen suggests that Hal's lines allude to Jesus's condemnation of the Jews:

Ye are of your father the devil, and the lustes of your father ye wil do: he hathe bene a murtherer from the beginning, and abode not in the trueth, because there is no truth in him. When he speaketh a lie, then speaketh he of his power: for he is a liar, and the father thereof. (John 8:44)

Has Hal picked up on Falstaff's blustering lie earlier in the scene that he and the other thieves bound "every man of them, or I am a Jew else, an 'Ebrew Jew" (2.4.172–3)? The Arden[3] note glosses "Jew" as "userer," but Hal's allusion suggests a better gloss would be "liar." Falstaff's question about the truth is usually explained as being proverbial, but it also recalls Pilate's question to Jesus in the same gospel Hal alludes to: "What is trueth?" (John 18:38) This would be an appropriate response to Falstaff's question and one the usually skeptical knight would probably understand. Equally important to the openness of Falstaff's lies, however, is that none of Falstaff's deceits, verbal or otherwise, causes real harm. His treatment of the conscripts has already been discussed. Falstaff's only other potentially serious offense is stealing money from the Canterbury pilgrims, but Hal pays them back (after stealing it from Falstaff, giving it back to him, and, presumably, participating in the carousing it would have paid for). And, for English Protestants, the pilgrims were engaged in a dubious enterprise to begin with.[53]

If Falstaff's conscripts have no great expectations, however much they are Lazarus-like or prodigal, the same cannot be said of Falstaff himself. His appropriations of Dives and Lazarus and the Prodigal Son are the only biblical allusions that emphasize the future as opposed to the static, timeless present. Falstaff's great expectation is that Hal will reward him when he is king. "Do not thou, when thou art king, hang a thief," pleads Falstaff to his young drinking companion, but he clearly hopes for more (*Part 1*, 1.2.58–9). Notoriously, when Hal does become king, Falstaff is rejected. A. C. Bradley pointed out that there are at least two reasons we resent Hal's behavior: first, he makes a public show of what could easily have been a private moment; second, he makes a pompous moralizing

---

[53] There are traders too, as well as pilgrims, "riding to London with fat purses" (1.2.120–1). The Chamberlain tells Gadshill of a "franklin in the Weald of Kent [who] hath brought with him three hundred marks in gold" (2.1.47). Their business is not subject to Protestant critique, but it is not entirely clear who the "Travellers" are that Falstaff and the others waylay in 2.2, pilgrims, traders, or both. In any case, the event is comic rather than serious, and whoever is robbed seems to be paid back by the prince.

sermon of it: "He had a right to turn away his former self, and his old companions with it, but he had no right to talk all of a sudden like a clergyman; and surely it was both ungenerous and insincere to speak of them as his 'misleaders,' as though in the days of Eastcheap and Gadshill he had been a weak and silly lad."[54] Even more disturbing, perhaps, is the sense that Hal learned how to talk like a clergyman from Falstaff, who frequently talks like one, and a Puritan one at that, but playfully, never with pomposity or self-righteous moralizing.

Interestingly, Hal alludes to the Bible as Falstaff does, with just as much interpretative freedom, but, whereas Falstaff is always primarily playful, Hal's play is deadly serious. There is a lot of playing throughout the *Henry* plays. In Eastcheap in *Part 1*, Hal plays his father, plays himself, and offers to play Percy. In *Henry V*, Hal promises the Dauphin, who has given him a mocking gift of tennis balls, "to play a set | Shall strike his father's crown into the hazard" (1.2.263–4). The promise is qualified by acknowledging "God's grace," but Hal's religious language here is part of playing another role: the anointed king, God's vicegerent. The invasion of France "lies within the will of God," but the play begins (in F)[55] with the Archbishop of Canterbury and the Bishop of Ely scheming to devise means of getting King Henry out of the country, distracting him from plans to seize the Church's wealth. Notably, one of the plans Henry has for the money he would appropriate from the Church is for the "relief of lazars and weak age, | Of indigent faint souls past corporal toil" (1.1.15–16). Lazars are the poor and diseased, the name deriving from the Lazarus of the parable. Henry, it seems, does not want to play Dives but to relieve the Lazaruses. But "God's will" distracts him from this charity, taking him rather to France, war, conquest, and power.

The clerics in *Henry V* acknowledge the king's remarkable reformation of character by means of biblical allusion:

> Consideration like an angel came
> And whipped the offending Adam out of him,
> Leaving his body as a paradise
> T'envelope and contain celestial spirits. (1.1.28–31)

---

[54] A. C. Bradley, "The Rejection of Falstaff," in Harold Bloom (ed.), *Sir John Falstaff* (Philadelphia: Chelsea House, 2004), 17–35, 22.

[55] *Henry V* is a case where the different playtexts matter in terms of biblical allusion. There are distinctly more of them in F than Q. 1.1 is only in F and adds a biblically rich, as well as Machiavellian, opening to the play. Other biblical allusions added in F include the notorious "babbled of green fields" and Herod and "the wives of Jewry" in the speech at Harfleur. Many of the biblical allusions in the treason scene of 2.2 are also missing in Q: "Another fall of man" (2.2.142) and the "desolation" of the kingdom (2.2.174). Given T. J. Craik's conclusion (*Henry V*, 28) that Q "is not an accurate record of a systematically cut version of the play," it is difficult to assess the significance of the missing biblical allusions.

Aspects of this allusion are discussed in Chapter 4. In this context, the point is that Falstaff is represented as the sinful Adam in the garden of the prince, expelled not by an actual angel but by the will of the prince himself (through "Consideration"). The relevant biblical context is not just Genesis but Ephesians, in which Paul orders "that ye cast of [off], concerning the conversation in time past, the olde man, which is corrupt through the deceivable lustes, And be renewed in the spirit of your minde, And put on the new man, which after God is created in righteousness and true holiness" (Eph. 4:22–4).[56] The Geneva gloss interprets the "olde man" as "all the natural corruption that is in us," our inheritance from Adam. As mentioned in Chapter 4, the baptismal rite included the prayer, adapted from Paul, "O merciful God, grant that the old Adam in these children may be so buried, that the new man may be raised up in them." But the old man cast out by the king is not Adam so much as Falstaff, and the redemption he promised in *Henry IV, Part 1*, a "reformation... | Redeeming the time when men think least I will" (1.2.203–7), is a calculated political move, not a spiritual conversion. Henry V has been called "an ideal Protestant hero," and his sermonizing rejection of Falstaff has been read in conjunction not only with Paul's Epistles but with the Elizabethan *Homily against Gluttonie and Dronkennes*.[57] This is the same Hal, however, who orders the throats of the French prisoners cut at Agincourt and who implicitly compares himself and his men to Herod and the soldiers who slaughtered the innocent children of Israel.[58] Before Harfleur, Henry gives a blisteringly vicious speech in which he promises rape, death, and destruction if the town is not surrendered:

> If not, why, in a moment look to see
> The blind and bloody soldier with foul hand
> Defile the locks of your shrill-shrieking daughters,
> Your fathers taken by the silver beards,
> And their most reverend heads dashed to the walls,[59]
> Your naked infants spitted upon pikes,
> Whiles the mad mothers with their howls confused
> Do break the clouds, as did the wives of Jewry
> At Herod's bloody-hunting slaughtermen. (3.3.33–43)

---

[56] See D. J. Palmer, "Casting off the Old Man: History and St Paul in 'Henry IV,'" *Critical Quarterly*, 12 (1970), 267–83.

[57] Michael Davies, "Falstaff's Lateness: Calvinism and the Protestant Hero in Henry V," *RES* 56/225 (2005), 351–78, 353.

[58] On Henry's order to kill the prisoners, see Norman Rabkin, *Shakespeare and the Problem of Meaning* (Chicago and London: University of Chicago Press, 1981), 53–5.

[59] The combination of infants and heads dashed against walls alludes to the vengeful close of Ps. 137 ("Blessed shall he be, that taketh thy children: and throweth them against the stones").

This nightmare out of Bosch or Brueghel does not come to pass, but the town surrenders not because of Henry's bloodthirsty rant but because they already know that the Dauphin's troops cannot reinforce and rescue them. Henry's speech has no practical effect, but it offers a picture of an unrestrained orgy of violence that is hard to get out of one's head even after the king has ordered "mercy to them all" (3.3.54).

The new King Henry seems exceptionally able, as a ruler, as a dispenser of justice (in his sentencing of the traitors in 2.2),[60] and as a military leader, but this is not the kind of "new man" Paul had in mind in Ephesians. But, if the fiercely pragmatic Henry is a disturbing parody of Paul's "new man," the Pauline perspective is itself subject to critique. As Joan Rees has argued, Shakespeare's Falstaff plays (including *Henry V*) can be read as "conducting an examination of the epistle of the Ephesians by the light of an experience of human nature."[61] Shakespeare's only use of the word "Ephesians" is in *Henry IV, Part 1*, when the page speaks of Falstaff supping in Eastcheap with his usual companions, "Ephesians...of the old church" (2.2.143).[62] As Arden[3] notes, the sense seems to be that these are unregenerate "old men," like the Ephesians Paul was trying to convert into "new men," but the term seems playful rather than seriously pejorative. Rees concludes, "not even St Paul can persuade Shakespeare that Prince Hal and his father are inevitably better men than the old reprobate, Falstaff."[63] Yet, as so often, even Shakespeare's skepticism is worked out in biblical terms. His critique of Paul takes part of its punch from his radical reading of Jesus's parable, in which fat man and thin man, Dives and Lazarus, are reversed. The thin Hal (in Falstaff's words, "you starveling, you eel-skin, you dried neat's tongue, you bull's pizzle, you stock-fish," *Henry IV, Part 1*, 2.4.231) comes into his inheritance of wealth and power and casts out the fat Falstaff, who, despite his obvious gluttony, is in fact the poor supplicant, as well as the

---

[60] There is a biblical background to this scene too. Henry's strategy in trapping the traitors is exactly that of the prophet Nathan in trapping King David into an admission of his sin. In both cases, a fictional scenario is presented that elicits a judgment from the guilty party; that judgment is then applied back on the judge. David condemns his own behavior, and the traitors condemn themselves to death. Henry also more specifically alludes to Ps. 137:5 ("If I forget thee, O Jerusalem, let my right hand forget her cunning"): "We...shall forget the office of our hand | Sooner than quittance of desert and merit" (2.2.33–5). As noted in Ch. 4, Henry likens this act of treason to "Another fall of man" (2.2.142). He also describes the future state of the kingdom, had the traitors succeeded, as a "desolation," the key word from Lamentations (2.2.174).

[61] Joan Rees, "Falstaff, St Paul, and the Hangman," *RES* 38/149 (1987): 14–22, 21.

[62] The Host uses "Ephesian," again the only instance in Shakespeare, in the same context in *Merry Wives*, to refer to himself, presumably in his capacity as innkeeper (4.5.15). According to the *OED*, neither form of the word was in use in this context before Shakespeare.

[63] Rees, "Falstaff," 22.

devoted friend. Given Falstaff's unquenchable thirst, one might again think him the parched Dives in hell, but, in Shakespeare's rewriting of the parable, it is the fat man who ascends to the bosom of Abraham, or, in this case, Arthur—perhaps an appropriate substitute for Falstaff's lost friend Hal, given the Tudor obsession with their Welsh lineage. Shakespeare complicates the parable of the Prodigal Son in similar fashion. Hal is the obvious prodigal, indulging in riotous living as a youth before returning to his father in remorse and being received with rejoicing. But the loose behavior of the original Prodigal Son was not coolly calculated to "falsify men's hopes" (1.2.201) so that his reformation would seem all the more brilliant. Falstaff is a prodigal too, if an odd one, but Shakespeare inverts the parable's father and son just as Falstaff and Hal did in their play in Eastcheap, the old Falstaff playing the young son Hal, and young Hal playing his father. Falstaff the prodigal father-figure comes to be welcomed and embraced by his "sweet boy" Hal, but is banished "on pain of death" (5.5.63). The "roasted Manningtree ox" (*Part 1*, 2.4.440) is denied the parable's fatted calf.

HENRY IV, PART 2

The Falstaff of *Henry IV, Part 2* is consistent with the same character in *Part 1*. Although Falstaff utters fewer biblical allusions in *Part 2* (seventeen out of sixty-five, according to Shaheen), he still alludes frequently, and irreverently, and his language is still that of the Martinist-style mock-Puritan. The Chief Justice, for example, tells Falstaff that "To punish you by the heels would amend the attention of your ears, and I care not if I do become your physician." Falstaff replies that "I am as poor as Job, my lord, but not so patient" (1.2.125). Falstaff's mental chain of association seems to move from the Justice's use of "physician" to the "patient" the Justice would make of him, and then from that word to the proverbial "patience" of Job (James 5:11). The wordplay also allows Falstaff another of his characteristic expressions of abjection, claiming Job's poverty, as well as, perhaps by implication, Job's innocent suffering. Falstaff also alludes to Job at the beginning of this scene, when he refers to the "brain of this foolish-compounded clay, man" (1.2.6). Job tells his friends, "Your memories may be compared unto ashes, and your bodies to bodies of clay" (Job 13:12), and the metaphor of bodies as clay (deriving ultimately from God's creation of man out of dust in Genesis 2) recurs throughout the book (Job 4:19, 10:9, 27:16, 33:6).

In the letter he writes to Hal urging him to "Repent at idle times as thou mayst," and which Hal reads aloud, Falstaff signs himself "Thine by yea and no" (2.2.122–4). This is a Puritan idiom, alluding to Matthew 5:37, where Jesus preaches from the mount, "let your communication be, Yea, yea: Nay, nay. For whatsoever is more then these, commeth of evil." The apostle James repeats this injunction in his epistle: "Let your yea, be yea, and your naye, naye, lest ye fall into condemnation" (James 5:12). References to yea and nay were common among Puritan writers. Perkins, in his *Golden Chaine*, writes that one of the principal abuses against God is "to sweare in common talke," citing as support "Mat.5.37. Let your communication be yea, yea, and nay, nay."[64] In *A Progresse of Pietie*, John Norden urged that "It is not inough to observe the letter of the law: For then wee may still continue manslayers in wrath towards our brethren, wee may commit adultery, by lusting we may sinne in our communication, exceeding yea and nay."[65] Even critics of Puritanism recognized Matthew 5:37 as an identifying catchphrase. In his *Survay of the Pretended Holy Discipline*, Richard Bancroft accuses Thomas Cartwright and the presenters of the Puritan *Admonition to the Parliament* of pride in their own learning, asking "is not this the lightnes, and fleshly minde, which the Apostle renounceth, in that they come thus unto us, with yea, and nay."[66] The passage in question, and iteration of the yea–nay rule, is 2 Corinthians 1:17, in which Paul writes, "When I therefore was thus minded, did I use lightnes? Or minde I those things which I minde, according to the flesh, that which shulde be, Yea, yea, and Nay, nay?" The sting of Bancroft's attack lies in his use of the Puritans' own idiom. Thomas Lodge's Nashean pamphlet *Wits Miserie and the Worlds Madnesse* includes a condemnation of the devil, Blasphemy:

He haunts ordinaries, and places of exercise, schooles and houses of learning, nay I fear me (would God it were a lie) there are more othes sworn in Poules in a day, than devout praiers said in it in a month: every shop hath one at least, beside the maister, to sweare to the price, and without an oth now adaies there is no buyeng or chaffare [trade]: faith and troth are the least hazard; yea and nay is a puritane.[67]

Finally, in the anti-Puritan play *A Knack to Know a Knave* (printed 1595), a Puritan (or "Precision") Priest describes the Puritan position, including the devotion to "yea and nay":

> And I among my brethren and my friends
> Doe still instruct them with my doctrine,
> And Yea and nay goes through the world with us.

---

[64] Perkins, *Golden chaine*, sig. H^r.   [65] Norden, *Progresse of Pietie*, fo. 20^v.

[66] Richard Bancroft, *A Survay of the Pretended Holy Discipline* (London: John Wolfe, 1591), 150. Collinson calls this tract "very nasty" ("Ecclesiastical Vitriol," 153).

[67] Thomas Lodge, *Wits Miserie and the Worlds Madnesse* (London: Adam Islip, 1596), 65.

> Fie, not an oath we sweare for twentie pound,
> Brethren (say we) take heed by Adams fal,
> For by his sinnes we are condemned all.
> Thus preach we still unto our brethren,
> Though in our heart we never meane the thing:
> Thus doe we blind the world with holinesse,
> And so by that are tearmed pure Precisians.[68]

Falstaff's "by yea and no" is thus not only an allusion to Paul but a mark of his mock-Puritan discourse.

Falstaff continues to turn Pauline allusions upside down, talking the Puritan talk to make fun of it. In the last scene with Hal in Eastcheap, Falstaff adopts yet another Puritan idiom, excusing his dispraise of Hal by claiming that he "dispraised him before the wicked," which is no sin (2.4.316). Hal retorts by asking who Falstaff counts among the wicked, starting with Doll, with whom he has been cuddling: "Is she of the wicked? Is thine hostess here of the wicked? Or is thy boy of the wicked? Or honest Bardolph, whose zeal burns in his nose, of the wicked?" (2.4.324–7). Of course they are, or at least there would be little doubt about a whore, the hostess of a seedy tavern, and a thief, but, since these are Falstaff's companions, Hal is challenging his hypocrisy, and in his own mock-Puritan terms. As mentioned earlier in the chapter, the "wicked" are referred to throughout the Bible. The Puritan *Admonition to the Parliament* contains numerous remarks about the wicked, as in its complaint about the abuses of the English Church, "throughe which thys long time brethren have bene at unnaturall warre and strife among themselves, to the hinderance of the gospel, to the joy of the wycked, and to the grefe and dismay of all those that professe Christes religion, and labor to attain Christian reformation."[69] Not surprisingly, Nashe exploited this idiom in his anti-Martinist pamphlets, including *A myrror for Martinists*, in which he complains about innovation in the Church: "But God for his mercie turne this awaie far from the mindes of his chosen, and let this bee rather the furie and madnesse of the wicked."[70] And in *An almond for a parrat*, Nashe attacks the Puritans (Precisians), citing their own condemnation of the wicked:

---

[68] William Kemp, *A most pleasant and merie new comedie, intituled, A knacke to knowe a knave* (London: Richard Jones, 1594), B2ᵛ. Robert Greene has been proposed as the author, but not conclusively. Hanspeter Born, *The Rare Wit and the Rude Groom: The Authorship of 'A Knack to Know a Knave' in Relation to Greene, Nashe, and Shakespeare* (Bern: Franke, 1971). The play was performed at least as early as 1592 (see Hunter, *English Drama*, 367–8).

[69] John Field, *An Admonition to the Parliament* ([Hemel Hempstead?: Printed by J. Stroud?, 1572]), sig. A8ᵛ.

[70] Nashe, *Myrror for Martinists*, 20.

Why, there is not a Presician in England that hath abused arte, or mistoken a metaphor but I haue his name in blacke and white, what say you to that zealous shéepebyter of your owne edition in Cambridge, that saide the wicked had a scabbe, a braune [callous], and a crust on their conscience, being so full of their wilie gilies, that we that are the true children of God can not tell how to concerne them.[71]

Hal's reference to Bardolph's burning "zeal" (continuing the running gag on his nose) draws in another Puritan watchword. Nashe writes that "Their zeale is hot, theyle plaie you sure," and that "under a great shew of holines and zeale, they thrust into the house of God, before the whole congregation, their contentous conceits and peevish affections."[72]

A few lines further in the tavern scene, Falstaff, in answer to Hal's challenge about his companions' wickedness, indicts the hostess "for suffering flesh to be eaten in thy house, contrary to the law," that law prohibiting the sale of meat during Lent (2.4.341–2). Hal tries to get in a riposte, beginning, "You, gentlewoman," but is interrupted by Doll, who says, perhaps puzzled by the suggestion of her own gentility, "What says your Grace?" This inspires Falstaff to a particularly blasphemous Pauline allusion: "His Grace says that which his flesh rebels against" (2.4.348). The allusion is to Galatians, "For the flesh lusteth against the Spirit, and the Spirit against the flesh" (5:17). Falstaff's primary meaning is rude, that Hal ("his Grace") says something (that Doll is a gentlewoman) that his flesh rebels against (since his "flesh," that is, his erection, proves Doll a whore, presumably since a gentlewoman would not arouse such a reaction?). There is more significance here too. Falstaff has often mocked Hal's "grace," both as royal title and as social or spiritual condition. "Grace thou wilt have none," says Falstaff in their first scene together in *Part 1*, "no, by my troth, not so much as will serve to be prologue to an egg and butter" (1.2.16–20), punning on yet another sense of "grace," the prayer before a meal. Here, though, Falstaff sets Hal's grace and his flesh in opposition, in good Pauline terms, but implicitly suggests a further tension between Hal's royal calling and his appetite for bodily pleasures in the fleshpots of Eastcheap. The Geneva note to Galatians 5:17 explains, "the natural man striveth against the Spirit of regeneration," which also neatly describes the ongoing dramatic conflict for Hal as to whether he will achieve his own regeneration or "reformation." It is also significant that "flesh" is a term usually associated with Falstaff throughout *Part 1*: "'Sblood, I'll not bear mine own flesh so far afoot again" (2.2.35–6), "this

---

[71] Nashe, *An almond for a parrat*, fo. 17ᵛ.
[72] Thomas Nashe, *Mar-Martine* (n.p., 1589), n.p.; *Myrror for Martinists*, 9.

huge hill of flesh" (2.4.237), "I have more flesh than another man" (3.3.165–6), "could not all this flesh keep in a little life?" (5.4.101–2).[73] Given this earlier association of Falstaff and flesh, even in *Part 2* we might interpret Hal's struggle as an internal psychomachia between the forces of "Grace," represented by his Grace the King, and the "flesh," represented by Falstaff.

Falstaff's last two Pauline allusions are spoken on the battlefield. First, when he encounters the rebel Colevile of the Dale, he blusters, "rouse up fear and trembling, and do observance to my mercy" (4.3.14–15). The hendiadys "fear and trembling" is biblical, once again from Ephesians: "Servants, be obedient unto them that are your masters, according to the flesh, with feare and trembling in singleness of your hearts as unto Christ" (6:5). The familiar emphasis on the flesh makes Ephesians all the more likely as the source of the allusion, though the phrase also appears in Philippians 2:12 ("so make an end of your owne salvation with feare and trembling").[74] Sixteenth-century uses of the phrase in print are exclusively from biblical or religious texts. Secondly, after turning Colevile over to Prince John, Falstaff says of this prince, "Good faith, this same young sober-blooded boy doth not love me, nor a man cannot make him laugh; but that's no marvel, he drinks no wine" (4.3.85–8). This is an unsurprising judgment from the high priest of sack, and Prince John is certainly a cold fish and a ruthlessly Machiavellian leader. There is a relevant biblical background to the drinking of wine: the Psalmist sings of "wine that maketh glad the heart of man" (104:15). Also, Jesus the son of Sirach writes that "Wine soberly drunken, is profitable for the life of man... Wine was made from the beginning to make men glad... Wine measurably drunken and in time, bringeth gladness and cherefulnes of the minde" (Ecclus. 31:27–8). And even Paul advises Timothy to "Drink no longer water, but use a litle wine for the stomakes sake, and thine often infirmities" (1 Tim. 5:23). The careful Bible reader might observe that the ellipses in the quotation from Ecclesiasticus above omit significant qualifications emphasizing moderation: "what is his life that is overcome with wine?" and "and not for drunkenness." Paul also recommends "a *litle* wine." In addition, a marginal note in the Geneva Bible points the reader to Proverbs, where one finds, "It is not for Kings, o Lemuel, it is not for Kings to

---

[73] One might even argue that Falstaff encapsulates "the world, the flesh, and the devil" that Christians prayed to be delivered from in the Litany of the Book of Common Prayer. Falstaff is certainly flesh, he says himself (role-playing Hal), "banish plump Jack, and banish all the world" (*Part 1*, 2.4.466–7), and Hal calls him (playing King Henry) "that old white-bearded Satan" (*Part 1*, 2.4.451).

[74] See also Ps. 55:5; Judith 2:28, 15:2; 1 Macc. 7:18; 2 Macc. 3:24; 1 Cor. 2:3; 2 Cor. 7:15.

drinke wine, nor for princes strong drink" (31:4). But in *Henry IV, Part 2*, Falstaff's Carnival spirit washes away such reservations. Like so much of Falstaff's language, his hymn to sack is also indebted to Nashe. His *Summers Last Will and Testament* was published only in 1600, but it had been performed in 1592. Shakespeare certainly knew the play and perhaps even performed in it, and there are strong parallels between Falstaff's speech on sack and Bacchus's praise of wine in Nashe.[75] In Nashe, Bacchus is condemned and rejected by Summer; in Shakespeare, Falstaff is rejected by Hal.

THE MERRY WIVES OF WINDSOR

The Falstaff of *The Merry Wives of Windsor* is not the same character as in the history plays. The play's use of biblical allusion marks a change in Falstaff's character and a shift in his relations with the rest of the dramatis personae, confirming Dover Wilson's argument that, when one is "studying the character of Falstaff, *The Merry Wives of Windsor* may be left out of account, that play being indubitably 'an unpremeditated sequel,' the hero of which is made to bear the name of Falstaff primarily for reasons of theatrical expediency, not of dramatic art."[76] Falstaff's name was the principal selling point of the play, placed first in the full printed title: *Syr* John Falstaff; *and the Merry Wives of Windsor*. On the other hand, Falstaff shared the title page with not only the wives, but with "*Syr* Hugh *the Welch Knight, Justice* Shallow, *and his wise Cousin M.* Slender" as well as "*the swaggering vaine of Aunctient* Pistoll, *and Corporall* Nym." Merry Wives contains thirty-odd biblical allusions (according to Shaheen), but only three of these are made by Falstaff. For example, he tells Pistol and Nim, in explanation of his plan to woo Mistress Ford, that her husband "hath a legion of angels" (1.3.50), or, in other words, has lots of money. This was a familiar pun on the coin known as the "angel" (since it bore an

---

[75] Katherine Duncan-Jones, "Shakespeare the Motley Player," *RES* 60/247 (2009), 723–43. Thomas Nashe, *A pleasant comedie, called Summers last will and testament* (London: Simon Stafford for Water Burre, 1600). For example, "So, I tell thee, give a soldier wine before he goes to battaile, it grinds out all gaps, it makes him forget all scarres and wounds, and fight in the thickest of his enemies, as though hee were but at foyles, amongst his fellows" (sig. F'). Falstaff states that sack "illumineth the face, which, as a beacon, gives warning to all the rest of this little kingdom, man, to arm; and then the vital commoners, and inland petty spirits, muster me all to their captain, the heart, who, great and puffed up with this retinue, doth any deed of courage; and this valour comes of sherries" (*Part 2*, 4.3.106–12).

[76] J. Dover Wilson, *The Fortunes of Falstaff* (Cambridge: Cambridge University Press, 1964), 5.

image of St Michael). Falstaff adds a more original allusion to Jesus's claim as he is arrested that, if he wished, he could "pray to my Father, and he wil give me mo then twelve legions of Angels" (Matt. 26:53). There may also be a further, punning allusion to "Legion," the name of the demon ("My name is Legion: for we are many") that Jesus exorcises into a herd of swine (Mark 5:1–13). Pistol after all responds, "As many devils attend her! [i.e., Mistress Ford, in parallel with her husband's 'angels']" (1.3.51). The point of Falstaff's allusions has perhaps to do with temptation (Christ's by Satan, Falstaff's by Ford's money; while Christ resists, Falstaff cheerfully succumbs), but this is not particularly clear.

Secondly, after Falstaff's first failure at wooing, having been squashed into a laundry basket and dunked in the Thames, Mistress Quickly nevertheless convinces him that Mistress Ford wants him to try again. He consents, but tells Quickly to ask Mistress Ford to "think what a man is. Let her consider his frailty, and then judge of my merit" (3.5.47–8). This sounds, at last, like the Falstaff of *Henry IV, Part 1*, misappropriating the biblical frailty of the flesh to describe his own physical vulnerability.[77] As already noted, Falstaff is frequently defined by his "flesh," and the linking of flesh and frailty is commonplace—perhaps ultimately deriving from Matthew 26:41 ("the flesh is weake")—as in Falstaff's own similar wordplay in *Part 1* (3.3.165–7). Ironically, Falstaff is speaking to a woman of what "a man is," while it is the woman who is traditionally (and biblically) the "weaker vessel" whom husbands should therefore honor (1 Pet. 3:7). Indeed, sometime shortly after writing *Merry Wives*, Shakespeare made Hamlet rail, "frailty thy name is woman" (*Hamlet*, 1.2.146). The reference to Falstaff's "merit" plays with theological language, as in *Part 1* (1.2.103–4). The joke here is meant to be that, for Protestants, justification is not by merit (that is, works) but by faith alone, and in his adulterous ambitions Falstaff is nothing if not faithless. (His works are not good either.)

Falstaff's final biblical allusion muddles together verses from 1 Samuel and Job. After his second comeuppance, having been forced to dress as a woman and then being beaten, Falstaff says to Ford (disguised as Brook) that when he is "in the shape of a man ... I fear not Goliath with a weaver's beam, because I know also life is a shuttle" (5.2.20–2). In other words, he asserts that he allowed the beating only because he was "in the shape of a woman." Goliath, the giant Philistine slain by David, carried a spear whose shaft "was like a weavers beam" (1 Sam. 17:7). The shuttle alludes to Job, who laments "My dayes are swifter than a weavers

---

[77] See the treatment of "frailty" in *Hamlet* in Ch. 4.

shuttle" (Job 7:6). The link between the passages, not explicitly made by Falstaff but available to anyone knowing both biblical passages, is the weaver, an especially appropriate figure given Falstaff's desire in *Part 1* to be a weaver and sing Psalms (2.4.126–7). Other characters call Falstaff "as slanderous as Satan," "as poor as Job," and "as wicked as [Job's] wife" (5.5.153–5), but Falstaff himself utters no further biblical allusions.[78] There are also in Falstaff's speeches far fewer of the Puritan-style religious idioms of the Henry IV plays. There are a few. For instance, he confesses facetiously to Pistol, "I am damned in hell for swearing to gentlemen my friends you were good soldiers and tall fellows" (2.2.8–10). He also swears "By the Lord" that Mistress Ford is a tyrant (3.3.51). He recounts his experience in the Thames, expressing his tendency to sink: "if the bottom were as deep as hell, I should down" (3.5.12). And he has one genuinely Falstaffian moment of mock-pious repentance, lamenting that "I never prospered since I forswore myself at primero" and promising, "if my wind were but long enough, I would repent" (4.5.94–6). But that is all.

One reason Falstaff no longer plays the stage Puritan may be that there is no longer any reason for him to. The Windsor of the play is already full of them, and biblical allusion is one of their dominant modes of discourse. Justice Shallow, Mistress Quickly, and Parson Evans, for instance, all allude to the Puritan "yea and nay": "by yea and no I do" (1.1.80), "the very yea and the no is" (1.4.88), "By yea and no" (4.2.182). Mistress Page laments the "wicked, wicked world" and exclaims against Falstaff, "What a Herod of Jewry is this!" (2.1.16).[79] Mistress Page also describes to Mistress Ford how her husband "curses all Eve's daughters" (4.2.21). Ford calls Page a fool because he "stands so firmly on his wife's frailty" (2.1.211). We expect Parson Evans to be ready with a biblical phrase, but he delightfully bungles his allusions. The most brilliant of these is the song he sings as he waits to duel with Dr Caius. First he warbles a verse of the famous Marlowe song, "Come live with me and be my love":[80]

---

[78] The Job allusion is another recollection of the Falstaff of the Henry plays, where, as we have seen, he describes himself as "poor as Job...but not so patient." As so often in *Merry Wives*, the wordplay in this instance involves gender reversal, Ford comparing Falstaff not only to Job but to his wife. In 4.2, Falstaff had to dress up as the old woman of Brentford.

[79] The allusion seems to be to the Herod of the mystery plays, famous for his villainous ranting (see Ch. 4). How exactly Falstaff is like Herod is a mystery, and that may be the point—Mistress Page simply likens him to the worst villain she can think of.

[80] On this poem, Sir Walter Raleigh's response, and the tradition they spawned, see Hamlin, "Replying to Raleigh's 'The Nymph's Reply': Allusion, Anti-Pastoral, and Four Centuries of Pastoral Invitations," in Christopher M. Armitage (ed.), *Sir Walter Raleigh: Literary and Visual Raleigh* (Manchester: Manchester University Press, forthcoming).

> To shallow rivers, to whose falls
> Melodious birds sings madrigals—
> There will we make our peds of roses
> And a thousand fragrant posies. (3.1.16–19)

Apart from a few minor Welshisms ("sings" and "peds"), Evans has this verse right, but as he repeats the verse his memory unravels:

> Melodious birds sing madrigals—
> Whenas I sat in Pabylon—
> And a thousand vagram posies. (3.1.22–4)

The last printed line in the Folio is "To shallow, etc.," suggesting Evans might go on with this marvelous mingle-mangle, perhaps improvising. "Pabylon," as mentioned above, is Babylon, and line 23 is the opening of Psalm 137 in the metrical version in the Sternhold and Hopkins psalter sung in parishes across England:

> When as we sat in Babylon,
> the rivers rounde about:
> And in remembraunce of Sion
> The teares for grief burst out.[81]

The only thing these songs have in common is, as Evans's countryman Fluellen might say, that there are rivers in both. Even the meters are different, as Evans would have discovered had he tried to sing more than one line of the Psalm ("Come live with me" is in iambic tetrameter and the Sternhold and Hopkins Psalm 137 in the common 8 and 6—alternating tetrameter and trimeter). To combine a seduction poem and a religious lament is wildly inappropriate, but it is a brilliant demonstration of Parson Evans's limitations as a clergyman, as well as perhaps a suggestion of the commonplace blurring of sacred and secular in popular culture. A similar but less dramatic blurring is referred to by Mistress Ford, when she compares the disjunct between Falstaff's disposition and his words to "the hundred psalms to the tune of 'Greensleeves'" (2.1.55–6). Many metrical Psalms were sung to popular secular tunes, both in England and on the Continent, leading some critics to call them "Geneva jigs." For Mistress Ford, the hypocritical Falstaff's proper words do not match his wicked inner character as seducer, just as the pious words of the Psalm do not match the tune of the seduction song to which it is set. No actual such use of the familiar Greensleeves tune has been found.[82]

---

[81] *The whole booke of Psalmes* (London: John Day, 1562), 350.
[82] On "Geneva jigs," see Quitslund, *Reformation in Rhyme*, 262–3.

The allusion to Psalm 137 in *Merry Wives* is diegetic, in that Evans could have made it intentionally, and Simple (who is with him) could have recognized it. It is clearly delivered unconsciously, however, which indicates a further distinction within the category of diegetic allusion. Diegetic and extradiegetic allusions are distinguished, above, on the basis of self-consciousness, whether the character alluding was aware of the allusion he or she was making. Among the examples of extradiegetic allusion cited were those of which the character could not possibly be conscious (pre-Christian settings, for instance), and those of which the character could have been, but clearly was not, conscious. Parson Evans's allusion seems a curious third type, in which the character might be conscious of the allusion, and clearly is not, but in which he really ought to be, and that negligent obliviousness is the main aspect of the humor.

Even if we might well expect to hear biblical allusions from Parson Evans, it is a surprise to hear so many from Pistol. Pistol speaks in allusions almost constantly in *Henry IV, Part 1*, but his allusions are usually classical in a heroic idiom borrowed from Elizabethan plays ("To Pluto's damned lake" or "feed and be fat, my fair Calipolis," 1.4.153, 175). In *Henry V*, which the latest editor of *Merry Wives* argues was written before it,[83] Pistol alludes more often to the Bible, perhaps because Falstaff himself is no longer present. Just before Falstaff's death, Pistol alliteratively reports, "The grave doth gape, and doting death is near" (2.1.61), perhaps alluding to Isaiah in the Bishops' Bible: "Therfore gapeth hell and openeth her mouth marveilous wyde, that their glorie, multitude, and wealth, with such as rejoyce in her, may descende into it" (Isa. 5:14). Isaiah 5 was the Old Testament Lesson at Matins on the Second Sunday in Advent. Later, Pistol draws on the marriage vows in asserting his rights to Mistress Quickly: "I have, and I will hold, the quondam Quickly" (2.1.79). Later still, Pistol's nasty call to arms may also be a biblical allusion:

> Let us to France, like horse-leaches, my boys,
> To suck, to suck, the very blood to suck! (2.3.53–4)

Horse-leaches crop up in Proverbs, where we are told, "The horse leache hathe two daughters which crie, Give, give" (Prov. 30:15). The point seems perhaps that even such a thing as a leach has essential needs and obligations, though the Geneva note offers a different explanation: "The leach hathe two forkes in her tongue, which here he calleth her two daughters, whereby she sucketh the blood: and is never satiate." Michael Cope took a more allegorical approach, interpreting the horse-leaches as

---

[83] Giorgio Melchiori (ed.), *The Merry Wives of Windsor*, 18–30.

"theeves and robbers, the covetous and usurers, the spoylers and extortioners, the whoremongers and adulterers, the gluttons and drunkards" and the two daughters, which he acknowledges are literally the two forks of the tongue, as "divers wayes and meanes to hurte, and to oppresse their neighbours, and to vexe themselves."[84] The verb "suck" is provided by the Geneva note, and, syntactically, Pistol's repeated "To suck, to suck" parallels the "Give, give" of the daughters (or the forks), however they are interpreted. Although the audience would readily understand the bloodsucking of a leach without any allusion, the biblical context would make clear the application to Pistol and his fellow "theeves and robbers." The verse also seems to have been relatively familiar, for in addition to Cope's and the Geneva Bible's commentaries on Proverbs, Robert Greene cites the verse in his advice to wayward youth, *Greenes never too late*: "He that hath the dropsie, drinketh while he bursteth and yet not; the Horseleach hath two daughters that never crie enough."[85] (Greene's point seems to be that the thirst of the dropsical man is as insatiable as the leaches'.)

In *Merry Wives*, Pistol is inexplicably the master of biblical allusion, as was his master Falstaff in *Henry IV, Part 1*. Even more curiously, his allusions are not only self-conscious but often clever. "He hears with ears" (1.1.136), Pistol replies, when Falstaff calls his name, alluding to the Litany (based on Psalm 44:1), "O God, we have hearde with our eares." That Parson Evans does not recognize the liturgy—"The tevil and his tam, what phrase is this?" (1.1.137)—seems to be the main joke; that Pistol does know it improves the joke. When Falstaff tells Nim and Pistol that he must steal to live—"There is no remedy, I must cony-catch, I must shift" (1.3.30–1)—Pistol supports him, saying, "Young ravens must have food" (1.3.32). In Psalm 147, God "feedeth the young ravens that call upon him" (Ps. 147:9), and in Job, God himself asks, rhetorically, "Who prepareth for the raven his meat, when his byrdes crye unto God, wandering for lacke of meat?" (Job 39:3). Are Falstaff and his men then like the ravens? Does God feed not only the carrion birds but thieves as well?[86] After Falstaff departs, Pistol grumbles, "Let vultures gripe thy guts! For

---

[84] Michael Cope, *A godly and learned exposition uppon the Proverbes of Solomon*, trans. M.O. (London: George Bishop, 1580), 617.

[85] Robert Greene, *Greenes never too late* (London: Thomas Orwin for N.L. and John Busbie, 1590), sig. C3ᵛ.

[86] Shaheen notes the similar allusion in *As You Like It*, when Adam says, "He that doth the ravens feed, | Yea, providently caters for the sparrow, | Be comfort to my age" (2.3.43–5). In this case, Shakespeare alludes more specifically to Luke 12:24, "Consider the ravens: for they nether sowe nor reape…yet God fedeth them." But the point of the allusion is the same as Pistol's, having to do with God's providential care for all creatures, however lowly, and the latter probably includes the gospel verse in its scope as well. (Luke himself, or Jesus, was much aware of Psalms and Job.)

gourd and fullam holds, | And high and low beguiles rich and poor" (1.3.82–3). His point seems to be that everyone can fall for gambling tricks, "gourd" and "fullam" are terms for loaded dice, which can be rigged to throw either high or low numbers ("tall-men and low-men").[87] Thus both the rich and poor can be beguiled by high and low. But Pistol is playing perversely with Psalm 49:2, "High and low, rich and poor, one with another," a popular phrase in sermons and commentaries, referring to all those who are called ("O Hear ye this, all ye people," Ps. 49:1). Pistol comes back to this verse later, in more straightforward fashion referring to the scope of Falstaff's amours: "He woos both high and low, both rich and poor, | Both young and old, one with another, Ford" (2.1.402–3). Pistol, Evans, the wives, and other citizens of Windsor allude to the Bible all the time, seriously and perversely, accurately and inaccurately, ingeniously and foolishly. Apparently in the 1620s Godfrey Goodman, Bishop of Gloucester, tried to impose a crucifix on the church at Windsor, but was blocked by the Puritan populace. "Hath not the town of Windsor sometimes received a rebuke for Puritanism?" he complained.[88] Shakespeare may have decided that Falstaff's role as a mock-Puritan was redundant in Windsor, since in reality they were all Puritans there already.[89] The result, however, is that Falstaff is a different and much reduced character in *Merry Wives* from the brilliant alluder and trickster of the *Henry* plays.

THEORETICAL CONCLUSIONS

One further aspect of Falstaff's biblical allusions needs to be clarified, and that is, whether they can properly be called allusions at all. As discussed in Chapter 3, allusion is sometimes defined as requiring a certain degree of covertness. Even the *OED* (4.) defines "allusion" as a "covert, implied, or indirect reference." By such a definition, Falstaff does not often allude but rather simply quotes or, to use Shaheen's neutral term, refers. Or, to use Falstaff's own term, iterates. There is nothing covert about saying someone is "as ragged as Lazarus in the painted cloth" or that they remind

---

[87] See *OED*. Anon., *No-body, and some-body* ([London]: [James Roberts] for John Trundle, 1606), sig. I2ᵛ. This interlude was staged *c*.1592.

[88] Cited in Margaret Aston, "Puritans and Iconoclasm, 1560–1660," in Christopher Durston and Jacqueline Eales (eds), *The Culture of English Puritanism, 1560–1700* (New York: St Martin's Press, 1996), 92–121, 107.

[89] Rhodes argues that "the number of scriptural and proverbial allusions in the play are vital in creating a kind of social atmosphere in which lechery can be treated both as an object of ridicule and as the road to damnation" and that "Falstaff has become a ritual scapegoat rather than Carnival celebrant" ("Shakespearean Grotesque," 127).

you of "Dives that lived in purple." Even when Falstaff argues "it is no sin for a man to labour in his vocation," he is being open and direct, requiring and expecting his listeners (and the audience) to recognize his travesty of Paul. But to distinguish such "references" from "allusions" proper, on the basis that one is open and obvious and the other covert and hidden, seems both wrong and methodologically impossible. For one thing, any allusion that is entirely covert does not allude, does not exist, since it has no perceptible trigger. One might theoretically speak of such a literary phenomenon as an allusion, but it would exist only in the mind of the author. Any allusion that is perceived by the reader, or audience, is at least to some degree open and available, otherwise it could not be detected. Since this is therefore a matter of degree rather than kind, it seems best to leave aside covertness as a defining characteristic of allusion, and say rather that allusions admit of different degress of overtness and covertness, just as they do of simplicity and complexity, or orthodoxy and heresy.

At the same time, though I do not want to distinguish Falstaff's quotations or references from allusions, I also do not want to suggest that they are not also quotations. If there is a sense among some critics that allusions must be covert, there is a more popular sense in which quotations must be accurate. Otherwise, it is misquotation.[90] Such a distinction fails to recognize that a misquotation cannot be a misquotation without also being at least partly a quotation. First, we recognize a word, phrase, or speech as a quotation, as the importation of some prior text into the present one. Then, we recognize the errors in the imported version of the text, and label it a misquotation. To speak of the process in this chronological way is probably an overstatement, since it often happens too quickly to separate out. The basic sense of the chronology seems accurate, however, and there are times when the process is much slower, when the reader does have to stop and think, or go to a reference work, before determining that a misquotation has been made. Allusion of Falstaff's sort involves misquotation that is deliberate, but the process for the reader is roughly the same as with a simple mistaken quotation. First, there is a recognition that something is being quoted, then one identifies the text being quoted, then one recognizes that it is actually misquoted. For allusion, though, there is a final stage of recognition: to understand the purpose of the misquotation, how the original is being manipulated, and

---

[90] See Julie Maxwell, "How the Renaissance (Mis)Used Sources: The Art of Misquotation," in Laurie Maguire (ed.), *How to Do Things with Shakespeare: New Approaches, New Essays* (Malden, MA; Blackwell, 2008), 54–76. Maxwell's "misquotation" is essentially the same as, or at least overlaps considerably with, allusion, when allusions are inaccurate, incomplete, out of context, or ironic.

what purposes—serious, comical, parodic, ironic—the manipulation might serve in the new context, which might be entirely different from the original context. In a sophisticated essay on quotation, Meir Sternberg argues that "to quote is to mediate and to mediate is to interfere," that all quotation involves "manifold shifts, if not reversals, of the original meaning and significance."[91]

Another reason for describing Falstaff's biblical references as allusions is that they work in the same ways his author's do: more often than not, as has been shown in Chapter 3, Shakespeare's allusions to the Bible, like Falstaff's, are ironic and contrastive; sometimes they are comical or even blasphemous. C. L. Barber writes of Falstaff that in the midst of his burlesque and mockery "an intelligence of the highest order is expressed" and "it is not always clear whether the intelligence is Falstaff's or the dramatist's."[92] A. L. Rowse proposed that Falstaff *is* Shakespeare.[93] Such bold claims are typically playful or polemical, but, in their contrastive and ironic use of biblical allusion, Falstaff and Shakespeare do have a striking amount in common.

---

[91] Meir Sternberg, "Proteus in Quotation-Land: Mimesis and the Forms of Reported Discourse," *Poetics Today*, 3/2 (1982), 107–56, 108.

[92] C. L. Barber, *Shakespeare's Festive Comedy: A Study of Dramatic Form and its Relation to Social Custom* (Princeton: Princeton University Press, 1959; repr. Cleveland and New York: World Publishing Company, 1963), 198.

[93] A. L. Rowse, *What Shakespeare Read—and Thought* (New York: Coward, McCann & Geoghegan, 1981), 110.

7

The Great Doom's Image: *Macbeth* and Apocalypse

In 1563, one year before William Shakespeare was born, his father John, as city alderman, was given the responsibility of whitewashing the wall paintings of the Guild Chapel in Stratford. To Protestants, religious art, including also statues, carvings, and stained-glass images, smacked of idolatry; it was especially condemned if it represented rejected Catholic doctrine. The most striking of the Guild Chapel mural paintings was its panoramic "Doom" or Last Judgment, painted above the chancel arch. This subject was by far the most popular among English church wall paintings. In the 1960s, a study listed seventy-eight such paintings surviving in churches across England, but more have been discovered since, including one at Coventry.[1] Such images depicted the Last Judgment as described in the Book of Revelation:

And I saw a great white throne, and one that sate on it, from whose face fled away both the earth and heaven, and their place was no more found. And I saw the dead, both great and small stand before God: and the books were opened, and another booke was opened, which is the booke of life, and the dead were judged of those things, which were written in the books, according to their works. And the sea gave up her dead, which were in her, and death and hell delivered up the dead, which were in them: and they were judged every man according to their works. And death and hell were cast into the lake of fire: this is the second death. And whosever was not found written in the booke of life, was cast into the lake of fire. (Rev. 20:11–15)

If John Shakespeare had the Guild Chapel Doom whitewashed in 1563, his son cannot have seen it. It might later have been described to him by

---

[1] A. Caiger-Smith, *English Mediaeval Mural Paintings* (Oxford, 1963), cited in Mary Lascelles, "*King Lear* and Doomsday," *SS* 26 (1973), 69–79, 73, n. 4. For recently uncovered paintings, see Anne Marshall, "The Doom, or Last Judgement, and the Weighing of Souls: An Introduction," at *Medieval Wall Painting and the English Parish Church: A Developing Catalogue* <http://www.paintedchurch.org/doomcon.htm> (accessed June 25, 2012.) For Coventry, see Miriam Gill and Richard K. Morris, "A Wall Painting of the Apocalypse in Coventry Rediscovered," *Burlington Magazine*, 143/1181 (August 2001), 467–73.

his father or someone else in the town; it was a dramatic and memorable painting, after all. It is also possible that the Doom was not whitewashed until a later date. In any case, Shakespeare could easily have seen similar paintings in London or elsewhere in the countryside. As Mary Lascelles points out, the accounts of the Guild Chamberlain (John Shakespeare's position) record a payment "for defaysing Ymages in the chapel" that does not specify which images were defaced. Lascelles notes that the Guild Chapel images of Thomas à Beckett and the True Cross would have been strongly offensive to Protestants, and were thus surely painted over; the Doom, however, may not have been, since such images were condemned only if they included references to intercession.[2] Painted Dooms, occasionally somewhat edited, survived elsewhere in the country. So when Macduff describes the body of the murdered Duncan as "great doom's image" in *Macbeth*, Shakespeare must have had in mind such an image. The Doom on the nave arch of the Guild Chapel included many bodies, some rising out of tombs on the left, and others dead, dying, and cast down into hell on the right.

Macbeth is pervaded by such imagery of the Apocalypse and by allusions to Revelation and other apocalyptic prophecies in the Bible. As such, the play exploited an English cultural obsession in the early seventeenth century: Christianity had been preoccupied with the End of Days since its earliest years, as evidenced by John's Revelation (written in *c.* CE 100), but interest intensified after the Reformation and especially so in England toward the end of the sixteenth and beginning of the seventeenth centuries. As Richard Bauckham observes, "Apocalypticism was Western Christendom's habitual response to historical crisis," and the Reformation, which splintered Western Christendom itself, was certainly a crisis.[3] Protestants frequently represented the Reformation in terms of the language and figures of Revelation, which was made easier by the coincidence that the book was originally written as a prophecy of the destruction of Rome. John's Rome in Revelation was not papal Rome, of course, but the Reformers' shift in identification from past to present was easy to make, especially give the obscurity of much of John's biblical allegory. The beast with seven heads could still figure the seven hills of Rome, since the geography had not changed, and the Pope could be the Antichrist as easily as could earlier Roman emperors. Other figures required more interpretive ingenuity. The Whore of Babylon, for instance, was given a triple tiara to indicate the papal crown in early Lutheran images like Lucas Cranach's illustrations to the Luther Bible.

---

[2] Lascelles, "'King Lear' and Doomsday," 74–5.
[3] Richard Bauckham, *Tudor Apocalypse* (Oxford: Sutton Courtenay Press, 1978), 233.

Fig. 7.1. Before the Reformation, early English church interiors were often decorated with brightly painted images depicting biblical scenes. A common subject was "Doom," or the Day of Judgment, such as the one above the chancel arch in the Guild Chapel, Stratford-upon-Avon, reconstructed in this 3D photograph. Christ judges from his throne, top center, while on the left side the elect rise from their earthly coffins, and on the right sinners topple into the furnaces of hell. John Shakespeare famously supervised the project of whitewashing the Guild Chapel's images. Courtesy Heritage Technology, Ltd, UK.

Her elaborate costume—she "was arrayed in purple and scarlet, and gilded with gold, and precious stones, and pearles, and had a cup of gold in her hand full of abomination, and filthiness of her fornication" (Rev. 17:4)—was easy to read in terms of the idolatrous trappings of Catholic worship, the embroidered copes and gowns, altarcloths, and the gold or silver chalices used in the Mass. That the woman was "drunken with the blood of Saintes" (Rev. 17:6) confirmed this, given the centrality of Eucharistic debates in Protestant–Catholic polemic; her cup contained blood just as Catholics believed the communion chalice did.

When the English Protestant exiles returned after the reign of Catholic Queen Mary, they interpreted their return in biblical terms; as the Jews after the Babylonian Exile returned to Jerusalem to build the new Temple, so English Protestants would return to England to establish a new church.[4] Queen Mary herself was described as Jezebel, the wicked queen who persuaded King Ahab to turn to idolatry and the persecution of the children of Israel (1 Kgs 21).[5] As the European conflict between Protestants and Catholics intensified, so did interest in interpreting Revelation. The year 1588, for instance—the year of the Spanish Armada—was predicted to be pivotal, because of a fifteenth-century prophecy that described an *annus mirabilis* in 88.[6] A bit of English doggerel was cited in William Perkins's *A Fruitfull Dialogue Concerning the End of the World* (1587):

> When after Christs birth there be expired,
> of hundreds fifteen, years eighty eight,
> Then comes the time of dangers to be feared,
> and all mankind with dolors it shall freight,
> For if the world in that yeare do not fall,
> if sea and land then perish ne decay.
> Yet Empires all, and Kingdomes alter shall,
> and man to ease himselfe shall have no way.[7]

The attack and defeat of the Spanish Armada seemed to confirm the momentousness of 88, even if the interpretations varied as to its ultimate meaning.

Subsequent historical crises, interpreted apocalyptically, included the death of Queen Elizabeth, the crowning of James I, and the Gunpowder Plot, which, like the Armada, was defeated.[8] There were also major outbreaks of plague in London in 1593 and 1603–4. John Davies of Hereford, in his verse remembrance of the plague of 1603, makes clear that at such times everyone had the Apocalypse vividly in mind:

---

[4] Bauckham, *Tudor Apocalypse*, 127, and Katharine R. Firth, *The Apocalyptic Tradition in Reformation Britain 1530–1645* (Oxford: Oxford University Press, 1979), ch. 3.

[5] Both John Knox and Christopher Goodman called Mary a Jezebel. See Dan G. Danner, "Resistance and the Ungodly Magistrate in the Sixteenth Century: The Marian Exiles," *Journal of the American Academy of Religion*, 49/3 (1981), 471–81.

[6] Bauckham, *Tudor Apocalypse*, ch. 9. Francis Bacon refers to this prophecy in his essay "Of Prophecies," writing: "There was also another prophecy, before the year of eighty-eight, which I do not well understand...It was generally conceived to be meant of the Spanish fleet, that came in eighty-eight" (Francis Bacon, *A Critical Edition of the Major Works*, ed. Brian Vickers [Oxford and New York: Oxford University Press, 1996], 413).

[7] Cited in Bryan W. Ball, *A Great Expectation: Eschatological Thought in English Protestantism to 1660* (Leiden: E. J. Brill, 1975), 22.

[8] In "Of Prophecies," Bacon also records a rhyme concerning Elizabeth: "When Hempe is sponne, England's done." "Hempe" was interpreted as the first initials of all the Tudors: Henry, Edward, Mary, Philip (of Spain, Mary's husband), and Elizabeth. Elizabeth's death did not result in England's destruction, Bacon noted, but it did pass away in the sense of becoming Britain, as England and Scotland were united by James I. *Major Works*, ed. Vickers, 413.

>   And all, almost, so fared through the Realme
>   As if their Soules the Judgement day were past.
>   This World was quite forgot; the World to come
>   Was still in minde; which for it was forgot,
>   Brought on our World this little day of Dome,
>   That choakt the Grave with this contageous Rot![9]

One result of the increasing interest in apocalyptic prophecies was a proliferation of publications interpreting Revelation and applying its prophecies to the last times.[10] These include Thomas Tymme's *The Figure of Antichrist, with the tokens of the end of the world* (1586), Lambert Daneau's *A treatise, touching Antichrist* (1589), Anthony Marten's *A second Sound, or Warning of the Trumpet unto Judgement* (1589), Thomas Rogers's *An Historical Dialogue touching Antichrist and Poperie* (1589), Hugh Broughton's *A concent of Scripture* (1590?) and his commentary on Daniel (1596), Lawrence Deios's *That the Pope is that Antichrist* (1590), John Napier's *Plaine Discovery of the whole Revelation of Saint John* (1593),[11] John Dove's *Sermon preached at Paul's Crosse the 3. Of November 1594, intreating of the second comming of Christ* (1594?), George Gifford's *Sermons upon the whole booke of Revelation* (1596), Arthur Dent's extremely popular *The ruine of Rome* (1603), and George Downame's *A treatise concerning antichrist* (1603), to cite only some of the works available in English. Further commentaries were available in Latin, by English as well as continental writers, and earlier works like John Bale's *Image of bothe Churches* (1548) remained in circulation.

Thomas Rogers's *Of the ende of this worlde and second coming of Christ*, first printed in 1577, was reprinted in 1578, 1582, and 1589. James I himself contributed to the bibliography on Revelation with his *Ane fruitfull meditatioun*. Published in Edinburgh in the Armada year of 1588, it was reprinted in 1603 in London after his accession to the English throne.[12] James wrote that, "of all the Scriptures, the buik of Revelation is maist meit for this our last age, as ane prophecie of the letter tyme."[13]

---

[9] John Davies of Hereford, *Humours heav'n on earth with the civile warres of death and fortune* (London: A[dam] I[slip], 1609), 232.

[10] Paul Christianson counts over one hundred apocalyptic treatises recorded in the STC printed between 1588 and 1628. *Reformers and Babylon: English Apocalyptic Vision from the Reformation to the Eve of the Civil War* (Toronto: University of Toronto Press, 1978), 94.

[11] Dedicated to his fellow Scot King James VI, Napier's book was reprinted 1594, 1611, 1641, 1645, as well as two editions in Dutch and four in French. Ball, *A Great Expectation*, 59.

[12] It was also translated into French (1589) and Latin (1596, 1603, 1608).

[13] James VI [and later I], *Ane fruitfull meditatioun contening ane plane and facill expositioun of ye 7.8.9 and 10 versis of the 20 chap. of the Revelation* (Edinburgh, 1589), sig. Aiii[r].

Perhaps the most influential commentary on Revelation was by Francis Junius. Published initially in Heidelberg in 1591, in Latin, it was translated into English as *Apocalypsis A briefe and learned commentarie upon the revelation of Saint John* (1592).[14] *Apocalypsis* was republished in 1596 and was also published with the Book of Revelation (separate from the rest of the Bible) in 1594 and 1600. Most importantly, Junius's vehemently anti-papal commentary replaced the notes of Laurence Tomson (based on Theodore Beza) in the Geneva Bible from 1602. Literary works also responded to the apocalyptic fervor: the first book of Spenser's *Faerie Queene* (1590), as well as his earlier translations for Jan van der Noot's *Theater for Worldlings* (1569), and Thomas Dekker's play *The Whore of Babylon* (1605). Shakespeare seems to have been especially interested in Revelation and the Apocalypse, since he alludes to it in several plays, including *Hamlet, King Lear, Othello, Antony and Cleopatra, All's Well that Ends Well, Richard II,* and *Richard III,* as well as *Macbeth*.[15]

BIBLICAL ALLUSIONS IN *MACBETH*

Macbeth contains over half a dozen allusions to Revelation; Shakespeare frequently interweaves them with allusions to the Crucifixion, Psalms, Old Testament and Apocryphal wisdom literature (Job, Ecclesiasticus), and the witch of Endor story from 1 Samuel. These interconnections reinforce the play's sense of apocalyptic doom. The Captain's comment about Macbeth and Banquo in battle memorializing "another Golgotha" (1.2.40)—referring to the "place of the skull" where Jesus is executed in Matthew 27:33—establishes the Crucifixion story as an allusive backdrop early in the play. Later, as Macbeth struggles to decide whether to murder Duncan, he says, "If it were done, when 'tis done, then 'twere well | It were done quickly" (1.7.1–2). Critics and editors often cite proverbs like "The thing done has an end" or "The thing that is done is

---

[14] Bauckham, *Tudor Apocalypse*, 138, though Bauckham confuses the editions of the *Apocalypsis* proper with the separate publications of the book of Revelation with Junius's commentary in the margins.

[15] Shaheen lists eight allusions each for *Richard II* and *Richard III*, seven for *All's Well*, and six for *Othello*. On *Hamlet*, for which Shaheen lists ten Revelation allusions, see David Kaula, "*Hamlet* and the Image of Both Churches," *SEL* 24/2 (1984), 241–55. On *King Lear* and *Antony and Cleopatra*, see Chs 8 and 5, Lascelles, "'King Lear' and Doomsday," as well as Joseph Wittreich, "'Image of that horror': the Apocalypse in *King Lear*," in C. A. Patrides and Joseph Wittreich (eds), *The Apocalypse in English Renaissance Thought and Literature* (Manchester: Manchester University Press, 1984), 175–206.

not to do," but these are not the same as Macbeth's phrases.[16] One might just as relevantly cite the repetitions of the verb "to do" in the General Confession's "We have left undone those things whiche we ought to have done, and we have done those things whiche we ought not to have done, and there is no health in us."[17] None of these phrases has Macbeth's "quickly," however, which serves as a trigger for an allusion to Jesus's words to Judas in John 13:27, "That thou doest, do quickely." The repeated, varied, forms of the verb "do" (technically polyptoton or ploce), the similar balanced syntax, and the same adjective mark the allusion. John 13 was recited every year during Holy Week, on Maundy Thursday, and the phrase is identical in the Geneva and the Bishops' Bibles.[18] Macbeth's betrayal of Duncan is thus marked as Judas-like, given that he is a friend and subject of the king.[19] As Macbeth says himself,

> He's here in double trust:
> First, as I am his kinsman and his subject,
> Strong both against the deed: then, as his host,
> Who should against his murderer shut the door,
> Not bear the knife myself. (1.7.12–16)

The murder of Duncan is a betrayal that violates several primal taboos, and for Christians the ultimate model of betrayal is Judas, as Dante acknowledged by placing him at the bottom of hell, chewed in perpetuity, as are Brutus and Cassius, in one of the three mouths of Satan.

There are a number of other allusions in *Macbeth* to the Crucifixion story. Some of these add to the sense of Duncan's murder as a type of Crucifixion. Macbeth's anxiety (and, later, Lady Macbeth's) about washing the blood off his hands—"Will all great Neptune's ocean wash this

---

[16] The first example is from *Macbeth*, ed. Braunmuller, referencing Robert W. Dent, *Shakespeare's Proverbial Language: An Index* (Berkeley and Los Angeles: University of California Press, 1981), the second from Frank Kermode, *Shakespeare's Language* (New York: Farrar, Straus, Giroux, 2000), 208 n., referencing M. P. Tilley, *A Dictionary of the Proverbs in England in the Sixteenth and Seventeenth Centuries* (Ann Arbor: University of Michigan Press, 1950).

[17] Morning Prayer (1559), in *BCP* 103.

[18] "Lessons proper for Holidays," in *BCP* 220.

[19] As Adrian Streete puts it, "Macbeth speaks Christ's words but carries out Judas's actions." "'What bloody man is that?': Questioning Biblical Typology in *Macbeth*," *Shakespeare*, 5/1 (2009), 18–35, 34, n. 16. Kermode (*Language*, 212, 215) notes the significant repetitions of "done" in the play. Lady Macbeth states "what's done, is done" (3.2.12), and then asks "What's to be done?" (3.2.44). Later, in her madness, she says, "what's done cannot be undone" (5.1.57–8). See also David L. Krantz, "The Sounds of Supernatural Soliciting in *Macbeth*," *SP* 100/3 (2003), 346–83. These repetitions relate to the play's preoccupation with the possibilities and consequences of human action and with time (past, present, future); the allusions to the Apocalypse are part of the play's exploration of time future.

blood | Clean from my hand?" (2.2.63–4)—alludes to Pilate's washing his hands of responsibility for Christ's execution in Matthew 27:24. Lady Macbeth responds, even more directly in the Pilate mode, "A little water clears us of this deed" (2.2.70), though her later cry when sleep-walking, "Out, damned spot!" (5.1.30), shows that she was as wrong as Pilate about the stain of guilt. Earlier, the witches greet Macbeth with the cry "All hail" (1.3.46 and after). As discussed in Chapter 4, Shakespeare almost always uses this phrase to allude to the traitorous greeting of Jesus by Judas in the garden of Gethsemane (in order to identify him to the soldiers), aligning whichever character speaks it with the archetypal betrayer; this wording does not appear in English Bibles, but it became conventional from its use in the York and Chester Cycles and other Mystery plays.[20] That the witches mean Macbeth harm, mean to betray him, seems clear enough, but to cast Macbeth as Christ is obviously problematic—how can he be both Christ and Judas? It is a contradiction that becomes even more marked at the end of the play.

Additional allusions to the Crucifixion story contribute to the general atmosphere of apocalyptic crisis in the play. For example, after the murder of Duncan, Ross remarks,

> By th 'clock 'tis day
> And yet dark night strangles the travelling lamp.
> Is't night's predominance, or the day's shame,
> That darkness does the face of earth entomb
> When living light should kiss it? (2.4.6–10)

Especially in the context of the other Crucifixion allusions, the unnatural darkness recalls the "darknes over al the land" from the sixth to the ninth hours until Jesus's death, when "the sunne was darkened" (Luke 23:44–5; see also Matt. 27:46, Mark 15:33).[21] The "living light" Ross refers to must be the sun, but for Christians the living light was Christ, identified by John as "the true light, which lighteth everie man that cometh into the

---

[20] Emrys Jones, *The Origins of Shakespeare* (Oxford: Clarendon Press, 1977; repr. 1978), 74–83. Other plays employing this allusion are *3 Henry VI* (5.7.33–4), *Richard II* (4.1.170), and *Julius Caesar* (2.2.58); on the latter two plays, and in other sixteenth-century printed works, see Chs 4 and 5. Braunmuller (*Macbeth*) makes the same point, probably based on Jones, in his note to 1.3.46.

[21] Peter Stallybrass notes that these events are taken, "more or less transformed," from the account of King Duff's murder in Holinshed's *Chronicles*. The way in which they are transformed, however, is to bring them into alignment with apocalyptic events in the Bible. Holinshed describes unusual darkness, and horses eating each other, as they are reported to do by Ross in 2.4, but no earthquake. The darkness in *Macbeth*, moreover, seems unnatural, perhaps like an eclipse, whereas in Holinshed the skies are simply cloudy. Peter Stallybrass, "*Macbeth* and Witchcraft," in John Russell Brown (ed.), *Focus on* Macbeth (Boston: Routledge, 1982), 189–209, 194.

worlde" (John 1:9) and his dual identity as son/sun was a commonplace. Jesus and his light were literally "entombed" in Joseph of Arimathea's "new tomb, which he had hewen out in a rocke" (Matt. 27:60). The point of these allusions seems to be to reinforce the sense of apocalyptic despair that Duncan's followers feel upon his murder, as they simultaneously elevate him to sainthood or godhood and describe their bereavement as a bottomless abyss. The apocalyptic imagery functions as a pivot, however, linking allusions to the Crucifixion and its aftermath with allusions to the destruction described in Revelation, because, in Macbeth's case, "when 'tis done," it *isn't* done.

As at the death of Jesus, for instance, darkness comes with the fifth angel in Revelation, who "powred out his vial upon the throne of the beast, and his kingdome waxed darke, and they gnewe their tongues for sorowe" (Rev. 16:10). This action fulfils the many terrible prophecies of darkness in the Old Testament: "For beholde, darkenes shal cover the earth, and grosse darkenes the people" (Isa. 60:2); "All the lights of heaven wil I make darke for thee, and bring darkenes upon thy land" (Ezek. 32:8); "The sunne shalbe turned into darkenes, and the moone into blood, before the great and the terrible daie of the Lord come" (Joel 2:31). In Revelation 6:12, it is specifically Joel's prophecy that is fulfilled: "the sunne was as blacke as sackecloth of here [hair], and the moone was like blood." Without a specific verbal link, the darkness Ross describes does not allude to the apocalyptic darkness of Revelation directly, but for a biblically literate audience, allusions to the darkness in Luke 23 also engage the prophecies of darkness in Isaiah, Ezekiel, Joel, and John of Patmos, since they are all linked typologically. This is what T. Grashop, in his "How to take profite by reading of the holy Scriptures," calls the "Agreement that one place of Scripture hath with an other."[22] The Geneva note at Joel 2:31 references Isaiah 13:10, Ezekiel 32:7, Matthew 24:29, as well as Joel 3:15. The passage in Matthew, like the analogous one in Luke 21:25 (referenced in the Geneva note, along with the usual prophetic verses), is Jesus's own prophecy of the Apocalypse, which cites in the margin Isaiah 13:10, Ezekiel 32:7, and Joel 2:31 and 3:15. Wherever readers might begin, the margins direct them to all the other typologically interconnected prophetic passages.

The Crucifixion story is most important to *Macbeth* because of its almost apocalyptic sense of crisis that extends the implications of one individual's death to all of humanity and the world. Thus, in response to Duncan's murder, Macduff exclaims,

---

[22] Included in many Geneva Bibles from 1579; see Ch. 1.

> Most sacrilegious murder hath broke ope
> The Lord's anointed temple and stole hence
> The life o'th'building. (2.3.60–2)

Kings are called "the Lord's anointed" throughout the Old Testament. But the temple image links a number of biblical passages. Paul describes Christians as "the Temple of the living God" (1 Cor. 6:16), for instance.[23] Jesus offers a cryptic prophecy of the Crucifixion in John 2:19 ("Destroye this temple, and in thre days I wil raise it up againe"), which is explained in 2:21: "But he spake of the temple of his bodie." After the death of Jesus, "the vaile of the Temple was rent in twayne" (Matt. 27:51). In Revelation, John writes that "the Temple of God was opened in heaven, and there was sene in his Temple, the Arke of his covenant: and there were lightnings, and voyces, and thondrings, and earthquake, and muche haile" (Rev. 11:19). In *Macbeth*, the earthquake comes as an omen before Duncan's murder, though Lennox can only report this secondhand, with some doubt: "Some say, the earth | Was feverous and did shake" (2.3.52–3). Macduff goes on to describe the murder as "great doom's image," the reference to the Last Judgment with which this chapter began.[24] Macduff's call to Malcolm and Banquo—"As from your graves, rise up and walk like sprites | To countenance this horror" (2.3.72–3)—alludes to the resurrection of the dead in Revelation ("I sawe the dead, both great and small stand before God," Rev. 20:12–13) as foretold in the gospels ("for that houre shal come in the which all that are in the graves, shal hear his voice," John 5:28). The final resurrection is also anticipated in the immediate aftermath of the Crucifixion, when because of the earthquake "the graves did open them selves, and many bodies of the Sainctes which slept, arose" (Matt. 27:52). Lady Macbeth enters, oddly calling the ringing bell "a hideous trumpet" (2.3.75). A. R. Braunmuller suggests this is a metaphor for the "alarum bell," but it is not a metaphor but rather an allusion to the trumpets of the Apocalypse: the "last trumpe" of 1 Corinthians 15, when "the dead shall ryse incorruptible," and the many trumpets blown by angels in Revelation (8:13, 9:1, 9:14, 10:7, etc).[25]

---

[23] J. Fosse notes this allusion, but not the links to other biblical passages: "The Lord's Anointed Temple: Study of Some Symbolic Patterns in *Macbeth*," *Cahiers élisabéthains*, 6 (1974), 15–22, 20. Fosse is interested in patterns of imagery rather than allusion.

[24] Later, in response to the line of kings called up by the witches, Macbeth asks, "will the line stretch out to the th'crack of doom?" (4.1.116). If the "glass" carried by the final figure in the prophetic procession (according to the Folio stage direction) was intended to reflect King James, that would reinforce the contemporary sense of imminent apocalypse when the play was first performed; the line stretches to the "crack of doom," i.e., the time of James I.

[25] As Braunmuller notes (*Macbeth*), this trumpet is anticipated by Macbeth's speculation that Duncan's "virtues | Will plead like angels, trumpet-tongued against | The deep damnation of his taking-off" (1.7.18–20).

Shakespeare, like his contemporaries, read the Bible typologically, interpreting New Testament events as fulfillment of Old Testament prophecies and foreshadowings.[26] This is evident in a very complex allusion in Macduff's first speech on leaving Duncan's bedchamber: "O horror, horror, horror, | Tongue nor heart cannot conceive, nor name thee" (2.3.57–8). The second line is similar to Paul's pronouncement in 1 Corinthians 2:9: "The things which the eye hathe not sene, nether eare hathe heard, nether came into mans heart, which God hath prepared for them that love him." To perceive the allusion one must remember both Paul and Shakespeare's previous use of it in *A Midsummer Night's Dream* (see Chapter 3). Bottom describes his experience with the faeries in a scrambled, synaesthetic parody of Paul's verse: "The eye of man hath not heard, the ear of man hath not seen, man's hand is not able to taste, his *tongue* to *conceive*, nor his heart to report, what my dream was" (4.1.205–14, emphasis added). The words "tongue" and "conceive" are not in the Corinthians passage.[27] Did they become part of the passage in Shakespeare's mind after he added them to the sequence of clauses pronounced by Bottom in *Midsummer*? The earlier allusion is the more explicit; the later one in *Macbeth* is briefer and more oblique, but clear enough, knowing Shakespeare's earlier play. Shakespeare may also have picked up the verb "conceive" from his extra-biblical reading. For instance, in *An Introduction to the loove of God. Accompted among the workes of S. Augustine*, the translator, Robert Fletcher, turns 1 Corinthians 2:9 into rough tetrameters:

> The hart of man cannot *conceave*,
>   the eye of man hath never seene:
> The Eare of man did never heare,
>   what things for these prepared hath bene.[28]

The same biblical passage is alluded to later, describing what the soul will have as

>   so passing excellent:
> as the eye of man hath never seene:
> Nor eare hath heard, nor yet *conceive*,
>   within the heart of man hath beene. (sig. G.ii.ʳ)

A couple of pages later, the passage is worked into the verse more loosely:

---

[26] On typology, see Ch. 4.
[27] The allusion in *Midsummer* is closest to the Bishops' Bible version or the Great Bible, not the Geneva. But no English translation has "tongue" and "conceive."
[28] Anon., *An Introduction to the loove of God. Accompted among the workes of S. Augustine* (London: Thomas Purfoote, 1581), sig. B.ʳ; emphasis added.

> His promise made to us is sealed,
>   of lasting love in greater sort:
> Then eyther can the *tongue* declare,
>   or else the Pen for trueth report. (sig. G.iii.ʳ, emphasis added)

This is almost doggerel verse, but it may be that Shakespeare picked up the translation at some point because of Augustine's name on the title or because the subject (the love of God, the joys of heaven) interested him. Fletcher is really just turning into meter an earlier prose translation of the same work by Edmund Roffen (also using "conceive" and "tongue"), published in 1574 and dedicated to Queen Elizabeth.

In any case, Bottom's allusion to divine mysteries makes sense (whether interpreted as a debased parody or as a secular epiphany),[29] whereas the allusion in *Macbeth* seems misplaced. Duncan's bleeding corpse is hardly one of the delights God has prepared for those who love him. The solution to this allusive puzzle lies in the margin to 1 Corinthians 2:9 in the Geneva Bible, where the reader would see the reference "*Isa. 64,4*." Paul appropriates Isaiah's language to describe the inscrutability of what God has prepared for the faithful: "For since the beginning of the worlde they have not heard nor understand with the eare, nether hathe the eye sene another God beside thee, which doeth so to him that waiteth for him" (Isa. 64:4). But, significantly, in Isaiah, this verse appears in the context of a supplication to God to punish the wicked and to let loose his wrath in terms much like Revelation's Apocalypse:

> Oh, that thou woldest breake the heavens, and come downe, and that the mountains might melt at thy presence. As the melting fyre burned, as the fyre caused the waters to boile, (that thou mightest declare thy Name to thy adversaries) the people did tremble at thy presence. (Isa. 64:1–2)

1 Corinthians 2:9 and Isaiah 64:4 were regularly quoted and cited together in writings on Revelation and the Apocalypse: for example, Thomas Rogers, *The General Session, conteining an apologie of the most comfortable doctrine concerning the ende of this World, and the second coming of Christ* (London 1581), 38; Leonard Wright, *A summons for sleepers* (London, 1589), 41–2; I. S., *Two treatises, one of the latter day of judgement: the other of the joyes of Heaven* (London, 1604), 95; William Perkins, *Lectures upon the three first chapters of the Revelation* (London, 1604), sig. Aᵛ. In his *An exposition of the Symbole or Creed of the Apostles* (Cambridge, 1595; reprinted in *A golden chaine*, London, 1600), Perkins writes, concerning the final resurrection, that "both the Prophet Esai and Saint Paul say, that *the eye hath not seene, and the eare hath not heard, neither came it into any*

---

[29] See Ch.3.

mans heart to thinke of those things which God hath prepared for those that love him."[30] Shakespeare's contemporaries were accustomed to thinking of these twin passages in the context of Apocalypse.

Perhaps most intriguingly, Sir Edward Phelips, the king's "serjeant-meane," opened the trial of Guy Fawkes and the other Gunpowder Plot conspirators by paraphrasing the verses, without citation:

> The matter that is now to be offered to you, my Lords the Commissioners, and to the trial of you, the Knights and Gentlemen of the Jury, is matter of treason; but of such horror, and monstrous nature, that before now,
>
>> The Tongue of Man never delivered,
>> The Ear of Man never heard,
>> The Heart of Man never conceived,
>> Nor the Malice of Hellish, or Earthly Devil ever practiced;
>> For, if it be abominable to murder the least,
>> If to touch God's Anointed be to oppose themselves against God,
>> If (by blood) to subvert Princes, States and Kingdoms, be hateful to God and Man [etc.].[31]

Not only does Shakespeare seem to have been aware of Phelip's speech (printed in 1606, but probably known about earlier, given the notoriety of the event), but it seems also possible that Phelips himself may have known Shakespeare's *A Midsummer Night's Dream*, and have been remembering Bottom's version of Paul rather than Paul himself. Phelips was in London in the 1590s (a Member of Parliament with an appointment at Middle Temple as well), and could have seen the play when it was first performed. But a "play of Robin goode-fellow," very likely *Midsummer*, was performed before King James, probably at Hampton Court, in January of 1604.[32] As King's serjeant, patronized by both the Earl of Dorset and Thomas Egerton, Lord Chancellor, Phelips might well have seen the play at court.[33] It is possible, of course, that Phelips could have picked up the key words "tongue" and "conceive" from Fletcher's or Roffen's translations of Augustine or somewhere else, as indeed Shakespeare might have. It seems unlikely that Shakespeare himself failed to note the allusion to 1 Corinthians 2:9 in the sensational Guy Fawkes trial to which *Macbeth* clearly alludes.

---

[30] William Perkins, *An exposition of the Symbole or Creed of the Apostles* (Cambridge: John Leggatt, 1595), 531 [misnumbered 532].
[31] *A true and perfect relation of the proceedings at the severall arraignments of the late most barbarous traitors* (London: Robert Barker, 1606), sig. C2.
[32] Gary Jay Williams, *Our Moonlight Revels:* A Midsummer Night's Dream *in the Theatre* (Iowa City: University of Iowa Press, 1997), 36–7.
[33] Information on Phelips, from Rebecca S. More, "Edward S. Phelips," *ODNB*.

The apocalyptic atmosphere surrounding the reaction to Duncan's death in 2.3 is prepared at the beginning of the scene by the famous Porter episode. Macbeth hears a knocking at the end of 2.2—four times in ten lines—after he has "done" the murder and Lady Macbeth has smeared blood on the grooms. The meaning of the knocking becomes clear in the next scene, as the Porter enters to answer the door of Macbeth's castle, Macduff and Lennox having arrived early in the morning at Duncan's command. The Porter obviously moves slowly in his appointed task, since he has time for a speech of sixteen lines, during which there are six further bouts of knocking. The speech opens with a consideration that, "if a man were porter of hell-gate, he should have old [i.e., much] turning the key" (2.3.1–2). The Porter, taking on the infernal role, calls, "Who's there i'th'name of Beelzebub?" and then proceeds to imagine a series of arrivals in hell: a ruined farmer who has killed himself, a thieving tailor, and, most famously, an "equivocator that could swear in both the scales against either scale, who committed treason enough for God's sake, yet could not equivocate to heaven" (2.3.7–9). The scene is one of low comedy, leading up to an exchange about drunkenness, urination, and sex, and was condemned by Coleridge, who was sure it was "written for the mob by some other hand."[34] In fact, the scene aligns perfectly with what comes before and after it and has serious implications beneath its bathetic humor. That Macbeth's castle is a kind of hell is the most obvious implication of the Porter's game of playing "devil-porter," and this is appropriate for several reasons.

First, and most obviously, Macbeth has just committed a hellish murder, about to be discovered by those closest to the victim. Second, a scene of condemned souls arriving in hell reinforces the sense of apocalyptic doom pervading the play. We may feel we have already been in hell from the opening scene of thunder, lightning, and demonic witches, and their return in 1.3, when Banquo's use of a familiar proverb connects them with the devil ("What, can the devil speak true?"). Revelation includes many images of hell, as well as doors, locks, and keys, as when, after the fifth Angel of the Apocalypse has blown his trumpet, John sees "a starre fall from heaven unto the earth, and to him was given the keye of the bottomles pit. And he opened the bottomles pit, and there arose the smoke of the pit, as the smoke of a great furnace, and the sunne, and the ayre were darkened by the smoke of the pit" (Rev. 9:1–2).[35] Later, an Angel comes down

---

[34] Samuel Taylor Coleridge, from the *Lectures*, in D. Nichol-Smith (ed.), *Shakespeare Criticism: A Selection 1623–1840* (London: Oxford University Press, 1916; repr. 1964), 266.

[35] Interpretations of the star falling from heaven vary (see Ch. 5), but a note in the 1560 Geneva Bible identifies the figure as the Pope, since he has a key as part of his insignia (evoking the keys figuratively given to Peter by Jesus at Matt. 16:9).

from heaven, "having the keye of the bottomles pit, and a great chaine in his hand. And he toke the dragon that olde serpent, which is the devil and Satan, and he bounde him a thousand yeres" (Rev. 20:1–2). The way into and out of hell, locked with a key, corresponds to the way into and out of heaven, also figured as a door. John is commanded to write on God's behalf to the Church of the Laodiceans, "Beholde, I stand at the dore, and knocke. If anie man heare my voice and open the dore, I wil come in unto him, and wil suppe with him, and he with me" (Rev. 3:20). This metaphor adapts one from Luke, where it is God who is on the inside, and the sinner who knocks:

> When the good man of the house is risen up, and hathe shut the dore, and ye beginne to stand without, and to knocke at the dore, saying, Lord, Lord, open to us, and he shal answer and say unto you, I knowe you not whence you are, Then shal ye beginne to say, We have eaten and drunke in thy presence, and thou hast taught in our stretes. But he shal say, I tel you, I know you not whence ye are: departe from me, all ye workers of iniquitie. (Luke 13:25–7)

The infernal atmosphere in *Macbeth* was created in its original performances not only by its words. Jonathan Gil Harris has argued that the standard stagecraft by which Shakespeare's theater created "thunder and lightning" was the squib, a firework made of dung and gunpowder that would not only have created "fog and filthy air" (1.1.11) but a lingering stink that would have given olfactory realism to Macbeth's invocation of the "dunnest smoke of hell" (1.5.49), a metaphor given concreteness in the Porter scene.[36] Harris goes on to suggest that the smell of the squibs would have conjured up two specific associations for the Jacobean theater audience. First, the recent Gunpowder Plot, in which thirty kegs of gunpowder were to have blown up the House of Parliament, and, second, the hellmouth of the Corpus Christi plays, whose sulphurous and fiery effects depended upon the same exploding devices. It has long been recognized that the Gunpowder Plot is alluded to by the Porter, since the Jesuit Henry Garnett, who used the alias "Farmer," was believed to be the author of *A Treatise of Equivocation*, a copy of which was found in the possession of one of the plotters (see also the allusions to 1 Corinthians 2:9, discussed above).[37] Equivocation, or mental reservation, was a means by which it was believed one could, without sin, withhold incriminating evidence under interrogation by revealing only part of the truth out loud, and the remainder in the mind to God. This argument was vehemently

---

[36] Jonathan Gil Harris, "The Smell of *Macbeth*," *SQ* 58/4 (2007), 465–86.
[37] Gary Wills, *Witches and Jesuits: Shakespeare's* Macbeth (New York and Oxford: Oxford University Press, 1995), ch. 5.

rejected by English Protestants. Harris suggests another dimension to *Macbeth*'s topicality. Intriguingly, these two associative contexts overlap. In a speech to Parliament published in 1605, James I himself describes the intended result of the plot in terms of the Apocalypse:

> ...so the earth as it were opened, should have sent forth of the bottome of the *Stygian* lake such sulphured smoke, furious flames, and fearefull thunder, as should have by their diabolicall *Domesday* destroyed and defaced, in the twinkling of an eye, not onely our present living Princes and people, but even our insensible Monuments reserved for future ages.[38]

Harris notes that James's reference to "*Domesday*" represents the plot as an anticipation of the final Apocalypse. It should be added that "the twinckling of an eye" does the same. Paul writes of the final resurrection: "In a moment, in the twinkling of an eye at the last trumpet: for the trumpet shal blowe, and the dead shal be raised up incorruptible, and we shalbe changed" (1 Cor. 15:52).

If *Macbeth* worked on the nose, it also worked on the ears, with effects beyond language. Kurt Schreyer argues that, like the smell of the squibs, the sound of the knocking on the castle gate also evokes the Mystery plays.[39] In the plays representing Christ's Harrowing of Hell (the apocryphal tale in which after his death he descends to hell, breaks open the gates, and releases the virtuous pagans), Christ repeats a cry based on Psalm 24:7, "Lift up your heads ye gates, and be ye lift up ye everlasting dores, and the King of glorie shal come in," which is accompanied by a huge racket. The gates of hell, constructed as a hell-mouth (see Fig. 7.2), come crashing down, with smoke produced by the same kind of squibs used on later stages. Building on Harris's argument, Schreyer suggests that *Macbeth*'s recreation of the hell of the Mystery plays depended on loud noise as well as on foul odors. He suggests, moreover, that the hell evoked is not just the hell of Revelation but that of Christ's Harrowing after the Crucifixion, though, as so often, these two seemingly separate events, biblical and biblical–apocryphal, are typologically equivalent. The apocryphal Harrowing of Hell, however, was rejected by Protestants as a papist fiction.

The infernal atmosphere of *Macbeth* is further reinforced by demonic apparitions, first the witches, then the ghost of Banquo. The witches, or weird sisters, set the tone of the play and set its plot in motion with their cryptic prophecies about the future to Macbeth and Banquo, prophecies

---

[38] James I, *His Maiesties Speech in This Last Session of Parliament*...(London: Robert Barker, 1605), sig. E3ᵛ, cited in Harris, "Smell of *Macbeth*," 474–5.

[39] Kurt Schreyer, " 'Here's a knocking indeed!': *Macbeth* and the *Harrowing of Hell*," *The Upstart Crow: A Shakespeare Journal*, 29 (2010–11), 26–43.

Fig. 7.2. In the Mystery plays representing the (apocryphal) tale of Christ's harrowing of Hell, the gates of Hell were constructed to look like a giant mouth. Another Hell-mouth, to which sinners of all ranks including bishops and monarchs, chained together, are fed, is part of a fifteenth-century Doom painting, one of the largest of its kind, above the chancel arch at the Church of St Thomas, Salisbury. (The painting was whitewashed in 1593, rediscovered in 1819, and restored in 1881. It was restored again in 1953.) © Amanda's Arcadia/Flickr/Getty Images.

that have been interpreted as themselves a kind of "equivocation," revealing partial truths while withholding critical details.[40] (As mentioned above, late-sixteenth- and early seventeenth-century England was also generally obsessed with prophecies, as part of the attempt to predict the end times.) The witches originated in Holinshed's account of Macbeth's murder of Duncan, where they are described first as "three women in strange and wild apparel, resembling creatures of the elder world," then as "either the Weird Sisters, that is (as ye would say), the goddesses of destiny, or else some nymphs or fairies endued with knowledge or prophecy by their necromantic science." There is also "a certain witch," who prophesies that Macbeth would never be killed until Birnam Wood came to Dunsinane, and there are also "certain wizards" who tell Macbeth to beware Macduff.[41] Shakespeare economizes, melding the witches and the weird sisters and putting all three prophecies in their mouths.

He also adds a second scene, 4.1, in which Macbeth seeks out the witches, after the appearance of Banquo's ghost, to discover what the future holds. This scene is modeled on Saul's visit to the witch of Endor in 1 Samuel.[42] Like Macbeth, Saul, the first king of Israel, is desperate to learn more about his future. God is no longer speaking to him, and God's prophet, Samuel, is dead, so he seeks out "a woman at Endor that hathe a familiar spirit" (1 Sam. 28:7; the page header in the Geneva Bible reads "Saul with the witch"). At Saul's insistence, the witch calls up the ghost of the prophet Samuel. After she has seen "gods ascending up out of the earth" (1 Sam. 28:13), Samuel's ghost appears and tells Saul that tomorrow in battle he will die. In *Macbeth*, three apparitions convey to him the prophecies from Holinshed. Then he asks whether Banquo's issue will "ever reign in this kingdom" (4.1.100–2). The stage direction indicates what Macbeth and the audience see: "A shew of eight Kings, and Banquo last, with a glasse [mirror] in his hand."[43] The woman/witch at Endor sees that Saul is deeply troubled and offers comfort, saying, "I pray thee, let me set a morsel of bread before thee, that thou maiest eat and get thee strength, and go on thy journey" (1 Sam. 28:22). The witches in *Macbeth*

---

[40] For example, Stallybrass, "*Macbeth* and Witchcraft," 199.

[41] Raphael Holinshed, *The First and Second Volumes of Chronicles*, ii. *The History of Scotland* (London, 1587). For a modernized edition of the relevant excerpts, see *Macbeth*, ed. Robert S. Miola, Norton Critical Edition (New York and London: W. W. Norton & Company, 2004), 101–8.

[42] H.W.B., "Saul and Macbeth," *Sewanee Review*, 1/3 (1893), 273–82; John Parker, "Shakespeare and the Geneva Bible: The Story of King Saul as a Source for *Macbeth*," *Tennessee Philological Bulletin*, 43 (2006), 6–23.

[43] Shakespeare, *Macbeth*, in *Mr William Shakespeares comedies, histories, & tragedies* (London: Isaac Jaggard and Ed. Blunt, 1623), 144 (three sections separately numbered). The stage direction in Braunmuller (*Macbeth*) is somewhat edited.

do not offer food, but Hecate does say, "Come, sisters, cheer we up his sprites, | And show the best of our delights" (4.1.126–7).[44] Macbeth also receives essentially the same prophecy that Saul does, even if it is too equivocal (in its reservation of key truths) for him to understand it: "none of woman born shall harm Macbeth" and "Macbeth shall never vanquished be until | Great Birnam Wood to high Dunsinane hill | Shall come against him" (4.1.79–80, 91–3). To Macbeth, this sounds like a wonderful prophecy of invulnerability; ironically, as he discovers, it is simply a prophecy of his death, after Malcolm's army has cut down Birnam Wood for camouflage and Macbeth has faced Macduff, "born" by Caesarean section.

Further allusions to the Saul story reinforce 1 Samuel as a significant context for the fall of a wicked king. Saul, like Macbeth, is beheaded after death (1 Sam. 31:9). Macduff's description of Duncan as "the Lord's anointed temple" may also be an ironic allusion to David's description of Saul as "the Lords Anointed" (1 Sam. 24:7). David has Saul, his king, in his power but refuses to kill him, despite Saul's ill treatment of him; by contrast, Macbeth is treated well by his king, yet he kills Duncan anyway.[45] As David begins his kingship after Saul's death, he travels to the city of Bahurim, where he encounters "a man of the family of Saul, named Shimei" (2 Sam. 16:5). Shimei throws stones at David and his men, and curses him, saying, "Come forthe, come forthe thou murtherer, and wicked man" (2 Sam. 16:7). The marginal note in the Geneva Bible states that the Hebrew rendered here as "murtherer" is, literally, "man of blood." George Peele was obviously aware of this, since he uses the phrase in his play *David and Bethsabe*, though in reference to David's general Joab rather than David himself: "Thou man of bloud, thou sepulchre of death."[46]

---

[44] This is perhaps the place to note that there has been much debate about the authorship of the Folio text (the only one surviving) of *Macbeth*. The songs in 3.5 and 4.1 are certainly by Middleton, since they appear in his play *The Witch*, but arguments have been made for more extensive addition and revision, including most of both of these scenes with Hecate. However, this debate does not affect the argument here, since, even if Hecate or 4.1 as a whole are Middleton's addition, the allusions to the Saul story remain. Whether conceived by Shakespeare or by Middleton (or both, the latter developing cues from the former), the allusions to Saul and the witch suit the play just the same. And the cultural context of 1610–11 (when Simon Forman saw the play, for which production Middleton may have revised it) was in fundamental ways similar to 1605–6. If anything, James I and his subjects were even more interested in the Apocalypse than they had been earlier. Even in 1616, James was speaking of "the latter daies drawing on." See Ball, *Great Expectation*, 1. On texts and dating, see Braunmuller (ed.), *Macbeth*, 255–63.

[45] Jane H. Jack, "Macbeth, King James, and the Bible," *ELH* 22/3 (1955), 173–93, 182–3.

[46] George Peele, *The love of King David and fair Bethsabe With the tragedie of Absalon* (London: Adam Islip, 1599), sig. H4ᵛ.

In Erasmus's *An exposicyon of the .xv. psalme*, on the other hand, it is David who is "a man of blode or blody man."[47] Shimei held David accountable for Saul's death. This was unjustified, but David was responsible for many other deaths, either at his own hands, or on his orders. For instance, David had Uriah killed in order to cover up his adultery with Uriah's wife Bathsheba. In his own words (so the tradition went), David accused himself of "blood-guiltiness" (Ps. 51:14). By law, whoever is guilty of blood will be bled: "whoso shedeth mans blood, by man shal his blood be shed" (Gen. 9:6), "for blood defileth the land: and the land can not be clensed of the blood that is shed therein, but by the blood of him that shed it" (Num. 35:33). As Christopher Hill has shown, the "man of blood" became a rallying cry during the seventeenth century in opposition to Charles I, providing biblical authority for overturning a blood-guilty king: "Because the people consented with the King in sheding innocent blood: therefore God destroyeth bothe the one and the other" (Geneva note to Judg. 9:24).[48]

Earlier Englishmen were also familiar with the biblical "man of blood," even if they had not yet applied the label to their king. Edwin Sandys, for instance, in a sermon published in 1585 but probably preached in 1570–6 when he was Bishop of London, stated that the story of God's preservation of David in the face Absalom's rebellion "may give us courage and strength against that man of bloud which at this day doth so cruelly persecute the professours of the Gospell, and so proudly take upon him to depose Christian princes and to place hypocrites in their roomes at his pleasure."[49] Duncan's captain is a "man of blood" only in the sense that he is covered in it (a "bloody man"), but the phrase applies much better to Macbeth, guilty (as Shimei thinks David is) of killing his king, as well as Banquo and Lady Macduff and her children. Blood is obviously one of

---

[47] Desiderius Erasmus, *An exposicyon of the .xv. psalme* [London: J. Waylande, 1537], sig. D7.

[48] Christopher Hill, *The English Bible and the Seventeenth-Century Revolution* (Harmondsworth: Penguin, 1993), 324–31. See also Patricia Crawford, "Charles Stuart, that Man of Blood," *Journal of British Studies*, 16/2 (1977), 41–61.

[49] Edwin Sandys, "A Sermon preached at Pauls Crosse at what time a maine treason was discovered," in *Sermons made by the most reverende Father in God, Edwin, Archbishop of Yorke* (London: Henrie Midleton for Thomas Charde, 1585), 364–5. The occasion of Sandys's sermon seems to be the Ridolfi plot to assassinate Elizabeth and put her cousin Mary Queen of Scots on the throne. See Mary Morrissey, *Politics and the Paul's Cross Sermons, 1558–1642* (Oxford: Oxford University Press, 2011), 75–78. There may be more candidates than one for Sandys's "man of blood," but Pope Pius V seems a good fit, since he issued the papal bull *Regnans in Excelsis* in 1570, excommunicating Elizabeth and encouraging her subjects to depose her. Sandys's use of the phrase is a little odd, however, since in 2 Samuel it refers to David, while Sandys's sermon is a condemnation of rebellion, implicitly placing the threatened Elizabeth in the position of David.

the pervasive images in the play, appearing on the dagger Macbeth thinks he sees, smeared on Duncan's grooms by Lady Macbeth, and recurring powerfully in the imaginations of Macbeth and Lady Macbeth: "make thick my blood" (1.5.41); "Will all great Neptune's ocean wash this blood | Clean from my hand?" (2.2.63–4); "I am in blood | Stepped in so far that should I wade no more, | Returning were as tedious as go o'er" (3.4.136–8). Macbeth's language draws on the passages about blood guilt in Genesis, Numbers, and elsewhere:

> It will have blood they say: blood will have blood.
> Stones have been known to move and trees to speak.
> Augures, and understood relations, have
> By maggot-pies, and choughs, and rooks brought forth
> The secret'st man of blood. (3.4.122–6)

But the real "man of blood" is Macbeth himself.

Returning to the witches, Shakespeare did not need to reach far for the allusion to Saul and Endor, since, as Peter Stallybrass notes, 1 Samuel 28 "was dealt with by nearly every Renaissance treatise on witchcraft."[50] The witch of Endor is mentioned, for instance, in Samuel Harsnett's *A declaration of egregious popish impostures* (1603), a book Shakespeare clearly knew, as well as more extensively in George Gifford's *A discourse of the subtell practices of devilles by witches and sorcerers* (1587).[51] Most interestingly, James I discussed the witch of Endor at length in his *Daemonologie* (1597, reprinted in Edinburgh and London in 1603).[52] Unlike Harsnett, who was debunking what he saw as papist magic tricks, James asserted the reality of the supernatural. Like other Protestant commentators, though, he clarified that the apparition produced by the witch of Endor could not actually have been the ghost of Samuel, however much it seemed so to Saul. Ludwig Lavater had made this clear in his *Of ghostes and spirites walking by nyght* (1572), stating that "very Samuell himself did not appear in soule and body, neither that his body was raised up by the sorcerers, which perchaunce then was rotten

---

[50] Stallybrass, "*Macbeth* and Witchcraft," 202.
[51] Samuel Harsnett, *A declaration of egregious popish impostures* (London: James Roberts, 1603), 153. Shakespeare draws on Harsnett for *King Lear*, in the names of demons used by Edgar as Poor Tom. See Stephen Greenblatt, *Shakespearean Negotiations: The Circulation of Social Energy in Renaissance England* (Berkeley and Los Angeles: University of California Press, 1988), ch. 4. George Gifford, *A discourse of the subtell practices of devilles by witches and sorcerers* (London: [By T. Orwin] for Toby Cooke, 1587), sigs. E3ᵛ–E4ᵛ.
[52] James VI [and later I], *Daemonologie* (Edinburgh: Robert Waldegrave, 1597), 2–4. Apparently, James wrote this work after his own experience with a treasonous plot against him by alleged witches. See James Sharpe, *Instruments of Darkness: Witchcraft in Early Modern England* (Philadelphia: University of Pennsylvania Press, 1997), 48.

and consumed unto dust in the earth, neither that his soule was called up, but rather some divelish spirite."[53] Lavater's book, reprinted in 1596, was a substantial study, including chapters intriguingly relevant to *Macbeth*, on "madde men, imagining things whiche in very deede are not," "Fearefull menne, [who] imagine that they see and heare straunge things," "That there happen straunge wonders and prognostications, and that sodayne noises and cracks and suche like, are hard before the death of men, before battaile, and before some notable alterations and changes," and that "Divells...sometimes they tell truth" (as in response to Banquo's question, "can the Devil speak true?"). Regarding the latter, Lavater notes in the title of another chapter that "suche kinde of apparitions are not to bee credited, and that wee oughte to bee verie circumspect in them." Shakespeare's ghost and witches were thus tapping into a deep cultural vein. Keith Thomas argues, furthermore, that "ghost-beliefs were also closely linked with the idea of witchcraft."[54] Certainly, Shakespeare's deceitful witches add evidence to Lavater's argument not to credit apparations.

But Shakespeare conveys less interest in the theology of ghosts than in their dramatic and psychological effect and, as such, the witches further the play's sense of apocalypse. Adrian Streete notes that early modern treatises on witchcraft emphasized not only witches' Satanic origins but their connection to end times as described in Revelation. In the words of an eminent modern scholar of witchcraft, "in early modern demonology, magicians and witches were in fact the precursors of the Antichrist, part of Satan's preparation for his arrival."[55] James I closes his *Daemonologie* with an explanation of why "divellishe practices" are so much increased in recent days: "the consummation of the worlde, and our deliverance drawing neare, makes Sathan to rage the more in his instruments, knowing his kingdome to be so neare an end."[56] In fact, witchcraft was believed to have been at the core of the Gunpowder Plot.

---

[53] Ludwig Lavater, *Of ghostes and spirites walking by nyght* (London: Henry Benneyman for Richard Watkyns, 1572), 127.

[54] Keith Thomas, *Religion and the Decline of Magic* (Harmondsworth: Penguin, 1971), 709. For one thing, the appearance of ghosts was often blamed on witches.

[55] Stuart Clark, *Thinking with Demons*, cited in Adrian Streete, "'What bloody man is that?' Questioning Biblical Typology in *Macbeth*," *Shakespeare*, 5/1 (2009). 18–35, 22. Streete makes the excellent point that the "Lord's anointed" allusion makes it difficult to determine whether Duncan is a Saul or a David and that this is "precisely the point" (p. 28). I would add that this allusive indeterminacy is equally true of Macbeth, who is connected by allusions at different points to both Saul and David, as well as to Judas, Christ, and Antichrist.

[56] James VI [and later I], *Daemonologie*, 81. Streete also notes this passage ("'What bloody man is that?,'" 22).

The plotters, led by Jesuits, were supposed to have devised their plan at a Black Mass, an event incorporated into Dekker's *Whore of Babylon*, and decried by Lancelot Andrewes in his 1606 sermon on the anniversary of the plot.[57] As Gary Wills points out, drawing on Harsnett's *Egregious Popish Imposters*, Elizabethan law held that participants in such a satanic ceremony were to be treated as witches.[58] Further, Samuel tells Saul, in condemning him for disobeying God's command, "rebellion is as the sinne of witchcraft" (1 Sam. 15:23).

WHO IS MACBETH?

What do all these allusions signify about Macbeth? Like the Gunpowder Plotters he is a traitor and rebel; like Saul and/or David he is a wicked king; like Judas he betrays his master. If Duncan is represented, however imperfectly, as a Christ-figure, though, Macbeth is not only a type of Judas, but, in the context of all the allusions to Revelation, even an Antichrist, or at least one of his instruments. Guy Fawkes and his co-conspirators were themselves described as "cursed instruments of Antichrist."[59] Macbeth as Antichrist is given a parodic Crucifixion by the righteous Macduff, who raises Macbeth's head on a pole. He tells Macbeth that he wants him to be, "as our rarer monsters are, | Painted upon a pole and underwrit, | 'Here may you see the tyrant'" (5.8.25–7), recalling in a grotesque parody Jesus's being hung on the cross with a sign above, "This is Jesus the King of the Jews" (Matt. 27:37). Macbeth is thus cast in several biblical roles (not always compatible with each other), as further biblical allusions suggest.

Duncan's death, for instance, is represented not only in terms of Christ's Crucifixion but in terms of the Fall. This is plain when Macbeth's castle is described by Duncan as "a pleasant seat" where, according to Banquo, the "temple-haunting martlet...Hath made his pendant bed and procreant cradle" (1.6.1–8), which alludes to Psalm 84:

> How pleasant is thy dwelling place,
>   O Lord of hostes to me:
> The tabernacles of thy grace,
>   how pleasant Lord they be:
> The sparrows find a roome to rest,
>   and save themselves from wrong:

---

[57] See Wills, *Witches and Jesuits*, 35–7.   [58] Wills, *Witches and Jesuits*, 36.
[59] Cornelius Burges to the House of Commons in November 1640, cited in Christopher Hill, *Antichrist in Seventeenth-Century England*, rev. edn (London and New York: Verso, 1990), 15.

> And eke the swallows hath a nest,
> wherein to keepe her young.[60]

This metrical version from the popular Sternhold and Hopkins psalter is closest to Banquo's language (instead of "pleasant," Geneva and other Bibles have "amiable"). The association of the martlet (a small bird like a swallow, whose nesting habits are also mentioned by Aragon in *Merchant*, 2.9.27) and the temple/tabernacle creates the connection with the psalm. Banquo says that the presence of the birds shows that "the heaven's breath | Smells wooingly here" (1.6.5).

Before Duncan arrives, however, Macbeth is urged by Lady Macbeth to "look like th'innocent flower, | But be the serpent under't" (1.5.63–4).[61] Malcolm's later statement to Macduff that "I shall tread upon the tyrant's head" (4.3.45) reinforces the comparison of Macbeth and the serpent, echoing God's promise to the serpent that Eve's offspring "shal breake thine head" (Gen. 3:15).[62] According to standard typological interpretations of this passage, that breaking of the serpent's head will occur at the Second Coming, as described in Revelation, when the serpent (or dragon, Satan) will be overcome by Eve's offspring, Jesus.

Macbeth is also like Adam, in that he is tempted by his wife to perform an act he knows is forbidden, the murder of Duncan, whose stabbed body looks like a "breach in nature" (2.3.106).[63] This phrase was not much in use before Shakespeare, though he himself had used it earlier in *King Lear* to refer to Lear's madness when Cordelia asks the doctor to "Cure this great breach in his abused nature" (4.7.15). After Shakespeare, the phrase appears in religious contexts referring to the effect of Adam and Eve's sin on mankind and indeed all the natural world.[64] In Augustine's *Of the Citie of God*, translated first into English in 1610, sin is described as a "second death," because "it followeth the first breach of nature, either betweene God and the soule, or this and the body."[65] Other examples of the Fall as

---

[60] Sternhold and Hopkins, cited in Shaheen, 625.

[61] Later, when it is Macbeth who is in the position of power, the serpent imagery is transferred to Banquo, after he is safely killed: "There the grown serpent lies" (3.4.29). Also, the escaped Fleance is the worm that "in time will venom breed" (4.3.30).

[62] See Philip C. Kolin, "Macbeth, Malcolm, and the Curse of the Serpent," *South Central Bulletin*, 43/4 (1974), 159–60. Kolin notes that, in Luke, Jesus promises the disciples that "I give unto you power to treade on serpents" (Luke 10:19).

[63] Paul N. Siegel notes that in *The City of God* Augustine argued that Adam had "transgressed not out of ignorance but out of love for Eve." ("Echoes of the Bible Story in 'Macbeth,'" *N&Q* 2 (April 1955), 142–3.)

[64] As Braunmuller (*Macbeth*) notes, the apocalyptic language of 2.3 is continued in the first murderer's description of the body of the murdered Banquo: "With twenty trenched gashes on his head, | The least a death to nature" (3.4.37).

[65] St Augustine, *Of the Citie of God*, trans. J.H. (London: George Eld, 1610), 471.

The Great Doom's Image 295

a "breach in nature" include sermons by Richard Warneford ("The Gospel teaches us how the Transgression and breach of Nature in *Adam* is to be repaired") and Hugh Knox ("we may infer the absolute necessity of a supernatural power and principle to mend and repair such a radical breach in our nature"), a treatise by Thomas Hartley (God "would repair that breach in nature which sin and the curse have made," referring to God as "the repairer of the breach" [Isa. 58:12]), and "On the Vicissitudes of Human Life," a poem by Nathan Withy:

> Lord, what is Man! we often read the first
> Was form'd by thy Almighty Hand with Dust;
> But ever since the Eden happy Reign,
> He's got by Sin, and then brought forth in Pain:
> Sorrow attends him the first Breath he draws,
> As if he'd made a Breach in Nature's Laws.[66]

Macbeth, who offers this description of Duncan's bloodied corpse, goes on to refer to the daggers of the attendants as "Unmannerly breeched with gore" (2.3.109). As Cleanth Brooks noted, earlier critics found this metaphor disturbing, William Warburton, Samuel Johnson, and William Seward all emending it ("reech'd," "drench'd," and "hatch'd," respectively) without any further justification. One nineteenth-century reader wrote, "A metaphor must not be far-fetched nor dwell upon the details of a disgusting picture, as in these lines."[67] Brooks notes the *Shakespeare Glossary* definition of "breeched" as "covered as with breeches," but neither he nor anyone else seems to have pursued the metaphor further. Two points seems relevant. First, to "breech" may mean to have on or put on breeches, but, as discussed in Chapter 4, in early modern England it was more specifically associated with the "breeching" of male children, when they were put into pants for the first time, thus marking their transition from (neuter) child to man.[68] The play contains numerous striking references to children, and Macbeth is obsessed, as is Lady Macbeth, with what it means to be a man. Macbeth speaks of "pity, like a naked newborn babe"

---

[66] Andrew Warneford, "Sermon I, John 12:28," in *Sermons of Various Subjects*, ii (York: Caesar Ward, 1758), 9. Hugh Knox, Sermon XX, "Creatures, broken cisterns: God alone, the fountain of living waters, from Jerem. ii, 12, 13," in *Select Sermons on Interesting Subjects*, ii (Glasgow: Robert & Andrew Foulis, 1726), 163. Thomas Hartley, *Paradise restored: or A Testimony to the Doctrine of the Blessed Millennium* (London: M. Richardson, 1764), 5. Nathaniel Withy, *Miscellaneous Poems*, 3rd edn (Wolverhampton: G. Smart, for the author, 1775), 11.

[67] Cleanth Brooks, *The Well-Wrought Urn: Studies in the Structure of Poetry* (San Diego, New York, and London: Harcourt Brace Jovanovich, 1947; repr. 1975), 30.

[68] Diane Purkiss, "Marvell, Boys, Girls, and Men: Should We Worry?" in Naomi J. Miller and Naomi Yavneh (eds), *Gender and Early Modern Constructions of Childhood* (Farnham and Burlington, VT: Ashgate, 2011), 181–92, 188.

(1.7.21), and Lady Macbeth vows that, if she had sworn to commit murder as Macbeth did, she would have "taken the babe that milks me" and "plucked my nipple from his boneless gums | And dashed the brains out" (1.7.55–8). (Lady Macbeth's famous lines allude to Psalm 137's more famous final curse, "Blessed shall he be that taketh and dasheth children against the stones.")[69] Just before the murder, Macbeth declares that he dares "do all that may become a man," to which Lady Macbeth responds, "When you durst do it, then you were a man" (1.7.46, 49). That the daggers are not just "breeched" but "unmannerly breeched" seems therefore striking. They have actually been "unmannerly breeched" in that it was the manly Lady Macbeth, not Macbeth himself, who dipped them in Duncan's blood. Does their unmannerliness also suggest that their "breeching" (in the child-rearing sense) has proved ineffectual, leaving them children, and not men, or the daggers of a child, not a man? A further association may help clarify Shakespeare's complex metaphor. Since at least the late eighteenth century, the Geneva Bible has been called the "Breeches Bible," because in Genesis 3, after Adam and Eve have eaten the forbidden fruit and known that they are naked, they "sewed fig tre leaves together, and made them selves breeches." (The Bishops' Bible has instead "aperns" or aprons.) Shakespeare was unlikely to have heard the Geneva referred to as the "Breeches Bible,"[70] but he certainly knew the passage for which it was nicknamed, since he alludes to it in *The Winter's Tale* when Leontes says that, when he looks on his son's face, "methoughts I did recoil | Twenty-three years, and saw myself unbreeched" (1.2.153–4). As discussed earlier, the lack of breeches alludes to a state of childish innocence analogous to Adam and Eve's naked state before the Fall, and described earlier in the play by Polixenes, when he speaks of himself and Leontes knowing not "the doctrine of ill doing" (1.2.69). Especially telling is Leontes's "unbreeched" state as when he had his "dagger muzzled" (1.2.155). When writing *The Winter's Tale*, Shakespeare evidently recalled his earlier metaphorical linking of breeches and daggers in the same biblical context of lost innocence and (male) violence. If the daggers in *Macbeth*, like Adam and Eve, have "committed" sin, then they are "breeched"—have "breeches" (perhaps literally the blood that covers them)—in order to cover their shameful nakedness. This biblical reading of the daggers may seem less of a stretch given that, a few lines later, Banquo tells everyone to go to their rooms and hide their "naked frailties"

---

[69] Geneva Bible, as quoted by Shaheen, 627. For more on this verse from Ps.137, see Hamlin, ch. 7.

[70] Henry Chapman, *A catalogue of several large collections and parcels of books, purchased since June 1785* [London, 1785], 30.

(2.3.119). "Frailty," as argued above, is a word that has specific connotations with humanity, especially women, after the Fall.[71] This interpretation may not satisfy those readers who demand that metaphors (or allusions) not be far-fetched, but it does suggest Shakespeare's choice of the word "breeched" was deliberate and complex.

If Macbeth plays both the serpent and Adam, he also takes a turn as Herod. Not only does Macbeth have Macduff's children murdered, a small-scale slaughter of innocents, but, like Herod, he also does so in response to a prophecy. The prophecy told by the wisemen to Herod is that the King of the Jews has been born (Matt. 2:1–2); the prophecy delivered by the wise women to Macbeth is that he should beware Macduff. In both cases, the murder of children results as the kings attempt to eliminate rival claimants to the throne. Macbeth also tries to have Fleance killed, who is in fact the child who, it is prophesied, will ultimately inherit the Scottish crown. Like the infant Jesus, Fleance escapes slaughter and eventually becomes king. The banquet scene in Macbeth may also derive from the Herod story, as told in the Mystery plays.[72] "The Death of Herod" from the Coventry Cycle, contains a banquet that Herod holds after hearing that the slaughter of the Jewish infants has been accomplished. At the banquet, however, Death appears, though nobody else but Herod notices him. After making a speech, Death, to the sound of trumpets, carries Herod off to hell. In *Macbeth*, the ghost of the dead Banquo appears at the banquet, and is seen only by Macbeth. Banquo's ghost is silent and leaves Macbeth where he is, but that may be appropriate since Scotland is represented as hell on earth already.

Such allusions give Macbeth's wickedness an almost cosmic dimension. Yet, despite the claims of critics who see Macbeth as a religious play, representing in orthodox terms the downfall of evil and the ultimate triumph of good, the play resists the simple moral binaries of standard treatises on the Apocalypse.[73] For one thing, there is no adequate "Christ" to oppose Macbeth's "Antichrist." Some critics have advanced Duncan, Malcolm, or even Macduff as candidates, or at least argued that these are the "good" characters in the play. They want Macbeth to be more of a traditional morality play than it really is. Duncan is relatively good, certainly more so

---

[71] In conjunction with Hamlet's "frailty thy name is woman," see Ch. 4.
[72] Jones, *Origins*, 80–3.
[73] Many critics interpret *Macbeth* as more or less orthodox in this respect, however different their approaches may be otherwise. See, e.g., Susan Snyder, "Theology as Tragedy in *Macbeth*," *Christianity and Literature*, 43/3–4 (1994), 289–300; Beatrice Batson, "The 'Horrid Deed' and its Consequences in the Tragedy of *Macbeth*," *Sewanee Theological Review*, 49/4 (2006), 431–42; John D. Cox, *Seeming Knowledge: Shakespeare and Skeptical Faith* (Waco, TX: Baylor University Press, 2007); Tom McAlindon, *Shakespeare's Tragic Cosmos* (Cambridge: Cambridge University Press, 1991).

than Macbeth, but he is obviously ineffectual, since his kingdom is in a perpetual state of rebellion, and he is a miserable judge of character, continually promoting the very men who betray him. In Holinshed, Macdonald (Macdonwald) calls him "a fainthearted milksop more meet to govern a sort of idle monks in some cloister than to have the rule of such valiant and hardy men of war as the Scots were."[74] Macduff calls Duncan "a most sainted king," but what kind of saint would respond to news that Macbeth has "unseamed [Macdonald] from the nave to th'chaps | And fixed his head upon our battlements" by calling Macbeth, "O valiant cousin, worthy gentleman!"? (1.2.22–4).[75]

Malcolm is even more suspect than Duncan. His response to the news that his father has been murdered is at best rather distant, at worst indifferent or even self-interested: "O, by whom?" (2.3.93). His test of Macduff in England by pretending to be utterly corrupt is bizarre, although it does follow Holinshed's account. The scene makes more sense, however, when read in parallel to the account in 1 Samuel of the creation of the first king of Israel. Israel demands a king, but God, through his prophet Samuel, tries to dissuade them, describing all that the king will demand of the people to satisfy his appetites: sons, daughters, fields and vineyards, produce, servants, and livestock (1 Sam. 8:9–18). Apart from being unnecessary, since God ought to be sufficient for Israel, kings are nothing but a burden to the people. Malcolm's "confession" of his faults to Macduff is an elaboration on Samuel's warning to the Israelites:

> When I shall tread upon the tyrant's head,
> Or wear it on my sword, yet my poor country
> Shall have more vices than it had before,
> More suffer, and more sundry ways than ever,
> By him that shall succeed. (4.3.45–9)

"Him that shall succeed" is Malcolm himself. He then confesses to unbridled lust, avarice, cruelty, and almost every other failing, persuading Macduff to despair for Scotland. Immediately Malcolm recants, singing Macduff's praises and assuring him:

> I put myself to thy direction and
> Unspeak mine own detraction, here abjure
> The taints and blames I laid upon myself,
> For strangers to my nature. (4.3.122–5)

---

[74] *Macbeth*, ed. Miola, 103.
[75] Millicent Bell notes that the heads of the Gunpowder Plot conspirators, boiled and tarred for preservation, were put on pikes on Tower Bridge, just down river from the Globe. *Shakespeare's Tragic Skepticism* (New Haven and London: Yale University Press, 2002), 196.

Readers and viewers of this scene may respond as Macduff does, after long silence: "Such welcome and unwelcome things at once, |'Tis hard to reconcile" (138–9). The warning against kings in 1 Samuel 8 was also one of the sources for Philisides's beast fable, "On Ister bank," in Sidney's *Arcadia*, a work Shakespeare knew, having borrowed a plot from it for *King Lear*.[76] The song tells of how the beasts asked Jove for a king. Jove warns them,

> Rulers will thinke all things made them to please,
> And soone forget the swincke [labor] due to their hire.[77]

The animals will not be dissuaded, but Jove stipulates that they must each give some quality of themselves to fashion this king. The king is Man, and from his creation springs faction, murder, exploitation, and tyranny. Malcolm may protest his own innocence, but he certainly wants to be king, and the point of Samuel's warning, as in Philisides's fable, is not that some king' are tyrants, but that they all are.

Macduff is the opponent who finally defeats Macbeth, but he too is a deeply flawed hero. For one thing, there is an unsettling sense of cyclical repetition in his putting Macbeth's head on a pole, since this is just what Macbeth himself did with Macdonald's head at the play's beginning. One rebel replaces another, and rebellion succeeds rebellion, each succeeding rebel beginning as a gentleman on whom the king builds an absolute trust (1.4.14–15).[78] Macduff's precipitous flight to England, leaving his family unprotected, troubles even Malcolm. Macduff's grief at the death of his wife and children is powerfully expressed in 4.3, with his stunned, repeated questions and his tender reference to "my pretty ones" and "my pretty chickens and their dam" (4.3.218–21), but no satisfactory explanation is offered as to why he had left them alone. Could he really be surprised? He tells Malcolm that in Scotland "new widows howl, new orphans cry" (4.3.5), widows and orphans being the standard biblical figure for innocent suffering. But Macduff seems not to realize that he has effectively widowed and orphaned his own family,

---

[76] The story of the Paphlagonian king was the basis for the Gloucester subplot. For Arcadia and 1 Sam. 8, see Blair Worden, *The Sound of Virtue: Sidney's Arcadia and Elizabethan Politics* (New Haven and London: Yale University Press, 1997), 268.

[77] Sir Philip Sidney, *The Countess of Pembroke's Arcadia*, ed. Maurice Evans (Harmondsworth: Penguin, 1977), 704–9.

[78] As Bell points out (*Shakespeare's Tragic Skepticism*, 193), Malcolm's attack on Macbeth, as well as being a foreign invasion (given his English troops), is in fact a rebellion, since Macbeth was legally made king by those who were presumably unaware of his murder of Duncan, and crowned at Scone. (Macbeth's position is thus analogous to Claudius's in *Hamlet*, an undiscovered murderer who is nevertheless lawfully crowned king.)

leaving them to howl and cry.[79] Even Lady Macduff is perplexed: "To leave his wife, to leave his babes, | His mansion, and his titles in a place | From whence himself does fly? He loves us not" (4.2.6–8). Moreoever, Lady Macduff is not the first woman to die because of Macduff. That he was "untimely ripped" from his mother presumably means that whoever did the ripping, on baby Macduff's behalf, killed her. This imagery also echoes, disturbingly, Macbeth's ripping of Macdonald at the play's beginning, when "he unseam'd him from the nave to th'chaps."

The end of the play offers little real consolation to us, even in terms of Apocalypse. It ends not with a bang but a whimper. Macbeth is defeated, but not by the forces of good, and no reign of peace is begun, despite Malcolm's conventional final pronouncements. As Braunmuller notes, Malcolm's promise that he will do all that needs to be done "in measure, time, and place" echoes Duncan's similar promise to Macbeth in 1.4. Furthermore, the greeting of Malcolm by Macduff and everyone else— "Hail, King of Scotland" (5.9.26)—sounds very like the witches' greeting to Macbeth, with an echo again of the betrayer Judas greeting Jesus. Indeed, it is certain Malcolm's genealogical line cannot continue, since we know from the witches that Fleance and his heirs will inherit the throne. And what of Donalbain, still hiding out in Ireland?[80]

Macbeth's perspective, dramatically the most interesting, is increasingly bleak. His most powerful expression of nihilistic despair is in response to the news of his wife's death, reported by the strikingly named Seyton (surely in the play's hellish landscape pronounced "Satan"), and marked by a cry of women, perhaps echoing in some ironic way the "great multitude of people, and of women, which bewailed and lamented" Christ (Luke 23:27). Macbeth laments:

> Tomorrow, and tomorrow, and tomorrow
> Creeps in this petty pace from day to day
> To the last syllable of recorded time;
> And all our yesterdays have lighted fools
> The way to dusty death. Out, out, brief candle,
> Life's but a walking shadow, a poor player
> That struts and frets his hour upon the stage
> And then is heard no more. It is a tale

---

[79] "We are fatherles, even without father, and our mothers are as widowes" (Lam. 5:3). In Ecclus. (35:14) it is said that God "despiseth not the desire of the fatherles, nor the widdow, when she powreth out her prayer." The fate of Lady Macduff and her children seems not to bear this out entirely, however.

[80] As Donald W. Foster notes, Malcolm might well say of Donalbain "what Macbeth once said of Fleance: his absence is material" ("Macbeth's War on Time," *ELR* 16/2 [1986], 319–42, 321).

> Told by an idiot, full of sound and fury
> Signifying nothing. (5.5.18–27)

Shakespeare here has penned a concentrated pastiche from the biblical wisdom books: Job, Ecclesiastes, several psalms, and the apocryphal book of Ecclesiasticus.[81] For example, the "dusty death" is from Psalm 22:15 ("thou shalt bring me into the dust of death"), the "brief candle" from Job 18:6 ("his candle shall be put out with him") or 21:17 ("How shal the candel of the wicked be put out?"), the "walking shadow" from Psalm 102:11 ("My days are gone like a shadow"), Job 8:9 ("For our days upon earth are but a shadow"), or especially Psalm 39:7 ("For man walketh in a vain shadow"). The "tale told," like the earlier reference in the play by the Old Man to "threescore and ten" (2.4.1), alludes to Psalm 90 ("we bring our years to an end, as it were a tale that is told") in combination with Ecclesiasticus 20:18 ("A man without grace is as a foolish tale which is ofte tolde"). The fretting probably also derives from Psalm 39, "thou makest his beauty to consume away, like as it were a moth fretting a garment" (Ps. 39:12). Psalms 39 and 90 are more broadly relevant to Macbeth's thinking in this speech and to the play as whole. Macbeth's appeal to the witches is essentially in the mode of Psalm 39:5, "Lord, let me know myne end, and the number of my daies: that I may be certified how long I have to live," and Psalm 90:12, "teach us to number our days." Macbeth's "yesterday" may echo Psalm 90:4, "For a thousand years in thy sight are but as yesterday." Some of these Bible passages were particularly familiar from their inclusion in the Book of Common Prayer's Burial Service: "he flyeth as it were a shadow"; "ashes to ashes, dust to dust." Macbeth's comforting prophecy—"none of woman born | Shall harm Macbeth" (4.1.79–80)—also alludes to the Burial Service: "Man that is born of a woman, hathe but a shorte tyme to lyve," which in turn derives from Job 14:1.[82] Macbeth reinforces the relevance of the liturgical–biblical source, when he kills Young Seward: "Thou wast born of woman" (5.7.12).

---

[81] The term "wisdom literature" dates only from the nineteenth century, according to the *OED*, and in the later twentieth century it was popularized especially by the work of Gerhard von Rad, *Wisdom in Israel*, trans. James D. Martin (Nashville: Abingdon Press, 1972).

[82] *BCP* 171–4. The prophecy in Holinshed (of "a certain witch") is that Macbeth "shall never be slain with man born of any woman" (Bullough, vii. 500), so Shakespeare's language is not much different from his source, but for his audience the allusion would be clear nevertheless. Macbeth's repetition of the prophecy is also closer to the biblical syntax ("no man that's born of woman | Shall e'er have power upon thee," 5.3.6–7). Moreover, Holinshed may himself have had the Book of Common Prayer in mind.

Scholars who have detected strains of skepticism in *Macbeth* have pointed to sources in Montaigne, Machiavelli, or classical writers like Lucian and Sextus Empiricus.[83] Yet Shakespeare could easily have found Macbeth's nihilism fully expressed in Ecclesiastes. "Tomorrow, and tomorrow, and tomorrow" uses the same empty repetition as "vanitie of vanities, all is vanitie" (Eccles. 1:2), and the Geneva's marginal note adds the final word of Macbeth's speech: "in this worlde all things are as vanitie and *nothing*." The repetitive "time for this and time for that" in Ecclesiastes 3 ("To all things there is an appointed time") is also relevant here, especially to Macbeth's comment, "There would have been a time for such a word" (5.5.16). Macbeth might have been encouraged to know that there is a "time to slay" as well as a "time to heale" (Eccles. 3:3), although his problem is really figuring out which is which. The Geneva editors were keen to clarify that the vanity lamented by Ecclesiastes applies only to this world, not to God. But an astute and skeptical Bible reader like Shakespeare could have found plenty of evidence to the contrary. Much of the wisdom of Ecclesiastes seems more compatible with both modern existentialism and ancient Epicureanism than with Christianity:

For the condition of the children of men, and the condition of beastes are even as one condition unto them. As the one dyeth, so dyeth the other: for they have all one breath, and there is no excellencie of man above the beast: for all is vanitie. All go to one place, and all was of the dust, and all shal returne to the dust. Who knoweth whether the spirit of man ascende upward, and the spirit of the beast descend downeward to the earth? (Eccles. 3:19–20).

I have sene all things in the daies of my vanitie: there is a juste man that perisheth in his justice, and there is a wicked man that continueth long in his malice. Be not thou just overmuch, nether make thy selfe over wise: wherefore shuldest thou be desolate? (Eccles. 7:17–18)

This is the evil among all that is done under the sunne, that there is one condition to all, and also the heart of the sonnes of men is ful of evil, and madnes is in their hearts whiles they live, and after that, they go to the dead. Surely, whoever is joined to all the living, there is hope: for it is better to a living dog, then to a dead lyon. (Eccles. 9:3–4)

The sunne riseth, and the sunne goeth downe, and draweth to his place, where he riseth. The winde goeth toward the South, and compasseth toward the North:

---

[83] Bell, introduction, in *Shakespeare's Tragic Skepticism*. Richard Strier also stresses the skepticism of anti-Catholic debunkers of witchcraft and demonism like Reginald Scott in *The Discoverie of Witchcraft* (London: [Henry Denham for] William Brome, 1584) and Samuel Harsnett (*A declaration of egregious popish impostures*). "Shakespeare and the Skeptics," *Religion & Literature*, 32/2 (2000), 171–96.

the wind goeth round about, and returneth by his circuites. All the rivers go into the sea, yet the sea is not ful: for the rivers go unto the place, whence thei returne, and go. (Eccles. 1:5–7)

This latter passage, which provided Ernest Hemingway with *The Sun Also Rises*, the title of his novel about waste and emptiness between the world wars, may lie behind Macbeth's expression of ennui after the "Tomorrow" speech: "I 'gin to be aweary of the sun | And wish th'estate o'th'world were now undone" (5.5.48–9).[84]

Despite its setting in a Christian Scotland, *Macbeth* seems hardly more Christian a play than *King Lear*. In fact, Shakespeare thoroughly expunges the explicitly Christian material from Holinshed's account: Duncan at his prayers, Macbeth's reform of the Church, getting priests to "attend their divine service according to their vocations," the bishops' role in the history of King Duff. There are apparently no bishops or priests in *Macbeth*, as there seems to be no Scottish church. And, though characters do mention God at several points, no one prays. Shakespeare does include the healing touch of Edward the Confessor, described by Malcolm as "most miraculous work," who also ascribes to him a "heavenly gift of prophecy" (4.3.149, 159). England's king may have had a kind of divinity (perhaps in an obligatory nod to James I?), but Scotland's kings apparently had no such gifts. Shakespeare's dechristianizing of Scotland goes along with Macbeth's critique of Christian time, with its sense of a specific future time when Christ will come again and "time should be no more" (Rev. 10:6). In Macbeth, on the contrary, time goes on, "tomorrow, and tomorrow, and tomorrow," and, despite the succession of one king by another, there seems "no new thing under the sun" (Eccles. 1:9).

It is significant that Shakespeare explores both conceptions of time— the teleological Christian salvation history and the endlessly empty cycles of Ecclesiastes—in terms of biblical allusion. It has been argued that Ecclesiastes provides a "critique of the wisdom tradition" within it, crucially contradicting the secure moral and providential perspective of more orthodox wisdom books like Proverbs and Ecclesiasticus.[85] (Job does too.) Ecclesiastes has this potentially subversive function within the

---

[84] Shaheen (641) suggests a possible reference to the Geneva note to Ps. 127, "He sheweth that the whole estate of the worlde...standeth by Gods mere providence," but the decay of the "estate of the world" is a commonplace in contemporary literature, especially of an apocalyptic sort.

[85] Katharine J. Dell, "Ecclesiastes as Wisdom: Consulting Early Interpreters," *Vetus Testamentum*, 44/3 (1994), 301–29, 303.

Jewish tradition, as well as in the context of the Christian Bible. The Bible provides plenty of support for the role of divine providence in shaping history, and for a final justice that will ultimately punish the wicked and reward the good. There are many voices in the Bible, however, and at least some of them raise serious questions about whether God really is in control, or cares, whether good will triumph over evil, and whether time will have an end. Some of these voices are ventriloquized in *Macbeth*.

8
The Patience of Lear: *King Lear* and Job

Humans have always suffered, but not all humans have suffered equally or at the same time, and suffering has probably never aligned perfectly with deserving, with only the wicked suffering, and in just proportion to their wickedness. For millennia, then, humans asked the same questions: "Why me? What have I done to deserve this?" A Christian believer, or any person of faith who believes in a good and just God by whose Providence all things are governed, may well expect an answer. For such a person there is in fact someone—God—who ought to know why anyone suffers. The question "Why me?" demands an answer in a way it need not for the nonbeliever. If God is indeed good and just, and if indeed he governs all things, then everything happens for a reason. And even if we can make no sense of our suffering, it must be a part of God's inscrutable plan that we simply cannot comprehend. To think otherwise is to call into question some aspect of God: his goodness, his justice, his power, or his very existence. This is why innocent suffering (and its converse, the prosperity of the wicked) is one of the critical theological problems.

Shakespeare's *King Lear* represents this problem in dramatic form. Samuel Johnson found the play disturbing for just this reason:

A play in which the wicked prosper, and the virtuous miscarry, may doubtless be good, because it is a just representation of the common events of human life; but, since all reasonable beings naturally love justice, I cannot easily be persuaded that the observation of justice makes a play worse; or that, if other excellencies are equal, the audience will not always rise better pleased from the final triumph of persecuted virtue.[1]

Johnson's eighteenth-century contemporaries clearly agreed, since they preferred Nahum Tate's happy-ending *King Lear* to Shakespeare's original. But Tate's version and Johnson's ideal "pleasant" tragedy avoid the essential questions about God's justice posed by *King Lear*, which even Johnson

---

[1] Cited in the New Variorum *King Lear*, ed. H. Howard Furness (Philadelphia: J. B. Lippincott & Co., 1880), 419.

recognized was a "just representation of the common events in human life." As Lear asks after Cordelia, the most innocent of the play's sufferers, has died, "Why should a dog, a horse, a rat have life | And thou no breath at all?" (5.3.305–6). Johnson records that, when he first read *King Lear*, he was "so shocked by *Cordelia's* death, that I know not whether I ever endured to read again the last scenes of the play till I undertook to revise them as an editor."[2]

Shakespeare's unpleasant ending was a deliberate choice, since he departed in this from his major sources. The anonymous play *The True Chronicle History of King Leir*, Shakespeare's most direct source for the Lear plot, ends differently: the wicked daughters and their husbands are defeated and driven off by the King of Gallia, and he and Cordella (*sic*) have the rule of England bestowed upon them by a grateful, loving (and living) Leir. Cordeilla (her name, like Lear's, has various spellings) does die in Geoffrey of Monmouth's account, but only years after the events recounted in the plays. As in the chronicle play, she and the King of Gaul defeat her sisters and brothers-in-law, and they return to England with Leir. He has three happy years before dying of old age, and Cordeilla continues to reign in peace. She does die badly, but only in a later episode, when she is taken prisoner by her sisters' sons and hangs herself in prison (an act of stoic heroism, quite different from her enforced and pointless hanging in Shakespeare). Holinshed tells essentially the same story, as do *The Mirrour for Magistrates* and Spenser's *Faerie Queene*. Why then does Shakespeare reject all the historical accounts in favor of an ending so much more bleak? An audience familiar with one of the other accounts of the story might well have wondered with Kent: "Is this the promised end?" (5.3.261).

To explore this question, it is useful to turn to another of Shakespeare's sources, the Book of Job. The comparison of Shakespeare's *King Lear* and the biblical Book of Job has become a critical commonplace. As early as 1949, G. Wilson Knight wrote that "*King Lear* is analogous to the Book of Job," but left the details of the analogy to be sketched out a decade later by John Holloway (*The Story of the Night*, 1961).[3] After remarking that the parallel between the two works "has seldom received much attention," Holloway notes a number of verbal points of contact and then concludes that the resemblance lies in the theme of patience in adversity: the protracted suffering of Lear derives from the prolonged

---

[2] Samuel Johnson, *Johnson on Shakespeare*, ed. Walter Raleigh (London: Oxford University Press, 1908; repr. 1952), 161–2.
[3] G. Wilson Knight, "The *Lear* Universe," in *The Wheel of Fire: Interpretations of Shakespearian Tragedy* (London: Methuen, 1930; repr. 1964), 191.

suffering of Job and his discussion of it with his friends.[4] By 1990, Arthur Kirsch could write that "the depiction of suffering in the play has often been compared to that in the Book of Job."[5] As well as Holloway, Kirsch cites Rosalie Colie's 1974 essay "The Energies of Endurance: Biblical Echo in *King Lear*," but he might have added others: W. R. Elton (King Lear *and the Gods*, 1966), for instance, and Kenneth Muir, who in 1984 went so far as to argue that "there is no doubt that Job was much in his mind while Shakespeare was writing *King Lear*."[6] More recent and extended discussions of Lear and Job include chapters in Steven Marx's *Shakespeare and the Bible* (2000) and Kenneth Gross's *Shakespeare's Noise* (2001) as well as Robert Pack's "King Lear and the Book of Job: Betrayal and Nothingness." Although it has developed considerably since the Second World War, the history of this idea may in fact pre-date the twentieth century. Charles Lamb wrote of Nahum Tate, author of the famous "Hollywood ending" revision of *King Lear* (Stanley Cavell's term), he "has put his hook into the nostrils of this Leviathan, for Garrick and his followers, the showmen of the scene, to draw the mighty beast about more easily."[7] The metaphor alludes to Job (in which God boasts that he can draw Leviathan with a hook).

Whenever it was first noted, however, the relationship between Job and *King Lear* is by now a familiar one. Yet the basic knowledge of *Lear*'s link to Job has been relatively undeveloped. For instance, Colie analyzes perceptively a number of important biblical allusions, but does not go beyond a few key passages, Gross restricts his discussion to the matter of cursing, and Marx, whose treatment is in some ways the most extensive, largely eschews critical analysis, reading the two books "in tandem" in a peculiar effort to produce a kind of contemporary midrash.[8] Pack's treatment

---

[4] John Holloway, *The Story of the Night: Studies in Shakespeare's Major Tragedies* (London: Routledge & Kegan Paul, 1961), 85.

[5] Arthur Kirsch, *The Passions of Shakespeare's Tragic Heroes* (Charlottesville, VA, and London: University Press of Virginia, 1990), 105.

[6] Rosalie L. Colie, "The Energies of Endurance: Biblical Echo in *King Lear*," in Colie and F. T. Flahiff (eds), *Some Facets of* King Lear: *Essays in Prismatic Criticism* (Toronto: University of Toronto Press, 1974), 117–44; W. R. Elton, King Lear *and the Gods* (San Marino, CA: Huntington Library, 1966), esp. 30, 68, 263; Kenneth Muir (ed.), King Lear: *Critical Essays* (New York and London: Garland Publishing, 1984), 289. John D. Rosenberg, in "Lear and his Comforters" (*Essays in Criticism*, 16/2 [1966], 135–46), casts *King Lear's* neo-Christian critics themselves in the role of Job's wishful-thinking but naive friends.

[7] Charles Lamb, cited in the New Variorum *King Lear*, ed. Furness, 421. Stanley Cavell, *Disowning Knowledge in Six Plays of Shakespeare* (Cambridge: Cambridge University Press, 1987), 68.

[8] Steven Marx, *Shakespeare and the Bible* (Oxford and New York: Oxford University Press, 2000), 59.

(from the perspective of a practicing poet), though intriguing, is entirely thematic.[9] As a result, a number of questions remain unasked and unanswered, questions of the sort posed throughout this book: Why did Shakespeare turn to the Book of Job when writing *King Lear*? What were his sources for the Job story and its interpretation? What place did Job have in Shakespeare's culture in the early years of the seventeenth century? And, finally, how does an awareness of *King Lear*'s relationship to Job affect our understanding of the play?

JOB AND LEAR: PREVIOUS PERFORMANCES

Despite the lack of conclusive evidence (we cannot ask Shakespeare himself), it is nevertheless possible to suggest how he might have arrived at the idea of drawing together the stories of Lear and Job. Theater history is often conjectural, because there is so much that scholars cannot know: when particular plays were written and performed, who performed them, certainly who saw them. Such conjecture must not be substituted for fact, but in the absence of facts it can still sometimes be useful and suggestive. Although they still disagree on particular points, scholars generally accept that Shakespeare knew the anonymous *The True Chronicle History of King Leir*, and that it was his principal source for his play. Its title is nearly identical to that of Shakespeare's 1608 Quarto, it was printed in 1605, and so it may have been read by Shakespeare before he wrote his own version; but it is possible that he already knew the anonymous play from an earlier performance.[10] When *King Leir* was played by the Queen's Men at the Rose in 1594, Shakespeare was active in the London theater, and it is reasonable to think he saw the play. This supposition is made more likely by arguments that Shakespeare had himself been a Queen's Man sometime during his mysterious "missing years," 1584–92.[11]

Yet Shakespeare's is the only version of the Lear story that alludes to Job. Although there were numerous Job plays in France, Germany, Spain, and Italy throughout the Middle Ages and Renaissance, his story seems not to have caught on similarly in England, despite the fact that there

---

[9] Robert Pack, "King Lear and the Book of Job: Betrayal and Nothingness," in *Willing to Choose: Volition and Storytelling in Shakespeare's Major Plays* (Sandpoint, ID: Lost Horse Press, 2007), 127–47. The essay was originally published in 1991.
[10] Richard Knowles, "How Shakespeare Knew *King Leir*," *SS* 55 (2002), 12–35; W. W. Greg, Review of *The Chronicle History of King Leir: The Original of Shakespeare's King Lear* by Sidney Lee, *Modern Language Review*, 5/4 (1910), 515–19.
[11] Scott McMillin and Sally-Beth MacLean, *The Queen's Men and their Plays* (Cambridge: Cambridge University Press, 1998), 160–6.

were plenty of other biblical dramas.[12] Nevertheless, there was apparently at least one Job play staged in sixteenth-century London: Richard Greene's *The History or Tragedy of Job*. The play has not survived, but it was entered in the Stationers' Register in 1594, the same year in which the anonymous *King Leir* was played at the Rose.[13] It has been suggested that Greene's Job might have been played by the Admiral's Men, who were staging another biblical drama, George Peele's *David and Bethsabe*, and that Ned Alleyn might have played both leading parts, Job and David.[14] It is also possible, however, that *Job* was a Queen's Men's play, since they presented other plays by Greene, including his *Friar Bacon and Friar Bungay* in 1594. If Greene wrote Job for the Queen's Men, and it was staged in 1594, then the same company was playing both *Job* and *King Leir*, and it is possible, moreover, that the two leading roles were played by the same actor. Even if this was not the case, Greene's *Job* and *King Leir* were being performed about the same time in London. If Shakespeare saw both plays, this may have given him the germ of the idea for a play in which these two figures were drawn into parallel.

Further inspiration for using the Job story to add complexity to his *King Lear* must have come from a play that Shakespeare certainly knew, Christopher Marlowe's *The Jew of Malta*. Written sometime between 1589 and 1592, *The Jew of Malta* was a major hit; it was performed seventeen times between 1592 and 1593 and was still popular in 1594, when it was entered in the Stationers' Register.[15] As mentioned above in Chapter 3, the play's allusions to Job are overt: the rich Jew, Barabas, having had his goods seized by the Christian rulers of Malta, curses his enemies, but is counseled to "be patient" by three friends, one of whom is named Temainte, which has been read as a variant of the tribe of Job's friend Eliphaz the Temanite (the tribe of Teman were Edomites, Gen. 36:11).[16] One of them urges, "Yet brother Barabas remember Job" (1.2.180). Barabas then launches into a comparison of himself to Job (concluding that he himself had been far richer than Job and is therefore more afflicted by his losses). Like Job, Barabas also curses his "fatall birth-day" and dismisses his friends (1.2.192). Marlowe's extraordinarily wicked Barabas is hardly a mirror of the perfect and upright Job, and Marlowe's allusive

---

[12] Leonard Siger, "The Image of Job in the Renaissance," Ph.D. diss (Johns Hopkins University, 1960), 230–53.
[13] Annaliese Connolly, "Peele's *David and Bethsabe*: Reconsidering Biblical Drama of the Long 1590s," *EMLS* Special Issue 16 (October 2007) 9.1–19.
[14] Connolly, "Peele's *David and Bethsabe*," para. 8.
[15] Roma Gill (ed.), *The Jew of Malta*, in *The Complete Works of Christopher Marlowe* (Oxford: Clarendon Press, 1995), iv, pp. xvi–xvii.
[16] 1.2.169, in Gill, ed. All citations are from this edition.

parallel is "cited in order to present Barabas as the opposite, as an Anti-Job, characterized by his *impatience* (l. 497), and choosing the road, not of Christian patience, but of its opposite, revenge."[17] As will be discussed below, Job himself is hardly patient, despite his reputation, but the idea of writing a play about an "Anti-Job" seems to have attracted Shakespeare.

A CONSTELLATION OF ALLUSIONS

The more one reads in Job, the likelier it seems that, as Muir suggested, Shakespeare had this book in mind and ear as he wrote *King Lear*. One of the play's more obvious allusions to the Book of Job (noted by Shaheen, Marx, Colie, and Holloway) is Gloucester's comment on the heath, when he and the old man leading him first encounter "Blind Tom," that he saw a person in the storm "Which made me think a man a worm" (4.1.35).[18] Although the Bible contains other comparisons of worms and men ("I am a worm and no man," for instance, in Psalm 22:6), such self-loathing worm references are particularly prominent in Job. For instance, Job's friend Bildad the Shuhite says that, if even the stars are unclean in God's eyes, then "How muche more man, a worme, even the sonne of man, which is but a worme?" (Job 25:6). Earlier in the book, Job himself states, "I shal say to corruption, Thou art my father, and to the worme, thou art my mother and my sister" (Job 17:14).

Colie cites several other allusions to Job, including Kent's remark in the stocks that "a good man's fortune may grow out at the heels" (2.2.157). (The expression "out at heels" means "worn out," so Kent is playing on both his "worn out" fortune and his actual heels, which are sticking out of the stocks and therefore the mark of his condition.) Similarly, Job complains to God that, figuratively speaking, "Thou puttest my feet also in the stockes, and lokest narrowly unto all my paths, and makest the printe thereof in the heeles of my fete" (Job 13:27).[19] Furthermore, when Lear is

---

[17] G. K. Hunter, "The Theology of Marlowe's *The Jew of Malta*," *Journal of the Warburg and Courtauld Institutes*, 27 (1964), 211–40, 219.

[18] More has been written about the different textual states of *King Lear* than about those of any of Shakespeare's other plays (see, e.g., Gary Taylor and Michael Warren (eds), *The Division of the Kingdoms: Shakespeare's Two Versions of* King Lear [Oxford: Clarendon Press, 1983]). The arguments for two entirely distinct and authorial versions of the play are not entirely convincing and, for the purposes of this article, not especially relevant. Passages present in only one or other version (Q and F) will be noted.

[19] The figure of Kent in stocks does have other possible sources, including Geoffrey Whitney's emblem on the "golden shackles" of courtly life, but these are not mutually incompatible. See Geoffrey Whitney, "*Aurea compedes*," in *A Choice of Emblemes and Other Devises* (Leyden: In the house of Christopher Plantyn by Francis Raphelengius, 1586), 202. The figure of a courtier in stocks obviously resembles *King Lear* 2.2, though Kent does not

out on the heath, he faces, according to the anonymous gentleman Kent encounters, a

> night wherein the cub-drawn bear would couch,
> The lion and the belly-pinched wolf
> Keep their fur dry... (3.1.12–14)[20]

Likewise, Elihu says in Job that, when God raises a storm, "Then the beasts go into the denne, and remaine in their places" (Job 37:8). Lear is also "a comrade to the wolf and owl" (2.2.399), just as Job is the "brother to the dragons, and a companion to the ostriches" (Job 30:29).[21] The allusion is perceptible even though the specific animals are changed. Colie's study is not exhaustive, however. Similarly, Job can also be heard behind Gloucester's fatalistic statement that "a man may rot even here" (5.2.8). Job says of people like himself who are persecuted by God: "Suche one consumeth like a roten thing" (33:28). Tellingly, this verse from Job immediately follows Job's statement about the stocks. The second half of this verse—"and as a garment that is motheaten"—also parallels *King Lear*, with its complex thematic treatment of clothing and nakedness.[22]

The intertextual relationship between Job and *King Lear* is a complicated one, mediated not just by overt allusions but also by additional biblical passages, and by non-biblical books that cite or comment on Job. As always, Shakespeare's reading practice corresponds with that described by T. Grashop in some Geneva Bibles and by George Herbert in "The H. Scriptures II," as discussed in Chapter 3. Herbert likens this approach to reading the Bible to a "constellation," in which different "stars" (passages) combine to make one bright shining, and meaningful, whole. In the case of Job, the most obvious such "motion" a reader would make is to the Epistle of James, which cites Job in its discussion of patience, the only other explicit biblical reference to Job being a passing mention in Ezekiel. The Geneva preface to Job ends by noting, "Ezekiel commendeth Job as a just man, Ezek. 14,14, and James setteth out his pacience for an example, Jam. 5,11." If the "motional" reading process Herbert described is applied to *King Lear*, one can perceive an allusive "constellation" in Gloucester's

---

actually look like a courtier in the scene, and the motto ("golden shackles") is not appropriate to the play. In the Arden[3] *King Lear* (note to 2.2.153–71), Foakes cites Maynard Mack's comment that Kent in the stocks is emblematic of "Virtue Locked Out," but neither critic cites an actual emblem.

[20] These lines are not in the Folio text.
[21] Colie, "Energies of Endurance," 130, 131.
[22] See Maurice Charney, "'We Put Fresh Garments on Him': Nakedness and Clothes in *King Lear*," in Colie and Flahiff (eds), *Some Facets*, 77–88.

and Job's aforementioned comments on rotting, Job's motheaten garment, and James's condemnation of rich men:

Go to now, ye riche men: wepe and howle for your miseries that shal come upon you. Your riches are corrupt: and your garments are motheaten. (James 5:1–2)

Furthermore, as does James, Lear condemns the rich using the metaphor of clothing:

> Thorough tatter'd clothes small vices do appear;
> Robes and furr'd gowns hide all. (4.6.166–7)

Moreover, Lear's "howl, howl, howl" (and another "howl" in the Quarto [5.3.255]) also echoes James's "wepe and howle for your miseries."[23]

There are further lights in the intertextual "constellation" linking *King Lear* and Job. *King Lear* echoes not only Job and James but also *The Sermons on Job* by John Calvin. They were translated into English by Arthur Golding, the translator of one of Shakespeare's most-used sources, Ovid's *Metamorphoses* (1565–7). Golding's translation of *The Sermons on Job* appeared in London in 1574 and sold well: there were five more editions in the next decade. At least two London parishes, St Botolph without Bishopsgate and St Andrew Holborn, purchased copies of Calvin's *Sermons* for the use of parishioners.[24]

Calvin's *Sermons* provided Shakespeare with some specific language for *King Lear* and seems to have influenced his choice of certain prevalent themes and imagery. In chapter 32 of Job, for instance, the brash, young Elihu condemns Job's three old friends, "because they colde not finde an answer, and yet condemned Job" (Job 32:3). In his commentary on this section, in which he develops the debate between youth and age, Calvin paraphrases Isaiah, who writes that, if the elderly do not act in the fear of God, "the aged shall not see any whit, and ... the wise shal become brutish and utterly dul." Calvin continues: "Now if God doe blinde the olde men, greate men, and such as are in authoritie after that sorte: what shall become of them (I pray you) if God give them not his holy spirite?"[25] Shakespeare's answer is that they end up alone and

---

[23] There is analogous howling in Isaiah, Jeremiah, and other prophets.
[24] Fiona Kisby, "Books in London Parish Churches before 1603: Some Preliminary Observations," in Caroline M. Barron and Jenny Stratford (eds), *The Church and Learning in Later Medieval Society: Essays in Honour of R. B. Dobson*, Proceedings of the 1999 Harlaxton Symposium (Donington: SHAUN TYAS, 2002), 305–26, 322–33.
[25] *The Sermons of M. John Calvin, upon the Booke of Job*, trans. Arthur Golding (London: [Henry Bynneman for] Lucas Harison and George Byshop [1574]), 620. On Elihu, Susan Schreiner points out that Calvin clearly identified with him, and argued that his words were not included in the criticism God directs at the friends in Job 42:7. Susan Schreiner, "Calvin as an Interpreter of Job," in Donald K. McKim (ed.), *Calvin and the Bible* (Cambridge: Cambridge University Press, 2006), 68–72.

suffering on the heath, like Gloucester and Lear. Blindness is a recurrent theme in the *Sermons on Job*, but Calvin also writes many times of God's stripping men naked: "I say, it becommeth us too suffer God too strippe us out of all, even to our bare and naked skynne, and to prepare oure selves to returne to our grave in the same state."[26] Lear, stripped of almost everything himself, sees the more literally "bare and naked" Edgar and comes to a conclusion similar to Calvin's: "Why, thou wert better in a grave than to answer with thy uncovered body this extremity of the skies. Is man no more than this?" (3.4.99–104). In a further image of nakedness, Job responds to the news that his children are dead: "Naked came I out of my mothers wombe, and naked shal I returne thether" (Job 1:21). When the blinded Gloucester and the mad Lear meet again on the heath, Lear similarly reminds Gloucester of the experience of leaving the womb:

> We came crying hither:
> Thou knowst the first time that we smell the air
> We wawl and cry. (4.6.174–5)

Calvin's ideas and imagery from his 101st sermon (on Job 27:19–28:9) underpin Lear's recognition scene with Edgar as Poor Tom:

Truely there are many even of the smallest and lowest things, which wee cannot conceyve, except God give us abilitie: according as wee see howe there are many simple idiotes (as man terme them) which know no more than brute beastes. Such manner of folke are set of God before our eyes as looking glasses, too humble us withall. When we see a starke idiot that hath no wit nor reason, it behoveth us to looke well upon him, for he is a mirror of our nature.[27]

Lear's encounter with Edgar works this way, as does his sympathy with the suffering of his Fool (both Tom and the Fool being "starke idiots" in their different ways). Lear turns from these particular "mirrours" to consider humanity in general, thinking of all the "poor, naked wretches" out in the storm, and recognizing that "I have ta'en too little care of this" (3.4.28, 32–3). In a later Job sermon, Calvin continues his meditation on how every man needs to consider the "starke idiot":

...but yet notwythstanding though he be a King, he must have brotherhood with the poorest shepeherds and neatherds in the world, except hee can put off his owne nature. And out of doubt, as for the cheefe and excellentest thing a king hathe in him, that is to say, manhood: hath not the shepehearde it aswell as hee?[28]

---

[26] *Sermons of Master John Calvin*, 33.
[27] *Sermons of Master John Calvin*, 421.
[28] *Sermons of Master John Calvin*, 554.

Lear is of course a king, as Job is not, and it is precisely his kinship with the poor that he finally recognizes in his meeting with Poor Tom. Lear longs to "put off his owne nature," since "Man's nature cannot carry | Th'affliction, nor the fear" of the storm (the one in his mind as well as the one on the heath). All he can actually "put off" are his clothes: "Off, off, you lendings: come, unbutton here" (3.2.48–9; 3.4.106–7). He recognizes the link between himself and Edgar that Calvin notes—his "manhood"—realizing that "man is no more than this":

> Thou ow'st the worm no silk, the beast no hide, the sheep no wool, the cat no perfume. Ha? Here's three on's us are sophisticated; thou art the thing itself. Unaccommodated man is no more but such a poor, bare, forked animal as thou art. (3.4.101–6)

But such a recognition seems beyond Lear's power to retain, and he continues to struggle against the "mortality" of which his hand smells, as he tells the blind Gloucester (4.6.129).

In addition to Golding's Calvin, there is another possible source for this speech by Lear in a sixteenth-century commentary on rejecting worldly goods that makes liberal reference to Job. The critical consensus has been that Lear's catalogue of animal products derives from Montaigne's essay "An Apologie of *Raymond Sebonde*":

> Miserable man; whom if you consider well what is he?...Truly, when I consider man all naked...and view his defects, his natural subjection, and manifold imperfections; I find we have had much more reason to hide and cover our nakedness, than any creature else. We may be excused for borrowing those [i.e., from those creatures] which nature had therein favored more than us, with their beauties to adorn us, and under their spoiles of wool, of haire, of feathers, and of silks to shroud us.[29]

John Florio's translation of Montaigne was published in 1603, so Shakespeare could have read it. But a similar passage appears in Edmund Bunny's protestantized version of Robert Parsons's *A Book of Christian Exercise*, which had already been immensely popular for twenty years:

> What vanitie is it then for us, to be so curious in apparel, and to take such pride therin, as we do? We rob and spoil al creatures almost in the world, to cover our

---

[29] *The Essayes of Michael Lord of Montaigne, Translated by John Florio*, 3 vols (London and Toronto: J. M. Dent; New York: E. P. Dutton, 1921), ii. 169, 181. The editorial interpolation is from *King Lear*, ed. Foakes, note to 3.4.101–3. On the relationship between Shakespeare and Montaigne, see Leo Salingar, "King Lear, Montaigne and Harsnett," in *Dramatic Form in Shakespeare and the Jacobeans* (Cambridge: Cambridge University Press, 1986), 107–39. Jonathan Bate also argues for the influence of Montaigne in this passage: *Soul of the Age: A Biography of the Mind of William Shakespeare* (New York: Random House, 2009), 365–6.

baks, and to adorn our bodies withal. From one, we take his wool: from another, his skin: from another, his fur: and from some other, their very excrements; as the silk, which is nothing els, but the excrements of woorms.[30]

The list of materials for clothing is similar in both Montaigne and Parsons, and perhaps simply makes sense in terms of contemporary garments, but, while Montaigne's list includes silk and wool, as Lear's does, it also includes feathers, which Lear's does not, and Parsons's "skin" is closer to Lear's "hide" than Montaigne's "haire." Furthermore, the syntax in Parsons is closer to Shakespeare's, stringing together clauses rather than just the nouns, as in Montaigne. Finally, the context in Parsons is telling. Seven pages earlier,[31] Parsons cites Job's "I said unto rottenness, thou art my father: and unto worms, you are my mother and sisters" (Job 17:14), so the reader would probably still have Job's worms in mind while reading about silk as the excrement of worms.

Parsons's immediate use for this quotation, however, is to support an argument against the vanity of nobility, the very argument Lear has come to in meeting Poor Tom: "He that wil behold the gentrie of his ancestors: let him look into their graves, and see whether Job saith truly or no" (that is, that rottenness is his father, worms his mother and sisters).[32] There follows, in the *Christian Exercise*, a discussion of fools, based on Paul's advice in 1 Corinthians that "The wisdom of this world is folly with God," and then a section on the vanity of beauty, concluding that "yet quickly commeth on old age, which riveleth the skin, draweth in the eies, setteth out the teeth, and so disfigureth the whole visage."[33] Then follows the aforementioned section on apparel, which begins by focusing on the lesson offered by a beggar, in appearance like Poor Tom:

---

[30] Robert Parsons, *A Booke of Christian Exercise... by R. P.* [Robert Parsons]. *Perused and accompanied now with a Treatise tending to Pacification: by Edm. Bunny* (London: N. Newton, and A. Hatfield, for John Wight, 1584), 293. All further citations will be from this edition, though the passages cited are identical in Parsons's *The First Book of Christian Exercise* ([Rouen], 1582). The similarity between these passages had been noted in passing in a little known essay by Christopher Devlin, "Hamlet's Divinity" (in *Hamlet's Divinity and Other Essays*, intro. C. V. Wedgwood [London: Rupert Hart-Davis, 1963], 41). On the curious history of Parsons's book, lightly protestantized by Bunny (the book was not polemically "Catholic" to begin with), see Robert McNulty, "The Protestant Version of Robert Parsons's *The First Booke of the Christian Exercise*," *HLQ* 22/4 (1959), 271–300. More recently, Brad Gregory argues that Bunny's adaptation of Parsons' was in fact more polemical than has been realized. See "The 'True and Zealouse Seruice of God': Robert Parsons, Edmund Bunny, and 'The First Booke of the Christian Exercise,'" *The Journal of Ecclesiastical History* 45/2 (1994), 231–69. A superb critical edition of Parsons's original edition has been edited by Victor Houliston, *Robert Persons SJ, The Christian Directory (1582)* (Leiden, Boston, and Cologne: Brill, 1998).

[31] Parsons, *A Booke of Christian Exercise*, 286.
[32] Parsons, *A Booke of Christian Exercise*, 286.
[33] Parsons, *A Booke of Christian Exercise*, 291.

If Adam had never fallen: we had never used apparel: for that apparel was devised to cover our shame of nakedness, and other infirmities contracted by that fal. Wherefore, we that take pride and glorie in apparel, do as much as if a begger should glorie and take pride of the old clouts that do cover his sores.[34]

Shakespeare seems to have Parsons in mind when writing Lear's speech to his daughters about nature, need, and clothing:

> Our basest beggars
> Are in the poorest thing superfluous;
> Allow not nature more than nature needs,
> Man's life is cheap as beast's. Thou art a Lady;
> If only to go warm were gorgeous,
> Why, nature needs not what thou gorgeous wear'st,
> Which scarcely keeps thee warm. (2.2.453–9)

Later, on the page following the passage on excrements, Parsons cites James 5:1–3 ("Now go to, you rich men: weep, and howl your miseries" etc.), and, on the same page, Job 1:21 ("We came in naked unto this world, and naked we must foorth again"), and Job 27:19–21 ("When the rich man dieth he shal take nothing with him, but shal close up his eies, and find nothing. Povertie shal lay hands upon him, and a tempest shal oppresse him in the night: a burning wind shal take him away, and a whirl wind shal snatch him from his place").

Several pages further on, Parsons turns his thoughts to "concupiscence of the flesh," and again cites several passages from Job, as well as the apocryphal book of Tobit. Tobit is a righteous Jew living in exile in Nineveh who is struck blind by bird droppings, which leads him to pray for death (see Fig. 8.1). His son, Tobias, after a long adventure, aided by the archangel Raphael, restores his father's sight with the gall of a fish. Parsons writes,

And old Tobias insinuateth yet another cause, when he saith; *What joy can I have or receive, seeing I sit heer in darknes?* Speaking literally of his corporal blindnes, but yet leaving it also to be understood of spiritual and internal darknes.[35]

Parsons's citation of Job and Tobias (or Tobit, as he is named in the Geneva Bible) together is no accident: the two figures were often linked as parallel exemplars of patient and righteous suffering, as in a poem by Robert Henryson (mixing up, as was common, the names of Tobit and Tobias):

---

[34] Parsons, *A Booke of Christian Exercise*, 292.
[35] Parsons, *A Booke of Christian Exercise*, 299.

Fig. 8.1. The apocryphal book of Tobit was extremely popular in the Renaissance, sung in ballads and cited even in the Book of Common Prayer. The pious Tobit was blinded by sparrows' droppings but then restored to sight by his son, Tobias, with the aid of the archangel Raphael and the gall of a fish. ("Tobit blinded by sparrow's droppings"; Dirk Volkertsz in *The Illustrated Bartsch*, lv.) © The Trustees of the British Museum.

> Job was moist riche, in writ we find,
> Thobe moist full of cheritie—
> Job wox peur and Thoby blynd,
> Baith temptit with adversitie:
> Sen blindes wes infirmitie,
> And povertie was naturall,
> Thairfoir in patience baith he and he
> Obeid and thankit God of all.[36]

Parsons's (or Henryson's) pairing of Job and Tobit, the beggar and the blind man, two biblical patterns of patience, is suggestive of Shakespeare's Lear and Gloucester (also of Poor Tom and Gloucester), though neither can necessarily be proven to be a direct source.[37]

If we return to Calvin's *Sermons on Job*, the Gloucester subplot contains further echoes of Golding's dedicatory epistle. For example, Gloucester blames the pernicious astrological influence of the "late eclipses of the sun and moon" for bringing about the conflicts he has witnessed:

Love cools, friendship falls off, brothers divide: in cities, mutinies; in countries, discord; in palaces, treason; and the bond cracked 'twixt son and father. This villain of mine comes under the prediction—there's son against father. The King falls from bias of nature—there's father against child. (1.2.106–12)

But the skeptical Edmund has a different perspective on Nature and privately dismisses his father's astrology as an "admirable evasion of whoremaster man":

This is the excellent foppery of the world, that when we are sick in fortune, often the surfeits of our own behaviour, we make guilty of our disasters the sun, the moon and the stars, as if we were villains on necessity, fools by heavenly compulsion, knaves, thieves and treachers by spherical predominance; drunkards, liars and adulterers by an enforced obedience of planetary influence; and all that we are evil in by a divine thrusting on. (1.2.118–26)

On the same subject, and in a passage that sounds similar to Edmund's critique, Golding criticizes those who, like Job, complain that their life is hard but who, unlike Job, search for some explanation besides God's will:

Do we look up to the hand that smiteth us? do wee consider the causes why they be layd upon us?...wee eyther...impute them to the influence of the

---

[36] Robert Henryson, "The Abbey Walk," ll.17–24, in *The Poems of Robert Henryson*, ed. Denton Fox (Oxford: Clarendon Press, 1981), 157.

[37] The more immediate source of King Lear's subplot is the story of the Paphlagonian King from Sidney's *Arcadia*, which has been recognized since at least Furness's 1880 Variorum edition. On the rich iconographic history that lies behind both Shakespeare's Gloucester and Sidney's Paphlagonian King, see Kahren Jones Hellerstedt, "The Blind Man and his Guide in Netherlandish Painting," *Simiolus*, 13/3–4 (1983), 163–81.

skies, or father them upon fortune, or attribute them unto men, or write them upon the unhappinesse of the tyme, or tie them to the place, or finally stand amazed at the afflictions themselves, surmizing any thing rather than the truthe, as who should say that God eyther could not or would not governe all things by his onely will and providence, which is as much as to denie that there is any God at all.[38]

Golding here identifies the perspectives of both Gloucester and Edmund. In Golding's interpretation of Calvin, however, both characters should be condemned: Gloucester for his superstitious belief in the "influence of the skies," and Edmund for denying there is "any God at all."[39] Shakespeare thus draws on a variety of sources—Job, James, Calvin, Golding, and Parsons—in fashioning his exploration of human suffering and providential justice.

THE PATTERN OF PATIENCE

Shakespeare's "constellation" of allusions to Job and its interpreters serves primarily to provide the audience with a familiar and authoritative "pattern of patience"—patience in its root sense of "suffering" (from the Latin *patiens* and ultimately *patior*, "to suffer"). Perhaps the clearest allusion to Job in *King Lear* is again "constellated" with Golding's Calvin and the Epistle of James. James urges his readers to be patient and cites the model of Job:

Behold we count them blessed which endure. Ye have heard of the pacience of Job, and have knowen what end the Lord made. For the Lord is verie pitiful and merciful. (James 5:11)

Shaheen hears James's statement behind Lear's cry that "I will be the pattern of all patience" (3.2.37).[40] But Shakespeare's specific wording is closer to Golding's dedication in Calvin's *Sermons*, in which Golding describes Job as "a perfect patern of patience."[41] (Calvin himself writes that "Job shoulde be set foorth unto us as a pattern," and that in him God has set us "a certaine portrayture of pacience."[42]

Lear may wish to be the "pattern of all patience," but the pattern had already been established for Shakespeare's audience by the proverbial

---

[38] *Sermons of Master John Calvin*, sig. aii.
[39] Elton describes and contextualizes both Gloucester's "pagan superstition" and Edmund's "pagan atheism." See King Lear *and the Gods*, chs 6 and 7.
[40] Shaheen, 611.
[41] *Sermons of Master John Calvin*, sig. A2ᵛ.
[42] *Sermons of Master John Calvin*, 27.

"patience of Job," a familiar idiom in early modern English.[43] Bartholomew Chappell, for instance, in his *Garden of Prudence* (1595), used the example of Job (along with David) to urge the rejection of worldy vanities and the patient acceptance of suffering:

> But if with want thou be opprest,
> if pinched eke with povertie,
> Let all by sufferance be redrest,
> when it shal please our God on hie,
> For *Job* by patience wan great praise,
> cruel *Pharoah* could not *David* daunt,
> By patient hope they both had ease,
> and al their foes could not once vaunt,
> Or say, loe here we have prevailed
> loe here is he, whom we subdued...[44]

As mentioned in Chapter 6, Falstaff makes humorous reference to Job's proverbial patience in Shakespeare's *Henry IV, Part 2*, admitting to the Lord Chief Justice, "I am as poor as Job, my lord, but not so patient" (1.2.101). A more conventional reference occurs in *The Conflict of Conscience* (1581), a "most lamentable Hystorie, of the desperation of Frauncis Spera, who forsooke the trueth of Gods Gospell, for feare of the losse of life and worldly goods" (long title), by Nathaniel Woodes, a Norwich vicar. Woodes interpreted Job's sufferings in the fashion made popular by Gregory the Great's *Moralia in Job*: whether Job deserved suffering is irrelevant, since suffering is a gift from God (and besides, he got everything back in the end):

> For trouble bring[s] forth pacience, from pacience dooth insue
> Experience, from experience Hope, of health the ankor true.
> Againe, oftimes, God doth provide, affliction for our gaine,
> As *Job* who after losse of goodes, had twice so much therefore:
> Sometime affliction is a meanes, to honor to attaine...[45]

Another straightforward reference to Job's patience occurs in Nicholas Breton's *The Soules immortall crowne consisting of seaven glorious graces* (1601; the fifth "grace" is entitled "The Praise of Patience"):

---

[43] See M. P. Tilley, *A Dictionary of the Proverbs in England in the Sixteenth and Seventeenth Centuries* (Ann Arbor: University of Michigan Press, 1950), J59.
[44] Bartholomew Chappell, *The Garden of Prudence* (London: Richard Johnes, 1595), sig. B2ʳ.
[45] Nathaniel Woodes, *An excellent new commedie intituled* [sic], *The conflict of conscience* (London: Richard Bradocke, 1581), 1.2.221–5 (sig. Biiʳ). On the title page, Woodes's "lamentable Hystorie" is actually announced as "An excellent new Commedie." On Gregory's *Moralia in Job*, see Susan E. Schreiner, *Where Shall Wisdom Be Found?: Calvin's Exegesis of Job from Medieval and Modern Perspectives* (Chicago and London: University of Chicago Press, 1994), ch. 1.

> By patience *David* had a Princely fame,
> And, *Job* his patience had a worthy praise:
> But Christ his patience hath a Glorious name,
> That ever lives to never ending daies.[46]

(Along with David, Job was traditionally interpreted as a type of Christ, which is significant for *King Lear*, as will be explained below.) Clearly, the virtue pre-eminently associated with Job in the sixteenth and seventeenth centuries was patience.

The virtue of patience is likewise prominent in *King Lear*. Lear's vow to be "the pattern of all patience" is one of six references to "patience," in addition to five references to other forms of the word, making it a keyword in the play. For example, Regan tells Lear, after he has complained about the indignity of his servant Gaius/Kent being in the stocks, "I pray you, sir, take patience" (2.4.327). Earlier, when Lear is railing against Goneril, Albany urges, "pray, sir, be patient" (1.4.254). For his own reasons, having more to do with staving off tears and madness than heeding his daughters, Lear himself desires to stay patient, saying (more to himself than anyone present) "I can be patient" and later calling, "you heavens, give me that patience, patience I need" (2.2.419, 460). Out on the heath, Kent (as Gaius) urges Lear to remember his promise that he "will be the pattern of all patience," saying, "Sir, where is the patience now | That you so oft have boasted to retain?" (3.6.57–8). In addition, characters other than Lear either demonstrate patience or are urged to do so. Before his deluded suicide attempt, Gloucester tells the gods that he will "shake patiently my great affliction off" (4.6.36). Gloucester seems to use "patience" in a sense of stoic suffering dispassionately born, though of course to commit suicide might well be considered an impatient act, as Edgar (disguised) reminds him, redefining the crucial term: "Bear free and patient thoughts" (4.6.80). Lear himself seconds Edgar's advice in the lines borrowed from Job cited above:

> Thou must be patient. We came crying hither:
> Thou knowst the first time that we smell the air
> We wawl and cry. (4.6.174–6)

By the final act, Albany's use of the word to Edmund is ironic: the long-scheming Edmund has been as patient (in waiting for the fruition of his plots and in "suffering" the consequences of bastardy) as anyone:

> Sir, by your patience,
> I hold you but a subject of this war,
> Not as a brother. (5.3.60–2)

---

[46] Nicholas Breton, *The Soules immortall crowne consisting of seaven glorious graces* (London: H. Lownes, 1601), [G2ᵛ].

Thus, Shakespeare connects Job and Lear through allusions involving patience. While Job proverbially is patient, however, Lear's patience is obviously lacking. On the other hand, it is important to realize that, despite the English proverb or James's Epistle, an attentive reader of Job must realize that Job is not that patient at all, a realization that troubled many early commentators, including Calvin.[47] The biblical Job does not go so far as to follow the advice of his wife, who tells him to "Blaspheme God and die," but he nevertheless curses the day he was born with an invective vehemence that rivals any of Lear's curses:

Let the daye perish, wherein I was borne, and the night when it was said, There is a manchild conceived.

Let that day be darkenes, and the shadowe of death staine it: let the cloude remaine upon it, and let them make it fearful as bitter day.

Let darkenes possesse that night, let it not be joined unto the dayes of the yere, nor let it come into the count of the monethes.

Yea, desolate be that night, and let no joye be in it. (Job 3:3–7)

In the Middle Ages, many retellings of the Job story, apparently disturbed by Job's intemperate passion, omitted his curses, as well as the colloquy with the three friends that follows.[48] The early modern Protestant attitude to passion was generally more accepting, thanks to various intellectual developments, and Job's outrage was not seen as necessarily blasphemous.[49] For instance, Samuel Rowlands used the example of Job both to counsel patience and to justify the open expression of grief by Mary at the foot of the Cross:

> If holy Job himselfe so patient bore,
> To give meeke care to many a grievous crosse,
> Destruction of his cattell, flockes, and store,
> Untill he heard his deerest childrens losse,
> And then his greefes extreamest did abound,
> Renting his garments, falling on the ground.
>
> Needs must (in mournfull sorrow's dire complaints)
> The blessed Virgin farre excell all other,
> What soule (with dolours ever so acquaints)

---

[47] See H. L. Ginsberg, "Job the Patient and Job the Impatient," *Conservative Judaism*, 21/3 (1967), 12–28.

[48] Siger, "Image of Job," 220 ff.

[49] On early modern attitudes to passion, in Erasmus and Luther as well as *King Lear*, see Richard Strier, "Against the Rule of Reason: Praise of Passion from Petrarch to Luther to Shakespeare to Herbert," in Gail Kern Paster et al. (eds), *Reading the Early Modern Passions: Essays in the Cultural History of Emotion* (Philadelphia: University of Pennsylvania Press, 2004), 23–42. Calvin, however, was as uncomfortable with passion as the Stoics, criticizing the excesses of both Job and David; see William Bouwsma, *John Calvin: A Sixteenth Century Portrait* (New York and Oxford: Oxford University Press, 1988), 94–6.

> As this most carefull comfort wanting Mother,
> To see her God, life, father, love and sonne,
> By bitt'rest torments unto death be donne.[50]

In other words, Job and Mary are linked by having one of the best-justified causes for grief, the death of a child, a cause that, at the end of Shakespeare's play, Lear also shares. Thus, Job and Lear are more alike than might at first appear to be the case. What seems at first a contrastive allusion—Lear suffers as Job does, but not patiently—turns out to be more complex: Job himself is not so patient after all, even if Calvin might wish him to be ("But by the way let us holde this for a rule, that to be pacient, it behoveth us to moderate our sorrow"[51]).

Moreover, in writing *King Lear*, Shakespeare seems to have had in mind the etymological relationship between patience, passion, and (Christ's) Passion, all of which derive from the same Latin root (*patior*, "to suffer").[52] That Shakespeare had the Latin in mind is supported by its actual inclusion in the play, in Lear's fear of "*Hysterica passio*" (2.2.246). There has been speculation about what medical condition Shakespeare had in mind and where he gained knowledge of it, but he may have particularly liked this disease because its name included the Latin root of the "patience" Lear desires, the "passion" that prevents him from attaining it, and the "Passion" of Christ that provides the model for Christian suffering.[53]

The only character who is genuinely patient is Cordelia: she suffers without complaint her father's curse, the hatred of her sisters, rejection by a suitor, banishment, defeat, and an ignominious death. In a scene cut from the Folio text, a Gentleman tells Kent how Cordelia took the news of her father's condition:

> It seemed she was a queen
> Over her passion, who, most rebel-like,
> Sought to be king o'er her...
> ...patience and sorrow strove
> Who should express her goodliest. (4.3.13–17)

---

[50] Samuel Rowlands, "*Mulier ecce Filius tuus*," in *The Betraying of Christ. Judas in Despaire. The Seven Words of Our Savior on the Crosse. With Other Poems on the Passion* (London: Adam Islip, 1598), sig. E4ᵛ.

[51] *Sermons of Master John Calvin*, 31.

[52] For a brilliant study of the history of these words and the ideas they represent, see Erich Auerbach, "*Passio* as Passion," trans. and intro. Martin Elsky, *Criticism*, 43/3 (2001), 295–308.

[53] The disease is also called "the mother" (as by Lear himself, 2.2.245) and is one associated exclusively with women; in a play with no mothers, and in which gender and procreation are much at issue, "*Hysterica passio*" has obvious thematic relevance. From the medical perspective, see Kaara L. Peterson, "*Historica Passio*: Early Modern Medicine, King Lear, and Editorial Practice," *SQ* 57/1 (2006), 1–22.

Cordelia's patience is not only appropriate to her character in general terms, but it also links her, through a number of prominent biblical allusions, to the Passion of Christ. For instance, in both Quarto and Folio Cordelia states to her absent parent, from whom she has been separated, "O dear father, | It is thy business I go about" (4.4.23–4). This is an allusion to Christ's remark to his parents in the Temple, where they found him after becoming separated: "Knewe ye not that I must go about my father's business?" (Luke 2:49). All the English Bibles from Tyndale on, as well as Erasmus's *Paraphrases*, use the phrase "I must go about my father's business" in this passage, and it appears frequently in sermons and other religious works. Luke 2:41–52 was also the gospel reading for the first Sunday after Epiphany.[54] Another example occurs when an anonymous gentleman states of the mad Lear (who has just fled the stage), "Thou hast one daughter | Who redeems nature from the general curse | Which twain have brought her to" (4.6.201–3). The twain in question are most obviously Goneril and Regan, who have "cursed" nature by their unnatural behavior, but, in biblical terms, the twain are Adam and Eve, whose sin brought a "general curse" (original sin) upon humanity, from which humanity is redeemed by the sacrifice of Christ. Though as a redeemer she is likened to Christ, Cordelia's redemption is a secular one: she redeems the anonymous gentleman's (and our) opinion of humanity, and she may redeem her father in some fashion, if we believe that Lear is a better man at the end of the play.[55] Lear further associates Cordelia with Christ in terms of their respective sacrifices, even if we are not quite sure what precise sacrifices Lear has in mind: "Upon such sacrifices, my Cordelia, | The gods themselves throw incense"(5.3.20–1).[56] Finally, the figure of the dead Cordelia in Lear's arms has been likened to a gender-inverted Pietà, a speculative suggestion that would nevertheless make visual sense on stage with Cordelia's qualities having been established as Christ-like (see Fig. 8.2).[57] This is not to say that Cordelia represents Christ allegorically, or is a "Christ-figure" in the sense critiqued by Richard Levin,[58] simply that she is

---

[54] *BCP* 284.

[55] Some, like Cavell, however, would argue that Lear does not learn enough from his experience, however changed he is in appearance and condition.

[56] Cordelia sacrifices her happiness, her freedom, and (later) her life in her efforts to help her father, but it is not clear this is what Lear has in mind. On this suggestive but puzzling passage, see Philip Brockbank's British Academy Shakespeare Lecture *"Upon Such Sacrifices"* (London: Oxford University Press, 1976).

[57] Katherine Goodland, "Inverting the Pietà in Shakespeare's *King Lear*," in Regina Buccola and Lisa Hopkins (eds), *Marian Moments in Early Modern British Drama* (Aldershot and Burlington, VT: Ashgate, 2007), 47–74.

[58] See Ch. 2.

Fig. 8.2. The Pietà, the image of the mourning Virgin Mary with the body of the dead Jesus in her lap, was one of the most familiar images of the Crucifixion story. The most famous sculpture, by Michelangelo, is in St Peter's in Rome. This less sophisticated relief of the scene nevertheless captures the essential iconography and conveys Mary's maternal grief. (Carved alabaster panel; England, fifteenth century.) ©The Victoria and Albert Museum.

similar to him in terms of her entirely innocent and patient suffering on another's account.

Ironically, a comparison between Lear himself and Christ is also implied by the allusive link between Lear and Job, since, as mentioned above, Job was a traditional type of Christ, the ultimate "pattern of patience" through his Passion.[59] More explicitly, Lear and Christ are linked by Edgar's exclamation in response to the mad Lear, "O thou side-piercing sight!" (4.6.85), which recalls the piercing of Christ's side by the soldier (John 19:34). Lear's mad scene would also be visually allusive on stage, if Lear wears a crown of wild flowers, as Cordelia suggests, and as many productions have staged it; such a crown of "burdock, hemlock, nettles" (4.4.3–6) suggests a crown of thorns more than flowers. Another association between

---

[59] On the iconographic relationship between Job and Christ, see G. von der Osten, "Job and Christ: The Development of a Devotional Image," *Journal of the Warburg and Courtauld Institutes*, 16/1–2 (1953), 153–8.

Lear and Christ is encouraged as Lear refers to his "pelican daughters" when he meets Edgar as Poor Tom (3.4.74). The pelican is another inhabitant of the wilderness (Ps. 102:6), which seems appropriate, but the reference is also to the popular myth that the pelican kills her young, grieves for them for three days, and then restores them to life by piercing her own breast and feeding them with her blood.[60] During the Middle Ages, this bit of imaginative nature lore acquired a Christian allegorical meaning, and the "pelican-in-her-piety" became a familiar symbol of the sacrifice of Christ (see Fig. 5.1). Shakespeare would have seen this common image in any number of places. (One example is on a carved and painted boss in Southwark Cathedral, then St Saviour's, where Shakespeare's brother is buried and a number of his theatrical colleagues were vestrymen.) However, in Lear's case, these allusions to Christ are mainly contrastive. Lear does not willingly feed his daughters with his own blood, as does the pelican; rather they are devouring him. The play is Lear's "Passion" in a more limited sense than it is Cordelia's; Lear suffers, but he does not suffer on anyone else's behalf, and he redeems no one. It is at the level of allusions that the patience, passion, and suffering (Passion) of Lear, Cordelia, Job, and Christ are at once drawn to our attention as well as contrasted with each other.

A HIDDEN GOD

Shakespeare explored the existential problems of suffering, providence, and divine justice using historical and literary sources, as one might gather from Bullough's *Narrative and Dramatic Sources of Shakespeare*. But to this constellation of secular authors should be added at least Job, the Epistle of James, Golding's translation of Calvin's *Sermons on Job*, and Bunny's edition of Parsons's *Booke of Christian Exercise*.[61] Situating the play in the context of Job and its interpretations reveals how *King Lear*, whatever the theological beliefs of its author, is firmly rooted in the ground of religious and biblical ideas. An awareness of *King Lear*'s many sources also reveals some sense of Shakespeare's reading practice and the gestation process of his plays. Finally, even if one remains skeptical about the influence of these sources on Shakespeare, knowing these works can help us understand

---

[60] For more on the pelican myth and its iconography, which Shakespeare alludes to in *Julius Caesar* as well, see Ch. 5.

[61] Additional biblical allusions lie outside the possible scope of this chapter. See, e.g., Susan Snyder, "*King Lear* and the Prodigal Son," *SQ* 17/4 (1966), 361–9, or Joseph Wittreich's *"Image of that Horror": History, Prophecy, and Apocalypse in King Lear* (San Marino: Huntington Library, 1984), which focuses on Revelation.

the cultural, intellectual, and theological contexts from which the play emerged in its own time and may affect our response to some interpretative debates about *King Lear*.

One long-standing interpretative debate, for instance, concerns whether the play is or is not "Christian," or whether it affirmed or challenged the prevailing Christian beliefs of its original audience. Elton's *King Lear and the Gods* has made naive "neo-Christian" readings (like Wilson Knight's) hard to take seriously, but more subtle Christian readings of the play persist. Seán Lawrence, for instance, assimilating Elton's analysis of *King Lear*'s characters as pagan or pre-Christian, has argued that the play's critique of religion is directed only at those specific religious views that in Christian terms are idolatrous.[62] René E. Fortin decides that *King Lear* is fundamentally ambivalent, subject only to a kind of "hermeneutical circularity." Fortin nevertheless allows that "the Christian reader who is responsive to the Biblical echoes of the play may view the play as an attempt to demythologize Christianity, to reassert the hiddenness of God against the presumptuous pieties and shallow rationalism of the Edgars and Albanies of the world."[63] This seems undeniable (Lawrence is perhaps a case in point). But the notion of the "hiddenness of God"—a kind of theological escape hatch—raises as many troubling questions for *King Lear* as it seems to answer.[64]

Luther and Calvin both believed in a God (the Father, the God of Judgment) who was profoundly alien to and hidden from humanity, although they also believed in a God (Christ, the Word) who was loving and infinitely merciful. It was precisely the kind of problems expressed in Job that led Luther to develop a theology of the *deus absconditus* ("hidden god"), a God whose nature, judgments, and justice were essentially unknowable. In *De servo arbitrio* (1525), his famous response to Erasmus's *De libero arbitrio*, Luther wrote about the problem of trying to reconcile human and divine notions of justice. We must simply recognize, he argues, that divine justice is beyond us and trust in faith over our limited reason, otherwise we may be led to dangerous speculations:

---

[62] Seán Lawrence, "'Gods that We Adore': The Divine in *King Lear*," *Renascence* 56/3 (2004), 143–59.

[63] René E. Fortin, "Hermeneutical Circularity and Christian Interpretations of *King Lear*," *SSt* 12 (1979), 121.

[64] This may seem a somewhat dismissive description of negative or apophatic theology, which attempts to describe God in terms of what cannot be said of him. Yet, from the perspective of the problem of evil and innocent suffering, the idea of a hidden God does seem a rather convenient and suspiciously irrefutable solution—suspicious in that any example of seeming injustice might be explained away by asserting that ultimate truth is hidden from us.

I will give an example to confirm this faith and console that evil eye which suspects God of injustice. As you can see, God so orders this corporal world in its external affairs that if you respect and follow the judgment of human reason, you are bound to say either that there is no God or that God is unjust. As the poet [Ovid, *Amores*] says, "Oft I am moved to think there are no gods!" For look at the prosperity the wicked enjoy and the adversity the good endure, and note how both proverbs and that parent of proverbs, experience, testify that the bigger the scoundrel the greater his luck.[65]

Luther then cites Job 12:6, "The tents of the ungodly are at peace," and goes on to say that we must remember that there is a life after this life in which all is set right. Despite the appearance of confidence here, however, it is clear elsewhere in Luther's writing that "there was terror in his encounter with the hidden, predestinating God and that the emotional, religious, or spiritual content of the experience burst the limits of the merely rational and conceptual."[66]

Calvin was similarly anxious, even terrified by "the sovereignty of Job's God," which made it difficult not to see God as a tyrant.[67] Calvin tried to quiet his anxieties by several means. First, the premiss of Job's perfection, with which the Book of Job begins, was simply unacceptable in terms of Reformation theology. Both the narrator and God himself, in the opening wager with Satan, describe Job as a man pre-eminently virtuous. In the Bishops' Bible Job is "perfect and just" (Job 1:1). "Perfect" accurately reflects the Hebrew word *tam*, but the idea that any man besides Christ could be perfect was irreconcilable with Calvin's understanding of original sin and human corruption after the Fall. For Calvin, Job, like any human, could not aspire to perfection; he could at best be "upright." (The Geneva translators followed his lead, calling Job "upright and just.") As a result, if Job is admitted to partake of original sin, he cannot be perfectly innocent, and if he is not innocent, his suffering cannot be entirely unmerited.[68]

---

[65] Martin Luther, "The Bondage of the Will," trans. Philip S. Watson in collaboration with Benjamin Drewery, in *Luther's Works* (American Edition), xxiii (Philadelphia: Fortress Press, 1972), 291.

[66] B. A. Gerrish, "'To the Unknown God': Luther and Calvin on the Hiddenness of God," *Journal of Religion*, 53/3 (July 1973), 274.

[67] Susan Schreiner, "Exegesis and Double Justice in Calvin's Sermons on Job," *Church History*, 58/3 (1989), 326. See also Schreiner, *Where Shall Wisdom Be Found?*, for a more extensive study. On Calvin's anxiety more generally, see Bouwsma, *John Calvin*, 32–48.

[68] Calvin and other commentators based their argument for Job's imperfection on several passages where he seems to admit his sinfulness, e.g., "And why doest thou not pardone my trespass? and take away mine iniquitie?" (Job 7:21), and "If I wolde justifie my self, mine owne mouth shal condemne me: if I wolde be perfite, he shal judge me wicked" (Job 9:20).

Calvin's most disturbing response to the problem of innocent suffering, as it appears in Job, was his theology of God's "double" or "secret" justice. Akin to Luther's concept of the *deus absconditus*, Calvin's idea was a means of reconciling divine providence with the obvious injustices of everyday life. Not only is God ultimately inscrutable and alien, but he operates by a principle of justice we cannot comprehend:

> There is also another kind of rightuousnesse which wee are lesse acquainted with: which is, when God handleth us, not according to his law, but according as he may do by right. And why so? Forasmuchas our Lord giveth us our lesson in his law, and commandeth us to do whatsoever is conteined there: although the same do farre passe al our power, and no man be able to performe the things that hee hath commaunded us: yet notwithstanding wee owe him yet more, and are further bound unto him: and the lawe is not so perfect and peerlesse a thing, as is the sayde infinite rightfulnesse of God, according as we have seene heretofore, that by that he could find unrighteousnesse in the Angels, and the very daysunne shoulde not bee cleere before him. Thus yee see how there is a perfecter rightuousnesse than the righteousnesse of the law. And so if God listed to use that: although a man had performed all that is conteyned in the lawe: yet should he not fayle to be condemned.[69]

In getting himself out of one theological bind, however, Calvin created further problems for himself. If God can operate according to a kind of justice that is above his own Law and essentially equivalent to his will, how can he escape the label of tyrant? Accordingly, Calvin, like his medieval predecessors commenting on Job, is reluctant to describe Job's suffering as "punishment," preferring to think of it as a test or even as a means of grace (since suffering may lead to spiritual improvement). As Susan Schreiner points out, "every time Calvin verges on saying that Job was judged for sins against God's secret justice, he switches vocabulary and says that God 'tested' Job according to 'another regard,' a 'higher cause,' or a 'secret intention,' namely as a model for future generations."[70] So in one sense, for Calvin, Job's story is not about justice at all. Golding takes this view further in his preface:

> God never forsaketh us in our troubles, but upholdeth and maynteyneth us even in our uttermoste extremeties, by a secret and incomprehensible woorking, not always seene of the worlde, nor presently perceyved of ourselves: and that his afflicting of us is not for anye hatred or ill will of purpose to destroy us, but of a fatherly loving kyndnesse, too make us knowe better both our selves and him....[71]

---

[69] *Sermons of Master John Calvin*, 451. Sermon 88 on Job 23:1–7, cited (in a different translation) in Schreiner, "Exegesis and Double Justice," 332.
[70] Schreiner, "Exegesis and Double Justice," 334.
[71] Golding, "Epistle to Leicester," in *Sermons of Master John Calvin*, sig. aii\.

Job himself would have had little patience for the false comfort of Golding or Calvin. Nor was he the only figure in the Bible who felt that God's plan was often not only difficult to discern but sometimes difficult to credit. Jeremiah questions, "wherefore doeth the waye of the wicked prosper?" and the Psalmist asks, "Then have I clensed my herte in vayne and washed my handes in innocency? All the daye long have I bene punished, and chastened every morning?" (Ps. 73:13–14). The complaint of Habakkuk is still more radical:

O Lord, how long shal I crye, and thou wilt not heare! Even crye out unto thee for violence, and thou wilt not helpe!

Why doest thou shewe me iniquitie, and cause me to beholde sorowe? for spoyling, and violence are before me: and there are [those] that raise up strife and contention.

Therefore the Law is dissolved, and judgement doeth never go forthe: for the wicked doeth compasse about the righteous: therefore wrong judgement procedeth. (Hab. 1:2–4)

Of those who pose such questions about innocent suffering and the prosperity of the wicked, Job is the only one who gets a definitive response, at least in the sense that it comes directly from God, speaking from a whirlwind. The problem is that God's answer is no answer at all. Job asks, why am I being punished since I have not sinned? God's "answer" is, "Where wast thou when I layed the fundacions of the earth? declare if thou hast understanding" (Job 38:4) and more of the same. In other words, who are you to ask such a question of me? However problematic God's non-answer, the response nevertheless comes directly from God himself, so Job is finally granted at least the audience he has demanded from the beginning. In legal terms, which Job often uses, he wants to bring his case before God and hear God's defense; Job is finally told that God is beyond any human jurisdiction. This seems to satisfy Job (perhaps especially since the comforters are chastised and his goods and health restored to him).

But *King Lear* is like Job without God's voice from the whirlwind. There are no answers, no voices from heaven, in *King Lear*. Instead, Gloucester says that the gods "kill us for their sport" (4.1.39). This is in fact what we see in Job, which begins with gaming—a heartless wager between God and Satan about the extent of Job's perfection. But there is no such explanatory "justification" in *King Lear*. Lear asks, "What is the cause of the thunder" (3.4.151). Yet, while God tells Job that he "hathe devided the spowtes for the rain or the way for the lightening of the thunders" (Job 38:25), Lear's thunder does not speak. Calvin writes about thunder and God's voice in his commentary on Elihu's statement, "Heare the sounde of [God's] voice, and the noyse that goeth out of his mouth" (Job 37:2). In Calvin's interpretation, Elihu refers not to the voice Job has just heard but to thunder more generally:

> This voyce [of God] is none other thing, than the same noise that is made by the thunder: neverthelesse it serveth too reprove men of their unthankfulnesse, in that they give not eare too Gods thundering: according also as it is a common proverbe when men play the madde men, too say that they are so lowde, that a man could not heare God thunder for them.[72]

Although Lear says that it is "the great gods | That keep this dreadful pudder o'er our heads," this seems mere wishful thinking (3.2.49–50). It is not evident that Lear actually hears any deity in the thunder, nor is it clear that we should either.

Another difference between Job and Lear is that, even before God answers out of the whirlwind, Job never doubts that God does exist. Job also believes that God is just and all-powerful. (If Job did not believe these things, his suffering would be less troubling.) But what does Lear believe in? Presumably not in a Christian God, since he lives before Christ's birth. Lear swears by Hecate, Jupiter, and Apollo, Roman deities who are certainly pre-Christian, yet Raphael Holinshed's *Chronicle*, another Shakespeare source, dates the beginning of Cordelia's reign from "the yeere of the world 3155, before the bylding of Rome 54." Leir's rule supposedly began in 3105, thus over a century before Rome was built, which makes it historically impossible that Leir could have heard of the Roman pantheon.[73] (All religious references in *King Lear*, whether Christian or not, are thus anachronistic to the play's historical/geographical setting.) When Lear curses Goneril, he invokes the goddess "Nature" (1.4.267). Does Lear believe he is addressing an actual deity? In a later curse, Lear addresses "You fen-sucked fogs" (2.2.356), but presumably he does not actually credit fogs with agency, any more than he does the winds, cataracts, and hurricanes in his storm speech on the heath (3.2.1–2). So, while Job actually expects, or at least hopes for, an answer to his question about divine justice, it is not clear whether Lear does.

Yet, like Job, *King Lear*'s audience does desire an answer, whether it comes from God or a character in the play. Which answer does the play finally privilege? Gloucester's, that the gods are cruel and sadistic? Edgar's, when he justifies to Edmund their father's blinding on the basis of his adultery?

---

[72] *Sermons of Master John Calvin*, 739.   [73] Bullough, vii. 319, 316.

> The gods are just and of our pleasant vices
> Make instruments to plague us:
> The dark and vicious place where thee he got
> Cost him his eyes. (5.3.168–71)

(This affirmation of divine justice has a comforting Old Testament ring, but, after the onstage horror of Gloucester's blinding, it has probably always struck audiences as pat and cruel;[74] even in an age when seditious libelers were mutilated and branded, and the heads of traitors were stuck on London Bridge, adulterers did not have their eyes gouged out.) What of the apparent atheism of Edmund? It may be that, as Lawrence suggests, *King Lear* represents merely a pagan world and has no implications for true-believing Christians. (Given its weight of biblical and religious allusions, this seems unlikely.) Or perhaps the God of *King Lear* is, as Fortin suggests, a Luther-inspired, inscrutable, hidden God, a *deus absconditus*. (It would be theologically appropriate, then, that there is no explanation for the suffering we see in the play.) Or perhaps, like Calvin, we should not expect the suffering of Gloucester, Lear, and Cordelia to seem just, since suffering is a blessing. Nor need it be justified to us, since God has his own "secret justice," which we cannot comprehend. This is Elton's conclusion about how Shakespeare's audience probably interpreted the play.

King Lear is as many faceted a play as has ever been written, and Shakespeare's audience was probably not homogenous in its response to these interpretative options. But Elton admits, importantly, that "an unhistorical, Christian-conditioned Renaissance author and audience could only with difficulty have objectively and detachedly viewed a presentation of religious problems without converting them to some extent into Christian terms," and he goes on to suggest that Shakespeare's "audience would have the more sympathetically regarded the heathen's difficulties with his gods insofar as the Jacobean age was experiencing an analogous crisis in religion and the idea of providence."[75] Calvin's theology was one way out of the religious crisis, though, as indicated above, it was not without its anxieties, anxieties that troubled Calvin in his reading of Job to the extent that he felt compelled to write 159 sermons on it: how does one distinguish between a God whose justice is inscrutable and one who is unjust? How does one distinguish between an absent God and one who simply does not exist? The answer for Calvin is faith, the same faith that seems to lie behind Christian or specifically Calvinist interpretations of *King Lear*.

---

[74] See Rosenberg, "Lear and his Comforters," 138–9.
[75] Elton, *King Lear and the Gods*, 338.

Faith, as the Epistle to the Hebrews puts it, "is the grounde of things which are hoped for, and the evidence of things which are not sene" (Heb. 11:1). In the theater, however, things seen tend to outweigh "things which are not sene," just as in the theater our emotional responses to the drama tend to outweigh our theological positions. Calvin would see Lear's suffering as justified in light of the overwhelming sin shared by all humanity. Yet, audiences have surely always seen *King Lear* as a tragedy, and many have felt, like Johnson, that the death of Cordelia is almost unbearable.[76] The closing lines of the play (whether spoken by Albany or Kent) urge us to "Speak what we feel, not what we ought to say" (5.3.323), and this point might be applied to the play's fundamental questions about God's justice and providence. What a good Protestant Christian "ought to say" in response to *King Lear* has been voiced by a number of critics, whether Christian, neo-Christian, or historicist. What we may "feel," though, is that all such readings are inadequate to the tragic power of Shakespeare's play. No theological argument proves convincing in the face of innocent suffering; neither Job's comforters, nor the voice from the whirlwind, nor commentators like Calvin provide a satisfying answer to Job's basic question, "Why me?" The questions posed by *King Lear* prove to be equally intractable. But this is probably because Shakespeare was a more skeptical reader of Job than was Calvin, and a skeptical reader of Calvin too, probing the anxieties about Job that the reformer was not quite able to argue away.

---

[76] The title page of the 1608 Quarto does advertise *King Lear* as a "true chronicle history," but no one in the audience would have failed to recognize that this version of the story has a tragic ending. Richard Dutton points out that the genre of chronicle history was a hybrid, "blended with romance materials—fantasies of love, of exile, of transformation, of the mingling of kings and commoners" ("'Methinks the Truth should Live from Age to Age': The Dating and Contexts of *Henry V*," *HLQ* 68/1–2 (2005), 173–204, 174–75. Yet Shakespeare's plays are almost invariably a generic mixture, and similar blending is evident in other tragedies: *Hamlet* and *Othello*, for instance. The printer of the Quarto, moreover, may in this case simply have wanted to capitalize on the popularity of the earlier "true chronicle history" of *King Leir*.

Conclusion

The four hundredth anniversary of the publication of the King James Bible (2011) has now passed, and the four hundredth anniversary of the death of William Shakespeare (2016) is on the horizon. The Victorians would have celebrated both events similarly, trumpeting the eternal glories and universal benefits of British civilization. But the King James Bible is now one translation among a multitude, churchgoing in Britain is on the wane, and the sun set on the Empire long ago. Shakespeare, however, remains vital. The celebration of the 2012 Olympics in London included *Globe to Globe*, featuring thirty-seven productions of Shakespeare plays in as many languages, including Swahili and sign language. As the BBC reported, among the productions were a "*King Lear* performed in Belarusian, *Hamlet* in Lithuanian and *Othello* re-interpreted through hip-hop."[1] Shakespeare is performed around the world, but especially in English-speaking countries. Centers of performance include Stratford and London, Washington, New York, and Chicago, Stratford (Canada), and Malkgulumbu, Australia. Film and television versions of the plays continue to be regularly produced, including most recently Julie Taymore's *The Tempest* (2010) and the BBC's *The Hollow Crown* (2012), the English history plays from *Richard II* through *Henry V*. The National Theatre production of *Timon of Athens* was broadcast in movie theaters across Britain and the United States in November 2012. Small company and amateur productions of Shakespeare must run into the hundreds if not thousands annually. In the United States, Shakespeare remains the one pre-twentieth-century author one can count on virtually all high-school students having read. In a weird way, Shakespeare has become something like the Bible of contemporary culture; everyone in Shakespeare's day knew the story of Adam and Eve and the serpent, while everyone today knows *Romeo and Juliet*. Yet how many of Shakespeare's millions of readers and viewers realize the extent to which he was a biblical writer?

There is widespread recognition of how much the English language has changed in four hundred years, and the extent to which this inhibits

---

[1] *BBC News* <http://www.bbc.co.uk/news/entertainment-arts-17811639> (accessed October 10, 2012.)

our comprehension of Shakespeare. We need teachers and editors to explain that in the sixteenth century "prevent" meant "anticipate," that to "halt" meant to "limp," and that "natural" could mean "foolish" as well as "according to nature." Scholars can also explain the now-obsolete use of the ethical dative in phrases like "I followed me close" (*Henry IV, Part 1*, 2.4.209–10), and the complex Elizabethan social distinctions between pronouns like "you" and "thou." Yet, readers and audiences have lost not only the lexical range of words but their allusive capacity as well. Even a single word like "frailty" (let alone "serpent" or "garden") had a specifically biblical and religious connotation for biblically literate early moderns. Phrases or sentences from familiar biblical passages, or even combinations of certain keywords, constitute allusions that add an entire level of significance to a speech or scene, evoking a biblical context that interacts with the dramatic context in the mind of the reader or audience member to produce meaning. Without these allusions, the plays mean less. My hope is that this book will provide readers, performers, and audiences with the means by which to engage in Shakespeare's plays more deeply, enabling them to grasp the meaning of the plays as fully as did Elizabethan and Jacobean audiences. To that end, I have tried to write for the educated general reader rather than just an academic community.

But *The Bible in Shakespeare* is aimed at the academic community as well, offering readings of the plays, but also arguments about the nature and history of the trope of allusion, a description of post-Reformation biblical culture, and a critical history of Shakespeare and the Bible. Biblical allusion has implications for editors of Shakespeare too, as well as readers, students, teachers, and critics. For example, several notorious textual cruces in *Hamlet*, *Othello*, and *Henry V* are resolved by considering Shakespeare's practice of biblical allusion; the arguments made here may not resolve all textual uncertainties, but they may at least aid in the critical debate.

Finally, I address those for whom Shakespeare means live action onstage (or screen). Biblical allusion was not obscure or even scholarly in Shakespeare's day. Everyone knew the Bible, and even the groundlings in the public theater would have understood some of Shakespeare's biblical allusions, eliciting a richer laugh, a sharper irony, or a more profound sense of loss. Obviously, it is impossible in any modern production fully to recapture the cultural context of the original performances. Still, an awareness of Shakespeare's biblical allusions provides an actor with another set of tools for unlocking and communicating a speech, and it should stimulate dramaturgs and directors in thinking through the dynamics of the play. For example, both Laurence Olivier and Kenneth Branagh cut the text of *Henry V* in their respective film versions. Olivier, not surprisingly given his post-war patriotism, omitted most of the appalling verbal violence of Henry's Harfleur speech (3.3.1–43). Branagh included more of that speech, but he omitted the allusion to "the wives of Jewry" howling "At Herod's bloody-hunting slaughtermen" (3.3.40–1). This diminishes the impact of the speech, since, as discussed in Chapter 4, the allusion does more than provide an example of violent slaughter: it potentially casts Henry himself in the role of Herod, which seriously compromises his status as right ruler and military hero. Of course, Branagh, like Olivier, may not have been comfortable with that degree of compromise to Henry's character.

The Bible in Shakespeare has by no means exhausted the topic of biblical allusion in Shakespeare. There are unquestionably more corners of early modern biblical culture to explore, more allusions to rediscover and interpret, and further connections to be made between Shakespeare's allusive practice and those of his contemporaries. To what extent, for instance, did Shakespeare influence the allusive practice of subsequent playwrights, especially those with whom he worked closely like Thomas Middleton and John Fletcher? Shakespeare's biblical allusions could also be examined in the context of non-dramatic literature, either preceding him (Spenser) or following (Milton). Moreover, Shakespeare's own non-dramatic writing contains biblical allusions that have been omitted from this study for reasons of space. The sonnets seem an especially rich ground for exploring biblical allusion.

Given the recently observed critical "turn to religion" in literary studies, and early modern studies in particular, and the widespread international celebration of the King James Bible anniversary, not to mention the dramatic global resurgence of interest in religious belief and practice, the time seems ripe for *The Bible in Shakespeare*.

Bibliography

Adelman, Janet, *The Common Liar: An Essay on* Antony and Cleopatra (New Haven and London: Yale University Press, 1973).

——, *Blood Relations: Christian and Jew in* The Merchant of Venice (Chicago: University of Chicago Press, 2008).

Alter, Robert, "Allusion and Literary Expression," in *The World of Biblical Literature* ([New York]: Basic Books, 1992), 107–30.

Anghiere, Pietro Martire d', *The history of travayle in the West and East Indies* (London: Richard Jugge, 1577).

Anon., *The Practice of Preaching* (London: William Jones, 1577).

——, *An Introduction to the looue of God. Accompted among the workes of S. Augustine* (London: Thomas Purfoote, 1581).

——, *A pleasant conceited historie, called The taming of a shrew* (London: Peter Short to be sold by Cutbert Burbie, 1594).

——, *The Whipping of Satyre* (London: John Flasket, 1601).

——, *No-body, and some-body* ([London]: [James Roberts] for John Trundle, 1606).

——, *A true and perfect relation of the proceedings at the severall arraignments of the late most barbarous traitors* (London: Robert Barker, 1606).

——, *An Imaginary Conversation Between Mr Phelps and D. Cumming. By the Ghost of Walter S. Landor* (n.p., 1865?).

——, "In the Editorial Perspective," *Flaming Sword*, 15/14 (February 22, 1901), 10.

——, "The Cipher Theory," *Cambrian*, 22 (Utica, NY, 1902), 247–8.

——, "The Baconian Method Applied to the Psalms," *Independent*, 74 (New York, January–June, 1913), 48.

Armin, Robert, *The history of the two maids of More-clacke with the life and simple maner of John in the hospital* (London: N.O. for Thomas Archer, 1609).

Armstrong, C. B., Letter, *The Times* [London], April 29, 1976, 17.

Aston, Margaret, *England's Iconoclasts* (Oxford and New York: Clarendon Press, 1988).

——, "The Bishops' Bible Illustrations," in *The Church and the Arts* (Oxford and Cambridge, MA: Published for the Ecclesiastical History Society by Blackwell Publishers, 1992), 267–85.

——, "Puritans and Iconoclasm, 1560–1660," in Christopher Durston and Jacqueline Eales (eds), *The Culture of English Puritanism, 1560–1700* (New York: St Martin's Press, 1996), 92–121.

Auerbach, Erich, "*Passio* as Passion," trans. and intro. Martin Elsky, *Criticism*, 43/3 (2001), 295–308.

Augustine, St, *Of the Citie of God*, trans. J.H. (London: George Eld, 1610).

Averell, William, *A Mervailous Combat of Contrarieties* (London: I. C[harlewood] for Thomas Hacket, 1588).

Aylmer, John, *Articles to be enquired of within the dioces of London, in the visitation of the Reverend Father in God, John Bishop of London* (London: [T. Orwin], 1589).

Babington, Thomas, Lord Macaulay, "John Dryden (January 1828)," in *Miscellaneous Writings and Speeches of Lord Macaulay*, ii. Online text prepared by Mike Alder and Sue Asscher, *Project Gutenberg* <http://www.gutenberg.org/ebooks/25903> (accessed November 21, 2012).

Bakhtin, Mikhail M., "Discourse in the Novel," in Michael Holquist (ed.), *The Dialogic Imagination: Four Essays*, trans. Caryl Emerson and Michael Holquist (Austin, TX: University of Texas Press, 1981), 269–422.

Bacon, Francis, "An Advertisement touching the Controversies of the Church, of England," in *Resuscitatio* (London: Sarah Griffin for William Lee, 1657), 162–79.

——, *A Critical Edition of the Major Works*, ed. Brian Vickers (Oxford and New York: Oxford University Press, 1996).

——, "Of Gardens," in *Francis Bacon: A Critical Edition of the Major Works*, ed. Brian Vickers (Oxford and New York: Oxford University Press, 1996), 430–5.

——, "Of Prophecies," in *A Critical Edition of the Major Works*, ed. Brian Vickers (Oxford and New York: Oxford University Press, 1996), 412–14.

Baldwin, Robert W., "A Bibliography of the Prodigal Son Theme in Art and Literature," *Bulletin of Bibliography*, 44 (September 1987), 167–71.

Baldwin, T. W., *William Shakspere's Small Latine and Lesse Greeke* (Urbana, IL: University of Illinois Press, 1944), i and ii; online reprint http://www.durer.press.illinois.edu/baldwin/ (accessed September 21, 2012).

Ball, Bryan W., *A Great Expectation: Eschatological Thought in English Protestantism to 1660* (Leiden: E. J. Brill, 1975).

Bancroft, Richard, *A Survay of the Pretended Holy Discipline* (London: John Wolfe, 1591).

Barber, C. L., *Shakespeare's Festive Comedy: A Study of Dramatic Form and its Relation to Social Custom* (Princeton: Princeton University Press, 1959; repr. Cleveland and New York: World Publishing Company, 1963).

Barkan, Leonard, *The Gods Made Flesh: Metamorphosis and the Pursuit of Paganism* (New Haven and London: Yale University Press, 1990).

——, "What did Shakespeare Read?" in Margreta de Grazia and Stanley Wells (eds), *The Cambridge Companion to Shakespeare* (Cambridge: Cambridge University Press, 2001), 31–48.

Barroll, Leeds, "The Allusive Tissue of *Antony and Cleopatra*," in Sara Munson Deats (ed.), *Antony and Cleopatra: New Critical Essays* (New York and London: Routledge, 2005), 275–90.

Barthes, Roland, "The Death of the Author," in *Image, Music, Text*, trans. Stephen Heath (New York: Hill and Wang, 1977), 142–8.

Bate, Jonathan, *Shakespeare and Ovid* (Oxford: Clarendon Press, 1993; repr. 2001).

———, *Soul of the Age: A Biography of the Mind of William Shakespeare* (New York: Random House, 2009).
Batson, Beatrice, "The 'Horrid Deed' and its Consequences in the Tragedy of *Macbeth*," *Sewanee Theological Review*, 49/4 (2006), 431–42.
Battenhouse, Roy W., *Shakespearean Tragedy: Its Art and its Christian Premises* (Bloomington and London: Indiana University Press, 1969).
———, "Falstaff as Parodist and Perhaps Holy Fool," *PMLA* 90/1 (1975), 32–52.
Bauckham, Richard, *Tudor Apocalypse* (Oxford: Sutton Courtenay Press, 1978).
Beard, Geoffrey, *Decorative Plasterwork in Great Britain* (London: Phaidon, 1975).
Bearman, Robert, "John Shakespeare: A Papist or Just Penniless?" *SQ* 56/4 (2005), 411–33.
———, "The Early Reformation Experience in a Warwickshire Town: Stratford-upon-Avon, 1530–1580," *Midlands History* (2007), 68–109.
Beck, Ervin, "Terence Improved: The Paradigm of the Prodigal Son in English Renaissance Comedy," *Renaissance Drama*, 6 (1973), 107–22.
Beckwith, Sarah, "Stephen Greenblatt's *Hamlet* and the Forms of Oblivion," *JMEMS* 33/2 (2003), 261–80.
Bell, Millicent, *Shakespeare's Tragic Skepticism* (New Haven and London: Yale University Press, 2002).
Belsey, Catherine, *Shakespeare and the Loss of Eden* (New Brunswick, NJ: Rutgers University Press, 1999).
Ben-Porat, Ziva, "The Poetics of Literary Allusion," *PTL* 1 (1976), 105–28.
Betteridge, Maurice, "The Bitter Notes: The Geneva Bible and its Annotations," *SCJ* 14/1 (1983), 41–62.
Biblia sacra vulgata, Clementine version, *DRBO.ORG* www.drbo.org.
[Biddulph, William], *The travels of certaine Englishmen into Africa, Asia, Troy, Bythinia, Thracia, and to the Blacke Sea* (London: Thomas Haveland for W. Aspley, 1609).
Birch, William J., *An Inquiry into the Philosophy and Religion of Shakspere* (London: C. Mitchell, 1848).
Black, Joseph L. (ed.), *The Martin Marprelate Tracts: A Modernized and Annotated Edition* (Cambridge: Cambridge University Press, 2008).
Blenerhasset, Thomas, *The seconde part of the Mirrour for magistrates* ([London]: Richard Webster, 1578).
Bloom, Harold, *The Map of Misreading* (New York: Oxford University Press, 1975; repr. 2003).
——— (ed.), *Modern Critical Interpretations: William Shakespeare's* Coriolanus (New York: Chelsea House, 1988).
Bloom, J. Harvey, *Shakespeare's Church* (London: T. Fisher Unwin, 1902).
The Book of Common Prayer: The Texts of 1549, 1559, and 1662, ed. Brian Cummings (Oxford: Oxford University Press, 2011).
Bond, Francis, *Wood Carvings in English Churches*, i. *Misericords* (London, New York, etc.: Henry Frowde, Oxford University Press, 1910).

Born, Hanspeter, *The Rare Wit and the Rude Groom: The Authorship of "A Knack to Know a Knave" in Relation to Greene, Nashe, and Shakespeare* (Bern: Franke, 1971).

Bouwsma, William, *John Calvin: A Sixteenth Century Portrait* (New York and Oxford: Oxford University Press, 1988).

Boyarin, Adrienne Williams, "Competing Biblical and Virgilian Allusions in Wyatt's 'Who So List to Hounte,'" *N&Q* 53/4 (2006), 417–21.

Brachlow, Stephen, *The Communion of the Saints: Radical Puritan and Separatist Ecclesiology 1570–1625* (1988).

Braden, Gordon, "Plutarch, Shakespeare, and the Alpha Males," in Charles Martindale and A. B. Taylor (eds), *Shakespeare and the Classics* (Cambridge: Cambridge University Press, 2004), 188–90.

Bradley, A. C., "The Rejection of Falstaff," in Harold Bloom (ed.), *Sir John Falstaff* (Philadelphia: Chelsea House, 2004), 17–35.

Bradshaw, Graham, *Misrepresentations: Shakespeare and the Materialists* (Ithaca, NY: Cornell University Press, 1993).

Breton, Nicholas, *The Soules immortall crowne consisting of seaven glorious graces* (London: H. Lownes, 1601).

Bridges, John, *A sermon, preached at Paules Crosse on the Monday in Whitson weeke Anno Domini. 1571* (London: Henry Binneman for Humfrey Toy, 1571).

Brockbank, Philip, *"Upon Such Sacrifices": British Academy Shakespeare Lecture* (London: Oxford University Press, 1976).

Brooks, Cleanth, *The Well-Wrought Urn: Studies in the Structure of Poetry* (San Diego, New York, and London: Harcourt Brace Jovanovich, 1947; repr. 1975).

Brown, James, ["J. B. Selkirk"], *Bible Truths with Shakespearean Parallels* (London: Hodder and Stoughton, 1862; 3rd edn, 1872).

Bryant, J. A., "Shakespeare Allegory: 'The Winter's Tale,'" *Sewanee Review*, 63/2 (1955), 202–22.

——, *Hippolyta's View: Some Christian Aspects of Shakespeare's Plays* (Lexington, KY: University of Kentucky Press, 1961).

Bullock, Charles, *Shakespeare's Debt to the Bible: with Memorial Illustrations* (London: "Hand and Heart" Publ., 1879).

Bullough, Geoffrey (ed.), *Narrative and Dramatic Sources of Shakespeare*, 8 vols (London: Routledge and Kegan Paul; New York: Columbia University Press, 1957–75).

Bunia, Remigius, "Diegesis and Representation: Beyond the Fictional World, on the Margins of Story and Narrative," *Poetics Today*, 31/4 (2010), 679–720.

Burckhardt, Sigurd, *Shakespearean Meanings* (Princeton: Princeton University Press, 1968).

Burgess, William, *The Bible in Shakspeare: A Study of the Relation of the Works of William Shakespeare to the Bible* (1903; repr. New York: Haskell House, 1968).

Burke, Kenneth, "*Coriolanus*—and the Delights of Faction," in Harold Bloom (ed.), *Modern Critical Interpretations: William Shakespeare's* Coriolanus (New York: Chelsea House, 1988), 33–50.

Burton, William, *A sermon preached in the Cathedrall Church in Norwich, the xxi. day of December, 1589* (London: Robert Waldegrave, 1590).

Bushnell, Rebecca, *Green Desire: Imagining Early Modern English Gardens* (Ithaca, NY: Cornell University Press, 2003).

Calvin, John, *The Psalmes of David and others. With M. John Calvins commentaries*, trans. Arthur Golding (London: [Thomas East and Henry Middleton: for Lucas Harison, and George Byshop], 1571).

———, *The Sermons of M. John Calvin, upon the Epistle of S. Paule too the Ephesians. Translated out of French into English by Arthur Golding* (London: [By Thomas Dawson] for Lucas Harison, and George Byshop, 1577).

———, *Sermons of Master John Calvin, upon the Booke of Job. Translated out of French by Arthur Golding* (London: [Henry Bynneman for] Lucas Harison and George Byshop, [1574]).

———, *A commentarie vpon the Epistle of Saint Paul to the Romanes*, trans. Christopher Rosdell (London: John Harison and George Bishop, 1583).

———, *A Harmonie upon the three Evangelists*, trans. E.P. (London: George Bishop, 1584).

Campbell, Thomas P., *Henry VIII and the Art of Majesty: Tapestries at the Tudor Court* (New Haven and London: Yale University Press, 2007).

Carlyle, Thomas, *On Heroes, Hero-Worship, and the Heroic in History*, ed. John C. Adams (Boston and New York: Houghton, Mifflin and Company; Cambridge, MA: Riverside Press, 1907).

Carter, Thomas, *Shakespeare and Holy Scripture with the Version He Used* (London: Hodder and Stoughton, 1905).

Caton, Mary Anne, "'Fables and fruit trenchers teach as much': English Banqueting Trenchers, c.1585–1662," *Magazine Antiques* (June 1, 2006), 112–19.

Cavell, Stanley, "*Coriolanus* and the Interpretation of Politics," in *Disowning Knowledge in Six Plays of Shakespeare* (Cambridge: Cambridge University Press, 1987), 143–78.

———, *Disowning Knowledge in Six Plays of Shakespeare* (Cambridge: Cambridge University Press, 1987).

Certaine sermons or Homilies, appointed to be read in churches, in the time of Queen Elizabeth I, 1547–1571/2 vols. in 1, facs. repr. of 1623 edn, intro. Mary Ellen Rickey and Thomas B. Stroup (Delmar, NY: Scholars' Facsimiles and Reprints, 1968).

Chambers, E. K., *William Shakespeare: A Study of Facts and Problems*, 2 vols (Oxford: Clarendon Press, 1930).

Chapman, Henry, *A catalogue of several large collections and parcels of books, purchased since June 1785* [London, 1785].

Chappell, Bartholomew, *The Garden of Prudence* (London: Richard Johnes, 1595).

Christianson, C. Paul, *The Riverside Gardens of Thomas More's London* (New Haven and London: Yale University Press, 2005).

Christianson, Paul, *Reformers and Babylon: English Apocalyptic Vision from the Reformation to the Eve of the Civil War* (Toronto: University of Toronto Press, 1978).

Churchyard, Thomas, *The Firste Parte of Churchyardes Chippes* (London: Thomas Marshe, 1575).
Clapham, Hennoch, *Three partes of Salomon his Song of Songs, expounded* (London: Valentine Sims for Edmund Mutton, 1603).
Clelia [Charles Downing], *God in Shakespeare: The Course of the Poet's Spiritual Life with his Reflections thereon and his Resultant Conception of his World-Personality Inductively Established by the Text*, 2nd edn (London: T. Fisher Unwin, 1901).
——, *The Messiahship of Shakespeare Sung and Expounded* (London: Greening, 1901).
——, *Great Pan Lives* (London: Luzac and Co., 1908).
Coghill, Nevill, "Comic Form in *Measure for Measure*", SS 8 (1955), 14–27.
Cohen, Simona, *Animals as Disguised Symbols in Renaissance Art* (Leiden: Brill, 2008).
Cohn, Norman, *The Pursuit of the Millennium: Revolutionary Millenarians and Mystical Anarchists of the Middle Ages* (London: Secker and Warburg, 1957, rev. Oxford University Press, 1970).
Cole, Howard C., "The Christian Context of *Measure for Measure*," *JEGP* 64/3 (1965), 425–51.
Colie, Rosalie L., "The Energies of Endurance: Biblical Echo in *King Lear*," in Rosalie Colie and F. T. Flahiff (eds), *Some Facets of* King Lear: *Essays in Prismatic Criticism* (Toronto: University of Toronto Press, 1974), 117–44.
——, *Shakespeare's Living Art* (Princeton: Princeton University Press, 1974).
Colie, Rosalie, and Flahiff, F. T. (eds), *Some Facets of* King Lear: *Essays in Prismatic Criticism* (Toronto: University of Toronto Press, 1974).
Collinson, Patrick, *The Elizabethan Puritan Movement* (Oxford: Clarendon Press, 1967).
——, *The Religion of Protestants: The Church in English Society 1559–1625* (Oxford: Clarendon Press, 1982).
——, "The Coherence of the Text: How it Hangeth Together: The Bible in Reformation England," in W. P. Stephens (ed.), *The Bible, the Reformation, and the Church* (Sheffield: Sheffield Academic Press, 1995), 84–108.
——, "Ecclesiastical Vitriol: Religious Satire in the 1590s and the Invention of Puritanism," in John Guy (ed.), *The Reign of Elizabeth I: Court and Culture in the Last Decade* (Cambridge and New York: Cambridge University Press, 1995), 150–70.
——, "Biblical Rhetoric: The English Nation and National Sentiment in the Prophetic Mode," in Claire McEachern and Debora Shuger (eds), *Religion and Culture in Renaissance England* (Cambridge: Cambridge University Press, 1997), 15–45.
Colton, G. Q., *Shakespeare and the Bible: Parallel passages and passages suggested by the Bible with the religious sentiments of Shakspeare* (New York: Knox, [*c.*1888]).
Colynet, Antony, *The true history of the civill warres of France* (London: [Thomas Orwin] for Thomas Woodcock, 1591).

Connolly, Annaliese, "Peele's *David and Bethsabe*: Reconsidering Biblical Drama of the Long 1590s," *EMLS* Special Issue 16 (October 2007), 9.1–19.
Cooper, Thomas, *Thesaurus linguae Romanae & Britannicae* (London: [Henry Denham], 1578).
Cope, Michael, *A godly and learned exposition uppon the Proverbes of Solomon*, trans. M.O. (London: George Bishop, 1580).
"The Cordewaners Play (The Agony and the Betrayal)," in *York Plays*, ed. Lucy Toulmin Smith (New York: Russell & Russell, 1963).
Cox, John D., *Seeming Knowledge: Shakespeare and Skeptical Faith* (Waco, TX: Baylor University Press, 2007).
Craig, Alexander, *The Poeticall Essayes* (London: William White, 1604).
Crawford, Patricia, "Charles Stuart, that Man of Blood," *Journal of British Studies*, 16/2 (1977), 41–61.
Crockett, Bryan, *The Play of Paradox: Stage and Sermon in Renaissance England* (Philadelphia: University of Pennsylvania Press, 1995).
Crowther-Heyck, Kathleen, "'Be Fruitful and Multiply': Genesis and Generation in Reformation Germany," *RQ* 55/3 (2002), 904–35.
Cubeta, Paul M., "Falstaff and the Art of Dying," *SEL* 27/2 (1987), 197–211.
Cummings, Anthony M., "Toward an Interpretation of the Sixteenth-Century Motet," *Journal of the American Musicological Society*, 34 (1981), 43–59.
D'Oench, Ellen G., *Prodigal Son Narratives 1480–1980* (New Haven: Yale University Art Gallery, 1995).
Danby, John F., "The Shakespearian Dialectic," *Scrutiny*, 16 (1949), 196–213.
Daniell, David, *The Bible in English: Its History and Influence* (New Haven: Yale University Press, 2003).
Danner, Dan G., "Resistance and the Ungodly Magistrate in the Sixteenth Century: The Marian Exiles," *Journal of the American Academy of Religion*, 49/3 (1981), 471–81.
Darlow, T. H., and Moule, H. F., rev. A. S. Herbert, *Historical Catalogue of Printed Editions of the English Bible 1525–1961* (London: British and Foreign Bible Society; New York: American Bible Society, 1968).
Davidson, Clifford, *History, Religion and Violence: Cultural Contexts for Medieval and Renaissance English Drama* (Aldershot: Ashgate, 2002).
Davies, John of Hereford, *Humours heav'n on earth with the civile warres of death and fortune* (London: A[dam] I[slip], 1609).
Davies, H. Neville, "Jacobean '*Antony and Cleopatra*,'" in John Drakakis (ed.), Antony and Cleopatra, New Casebooks (New York: St Martins Press, 1994), 126–65.
Davies, Michael, "Falstaff's Lateness: Calvinism and the Protestant Hero in *Henry V*," *RES* 56/225 (2005), 351–78.
Dell, Katharine J., "Ecclesiastes as Wisdom: Consulting Early Interpreters," *Vetus Testamentum*, 44/3 (1994), 301–29.
Dennis, Carl, "'All's Well that Ends Well' and the Meaning of 'Agape,'" *Philological Quarterly*, 50/1 (1971), 175–84.
Dent, Robert W., *Shakespeare's Proverbial Language: An Index* (Berkeley and Los Angeles: University of California Press, 1981).

Dethicke, Henry, "To the righte honourable and his singular good Lord, Sir William Cecill," in Dydymus Mountaine [Thomas Hill], *The gardeners labyrinth* (London: Henry Bynneman, 1577).

Devlin, Christopher, *Hamlet's Divinity and Other Essays*, intro. C. V. Wedgwood (London: Rupert Hart-Davis, 1963).

Dodds, Gregory D., *Exploiting Erasmus: The Erasmian Legacy and Religious Change in Early Modern England* (Toronto: University of Toronto Press, 2009).

Doebler, John, "*The Knight of the Burning Pestle* and the Prodigal Son Plays," *SEL* 5/2 (1965), 333–44.

——, *Shakespeare's Speaking Pictures* (Albuquerque: University of New Mexico Press, 1974).

Donne, John, *Devotions upon Emergent Occasions together with Death's Duell* (Ann Arbor: University of Michigan Press, 1959).

Dove, John, *A sermon preached at Pauls Crosse, the 3 of November 1594* (London: V.S. for William Jaggard, [1594?]).

Drayton, Michael, *Poly-Olbion* (London: M. Lownes, J. Browne, J. Helme, J. Busbie, 1612).

Dryden, John, *From the Prologue to* The Tempest, or The Enchanted Island, 1667, *published* 1670, and *From the Prologue to* Aureng-Zebe, 1675, *published* 1676, in D. Nichol Smith (ed.), *Shakespeare Criticism: A Selection, 1623–1840* (London: Oxford University Press, 1916; repr. 1964), 22–3.

Du Bartas, Guillaume de Salluste, *Du Bartas his devine weekes and workes translated: and dedicated to the Kings most excellent Maiestie by Josuah Sylvester* (London: Humfrey Lounes, 1611).

Duncan-Jones, Katherine, "Shakespeare the Motley Player," *RES* 60/247 (2009), 723–43.

Dutton, Richard A., *Licensing, Censorship, and Authoship in Early Modern England* (Basingstoke: Palgrave, 2000).

——, "'Methinks the Truth Should Live from Age to Age': The Dating and Contexts of *Henry V*," *HLQ* 68/1–2 (2005), 173–204.

——, Findlay, Alison, and Wilson, Richard (eds), *Region, Religion, and Patronage: Lancastrian Shakespeare* (Manchester and New York: Manchester University Press, 2003).

——, Findlay, Alison, and Wilson, Richard (eds), *Theatre and Religion: Lancastrian Shakespeare* (Manchester and New York: Manchester University Press, 2003).

Eaton, T. R., *Shakespeare and the Bible: Showing How the Great Dramatist Was Indebted to Holy Writ for his Profound Knowledge of Human Nature* (London: James Blackwood, 1858).

Edwards, John, *A Discourse concerning the authority, stile, and perfection of the books of the Old and New-Testament* (London: Richard Wilkin, 1693).

Eliot, T. S., "Philip Massinger," in *Selected Essays*, new edn (New York: Harcourt, Brace & World, Inc., 1960), 205–33.

Elton, William R., King Lear *and the Gods* (San Marino, CA: Huntington Library, 1966).

Elvins, Mark T., *Catholic Trivia: Our Forgotten Heritage* (Leominster: Gracewing, 2002; first pub. Harper Collins, 1992).
Emerson, Ralph Waldo, *Representative Men*, in *The Complete Works of Ralph Waldo Emerson*, iv (Boston and New York: Houghton, Mifflin and Company, 1903–4).
Erasmus, Desiderius, *Apophthegmes*, trans. Nicolas Udall (London: Richard Grafton, 1542).
——, *An exposicyon of the .xv. psalme* [London: J. Waylande, 1537].
——, *The first tome or volume of the Paraphrase of Erasmus vpon the Newe Testamente* (London: Edwarde Whitchurch, 1548).
——, *The praise of Folie, Moriae Encomium, a booke made in latine by that greet clerke Erasmus Roterodame* (London: Thomas Berthelet, 1549).
——, *The seconde tome or volume of the Paraphrase of Erasmus upon the Newe Testament* (London: Edward Whitchurch, 1549).
Evenden, Elizabeth, *Patents, Pictures and Patronage: John Day and the Tudor Book Trade* (Aldershot and Burlington, VT: Ashgate, 2008).
Evett, David, "Types of King David in Shakespeare's Lancastrian Tetralogy," *SSt* 14 (1981), 139–61.
Ferguson, Frances, *Trope and Allegory: Themes Common to Dante and Shakespeare* (Athens, GA: University of Georgia Press, 1977).
Fermor, Noel, Letter, *The Times* [London], April 27, 1976, 15.
Field, John, *An Admonition to the Parliament* ([Hemel Hempstead?: Printed by J. Stroud?, 1572]).
——, *A caveat for Parsons Howlet concerning his untimely flight* (London: Robert Waldegrave for Thomas Man and Toby Smith, [1581]).
Fike, Matthew, "Dives and Lazarus in *The Henriad*," *Renascence*, 55/4 (2003), 279–91.
Fincham, Kenneth, "The King, the Bishops, the Parishes and the KJV," conference paper at "An Anglo-American History of the KJV," Folger Shakespeare Library, Washington, September 30, 2011.
Firth, Katharine R., *The Apocalyptic Tradition in Reformation Britain 1530–1645* (Oxford: Oxford University Press, 1979).
Fisch, Harold, *The Biblical Presence in Shakespeare, Milton, and Blake: A Comparative Study* (Oxford: Clarendon Press, 1999).
Fissell, Mary E., "The Politics of Reproduction in the English Reformation," *Representations*, 87 (2004), 43–81.
Fletcher, Joseph, *Christes bloodie sweat, or the Sonne of God in his agonie* (London: Ralph Blower, 1613).
Foirades/Fizzles: Echo and Allusion in the Art of Jasper Johns ([Los Angeles]: Grunwald Center for the Graphic Arts: Wight Art Gallery, University of California, Los Angeles, 1987).
Folger Shakespeare Library Website <http://www.folger.edu/html/exhibitions/fakes_forgeries/FFFmulberry.asp> (accessed December 15, 2011).
Fortin, René E., "Hermeneutical Circularity and Christian Interpretations of *King Lear*," *SSt* 12 (1979), 121.

Fosse, J., "The Lord's Anointed Temple: Study of Some Symbolic Patterns in *Macbeth*," *Cahiers élisabéthains*, 6 (1974), 15–22.

Foster, Donald W., "Macbeth's War on Time," *ELR* 16/2 (1986), 319–42.

Foucault, Michel, "What is an Author?" in Donald F. Bouchard (ed.), *Language, Counter-Memory, Practice: Selected Essays and Interviews by Michel Foucault* (Ithaca, NY: Cornell University Press, 1977), 113–38.

Foulkes, Richard, "'Every Good Gift from Above': Archbishop Trench's Tercentenary Sermon," *Shakespeare and Religions*, SS 54, ed. Peter Holland (Cambridge: Cambridge University Press, 2001), 80–8.

——, "William Shakespeare: The Model Victorian Protestant," *Shakespeare*, 5/1 (2009), 68–81.

Fox, Adam, *Oral and Literate Culture in England, 1500–1700* (Oxford: Clarendon Press, 2000).

Frye, Northrop, *Words with Power: Being a Second Study of the Bible and Literature* (San Diego, New York, and London: Harcourt Brace Jovanovich, 1990).

Frye, Roland Mushat, *Shakespeare and Christian Doctrine* (Princeton: Princeton University Press, 1963).

Fulke, William, *Praelections upon the sacred and holy Revelation of S. John* (London: Thomas Purfoote, 1573).

Garganigo, Alex, "*Coriolanus*, the Union Controversy, and Access to the Royal Person," *SEL* 42/2 (2002), 335–59.

Garner, Richard, *From Homer to Tragedy: The Art of Allusion in Greek Poetry* (London: Routledge, 1990).

Garrick, David, *Shakespeare's Garland* (London: T. Becket and P. A. de Hondt, 1769).

Gerard, John, *The herball or Generall historie of plantes* (London: [Edm. Bollifant for Bonham Norton and] John Norton, 1597).

Gerrish, B. A., "'To the Unknown God': Luther and Calvin on the Hiddenness of God," *Journal of Religion*, 53/3 (July 1973), 274.

Gibson, Michael Francis, *The Mill and the Cross: Peter Bruegel's "Way to Calvary"* (Lausanne: Acatos, 2000).

Gifford, William, "Time and Place in Donne's Sermons," *PMLA* 82/5 (1967), 388–98.

Gill, Miriam, and Morris, Richard K., "A Wall Painting of the Apocalypse in Coventry Rediscovered," *Burlington Magazine*, 143/1181 (August 2001), 467–73.

Ginsberg, H. L., "Job the Patient and Job the Impatient," Conservative Judaism, 21/3 (1967), 12–28.

Goldberg, Jonathan, "Romeo and Juliet's Open Rs," in *Shakespeare's Hand* (Minneapolis: University of Minnesota Press, 2003), 271–85.

Gombrich, E. H., *Art and Illusion: A Study of the Psychology of Pictorial Representation* (Princeton: Princeton University Press, 1969).

Goodland, Katherine, "Inverting the Pietà in Shakespeare's *King Lear*," in Regina Buccola and Lisa Hopkins (eds), *Marian Moments in Early Modern British Drama* (Aldershot and Burlington, VT: Ashgate, 2007), 47–74.

Grashop, T., "How to Take Profit by Reading of the Holy Scripture," in *The Bible that is, the Holy Scriptures* [Geneva–Tomson–Junius] (London: Robert Barker, 1603).
Gray, Jonathan, *Watching with the Simpsons: Television, Parody, and Intertextuality* (New York: Routledge, 2006).
——, "'Simpsons Did It!': South Park and the Intertextuality of Contemporary Animation," *Studies in American Humor*, 3/17 (2008), 19–34.
Graziani, René, "M. Marcadé and the Dance of Death: *Love's Labour's Lost* V.2.705–711," in Felicia Hardison Londré (ed.), Love's Labour's Lost: *Critical Essays* (New York and London: Garland Publishing, 1997), 301–4.
Green, Ian, *Print and Protestantism in Early Modern England* (Oxford: Oxford University Press, 2000).
Greenblatt, Stephen, *Renaissance Self-Fashioning: From More to Shakespeare* (Chicago and London: University of Chicago Press, 1980).
——, "Shakespeare and the Exorcists," in Patricia Parker and Geoffrey Hartman (eds), *Shakespeare and the Question of Theory* (New York and London: Methuen, 1985), 163–86.
——, *Shakespearean Negotiations: The Circulation of Social Energy in Renaissance England* (Berkeley and Los Angeles: University of California Press, 1988).
——, *Hamlet and Purgatory* (Princeton: Princeton University Press, 2001).
——, *Will in the World: How Shakespeare became Shakespeare* (New York: W. W. Norton, 2004).
Greene, Richard L. (ed.), *The Early English Carols* (Oxford: Clarendon Press, 1935).
Greene, Robert, *Greenes never too late* (London: Thomas Orwin for N.L. and John Busbie, 1590).
——, *A quip for an upstart courtier* (London: John Wolfe, 1592).
——, *The honorable historie of frier Bacon, and frier Bongay* (London: [Adam Islip] for Edward White, 1594).
Greene, Thomas M., *The Descent from Heaven: A Study in Epic Continuity* (New Haven and London: Yale University Press, 1963).
——, *The Light in Troy: Imitation and Discovery in Renaissance Poetry* (New Haven and London: Yale University Press, 1982).
——, "History and Anachronism," in Gary Saul Morson (ed.), *Literature and History: Theoretical Problems and Russian Case Studies* (Stanford: Stanford University Press, 1986), 205–20.
Greenfield, Thelma N., "*A Midsummer Night's Dream* and *The Praise of Folly*," *Comparative Literature*, 20/3 (1968), 236–44.
Greg, W. W., Review of *The Chronicle History of King Leir*: The Original of Shakespeare's *King Lear* by Sidney Lee, *Modern Language Review*, 5/4 (1910), 515–19.
Gregory, Brad, "The 'True and Zealouse Service of God': Robert Parsons, Edmund Bunny, and 'The First Booke of the Christian Exercise,'" *Journal of Ecclesiastical History*, 45/2 (1994), 231–69.
Griffith, Elizabeth, *The Morality of Shakespeare's Drama Illustrated* (London: T. Cadell, 1775).

Grosse, Kenneth, *Shylock is Shakespeare* (Chicago: University of Chicago Press, 2006).
Groves, Beatrice, "'Now Wole I a Newe Game Begynne': Staging Suffering in *King Lear*, the Mystery Plays and Grotius's *Christus Patiens*," *Medieval and Renaissance Drama in England*, 20 (2007), 136–50.
——, "Shakespeare's Sonnets and the Genevan Marginalia," *Essays in Criticism*, 57/2 (2007), 114–28.
——, *Texts and Traditions: Religion in Shakespeare 1592–1604* (Oxford: Clarendon Press, 2007).
Gurr, Andrew, *Playgoing in Shakespeare's London*, 3rd edn (Cambridge: Cambridge University Press, 2004).
Haddon, Walter, *Against Jerome Osorius Byshopp of Silvane in Portingall* (London: John Day, 1581).
[Hake, Edward] E.H., *A touchestone for this time present expressly declaring such ruines, enormities, and abuses as trouble the Churche of God and our Christian common wealth at this daye* (London: [W. Williamson] for Thomas Hacket, 1574).
Hall, Joseph, *The Kings Prophecie* (London: Symon Waterton, 1603).
Halliwell, J. O., *An Attempt to Discover Which Version of the Bible Was That Ordinarily Used by Shakespeare* (London: Privately Printed, 1867).
Hamlin, Hannibal, "The Bible, *Coriolanus*, and Shakespeare's Modes of Allusion," in Jennifer Lewin (ed.), *Never Again Would Birds' Song Be the Same: Essays in Early Modern and Modern Poetry in Honor of John Hollander* (New Haven: Beinecke Library, Yale University, 2002), 73–91.
——, *Psalm Culture and Early Modern English Literature* (Cambridge: Cambridge University Press, 2004).
——, Review of *Catholic Theology in Shakespeare's Plays*, by David Beauregard, *SQ* 59/4 (2009), 24–6.
——, "Replying to Raleigh's 'The Nymph's Reply': Allusion, Anti-Pastoral, and Four Centuries of Pastoral Invitations," in Christopher M. Armitage (ed.), *Sir Walter Raleigh: Literary and Visual Raleigh* (Manchester: Manchester University Press, forthcoming).
Hamling, Tara, *Decorating the "Godly" Household: Religious Art in Post-Reformation Britain* (New Haven and London: Yale University Press, 2010).
——, "Guides to Godliness: From Print to Plaster," in Michael Hunter (ed.), *Printed Images in Early Modern Britain: Essays in Interpretation* (Farnham, Surrey; Burlington, VT: Ashgate, 2010), 65–85.
Harris, Jonathan Gil, "The Smell of *Macbeth*," *SQ* 58/4 (2007), 465–86.
Harsnett, Samuel, *A declaration of egregious popish impostures* (London: James Roberts, 1603).
Hartley, Thomas, *Paradise restored: or A Testimony to the Doctrine of the Blessed Millennium* (London: M. Richardson, 1764).
Harwood, Stacey, "Poetry in Movies: A Partial List," *Poets.org* <http://www.poets.org/viewmedia.php/prmMID/19359> (accessed October 12, 2012).
Hassel, R. Chris, Jr, *Renaissance Drama & the English Church Year* (Lincoln, NE: University of Nebraska Press, 1979).

——, Jr, *Faith and Folly in Shakespeare's Romantic Comedies* (Athens, GA: University of Georgia Press, 1980).
Heather, P. J., "Animal Beliefs" (Continued), *Folklore*, 52/3 (1941), 217.
Helgerson, Richard, *The Elizabethan Prodigals* (Berkeley, Los Angeles, and London: University of California Press, 1976).
Hellerstedt, Kahren Jones, "The Blind Man and his Guide in Netherlandish Painting," *Simiolus*, 13/3–4 (1983), 163–81.
Henryson, Robert, *The Poems of Robert Henryson*, ed. Denton Fox (Oxford: Clarendon Press, 1981).
Herbert, George, *The Works of George Herbert*, ed. F. E. Hutchinson (Oxford: Clarendon Press, 1941).
Heresbach, Conrad, *Foure Bookes of Husbandry*, trans. Barnabe Googe (London: Richard Watkins, 1577).
Herr, Alan Fager, *The Elizabethan Sermon: A Survey and a Bibliography* (Philadelphia: University of Pennsylvania, 1940; repr. New York: Octagon Books, 1969).
Hill, Christopher, *Antichrist in Seventeenth-Century England*, rev. edn (London and New York: Verso, 1990).
——, *The English Bible and the Seventeenth-Century Revolution* (Harmondsworth: Penguin, 1993), 324–31.
Hirschfeld, Heather, "Hamlet's 'First Corse': Repetition, Trauma, and the Displacement of Redemptive Typology," *SQ* 54/4 (2004), 424–48.
Hodson, Bishop Mark, Letter, *The Times* [London], April 24, 1976, 12.
The. holie. Bible conteynyng the olde Testament and the newe [The Bishops' Bible] (London: Richard Jugge, 1568), *EEBO*.
Holinshed, Raphael, *The First and Second Volumes of Chronicles*, ii. *The History of Scotland* (London, 1587).
Holland, Norman, "*Measure for Measure*: The Duke and the Prince," *Comparative Literature*, 11/1 (1959), 16–20.
Hollander, John, *The Figure of Echo: A Mode of Allusion in Milton and After* (Berkeley: University of California Press, 1981).
Holloway, John, *The Story of the Night: Studies in Shakespeare's Major Tragedies* (London: Routledge & Kegan Paul, 1961).
Holmes, Wilfrid, *The fall and evill successe of Rebellion* (London: Henry Binneman, 1572).
The Holy Bible conteyning the Olde Testament and the Newe [Geneva–Tomson Bible] (London: Christopher Barker, 1595).
Honan, Park, *Christopher Marlowe: Poet and Spy* (Oxford and New York: Oxford University Press, 2005).
Hopkinson, William, *A preparation into the waye of lyfe* (London: Robert Waldegrave, 1581).
Horace, *The Epistles of Horace: A Bilingual Edition*, trans. David Ferry (New York: Farrar, Straus and Giroux, 2001).
Hunt, Arnold, *Past and Present*, 161 (1998), 39–83.
——, *The Art of Hearing: English Preachers and their Audiences, 1590–1640* (Cambridge: Cambridge University Press, 2010).

Hunt, Maurice, *Shakespeare's Romance of the Word* (Lewisburg: Bucknell University Press, 1990).
—— , *Shakespeare's Religious Allusiveness: Its Play and Tolerance* (Aldershot and Burlington, VT: Ashgate, 2004).
Hunter, G. K., "The Theology of Marlowe's *The Jew of Malta*," *Journal of the Warburg and Courtauld Institutes*, 27 (1964), 211–40.
—— , *English Drama 1586–1642: The Age of Shakespeare* (Oxford: Clarendon Press, 1997).
Hunter, Michael, "Introduction," in Hunter (ed.), *Printed Images in Early Modern Britain: Essays in Interpretation* (Farnham and Burlington, VT: Ashgate, 2010), 1–22.
—— (ed.), *Printed Images in Early Modern Britain: Essays in Interpretation* (Farnham, Surrey; Burlington, VT: Ashgate, 2010).
H. W. B., "Saul and Macbeth," *Sewanee Review*, 1/3 (1893), 273–82.
Injunctions geven by the Quenes Majestie anno Domini MD.LIX. (London: Richard Jugge and John Cawood, 1559).
Irwin, William, "What Is an Allusion?" *Journal of Aesthetics and Art Criticism*, 59/3 (2001), 287–97.
—— , and Lombardo, J. R., "The Simpsons and Allusion: 'The Worst Essay Ever,'" in William Irwin, Mark T. Conar, and Aeon J. Skoble (eds), *The Simpsons and Philosophy: The D'Oh of Homer* (Chicago: Open Court, 2001), n.p.
Jack, Jane H., "Macbeth, King James, and the Bible," *ELH* 22/3 (1955), 173–93.
Jackson, Ken, and Marotti, Arthur F., "The Turn to Religion in Early Modern English Studies," *Criticism*, 46/1 (2004), 167–90.
James VI [and later I], *Ane fruitfull meditatioun contening ane plane and facill expositioun of ye 7.8.9 and 10 versis of the 20 chap. of the Revelation* (Edinburgh, 1589).
—— VI [and later I], *Daemonologie* (Edinburgh: Robert Waldegrave, 1597).
James, Heather, *Shakespeare's Troy: Drama, Politics, and the Translation of Empire* (Cambridge and New York: Cambridge University Press, 1997).
Jehne, Martin, "History's Alternative Caesars: *Julius Caesar* and Current Historiography," in Horst Zander (ed.), Julius Caesar*: New Critical Essays* (New York and London: Routledge, 2005), 59–70.
Jensen, Phebe, *Religion and Revelry in Shakespeare's World* (Cambridge: Cambridge University Press, 2008).
Johnson, Samuel, *Johnson on Shakespeare*, ed. Walter Raleigh (London: Oxford University Press, 1908; repr. 1952).
—— , "From the Edition of Shakespeare's Works, 1765," in D. Nichol-Smith (ed.), *Shakespeare Criticism: A Selection 1623–1840* (London: Oxford University Press, 1916; repr. 1964), 117.
Jones, Emrys, *The Origins of Shakespeare* (Oxford: Clarendon Press, 1977; repr. 1978).
Jones, Malcolm, *The Print in Early Modern England: An Historical Oversight* (New Haven and London: Yale University Press, 2010).
Jonson, Ben, *Bartholomew Fair*, ed. G. R. Hibbard, New Mermaids (London: A&C Black; New York: W. W. Norton, 1977; repr. 1994).

Jorgensen, Paul A., *Redeeming Shakespeare's Words* (Berkeley and Los Angeles: University of California Press, 1962).
Junius, Francis, *Apocalypsis A briefe and learned commentarie upon the revelation of Saint John* (London: Richard Field for Robert Dexter, 1592).
——, *The Apocalyps, or Revelation of S. John the apostle and evangelist of our Lord Jesus Christ* (Cambridge: John Legat, 1596).
Kallendorf, Craig, "From Virgil to Vida: The Poeta Theologus in Italian Renaissance Commentary," *Journal of the History of Ideas*, 56/1 (1995), 41–62.
Kaula, David, "Hamlet and the Image of Both Churches," *SEL* 24/2 (1984), 241–55.
Kemp, William, *A most pleasant and merie new comedie, intituled, A knacke to knowe a knave* (London: Richard Jones, 1594).
Kennedy, William, *The Site of Petrarchism: Early Modern National Sentiment in Italy, France, and England* (Baltimore: Johns Hopkins Univerity Press, 2003).
Kermode, Frank, *Shakespeare's Language* (New York: Farrar, Straus, Giroux, 2000).
——, "The Mature Comedies," in *Shakespeare, Spenser, Donne* (first edn, 1971; repr. Abingdon: Routledge, 2005).
Kezar, Dennis, "*Julius Caesar*'s Analogue Clock and the Accents of History," in Horst Zander (ed.), *Julius Caesar: New Critical Essays* (New York and London: Routledge, 2005), 241–55.
Kim, Hyun-Ah, *Humanism and the Reform of Sacred Music in Early Modern England: John Merbecke the Orator and* The Booke of Common Praier Noted *(1550)* (Aldershot and Birmingham, VT: Ashgate, 2008).
Kirsch, Arthur, *The Passions of Shakespeare's Tragic Heroes* (Charlottesville, VA, and London: University Press of Virginia, 1990).
Kisby, Fiona, "Books in London Parish Churches before 1603: Some Preliminary Observations," in Caroline M. Barron and Jenny Stratford (eds), *The Church and Learning in Later Medieval Society: Essays in Honour of R. B. Dobson*, Proceedings of the 1999 Harlaxton Symposium (Donington: SHAUN TYAS, 2002), 305–26.
Knapp, Jeffrey, *Shakespeare's Tribe: Church, Nation, and Theater in Renaissance England* (Chicago and London: University of Chicago Press, 2002).
Knight, G. Wilson, *The Wheel of Fire: Interpretations of Shakespearian Tragedy* (London: Methuen, 1930; repr. 1964).
Knowles, Richard, "How Shakespeare Knew *King Leir*," *SS* 55 (2002), 12–35.
Knox, Hugh, Sermon XX, "Creatures, broken cisterns: God alone, the fountain of living waters, from Jerem. ii, 12, 13," in *Select Sermons on Interesting Subjects*, ii (Glasgow: Robert & Amdrew Foulis, 1726), 143–65.
Kolin, Philip C., "Macbeth, Malcolm, and the Curse of the Serpent," *South Central Bulletin*, 43/4 (1974), 159–60.
Krantz, David L., "The Sounds of Supernatural Soliciting in *Macbeth*," *SP* 100/3 (2003), 346–83.
Kristeva, Julia, "Word, Dialogue, and the Novel," in Leon S. Roudiez (ed.), *Desire in Language: A Semiotic Approach to Literature and Art*, trans. Thomas Gora, Alice Jardine, and Leon S. Roudiez (New York: Columbia University Press, 1980), 64–92.

Kristeva, Julia, *Revolution in Poetic Language*, trans. Margaret Waller (New York: Columbia University Press, 1984).

Kuchar, Gary, *The Poetry of Religious Sorrow in England* (Cambridge: Cambridge University Press, 2011).

Kugel, James, *The Bible As It Was* (Cambridge, MA: Harvard University Press, 1997).

Kyd, Thomas, *The Spanish Tragedy*, ed. J. R. Mulryne, New Mermaids, 2nd edn, (London: A&C Black; New York: W. W. Norton, 1989; repr. 2000).

Lake, Peter, *Anglicans and Puritans? Presbyterianism and English Conformist Thought from Whitgift to Hooker* (London: Unwin Hyman, 1988).

——, and Questier, Michael, "Appropriation and Rhetoric under the Gallows: Puritans, Romanists and the State in Early Modern England," *Past & Present*, 153 (1996), 64–107.

——, with Questier, Michael, *The Antichrist's Lewd Hat: Protestants, Papists & Players in Post-Reformation England* (New Haven and London: Yale University Press, 2002).

Lancashire, Ian, "A Brief History of the Homilies" (Toronto: Web Development Group, University of Toronto, 1994, 1997) <http://www.library.utoronto.ca/utel/ret/homilies/elizhom3.html> (accessed September 21, 2012).

[Lane, John] J.L., *An elegie upon the death of the high and renowned princesse* (London: [W. White] for John Deane, 1603).

Lanquet, Thomas, Cooper, Thomas, and Crowley, Robert, *An epitome of chronicles Conteyninge the whole discourse of the histories as well of this realme of England, as al other cou[n]treys* (London: [William Seres for] Thomas Marshe, 1559).

Laporte, Charles, "The Bard, the Bible, and the Shakespeare Question," *ELH* 74 (2007), 609–28.

——, "The Devotional Texts of Victorian Bardolatry," in Travis DeCook and Alan Galey (eds), *Shakespeare, the Bible, and the Form of the Book: Contested Scriptures* (New York and Abingdon: Routledge, 2012), 143–59.

Lascelles, Mary, *Shakespeare's Measure for Measure* (London: University of London, Athlone Press, 1953).

——, "*King Lear* and Doomsday," *SS* 26 (1973), 69–79.

Lavater, Ludwig, *Of ghostes and spirites walking by nyght* (London: Henry Benneyman for Richard Watkyns, 1572).

Lawrence, Seán, "'Gods that We Adore': The Divine in *King Lear*," *Renascence*, 56/3 (2004), 143–59.

Le Huray, Peter, *Music and the Reformation in England 1549–1660* (London: Herbert Jenkins, 1967; repr. Cambridge: Cambridge University Press, 1978).

Leggatt, Alexander, *Shakespeare's Political Drama* (London and New York: Routledge, 1988).

Levin, Richard, "On Fluellen's Figures, Christ Figures, and James Figures," *PMLA* 89/2 (1974), 302–11.

——, "The Relation of External Evidence to the Allegorical and Thematic Interpretation of Shakespeare," *SSt* 13 (1980), 1–29.

Lewalski, Barbara K., "Biblical Allusion and Allegory in *The Merchant of Venice*," *SQ* 13/3 (1962), 327–43.
Lodge, Thomas, *Wits Miserie, and the Worlds Madnesse* (London: Adam Islip, 1596).
Lok, Henry, *Ecclesiastes, otherwise called The preacher* (London: Richard Field, 1597).
Lupset, Thomas, *A compendious and a very fruteful treatyse, teachynge the waye of dyenge well* (London: Thomas Berthelet, 1541).
Lupton, Julia Reinhard, *Citizen–Saints: Shakespeare and Political Theology* (Chicago and London: University of Chicago Press, 2005).
Lupton, Lewis, *A History of the Geneva Bible*, vi. *Hope's Anchor* (London: Olive Tree, 1974).
Luther, Martin, *An exposicion upon the songe of the blessed virgine Mary*, trans. John Hollybush ([Southwark: J. Nicholson], 1538).
———, "The Bondage of the Will," trans. Philip S. Watson in collaboration with Benjamin Drewery, in *Luther's Works*, American Edition, xxiii (Philadelphia: Fortress Press, 1972).
McAlindon, Tom, *Shakespeare's Tragic Cosmos* (Cambridge: Cambridge University Press, 1991).
McCullough, Peter E., *Sermons at Court: Politics and Religion in Elizabethan and Jacobean Preaching* (Cambridge: Cambridge University Press, 1998).
———, Adlington, Hugh, and Rhatigan, Emma (eds), *The Oxford Handbook to the Early Modern Sermon* (Oxford: Oxford University Press, 2011).
McFall, E. K., "*Macbeth* and Dante's *Inferno*," *N&Q* (December 2006), 490–4.
Machacek, Gregory, "Allusion," *PMLA* 122/2 (2007), 522–36.
McKerrow, R. B., and Ferguson, F. S., *Title-Page Borders Used in England and Scotland, 1485–1640* (London: Printed for the Bibliographical Society at the Oxford University Press, 1932).
MacLure, Millar, *The Paul's Cross Sermons, 1534–1642* (Toronto: University of Toronto Press, 1958).
McMillin, Scott, and MacLean, Sally-Beth, *The Queen's Men and their Plays* (Cambridge: Cambridge University Press, 1998).
McNulty, Robert, "The Protestant Version of Robert Parsons' *The First Booke of the Christian Exercise*," *HLQ* 22/4 (1959), 271–300.
Malcolm, W. H., *Shakspere and Holy Writ: Parallel Passages, Tabularly Arranged*, with foreword by F. J. Furnivall (London: Marcus Ward & Co., 1881).
Malin, Eric S., *Godless Shakespeare* (London and New York: Continuum, 2007).
Manguel, Alberto, *The Library at Night* (New Haven and London: Yale University Press, 2006).
Manley, Lawrence, *Literature and Culture in Early Modern London* (Cambridge: Cambridge University Press, 1995).
Mann, Isabel Roome, "The Garrick Jubilee at Stratford-Upon-Avon," *SQ* 1/3 (1950), 128–34.

Marlowe, Christopher, *Dr Faustus: Based on the A Text*, ed. Roma Gill, New Mermaids (London: A&C Black; New York: W. W. Norton, 1968; 2nd edn, 1989).

——, *The Jew of Malta*, ed. Roma Gill, in *The Complete Works of Christopher Marlowe*, iv (Oxford: Clarendon Press, 1995).

Marnix van St Aldegonde, Philips van, *The bee hive of the Romishe Church* (London: Thomas Dawson for John Stell, 1579).

Marotti, Arthur F., and Jackson, Ken (eds), *Shakespeare and Religion: Early Modern and Postmodern Perspectives* (Notre Dame, IN: University of Notre Dame Press, 2011).

Marshall, Anne, "The Doom, or Last Judgement, and the Weighing of Souls: An Introduction," at *Medieval Wall Painting and the English Parish Church: A Developing Catalogue* <http://www.paintedchurch.org/doomcon.htm> (accessed June 25, 2012.)

Marvell, Andrew, *The Poems of Andrew Marvell*, ed. Nigel Smith, rev. edn (Harlow and New York: Pearson Longman, 2007).

Marx, Steven, *Shakespeare and the Bible* (Oxford and New York: Oxford University Press, 2000).

Masten, Jeffrey, "Playwrighting: Authorship and Collaboration," in John D. Cox and David Scott Kaston (eds), *A New History of English Drama* (New York: Columbia University Press, 1997), 357–82.

Matus, Irvin Leigh, "An Early Reference to the Coventry Mystery Plays in Shakespeare?" *SQ* 40/2 (1989), 196–7.

Maveety, Stanley R., "A Second Fall of Cursed Man: Bold Metaphor in *Richard II*," *JEGP* 72 (1973), 175–93.

Maxwell, Julie, "How the Renaissance (Mis)Used Sources: The Art of Misquotation," in Laurie Maguire (ed.), *How to Do Things with Shakespeare: New Approaches, New Essays*. (Malden, MA; Blackwell, 2008), 54–76.

Mayer, Jean-Christophe, *Shakespeare's Hybrid Faith: History, Religion, and the Stage* (Basingstoke and New York: Palgrave Macmillan, 2007).

Mears, Natalie, "Public Worship and Political Participation in Elizabethan England," *Journal of British Studies*, 51/1 (2012), 4–25.

Mebane, John S., "'Impious War': Religion and the Ideology of Warfare in *Henry V*," *SP* 104/2 (2007), 250–66.

Mehl, Dieter, "*The London Prodigal* as Jacobean City Comedy," in Dieter Mehl, Angela Stock, and Anne-Julia Zwierlein (eds), *Plotting Early Modern London: New Essays on Jacobean City Comedy* (Aldershot: Ashgate, 2004), 165–76.

Merchant, Carolyn, *The Death of Nature: Women, Ecology, and the Scientific Revolution* (San Francisco: Harper and Row, 1980).

Miller, Shannon, "Topicality and Subversion in William Shakespeare's *Coriolanus*," *SEL* 32/2 (1992), 287–310.

Milton, John, *The Riverside Milton*, ed. Roy Flannagan (Boston and New York: Houghton Mifflin, 1998).

Miola, Robert, *Shakespeare's Rome* (Cambridge and New York: Cambridge University Press, 1983).

——, *Shakespeare's Reading* (Oxford and New York: Oxford University Press, 2000).
Molekamp, Femke, "Using a Collection to Discover Reading Practices: The British Library Geneva Bibles and a History of their Early Modern Readers," *Electronic British Library Journal* (2006), 1–13.
——, "'Of the Incomparable Treasure of the Holy Scriptures': The Geneva Bible in the Early Modern Household," in Matthew Dimmock and Andrew Hadfield (eds), *Literature and Popular Culture in Early Modern England* (Farnham and Burlington, VT: Ashgate, 2009), 121–36.
Montaigne, Michel de, *The Essayes of Michael Lord of Montaigne, Translated by John Florio*, 3 vols (London and Toronto: J. M. Dent; New York: E. P. Dutton, 1921).
Montrose, Louis, *The Purpose of Playing: Shakespeare and the Cultural Politics of Elizabethan England* (Chicago: University of Chicago Press, 1996).
More, Sir Thomas, *A dyaloge of syr Thomas More knyghte... Wyth many othere thyngys touching the pestylent sect of Luther and Tyndale, by the tone bygone in Sarony [sic], and by tother laboryed to be brought in to Englond* (London: [J. Rastell], 1529).
——, *The apologye of syr Thomas More knyght* (London: W. Rastell, 1533).
Morrall, Andrew, "Protestant Pots: Morality and Social Ritual in the Early Modern Home," *Journal of Design History*, 15/4 (2002), 263–73.
——, and Watt, Melinda (eds), *English Embroidery from the Metropolitan Museum of Art, 1580–1700* (New Haven and London: Yale University Press, 2008).
Morris, Helen, "Shakespeare and Dürer's Apocalypse," *SSt* 4 (1968), 252–62.
——, "Queen Elizabeth I 'Shadowed' in *Cleopatra*," *HLQ* 32 (1969), 271–8.
Morrissey, Mary, *Politics and the Paul's Cross Sermon, 1558–1642* (Oxford and New York: Oxford University Press, 2011).
Muir, Kenneth (ed.), *King Lear: Critical Essays* (New York and London: Garland Publishing, 1984).
Muller, Ghislain, *Was Shakespeare a Jew?: Uncovering the Marrano Influences in his Life and Writing* (Lewiston, NY: Edwin Mellen Press, 2001).
Munday, Anthony, *Palmerin D'Oliva The mirrour of nobilitie* (London: J. Charlewood, for William Wright, 1588).
——, Chettle, Henry, et al., *Sir Thomas More*, ed. John Jowett, Arden (London: Methuen Drama, A&C Black, 2011).
Munkelt, Marga, "Recent Film, Stage and Critical Interpretations," in *Julius Caesar*, ed. Martin Spevack, New Cambridge Shakespeare (Cambridge and New York: Cambridge University Press, 1988), 46–8.
Nagel, Alexander, and Wood, Christopher, *Anachronic Renaissance* (New York: Zone Books, 2010).
Napier, John, *A plaine discouery of the whole Revelation of Saint John* (Edinburgh: Robert Waldgrave, 1593).
Nashe, Thomas, *An Almond for a Parrat* (London?: n.p., 1589).

Nashe, Thomas, *Mar-Martine* (n.p, 1589).

——, *A myrror for Martinists, and all other schismatiques* (London: John Wolfe, 1590).

——, *Christes Teares over Jerusalem* (London: James Roberts, 1593).

——, *Have with You to Saffron-Walden* (London: John Danter, 1596).

——, *A pleasant comedie, called Summers last will and testament* (London: Simon Stafford for Water Burre, 1600).

——, *The Works of Thomas Nashe*, ed. Ronald B. McKerrow; repr. with corrections and supplementary notes by F. P. Wilson (Oxford: Blackwell, 1958), vols. 1 and 2.

Nausea, Friedrich, *A Bright Burning Beacon, forewarning all wise Virgins to trim their lampes against the coming of the Bridegroom*, trans. Abraham Fleming (London: Henrie Denham, 1580).

Naylor, B. S., *Time and Truth reconciling the moral and religious world of Shakespeare; the greatest Poet and Dramatist, the greatest Moral-philosopher and Philanthropist, that ever lived in the tide of times: whose greatness, like an Alpine-avalanche, continues increasing and increasing and increasing, as the wonderful revelations of his overwhelming Genuis roll down the steep of time* (London: W. Kent & Co., 1854).

The New Testament of Jesus Christ (Rheims: John Fogny, 1582).

Nicholl, Charles, *The Lodger Shakespeare: His Life on Silver Street* (New York: Viking, 2008).

Nicholson, Samuel, *Acolastus* (London: John Baylie, 1600).

Noble, Richmond, *Shakespeare's Biblical Knowledge and Use of the Book of Common Prayer* (London: Society for Promoting Christian Knowledge; New York: Macmillan, 1935).

Norden, John, *A mirrour for the multitude* (London: John Windet, 1586).

——, *A Progresse of Pietie* (London: J. Windet for J. Oxenbridge, 1596).

Norton, David, "'Proofs of Holy Writ': Myths of the Authorized Version: Kipling and the Bible," *Kipling Journal* (December 1989), 18–27.

—— (ed.), *The Bible: King James Version with The Apocrypha* (London: Penguin, 2006).

——, *A History of the English Bible as Literature* (Cambridge: Cambridge University Press, 2000).

Nuttall, A. D., "*Measure for Measure*: Quid Pro Quo?" *SSt* 4 (1968), 231–51.

O'Brien, Mark, *When Adam Delved and Eve Span: A History of the Peasants' Revolt of 1381* (Cheltenham: New Clarion, 2004).

O'Connell, Michael, "Vital Cultural Practices: Shakespeare and the Mysteries," *JMEMS* 29/1 (1999), 149–68.

Osten, G. von der, "Job and Christ: The Development of a Devotional Image," *Journal of the Warburg and Courtauld Institutes*, 16/1–2 (1953), 153–8.

Ostovich, Helen, "'Here in this garden': The Iconography of the Virgin Queen in Shakespeare's *Richard II*," in Regina Buccola and Lisa Hopkins (eds.), *Marian Moments in Early Modern British Drama* (Aldersgate: Ashgate, 2007), 21–34.

Ovid's Metamorphoses Translated by Arthur Golding, ed. Madeleine Forey (Baltimore: Johns Hopkins University Press, 2002).
Pack, Robert, "*King Lear* and the Book of Job: Betrayal and Nothingness," in *Willing to Choose: Volition & Storytelling in Shakespeare's Major Plays* (Sandpoint, ID: Lost Horse Press, 2007), 127–47.
Palmer, D. J., "Casting off the Old Man: History and St Paul in 'Henry IV,'" *Critical Quarterly*, 12 (1970), 267–83.
Parker, John, "Shakespeare and the Geneva Bible: The Story of King Saul as a Source for *Macbeth*," *Tennessee Philological Bulletin*, 43 (2006), 6–23.
Parker, Roscoe E., "The Reputation of Herod in Early English Literature," *Speculum*, 8/1 (1933), 59–67.
Parsons, Robert, *The first booke of the Christian exercise* ([Rouen], 1582).
——, *A Booke of Christian Exercise . . . by R.P.* [Robert Parsons]. *Perused and accompanied now with a Treatise tending to Pacification: by Edm. Bunny* (London: N. Newton, and A. Hatfield, for John Wight, 1584).
——, *The seconde parte of the booke of Christian exercise, appertayning to resolution. Or a Christian directorie, guiding all men to their salvation* (London: John Charlwoode and [i.e. for] Simon Waterson, 1590).
——, *Robert Persons, SJ, The Christian Directory (1582)*, ed. Victor Houliston (Leiden, Boston, and Cologne: Brill, 1998).
Patterson, Annabel, "Bottom's Up: Festive Theory in *A Midsummer Night's Dream*," in Dorothea Kehler (ed.), A Midsummer Night's Dream: *Critical Essays* (New York: Garland, 1998), 165–78.
Paulus, Irena, "Stanley Kubrick's Revolution in the Usage of Film Music: *2001: A Space Odyssey* (1968)," *International Review of the Aesthetics and Sociology of Music*, 40/1 (2009), 99–127.
Peele, George, *The love of King David and fair Bethsabe With the tragedie of Absalon* (London: Adam Islip, 1599).
Peri, Carmella, "On Alluding," *Poetics*, 7 (1978), 289–307.
Perkins, William, *A treatise tending vnto a declaration whether a man be in the estate of damnation or in the estate of grace* (London: R. Robinson for T. Gubbin and I. Porter, 1590).
——, *A golden chaine, or the description of theologie containing the order of the causes of salvation and damnation, according to Gods woord* (London: Edward Alde, 1591).
——, *An exposition of the Symbole or Creed of the Apostles* (Cambridge: John Legatt, 1595).
——, *The combat betweene Christ and the Divell displayed* (London: Melchisedech Bradwood for E. E[dgar], 1606).
Peterson, Kaara L., "*Historica Passio*: Early Modern Medicine, *King Lear*, and Editorial Practice," *SQ* 57/1 (2006), 1–22.
Petrarca, Francesco, *Petrarch's Lyric Poems: The Rime sparse and Other Lyrics*, trans. and ed. Robert M. Durling (Cambridge, MA: Harvard University Press, 1976).
Pettie, George, *A petite pallace of Pettie his pleasure* (London: R. W[atkins], 1576).

Pigman, G. W., III, "Versions of Imitation in the Renaissance," *RQ* 33/1 (1980), 1–32.
Plumptre, Charles J., *The Religion and Morality of Shakespeare's Works* (London: Sunday Lecture Society, 1873).
Plutarch, *The Lives of the Noble Grecians and Romans*, trans. Sir Thomas North, ed. Roland Baughman (New York: Heritage Press, 1941).
Pollen, Burton R., "Hamlet, a Successful Suicide," *SSt* 1 (1965), 240–60.
Poole, Kristen, "Saints Alive! Falstaff, Martin Marprelate, and the Staging of Puritanism," *SQ* 46/1 (1995), 47–75.
Potter, Lois, *The Life of William Shakespeare: A Critical Biography* (Malden, MA: Wiley-Blackwell, 2012).
[Pritchard, Thomas], *The schoole of honest and vertuous lyfe profitable and necessary for all estates and degrees, to be trayned in* (London: [William How for] Richard Iohnes, [1579]).
Pucci, Joseph, *The Full-Knowing Reader: Allusion and the Power of the Reader in the Western Literary Tradition* (New Haven and London: Yale University Press, 1998).
Pugliatti, Paola, *Shakespeare the Historian* (New York: St Martin's Press, 1996).
Pullman, Philip, *The Golden Compass* (New York: Dell Laurel-Leaf, 1995).
Purkiss, Diane, "Marvell, Boys, Girls, and Men: Should We Worry?" in Naomi J. Miller and Naomi Yavneh (eds), *Gender and Early Modern Constructions of Childhood* (Farnham and Burlington, VT: Ashgate, 2011), 181–92.
Puttenham, George, *The Art of English Poesy: A Critical Edition*, ed. Frank Whigham and Wayne A. Rebhorn (Ithaca, NY, and London: Cornell University Press, 2007).
Quitslund, Beth, *The Reformation in Rhyme: Sternhold, Hopkins and the English Metrical Psalter, 1547–1603* (Aldershot and Burlington, VT: Ashgate, 2008).
Rabkin, Norman, *Shakespeare and the Problem of Meaning* (Chicago and London: University of Chicago Press, 1981).
——, "Either/Or: Responding to *Henry V*," in Harold Bloom (ed.), *Modern Critical Interpretations: Shakespeare's* Henry V (New York, New Haven, and Philadelphia: Chelsea House, 1988), 35–59.
Rackin, Phyllis, "Temporality, Anachronism, and Presence in Shakespeare's English Histories," *Renaissance Drama*, 17 (1986), 101–23.
——, *Stages of History: Shakespeare's English Chronicles* (Ithaca, NY: Cornell University Press, 1990).
Rad, Gerhard von, *Wisdom in Israel*, trans. James D. Martin (Nashville: Abingdon Press, 1972).
Ramsey, Jarold W., "Timon's Imitation of Christ," *SSt* 2 (1966), 162–73.
Read, Herbert, *English Stained Glass* (London and New York: G. P. Putnam's Sons, 1926).
Rebhorn, Wayne, "The Crisis of the Aristocracy in *Julius Caesar*," in Richard Wilson (ed.), *Julius Caesar:* New Casebooks (Houndsmills, Hampshire, and New York: Palgrave, 2002), 29–54.
Rees, Joan, "Falstaff, St Paul, and the Hangman," *RES* 38/149 (1987), 14–22.
Reynolds, Christopher A., *Motives for Allusion: Context and Content in Nineteenth-Century Music* (Cambridge, MA: Harvard University Press, 2003).

Rhinehart, Keith, "Shakespeare's Cleopatra and England's Elizabeth," *SQ* 23 (1972), 81–6.

Rhodes, Neil, "Shakesperean Grotesque: The Falstaff Plays," in Georgia Brown (ed.), *Thomas Nashe* (Aldershot: Ashgate, 2011), 47–93.

Richardson, Peter, *Herod: King of the Jews, Friend of the Romans* (Columbia, SC: University of South Carolina Press, 1996).

Rickert, Edith (ed.), *Ancient English Christmas Carols, 1400–1700* (New York: Duffield and Company, 1915).

Ricks, Christopher, *Allusion to the Poets* (Oxford: Oxford University Press, 2002).

Rio, A. F., *Shakespeare* (Paris: Charles Douniol, 1864).

Robbins, R. H., "Shakespeare and Psalm 46: An Accumulation of Coincidences," *N&Q* 50/1 (March 2003), 58–60.

Roberts, Josephine A., and Gaines, James F., "Kyd and Garnier: The Art of Amendment," *Comparative Literature*, 31/ 2 (1979), 124–33.

Robson, Mark, "Looking with Ears, Hearing with Eyes: Shakespeare and the Ear of the Early Modern," *EMLS* 7/1 (2001), 10.1–23.

Rogerson, Margaret, "English Puppets and the Survival of Religious Theatre," *Theatre Notebook*, 52/2 (1998), 91–111.

Rollins, Hyder E. (ed.), *Old English Ballads, 1553–1625* (Cambridge: Cambridge Universiyt Press, 1920).

Ronan, Clifford, *"Antike Roman": Power Symbology and the Roman Play in Early Modern England, 1585–1635* (Athens, GA, and London: University of Georgia Press, 1995).

Rosenberg, John D., "Lear and his Comforters," *Essays in Criticism*, 16/2 (1966), 135–46.

Ross, Stephanie, "Art and Allusion," *Journal of Aesthetics and Art Criticism*, 40/1 (1981), 59–70.

Rowlands, Samuel, *The Betraying of Christ. Judas in Despaire. The Seven Words of Our Savior on the Crosse. With Other Poems on the Passion* (London: Adam Islip, 1598).

Rowse, A. L., *What Shakespeare Read—and Thought* (New York: Coward, McCann & Geoghegan, 1981).

Rubinstein, Frankie, *A Dictionary of Shakespeare's Puns and their Sexual Significance* (Houndsmills and London: Macmillan, 1984).

Rushforth, G. McN., *Medieval Christian Imagery as Illustrated by the Painted Windows of Great Malvern Priory Church Worcestershire* (Oxford: Clarendon Press, 1936).

Salingar, Leo, "King Lear, Montaigne and Harsnett," in *Dramatic Form in Shakespeare and the Jacobeans* (Cambridge: Cambridge University Press, 1986), 107–39.

Sandys, Edwin, *Sermons made by the most reverende Father in God, Edwin, Archbishop of Yorke* (London: Henrie Midleton for Thomas Charde, 1585).

Saussure, Ferdinand de, *Cours de linguistique générale*, in *Revue des langues romanes*, 59 (1916).

Schreiner, Susan, "Exegesis and Double Justice in Calvin's Sermons on Job," *Church History*, 58/3 (1989), 326.

———, *Where Shall Wisdom Be Found?: Calvin's Exegesis of Job from Medieval and Modern Perspectives* (Chicago and London: University of Chicago Press, 1994).

———, "Calvin as an Interpreter of Job," in Donald K. McKim (ed.), *Calvin and the Bible* (Cambridge: Cambridge University Press, 2006), 68–72.

Schreyer, Kurt, " 'Here's a knocking indeed!': *Macbeth* and the *Harrowing of Hell*," *The Upstart Crow: A Shakespeare Journal*, 29 (2010–11), 26–43.

Scott, Reginald, *The Discoverie of Witchcraft* (London: [Henry Denham for] William Brome, 1584).

Scoufos, Alice-Lyle, *Shakespeare's Typological Satire: A Study of the Falstaff–Oldcastle Problem* (Athens, OH: Ohio University Press, 1979).

Scoville, Chester N., *Saints and the Audience in Middle English Biblical Drama* (Toronto: University of Toronto Press, 2004).

Seaton, Ethel, "*Antony and Cleopatra* and the Book of Revelation," *RES* 22/87 (1946), 219–24.

Seymour, Henry, "Illustrations of Baconian Cyphers," *Baconiana*, 3rd edn, 17 (1924), 256–75.

Shaheen, Naseeb, "Shakespeare and the Tomson New Testament," *N&Q* 42/3 (1995), 290–1.

———, *Biblical References in Shakespeare's Plays* (Newark: University of Delaware Press; London: Associated University Presses, 1999).

Shakespeare, William, *The History of Henrie the Fourth* (London: P[Eter] S[Hort] for Andrew Wise, 1598).

———, *Mr William Shakespeares comedies, histories, & tragedies* (London: Isaac Jaggard and Ed. Blunt, 1623).

———, *The Works of William Shakespeare. In ten volumes. Publish'd by Mr. Pope and Dr. Sewell* (London: J. Knapton, J. Darby, A. Bettesworth, J. Tonson, F. Fayram, W. Mears, J. Pemberton, J. Osborn and T. Longman, B. Motte, C. Rivington, F. Clay, J. Batley, RI. JA. And B. Wellington, 1728), vol. 2.

———, *The Works of Shakespeare in Seven Volumes*, ed. Lewis Theobald (London: A. Bettesworth and C. Hitch, J. Tonson, F. Clay, W. Feales, and R. Wellington, 1733).

———, *The Complete Works of William Shakespeare; Revised from the original editions: with a Memoir, and Essay on his Genius by Barry Cornwall*, iii (London: London Printing Company, 1870).

———, The New Variorum *King Lear*, ed. H. Howard Furness (Philadelphia: J. B. Lippincott & Co., 1880).

———, *Henry V*, ed. J. Dover Wilson (Cambridge: Cambridge University Press, 1947).

———, *The First Part of the History of Henry IV*, ed. J. Dover Wilson (Cambridge: Cambridge University Press, 1964).

———, *The Complete Works*, ed. Alfred Harbage, The Pelican Text Revised (New York: Viking Press, 1969; repr. 1977).

——, *Shakespeare's Sonnets*, ed. Stephen Booth (New Haven and London: Yale University Press, 1977).

——, *Hamlet*, ed. Harold Jenkins, Arden² (London and New York: Methuen, 1982).

——, *Julius Caesar*, ed. Arthur Humphreys (Oxford: Clarendon Press, 1984).

——, *Coriolanus*, ed. Philip Brockbank, Arden² (Methuen, 1976; repr. London and New York: Routledge, 1988).

——, *Julius Caesar*, ed. Martin Spevack, New Cambridge Shakespeare (Cambridge and New York: Cambridge University Press, 1988).

——, *Coriolanus*, ed. and intro. R. B. Parker (Oxford and New York: Oxford University Press, 1994).

——, *The Winter's Tale*, ed. Stephen Orgel, Oxford Shakespeare (Oxford and New York: Oxford University Press, 1996).

——, *King Lear*, ed. R. A. Foakes, Arden³ (Walton-on-Thames, Surrey: Thomas Nelson and Sons, 1997).

——, *Macbeth*, ed. A. R. Braunmuller, New Cambridge Shakespeare (Cambridge: Cambridge University Press, 1997).

——, *Othello*, ed. E. A. J. Honigmann, Arden³ (Walton-on-Thames: Thomas Nelson and Sons Ltd., 1997).

——, *Julius Caesar*, ed. David Daniell, Arden³ (Walden-on-Thames: Thomas Nelson and Sons, 1998).

——, *Pericles*, ed. Doreen DelVecchio and Antony Hammond, New Cambridge Shakespeare (Cambridge: Cambridge University Press, 1998).

——, *Love's Labour's Lost*, ed. H. R. Woudhuysen, Arden³ (Walton-on-Thames, Surrey: Thomas Nelson and Sons, 1998).

——, *The Merry Wives of Windsor*, ed. Giorgio Melchiori, Arden³ (London: Thomson Learning, 2000).

——, *Romeo and Juliet*, ed. Jill L. Levenson, Oxford Shakespeare (Oxford and New York: Oxford University Press, 2000).

——, *Henry V*, ed. T. W. Craik, Arden³ (Routledge, 1995; repr. London: Thomson Learning, 2001).

——, *Antony and Cleopatra*, ed. John Wilders, Arden³ (Routledge, 1995; repr. London: Thomas Learning, 2002).

——, *King Henry IV, Part 1*, ed. David Scott Kastan, Arden³ (London: Thomson Learning, 2002).

——, *King Richard II*, ed. Charles R. Forker, Arden³ (London: Thomson Learning, 2002).

——, *Macbeth*, ed. Robert S. Miola, Norton Critical Edition (New York and London: W. W. Norton & Company, 2004).

——, *Pericles*, ed. Suzanne Gossett, Arden³ (London: Thomson Learning, 2004).

——, *King Henry IV Part 2*, ed. A. R. Humphyreys, Arden² (Methuen & Co., 1981; repr. London: Thomas Learning, 2005).

——, *Cymbeline*, ed. Martin Butler, New Cambridge Shakespeare (Cambridge: Cambridge University Press, 2005; repr. 2006).

Shakespeare, William, *Timon of Athens*, ed. Anthony B. Dawson and Gretchen E. Minton, Arden³ (London: Cengage Learning, 2008).
——, *The Merchant of Venice*, ed. John Drakakis, Arden³ (London: A & C Black Publishers Ltd., 2010).
"Shakespeare's World in 100 Objects," *Shakespeare Birthplace Trust* (website) <http://www.findingshakespeare.co.uk/shakespeares-world-in-100-objects-number-15-a-painted-cloth> (accessed December 15, 2011).
Shapiro, James, *Shakespeare and the Jews* (New York: Columbia University Press, 1996).
——, A Year in the Life of William Shakespeare: 1599 (New York: HarperCollins, 2005).
Sharpe, James, *Instruments of Darkness: Witchcraft in Early Modern England* (Philadelphia: University of Pennsylvania Press, 1997).
Shelford, Robert, "A Sermon shewing how we ought to behave our selves in Gods house," in *Five pious and learned discourses* (Cambridge: [Thomas Buck and Roger Daniel], 1635).
Shell, Alison, *Shakespeare and Religion* (London: Arden Shakespeare, 2011).
Shell, Marc, "The Wether and the Ewe: Verbal Usury in *The Merchant of Venice*," *Kenyon Review*, 1/4 (1979), 65–92.
Shenk, Linda, *Learned Queen: The Image of Elizabeth I in Politics and Poetry* (New York: Palgrave Macmillan, 2010).
Sherman, William H., *Used Books: Marking Readers in Renaissance England* (Philadelphia: University of Pennsylvania, 2008).
Shrank, Cathy, "Civility and the City in *Coriolanus*," *SQ* 54/4 (2003), 406–23.
Shuger, Debora K., *Habits of Thought in the English Renaissance: Religion, Politics, and the Dominant Culture* (Berkeley and Los Angeles: University of California Press, 1990).
——, *Political Theologies in Shakespeare's England: The Sacred and the State in* Measure for Measure (Basingstoke: Palgrave, 2001).
Sidney, Sir Philip, *The Countess of Pembroke's Arcadia*, ed. Maurice Evans (Harmondworth: Penguin, 1977).
Siegel, Paul N., "English Humanism and the New Tudor Aristocracy," *Journal of the History of Ideas*, 13/4 (1952), 450–68.
——, "Echoes of the Bible Story in 'Macbeth,'" *N&Q* (April 1955), 142–3.
——, "Christianity and the Religion of Love in *Romeo and Juliet*," *SQ* 12/4 (1961), 371–92.
Siger, Leonard, "The Image of Job in the Renaissance," Ph.D. diss. (Johns Hopkins University, 1960).
Sims, James H., *Dramatic Uses of Biblical Allusions in Marlowe and Shakespeare* (Gainesville, FL: University of Florida Press, 1966).
Smith, Bruce R., *The Acoustic World of Early Modern England: Attending to the O-Factor* (Chicago and London: University of Chicago Press, 1999).
Smith, D. Nichol (ed.), *Shakespeare Criticism: A Selection, 1623–1840* (London: Oxford University Press, 1916; repr. 1964).

Smith, Henry, *A treatise of the Lords supper in two sermons* (London: R. Field, 1591).
———, *The sinfull mans search: or seeking of God* (London: [by T. Scarlet] for Cuthbert Burby, 1592).
Snyder, Susan, "*King Lear* and the Prodigal Son," *SQ* 17/4 (1966), 361–9.
———, "Theology as Tragedy in *Macbeth*," *Christianity and Literature*, 43/3–4 (1994), 289–300.
Sohmer, Steve, *Shakespeare's Mystery Play: The Opening of the Globe Theatre 1599* (Manchester and New York: Manchester University Press, 1999).
Speed, John, *The theatre of the empire of Great Britaine* (London: [William Hall] for John Sudbury and Georg Humble, 1612).
Spencer, T. J. B. (ed. and intro.), *Shakespeare's Plutarch* (Harmondsworth: Penguin, 1964).
Spenser, Edmund, *The Yale Edition of the Shorter Poems of Edmund Spenser*, ed. William A. Oram et al. (New Haven and London: Yale University Press, 1989).
———, *The Faerie Queene*, ed. A. C. Hamilton, text ed. Hiroshi Yamashita and Toshiyuki Suzuki (London and New York: Longman, 2001).
Spurgeon, Caroline, *Shakespeare's Imagery and What It Tells Us* (New York: Macmillan; Cambridge: Cambridge University Press, 1936).
Stallybrass, Peter, "*Macbeth* and Witchcraft," in John Russell Brown (ed.), *Focus on* Macbeth (Boston: Routledge, 1982), 189–209.
———, "Books and Scrolls: Navigating the Bible," in Jennifer Andersen and Elizabeth Sauer (eds), *Books and Readers in Early Modern England: Material Studies* (Philadelphia: University of Pennsylvania Press, 2002), 42–79.
Steinmetz, David C., *Calvin in Context*, 2nd edn (Oxford and New York: Oxford University Press, 2010).
Sternberg, Meir, "Proteus in Quotation-Land: Mimesis and the Forms of Reported Discourse," *Poetics Today*, 3/2 (1982), 107–56.
Stevenson, David L., *The Achievement of Shakespeare's* Measure for Measure (Ithaca, NY: Cornell University Press, 1966).
Stewart, Stanley, *The Enclosed Garden: The Tradition and the Image in Seventeenth-Century Poetry* (Madison: University of Wisconsin Press, 1966).
Streete, Adrian, "'What bloody man is that?' Questioning Biblical Typology in *Macbeth*," *Shakespeare*, 5/1 (2009), 18–35.
Strier, Richard, "Shakespeare and the Skeptics," *Religion & Literature* 32:2 (2000): 171–96.
———, "Against the Rule of Reason: Praise of Passion from Petrarch to Luther to Shakespeare to Herbert," in Gail Kern Paster et al. (eds.), *Reading the Early Modern Passions: Essays in the Cultural History of Emotion* (Philadelphia: University of Pennsylvania Press, 2004), 23–42.
Strong, Roy, *Portraits of Queen Elizabeth I* (Oxford: Clarendon Press, 1963).
Stroup, Thomas B., "Bottom's Name and his Epiphany," *SQ* 29/1 (1978), 79–82.

The Summe of the Conference betwene John Rainoldes and John Hart (London: [John Wolfe], 1584).
Summersgill, Travis L., "The Influence of the Marprelate Controversy upon the Style of Thomas Nashe," *SP* 48/2 (1951), 145–60.
Summit, Jennifer *Memory's Library: Medieval Books in Early Modern England* (Chicago: University of Chicago Press, 2008).
Swinburne, Charles Alfred, *Sacred & Shakespearean Affinities, being analogies between the writings of the Psalmists and of Shakespeare* (London: Bickers and Son, 1890).
Synesius of Cyrene, Bishop of Ptolemais, *Paradoxe, Proving by reason and example, that Baldnesse is much better than bushie haire*, trans. Abraham Fleming (London: H. Denham, 1579).
Taine, H. A., *A History of English Literature*, trans. H. van Laun, *Catholic World* 15:85 (1872), 1–17.
Targoff, Ramie, *Common Prayer: The Language of Public Devotion in Early Modern England* (Chicago: Chicago University Press, 2001).
Taylor, Gary, "The Fortunes of Oldcastle," *SS* 38 (1985), 85–100.
——, and Warren, Michael (eds), *The Division of the Kingdoms: Shakespeare's Two Versions of* King Lear (Oxford: Clarendon Press, 1983).
Taylor, Jeremy, *Dekas embolimaios* (London: R. Royston, 1667).
Taylor, Michael, "'As You Like It': The Penalty of Adam," *Critical Quarterly*, 15/1 (1973), 76–80.
Theobald, Lewis, *Shakespeare restored: or, a specimen of the many errors, as well committed, as unamended, by Mr Pope in his late edition of this poet* (London, 1726).
Thomas, Keith, *Religion and the Decline of Magic* (Harmondsworth: Penguin, 1971).
Tilley, M. P., *A Dictionary of the Proverbs in England in the Sixteenth and Seventeenth Centuries* (Ann Arbor: University of Michigan Press, 1950).
Timmins, J. F., *The Poet–Priest: Shakespearian Sermons Compiled for the Use of Students and Public Readers* (London: J. Blackwood & Co., 1880).
Tippens, Darryl, "Shakespeare and the Prodigal Son Tradition," *Explorations in Renaissance Culture*, 14 (1988), 57–77.
Tobin, J. J. M., "*Hamlet* and *Christ's Teares over Jerusalem*," *Aligarh Journal of English Studies*, 6/2 (1981), 158–67.
——, "*Macbeth* and *Christ's Teares over Jerusalem*," *Aligarh Journal of English Studies*, 7/1 (1982), 72–8.
——, "Antony, Brutus, and *Christ's Tears over Jerusalem*," *N&Q* 45/3 (September, 1998), 324–31.
——, "Nashe and Iago," *N&Q* 50/1 (March 2003), 47–50.
Toole, William B., *Shakespeare's Problem Plays: Studies in Form and Meaning* (The Hague and New York: Mouton, Humanities, 1965).
The Towneley Plays, ed. A. W. Pollard and Eugen Kölbing, Early English Text Society (London: Kegan Paul, Trench, Trübner & Co., 1897).
Tuke, Thomas, *A discourse of death, bodily, ghostly, and eternall* (London: William Stansbie for George Norton, 1613).

Tyacke, Nicholas, *Anti-Calvinists: The Rise of English Arminianism c.1590–1640* (Oxford: Clarendon Press, 1987).
Udall, Nicholas, *Floures for Latine spekynge selected and gathered oute of Terence* (London: Tho. Bertheleti, 1534).
Velz, John W., "The Ancient World in Shakespeare: Authenticity or Anachronism? A Retrospect," *SS* 31 (1978), 1–12.
Velz, John W., "England as Eden in *Richard II*," in Beatrice Batson (ed.), *Shakespeare's Second Historical Tetralogy: Some Christian Features* (West Cornwall, CT: Locust Hill Press, 2004), 129–46.
Vickers, Brian, *Appropriating Shakespeare: Contemporary Critical Quarrels* (New Haven and London: Yale University Press, 1993).
Virgil, *Georgics*, in *Virgil*, i, ed. Rushton Fairclough, H. Loeb Classic Library (Cambridge: Harvard University Press, 1965).
——, *The Eclogues*, trans. and ed. Guy Lee (Harmondsworth: Penguin, 1980; rev. 1984).
——, *The Eclogues of Virgil*, trans. David Ferry (New York: Farrar, Strauss and Giroux, 1999).
Waddington, Raymond, "Moralizing the Spectacle: Dramatic Emblems in *As You Like It*," *SQ* 33/2 (1982), 156.
Wallace-Hadrill, Andrew, *Past and Present*, 95 (1982), 19–36.
Walsham, Alexandra, *Church Papists: Catholicism, Conformity, and Confessional Polemic in Early Modern England* (Woodbridge: Published for the Royal Historical Society by Boydell Press, 1993).
Warneford, Richard, "Sermon I, John 12:28," in *Sermons of Various Subjects*, ii (York: Caesar Ward, 1758), 1–14.
Watson, Sir Frederick Beilby, *Religious and Moral Sentences Culled from the Works of Shakespeare, Compared with Sacred Passages Drawn from Holy Writ* (London: Calkin & Budd, 1843).
Watson, Robert N., and Dickey, Stephen, "Wherefore Art Thou Tereu? Juliet and the Legacy of Rape," *RQ* 58 (2005), 127–56.
Watt, Tessa, *Cheap Print and Popular Piety, 1550–1640* (Cambridge: Cambridge University Press, 1991).
Watts, Cedric, "Fundamental Editing: In *A Midsummer Night's Dream*, Does 'Bottom' Mean 'Bum'? And How about 'Arse' and 'Ass'?," *Anglistica Pisana*, 3/1 (2006), 215–22.
Waugaman, Richard, "The Sternhold and Hopkins *Whole Book of the Psalms* is a Major Source for the Works of Shakespeare," *N&Q* 56/4 (2009), 595–604.
Webber, Clifford, "Intimations of Dido and Cleopatra in Contemporary Portrayals of Elizabeth I," *SP* 96/2 (1999), 127–43.
Wells, Stanley, *Shakespeare for All Time* (Oxford: Oxford University Press, 2003).
Wells-Cole, Anthony, *Art and Decoration in Elizabethan and Jacobean England: The Influence of Continental Prints, 1558–1625* (New Haven and London: Yale University Press, 1997).

Wetzsteon, R., "Allusion," in *The Princeton Encyclopedia of Poetry & Poetics*, 4th edn (Princeton and Oxford: Princeton University Press, 2012).
The Whole Booke of Psalmes (London: John Day, 1562).
White, Paul Whitfield, *Drama and Religion in English Provincial Society, 1485–1660* (Cambridge: Cambridge University Press, 2008).
Whitney, Geoffrey, *A Choice of Emblemes and Other Devises* (Leyden: In the house of Christopher Plantyn by Francis Raphelengius, 1586).
Wilders, John, *The Lost Garden* (Totowa, NJ: Rowman and Littlefield, 1978).
Wilkins, George, *The miseries of inforst mariage* (London: George Vincent, 1607)
———, *The Painfull Adventures of Pericles Prince of Tyre* (London: T. P[urfoot] for Nat: Butter, 1608)
Williams, Arnold, *The Common Expositor: An Account of the Commentaries on Genesis, 1527–1633* (Chapel Hill: University of North Carolina Press, 1948).
Williams, Gary Jay, *Our Moonlight Revels: A Midsummer Night's Dream in the Theatre* (Iowa City: University of Iowa Press, 1997).
Williams, George Walton, "Still Babbling of Green Fields: Mr Greenfields and the Twenty-third Psalm," in Lois Potter and Arthur F. Kinney (eds), *Shakespeare: Text and Theater: Essays in Honor of Jay L. Halio* (Newark: University of Delaware Press; London: Associated University Presses, 1999), 45–61.
Williams, Richard L., "Censorship and Self-Censorship in Late Sixteenth-Century English Book Illustration," in Michael Hunter (ed.), *Printed Images in Early Modern Britain: Essays in Interpretation* (Farnham, Surrey; Burlington, VT: Ashgate, 2010), 43–63.
Williams, Simon, *Shakespeare on the German Stage,* i. *1586–1914* (Cambridge: Cambridge University Press, 1990; repr. 2004).
Wills, Gary, *Witches and Jesuits: Shakespeare's* Macbeth (New York and Oxford: Oxford University Press, 1995).
Wilson, J. Dover, *The Fortunes of Falstaff* (Cambridge: Cambridge University Press, 1964).
Wilson, Robert F., "God's Secrets and Bottom's Name: A Reply," *SQ* 30/3 (1979), 407–8.
Wilson, Richard, *Secret Shakespeare: Studies in Theatre, Religion, and Resistance* (Manchester and New York: Manchester University Press, 2004).
Wimsatt, W. K., Jr, and Beardsley, Monroe C., "The Intentional Fallacy," in W. K. Wimsatt Jr, *The Verbal Icon: Studies in the Meaning of Poetry* (Lexington, KY: University of Kentucky Press, 1954), 3–20.
Withy, Nathaniel, *Miscellaneous Poems*, 3rd edn (Wolverhampton: G. Smart, for the author, 1775).
Wittreich, Joseph, "'Image of that horror': The Apocalypse in *King Lear*," in C. A. Patrides and Joseph A. Wittreich (eds.), *The Apocalypse in English Renaissance Thought and Literature* (Manchester: Manchester University Press, 1984), 175–206.
———, *"Image of that Horror": History, Prophecy, and Apocalypse in King Lear* (San Marino: Huntington Library, 1984).

Womack, Peter, "Shakespeare and the Sea of Stories," *JMEMS* 29/1 (1999), 169–87.
Woodes, Nathaniel, *An excellent new commedie intitutled* [sic], *The conflict of conscience* (London: Richard Bradocke, 1581).
Worden, Blair, *The Sound of Virtue: Sidney's Arcadia and Elizabethan Politics* (New Haven and London: Yale University Press, 1997).
Wordsworth, Charles, *Shakespeare's Knowledge and Use of the Bible*, 4th edn, rev. (London and Sydney: Eden, Remington & Co Publishers, 1864).
Wright, Daniel L., *Anglican Shakespeare: Elizabethan Orthodoxy in the Great Histories* (Vancouver, WA: Pacific-Columbia Books, 1993).
Wright, Nicholas Thomas, *The Resurrection of the Son of God* (Minneapolis: Fortress Press, 2003).
Wyatt, Sir Thomas, *The Complete Poems*, ed. R. A. Rebholz (Harmondsworth: Penguin, 1978).
Wymer, Rowland, "Shakespeare and the Mystery Cycles," *ELR* 34/3 (2004), 265–85.
Wyrick, Deborah Baker, "The Ass Motif in *The Comedy of Errors* and *A Midsummer Night's Dream*," *SQ* 33/4 (1982), 432–48.
York Plays, ed. Lucy Toulmin Smith (New York: Russell & Russell, 1963).
Young, Alan R., *The English Prodigal Son Plays: A Theatrical Fashion of the Sixteenth and Seventeenth Centuries* (Salzburg: Institut für Anglistik und Amerikanistik, Universität Salzburg, 1979).

Index

Italic page numbers signify pages containing artwork

Abbott, George 34
Admonition to Parliament 258–9
Advent 266
Agamben, Giorgio 75
allegory 68, 87, 120, 136, 140, 160, 182, 266, 272, 324, 326
Alleyn, Ned 309
allusion
  and anachronism, *see* anachronism
  and *imitatio* 78–80
  and intertextuality 67, 81–3
  critical history on Shakespeare's biblical allusion 29, 43, 44–6, 49–50, 51, 52–3, 54, 55, 56, 62, 63–7
  definitions 80–5
  diegetic and extradiegetic (conscious and unconscious) 108, 112–15, 120, 138–40, 170, 182, 197, 231–4, 266–7
  history of 44, 78–9, 85
  in Bible 88–95
  in Classical literature 78–9, 86
  terminology 64–5, 66, 77–85
  theory of 41–2, 65–6, 71, 77–85
Amyot, Jacques 180
anachronism 4, 84, 114–15, 158, 170, 179–230, 331
Anders, Henry R. D. 33
Andrewes, Lancelot 14, 36, 293
apocalypse 74, 86, 217–22, 225–30, 271–304
Arbuthnot, George 52
Ariosto, Ludovico 79
Aristotle 78, 199
Armin, Robert 117–18
Augustine, St 19, 93, 141, 171, 281–3, 294

Bacon, Francis 61, 127, 237
Badiou, Paul 75
Bakhtin, Mikhail 82
Baldwin, T. W. 29–31
Bale, John 275
Balechouse, John 22
ballads 4, 28–9, 73, 108, 130, 132, 244, *317: Fig. 8.1*
Bancroft, Richard 258
Barber, C.L. 270

bardolatry 46–59
Barkan, Leonard 34
Barlow, William 37
Bartas, Guillaume Du 144
Barthes, Roland 80
Bate, Jonathan 13, 34, 108, 123, 166, 182, 230
Battenhouse, Roy W. 70, 251
Bauckham, Richard 272
Beardsley, Monroe C. 80
Beaumont, Francis 23, 234
  Knight of the Burning Pestle, The 23
Beauregard, David 75
Beham, Sebald 72
Bell, James 51
Bethell, S.L. 69
Bettes, John, the Elder, 27
Beza, Theodore 10, 30–1, 127, 276
Bible
  commentaries 32–5, 82, 87–8, 95, 104, 178, 218–21, 229, 267–8, 275–6, 312, 314, 330
  see also individual authors, sermons
  images and art 4, 12, 22–8, *24: Fig. 1.1, 25: Fig. 1.2,* 30, 42, 72, 73, 130–1, *131: Fig. 4.1,* 133, 159–60, *160: Fig. 4.2, 165: Fig. 4.3,* 204 n., *190: Fig. 5.1, 206: Fig. 5.2,* 220, *227: Fig. 5.3,* 244–5, *245: Fig. 6.1, 247: Fig. 6.2,* 248, 268, 271–3, *273: Fig. 7.1, 287: Fig. 7.2, 317: Fig. 8.1, 325: Fig. 8.2*
  persons and places
    Aaron 71
    Abraham 22, 103, 246, 247, 248, 251, 257
    Abraham and Isaac 23, 89, 91–2, 192
    Absalom 290
    Adam 46, 63, 71, 90, 119, 128, 132–4, 136–44, 146–7, 149, 152–5, 159, 161, 170, 243, 255, 294
    Eve 128, 132–4, 136, 155, 159–61, 169, 175, 225, 294
    Adam and Eve 20, 23, 24, 25, 28, 77, 78, 83, 112, 127–78, 224, 296–7, 334

Antichrist 38, 219, 221, 222, 292, 293, 297
Babylon 97, 118, 140–1, 273
Barabbas 100
Cain and Abel 71, 74, 83, 140, 153, 154
Calvary 69, 208
Daniel 28, 94, 118
David 20, 71, 74, 90, 112, 119, 289–90, 293, 320, 321
David and Bathsheba 22, 28, 120
David and Goliath 45, 53, 263
Devil (Satan, Lucifer) 91, 101, 149, 158, 169, 219, 221, 222, 241, 263, 264, 277, 285, 292, 294, 300, 328, 330
Eden 127–78
Egypt 91, 100
Elias 23
Elihu 330–1
Esther 22
Ezekiel 23
Gabriel 93–4, 160, 166
Gethsemane, Garden of 139, 187, 196, 204, 223, 278
God 18, 19, 20, 21, 26, 27, 37, 41, 48–9, 50, 52, 54–5, 57, 68, 86, 87, 88, 89, 90, 91, 92, 95, 97, 98, 99, 100–1, 104, 106, 108–11, 116, 118, 119, 121–2, 127, 128, 129, 131, 133, 134, 137, 139, 140, 142, 143–4, 149, 150, 152, 154, 155, 157, 160, 171, 174, 175, 176, 185, 187, 191, 193, 200, 201, 202, 205, 209, 211, 212, 213, 214, 217, 218–19, 222, 239, 240, 241, 247, 250, 252, 254, 255, 257, 258, 259, 260, 267, 271, 280, 281, 282, 283, 284, 285, 288, 290, 293, 294–5, 298, 302, 303–4, 305, 307, 310, 311, 312, 313, 315, 318, 319, 320, 322, 323, 326–33
Golgotha 276
Habakkuk 330
Hagar 92
Herod Antipas 26, 89, 91, 104, 147, 150, 216, 264, 297, 336
Herod the Great 215
Isaac 71, 102, 119
Ishmael 91
Jacob 94, 102–3, 113, 119
Jacob and Esau 74, 102, 232
Jehovah 199–200, 208–9
Jephtha 28, 89, 113, 150

Jephthah's daughter 45, 89, 113, 150
Jeremiah 71, 330
Jerusalem 53, 140–3, 273
Jesus (Christ, Jesus Christ) 20, 21, 28, 68, 69–73, 87, 90, 91, 94–5, 99, 100, 103–4, 107, 112, 113, 114, 119, 122, 128, 129, 132, 133, 138–40, 160, 174, 175, 180, 182, 183, 184–97, 198–214, 215–23, 225–8, 233, 243, 252, 263, 277–80, 293, 294, 297, 300, 303
Jezebel 274
Job 5, 28, 51, 100, 119, 243, 257, 264, 303, 305–33
Joel 279
John of Patmos 279
John the Baptist 26, 150, 209, 216
Jonah 71, 91, 119, 120–2
Joseph (father of Jesus) 71, 174
Joseph (son of Jacob) 71, 88, 243
Joseph of Arimathea 279
Joshua 23
Judas 71, 113, 115, 119, 138–40, 187–8, 195, 197, 222–3, 232–3, 277, 293
Judith 26, 28
Lazarus, *see* Parable of Dives and Lazarus
Legion 103, 263
Lot 89–90
Mary (mother of Jesus, Virgin) 93, 95, 99, 114, 132, 159–66, 174, 225–7, 227: Fig. 5.3, 322–3, 325: Fig. 8.2
Mary Magdalene 79
Melchisedech 71, 119
Moses 23, 71, 90, 91, 100, 107, 119
Nebuchadnezzar 45, 118
Noah 71, 88
Paul 20, 22, 23, 27, 31, 55, 65, 75, 91–2, 104–5, 108–12, 127, 143, 157, 175, 185, 211, 237, 239, 242–3, 255, 256, 261, 269, 280, 281–2, 315, 321, 323–6
Peter 105, 139, 195, 202, 223
Pharaoh 91, 243
Pharisees 196
Philip 32, 92
Pilate 45, 71, 138–40, 187, 203, 205, 253, 278
Rebecca 102
Salome 26
Samson 45, 71, 149
Samuel 112, 276, 288, 293, 298–9

Sarah 92
Saul 112, 288–91, 293
serpent 24, 130–1, 154, 169, 224–5, 285, 294, 297, 334, 335
Sodom and Gomorrah 89–90, 200, 209
Solomon 28, 29, 53, 71, 114, 149
Susanna and the Elders 22, 23, 28
Tobit/ Tobias 28, 316–18, *317: Fig. 8.1*
witch of Endor 276, 288, 291
whore of Babylon 219–20, 226–7, 272
woman clothed with the sun 164, *165: Fig. 4.3*, 226–7, *227: Fig. 5.3*
Zacharius 86
stories and episodes
Babel, Fall of 97
Creation 27, 63, 88, 97, 127, 131, 134
Expulsion 130 n., 142, 159, 177
Flight into Egypt *24: Fig. 1.1*
Flood 88
Last Supper 115, 188–9, 223
Nativity 27, 68, 104, 129, 174, 215–17
Parable of Dives and Lazarus (Lazarus, see) 20, 22, 23, 28, 45, 244, 246–8, *247: Fig. 6.2*, 251–4, 256–7, 268–9
Parable of the Lost Sheep 20
Parable of the Prodigal Son 5, 22, 24, 25, 27, 45, 55, 68, 72, 73, 113, 136, 143, 151, 244–6, *245: Fig. 6.1*, 248, 252–4, 257
Passion/ Crucifixion 22, 24, 27, 112, 129, 138, 140, 180, 189–90, 192, 203–8, 222, 276–80, 286, 293, 323–6
Ten Commandments 26
translations
Bishops' Bible 10, 12, 15, 16, 17, 18, 27, 29, 30, 33, 63, 65, 102, 105, 107, 109, 133, 196, 277, 296
Coverdale Bible 9, 109
Geneva Bible 9, 10, 11, 12, 15, 16, 17, 18, 27, 29, 30, 32, 33, 34, 55, 62, 63, 64, 65, 66, 93, 94, 97, 98, 100, 102, 107, 109, 127, 150, 160, 173, 175, 185, 187, 192, 193, 220, 221, 222, 226, 255, 260, 261, 267, 277, 279, 282, 288, 289, 296, 302, 310, 316
Geneva-Tomson Bible 10–11, 127, 186, 233, 276

Geneva-Tomson-Junius Bible 11
Great Bible 9, 12, 15, 64
King James Bible (or Authorized Version) 15, 16, 33, 53, 55, 56, 59–62, 63, 64, 67, 93, 105, 334, 336
Tyndale translations 9, 16, 31, 64, 93, 109, 187, 217, 324
Rheims New Testament 64, 95
Vulgate Bible 11, 16, 30–1, 79, 98, 113, 159–60, 244
Wycliffite Bible 64
Bickersteth, Geoffrey L. 69
Bilson, Thomas 37
Bloom, Harold 82, 213
Boccaccio, Giovanni 134
Boiardo, Matteo 79
Boleyn, Anne 79
Book of Common Prayer 14–15, 17, 18, 20, 33, 34, 39, 41, 63, 65, 105, 113, 116, *317: Fig. 8.1*
Baptism 13, 20–1, 127, 191, 238, 255
Burial 20–1, 105, 128, 301
Commination against Sinners (Ash Wednesday) 14
Communion 14, 20, 50, 211
Evening Prayer (Evensong) 14, 19, 20, 50, 127
General Confession 20, 277
The Litany 20, 50
Matrimony (Marriage) 20–1, 105, 128, 266
Morning Prayer (Matins) 14, 19, 21, 37, 50, 127, 266
Te Deum 113
Thanksgiving of Women after Childbirth (Churching of Women) 128
Visitation of the Sick 128
see also Coverdale, Miles; liturgy
Bradley, A.C. 253
Bradshaw, Graham 146
Braithwaite, Richard 26
Branagh, Kenneth 335–6
Braunmuller, A.R. 280, 300
Breton, Nicholas 320
Bridges, John 188
Bright, Timothy 34
Brockbank, Philip 198, 201, 203
Brooke, Arthur 161
Brooke, William 236
Brooks, Cleanth 295
Broughton, Hugh 34, 275
Brown, James, of Selkirk ("J.B. Selkirk") 52

Brueghel, Pieter, the Elder 180, 256
Bryant, J.A. 69–70, 71, 74
Buckeridge, John 36
Bullingham, Nicholas 15
Bullock, Charles 51, 52
Bullough, Geoffrey 36, 195, 326
Bunny, Edmund 35, 314–15, 326
Burckhardt, Sigurd 179–80
Burgess, Anthony 60
Burgess, William 5
Burke, Kenneth 213
Burton, William 30, 34
Bushnell, Rebecca 177
Butler, Martin 169–70

Caesar, Augustus 148, 183, 215
Caesar, Julius 180, 182, 184–97, 214
Calepino, Ambrogio 31
Callimachus 78
Calvin, John 10, 11, 17, 34, 35, 87, 99, 148, 327–33
   Commentaries on Psalms 34, 157, 251
   Institutes 34
   Sermons on Ephesians 34, 157–8, 161
   Sermons on Job 35, 55, 157, 312–4, 318–19, 322, 326
Camden, William 133
Camerarius, Joachim 127
Carlyle, Thomas 47–8
carols 99, 131–2, 160
Carter, Thomas 64, 65, 66
Cartwright, Thomas 258
Case, R.H. 201
Cassiodorus 88, 95
Catullus 78, 79
Cavell, Stanley 198, 209, 307
Cecil, Robert 177
Cecil, William 177
Chaloner, Thomas 110
Chapel Royal, *see* churches
Chapman, George 72
Chappell, Bartholomew 320
Charles I 290
Charles V, Holy Roman Emperor 181
Chaucer, Geoffrey 83–4, 118
Cheke, John 29
childbirth 4, 133, 174–7
Chillingworth, William 14
Christ figures 70–2, 119, 139
Christmas 21, 38, 129
   twelve days of 21
churches 9, 12, 15–18, 22, 33, 41, 130, 271
   Chapel Royal 14, 21
   Guild Chapel, Stratford-upon-Avon 271–3, *273: Fig. 7.1*
   Holy Trinity, Stratford-upon-Avon 13, 36
   St Helen's Bishopsgate, London 14
   St Olave's, London 14, 36
   St Paul's, London 26
   St Saviour's, Southwark 14, 36, 326
Churchyard, Thomas 191
Chytraeus, David 109
Cicero 78, 181
Clelia, *see* Downing, Charles
Coghill, Nevill 70
Cole, Howard C. 70
Coleridge, Samuel Taylor 284
Colie, Rosalie L. 307, 310
Collaert, Adrian 72
Collyer, Robert 52
Colton, G.Q. 52, 55–6
Cooper, Thomas 31, 134
Cope, Michael 266–7
Corpus Christi Plays, *see* Mystery Plays
Coverdale, Miles 9, 16–17, 188
   psalter 17, 18, 65, 116
   see also Bible, translations
Craig, Alexander 135
Cranach, Lucas, the Elder 180, 220, 272
Cranach, Lucas, the Younger 180
Crockett, Bryan 40
Cromwell, Thomas 181
Crowley, Robert 134
Cubeta, Paul 248, 250
curriculum, *see* education

D'Oench, Ellen G. 72
Danby, John F. 69
Daneau, Lambert 229, 275
Daniell, David 184, 185, 193, 194
Dante 47, 195, 277
Davies, John, of Hereford 274
Davies, Richard 58
Day, John 27
Day, Richard 27, 158
Deios, Laurence 229, 275
Dekker, Thomas 73, 229, 237, 276, 293
Dennis, Carl 70
Dent, Arthur 229, 275
Dethicke, Henry 176
Dickey, Stephen 162
Disobedient Child, The 244
Dodd, William 49
Donne, John 1, 37, 166
Doom (Last Judgment) 271–3, *273: Fig. 7.1*, 287: *Fig. 7.2*
Douglas, Gavin 181
Dove, John 38, 275
Dove, Thomas 36

Index

Dowden, Edward 179
Downame, George 275
Downing, Charles ("Clelia") 57
Drayton, Michael 85–6, 95, 235
Dryden, John 46
Dürer, Albrecht 72, 205, *227: Fig. 5.3, 245: Fig. 6.1*
Dutton, Richard 145–6, 182

Easter 37, 129
Eaton, T.E. 50–1
Edgeworth, Roger 87
education 3, 29–32, 42, 65, 84
Edward the Confessor 303
Egerton, Stephen 39–40
Egerton, Thomas 283
Eliot, George 58
Eliot, T.S. 67, 78, 84
Elizabeth I 15, 130, 135, 145, 188, 229, 274
Elton, William R. 69–70, 307, 327, 332
Elyot, Thomas 29
embroidery 4, 23, *24: Fig. 1.1*, 130, 273
Emerson, Ralph Waldo 48
Empiricus, Sextus 302
Empson, William 67, 69
Epiphany 21, 324
Erasmus, Desiderius 29, 30–1, 33, 78, 86, 290, 327
  Novum Instrumentum 30–1
  Paraphrases 33, 71, 86, 109, 202, 218, 221, 324
  The Praise of Folly 110–11
Essex, Robert Devereux, Earl of 182, 198
Estienne, Robert 11
Eucharist 190–1, 273; *see also* Book of Common Prayer, Communion

Fall, The 23, 63, 127–78, 224, 243, 293, 294, 296–7, 328
Fawkes, Guy 283, 293
Field, John 188
Field, Richard 34
Fike, Matthew 251–2
Fisch, Harold 224
Fissell, Mary 174
Flaming Sword, The 60
Fleming, Abraham 94
Fletcher, John 14, 36, 234, 336
Fletcher, Joseph 205
Fletcher, Richard 36
Fletcher, Robert 281–3
Florio, John 314
Folger Shakespeare Library 53
Fortin, René E. 327

Foucault, Michel 80
Foulkes, Richard 59
Foxe, John 33, 36, 37
Friedman, William and Elizabeth 61
Fripp, Edgar I. 69
Frye, Roland Mushat 69–70
Fulke, William 220
Furnivall, F.J. 58

Galle, Philips 27
gardens and gardening 4, 127, 136–7, 145–7, 148–9, 154, 159–67, *165: Fig. 4.2*, 167–71, 173–7, 255, 335
  see also Bible, Eden
  Bible, Gethsemane
  Hesperides
  hortus conclusus
Gardiner, Stephen 87
Garnet, Henry 285
Garnier, Robert 181
Garrick, David 47, 48, 307
Gascoigne, George 72, 244
Geoffrey of Monmouth 306
Gerard, John 177
Gifford, George 34, 229, 275, 291
Ginsburg, Christian 52
Godet, Giles 27
Goethe, Johann Wolfgang von 48
Goldberg, Jonathan 163–4
Golding, Arthur 35, 152, 157, 158, 160, 312, 314, 318–19, 326, 329–30
Good Friday 222
Goodman, Godfrey 268
Goodspeed, George S. 51
Googe, Barnaby 176
Gough, Robert 14
Grashop, T. 32, 33, 36, 38, 93, 279, 311
Greenblatt, Stephen 35, 74, 75, 81, 82
Greene, Robert 169, 236–7, 244, 267, 309
Greene, Thomas M. 166, 181
Gregory I, Pope 320
Gregory XIII, Pope 180
Griffith, Elizabeth 45–6
Gross, Kenneth 307
Guild Chapel, Stratford-upon-Avon, *see* churches
Gunpowder Plot 229, 274, 283, 285, 292–3

Hake, Edward 155
Hall, Edward 83
Hall, Joseph 135
Halliwell, J.O. 62
Hamling, Tara 23, 26

Harris, Jonathan Gil 285–6
Harsnett, Samuel 35–6, 291, 293
Hartley, Thomas 295
Harvey, Gabriel 29, 240
Harvey, Richard 240
Hassell, R. Chris, Jr. 21
Heemskerck, Maarten van 27
Helgerson, Richard 72, 244
Hell, harrowing of 286–7, *287: Fig. 7.2*
hellmouth 285–7, *287: Fig. 7.2*
Hemingway, Ernest 303
Henry VIII 15, 22, 79, 115, 147
Henryson, Robert 316, 318
Henslowe, Philip 14
Herbert, George 1, 2, 93, 311
Hercules 106–7, 167–8, 205
Heresbachius, Conradus 176
Hesperides, Garden of 167–8, 169
Heywood, Thomas 73
Hill, Christopher 290
history 133–47, 179–83, 229–30, 303–4
  see also anachronism
Hodson, Mark 60
Holinshed, Raphael 5, 83, 146, 288, 298, 303, 305, 331
Holland, Norman 70
Hollander, John 84
Holloway, John 306, 310
Holmes, Wilfrid 144
Holy Trinity Church, Stratford-upon-Avon, *see* churches
Holy Week 129, 192, 277
Homer 79, 86, 166
Homilies, Book of 36, 89, 104, 105, 128–30, 144, 149–50, 191, 255
Hooker, Richard 34, 37
Horace 78, 148
hortus conclusus 159–64, *160: Fig. 4.2*
Humphreys, Arthur 184
Hunt, Maurice 74
Huntington, Frederick D. 52
Hutchinson, Roger 109

Imaginary Conversation between Mr. Phelps and Dr. Cummings, An 57
Irving, Washington 47

James I, and VI 199, 215, 229, 274, 275, 283, 286, 291, 292, 303
James, Heather 123
Jenkins, Harold 105
Jerome, St 30
Jewel, John 37, 87
Johnson, Samuel 44, 46–7, 159, 251, 295, 305

Jones, Malcolm 27
Jonson, Ben 1, 21, 31, 60, 72, 73, 170
  Bartholomew Fair 28, 237
Junius, Francis 11, 219, 221, 222, 229, 276

Kermode, Frank 110
King Leir, The True Chronicle History of 306, 308–9
Kipling, Rudyard 58, 59–60
Kirsch, Arthur 307
Knack to Know a Knave, A 258
Knapp, Jeffrey 74
Knight, G. Wilson 67–70, 306, 327
Knox, Hugh 295
Knox, John 34
Kristeva, Julia 81–2, 83
Kugel, James 32, 83
Kyd, Thomas 96–7, 100, 181
  The Spanish Tragedy 96–7, 182

Lake, Arthur 37
Lamb, Charles 307
Lambert, Franz 109
Lane, John 135
Langton, Stephen 11
Lanquet, Thomas 134
LaPorte, Charles 56
Lascelles, Mary 70, 272
Lavater, Ludwig 291–2
Lavender, Theophilus 121
Lawrence, Seán 327, 332
Leggatt, Alexander 203
Lent 21, 127, 260
Levin, Richard 70–2, 324
Lewalski, Barbara K. 70
Leyden, Lucas van 72
liturgy 16–22, 50, 65–6, 104, 128, 151, 181, 216, 267; *see also* Book of Common Prayer
Lodge, Thomas 135, 152, 244, 258
Lok, Henry 34, 243
London Prodigal, The 72
Lothian, John M. 69
Lucian 302
Lucretius 83
Lusty Juventus 244
Luther, Martin 14, 17, 34, 86, 99, 114, 148, 272, 327–9
Lydgate, John 134
Lyly, John 72, 236–7, 240, 244

Macaulay, Thomas Babington, Lord 58
Machacek, Gregory 83
Machiavelli, Niccolò 302

Index

MacLure, Millar 40
Malcolm, W.H. 58
Malone, Edmund 59
Manguel, Alberto 81
Mantuan 78
Marlowe, Christopher 1, 18, 29, 73, 96, 97–100, 264
  Doctor Faustus 96, 97–8
  The Jew of Malta 96, 99–100, 102, 309
Marprelate, Martin 236–7, 239, 257, 259
marriage 4, 10, 20–1, 69, 92, 105, 107, 112, 115, 128, 133, 148, 155–6, 160, 166–7, 170–1, 174–7, 215, 230–1, 266
Marshall, Cynthia 74
Marston, John 72
Marten, Anthony 275
Marvell, Andrew 148
Marx, Steven 34, 73, 307, 310
Mary I 9, 12, 273–4
Massinger, Philip 14
Maundy Thursday 277
Maxey, Anthony 37
Mayer, Jean-Christophe 74
Mebane, John S. 146
Melville, Herman 77
Middleton, Thomas 21, 72, 237, 336
Milton, John 2, 48, 148, 170, 336
Milward, Peter 75, 187
Miola, Robert 31–2, 34
Mirrour for Magistrates, The 133, 134, 154, 306
Moffett, Peter 34
Montaigne, Michel de 302, 314–15
Montrose, Louis 111
More, Thomas 86, 109
Morgann, Maurice 234
Morrison, George H. 71
Mostaert, Jan *206: Fig. 5.2*
Muir, Kenneth 307, 310
Munday, Anthony 156, 235, 236–7
Mystery Plays 104, 119 n., 130–1, 138 n., 174, 181, 187–8, 196, 204–5, 217, 225, 264 n., 278, 285–7, *287: Fig. 7.2*, 297

Napier, John 218, 221, 229, 275
Nashe, Thomas 1, 37, 39, 142, 236–7, 239–42, 259–60, 262
Naylor, B.S. 56–7
New York Times, The 77
Nice Wanton 244
Nicholson, Samuel 168
Noble, Richmond 29, 30, 64–6, 74
Noot, Jan van der 276

Norden, John 188, 241, 258
North, Thomas 180, 202
Norton, David 56
Nuttall, A.D. 70

Ocland, Christopher 229
Oldcastle, John 235–6
Olivier, Laurence 335–6
Ovid 328
  Metamorphoses 2, 3, 5, 35, 108, 116, 123, 152, 157, 162, 166, 168, 170, 312

Pack, Robert 307
painted cloths 22–3, 73, 247, 268
paintings, wall 4, 22–3, 130, 244, 271
Palmer, Thomas 234–5
paradise 46, 128, 129, 135, 142, 144–5, 149, 150–2, 156, 163, 176, 177; *see also* Bible, Eden
Parker, Matthew 10, 12, 15, 33
Parker, R.B. 198
Parsons, Robert 35, 58, 83, 215, 314–19, 326
Patterson, Annabel 111
Paul's Cross 36–7, 38, 40, 188
Paynell, Thomas 109
Peele, George 289, 309
pelican in her piety *190: Fig. 5.1*, 326
Pencz, Georg *247: Fig. 6.2*
Perkins, William 34, 155, 229, 239, 258, 274, 282
Petrarch 79, 163–4
Pettie, George 156
Phelips, Edward 283
Philips, Edward 36
Phillips, Augustine 14
pietà 28, 324–5, *325: Fig. 8.2*
Pindar 78
Plato 110, 148
Plautus 167
Playfere, Thomas 37
Plumptre, Charles J. 52
Plutarch 5, 34, 182–4, 189, 193, 195, 197, 199, 202–3, 204, 208, 209, 212, 217, 225
Pollen, Burton R. 70
Poole, Kristen 236
Pope, Alexander 44–5
Pound, Ezra 78
Pownall, Alfred 51
preaching, *see* sermons
printers and printing 11–12, 16, 27–8, 34–5, 37, 39, 83–4, 236
prints 26–8, 72

Procter, William 52
Prodigal Son, The (play) 72
proverbs (English) 26 n., 101 n., 117, 143 n., 184, 241, 253, 276–7, 284, 319–20, 322, 328, 331
Psalm 46
  cipher 60–2
Psalms, metrical 265; *see also* Sternhold and Hopkins
Pucci, Joseph 85, 92
Pugliatti, Paola 146
Pullman, Philip 177
puppet plays 4, 130
Puritans and Puritanism 2, 40, 64, 236–9, 249, 254, 257–60, 264, 268
Puttenham, George 238

Quitslund, Beth 249

Rabkin, Norman 146
Rainoldes, John 95
Raleigh, Walter 58, 133, 198
Ramsey, Jarold W. 70
Raphael, D.D. 61
Rayndale, Thomas 174
Rees, Joan 256
Ridley, Nicholas 87
Rio, A.F. 59
Roffen, Edmund 282
Rogers, Thomas 275, 282
Ronan, Clifford 197
Rosdell, Christopher 87
Rowlands, Samuel 188, 322
Rowse, A.L. 270

Sackville, Thomas 283
Sadelet, Johannes 72
Sanders, Nicholas 87
Sandys, Edwin 15, 40, 158, 290
Sannazaro, Jacopo 78
Saussure, Ferdinand de 83
schooling, *see* education
Schreiner, Susan 329
Schreyer, Kurt 286
Scott, Reginald 36
Seaton, Ethel 221
Second Shepherd's Play, The 181
Selden, John 85–6, 95
Selkirk, J.B., *see* Brown, James, of Selkirk
Seneca 181
  Tragedies 2, 3, 79
sermons 14, 32–3, 36–42, 52, 65, 82, 87, 104, 128, 244, 268, 324, *see also* individual authors
Seward, William 295

Seymour, Henry 61
Shaheen, Naseeb 17, 29, 64, 66–7, 105, 116, 194, 195, 207, 212, 218, 237, 242, 246, 257, 262, 268, 310, 319
Shakespeare Jubilee 47
Shakespeare, Edmund 14
Shakespeare, John 13, 58–9, 271–3, *273: Fig. 7.1*
Shakespeare, William
  church going 13–22, 36–7
  education 29–32
  plays
    All's Well That Ends Well 45, 49–50, 53, 118, 276
    Antony and Cleopatra 4, 18, 63, 183, 214–30, 276
    As You Like It 3, 9–10, 44, 53–4, 55, 62, 72, 151–4, 244
    Comedy of Errors 21, 123
    Coriolanus 4, 63, 117, 194, 197–214
    Cymbeline 63, 119, 169–71
    Hamlet 3, 4, 46, 74, 75, 96, 105, 113–14, 119–20, 123, 153, 154–61, 190, 263, 264, 276, 335
    Henry IV, Part 1 4, 23, 44, 72, 143, 146, 156, 159, 234–46, 249, 251–7, 260, 263, 266, 267, 335
    Henry IV, Part 2 4, 18, 22, 144, 234, 241, 244, 247, 249, 250, 252, 257–62, 320
    Henry V 46, 63, 113, 116, 144, 145–6, 147, 182, 234, 246, 248, 250, 254, 266, 335
    Henry VI, Part 1 136
    Henry VI, Part 2 136
    Henry VI, Part 3 45, 113, 119, 187, 233
    Henry VIII 59, 117, 184
    Julius Caesar 4, 179, 184–97, 199, 202, 203, 214, 222, 223
    King John 51, 64, 184, 303
    King Lear 5, 21, 35, 45, 63, 67, 69, 72, 117, 231, 276, 294, 299, 305–33
    Love's Labour's Lost 4, 15, 30, 45, 73, 148–51, 172
    Macbeth 5, 51, 187, 271–304
    Measure for Measure 21, 53, 63, 67–9, 73, 122–3, 182
    The Merchant of Venice 3, 16, 44–5, 46, 50, 55, 69, 71, 73, 102–4, 107, 113, 123, 161, 231–2, 246, 294
    The Merry Wives of Windsor 3, 18–19, 22, 45, 234, 242, 244, 262–8

Index

A Midsummer Night's Dream 21, 50, 63, 65, 107–12, 167, 170, 231, 281
Othello 10, 18, 63, 69, 100–1, 113, 213, 230, 231, 276, 335
Pericles 120–2, 167–9, 231
The Play of Sir Thomas More 104
The Rape of Lucrece 184–5
Richard II 4, 45, 54, 71, 135, 136–42, 186, 276
Richard III 64, 117, 276
Romeo and Juliet 118, 161–7
The Taming of the Shrew 63, 105
The Tempest 3, 63, 73, 116
Timon of Athens 17, 51, 117, 119
Titus Andronicus 3, 115, 118, 159
Troilus and Cressida 97–8
Twelfth Night 21, 44
Two Gentlemen of Verona 113
Venus and Adonis 34
The Winter's Tale 4, 17, 28, 46, 69, 75, 101–3, 156, 171–7, 296
Shapiro, James 14
Shelford, Robert 41
Sidney, Philip 72, 244, 299
Siegel, Paul N. 69–70
Simpsons, The 41
Sims, James H. 73–4
Smith, Bruce R. 28
Smith, Henry 34, 38, 191
Southwark, London 14
Spanish Armada 274, 275
Speed, John 135
Spence, Sarah 92
Spencer, T.J.B. 183
Spenser, Edmund 1, 2, 84, 98–9, 191, 205, 241, 336
The Faerie Queene 98–9, 155, 169, 276, 306
St Helen's Bishopsgate, London, *see* churches
St Mary's Spital (hospital) 37
St Olave's, London, *see* churches
St Paul's, London, *see* churches
St Saviour's, Southwark, *see* churches
Stallybrass, Peter 291
Stationers' Register 26–7, 309
Sternhold and Hopkins (*The Whole Booke of Psalmes*) 17, 18, 39, 265, 294
Stevenson, David L. 70
Strauss, David 58
Streete, Adrian 292
Stroup, Thomas 109–10
Stubbes, Philip 37, 242
Surrey, Henry Howard, earl of 79

Swinburne, Algernon Charles 58
Swinburne, Charles Alfred 53–5
Symonds, William 229
syncretism 106, 148, 152, 168, 215, 225 n.
Synesius 94

Taming of a Shrew, The 30
tapestries 22, *24: Fig. 1.1*, 248
Tasso, Torquato 79
Tate, Nahum 305, 307
Taylor, Jeremy 168
Tennyson, Alfred, Lord 169
Terence 167
Theobald, Lewis 44–6, 250
Theocritus 78
Thomas, Keith 292
Times [London], *The* 77
Timmins, J.F. 57
Tomson, Laurence 10, 127, 276, *see also* Bible, Geneva-Tomson; Bible, Geneva-Tomson-Junius
Toole, William B. 70
Total Film 179
Tottel, Richard 134
Trench, Richard Chenevix 52
Tweed, Cyrus 60
Tyler, Wat 136
Tymme, Thomas 275
Tyndale, William 9, 16, 31, 86, *see also* Bible, Tyndale
typology 71–2, 90–1, 94 n., 100, 112, 119, 122, 139, 141, 154, 160, 166, 169 n., 192, 225, 281, 293, 321, 325

Udall, Nicholas 86

Vair, Guillaume du 34
Vautrollier, Thomas 34
Virgil 78, 79, 148, 215
Aeneid 2, 123, 166, 181
Georgics 186

Wallace-Hadrill, Andrew 148
Warburton, William 295
Warneford, Richard 295
Wars of the Roses 135, 147
Watson, Robert 162
Watson, Sir Frederick Beilby 49–50, 51, 52, 58
Watt, Tessa 22, 28, 72
Webbe, George 39
Wells, Stanley 13
Whipping of Satyre, The 235

Whitaker, Virgil 34
White, Paul Whitfield 187
Whitney, Geoffrey 153, 170, *190: Fig. 5.1*
Whittingham, William 11
Wilders, John 222
Wilkins, George 168
  *Miseries of an Enforced Marriage,
  The* 23
Wills, Gary 293
Wilson, J. Dover 69, 250–1, 262
Wilson, Richard 75

Wimsatt, W.K. 80
Withy, Nathan 295
Woodes, Nathaniel 320
Wordsworth, Charles 51, 62–4, 65, 66
Wright, Leonard 282
Wyatt, Thomas 79, 181
Wyclif, John 236
Wymer, Rowland 187

Young, Alan 72